A Psycho-Spiritual View on the Message of Jesus in the Gospels

Studies in Biblical Literature

Hemchand Gossai
General Editor

Vol. 128

PETER LANG
New York • Washington, D.C./Baltimore • Bern
Frankfurt • Berlin • Brussels • Vienna • Oxford

Wali van Lohuizen

A Psycho-Spiritual View on the Message of Jesus in the Gospels

Presence and Transformation in Some Logia as a Sign of Mysticism

PETER LANG
New York • Washington, D.C./Baltimore • Bern
Frankfurt • Berlin • Brussels • Vienna • Oxford

Library of Congress Cataloging-in-Publication Data
Lohuizen, Wali van.
A psycho-spiritual view on the message of Jesus in the Gospels:
presence and transformation in some logia as a sign of mysticism / Wali van Lohuizen.
p. cm. — (Studies in biblical literature; v. 128)
Includes bibliographical references and index.
1. Kingdom of God. 2. Jesus Christ—Kingdom. 3. Mysticism. 4. Spirituality.
5. Jesus Christ—Words. 6. Bible. N.T. Gospels—Criticism,
interpretation, etc. 7. Psychology, Religious. I. Title.
BT94.L64   231.7'2—dc22   2010023345
ISBN 978-1-4331-0658-3
ISSN 1089-0645

Bibliographic information published by **Die Deutsche Nationalbibliothek**.
Die Deutsche Nationalbibliothek lists this publication in the "Deutsche
Nationalbibliografie"; detailed bibliographic data is available
on the Internet at http://dnb.d-nb.de/.

Author photo © Kadir van Lohuizen / NOOR

The paper in this book meets the guidelines for permanence and durability
of the Committee on Production Guidelines for Book Longevity
of the Council of Library Resources.

© 2011 Peter Lang Publishing, Inc., New York
29 Broadway, 18th floor, New York, NY 10006
www.peterlang.com

All rights reserved.
Reprint or reproduction, even partially, in all forms such as microfilm,
xerography, microfiche, microcard, and offset strictly prohibited.

Printed in Germany

Contents

Book Marker: *What to Read* xi
Selected Abbreviations xiii
Preface xv
Editor's Preface xxi

Part One
What Is It About?

Chapter One: Introduction 3
    This Study 4
    The Process of Investigation 5
    Toward a Conceptual Framework 8
    The Quest for Jesus 10
    Program of the Book 18
    Postscript 22
    A Note on the Selection of the Logia Analyzed 22

Chapter Two: In Search of Mysticism: Framing the Concept 23
    Introduction: What Is Mysticism? 23
    The Handbooks 33
    Some Testimonies 36
    Mysticism in the Gospels? 42
    Conclusions 46

Chapter Three: Biblical Criticism: The Case of the Jesus Logia 47
    Introduction 47
    Sacred Texts 48
    The Logia: A Genre 53
    Implications of Method for NT Criticism 68
    Annex 1: Methodology Revisited 74
    Conclusions 76
    Annex 2: Greek and Aramaic 76

Part Two
The Kingdom of God: A Spiritual Interpretation

Introducing the Kingdom of God 81

Chapter Four: The Kingdom of God: *Eschaton*, Polity, Inner Reality? 83
    Introduction 83

The *Eschaton*? 84
Conclusions 93

Chapter Five: What Is a Kingdom? The Glory of the Kingdom Restored 94
    Kingdom 94
    Kingship 96
    Inner Strength 97
    Partaking 99
    Conclusions 99

Chapter Six: The Kingdom in the Gospels: 'When'? 100
    Introduction 100
    When?: Mk 1.14-15: The Text 102
    Intermezzi 106
    Near or Arrived? 109
    Conclusions 113

Chapter Seven: The Kingdom in the Gospels: 'Where'? 114
    The Scene 114
    The Kingdom Is Inside 116
    Observations 117
    Inside, or in the Midst Of? 120
    Where Do We Stand? 122
    Conclusions 123

Chapter Eight: The Kingdom in the Gospels: 'What' Is It? 125
    Introduction 125
    The *mustêrion* 126
    The Sower Parable 131
    Parables on the Kingdom of God 134
    Summary and Conclusions 137

Chapter Nine: The Kingdom in the Gospels: 'For Whom' 139
    Introduction 139
    'As a Little Child', *hôs paidion* 139
    'Poor in spirit', or: Craving for the Spirit? 148
    Transformation 155
    Conclusions: What Is Needed to Connect to the Kingdom of God? 161

Concluding Part Two: The Kingdom of God: A Spiritual Interpretation 162
    Summarizing 164

CONTENTS

Part Three
Transformation: The Psyche

Introduction 169

Chapter Ten: Transformation of the Self: What Is the Self, the *psuchê*? 172
    Introduction: Does *psuchê* Signify 'Life' 172
    Analysis 173
    Greek-Hellenistic Influences 178
    Another Paradigm? 180
    Conclusions 182
    Annex 3: Classification of the Occurrences of *psuchê* in the Gospels 183
    Annex 4: Some Literature Reviewed 184

Chapter Eleven: *Metanoia* as Transformation 187
    Introduction: Mk 1.15 par 187
    Terms and Concepts 189
    Continuity 196
    Change, Conversion, Transformation 200
    Metanoia as Transformation 201
    Sin and Forgiveness 204
    The Other Logia 207
    Conclusions 211

Chapter Twelve: Laying Down One's Life? The Good Shepherd and
    Other Pericopes in John: *"tên psuchên tithêmi"* 213
    Introduction 213
    What is the Meaning of *psuchê* and *tithêmi*? 216
    What is it that Jesus Wants to Communicate? 218
    Comments 221
    Conclusion: To Dedicate 223

Chapter Thirteen: To Lose One's *psuchê*, or to Save It? 224
    Logia about Saving or Losing the *psuchê* 224
    Psycho-Spiritual Transformation 229
    Conclusions 232

Chapter Fourteen: The Multifariousness of *psuchê*: The Other Pericopes 233
    Emotional Aspects of *psuchê* 233
    Physical Aspects 236
    Conclusions 241

Concluding Part Three: Transformation: The Psyche 242

Part Four
Explorations in the Field of *Pneuma*, Spirit

Introduction 247

Chapter Fifteen: The Concept of *pneuma* in the Gospels and Its Forms 249
    'The Spirit' or 'Spirit': *pneuma (hagion) / to pneuma ([to] hagion)* 249
    Is 'Spirit' a Feasible Translation of the Anarthrous *pneuma*? 254
    What is 'Spirit'? 256
    What is 'the Spirit'? 259
    Conclusion 261

Chapter Sixteen: Being in Spirit: A Case Study on the Pericopes in the
    Synoptics with '*en pneumati*' 264
    Introduction 264
    Being in Spirit: *en pneumati;* the Gospels 265
    Discussion 270
    Other NT Texts..274
    An Inquiry into Literature..277
    Conclusions 280
    Annex 5: The Texts Analyzed 281

Chapter Seventeen: The Words from the Cross: A Scene of Serenity 288
    Introduction 288
    The Scene at the Cross in John 289
    And in the Synoptic Gospels..295
    Evaluation and Conclusions...297

Chapter Eighteen: Rendering *ekstasis* in the NT 299
    Introduction 299
    Ecstasy: Term and Concept, Greek and English 301
    Ekstasis in the NT: A Presentation..308
    Comments 312
    Some Issues..315
    Evaluation and Conclusions...320

Concluding Part Four: Explorations in the Field of *pneuma*, Spirit............................322
    Summary 322

Part Five
What It Was About

Conclusions 329
    Approach 329
    Analysis 333

Mysticism	337
Evaluation	338
Synthesis	340
Annex 6: Summaries of the Outcomes of the Case Studies	342
Bibliography	353
Index	371

* * *

Transcription of the Greek

Transcription follows current practice with the following particulars:
- η as ê, like in English th*e*re
- υ as u (not as the usual y), pronounced like in English upper or in German *über*
- χ as ch, pronounced as a guttural h, or as in German *hoch*
- ω as ô, like in English *o*r

Book marker: *What to read*

For getting aquainted:
    Part V
For an overview:
    Chapter 1 and the introductions ands conclusions of Parts II, III, and IV
For conceptual studies:
    Chapter 10 on *psuchê*
    Chapter 15 on *pneuma*
    Chapters 4, 5, 8, and 9 on the Kingdom of God
For case studies of terms and concepts:
    Chapters 6 and 7 on the when and where of the Kingdom of God
    Chapter 11 on *metanoia*: repentance or change of mind-and-heart
    Chapters 12, 13 and 14 on the use and meaning of *psuchê*: laying down one's life, saving or losing life
    Chapters 16 on *pneuma*, spirit, and 18 on *ekstasis*
For background studies:
    Chapter 2 in mysticism
    Chapter 3 on Bible criticism

Selected Abbreviations

BDAG	see Bibliography: Bauer
JBL	Journal of Biblical Literature
JSHJ	Journal for the Study of the Historical Jesus
JSNT	Journal for the Study of the New Testament
RBL	Review of Biblical Literature
TDNT	see Bibliography: Kittel
WNT	see Bibliography: Bauer
ZNW	Zeitschrift für die neutestamentliche Wissenschaft und die Kunde der älteren Kirche
Mt	Gospel of Matthew
Mk	Gospel of Mark
Lk	Gospel of Luke
Jn	Gospel of John
Th	Gospel of Thomas
par	parallel texts in other gospels, e.g. Mk 8.35 par

Source Materials
NA27 *Novum Testamentum Graece* (NA27), DBG 1984
LXX   *Septuaginta: id est Vetus Testamentum graece iuxta LXX interpretes*, DBG 1979
Kurt Aland (ed.), *Synopsis of the Four Gospels*, DBG 1993

Preface

> *Veni Sancte Spiritus*
> *Reple tuorum corda fidelium*
> *Et tui amoris in eis ignem*
> *Accende*
> W.A. Mozart K 47 [1]

Paul, in closing his first letter to the Thessalonians, writes twice about the spirit. "May God himself, the God of peace, sanctify you through and through. May your whole spirit, soul and body be kept blameless..."[2] Using this concept he characterizes people as 'pneumatics' (spiritual people), as 'psychics'[3] and even as 'sarkics' ('fleshly' people')[4]. Is this a categorization, or maybe rather a differentiation according to the individual's understanding, wisdom and level of consciousness? Elaine Pagels, in her *The Gnostic Paul*[5], awoke my vivid interest in Christian anthropology where she analyzes these passages on *pneuma*, spirit, and *psuchê*, soul. Then I started wondering what Jesus in his logia in the canonical Gospels is saying about the human psyche and spirit. Soon sayings on the Kingdom of God challenged my interest for their transformative power. Gradually it dawned on me that in many of the sayings there might be hidden some measure of mysticism where spirit is functioning inside the human being.

This book is about some important sayings of Jesus, the logia. It is about mysticism in his words, and it dives into the concept of the *basileia tou theou*, the Kingdom of God: an inner potential. It is the essence of his message, further explained in many of his sayings. In the same line Jesus incites the individual to transform the psyche (*metanoia, psuchê*) and search for spirit (*pneuma*).

Where else does one find the Message of Jesus, the *euaggelion*, the good message, but in his very words, sayings, the logia? Logia are, or at least are taken

---

1 *The writing of this book and its contemplation*
sometimes experienced the blessing of this musical call for inspiration:
divine music of happiness, touching the soul and immersing the mind
in holy spirit (see Mk 1.8), filling the heart.

Compare also the phrase *hôs to paidion* 'as a little child' (Lk 18.17; see chapter 9): Mozart composed K 47 when 12 years of age (: 'Lofty and imposing, despite its primitiveness' (Alfred Einstein, *Mozart*, 1946, London: Panther 1971, 335).

2   1 Thess 5.28.
3   1 Cor 2.14-16.
4   1 Cor 3.1.
5   Pagels 1975, 59.

as, the words of Jesus as remembered by Jesus' contemporaries, and as they have been passed on by the evangelists. What purport did these words convey?

In a way this book is a collection of considered essays, *capita selecta*. The major part consists of semantic analyses of crucial terms, i.e. case studies of pericopes with specific terms like psyche, spirit, repentance, kingdom, and faith. One or the other reader may consider them rather dry analyses, but they turn into fascinating explorations. Explorations indeed of what turned out to touch some important fields of Christian faith and human understanding, religion and mysticism. An issue will be whether Jesus was a mystic. The explorations will lead to fresh views into what religion and mysticism can contribute to individual lives and to our present-day society. It is a plea for looking beyond (post-)modernity, enlightenment and rationality by imbuing our understandings with new insights of the beyond, and with a feed-back to 'traditional' religion.

These case studies grew out of a personal interest in religion and mysticism, in terms of both knowledge and experience as well as out of an amazement sensed already at a young age: what is the message Jesus is telling? As a violinist I experienced the spirit in performances of the Passions of Bach. In terms of the written word I was attracted to the Gospels, also out of interest in language and semantics. I started to study the term *psuchê* in the words of Jesus, wondering why so often it is rendered as life, and giving up life. However, I was not yet aware that it would lead to such other understanding. Another term even more challenging took my vivid interest, the concept of spirit, or *pneuma*.

When taking an early retirement from my scholarly work in urban and regional planning and from my chair as a professor, among others, in the methodology of utilization-focused research, I found a fascinating call in the field that resulted in this book, triggered by the challenging books on *The Gnostic Gospels* and *The Gnostic Paul* by Elaine Pagels. It was as a late vocation. I got rewarding teachings in the discipline by the NT professor of Leiden University, H.J. de Jonge. The contents of this book has grown through a long process. I took up my earlier field of interest in Jesus and mysticism, and started to study the logia. Thus, in the course of time some eight papers were produced and presented at meetings of the SBL (both the Annual and the International Meetings) and of the EABS, over the years 2000-2006. Each of these contributed to this work. Some twelve years of actual research and contemplation have now resulted in this book.

How did it come about? The system of the book had not yet developed to what it is now at the time I selected the topics of my papers step by step. I was not in search of mysticism as a guiding principle then. That option developed only gradually when it appeared as if out of itself. My early fascination got new energy by further study of concepts like *pneuma* (spirit) and its role in the Gospels, or by wondering what could be meant by e.g. 'laying down one's life' (*psuchê*). More and more I got caught by the logia of Jesus. This continued interest was prompted by what they were saying but also because of their supposed role in the period before the Gospels were composed, and during their composition.

Only step by step the focus of the work became manifest: what role, for example, does 'spirit' have in the Gospels considering that it is the central concept of spirituality and mysticism? *Pneuma* as a sacred entity outside human reach but also as a human quality endowed to the human in God's very act of creation when blowing his breath, his spirit, his *pneuma* onto the human being, making him into a living soul. Another instance the way the argument developed was in wondering about the Kingdom of God. Is it a future entity or rather an inner Presence, where the Kingdom of God may be standing for God's indwelling spirit? It is important to consider the value of such a statement. Is there one single interpretation of the Jesus logia? Or does mysticism teach wisdom? Is it not so that inspired sacred words require a multi-layer interpretation? Indeed, interpretation on many levels will probably affect translation. This book suggests there may be a number of cases where important words of Jesus may carry different meanings, like *psuchê*, or *metanoia*, 'poor in spirit', *dunamis*, *ekstasis*, and others.

Gradually during the empirical case studies awareness grew that the analytical outcomes of these case studies supposed wider contexts. Could it be that there was mysticism hiding in the simple words of Jesus? How is it possible to detect them?

A study of mysticism has been done in order to trace some key words that function as signs of mysticism, to be applied to the sayings during my explorations when working on the case studies. This is one of the contexts.

The other context is about methodology. What Jesus said had been remembered and collected in 'sayings Gospels' orally. They were later written down. What is the anthropology of Jesus: who is the human being? Has he been created in the image of God, or rather the fallen man subject to cardinal sin? What was the purport of Jesus' words? Could it be that he brought a message of God, of a divine Kingdom inside the human being? This idea led me to another type of study: what was the role of Jesus? What is mysticism? How did his words echo in early Christianity? Each of these a vast field, reduced in this study to construct its framework, supported by the rich array of the historical Jesus research.

Therefore, the system of the book distinguishes two approaches: the analytical case studies, and an overarching framework. The case studies are grouped together in three Parts: the Kingdom of God (II), transformation and the psyche (III), and the spirit (IV). The general framework consists of two main bodies. One is about mysticism and is discussed in chapter 2, the other about methodology and is discussed in chapter 3.

The basic idea of this book, therefore, is that the message of Jesus is to be found in his sayings: the logia. It can be traced by some new approaches in NT criticism, and by a fresh attitude to Jesus whose image has suffered from modernity and secularism at the cost of his spiritual grandeur, his essence. Fortunately there is some counter-movement trying to retreat from modernity and secular criticism and find a new way back to Jesus. This book contributes to this counter-movement, in a new way, far from dogmatism, doctrines, church history, and confession, finding spirit back in the teachings of Jesus, in some of his sayings, his logia.

Now that I have arrived at the end of this long and rewarding expedition I want to express my appreciation and gratefulness to the following persons. I have loved the contact and the scarce moments of exchange I could have with you, my friends and colleagues during my solitary expedition over these many years.

Elaine Pagels has figured at the very roots of this book. Her groundbreaking studies *The Gnostic Gospels* and *The Gnostic Paul*, published as early as the 1970s, have made a huge impact. Later she confirmed the idea of studying the *psuchê* when I did my first hesitating steps in this direction. I had the great pleasure of meeting her in the early 1990's in Princeton when I accompanied my wife when she was a Summer Visitor of the Institute for Advanced Study. Henk-Jan de Jonge has guided me as a beginning student of the NT. Gerard Luttikhuizen, Bas van Os, Riemer Roukema, and other members of the Gnosticism discussion group in the Netherlands have offered me their stimulating critique. Gert Bos, Otto Duintjer, Frans Jorna, Pieter Oussoren and Huub Welzen obliged me when offering their time and energy to comment on early drafts of parts of the book. Phil Korsak did so when commenting so positively on some of my papers at SBL meetings. Bert Jan Lietaert Peerbolte helped me in accommodating in the EABS. Miodrag Mičovič offered his efficient technical abilities whenever asked. Our son Kadir took pains to provide the photograph on the cover.

The book would not have been but by the stimulating welcome of my initial proposal by the publisher, and later the heart-warming and professional cooperation of Heidi Burns, Nicole Grazioso and Jackie Pavlovic of Peter Lang's series *Studies in Biblical Literature*, guiding me through all sorts of intricacies with a friendly patience.

Mab van Lohuizen-Mulder, my beloved wife and life's partner, has played significant roles during the complete process. Moreover, she has functioned as an eye-opener to this sort of study—independent, critical, creative, constructive—during her own ground-breaking Ph.D. research work, first on

PREFACE

Raphael, then on Late Antique and Early Christian art and Early Islamic art. She has been a loving and understanding critic, a strong support, and an active stimulant, during my initially hesitant explorative steps. Finally I am indebted to Universal Sufism where I found my life's sustenance from early age onward. My late parents both have been creative and supportive to my life in many respects: offering opportunities, nurturing idealism, spiritual inspiration, a Christian basis, and precious memories. My father initiated scholarly research and planning in urbanism, whose footsteps have been guiding me.

My e-mail address:
vanlohuizens@xs4all.nl

Editor's Preface

More than ever the horizons in biblical literature are being expanded beyond that which is immediately imagined; important new methodological, theological, and hermeneutical directions are being explored, often resulting in significant contributions to the world of biblical scholarship. It is an exciting time for the academy as engagement in biblical studies continues to be heightened.

This series seeks to make available to scholars and institutions, scholarship of a high order, and which will make a significant contribution to the ongoing biblical discourse. This series includes established and innovative directions, covering general and particular areas in biblical study. For every volume considered for this series, we explore the question as to whether the study will push the horizons of biblical scholarship. The answer must be yes for inclusion.

In this volume Van Lohuizen examines in detail a select group of the *logia* of Jesus with a particular focus on the mystical component within them. The author argues that these sayings of Jesus reflect a quality of mysticism specifically in terms of Presence and Transformation that portrays the message of Jesus in a psycho-spiritual perspective. Within the Jesus sayings that he examines, there are four principal Greek concepts that are foundational: *psuchê, pneuma, metanoia,* and *basileia tou theou* (Kingdom of God). Van Lohuizen concludes that Jesus' role is primarily that of a mystic and messenger of God. Scholars who are engaged in this area of biblical scholarship will find much here to examine, reflect on, challenge and I believe above all allow for a serious expansion of the discourse on Jesus logia.

The horizon has been expanded.

Hemchand Gossai
Series Editor

PART ONE
What Is It About?

CHAPTER ONE
Introduction

> *May your whole spirit, soul and body be kept blameless*
> 1 Thess 5.23

The title of the book, *A Psycho-Spiritual View on the Message of Jesus: Presence and Transformation in Some Logia as a Sign of Mysticism*, represents its program. It is about Jesus, viewed here as a Messenger of God. It is about his Message. The message of Jesus can be traced in some of his sayings: in the logia.[1] Jesus can also be viewed as a mystic. Key concepts of mysticism are divine presence and transformation. This study therefore studies some of the logia as his message by tracing presence and transformation as signs of his mysticism. The hypothesis of this work is that these two concepts constitute the nucleus of some of the most important logia of Jesus. The view expressed in this work is that the message of Jesus as contained in these logia requires a psycho-spiritual interpretation. Spiritual, as his words are spirit. Psychological, as it calls for transformation of the psyche, the self, oneself. Indeed, this transformation is feasible only when the spirit guides. What is spirit (*pneuma*)? Is it not the breath of God inhaled by 'man' at creation? Could it be a repeated reality at each birth? Is it the human being created in His image? It is the spirit that is the Kingdom of God, a divine Presence, indwelling in each human being in need of being called to awaken: bold statements, indications of what mysticism is conveying.

In that sense this book is about mysticism. It is about Jesus. It is about the mysticism of Jesus, and it is about his words, his logia. The logia are witnesses of the Message (*euaggelion*) of Jesus, they form, as it were, the 'word' of God. The book therefore is about words. At the same time, words can never tell the truth: they substitute *arrhêta rhêmata*[2]: words that can't be worded. Words, in mysticism are signs toward truth. Therefore words may contain various meanings, seemingly contrary ones, in reality aspects of the same, different dimensions that in combination offer an unexpected vision on Reality.

---

1 Logion: "a usually short pointed pregnant saying or observation, esp. by a religious teacher" (*Webster's*). In Jesus research it generally is used for the items of sayings collections, in particular the sayings Gospels of Q and *Th*. In this work 'logion' is applied to sayings by Jesus taken independently from the narrative context, or as a saying per se. Moreover, a logion is more concise than a saying, which sometimes expands into a discourse.
2 2 Cor 12.4.

This Study

This study opens new views on the historical Jesus. The key to it lies in six specific assumptions[3] by which the explorations in the book have been guided. One, Jesus' role: he is seen primarily in the perspective of his being *a mystic and messenger of God*—rather than taking the socio-cultural and historical context (within the scope of Modernity)—as keys to understand him: verticality versus horizontality. Two, the gate to know his message is found in some of *the logia* rather than in the narratives of the Gospels or in christological and eschatological interpretations. Three, *an analysis of key terms* of important concepts discloses new meanings that are helpful in understanding the message and its mysticism. Four, a better understanding of *mysticism* leads to a different interpretation of his teachings, with divine presence and transformation being the key to trace mysticism in the logia. Five, the words of Jesus are *sacred words* and therefore stand in a specific perspective. Six, the analysis of some key terms leads to a *psycho-spiritual view* on the Message of Jesus. To sum up. The following three statements contain the intention of the book, and indicate the pillars on which the book is built:

> Jesus is a mystic and a messenger. His mysticism, like most mysticism, is characterized by the two concepts of Presence and Transformation
>
> The Jesus logia as sacred words are the key to the various doors for understanding the good message
>
> Some crucial terms in the logia are to be understood on different levels of understanding.

* * *

The central issue of this book is whether some important sayings by Jesus reflect mysticism in terms of presence and transformation.

Part of this exploration is an analysis of these sayings and of some key words in them, being alert for implied alternative meanings and for possible inconsistencies in translated texts.

* * *

This is a clear statement of the basic assumption made and of the approach taken. It distinguishes this study from many others. For some the Christian tradition as developed in Church and in systematic theology is a lead (Dunn 2003, 2005). Others, on the contrary, try and remove everything confessional as

---

3   To be distinguished from a preconceived idea which goes without adequate evidence or through prejudice: 'held to his preconceived opinion despite the new evidence' (*Webster's*).

blinding objective research ('faith is a hindrance'[4]) (much of the Third Quest scholars do). Again others maintain that a real understanding of Jesus as a historical figure cannot but recognize him as Christ ('Hurtado'[5]), criticized by others.[6] This study's focus is on Jesus as a mystic and messenger, and wonders if these qualities are to be found in his words. The search will be guided, as far as is within my reach, by the best principles of academia.

After this background philosophy this introductory chapter continues with laying out the process of the investigation, followed by some aspects of the conceptual framework of the study. Finally the program of the individual chapters will be laid out.

The Process of Investigation

Questions as these require an objectifying analysis next to spiritual synthesis, based on existential experiences shared in inter-subjectivity. My subjective understanding based on these objectifying studies results in a sense that many of the Jesus logia betray a measure of mysticism. This mysticism is moderate indeed, conceived as a Path toward God rather than as a peak experience out of the blue. How does one define mysticism in order to trace it? Defining mysticism is a *contradictio in terminis*. However, through an exploration of mysticism two concepts have been found to be central to this path: presence and transformation, presence as a sense of the divine, transformation as a precondition and as a concomitant process of changes of self. Both these concepts have been used in order to explore the possible mysticism in some logia by Jesus. This is a first and rough map of this study. How was it tackled?

The work on the topic started when I began wondering about concepts like *psuchê, pneuma, metanoia*. These first studies were pure analyses of the respective term: its incidence, its literal meaning as to dictionaries, its use in current translations, and its sense as found in scholarly literature. It was a bottom-up approach, from facts to insight. Gradually, though, an awareness grew that there might be more around than what was resulting from this exploration.

When I worked on the research on the Kingdom of God, the *basileia tou theou*, it dawned upon me that indeed I was travelling in the domain of mysticism. For the next paper, then, I went on the quest of what mysticism is about. A sort of common denominator emerged as a result: presence and transformation: living in a divine domain (presence, the Kingdom of God), and

---

4   A label by Dunn (2005)
5   Hurtado 2003.
6   A methodological discussion is found in Reiser 2005.

transformation of the self as a precondition as well as an outcome of that presence.

This result made me return to the earlier work in order to see whether these terms could be traced in the logia on *pneuma, psuchê, metanoia*, and others: a top-down approach. When this approach worked out positively, an overall framework developed in two ways. One was the recognition of the concepts of presence and transformation as signs of mysticism in the Jesus logia. Then the surmise developed that this was the very message, the *euaggelion*, that Jesus proclaimed: the presence of the divine domain, and transformation (*metanoia*) of the self (*psuchê*) as its condition as well as its effect. The present work, therefore, is about a psycho-spiritual view on the Message of Jesus. It searches selected logia on traces of mysticism.

In this way the expedition resulting in this book worked its way both bottom-up and top-down. Bottom-up is the way of the semantic analyses; top-down the framework of mysticism to interpret them.

Bottom-up

The former is a scrupulous empirical analysis of words or word groups in the framework of a pericope (or passage), trying to find out what the word (group) may signify, in the first place linguistically, based on the handbooks like BDAG and TDNT, and on scholarly literature. To some degree it is semantic in character. This approach is supported, be it ex post, by Barton's concept of 'plain sense' (Barton, *The nature of biblical criticism, 2007)*. It is a semantic or linguistic and literary operation first and foremost, only indirectly concerned with the original, the intended, the historical, or the literary meaning" (101): thus, it is purely bottom-up. The empirical analysis has been done principally on the terms mentioned above—a selection that gradually took form, without pre-set criteria. In some cases the topic was triggered by an SBL Meeting sections' program. One of the motivating forces was a lively interest in these and other terms and concepts, and in their translations—that often triggered curiosity as to their meaningful relationship to the Greek originals. A little fore-taste of what is to come in this book was presented in the opening paragraph. The bottom-up exercise resulted in a number of case studies around the selected terms mentioned, directed to 'plane sense' research focused on the semantic aspect at the cost of the theological interpretation. The case studies, therefore, do not figure as monographs or as state-of-the-art reports. Yet, they constitute the main body of this study, its core indeed.

This line of research resulted in alternative understandings and insights for a number of terms and concepts. Hence the need of hypotheses evolved to help frame alternative readings:

Top-down

This method led to the other approach, the top-down. Several hypotheses or thought constructs of a non-empirical nature were formed in a gradual process of gaining insight. They serve as a possible framework to see in what way the outcomes of the bottom-up exercise make sense. They do not function as proof, nor will they be subject to proving. Rather they will serve to search for a measure of plausibility in the arguments of this book. Referring to the six assumptions in the opening paragraph, four lines of this approach are distinguished. One is that some of the Jesus logia exhibit a measure of mysticism. The second is about the centrality of some of the Jesus logia (sayings). Closely related is the third, the sacredness of these sayings. Finally, the figure of Jesus is viewed as an independent messenger of God, independent (to some degree) of his Jewish context and of the Hellenistic environment. These hypotheses function as lines of approach.

The Lines of Approach

- The central hypothesis is that a number of Jesus logia may exhibit traces of *mysticism*. The explorations in this book will confirm this for a large number of such pericopes. But that is anticipating on the work to be done in the next many chapters (6 through 18). What mysticism is supposed to be will be made operational empirically (chapter 2). The idea to look for mysticism originated, on the one hand, in the awareness that essentially mysticism is the core of religion and of major religions: why not present in the words of Jesus? And on the other hand as the understanding that here the sense of experiencing the divine is to be found.

- The present study focuses on selected *logia* by Jesus. Such a logion will be taken as an independent text, sensible in itself. It does not take the context of the narrative as the prime frame within which to understand it. And it leaves explanatory determinants derived from biblical theology aside. It will be proposed to treat the logia as a literary genre of its own. For the methodology adopted, see chapter 3.

- Words[7] of Jesus are conceived as sacred words, as part of an inspirational message. Related to this point of departure is the understanding that the logia in principle represent inspired sacred speech. If not 'the word of God', divine inspiration is the force behind it, making the words living words. Interpretation needs to be adequate to it. See next section.

---

7   The concept 'word' has acquired specific meanings in theology, like in the phrase the Bible being the Word of God. Schaper (2009b, 279), in my understanding, considers the ban on images of God by a writing God in the OT as a legitimation of the Word as divine. Has that Word now become as strongly fixed as a sculpture? If so, shouldn't it therefore be equally subjected to this ban? Where is the fluency of water, the 'shapeability of air or wind, *pneuma*, breath? Schaper (279) speaks of "the biblical rejection of the plastic representation of the deity." My point is that a right understanding of the logia requires a fluid approach to the text, *as if it is spirit*.

- Jesus as a messenger, and various other roles have been attributed to him, too. Apart from christology with all its orthodox implications, modern views depict him as a wandering sage, a Jewish rabbi, a healer and exorcist, a political revolutionary, a social reformer, the promised messiah, and still more. What did escape attention is the Messenger Jesus. Jesus as the Messenger of his time (and of all times), bringing the (good) message (*euaggelion*). It seems useful to take the history of religions as the context. See further down.

The elements of these lines will be explained in chapters 2 (mysticism) and 3 (bible criticism).

Toward a Conceptual Framework

Therefore two important items have to be discussed. One is the idea of treating the logia as the object of research, and its sacredness. The other is to situate the idea of Jesus as a mystic and a messenger in the ongoing discourse on the historical Jesus: the quest for Jesus.

Logia as an Independent Sacred Message[8] [9]

This book focuses on the logia by Jesus, in the first place in the Synoptics. It takes the following strand of thought. The logia are signatures for tracing the message (*euaggelion*) of Jesus and his mysticism. In principle they represent the oldest texts as remembered by the close circle around Jesus, and later incorporated in the narratives of the respective Gospels. Later each of the evangelists has selected those logia that each considered essential for his narrative as remembered in his particular early-Christian community. In this way they were contextualized when woven into the narratives of the evangelists. The narrative was constituted to contain the story of Jesus' acts and what happened around his words, told and written for their audiences, various early Christian communities. In the process the logia were included in the Gospel narrative and thus contextualized when woven into the narratives of the evangelists—each having his own story to tell to his particular audience, one of the various groups of the earliest Christians.[10] This happened over the decades in the period

---

8   Koester (*Ancient Christian Gospels: their history and development*, 1990) has functioned as an early incentive to me, in the first place by his focus on sayings, and by his broadening outlook on early Christianity.
9   This section summarizes one of the arguments expounded in chapter 3, section *The Logia As genre*.
10 Initially these groupings ('voluntary associations', sociologically spoken) were informal gatherings to join together, socially, religiously. They were not sects. (Harland 2009, 25–47; 27. Kloppenborg (2006, 323–38; 327–29) discusses the idea association (in relation to the Jesus movement) in the more formal context of professional organizations and more fixed religious entities.

INTRODUCTION

between the crucifixion in the mid-thirties and the 'Gospel period', the period from 70 till about 100, and even later. Gradually this gap in the search for the historical Jesus is filling. By the way, to my knowledge another gap remains open to impartial research, the period of his life story between the time when he was twelve years old and the beginning of his mission around his thirtieth birthday.

It must be assumed that in the process of transmitting texts they may have undergone changes, both minor and major. However, these logia must have been considered sacred words, the very words of the Master, that were to be conserved as authentically as possible: a sacred treasure, out of reverence, of being aware of their sanctity, of understanding that these words conveyed a power, a *dunamis*, a strength, an energy that was unequalled: the living word. This book takes the logia as they are, without the context; comparable to Q and Th, 'decontextualized' as it were, appearing as 'aphorisms,'[11] as logia.

This study takes the logia *per se*, more or less as a sayings Gospel, a term used for the so-called Q Gospel, and for the Gospel of Thomas—which as the only ones contain almost nothing but sayings by Jesus, logia therefore.

This book is born out of wondering, both in the sense of amazement and in the sense of doubt, an attitude of awe toward the words of Jesus, his message. At the same time it is written in a critical attitude toward the rendering of these words, in three senses: what does the Greek word say semantically,[12] How is it translated, and how is it perceived in specific understandings (theologically, others)? Another aspect is a sound sense of doubt with a foundation of trust, *gnosis*, of inner knowledge. Semantic studies are rare and rather technical. In the perspective of spirituality I have found unexpected opportunities where new meanings open up. Sometimes a new alternative is found, sometimes a new perspective changes the scene. Alternatively, a current interpretation is confirmed but with a new depth of meaning.

The logia to be analyzed are seen here as teaching, as revelation, as inspiration. Where else should one find the Message of Jesus, the *euaggelion*, the good message? Logia are, or at least are taken as (a selection of), the words of Jesus, as remembered by the witnesses of Jesus alive, as passed on to the evangelists. The words are taken here as the best available when making the (idle) search for his *ipsissima verba* (Jeremias): literal, authenticated words by Jesus. Whatever its authenticity each logion must have undergone changes over the decades since it had been pronounced, the period generally called the post-

---

11 An aphorism is "a terse and often ingenious formulation of a truth or sentiment, usually in a single sentence" (*Webster's*, sub 2). Aphorisms, sayings and logia are used as synonyms. Occasionally this word is used as a synonym for logion or saying. Included in this approach are the categories of 'apothegm,' 'pronouncement story,' or *chreia* (Hurtado 261).
12 *Webster's*: Semantics, sub 1a: the study of meanings of words and forms.

Easter period, i.e., in the period between the crucifixion in the mid-thirties and the 'Gospel period'.[13] What Jesus had said, one may assume, was considered sacred, words of utter value, words from the mouth of the revered and beloved teacher. What else to do for his contemporaries than to conserve them as authentically as possible, as a sacred treasure, out of reverence, out of being aware of their sanctity, of understanding that these words conveyed a power, a *dunamis*, a strength, a presence, a spirit, an energy that was unequalled: the living word.

It seems worthwhile to take these logia as such, to de-contextualize them from the narrative and the situations and conditions depicted there. It may well be that the logia have been traditioned as entities of their own, next to the narratives remembered as such. Rather the oral tradition of the logia must have had priority, both in care taken and in which time they were registered. Therefore, this book tries to take them as logia, de-contextualized from the narrative of the Gospels, appearing as 'aphorisms', words that are be taken as such, without a context, similar to *Q* or *Th*.

The Quest for Jesus

During the explorations on *basileia, psuchê, pneuma,* and other terms, and the concepts behind these, it occurred to me that quite a few of these logia betray a measure of spirituality of the mysticism type: divine presence, transformation. Jesus as a mystic. Even more: Jesus as a messenger, as the messenger of that time (and of all times?), bringing a divine Message, the *euaggelion*: the Kingdom of God is within you (see Part II), one can be in spirit (or the spirit may be in one) (see Part IV); the self is to be transformed in the 'Self' (Part III). A messenger, incomparably comparable to other messengers in humanity's history. Little of this can be found in the scholarly literature of at least the last hundred years or so.

> In the history of Jesus research three 'quests' have been identified, all focusing on the search for the identity of Jesus, with a strong focus on the 'historical Jesus.' Delimitations between the types vary.[14] Initially, before the 'quests,' the 'historical' Jesus coincided with the doctrinal Jesus of the Church, whether Roman- or Eastern Catholic, or Protestant, in all diverse denominations.

---

13   For example, Focant (2009, 18): "les experiences pasquales ont en effet provoqué une nouvelle compréhension et un relecture de la vie antérieure de Jésus»: the words of Jesus were understood differently after Eastern, and his words read again, causing a re-interpretation.

14   My rendering of this search depends heavily on six sources, in random order: Dunn 2003, ch. 5, 67–97, Weren 2008, 367–75, Soulen 2001, 153–56, Robinson, 2007, Pagels 1981, Funk 1993.

INTRODUCTION

Since the 18th century, Modernism and the neo-Liberal (Protestant) *(first) quest* were prevailing. For this quest the tools of historical inquiry and the Gospel material available were considered wholly adequate for finding the resulting wise teacher behind the theologized Gospel portrayals and the dogmatic Christ of faith. Though methodologically this period has been fruitful, historically it suffered from subjective views on Jesus, coloring the outcomes of many of the studies in this line. It was Albert Schweitzer, among a few other great scholars, who with his 'Leben Jesu Forschung' broke with the liberal historiography and grounded the Jesus research on a supposedly firmer scholarly foundation, concluding Jesus to be the eschatological preacher, replacing the old picture of Jesus as a moral and religious teacher.[15]

Eschatological interpretations thus prevailed in the first half of last century, and it did not disappear at all since. Bultmann, a brilliant scholar and empiricist, although he had pre-set ideas,[16] continued on the eschatological avenue some forty years later and thus finished the first quest). See chapter 4.

On the other hand, Bultmann was one of the great scholars who developed *the second quest* by a significant break when he adopted Barth's kerygmatic theology: the heavenly kerygmatic Jesus overtook the earthly Jesus. In terms of the history of Jesus quest, he left the unfruitful search for the historical Jesus in favor of the search after his message, narrowing it down to the kerygma,[17] more Pauline than Jesus-founded (see also chapter 4). Unfortunately, he narrowed down Jesus to an eschatologist to the detriment of 'Jesus as moral and religious exemplar.'[18] Irresistibly—in a concurring other second quest (initiated by James Robinson in 1959[19]), by some named the new quest[20]—the historical Jesus resurfaced when scholars returned to the issue of historicity. In search of the authenticity of his words they created criteria to apply to texts. He may be seen as the precursor of the *third quest*.

The beginnings of the third quest (onward from the 1980s) were summarized in 1995 by Ben Whitherington III in an excellent treatment.[21] The threefold common thread in the overwhelming variety of studies he summarizes is (1) 'the search for a common object: knowledge about an ancient person,' (2) 'to place Jesus more firmly in his social and economic setting,' (3) a 'desire to say something new and fresh' (247),[22] this latter point being also one of the outcomes of this work. In some sense, it returned to the first quest in its Schweitzerian "depiction of a prophet of the end time in the context of Jewish eschatological expectation" (N.T. Wright, 1982).[23] Soon, however, it reversed

---

15 Schweitzer 1906.
16 Bultmann 1948.
17 *Kerugma*, literally proclamation, was the activity of Jesus when he proclaimed the Kingdom of God. In Acts and the Pauline letters, it is used in a quite different interpretation in the concept of Gospel as defined by Paul that is strongly divergent from the sense of the message in the words of Jesus. See further Soulen&Soulen 93–94.
18 Soulen & Soulen 154.
19 Robinson, 1959.
20 Soulen 154.
21 Witherington 1995.
22 See also the excellent overview in Theissen 2002, 141–52.
23 Soulen 2001, 155.

itself and, supported by many authors, Jesus emerged as a non-eschatological Jesus. It initiated the view to interpret Jesus and his words and deeds primarily in his being a Jew, grounded in the social and economic setting of the time as well as in the Jewish culture and religion. Theissen et al. summarize the third quest as seeking a 'contextual Jesus.'[24] In my view, the recurring underlying theme of this quest is its expression of modernity and thus often its secular approach. This dynamic is expressed in Jesus as a human being, as a 'regular' Jew, as one uttering words that attest human wisdom, the Gospel texts as literature, religion as a human construct.[25] Secular, notwithstanding the recognition that the figure of Jesus cannot be understood apart from the strongly religious character of the society he lived in. Robinson and his school played a significant and enduring role in the Jesus research, both on Th[26] and on Q. He is often underrated due to controversies over Q. This eminent scholar with his famous Claremont institution through a minute analysis of the Q texts unearths Jesus (again) as the moral and ethical idealist, who calls for reforming humanity and society on a basis of humaneness in full trust of God as guiding us.[27] He does so by identifying the logia of Jesus in Q as the closest approximation of the very words of Jesus. More about Q in chapter 3.

What image of Jesus resulted from the often excellent studies of the third quest, sometimes dubbed 'secular'[28]? The picture is highly diverse as are the studies in their respective starting points, their intent, methods applied, their background philosophy, and therefore their outcomes. To mention a few: the Jesus Seminar finds but a few sayings authentic, a Jesus that is rather down to earth.[29] Dominic Crossan, an outstanding analyst of the historical Jesus calls him a Jewish peasant.[30] He and many others tend to see Jesus as 'a marginal Jew or a Jewish messiah,' a view that has become rather dominating.[31] Burton Mack typifies the quest for the historical Jesus as demythologizing.[32] Gerd Theissen characterizes Jesus as the prophet of social change.[33],[34] James Dunn sees Jesus as the eschatological spokesman of God.[35] Dunn is one of the

---

24 Theissen 2002 144.
25 Theissen 2002, 142f sub 1 and 2. In Dutch theology this trend of Modernity has been expressed quite strongly by the Reformed theologian, H.M. Kuitert (1999, 2002).
26 He has played a significant role in the history of the publication of Th.
27 E.g., Robinson 2007, 224–34.
28 Theissen 2002, 142f, sub 1 and 2 referring to the third quest being secular.
29 Funk 1993 treats the words of Jesus.
30 John Dominic Crossan, *The Historical Jesus: The Life of a Mediterranean Jewish Peasant*, HarperSanFrancisco, San Francisco 1991, or his *The Birth of Christianity: Discovering What Happened in the Years Immediately after the Execution of Jesus*, same, 1998.
31 Ben Witherington III in *The Jesus Quest* 1995 presents documentation on John P. Meier (197–213), James Dunn (215–16), Marinus de Jonge (216–18), Markus Bockmühl (218), and N.T. Wright 219–32. All these figure in the chapter 8 'Jesus: Marginal Jew or Jewish Messiah (197–232).
32 Mack 1993.
33 Witherington1995, 137–45.
34 E.g., Theissen 2002, and earlier pioneering works by him.
35 Dunn, 2003, 62. Thus he returns to the main stream of the first half 20th century when eschatology dominated.

INTRODUCTION

principal spokesmen in today's Jesus quest.[36] E.P. Sanders also returns to eschatology calling Jesus the eschatological prophet.[37] Evans (2006, 35, 39), in assessing the third quest, concludes: "Perhaps the most important gain is in a renewed appreciation of the Judaic character of Jesus, his mission, and his world".

Parallel to the quest for the historical Jesus, a significant role was played by the group that worked on 'redescribing Christian origins': what happened after the crucifixion among Christians: was proto-orthodoxy paramount and the only way? Starting in 1992 a ground-breaking series of seminars and papers was produced under the aegis of SBL. Its purpose was to bring under discussion the paradigm of traditional Christian 'myths': what is it that really happened in those early years. Its work ended successfully with a voluminous report.[38] Furthermore, this group entertained a modernist and secular view on Christian history.

It appears, however, that a new turn in the Jesus quest has started. Apart from a trend to revivify the traditional paradigm in a modernized version, the moral-ethical message of Jesus is coming to the fore again. Robinson, when speaking to the general public, summarizes Jesus' message as: "...trust God to look out for you by providing people who will care for you, and listen to him when he calls on you to provide for them. God is somebody whom you can trust, so give it a try."[39] Thus, he revivifies the moral-ethical side of Jesus' message. Borg is another scholar working in this line (see chapter 4).

Maybe more than ever before, the variety of results is as impressive as that of the points of departure. This interpretation was reinforced in the course of time when another dimension was added by incorporating a wide range of disciplines, that both broadened and deepened the Jesus research into a multidisciplinary undertaking. In terms of both quantity and quality, this third quest constitutes a tsunami of studies, often of highest quality.

At the same time, one must state that both incomprehensibly (in essence) and naturally (as to present-day culture), mysticism is a dimension that is missing in these studies, completely or at least to a great extent. Modernity is paramount.[40]

Jesus: A Mystic, A Messenger?

Where is this study to be located in the historical Jesus discourse? Is it located within the third quest, or is it a maverick? How does one of the assumptions of the study, Jesus being a mystic and a messenger, fit in? Technically the question of mysticism will be answered by finding key words that indicate whether a text

---

36 Ibidem, *passim* and Dunn 2005.
37 Witherington 1995,118-32, referring to E. P. Sanders 1985.
38 Cameron, Miller (ed): *Redescribing Christian Origins,* 2004.
39 Robinson 2005, viii.
40 Major exceptions are Marcus Borg (to some extent) and Elaine Pagels; more about their view on spirituality and Jesus below and in chapter 4.

may be considered mystical (chapter 2). Conceptually, we will gain insight gradually while progressing in this study, chapter by chapter.

The issue of Jesus being a messenger is largely a matter of definition and assumption. He is the bringer of the message of the Kingdom of God, the *euaggelion*, the (good) message. In terms of the history of religion he is the messenger of Christianity. Task and role of each of the great messengers of the world has been a renewal of religion, often but hidden, through mysticism: to call people to remember one's origin as sons and daughters of God.[41] Admittedly, though, there is no way to make that claim plausible through analyzing the words of Jesus. The third quest does not offer openings to that position either. However, the novelty of his message as expressed in his logia— breaking through the traditional Jewish religious context—makes one think that it is not plausible either to limit his role and his being to a sage—or any other characteristic to be mentioned. His greatness and grandeur filters through his 'simple' words and acts. The reader has to wait and see what arguments the study will produce in the course of this expedition.

What is the present-day context in which my assumption is positioned? What is the broader view on religion and spirituality in Western culture? Already for decades new views appear, in which a new search has been tackled on the question: who is Jesus, what do his words mean, what is the significance of Jesus, apart from the classification of the previous section? NT scholarship in an open spirit is engaging in this quest, as we have seen in the previous section where method and object were in focus. At the moment two currents, with many shades in between, are prominent. The one, mainly the third quest, is critical as to the historicity of parts of the Gospel texts and therefore regarding the traditional image of Jesus and of his pronouncements. The traditional image involves trying to imagine or even reconstructing the role and position of Jesus as a Jew in the first century, as a wandering Cynic, or as a healer and exorcist, as a Mediterranean farmer, as a carpenter, as a teaching rabbi or a sage, as the coming messiah, or as an eschatologist and apocalyptic.[42] Philosophically and methodically these studies belong to modernity, and in a sense, therefore, are secular. The other current, possibly termed confessional, though takes this critique seriously, seeks to re-find and re-found orthodox Christianity through selected findings of that same critical research, and reformulates traditional dogmas.[43] Undeniably the two currents intertwine and thus blur the contrast.

---

41 Interest in other religions has been rising. Some publications explore differences and similarities among Jesus and other messengers. Borg (1997, *Jesus and Buddha*) places sayings of Jesus and Buddha on various items next to one another.
42 Crossan 1991. Also Dunn 2003.
43 For example Larry W. Hurtado in his authoritative work *Lord Jesus Christ: Devotion to Jesus in Earliest Christianity*, 2003, represents the typical Christological look, in which he has

Within the third quest the most critical line has unearthed information that supports the view of Jesus as a mystic. Or at least has stripped the eschatological Jesus of his other-worldly image.

This present study avoids classification in either of these two currents: it is neither secular (in my definition; see above) nor confessional. Again, does my approach belong to the third quest?

> A way of answering this question is to ask whether the approach of this study meets the criteria of Witherington, as rendered above? The answer is yes and no. It does claim to offer something 'new and fresh' (criterion three). It does not fit in his second one, putting the social and economic setting as framework for interpretation. It partly fits to the first criterion as it does search for knowledge about Jesus, checked for historicity. But it does not as to its object, which is not Jesus as 'an ancient historical figure.'

What do we know of Jesus except through the Gospels and the saying collections? We just have a snapshot of a few years of his life—in his thirties. The Gospels are tacit about his teens and twenties. A glimpse of his knowledge and understanding on his 12th birthday is given in Lk 2.46–47 and 52.[44] Is it too audacious to submit that the long period between his 15th and his 30th birthday was devoted to a specific education: knowledge of this world, knowledge of the spirit (*gnosis*)? The Gospels do not refer to it, understandably: their story is focused on passion and resurrection, on Christ and the eschaton.

While, on the one hand, it is feasible to fit this study in the third quest at least partially, some of its essential characteristics make it peculiar. My point is, through an empirical study of the logia on selected items, to find out if these logia contain traces of mysticism, in terms of presence and transformation. It does not, however, impose a pre-set idea on the work. In addition, it does not search systematically for the historic Jesus as 'an ancient person,' or in the first century Jewish context—religious, socio-economic, and cultural. Whilst not denying the importance of these points, my underlying question is whether from these logia he appears as a mystic and possibly as a messenger of God. In that

---

integrated skilfully the findings of many third-quest studies. His argument centers around devotion for Christ. Only the canonical Gospels represent 'the word'. Comment: Though he recognizes Q as an authentic first-century 'Jesus book' (256), earlier than the canonical books of Mt and Lk (for which it served as a source); to him it is just a saying collection that only gains authority in the Gospels. Another major work in the classical line is James D.G.Dunn's *Jesus Remembered* (2003).

44 We have two clues: Lk 2.46–47 and 2.52. Jesus, sitting in the temple and listening to the teachers and asking them questions, 'amazing them … for his understanding and his answers,' for two long days. And after that, Lk adds, he grew in wisdom and maturity (*hêlikia*, BDAG 2b).' In view of this and his later words and acts, and in view of his professed mission, what has happened in this period? Some higher form of education? A period of 'monastic' training? Qumran? Abroad?

sense this book does not fit in the third quest literature, if only because it is not secular.

Now let us make a turn. Take—even for a moment—Jesus as a mystic, as a messenger of God, his words being sacred. Doing this trustworthily creates a milieu of understanding, very different from what is current, of what is *communis opinio*.[45] That is what this study does. Are we then returning to the old days of traditional religion? Or to the concept of 'liberal lives of Jesus'[46] where one "attempted to limit the explanation of Jesus' actions and the events of his life (*sic*: again without his words!, WvL) to natural, psychological causes and motivations"[47]?

Vertical versus Horizontal

In my interpretation most of the positions taken in Jesus research put what I preliminarily call horizontality central. Inter-human relations stand out in this dimension: that is what matters in the message of Jesus, apart from eschatological traits. It is also the dimension where Jesus is understood in his socio-cultural and religious context: first-century Palestine.

What will be found in the logia studied on the contrary is a sense of verticality, where a more direct connection with the divine is considered central. In what sense? In the sense of the Kingdom of God being present, of a positive role of the spirit (*pneuma*), in an interaction with one's mind-and-heart (*psuchê*) that effects transformation, qualities discussed in the main body of this study. They are positions that touch mysticism. In this spiritual line some authors are found, like Marcus Borg (see chapter 4) and Geza Vermes ('Jesus the *chasid*'),[48] a *chasid* here probably seen as a realized mystic rather than as a rather ultra-orthodox religious figure. Also Elaine Pagels, who in her works came to discover the spiritual dimension of the Gospels, differentiates between belief, trust, and experience.[49] In her initial works, she is fascinated by gnosticism, in the Gospels, in Paul,[50] a gnosticism that is closer to mysticism than the later mythological

---

45 It is this sort of view—narrowing the study to one dimension only—that Dunn contests in, e.g., his *New Perspective* 58 and in his *Jesus remembered* Part One, when arguing for placing Jesus in both his Jewish and his socio-cultural context.
46 Schweitzer quoted by Soulen 2001, 153.
47 Soulen 153f.
48 Witherington 1995, 108–12, based on Geza Vermes, "Jesus the Jew", in Charlesworth (ed), *Jesus' Jewishness*, 1991.
49 Modern scholarship tends to neglect the spiritual aspect as a category of its own. For example, Kowalski (1996, 150) writes that John's message is ecclesiological, christological, soteriological, and theological. There is no mention of a spiritual or mystic message.
50 Pagels 1975/1992, 1981, 2003.

INTRODUCTION

excrescences, causing misunderstandings as to what may be called Christian or heretic.

My approach is close to those of Borg and Pagels, a view to be illustrated in chapter 4. Even so it is different. What is essential in this study are two factors: placing the logia in the focus, and conceiving Jesus as a mystic and messenger of God, a spiritual approach therefore in a search for mysticism.

This mystical dimension has not been recognized, or rather ignored completely to my knowledge, ever since Harnack's famous lecture series from 1899 to 1900 (for a crucial text of his, see chapter 4). My approach, though taking elements of the three quests, will be different, based as it is on a spiritual dimension in the words of Jesus. The full swing of this approach will become clear only gradually, during the complete process of exploration. He is viewed as the world Messenger, as the founder, maybe, of the Kingdom of God in the human heart as an inner reality, transforming the *psuchê*, and recognizing (the) spirit (*pneuma*).

Parallel to the quest of the historical Jesus, another current has developed in our Western culture over the past decades. It is a new discovery of spirituality, not in theory but rather in a quest to re-find its genuine focus on experience. Here a new perspective for the debate emerges. In this search for spirituality a new genuine desire for mysticism can be traced. It is a search for mysticism as a rediscovered human potential, as an essential—though often covered and un(der)developed—quality of the human being. It started in the 1960s and 1970s inspired by Eastern religions and by new currents in psychology. Parts of it went astray into aspects of the movement called the New Age, misunderstanding and misusing mysticism. For about the past two decades, Christian mysticism has been undergoing a period of being rediscovered: its traditions, literature, and tools. In the process one would expect that the logical question, 'is Jesus a mystic?' would be prominent. However, amazingly this issue is hardly raised, let alone answered, especially in scholarly work. Moreover, in publications about Christian mysticism, who is missing? Jesus! Practically no study of Christian mysticism includes sayings of Jesus. There is a strange incapacity to integrate the mysticism of Jesus into Christianity, to understand the mysticism of Jesus.

However, his message is mysticism indeed, a mysticism that is not defined or described as such. It is not the mystical texts of the world-famous mystics, like Teresa of Avila, Ruusbroec, Juan de la Cruz, Jelaluddin Rumi, and so many others who tell about their experiences with the divine, in the divine atmosphere. Hidden in and behind the words of Jesus, the *mustêrion*, one finds pure mysticism as his utterances originate from a realized union with God, that try to call on humanity to open up, to learn about the Kingdom that is inside and a call for transformation of the self.

Jesus does not tell about mysticism, what it is, nor does he communicate his experiences, his communications with God. What he does is to direct man to the spiritual path, to transform in order to reach some awareness of the divine Presence.

Therefore his mysticism does not speak about what is commonly known as uniting with God. That is what I call apex mysticism, experiences that are not common to people. Identifying mysticism with these exceptional experiences is like telling that the essence of sport is becoming a world champion. The joy of sport is in doing what is within one's reach, the degree of talent one is endowed with, and to develop and train that potentiality. Jesus is portraying the way of mysticism for everybody who seeks the light, who is desperately in search of the spirit (Mt 5.3 par), who is prepared to cultivate the heart to the effect that it is pure (Mt 5.8): such are the ones whose is the Kingdom of God, who may 'see' God.

The motive behind all this is the need to re-evaluate the role of Jesus of Nazareth. If we are not happy with the image of Jesus as the sage, the rabbi, the healer, the exorcist, the coming Messiah, the apocalyptic, what sort of person he then really was? Are we satisfied with a teacher of morals and of do's and don'ts? Is it not the natural longing of the human being to relate to God, in his grandeur, in its intimacy? In the present investigation are traces of his role as such a mystic and as a messenger, the one who brings the Message of God, the perpetual reminder of mankind by God to individuals' close relationship to God. The other roles and the 'worldly' context must be recognized in understanding Jesus, but is secondary at best when explaining the Message. It is a devaluation of Jesus not to recognize him as the Messenger of his time, of all times. This position is not an a priori fixed axiom. It is a hypothesis that will be regarded during this investigation, in a process of mutuality: the hypothesis may change words in order to sharpen the argument as well as its contents. The aim of my Jesus research is to clarify which interpretation of him can be reconciled with the primary materials and which cannot. My pretense is to open a new challenge in taking the logia as the primary source material, and thus offering a new interpretative perspective.

Program of the Book

Let us see how the argument unrolls in the chapters that follow.

Chapter 2 is a treatment of mysticism in order to find concepts expressed in terms in order to locate mysticism in the logia. It will discuss the nature of mysticism, referring to a small selection of literature out of the voluminous stream, and taking the reader back to early Christianity. Mysticism will be described as referring to a 'reality beyond', beyond sensory perception and therefore refuting some of the rationality based on sensory perception. We will find two substantive characteristics that consequently will be used throughout the book: Transformation and Presence.

Mysticism literature is discerned into three categories: texts pronounced from a mystical consciousness though not about the experience (e.g., the Jesus *logia*), primary witnesses describing a mystical experience of the subject (e.g., John of the Cross), and texts discussing the two former ones though mostly limited to the second type (e.g., Underhill).

Chapter 3 will then discuss the consequences of analyzing mystical texts for Bible criticism. Furthermore, if the logia are taken as units per se, what does this approach mean in terms of method? Do spiritual and sacred texts revealing a 'reality beyond,' like the *logia* of Jesus, require a category of its own in Bible criticism? It is contended that in some yet crucial respects they do require an approach different from a narrative, from a philosophical statement, from a rational argument, even from a poem. The nature of the 'reality beyond' is as it were a reality with a dimension added, a three-dimensional object cannot be understood by a two-dimensional methodology. In that other dimension other rules govern, added to the ones generally known in order to reach understanding and insight. Their meaning may be approached, however, by applying extra tools in hermeneutics and Bible criticism. One is multi-interpretability, maybe referring to literary criticism on poetry. One of the proposals to be discussed is whether the *logia* constitute a *genre per se*, well differentiated from the narrative.

With Part II the book then arrives at the substance, the *capita selecta* part: concepts and terms that in the light of mysticism and spirituality may acquire a new meaning.

Chapters 4 to 10 place the concept of the Kingdom of God in the center of the argument. Do we find Presence represented? What about Transformation? The issue will be tackled whether the Kingdom of God is eschatological, or did it refer to a nearby political event? Or does Jesus announce it as having arrived here and now? And if so where? Alternatively, it is suggested, is the kingdom of God a state of spiritual consciousness rather than an event? For the question what the Kingdom is one will find the closest approximation in the parables about the Kingdom. What did Jesus tell how to reach it, for whom is it meant really speaking, and how to relate.

The discussion on Transformation is continued in Part III on transformation and the psyche. Chapter 10 is introductory, asking what is the *psuchê?* The word group *metanoia / metanoein* is the object of chapter 11. Traditionally it is translated as repentance, penitence, conversion, *Busse*. Confrontation with its use in some *logia* rather invites to render it by change of mind and heart, as a transformation of the psyche, in the light of the divine. This is supported by the primary meaning of *metanoia*.

Chapters 12 and 13 will directly address the term *psuchê*, first in some principal texts in Jn. The phrase *psuchên tithêmi*, generally rendered as to lay down one's life, is critically analyzed resulting in an alternative proposal. Included is the so-called Good Shepherd pericope (Jn 10) and related texts in John 13 and 15. Then also the phrase saving or losing life in its many variants (Mk 8.35par) will be questioned. It will be argued that *psuchê* in these and quite a few other cases may quite naturally be translated as self, or as psyche, or mind-and-heart, rather than life. Here Transformation again is the central issue. The discussion of *psuchê* ends with chapter 14 where the other texts with the term will be covered.

Part IV discusses the concept of spirit. Different from Parts II and III, it does not focus on Jesus' logia. Moreover, some chapters will cover a wider field of analysis, including Jn and other some other books of the NT. The discussion moves to Presence more directly: presence of the Spirit, a presence experienced outwardly, a presence experienced inwardly. The issue will be explored by four approaches, *capita selecta* each on a different topic. After looking at the concept *pneuma* in general (chapter 15) the challenging expression *en pneumati* is analyzed in chapter 16. I propose it to be understood as '(being) in spirit' rather than 'by the spirit': a literal rendering of *en*. Baptism is immersing in holy spirit rather than baptizing with the Holy Spirit. Has the anarthrous use in Greek of (holy) spirit been interpreted satisfyingly? Spirit may refer in fewer cases to the Holy Spirit than is mostly done. Chapter 17 is an essay-like attempt to interpret the words on the cross relating to *pneuma*. What was Jesus' condition? Did the suffering overwhelm him, or did his spirit-consciousness already have the overhand? The scene at the cross is seen as one of dignity and serenity rather than drama.

Chapter 18 finally adds a discussion on *ekstasis* as an expression of spirit inside, or does it refer to being out-of-order? Here it is understood as a state of heightened consciousness, a working of the spirit through the individual. A good case is with the women at the grave when they realize that a miracle is happening (Mk 16:8)? Is ecstasy spiritual or psychic?

The book ends with a summary and conclusions in chapter 19 where the main issues are summarized and conclusions drawn.

> A word about the option to select both *psuchê* and *pneuma*. Each of these fields has been neglected in Western theology and NT criticism since decades. Practically no attention has been paid to the relationship of these concepts. a *horror vacui* seems to exist to recognize the sacred of the spirit, and of the humanity of the psyche, often out of fear of identification with the Platonic soul.[51]

---

51 I made a rapid consultation of the writings of some Apostolic Fathers (Loeb edition, by B, Ehrman, ed). Nowhere does one find *psuchê* as life but often as a definite aspect of the

The reader will be confronted with compelling issues. Spirit: human or divine? Is the psyche as an intrinsic aspect of the human being yet with its own dynamics of transformation? Does one find repentance in the logia? What is the purport of sin? What is forgiving? The Kingdom of God, where is it? When does it come? Here and now, or at the end of times? What is a kingdom, a realm or a state of consciousness? What does it mean, to believe? What is baptism other than being immersed in spirit?

It is intriguing to have found a number of cases where the primary or at least a possible alternative meaning of a term seems to have been neglected in the main current translations. This the more so as the alternative or even primary meaning seems to be at odds with theology and Church doctrines, yet appears so logical and natural: the kingdom has arrived rather than being at hand; it is inside rather than among you; Jesus and others do things (being) in spirit rather than by the spirit; the shepherd rather dedicates his self to the sheep rather than to die, and so does Jesus ask his disciples to love one another dedicating themselves to one another rather than giving their lives. Jesus calls for a spiritual change of mind in view of the arrival of the kingdom rather than presupposing sin that needs penitence.[52]

The perspective offered is different from the current ones. One is about the Kingdom at the end of times, the parousia (or second coming of the glorified Christ), the saving message of passion, cross, death, resurrection and the forgiveness of sin. Another one is the moral message of love, renunciation and service worded in the Sermon on the Mount (and its Lukan parallel Sermon on the Plain), centering around the Beatitudes. 'The uniqueness and finality of Christianity finds a basis in the apocalyptic understanding of Jesus', is an often heard statement.[53] I hope in this study to put another view in parallel, where the message of Jesus tells that the divine has been given to the human being in his heart, and that this is a universal message.

These issues are presented here as a series of hypotheses, based on more than a decade of research and meditation on the inspired texts in the Gospels found in the Bible and in the Gospel of Thomas. The work will shed fresh light on these biblical concepts, adding to a better understanding in the context of present-day needs, and highlighting spirituality as central to daily life. The

---

human being. *Pneuma* often refers to a person's spirit: Barnabas, *Epistles*; Shepherd of Hermas, *Entolai*

52 George Aichele's *The control of biblical meaning: canon as semiotic mechanism*, 2001 I got hold of only recently. I could not include it in my explorations. But it is precisely to the point. The synopsis asks 'how the canon influences the meaning of the text'. 'Could texts be "liberated" from the canon'? 'How does a canon influence or create ideology and culture?' 'How form and function of canon both reveals and conceals texts from its readers'.

53 Kent Brower in his review in *JSNT* (28,5, 2006) of John S. Kloppenborg, *Apocalypticism, Anti-Semitism and the Historical Jesus*, T&T Clark, London 2005.

results of this study do not pretend more than a couple of suggestions how texts from the Gospels may be viewed in an alternative way as compared to current interpretations. It is hoped that some of these proposals will be taken up in scholarly discussions.

Postscript

This study touches upon many fields, each having a rich record of noteworthy studies. I have taken the audacity to tackle some issues leaving alone the broader context of the fields. I apologize therefore for neglecting important studies.

I am aware that some of my findings appear to contradict elements of Christian faith, doctrine and research, cherished for two thousand years. It is embarrassing. Two words on that issue: One is that likewise over these two thousand years mysticism has been denied in leading circles of both Church and academia—it needs to be detected and restored. This is a humble contribution. The other word is that these findings resulted from impartial empirical studies of terms and concepts.

Whatever in this study is proposed—as a new line of thought, a hypothesis, a method, an object, an outcome—it serves as a suggestion to take in consideration either as supplementary or as an alternative. Its pretense is neither to replace any scholarly result or view in the Jesus research nor to reject it. I defend this non-competitive attitude / position out of respect, and because to me this 'matter' is so 'immaterial' that no final conclusion is within reach: spirit is intangible to logic, reason, and considerate understanding. Yet one must apply each of these, while respecting the sacred. The words of Jesus are multi-layered, and therefore multi-interpretable—to the extent of one being able to 'see' and to 'hear.' For a closer analysis of the concepts of seeing and hearing, see chapter 8, section on the Sower.

* * *

A Note on the Selection of the Logia Analyzed

The criteria for selecting the logia to be studied in this work have been chosen independent of, and prior to, the search of mysticism in them.

The logia containing *psuchê, metanoia,* and *pneuma* are complete representations of the respective terms in the Gospels. Those with *ekstasis* include the whole NT. The logia with *basileia tou theou* (the Kingdom of God) are selected on the criteria of being non-eschatological and non-secular (see page 98 note 3).

CHAPTER TWO
In Search of Mysticism: Framing the Concept

Let Thy wish become my desire,
Let Thy will become my deed,
Let Thy word become my speech, Beloved,
And Thy love become my creed.

Let my plant bring forth Thy flowers,
Let my fruits produce Thy seed,
Let my heart become Thy lute, Beloved,
And my body Thy flute of reed.[1]

Introduction: What is Mysticism?

If one is looking for mysticism in the logia of Jesus, the first question to answer is, what is mysticism. Quite often it is considered a peak experience of union, unity, being unified, at another level of consciousness than the ordinary, a one-time event, often not repeatable, reserved as it were for some individuals: an experience beyond presence. I want to challenge this position on at least two principal points because this view is one-sided and does not do justice to a wider sense of mysticism. One point is, though recognizing the peak experience as the most outstanding characteristic of mysticism, to see that experiences also appear at different and 'lower' levels of consciousness. Consciousness may transform at different levels, thus effecting an awareness of presence on some level of consciousness. Moreover, and that is the other point, it is a path of development and a process of transformation of the self, rather than limiting it to a particular status of consciousness.

This chapter does not pretend to be a treatise on mysticism. The object is threefold: to begin mysticism is defined, succeeded by a search for key terms as signs of mysticism; third a reconnaissance of what is being said about mysticism in the Gospels follows.

The first objective is to try and answer a few questions. This step is accomplished in a concise exploration of the phenomenon, answering questions

---

A first draft was read at the EABS Meeting, section New Testament, Dresden 2005.

1   Inayat Khan, *The Dance of the Soul: Vadan*, Delhi, Motilal Banarsidass 1993, 147. Also: idem, *Gayan, Vadan, Nirtan*, Barrie and Rockliff, London.

such as what mysticism is, and how it manifests itself. Is it a phenomenon of the psyche or of the spirit? How does it relate to religion? Is it knowledge, or experience, or a state of consciousness? If one seeks for literature, one will find three types of publications: theoretical statements *on* mysticism, reports relating experiences *about* it, and statements that emanate *from* a mystic state but do not report about it: texts on, about, and from mysticism.

The second object is an exploration in 'publications on (section Handbooks) and in 'publications about' (section Testimonies) in order to find key terms that can function as signs of mysticism in logia.

The third object is an exploration of what has been said from mysticism in the Gospels and the logia.

Some Questions

When trying to define mysticism one needs wondering. When asking what mysticism is, one will find that it is difficult if not impossible to define it if one wants to do justice to the phenomenon.[2] Defining mysticism is an elusive enterprise, yet it is about a most essential endeavor of humanity. Here is what *Webster's* has to say.[3] It describes mysticism as an experience (sub 1) and as a theory (sub 2)—to both of which I subscribe—apart from sometimes being understood as just a vague speculation (sub 3)—which I reject as being pseudo-mysticism. Experience refers to "mystical union or direct communion with ultimate reality reported by mystics." Theory refers to the idea that "direct knowledge of God, of spiritual truth, of ultimate reality or comparable matters is attainable through immediate intuition, insight, or illumination and in a way differing from ordinary sense perception or ratiocination." Elsewhere[4] it is said that "[m]ysticism is the study of ways in which the largely hidden aspects of God's nature have been approached and understood". And: "…the nature of divine truths, which are both abstract and personal [!], tend to elude clear definition and objective research." That is enough to start with, provided one keeps in mind that speaking about mysticism cannot be but by stammering[5].

Its manifestation

Mysticism may present itself in, and to, the individual in two ways. One is a spontaneous manifestation of spirit: the way that is generally known as mysticism through the testimonies of the 'recognized' mystics when they speak

---

2   McGinn 1991 argues in a consistent way throughout the 600 odd pages that defining mysticism is an elusive enterprise.
3   *Webster's Third New International Dictionary*, 3 vols,
4   John Bowden, *Christianity: the complete guide*. 2005, 817.
5   Erik van Ruysbeek, *Mystiek en mysterie*, 1992 (Mysticism and mystery).

of a state of elevated consciousness. The other is going the Path, a gradual discovery of both the great Presence and of one's inner self. This does not happen but through processes of gradual transformation. All this involves an active managing of the psyche, in an involved relationship with the spirit so as to create conditions for the spirit to manifest transformation. On the other side, spirit, when manifesting itself, transforms the psyche spontaneously. It is an intertwining process: a psycho-spiritual process.[6]

Mysticism is getting to 'know' the Presence, inside, outside, beyond, the All, the One. This process of 'knowing' that surpasses rationality[7] as the ultimate criterion, is a process of evolving consciousness, necessarily implying transformations of the psyche as the human instrument of mind and heart.[8] *Mysticism thus is not a tradition, it is an actual real fresh phenomenon, each time a person experiences a Presence—inside, outside, beyond—and a Transformation of self.* Presence, here to be understood as numinous,[9] as a divine presence.

What about the psyche?

The title of this book,—*A Psycho-Spiritual View on the Message of Jesus in the Gospels: Presence and Transformation in Some Logia as a Sign of Mysticism*—announces as its main topic the development of a psycho-spiritual view (on the Message of Jesus). What is psycho-spiritual? What is its relation with mysticism? What is spirituality?[10] What has it to do with the psyche? The sayings of Jesus, the logia, exhibit a clear call for transformation, often implicit and sometimes

---

6 Pike, *Mystic Union* (1992) speaks of mysticism as spiritual closeness [Presence!], and differentiates between the prayer of quiet, the prayer of full union, and rapture. Prayer, obviously to be understood as an inner realization, sort of meditation. He refers to 'recollection as prayer.' Interestingly, I add, this is similar to the Islamic remembrance, dhikr or zikr (p. 1).

7 Is mysticism subject to rationality? In case one cannot explain religion or mysticism rationally, one must accept that these are experiential existential realities (Michiel Leezenberg 2007, on ratio and religion).

8 Knowing and knowledge on an altered state of consciousness refer to *gnosis*. Gnosticism claims the term *gnosis* as a sort of technical term. However, it should be understood in a wider and more basic sense: inner knowledge. It is frequent in the Gospels and an important term in the writings of Paul and should be understood in this spiritual sense. Whilst it is accepted as 'knowledge' in the NT, in the same breath it is rejected as 'gnosis' in extra-canonical works.

9 *Webster's:* As adjective, sub 2: "filled with a sense of the presence of divinity: holy." It even mentions the transubstantiation during Mass as numinous. As noun: "an unseen but majestic presence." The *Webster's* seems to display spiritual insight.

10 Spirituality is the wider term and consequently less concentrated than mysticism. Besides being used at random in New Age circles it includes rituals, doctrines, confession, a community, but not necessarily the individual's going the Path towards realization.

explicit. They indicate what is to be transformed is the psyche, but in a framework of spirituality.

Part III will take the psyche as its subject where it will be argued that the Greek *psuchê* often stands for 'psyche' rather than for 'life,' for 'self' or as a pronoun. There is an overall agreement that the human being is a complete and indivisible whole, in the tradition of most of the OT. In intertestamental times, however, the idea spread that man is constituted of body and psyche (and optionally: spirit). It is to be found in the Gospels (see Part III), in the Epistles, and certainly in Apostolic Fathers, like Origen.[11] Here is a concise overview of the use of *psuchê* in the Epistles quoted. Particularly challenging are the pericopes where *psuchê* stands combined with *pneuma* and/or *soma / sarx*.

Psuchê as mind, or heart, or psyche, or soul: Eph 6.6 (heart), Col 3.23 (put yourselves [soul] into it), 1 Th 2.8 (our own selves [minds]), Hebr 6.19 (hope as an anchor of the soul), 10.39 (I prefer my "who are of faith for securing the psyche" over NSAV's "those who have faith and so are saved", 13.7 ("keeping watch over your souls").

Psuchê with *pneuma*: 1 Cor 15.45,[12] Phil 1.27b,[13] Hebr 4.12 (dividing soul from spirit),

---

11 Origen (ca 185–ca 251) distinguishes three levels in the human: body, soul, and spirit. One's level of consciousness (level of anagogic reading, ascension to God) defines the level of interpretation of the text. Origen discloses some of the essentials of the mystic path. "Following the formula of St. Paul, Origen thus identifies three levels in the human person—body, soul, and spirit—and sees the true relation of these three components realized through personal appropriation of the scriptural message at three levels. The encounter with the text provides the spiritual education by which we reach the true goal of life." Thus, Origen seems to suggest that understanding of scripture implies doing so on all three levels. This means that a person must develop step by step in a process of spiritual education to reach the true goal of life. The first level consists in determining the literal sense of the words, both grammatically and in terms of historical reality. Even the grammatical meaning "carries a deeper message for the believers" [!]. According to Origen, there is "the necessity to move beyond the 'letter that kills' to the second level (corresponding to the soul) for the moral meaning and to the third level (corresponding to the spirit) for the mystical meaning of the scriptures." The teaching is through the Logos. Origen "is the first Christian to describe the personal appropriation of the teaching of the Logos as an anagogic reading, one designed to lift the soul above. (…) The goal of interpretation is to realize the Bible's teaching through one's own ascension to God, a process that Origen once expressed as wishing 'to gallop through the vast spaces of mystic and spiritual understanding' (Commentary on Romans 7.11)." Based on Bernard McGinn, Patricia McGinn, *Early Christian Mystics* 2003, p. 24f. See also B. McGinn, *The Presence of God*, 1991.

12 "… became a living being [soul],…became a life-giving spirit." There is more to it. V.4a *speiretai sôma psuchikon, egeiretai sôma pneumatikon* (NRSV: it is sown a physical body, it is raised a spiritual body, where NRSV translates the *psuchikon* as physical where the Greek says psychic. Paul makes clear that the two bodies are juxtaposed: "If there is a physical body there is also a spiritual body" (v. 44b). Seemingly Paul puts it in a temporal perspective, but spiritually it can be understood in terms of self-development. Paul juxtaposes spirit and psyche (dichotomy) more often, e.g., when speaking of *psuchikoi* and *pneumatikoi*: people who live in their psyche versus those who live in their spirit (1 Cor 2.14–16). A little further

Psuchê with *soma / sarx*: 1 Cor 3.1, 3 (you as spiritual people versus people of the flesh[14])

Psuchê together with *soma* and *pneuma*: 1 Thess 5.23[15]

NOTE. Left out are those cases where *psuchê* obviously stands for life or indicates a personal pronoun. Translations are NRSV unless otherwise indicated. Square brackets indicate my preference.

What do we find? The sources that were consulted confirm the human being as an integral whole, yet consisting of parts that can be discerned clearly: body, psyche (mind), and spirit, each with clearly different functions. Challenging would it be to find out their relationships further. Here it would lead too far. The dual combinations in the presentation above might suggest that other combinations are implied. *Psuchê* combines with *pneuma* as it does with *sarx / soma*, and there is one case where the three are related.[16]

This exposition forms a background to find out if *psuchê* and *pneuma* are present in the logia of Jesus, and if it can be made plausible. This enterprise is quite precarious in that the general understanding is that spirit is not a component of the human being, and *psuchê* stands for the complete human being. Throughout this book, these concepts will be explored, mainly in the form of the terms *psuchê* and *pneuma*, respectively. Jesus' announcements of the Kingdom as the Message will be another essential concept on the way of understanding the mysticism of Jesus.

It therefore is proposed to view mysticism primarily as the psycho-spiritual path towards God, a process of a growing awareness of God's presence in the world, in nature, in humanity, in a person, beyond and yet present, around, above, outside, inside, unseen yet to be seen, unheard yet to be heard. In other words, it is a process where *psuchê* and *pneuma* are intertwined. Is this what mysticism generally may be considered to be? Is this view compatible with the teachings of Jesus? The answer is yes when one looks at Jesus in his unitary relation to God. However, how can mysticism and Jesus be aligned? People have

---

he completes it to a trichotomy when writing to the brothers "as to sarkics (*sarnikoi, sarkikoi*)(i.e., of the flesh), those immature in Christ". (1 Cor 3.1–33). Both adjectives (*sarnikos, sarkikos*) stand for "being material or belonging to the physical realm, material, physical, human, fleshly; pertaining to being human at a disappointing level of behavior or characteristics" (BDAG).

13 "… standing firm in one spirit, striving…with one mind …."
14 V. 3.3: "as long as there is jealousy and quarreling among you are you not of the flesh, …?"
15 "May your spirit and soul and body be kept sound (or: complete) and blameless."
16 Teresa of Ávila, the great 16th c mystic, speaks of two inhabitants of the interior castle, one is God, the other the soul: "God (in noncorporeal form) and soul are both within the soul" (Pyke *Mystic Union* 8). She differentiates between the soul as a domain, an abiding place, and the soul as an entity, the essential part of the soul . According to Christian doctrine, the latter is the entity that departs from the body at death and remains elsewhere forever more (ibid., 6). Here is a text of a recognized Christian mystic who recognizes the divine in the human.

often recoiled from making the relation explicit. The alignment has frequently and enduringly been seen as a *contradictio in terminis*: the two do not go together. In my view this attitude is the result of misunderstanding mysticism. It has often and consistently been seen as something foreign, beyond reality, either as a peak experience or even as a psychiatric aberration. Even more important, doctrines and the Church have often excluded even the possibility for a human being to come so close to God. The chasm between God and the fallen Adam is unbridgeable for human initiative, it says. Apart from that, it is significant that all major works on mysticism fail to recognize the mysticism of and in the message of Jesus.[17]

Religion and consciousness[18]

It is often said that mysticism is the heart of religion, indeed of all religions,[19]

---

17   Quarles 2005 explores Jesus as a *merkabah* mystic. This idea reflects a concept of mysticism that is not the one I adopt in this study. Even if this type of mysticism were in existence and practiced in the first century—no conclusive evidence is available—(page 10) one does not (in my opinion) find indications in the Jesus logia.
18   McGinn 1991 (*Foundations*, Appendix, 265–343) offers a few insights (his page numbers in brackets):
   - Rudolf Otto (*Das Heilige*, 1917) "comes close to identifying mysticism if not with the core at least with the acme or goal of religion [!] (327).
   - The essence of religion is identical to the mystical: Schuon, *The Transcendent Unity of Religions*, 1984, Huston Smith, *Forgotten Truth*, 1976, Seyyed Hossein Nasr, *Knowledge and the Sacred*, 1981 (331).
   - Freud expresses about the same: the 'oceanic feeling' of the mystic and novelist Romain Rolland constitutes the essence of religion (332).
   - Gerardus van der Leeuw, the great Dutch scholar of the phenomenology of religion (*Phänomenologie der Religion*, 1933), saw mysticism as a universal phenomenon, "one of the forms of inward action demonstrating the reciprocal operation of the subject and object of religion ..." (333).
   - Gershom Sholem (*Major Trends in Jewish Mysticism*, New York 1961) quotes Rufus Jones who defined mysticism as "the type of religion which puts emphasis on immediate awareness of relation with God." He refuses to restrict mysticism to the experience of union with God (334–35), to which I of course fully agree.
   - Robert Zaehner, one of the great scholars in this field, seems to express the same, though differentiating between types of experience that seem to exclude one another, criticized by more unifying scholars like W. T. Stace, Ninian Smart, Ph. Almond (339).
   - For developments in mysticism see e.g. the current International Series in the Psychology of Religion. Two recent volumes are J. A. Beelzen, A. Geels, *Mysticism, a variety of psychological perspectives* 2003, and R. W. Hood Jr., *Dimensions of Mystical Experiences: Empirical Studies and Psychological Links* 2001.
   - For more, see McGinn's Appendix, and the overwhelming amount of literature that is published since last century.
      "Mysticism is at the root of all religion, and all the higher religions have their mystical expressions." It is the 'perennial philosophy' (F. C. Happold, *Mysticism: A Study and an*

and it is equally often denied. This denial may be radical: it is not religion. Or one says, it is an epiphenomenon only. Anyhow, it is a phenomenon that calls for attention: mysticism is a central issue in theology.[20] "Is a mystic religious? He is religious in the real sense of the word.... [M]ysticism is deeper than religion; in other words mysticism is the soul of religion. a person who follows a religion follows its form; the one who touches mysticism touches the spirit of religion. Religion with mysticism is living, without mysticism it is dead."[21] Mysticism is the nucleus of spirituality. The logia of Jesus are the heart of his message and thus are the guides on the path of finding spirituality. Religion, in the view entertained in this work, makes a call to humanity, both individually and at large, to become conscious of God, and to realize one's relation to him, a relationship that is both full of reverence and deeply intimate. Mysticism is both the path leading in that direction and its fulfillment. After all, it implies becoming aware of the divine. At each and every step on the path, in all stages, again and again this awareness increases in intensity. It leads to a rise of consciousness, to a widening and deepening of it. One becomes aware that there is more reality than what can be perceived through the senses. There is more than one experiences in one's emotions: expressions of the psyche. On the way, one may experience a gradual awakening to a reality beyond, and yet so near that it feels as immediate: expressions of the spirit. It is of a different dimension, a sort of presence, though one does not know of what. Gradually one may grasp that it is a manifestation of the realm of spirit, beyond the physical and beyond the psyche. Then the presence becomes Presence. What used to be experiences, when in the realms of body and psyche, is now perceived as a state of consciousness. Experience is temporal, whereas consciousness is more enduring. An experience finishes when the object passes. Consciousness when evoked by an internal or outer agent may remain after the agent is past. This state may be active, or it may be in the area where it slumbers in the active mind but reigns in the sub-active mind.[22] In this process one becomes aware of a reality more subtle than the senses can perceive. With the rising consciousness transformations start to take place. Transformation is the parole on this path. The mystic path is one of transformation. Some of these transformations come about by itself, without any action on the part of the subject. They will be of a spiritual nature. Others will happen only when the subject creates the necessary conditions for them to come about. They are on the level of the psyche: mind and heart. The effect is that the spirit can do its work.

Anthology, 1963). Huston Smith (2001, 28–29) describes vividly the natural longing for the Other, for expansion, and in all religions.

20 Karl Rahner and Hans Urs von Balthasar are in agreement regarding this question (McGinn, *Foundations*, 285–89).

21 Khan 1989, vol. XI 223.

22 See McGinn and Underhill later in this chapter. Borg, see ch. 4.

Is mysticism extra-worldly? Both tradition and history seem to affirm this question. Mystics often have sought solitude or communities apart from the world. Even so, how can one love God and deny one's fellow brothers and sisters? How can one strive after unity and dismiss one's fellow human? How can one experience presence and reject one's neighbor? As to the message of Jesus, it was pure mysticism, a mysticism of love: to judge no one, to forgive everyone, to develop that quality in oneself.[23]

Practice, therefore, has often been different. It will be our task to see what the logia can tell us about how mysticism in the world and in daily life may be a fruitful thing.

A Side-Remark

Some take mysticism primarily as vision mysticism, referring to the schools and traditions reporting about visions, like in Hellenism, in Plato's Phaidros, in Judaism (merkabah mysticism, the celestial journey. For example Paul (2 Cor 3.18): "the vision of the Glory initiates a metamorphosis into the divine likeness"; also other pericopes testify of 'being transformed in Christ'[24]). This is an important phenomenon. Yet, this vision mysticism is not its core. We do not find it but sporadically in the Gospels. The frequent call by Jesus to the right seeing does not, in my opinion, refer to vision mysticism, but to an inner maturing. It has always been tempting to address mysticism in terms of the book of Revelation with its imagery that tends to mythologizing.

Knowledge, Experience and Consciousness

When searching for the sense of mysticism, and before diving into the handbooks, the question arises if books are the right source to quench the thirst for this sort of knowledge. Libraries have been filled with books on mysticism. However, is mysticism to write or to philosophize about? Is it sensible to examine it systematically and rationally? Mysticism is the ultimate drive in humans to attain ultimate knowledge. Then, though, what is knowledge? In our cultures it goes without saying that knowledge is rational knowledge or knowledge acquired by experience through the five senses. It functions on the physicallevel. At the spiritual level it is experiential knowledge also, but in a state much deeper than the ordinary experience. It is a reality, which on its higher levels extends beyond feeling and even beyond emotion, yet as real as anything—a type of knowledge that transforms one's being. This is what the term gnosis (*gnôsis*) essentially tells.[25] It is being lifted to higher spheres,

---

23 Inayat Khan, in an unpublished paper on the Message from the 1920s
24 DeConick, *Voices of the Mystics*, 2001, 64 and elsewhere.
25 Gnosis is usually associated with gnosticism, a spiritual movement in the beginnings of the first millennium. It says it has the gnosis. And this is understood as to belong to gnosticism exclusively. My interpretation is that gnosticism is a system with a cosmos of myths, revelations, narratives, symbologies around the basic concept of *gnosis*—which in reality

ultimately meeting with the divine, uniting with the One, the All. From it springs the basic universal dynamic potentiality that is love—at the same time its motivating power. Mystics through the ages and cultures have found this encompassing power the essence of the new consciousness that came to them. This 'knowledge' is so intense and of such completely different nature that sometimes it was called 'the cloud of unknowing.'[26] "The true knowledge of God appears then as an unknowing."[27] Alternatively, "to know him through unknowing, in a union that rises above all intellect."[28] "Mysticism, therefore, may be considered as the essence of all knowledge," says a twentieth-century mystic.[29] The Gospel of John clarifies 'knowledge' by introducing 'sight,' "[s]eeing God, which is a special way of knowing him, is an essential part of John's message"[30]

Near-Death Experiences (NDE)

The introduction of consciousness rather than experience as the central term is of significance for understanding mysticism. In neuroscience and brain research, two closely related fields, consciousness is a hot issue but has not yet been explained, notwithstanding intense research projects the world over. From another scientific side new light is being thrown on what human consciousness is. In a major study in the medical field patients have been interrogated.[31] This was done after successful resuscitations following a cardiac arrest asking about what they remembered. It was found that they reported experiences precisely in the period they could not, due to their physical situation. That they could was highly remarkable as these experiences occurred precisely during the short period that the brain was absolutely inactive with a flat EEG: zero activity of the brain, no capacity of memory. Yet they report exceptional experiences, which have become known as near-death experiences (NDE), experiences that appear as if coming from a world beyond. These patients report experiences that are largely congruous with one another. But invariably the subjects make clear that what happened cannot be expressed adequately in words: ineffability. Herein there is striking similarity with testimonies of mystics: an intense supernatural light, a powerful awareness of peace and happiness, a 'knowing' beyond the senses. The reports of these patients have caused some scientists to conclude that human consciousness can operate outside the brain, at the moment that the brain cannot function in any way. Yet that

---

refers to the realized awareness of God, or the Spirit. In gnosticism, this concept has been moved to the background.
26 An anonymous 14th c English book. It stands in the tradition of negative theology. Cf Pseudo-Dionysius the Areopagite, and of John of the Cross' dark night.
27 Clément 1982, 231, referring to Augustine.
28 Dionysius the Areopagite, *Divine Names* VII,3 (PG 3,872) quoted by Clément 231.
29 Khan 1989 vol. X, 13.
30 McGinn 76.
31 Pim van Lommel, "Near-Death Experiences in Survivors of Cardiac Arrest: A Prospective Study in the Netherlands," *The Lancet* 358 (2001), 2039–45. The article has been expanded to a book as *Consciousness beyond life*, 2010 (forthcoming in German, French and others). Original title *Eindeloos Bewustzijn*, 2007.

brain, or is it the mind?, remembers what had happened during that period of zero activity. Others remain skeptical, like so many rationalists' attitude towards mysticism.

Closely related is a study by Arie Bos[32]. He discusses the position of mystical experiences in relation to science and to consciousness. How does self-consciousness relate to expanded consciousness?

Three Types of Text

How can one become acquainted with mysticism? Where can one read about it? Or rather, where can one 'read mysticism,' a direct experience? As mentioned earlier, three fields present themselves, yet they are three very different types of texts that may instruct one in mysticism.

- The first type includes treatises *on* mysticism. Typically they are written by an author who is not a mystic; some cases will be treated below (Handbooks). These books provide important materials to acknowledge the keywords we are seeking.
- The second type contains what generally is called mystical texts, it reports *about* mysticism. Here one will find testimonies of mystics who tell us of their experiences, of what happened to them in their higher states of consciousness. These are testimonies of mysticism.
- The third type is very different. It is not literature explaining mysticism, nor does it testify of experiences and or of states of consciousness. These texts contain 'words' originating in the source of mysticism directed to an audience, often 'disciples.' They originate from a mystic consciousness, pronounced from a deep awareness of presence. They do not speak about mysticism or states of consciousness: they originate *from* mysticism. What is their goal? They are aimed at calling others to understand Reality. It is a reminder of what may be concealed in a hidden state of consciousness. At the same time a push to move forward, a stimulus to transform, a call to open up, a call to recognize the Kingdom of God, here and now, inside as well as outside. Such, I have found, are many of the 'words' of Jesus, the logia, it is a revelation of the Logos in human terms in order to make it understandable and manageable for humans. That is the hypothesis underlying this work. If we find the key concepts, still to be identified, in some of the words of Jesus, then we may conclude to find mysticism in his Message.

Mysticism often has been seen as something extraneous, even as magic. The Church has seen it as heterodox now and then. It would not harmonize with the catechism. *Sola scriptura* was seen as opposed to experience and to raising the consciousness while taking Scripture in a literary sense. *Sola fide* on the other hand tended to neglect the sacred word; the words of the confession are taken for faith. Bultmann for example rejects mysticism, as by faith (*Glauben*) alone is it possible that one is drawn to God or Christ[33]. Faith, then, is menaced when reduced to testifying an ideology.

---

32 Arie Bos, *Hoe de stof de geest kreeg*, Zeist 2008 (the evolutionary relation between matter, mind, and spirit).
33 Bultmann 1948, 437. Also 312, 328, 403.

However, in our societies there is a strong upward surge of the spirit. Mysticism increasingly is viewed as a spiritual reality, and already for decades. Attention is increasing. Nevertheless wide circles have constantly rejected it as either just religious, or something contrary to religion. It was not accepted, and this is continuing. That is the case for many Christian denominations, especially Protestantism,[34] as well as for many advocates of contemporary Enlightenment and Modernism, in the sense of absolute rationality. The acceptance, however, does not stretch to include the Gospels or the logia. In this book it will be shown that central concepts of mysticism do figure in these texts. They even can be interpreted to form a key to an alternative understanding of the logia.

The 'Handbooks'[35]

> *Out of the united (Einigen) comes the One only (Einzige),*
> *Out of the All-One (All-einigen) the Alone (Allein-ige)…*
> *The relationship of original immanence…passes,*
> *And is transformed into complete transcendence.*[36]

The first work to be consulted is McGinn's masterly work,[37] the first volume dating from 1991 on the origins of (Western) Christian mysticism. He, rightly

---

34 Peter Hicks makes a good case in favor of mysticism in Protestantism ("Fathoming the Unfathomable," in: Partridge and Gabriel, *Mysticisms* 342
35 Some other valuable titles on mysticism, in a subjective selection, and in random order:
 - J. de Marquette, *Introduction à la mystique comparée*, 1956. English edition *Introduction to Comparative Mysticism*, Duncan 1948.
 - O. Clément, *The roots of Christian Mysticism: text and commentary*, New City, London etc. 1993, 1994. Originally in French: *Sources*, 1982.
 - Bruno Borchert, *Mystiek: Geschiedenis en uitdaging* (Mysticism: history and challenge), 1989.
 - Albert Schweitzer, *Die Mystik des Apostel Paulus*, 1980.
 - Dorothee Sölle, *Mystik und Widerstand*, 1997.
 - J. Baars et al. (eds), *Encyclopedie van de Mystiek*, 2003.
 - Inayat Khan, *Philosophy, Psychology, Mysticism*, 1990. Also by Barrie&Rockliff, 1964.
 - Boris Todoroff, *Een verlangen naar eenheid*, 2006 (A longing for unity).
 - April D. DeConick, *Voices of the Mystics*, 2001.
 - Richard Woods (ed), *Understanding Mysticism*, 1980, a rich and multi-faceted reader by important authors, like Underhill (1911), Zaehner, Staal (1975), Scholem (1961), William James (1902), Deikman, Bergson, Auden, and many others.
 - Christopher Partridge and Theodore Gabriel (ed), *Mysticism East and West: Studies in Mystical Experience*, 2003.
36 Rudolf Otto, *Mysticism East and West*, New York 1932, p. 52 / *West-östliche Mystik*, Gotha 1926, p. 69. Quoted by Steven T. Katz (ed), *Mysticism and Religious Traditions*, 1983, p. 198.

in my view, refuses to define mysticism. Indeed, one of the primary characteristics of mystical consciousness is its ineffability.[38] How then is this state to be described? And, a fortiori, how to capture mysticism in all its width and depth by words? He (p. xix) offers a good start when describing (not: defining) mysticism "as involving an immediate consciousness of the presence of God." This is "a central claim that appears in almost all mystical texts." "[T]heir mode of access to God is radically different from that found in ordinary consciousness, even from the awareness of God gained through the usual religious activities of prayer, sacraments, and other rituals" because these are "not in any direct and immediate fashion."

McGinn effectively proposes to rather call such experiential knowledge a state of raised consciousness, "the consciousness of divine presence."[39] He calls it "some of the major issues that govern the account of mysticism." He objects to calling it just experience, as this however intense is passing: experience is a something that one *has* rather than *being* it. Consciousness is a state of being where one *is*, with which one identifies completely. It is a presence. Here we find one of the key-concepts of this book: Presence.

So, mysticism is a state, a condition, and of the highest sort? Yes, but it is much vaster. Otherwise, if presented in this way, it would preclude the *path towards* that state of consciousness and thus not include other states of consciousness somewhere between the normal consciousness based on conceiving by the senses and controlled by rationality. Therefore, the concept of transformation would wrongly be missing.

Evelyn Underhill

Quite different is Evelyn Underhill's classic *Mysticism* of 1911, reprinted time and again.[40] She describes mysticism as "the nature and *development* [emphasis added] of man's spiritual consciousness [!!]" (the subtitle of her book). Thus, it belongs to human nature, yet needs to be developed in the individual, like other faculties, in a process of transformation. Alternatively, in her more elaborate definition (p.xiv), "[Mysticism is] the expression of the *innate tendency* (italics, WvL) of the human spirit towards complete harmony with the transcendental

---

37　Bernard McGinn, *The Foundations of Mysticism: Origins to the Fifth Century*, part of a four-volume series *The Presence of God: a History of Western Mysticism*. Crossroad, New York 1991–2002.
38　James, *Varieties*, 380.
39　McGinn, xiii
40　Evelyn Underhill, *Mysticism: a Study of the Nature and Development of Man's Spiritual Consciousness*, Methuen, London 1911/1960. Latest publication as *Mysticism, the Nature and Development of Spiritual Consciousness*, OneWorld, Oxford 1999. She wrote proficiently on the subject.

order; whatever be the theological formula under which that is understood…"; "…and in the experience called 'mystic union', it attains its end." "…this is a genuine life process and not an intellectual speculation…." One of the main characteristics of the mystical consciousness is "[a] joyous apprehension of the Absolute, 'the practice of the Presence of God'" (240 and *passim*). Sometimes, she tells, the mystic experience occurs all of a sudden, God's grace descending, the divine presence enveloping. It is a 'peak experience.' Thus mystical texts are often reflections of such an experience.

However, mostly mysticism is a gradual process rather than a rare summit experience, a view adopted rather generally.[41] What counts is the process of transformation on the spiritual level, of development (Underhill, quoted above), a process of alternating phases of light and shade, in various intensities. What is needed also is an appropriate psychological make-up, a transformation of the 'self' into the 'Self'. It starts as transformation on the level of the psyche (91, 402, 413ff). Mysticism covers all phases of this inner development. She proves mysticism to be a universal religious, spiritual phenomenon that is rooted in the human soul. Moreover, mysticism contains a practical approach to living a spiritual life, even while living a worldly life at the same time, when we are capable of building "the soul's house, that interior dwelling-place which we all possess, for the upkeep of which we are responsible—a place in which we can meet God" (*The Essentials*,[42] p. 187). Cf Paul: "Do you not know that you are God's temple and that God's Spirit dwells in you?" (1 Cor 3.16).

Thus, the two key concepts of presence and transformation are found in her penetrating rendering.

William James[43]

The reason to include the medical doctor, philosopher, and psychologist William James in our argument is his recognition of the genuineness of the mystic experience though on the other hand classifying it among the various religious experiences on the human level. Essential to him is the awareness of the consciousness as a "sudden realization of the immediate presence of God" (393); it is the paramount state of mystical consciousness. "[T]o the medical mind these ecstasies—he refers to experiences of Teresa of Avila—signify nothing but suggested and imitated hypnoid states, on an intellectual basis of superstition, and a corporeal one of degeneration and hysteria" (413). They may appear like

---

41　E.g., "Spiritual union with the divine" (Everett Ferguson (ed), *Encyclopedia of Early Christianity*, Garland, New York / London 1990, 632); further abbreviated as EEC.
42　Evelyn Underhill, *The essentials of mysticism and other essays*, 1995.
43　William James, *The Varieties of Religious Experience: A Study in Human Nature*, 1902; here: Penguin Classics 1985. His lectures are contemporaneous with Von Harnack (see chapter 4), which also are favorable about the genuineness of mysticism.

that, he says, but one should "inquire into their fruits of life"(413), such as the soul rendered more energetic, optimism prevails, a reconciling mood, a unifying tendency, a tendency to the 'yes-function', a consciousness that is passing from less to more, from smallness into vastness, from unrest to rest, and finally overcoming the usual barriers between the individual and the Absolute (415f), a description that reminds one of the near-death experiences. This text represents the concept of transformation, whilst the earlier quote signalizes the concept of presence.

James again mistakes mysticism as only the absolute culminating top experience, whilst it is of paramount importance to include in the term the mystic path, the development of human nature toward this expansion of consciousness. Musing about the reality of such experiences, he suggests that one should entertain the supposition that "mystical states may…possibly be such superior points of view, windows through which the mind looks out upon a more extensive and inclusive world" (428). He concludes that these experiences are absolutely authoritative for the individual to whom these states come. But outsiders of such experience need not accept any of these uncritically. However, these states "break down the authority of the non-mystical or rationalistic consciousness, based upon the understanding and the senses only. They show it to be only one kind of consciousness" (422–23). Some of these characteristics are of importance for our argument. One is the ineffability of mystical states: they cannot be said. Two is the noetic quality: mystical states are also states of knowledge (380).

James makes clear that there is no comparison whatsoever with pathological states of consciousness or with those brought about by intoxicants. They are, in my terminology, wrong workings of the physical and of the psychic consciousness, respectively.

Some Testimonies

Here are some of the expressions of the second type text on mysticism: testimonies of mystics about that state of consciousness. Many of these I have selected from an anthology of early Christian mysticism texts, collected by Olivier Clément[44]. He has brought together many convincing sources from early Christianity. I give a few quotations from his chapter on 'enstasy-ecstasy' (pp. 230–269).

- Augustine (354–430)
  God is both within and high:

---

44 Clément 1982.

Augustine (*Confessiones*): "*Tu autem, Domine, eras interior intimo meo et superior summo meo*" (But Thou, Lord, wast more within me than my innermost being, and higher than my highest being [trans., WvL]. "God who is inaccessible and quite suddenly perceptible to the heart with an overwhelming immediacy...glimpsed as an 'abyss of inner joy' and as the Other, as my Creator, in whose presence I am and who is speaking to me." (quoted by Clément 230–231)

- Gregory of Nissa (331/40–ca. 395)
  God's energy is within. See in yourself the One you are seeking (*Homilies on the Beatitudes, 6*)
  He discloses the source of this energy: "He who formed you put in your being an immense power. ... he enclosed in you the image of his perfection." "... the inward part of the personality ..., once rid of the rust that hid its beauty, will rediscover the first likeness and be real.... So when people look at themselves they will see in themselves the One they are seeking.... When the sun is looked at in a mirror...the sun's brightness is seen in the mirror exactly as if the sun's disc itself were being looked at.... The divine image will shine brightly in us in Christ Jesus our Lord..." (quoted by Clément 237). Clément comments that although the essence of God is inaccessible that very essence is made inexhaustibly capable of being shared in (237).

- Pseudo-Dionysius the Areopagite (fl. 500) and Maximus the Confessor (580–662), as summarized by Clément:
  "God is altogether shared and altogether unshareable" (238).

- Pseudo-Dionysius the Areopagite (in a summary by Clément): "all 'essence' is surpassed, by God in a 'trans-descent', by the human being in a 'trans-ascent'. There is now only an inexpressible communion of persons" (247).

- Ignatius of Antioch (early 2nd c), speaks about the 'abiding' or 'indwelling' of God in us. His 'indwelling' makes us temples of God. (Clément 249).

- "The spiritual homeland...is within. The sun that shines there is the light of the Trinity." (Isaac of Niniveh (d. ca. 700), *Ascetic Treatises*) (253).

- "... as soon as He came within He roused my sleeping soul, He stirred and softened and wounded my heart, for it was hard and stony and poor in health" (Bernard de Clairvaux, 1090–1153).[45]

- Into my heart's night / Along a narrow way / I groped; and lo! the light / An infinite land of day. (Jelaluddin Rumi, 1207–1273).[46]

- Oh night that was my guide!   *!Oh noche que guiaste!;*
  oh night dearer than the morning's pride, *!oh noche amable másque la alborada!;*
  oh night that joined   *!oh noche che juntaste*
  Beloved to beloved   *Amado con amada,*
  transfiguring beloved into the Beloved.   *amada en el Amado transformada!*
                       (Juan de la Cruz)[47]

---

45 From his *Sermon on the Song of Songs* (Happold 1963, 205).
46 In F. C. Happold, 1963, 227.
47 In F. C. Happold,, 1963, 326. Spanish original in *Fuente*, 1991, 38. Translation partly mine, WvL.

- Consider the treasure thou hast within thee; the Saviour of the world, the eternal Word of God lies hid in thee, as a spark of the divine nature which is to…generate the life of Heaven again in thy soul.

  For this turning to the light and Spirit of God within thee is thy only true turning to God; there is no other way of finding Him but in that place where He dwelleth in thee (William Law).[48]

- Dieu incline le coeur de ceux qu'Il aime.
  Deus inclinat corda eorum.
  Celui qui L'aime.
  Celui qu'Il aime.

  (Blaise Pascal)[49]

- Nature is an infinite sphere of which the center is everywhere and the circumpherence is nowhere

  (Blaise Pascal)[50]

'Of the Eternal Birth'
"The soul that would experience this birth must detach herself from all outward things: within herself completely at one with herself…You must have an exalted mind and a burning heart in which, nevertheless, reign silence and stillness."

(Meister Eckhart)[51]

From these few references we learn that essential concepts were engrained in (early) Christianity, like 'the divine being is close to the human being', or the possibility to experience the fullness of divine presence, and the need to transform in order to be prepared as well as becoming transformed by that very presence.

Thus, apart from presence, these mystics have endowed us with precious testimonies about transformation, often in the form of instructions and admonitions. The essence is to transform mind and heart, purifying them to the effect of being in a condition to perceive the spirit. Clément offers another impressive anthology in his chapter 'Passions transfigured, thought transcended' (166–77).

Now a few modern statements, taken at random from the huge amount of information (some with comments by this author).

> My device—if any
> *Numen semper adest.*
> In that case: if uneasy—why?
> Dag Hammerskjöld[52]

---

48 William Law (1686–1762), *The Spirit of Prayer*. In F. C. Happold 1963, 346.
49 *Pensées*, Livre de Poche 1962, 440. In his handwritten text this saying was scratched out.
52 Quoted in Laurent Dick, *Antarctica,* Tielt: Lannoo 2008, without reference..
51 Quoted by Dag Hammerskjöld 1964, dated Christmas Day, December 25, 1956. He was UNO Secretary General

What follows is in German: Buber's language is a gem itself:

> Das Grundwort Ich-Es ist nicht vom Übel—wie die Materie nicht vom Übel ist. Es ist vom Übel—wie die Materie, die sich anmasst, das Seiende zu sein. Wenn der Mensch es walten lässt, überwuchert ihn die unablässig wachsende Eswelt, entwirklicht sich ihm das eigene Ich, bis der Alp über ihm und das Gespenst in ihm einander das Geständnis ihrer Unerlöstheit zuraunen.
>
> Martin Buber[53]

> To experience the attraction of God, to be sensible of the beauty…is the highest and…the most complete of our 'passivities of growth.'
>
> Teilhard de Chardin[54]

> Yes, Lord, not only the ray that strikes the surface, but the ray that penetrates, not only your Epiphany, Jesus, but your *diaphany*.
>
> Teilhard de Chardin[55]

The (revolutionary) Roman-Catholic catechism of 1966 (!), related to Vaticanum II, published by the Dutch bishops[56] has some amazingly similar answers. It says that in the mystic prayer one experiences "the nearness of God's power and love." It is a radiant presence, a 'sublime commonness.'[57]

Teresa of Avila is quoted saying that we may imagine inner man as a castle whose central room, located at the deepest level, is where God is living. There one is permeated with the silent knowing that God is within you. At the same time you are living in the earthly reality that has become magnificent realizing that God is the ineffable heart of all reality (Catechismus 1966, 374).[58] The question if mysticism is also for the common man or woman is answered in the affirmative.

---

52 Hammerskjöld 1964, dated November 17, 1956.. Published by Faber & Faber, London 1964.
53 *Ich und Du*, Philipp Reclam jun,, Stuttgart 1983, 1995, 44.
54 Teilhard de Chardin, *The Divine Milieu* 1960, 131.
55 Ibid.
56 *De nieuwe catechismus* , Hilversum: Brand1966, 373f .
57 I have searched in vain the present official Vatican catechism for similar expressions. Section 2014—the only one mentioned in the subject index related to mysticism—mentions union with Christ only; its working is through the sacraments specifically; and it is suggested that it is granted to some only (*Catechism of the Catholic Church*, London 1994/2003).
58 Quoted literally: "… de allerhoogste gebedsgenade…[is] een sublieme gewoonheid [nl zonder symptomen, of zonder er betekenis aan de hechten]. Teresa van Avila heeft een boek geschreven, waarin de innerlijke mens wordt voorgesteld als een kasteel met zeven verblijven. Verblijf na verblijf voert dieper en dieper naar de zevende kamer, waar God—dat is Christus—woont. Zijn aanwezigheid is in heel het kasteel te bespeuren, maar ben je in dat midden gekomen, diep in je eigen werkelijkheid, dan word je geheel doorstroomd van het stille gevoel dat God in je is. Je leeft in de aardse werkelijkheid, die prachtig is geworden omdat je beseft dat God het onuitsprekelijke hart van alle werkelijkheid is."

The great mystics have worded it in a way that has brought mankind to the awareness of the divine presence. Essential is that the experience will be integrated in one's life—a life that may be transformed by the light discovered. Mysticism is the mystic *way*.

- Bruno Borchert, a contemporary Dutch mystic, in his excellent overview of mysticism[59], obviously inspired by his own experiences, stresses the essential nature of mysticism. The yearning of the soul is universal. Mostly it is covered and remains unaware, but it may break out and reach a peak experience when brought into contact with the divine, within or without, in nature or in church. At the same time it brought about the great misunderstanding that mysticism is a rarity, only granted to some souls who are the beloveds of God. Others have concluded that it is human madness, a psychiatric illness. Yet it is a universal human capacity, laid down in everyone's heart as a potentiality to be awakened. Essential is that the experience does not remain isolated and momentary, but will be integrated in one's life—a life that may be transformed by the light discovered. That one is capable of rooting the experience in one's mind, heart and body. Mysticism is the mystic *way*.

- Friedrich Heiler[60]: "Das ganze Leben ist (für die grossen Frommen) 'ein einziges zusammenhängendes grosses Gebet (*mia sunaptomenê euchê*), wie ein schönes Wort des Origenes lautet'"(1923, 223-4; Origenes *De or.,* I,12).

    In his classic on prayer he defines the mystic prayer as the culmination of prayer: "die selbstvergessene, in Gott versunkene Anbetung" (p.46). Although not speaking specifically about mystics, what mysticism is about is expressed by Heiler, though he pays little attention to mysticism in the NT. He is of the opinion that Christian mysticism is formed under the influence of neo-platonism and of Pseudo Dionysios (233). Although he does justice to mysticism as such he nevertheless dichotomizes mysticism and the 'prophetische Frommigkeit', trying to emphasize the differences rather than showing how the two both balance and complement each other (248–283).

    Although he suggests that mysticism is static as compared to the dynamics of the personal-prophetic religious practice, in the table on mystic prayer (312-3) it is obvious that mystic practice is characterized by development rather than by either a static being-in-oneself or by momentary ecstatic eruptions. This dynamics of the mystic path gradually integrating the somatic, the psychic and the spiritual is the main characteristic of genuine mysticism. This is the mysticism of Jesus walking on the earth, of Paul, of the great religious geniuses.

- Albert Schweitzer in his 1930 book on the mysticism of Paul[61] indicates mysticism as follows: "wo ein Menschenwesen die Trennung zwischen irdisch und überirdisch, zeitlich und ewig als überwunden ansieht und sich selber, noch in dem Irdischen und Zeitlichen stehend, als zum Überirdischen und Ewigen eingegangen erlebt" (p.1).

    Also Schweitzer does not take pains to see whether the synoptic Gospels contain mysticism. In his first chapter he makes clear how important mysticism is in religion, and how it penetrates even 'the originally naive-dualistic Christianity, and then refers to the

---

59 Bruno Borchert, *Mystiek: geschiedenis en uitdaging* ('Mysticism: history and challenge'), 1989.
60 Friedrich Heiler, *Das Gebet* 1923, 5 ('Prayer: a study in the history and psychology of religion').
61 Albert Schweitzer, *Die Mystik des Apostel Paulus*, 1980.

well-known Christian mystics of all ages. His book focuses on the mysticism of Paul and wonders about its special character as it does not focus on God but on Christ as a means to communicate with God. Paul is the only one who knows only Christ mysticism and no God mysticism. Compare this to Jn where both are there. The book discusses the issue at length. Mysticism as a dynamic process in human life is not the issue because of the eschatological perspective.

- Dorothee Sölle (*Mystik und Widerstand*,1997) clarifies how mysticism seems to be world-negating, yet in its true manifestations is positive to life here and now, but requires men to be open to transformation, to recognize the deep longing for discovering one's true self. Mysticism is a path to be traveled, step by step.

And here is a voice, altogether different:

Bultmann in his *Theologie des Neuen Testaments* (UTB, Tübingen 1984[9]) does not honor mysticism in any way. On the contrary he opposes it, sometimes implicitly, sometimes explicitly. Wherever texts might be interpreted as mystical he argues to the contrary. For example, he admits that the text in Jn 17:22f originates in the tradition of mystic language. But these words do not refer to "einem mystischen Verhältnis zwischen Jesus und die Seinen". Rather they have to be understood as "die der Welt entnommene eschatologische Existenz der Gläubenden. Diese Existenz ist aber nur im Glauben wirklich *und nicht in einem direkten Verhältnis zu Jesus oder zu Gott*" (emphasis by Bultmann) (p.436f, § 50.6). As if the one excludes the other. *Pisteuein* is existential. To believe is not a statement. It is a total rendering oneself into the person or thing one believes in. *Pisteuein* is not merely believing, its other and maybe more basic meaning is trusting. To have belief and/or faith in somebody (or something) is to trust, to throw oneself completely into the arms of the beloved. Does not Jesus in other pericopes in the same great speech speak about the love between his Father and himself, and between himself and the disciples, and among the disciples (Jn 15:9-17)? Is this *pisteuein* somehow and intimately related to love? Both make oneself to render oneself completely and unconditionally to the other. This love may be considered to be the foundation of faith.

In Jn 14:8ff unity between Jesus as son and his Father is discussed between Jesus and Philip. In explaining the pericope Bultmann quasi apologizes the use of this terminology, because it seems related to "der Formel des gnostischen Mythos", and a little further he says, obviously "Formeln der Mystik müssen dazu dienen, die Einheit zu beschreiben" (p.402, § 47.1). He argues that "in allen diesen Wendungen weder Mythologie noch Mystik vorliegt" because of the further reply to Philip "die das *egô en tôi patri*; *kai ho patêr en emoi* exegesiert: *ta rhêmata ha egô legô humin ap emautou ou lalô; ho de patêr ho en emoi menôn poiei ta erga mou* (14:10) (p.403, § 47.1). It seems to me that the latter phrase is even more mystic in character: it is God who speaks and acts through Jesus as a consequence of the full unity between them. Similarly in the expression *einai en Christôi*. Bultmann argues "Das *en Christôi*, weit entfernt eine Formel für mystische Verbundenheit zu sein, ist primär eine ekklesiologische Formel…" (p.312, § 34.3). He mistakes the deep sense the phrase had and still has for many of the faithful. In § 36.3 (p. 328) he however confirms the same exegesis when saying that it does not refer to "eines individuellen mystischen Christusverhältnisses".

Sic.

And finally a modern Sufi, Inayat Khan:

You are my life, it is in you that I live,
From you I borrow life and you do I give;
O my soul and spirit, you I adore,
I live in you, so do I live ever more.
You are in me and in you do I live,
Still you are my King and my sins you forgive.
You are the Present and Future and Past
I lost myself, but I have found you at last.[62]

To Resume

Mysticism in realization (versus when it is written about) is about an overwhelming experience in the deeper levels of consciousness, in a genuine transformation process of the soul, an experience of inspiration if not revelation from the 'other' world. Here spirituality presents itself not as theory but as a reality, in union with *das ganz Andere* (Otto), *fascinans et tremendum,* yet so intimate. Often it is referred to as fear. I prefer to understand it as awe, which is fascinating and makes one tremble. Viewed in this way, it is a positive uplifting experience. It is about an awe-arising intimate awareness of the Presence of the Divine around, and of a true connection to the spirit-within. The sacred becomes a living entity. What happens in a mystic experience is a transformation of the self: a rise to a higher level of consciousness. At the same time, transforming the self, or at least a serious willingness to do so, is a prerequisite of experiencing mysticism, of rising to that other consciousness.

Therefore, transformation and presence are confirmed as the key concepts of mysticism.

Mysticism in the Gospels?

Having introduced mysticism the question arises if it is to be found in the Gospels? Consulting any history of Christian mysticism it seems that the answer is negative. It is hardly possible to find studies in which Jesus is presented among the founders of mysticism, nor is he seen as one of its representatives.[63] Moreover, he does not figure in any anthology but one,[64] and the Gospels are not treated as containing texts that testify of mysticism, except (passages in) the

---

62 Hazrat Inayat Khan, *The Dance of the Soul: Nirtan,* 1993, 247.
63 However, EEC (633) underscores that "[t]he roots of Christian mysticism appear in the NT, particularly in the teachings of Paul and John concerning union with Christ and the experience of God's presence [!] and love."
64 Andrew Harvey (ed), *Teachings of the Christian Mystics,* 1998.

IN SEARCH OF MYSTICISM: FRAMING THE CONCEPT   43

Gospel of John. Is Jesus not a mystic indeed?[65] Or is mysticism only mysticism if labeled as such?

McGinn (1991, chapters 4–7) considers Christian mysticism to start in the fourth century only, with Augustine and the founding of monasticism. Yet he does not deny mystical elements in the first centuries after Christ. He finds one of the foundations of Christian mysticism in the Judaism of the Second Temple period and in the LXX in which the Psalms and the Song of Songs were favorites exemplifying the stages of human transformation on the way to experience divine presence. Another foundation was in Hellenism with its profound contemplative experience. Even so, a third source, of course, was found in the NT. "[C]ertain NT texts were plausibly interpreted as guides for the mystical life," says McGinn. Significantly, he adds but "as early as the late second century C.E.", 'only', I add. Is it true that there was no mysticism right from the beginning? Seen from the point of view of the proto-orthodox church, yes, probably. Spiritual duality and a complete focus on Christology dominated.[66] Moreover, God mysticism was transformed into Christ mysticism (Schweitzer)—though of course it remains mysticism. However, the great difference, as it was interpreted, is not about Jesus but about Christ.

What about the period from the mid-first century, the period from just after Jesus was active, to the late second century? What did the various Christian groupings 'do' with the intrinsic human need of spirituality and the drive to the One? Did the implicit mysticism contained in the Jesus logia remain undiscovered? Or were there other groupings of Christians who did discover this treasure? Certainly the ones who collected the sayings in what became the Gospel of Thomas, or that of Q. And what about Paul's mysticism, or gnosticism as Elaine Pagels termed it[67]? Certainly his 'trichotomy' of body, psyche, and spirit (1 Thess 5.23) is an indication in that direction. Even more his passages on the persons living in the consciousness of the spirit: the *pneumatikoi* versus the persons living in the consciousness of the psyche: the *psuchikoi*.[68] The latter term is often translated as 'natural', misinterpreting the meaning of *psuchê*.

---

65 René Bütler (*Die Mystik der Welt*, 1992) criticizes this approach. "Die Religionsstifter oder die Autoren der heiligen Schriften…haben die Offenbarung empfangen durch einen Akt, den man als unmittelbaren Gotteserfahrung ansprechen muss…. Am Anfang jeder Religion…steht demnach die Mystik …"(21) "Die Nichtberücksichtigung von heiligen Schriften wie zum Beispiel der Evangelien des Neuen Testaments würde einen erheblichen Verlust bedeuten" (9).
66 Here in the sense of condensing Christianity to suffering, the cross, the rising, and the glorification, in the form of the teachings of Paul.
67 Pagels 1992.
68 1 Cor 3.16.

Were then the Gospels not understood by their readers as (in part?) voicing mysticism? Didn't one trace mysticism in the logia? McGinn is not convinced that one did. He only finds that from the late second century onward texts from the NT were explained as mystical. They were seen as an interpreted manual on what later would be called the mystical way (7). Rather, early Christians experienced divine presence in the person of Jesus, rather than in God. It "was accessible through the community and its sacramental rituals, particularly in baptism as foundation and Eucharist as crown" (6). The presence of God was not primarily sought in the teachings of Jesus but rather in Jesus as being himself the presence of God (chapter 3). McGinn may be the victim of misguidance in that some Christian grouping considered only the canonical Gospels as Scripture. What about the circle from which later on the Gospel of Thomas emerged? What about Q?

In the proto-orthodox groupings, contact with the divine presence was to be sought in the confession of faith and in the ritual of baptism. "Jesus the preacher of the message [of the Kingdom of God] became Jesus the preached message and soon Jesus the written message…, especially the account of his sacrificial death and rising…." (63). Moreover, of course, Jesus would be present only at the *parousia*, when Jesus would return on earth, manifesting his divinity" (62f). The references to pericopes in the Synoptics later interpreted as mysticism are scant.

Even so, McGinn acknowledges mystical elements in the scriptures of the first century: John and Paul, and with early Christian writers. However, he refuses to take these authors as mystics when compared to Augustine or Origen. These elements have constituted the basis of the later Christian mysticism, he admits. 'Even' some texts in the Synoptics can be interpreted as close to some elements of mysticism. Essential to an approach that may trace mysticism in the Gospels is a 'spiritual reading' (66, also 68 and so on). My comment to his approach is that he takes the later Christian mysticism as the element that defines mysticism in the Gospels. Would he call Jesus a mystic? It is not be found in his chapter. Hesitatingly he seems to admit that some pericopes could reveal mysticism, like Mt 10.28 par, Mt 11.27 and Lk 10.22. This selection is in line with his view presented above. The latter two pericopes refer principally to the relation between Jesus and God, not about the perspective for humans. The first pericope, "Anyone who does not take up his cross and follow in my footsteps is not worthy of me"[69] is not specifically mystical and if so, is thought to refer to martyrdom and Christology rather than to union with God.

---

69 The quotation is in McGinn's version. Two comments. It is not Mt 10.28 but 16.24. The RSV says, "If any man would come after me, let him deny himself and take up his cross and follow me".

The transfiguration[70] is rightly interpreted as mysticism (67), but rather than referring to possibilities for contact with the Presence McGinn tells about it as a unique occurrence privileged to Jesus alone. Yes, it is brought as comparable to the peak experience as described by the famous mystics but it is not carried onward to what it may imply for our understanding of mysticism.

> For the disciples it happened as an initiation. Jesus took some of the disciples and climbed a high mountain. Then something occurred through which Jesus' "face shone like the sun, and his garments became dazzling white". The disciples "fell to the ground, and were filled with awe."[71] ...Jesus came and touched them, saying, 'Awake, and have no fear'" (Mt version, NSAV). Mark and Luke have slightly different versions, Luke adding that the disciples kept silence over this occurrence.[72]

Significantly, McGinn's paragraph on the synoptic Gospels covers not even two pages. That is different for the Gospel of John (74–79). The main line in McGinn's argument is continued when discussing this Gospel. Rather than straightly acknowledging its mysticism, he prefers to treat it as interpretations by later Christians. It is as if he himself has not come to terms with Jesus as a mystic. However, from the quotations he gives it is clear that this Gospel abounds with texts that are mystical. It is no exaggeration to posit that it is mysticism itself. This interpretation does not refer to the union between God and Jesus only. Time and again, and this is acknowledged by McGinn, it is a call "to a deeper understanding of the meaning of that life through an enlightenment whose goal is an experience of union with God through Christ begun in this life and completed in the next," rather than only "conversion and participation in the new community and its sacramental life"(75).[73] If we take the *paraklêtos* to be the Spirit in Jn we find a clear reference of the Spirit's indwelling in the disciples (Jn 14.17).

The question remains: is Jesus a mystic? McGinn does not answer explicitly, as we have seen. The answer must even be negative if we go by any list of Christian mystics: he does not figure there. Yet if anybody should be 'on the list,' it is Jesus. Even if we consult anthologies of Christian mysticism, we will not find any that includes Jesus' words, except the one mentioned. Three reasons may explain this remarkable failing. One is the general conception that a text is mystical when it describes an experience of union with God, or of knowing the divine Presence. This indeed is hardly the case in the Gospels

---

70 Mt 17.1–9, Mk 9.2–10, Lk 9.28–36.
71 My translation of the verb *ephobêthêsan*, awe being a more adequate rendering of *phobos*. NSAV says, 'were overcome by fear'.
72 There are some parallels with Mk 16.1–8. See the relative section in chapter 18.
73 McGinn presents this passage on conversion and participation as invitations by Jesus to his followers. Does Jesus in Jn call for conversion and participation in a community that was to come into existence? I doubt whether he did so, even in intention.

(except Jn). The other is that in handbooks mysticism is defined in a way that makes one forget to look back at the logia. It got as it were 'institutionalized' in the Middle Ages, the period considered the period of its highest blossoming. In those terms it might be difficult to find mysticism in the logia. Moreover, the third reason, confession and catechism deny mysticism and make people afraid of it.

In the important Dutch language *Encyclopedie van de Mystiek*[74] a chapter by Huub Welzen is devoted to mysticism in the NT (521–38). Texts in the NT have inspired mystics how to describe their experiences, 'as sources to phrase their experiences' (particularly when it concerns processes of transformation or about 'meeting the Supreme' (521). Here we find the key concepts of presence and transformation again. Examples: the Sermon on the Mount, the Lord's Prayer. Another point he makes is that these texts take on the function to give guidance to the mystic process of readers. This, it seems to me, is the genuine function of scripture texts. He writes that in present-day Bible exegesis NT texts are seen as more 'performative' than 'informative.' Their intent is the message to be effective to the reader rather than to inform him about historical, dogmatic, or other facts. This even applies to narrative texts, a viewpoint that I subscribe fully (524). Performative may be interpreted also in a different way: he, like McGinn, takes the texts as performances: the persons and acts of the principal figures, like Jesus, Paul, and others, are as examples to follow, or even to reproduce within the limits of reality (525ff.). What is missing is the inner meaning of crucial texts. For example, Mk 8.35 is used as indicating Jesus' future passion rather than instructing his disciples to transform their psyche. In chapter 14 this issue will be developed. In his discussion of the Gospel of John its mysticism, in the view of Welten, is centered on the relation of God and Jesus rather than explicating its relevance for the human being.

In this way the direct message about the Kingdom as an inner presence in the Synoptics was pushed to the background, and ultimately forgotten.

Conclusions

Mysticism is found to be essential to spirituality and religion.[75] The present exploration of how to recognize it has led to identifying key concepts of mysticism that serve as signposts. Presence and transformation are typical and characteristic concepts to be used as sensible indicators for a text to contain mysticism. They will be applied in the further analysis of the logia.

---

74 J. Baars et al. (eds), *Encyclopedie van de Mystiek*, 2003.
75 See Duintjer 2007 (and his co-authors) for an account of the inner path in the world.

CHAPTER THREE
Biblical Criticism: The Case of the Jesus Logia
Meaning Beyond The Word

Introduction

In the first chapter we have set our goal—tracing mysticism in the logia, and its impact on interpretation. The previous chapter has explored what mysticism is, in two ways. First, key words for recognizing mysticism in a text were traced, resulting in the two keywords Presence and Transformation. Second, it resulted in the insight that the language of mysticism, here understood as 'sacred' text, primarily works on an expanded level of consciousness where words, sentences, and arguments function as signs for an essential meaning. Logic and rationality are not the way to understand; they are as primitive means to render a reality that withdraws from this material, mental and emotional world into an expanded consciousness.

This chapter, therefore, charts the consequences of the foregoing for the methodology of this study, at the same time deepening the concept of what sacred texts are. Questions will be asked like the following. Is sacred text different from normal text? Do we treat it in the same way as we do with regular literary texts? Are logia distinct from narrative text? What about the origin of pronouncements of Jesus? Moreover, the logia form has to be explained in context.

The substance matter of this chapter, therefore, is not methodology. It does not attend to the relevant literature. What is at stake are the logia as sacred text. Does its character have implications for understanding and interpretation[1] and the concomitant translation? An alternative approach will be explored. The outcome may be relevant as an extra to existing Bible criticisms.

A lead issue for this chapter then is to recognize the distinct character of sayings versus the narrative, and to formulate the requirements methodology (as the systematic study of methods) has to meet to do the work. The sayings that will be in focus are the logia, sayings by Jesus with a particular purport. That is the central object of this book. They will be viewed as text entities *per se*, rather than as parts of a narrative, and therefore they need to be treated differently.

An initial draft was read at the SBL International Meeting, Groningen 2004.

1   I will generally prefer 'interpretation' over 'exegesis', the latter seeking objectivity, the former intersubjectivity.

This is all the more the case as these logia plausibly are close to what Jesus has said. These logia will be studied from a definite perspective. They will be considered inspired, or even revealed, words stemming from the divine. Chapter 1 has spelled out the hypotheses and the approach chosen. How does that approach relate to current NT criticism? On one point at least it does not. One of the principles of current NT critique is that Gospel texts, or the logia for that matter, are literary texts as any. Any literary criticism thus is applicable.

This leads to the question whether the ancient view of texts being sacred—a view largely lost, even sometimes in Christian communities—is worth to be reconsidered. Does this imply inspiration or even revelation? If so, are the logia such texts? What is sacred? Issues like authenticity, discussions about earlier traditions, and whether oral or written and the like will be touched summarily. A second issue is how these and other questions relate to the existing types of NT criticism. To what extent available Bible criticisms are appropriate for this specific object? Is the peculiarity of the logia such that they require a methodology of interpretation that is distinct? Which adaptations may be appropriate?

Thus, this chapter focuses on the relationship between sacred texts (NT, Gospels, *logia*) and current hermeneutics, exegesis, and Bible criticisms (as methods).[2] Do methodologies do justice to salient characteristics of sacred texts? Sacred texts reveal a sacred message. To understand, a spiritual / mystic approach is needed. Some crucial characteristics will be named.

These characteristics will be confronted with current methodology. Usually three or four approaches are used to understand sacred texts: literal, symbolical, esoteric, and mystical. It is taken that the symbolical and mystic approaches best serve the understanding of sacred texts. Current criticisms remain valuable but are in need of additional perspective to serve the cause. The deconstructive criticism appears offering interesting perspectives, provided the spiritual outlook is taken into account.

Sacred Texts

What is religion? In line with what we found about mysticism religion is conceived as a phenomenon that is neither about knowledge nor about rituals or dogmas. Its foremost function is raising the consciousness of the subject and the community to the divine, to the connection to God and (the holy) spirit, both around and inside. It is about the light that we do not know but may sense, about a world we have heard about and that we may visualize, a reality beyond

---

[2] Exegesis is the actual interpretation of a sacred text, the bringing out of its meaning. Hermeneutics is the study and establishment of the principles of exegesis. Bible criticism its tool box. Together they form the methodology. See Soulen, *Biblical Criticism*, 2001.

we have read about and that we may suspect. Do exegesis, hermeneutics and Bible criticism serve to lift a tip of the veil? Are they in a position to look beyond the literary scene: literal in terms of verbal as well as of literature (*littéraire*)?

However, increasingly a tendency prevails to consider religion a human construct denying its revelatory nature.[3] This tendency flows from the secular interpretation of Enlightenment and Modernity. However, throughout history the 'beyond' has been recognized. Even today, mainly backstage, the awareness of the sacred transpires here and there. Historically, behind the myths explaining natural phenomena, there was always an awareness of a spiritual reality. This was conveyed intuitively but above all by inspirational persons conveying a message from beyond, from the divine, from God. Differences and distinctions appeared as mystics and messengers conveyed this in human words in different cultures in different periods of history. This is what I call the 'Message', divine inspiration communicated to the 'messengers' of great religions, and in this study to Jesus. Differences abound and are to be attributed to contexts of time and culture, to human wordings. Communities have often regarded their own tradition sacrosanct: the Word of God, literally, word for word, unique. However, analysis of the history of these sacred texts has made it clear that the wordings of these messages manifest the cultural and historical realities of the time. This of course is a fact established by Bible research as well as by studies of other religions. However, this development has crossed the threshold of what religion is. Consequently in some circles—and they increase in number and size—the Bible is no longer seen as the Word of God. It is now viewed as a human construct originating from different periods authored by different individuals, or the result of accrescent texts: myths, narratives, poetry, and fantasies. The sacred is relegated to the realm of rituals and human fantasy, imagination and myth. However, "sacred writings…stand apart; the language in which they were originally expressed is crucial to their deepest meaning."[4]

The approach of this book is different. It does not contribute to re-establish the traditional dictum of the Bible being the Word of God. However, I do want to recognize that significant parts of the Gospels, and specifically the logia unmistakably speak a language different from the ordinary.

---

3   H. M. Kuitert, *Voor een tijd een plaats van God*, 2002: religion is about the human being, and *Jezus: nalatenschap van het Christendom*, 1998. His pilgrimage to a disenchanted Jesus and Christian faith is best illustrated by his 1992 published book called 'The overall doubted Christian faith.' Kuitert is the icon of a critical current in Dutch Reformed theology, who in a long pilgrimage concluded that the Gospels are a human construct, and the figure of Jesus the outcome of varying views. 'Man was here prior to God'. He is a major representative of this present-day (post-) modernist view. Similarly the Bible is not God's word but consists of human stories embedded in specific cultures.
4   Rajak 2009, 1139 writing about the language of the LXX.

Sacred texts typically are inspired if not revealed texts. Sacred is what is coming from the world beyond, which is not perceivable by the senses, yet testifies of an experience of a reality beyond the real, a reality as if being an eyewitness. They appeal as it were to the 'conscience' as being true: an appeal to some remembrance from beyond, causing a happiness that transcends joy and pleasure: *makarios*: blessed, blissful, sacred, the central word of the Beatitudes (Mt 5). The 'sacred', as it is perceived, may be defined in terms of expanded consciousness.[5]

What is a revealed text? It is a message coming from Beyond through a human channel. It is expanded inspiration. In-spir-ation is when the spirit is breathed into the psyche. Spirit is sacred, and therefore holy spirit. It exceeds the realm of the psyche and the emotional as it originates in another sphere. That is what mystics, prophets and messengers testify on occasions, through the ages, through all cultures, through the great religions. For Christianity of course its culmination is the spiritual message by Jesus, the great mystic and messenger.

How come that the words of Jesus in the logia differ so much from most writings by other mystics? Is he a mystic? Mystics write about their experience. Jesus speaks being in spirit, from a state of consciousness originating from the experience of presence and transformation, in a direct and enduring relationship with God. Consequently the difference between the logia and the narrative of the Gospel is that in the logia we trace words of Jesus himself. Even if not verbally authentic, they stem from an old, established tradition. From the previous chapter we understand that mysticism in realization (versus when it is written about) is about an overwhelming experience in the deeper levels of consciousness, in a genuine transformation process of the soul, an experience of inspiration if not revelation from the 'other' world. Here spirituality presents itself not as theory but as a reality, in union with *das ganz Andere* (Otto). It is about an awe-arising intimate awareness of the Divine around, and of a true connection of the spirit-within with it. The sacred becomes a living entity. The previous chapter has given some fine proofs of texts, both on and about mysticism.

Many sacred texts convey essentials from that 'other' world, or about the way toward it. Such text stems from a higher consciousness that has been attuned by the Spirit. It makes an appeal to the spirit in the reader to the effect

---

5   Cf the Near-death experiences (NDE), where experiences are reported that are not the result of sensory perception, yet are real-world experiences of the subjects that have a lasting positive impact on the mentality (psyche) of the subjects. Moreover, they are verifiable in terms of repeated patterns among the subjects and of their descriptions of these experiences. The reality of this phenomenon has been found to occur during cardiac arrest when all brain functions are flat. It has been reported scientifically. See the paragraph on NDE in the previous chapter.

of awakening to the essence of the text. This mostly happens implicitly, i.e., the individual who is open to the hidden message will receive and understand it.[6] In this way different interpretations (and consequently different translations) may exist next to one another.

Bible criticisms and hermeneutics have as a task to study sacred texts. One of the ends is to find the most plausible interpretation. As to sacred texts the task of methodology is to find ways of revealing the hidden treasures, not on the experiential level but for understanding the text in its spiritual intent, that is: not merely philosophically, logically, or even theologically. This is not simple, as direct interpretational methods do not apply right away as *the* critical method. It is logical indeed that such texts are not logical.

> It is current practice to place sacred texts in context, and thus to understand them. To derive the sense of sacred texts from iconographical images and historical concepts from outside. Or to trace the meaning back through methods of intertextuality. All of this does make sense but within boundaries. Spiritual and mystical texts indeed are not traditioned, they do not derive from literal expressions. Rather they are spontaneous expressions of inborn qualities and images and concepts whose source is in the spirit.

The point is that texts of this sort do not answer the characteristics neither of philosophy nor of theology. Inner experiences on the path or a mystical state of being in its essence cannot be transmitted by words. Neither are they systematic. Witnesses tell there is no language to express the reality beyond, yet so near. If words are used, as of necessity they will be understood in their current every-day meaning. That is also the problem when trying to understand the near-death experiences.

* * *

> How is this to be understood? It is like trying by a two-dimensional picture of a grandiose mountain landscape to share with another the overwhelming experience when you yourself were there, completely surrounded by beauty, captured by awe, silenced by a Presence. And especially so when the other does not know the third dimension, and is in no position even to imagine what you want to share. And how would you explain a deeply felt silence, other than in 'negative' terms, when the listener never did experience positively a real silence?

* * *

What methodology can do is to recognize this situation as tense and face it: how to deal rationally with what exceeds rationality. It is done here by assuming that

---

6   Another way of transmitting the sacred is not by talking about it but being touched by the sacred so that what one says may be illuminated with the light of knowing to be united. Or in direct contact with a person who has absorbed the sacred and radiates it.

the spiritual is part of human nature. It is within human capacity. Mystics, prophets, and messengers have tried to depict that reality in words, in silence, in presence and otherwise, in order to call on the potential of soul and spirit in each human being to understand. It perhaps is an innate faculty that often is buried, neglected, or atrophied. However, it can be developed in that process of transformation mentioned earlier. But when these words then are interpreted in the usual concepts of the 'second dimension' the text tends to lose its prime meaning and energy, whilst on other levels the text remains meaningful. Thus, more than one interpretation is valid: they are polysemic. Characteristically therefore they would have more than one layer of understanding: literal, psychological, spiritual / mystical, or symbolical. Such texts thus are characterized as being multi-interpretable, because multi-layered. Therefore they cannot be handled in the same way as a text of philosophy or literature is interpreted.[7] Methodology unfortunately has not differentiated between 'ordinary' and sacred texts. In sacred texts, the words of a passage are considered *indications* of meaning (one term, several concepts) rather than one established and codified meaning (one term, one concept). The reason is that such texts originate from a different level of consciousness than the regular one and therefore need a similar level in the reader, presuming a change in the reader, and consequently in the interpreter, and eventually the translator. The crux is that 'normal' texts are in human words about human conditions while sacred texts deal with transcendent and immanent realities in human words.

Even stronger is the notion that 'things' cannot be expressed in words, or in words that cannot be said because they belong to another world, or to another dimension. Things of the third dimension cannot be expressed in terms of the second. Paul's *arrhêta rhêmata* (2 Cor 12.4) refer to a reality beyond comprehension: he heard words that can't be worded, unutterable words.[8] Mostly it is interpreted as things that are forbidden to convey. Yet Paul tells that he heard them. It is mysticism. This concept will be further discussed in chapter 8 in the section on hearing and 'hearing'.

---

[7] Gordley 2010 reviews the excellent book by Peter Leithart 2009 (not available to me). It offers insights and tools relevant to what this chapter stands for. Leithart proposes to go beyond 'the skeletal notion of meaning: the meaning of a text is not fixed but mutable' (46). Be alert that a covert sense may be lurking under the surface of the overt (86). He argues for sensitivity to the evocative power of words and their connotations (end of chapter 3). "A good interpreter…must also develop an ear for the multiple melodies …" (144). Much of these suggestions will return in my observations and proposals further down.

[8] See Lietaert Peerbolte 2008, 164 who in his insightful chapter connects this phrase of Paul to mysticism.

* * *

In order to help understand this argument we may take a poem as example. One person may take it literally. Another will understand it symbolically, and appreciate the skill and beauty of expression in that sense. A third one may see a different symbology. Yet another may be struck inwardly so as to be captured and transformed. A traditional Sufi love poem, e.g., is very concrete in terms of worldly love. Symbolically, though, it obviously refers to love for God. Apart from understanding it mentally or emotionally, it reaches beyond: one is moved by it spiritually and brought to a high state of consciousness so as to participate in that love. Subsequently one realizes that the words of the poem are merely suggesting the reality beyond. Even a master poet cannot find words that are adequate to the experience he desires so fervently to express.

* * *

Concluding,

- *sacred texts transmit from a transcendent reality, reflected and translated in human words: a 'voice from beyond', sometimes to the degree of a* mustêrion
- *their meaning often is multilayered (dimensions)*
- *reading and interpreting therefore requires an open mind and spirit*
- *they differ from regular texts in power, in bearing, in tone.*

The Logia: A Genre

Logia are the prime source material for understanding the message of Jesus.

The Jesus logia as they appear in the Bible are an intrinsic part of the Gospels. Throughout two thousand years of history, the Gospels have been seen as the only scripture about Jesus: the unique document about Jesus and his Message, often seen as 'the Word of God'. Nowadays an interest is developing for the logia of Jesus, the sayings. There is even a tendency to define these under the heading of a genre of its own: the genre of the sayings Gospel. This dynamic has occurred because of the appearance of the Gospel of Thomas, by the growing attention for the significance of the sayings Gospel of Q, and third by the shift of attention from the Gospel narratives to the words of Jesus.

The discovery of the Gospel of Thomas in 1945 has had an enormous impact. After a modest and incredulous start—'just one of the gnostic documents of the Nag Hammadi library'—in the last few decades an impressive tsunami of scholarly publications has flooded the landscape of NT scholarship, uprooting many hedged certainties. Its impact is twofold. One is the message it contains. Instead of a focus on Christology and associated themes, it teaches about psycho-spiritual development in the framework of realized mysticism. It does not talk about eschatology,[9] passion, or resurrection, let alone redemption. The other impact is the recognition that it simply represents a different Gospel genre: it is not a narrative but a sayings Gospel. Th consists exclusively of logia, words of Jesus. Although most scholars give a fairly late date to the final redaction (second century), there is a widespread conviction that it stands in a long line of a tradition of its own, first an oral and later a written tradition. Some hold that the text as we know it now may well reflect its original content, dating from the first decades after Jesus' death.

This Thomas tradition operated next to and apart from a variety of other groupings among whom the proto-orthodox. Multiformity of Jesus groups belonging to different traditions was the standard pattern, as most scholars agree nowadays, opposed to the centuries-long supposition of the one and single Church that became multiform by schisms and the like only later.

Q and Thomas[10]

Even more interesting for this study is the Sayings Gospel of Q. It is a first-century Jesus book, a virtual book, to be sure, as it never was found. However, it is definitely earlier than the canonical Gospels, many maintain. Many others do not see Q but as of a technical instrument in criticism. What is the issue? Though NT scholars had been aware of a supposed collection of sayings all the time since the 1830s, it remained the domain of specialists. But what is it? In search for the history of the Synoptics remarkable similarities in the Gospel texts were found. The issue at stake is called the Two Source (or Two Document) Hypothesis as part of the so-called Synoptic Problem.[11] What is it? Much of the

---

9   DeConick (2005, 113) is of a different opinion. She demonstrates that especially the oldest layer of Th ('the kernel speeches'), generally considered mystical, should be understood as referring to the eschaton.
10 The issue of Q and Th, of sayings as an independent tradition, and the jump in focus from the canonical Gospels to the broad field of ancient Christian Gospels has been highly significant for fresh views on early Christianity as well as on Jesus. One of the key figures in this development has been Helmut Koester. See Koester 1990.
11 Literature abounds. Dunn (2003, 41–45) offers a fair insight in this complicate issue that has stood central in NT criticism. It is widely adopted but it continues to be challenged (e.g., Mark Goodacre and Perrin, 2004).
    Evan Powell (2006, chapter 7) offers a technical argument against the Two Document (or Source) Hypothesis. She concludes that the Q solution is superfluous. No primitive sayings collection can be thought to go back to Jesus. The original Jesus movement was an overt political movement that was toned down in the Synoptic tradition in order to make it more favourable to Rome. Jesus thus advocated an anti-establishment message in favour of the poor and against Roman imperialism and Jewish wealth. See its review by Jim West, *RBL* June 1, 2007.
    Burkett, in two well-considered books (2004, 2009), concludes in favour of Q. He suggests a different stand, and on good grounds, "… no Synoptic Gospel depended upon any other,

materials in Mt and Lk are the same almost verbally, some of which could be traced back to Mk, the oldest Gospel. However, for other texts the similarities were so great that one could not but suppose a common external source: no other way to explain the similarities. It was decided among scholars to hypothesize a lost source, a *Quelle*, and they nicknamed it Q (for *Quelle*), containing all texts common to Mt and Lk but not in Mk. Only step by step it got accepted as something more than an analytic tool, a Sayings Gospel. "Many New Testament scholars resisted the idea of Q because they thought there was no other example of the genre in early Christian literature and thus could not imagine why early Christians would have written such a text."[12] Then appeared the Gospel of Thomas, a sayings Gospel, demonstrating the reality of the genre. The hypothesis of a sayings Gospel has been attacked and discussed over and over again, but it has stood the time. Q as a material document is a hypothesis as no manuscript was ever found. However, through arduous study by scholars like Robinson, Kloppenborg, Mack, Hoffman, and others, it is widely accepted now: here an independent tradition is speaking.[13]

The most important and unique features, though, are its style and content. Contrary to the Gospel texts at large that are narrative the Q texts consist almost exclusively of sayings of Jesus: the style is not narrative but a collection of just sayings, a genre in itself. This phenomenon is new in Gospel land, although it is known to everybody but often goes unnoticed as to its implications. The implications initially have not been seen, then attacked,[14] and finally accepted at least in some circles. Another feature is the contents. Q does not mention the

---

   but all depended upon a set of earlier sources …". This option feeds upon the basic idea that the written Gospels were the result of a long process of transmitting. See the section on the oral tradition. A further treatment of the issue exceeds the framework of this chapter, and indeed of this book.
12 Mack 1993, 16.
13 The great names of the Q project are Robinson (2000, 2005, 2007), Kloppenborg (2000, 2008, also co-author of Robinson 2000), Mack 1993. Other titles, among many, Tuckett 1996, Allison 1997. The final presentation of the Q text is in Robinson et al. 2000, a critical edition with synopsis, and *the* description of the history of the International Q Project. Kloppenborg's *Excavating Q* (2000) gives a complete picture of the Q issue.
14 I will not present the counterevidence, with one exception. Jens Schröter (*Von Jesus zum Neuen Testament*, Mohr Siebeck, Tübingen 2007, 104 and chapter 5) argues: "eine plausibele Rekonstruktion der Geschichte Jesu ergibt sich nur dort wo die beiden Pole zusammengehalten werden": 'Wortüberlieferung' und 'Erzählungsüberlieferung'. In that connection Schröter finds that in the past decades the importance of Q over Mk has been overrated. My critique to him is that the word traditionally has been interpreted in the framework of the narrative, rather than taking the word as belonging to an autonomous tradition that later got incorporated in the narrative, whether or not adapted to the narrative. Consequently it will be necessary to disconnect sayings from narrative. Of course, in the case that the Gospel as such is object of analysis, Schröter's requirement is valid.

crucifixion, there is no word predicting Jesus' death, neither does it refer to an atoning effect of Jesus' death nor to the resurrection. In the oldest layer it does not contain anything on the eschaton, a striking resemblance to Th, and a meaningful one: what did these early Christian communities conserve as the message of Jesus?

Acceptance of Q and recognition of Th had huge implications. Luttikhuizen (2002, 54), in his Dutch-language work on the pluriformity of earliest Christianity, observes that part of the Thomas logia are similar to the logia in the Gospels, others do not, but display an esoteric or Gnostic [mystical] character. This strengthens the assumption made above that the Synoptics have selected logia from a richer array. Thomas testifies of the character of these as mystical.

What does it mean when one tries to redefine the message of Jesus if one would disregard christology, crucifixion, resurrection, and eschatology? It is like revolution when seen from the (proto-)orthodox point of view. The Gospels within the complete New Testament focus on it, it is the leading thread. For the Church it seems to be the central issue of faith: one confesses to it. This book will not venture into this tricky issue but it is clear that it changes the drama, not just the décor. Part II on the Kingdom of God will look at some aspects of it. What does it mean if one would take the saying (logia) as the message? This study will not tackle the question but try and see what emerges from the logia on the topics analyzed. What does it imply for Christology? "Christology and the elaboration of the singular and unique character of Jesus was not a major preoccupation of the [early] Jesus people" according to Q, "a point of view customary for scholars of most stripes"[15] It was indeed not for Q, continues Kloppenborg, one of the prime scholars of Q: "The fields of Christology, the elaboration of the nature of the kingdom, of futuristic or presentist eschatology rather inhere in contemporary theological habits: it is more a meta-debate about theological authority"[16]

> Orthodox scholars, therefore, have wrestled with Q as an authoritative collection, let alone to view it as an independent sayings Gospel. Q does not submit Christological claims, admits Hurtado.[17] He, a highly esteemed NT Christological scholar, recognizes these features of Q, style and contents, and agrees with Kloppenborg that Q therefore does contain evidence of a very early distinctive form of Christianity (219). Yet he denies the implications for what the Jesus community was like, for he claims a continuity between the Gospels and early Christianity[18] (till 170 CE), playing down the

---

15 Kloppenborg 2007, 359–59, referring to Melanie Johnson-De Baufre, *Jesus Among her Children*, Harvard UP, Harvard 2006.
16 Ibid.
17 Hurtado 2003, 218.
18 Like Käsemann in 1953, quoted by James M. Robinson, *Kerygma und historischer Jesus*, Zwingli, Zürich / Stuttgart 1960, 11.

characteristics of Q, playing down the gap between the teachings of Jesus and those of Paul, for example. His statement that "Christological beliefs…were common currency in Christian circles from a very early point onward" (232) seems at odds with what we just learned as his view on Q.

My conclusion, therefore, is to recognize Q, and *mutatis mutandis* Th for that matter, as authentic and early witnesses of the Jesus message, conserved carefully and devotedly as an intimate treasure, private as well as community-wise, that serves as a trustworthy source of knowledge of Jesus. It is then recognized that in early Christianity teachings of Jesus were conserved in the form of sayings, logia. In these the words of Jesus and his message resound.[19]

However, there is more to it of course. The Gospel texts have been written decades after Jesus. In how far did the period after the crucifixion influence the texts? Hurtado (2003, 71) signalizes developments that may have affected the texts: "The early Christian sources all indicate that after Jesus' execution there was a significant reformulation of the faith of his followers and a new and powerful sense of revelation, these things connected to religious experiences that were perceived by recipients to have a new quality and frequency in their lives." Probably he refers to the Pauline writings and to passages in Acts as an aftermath of crucifixion and resurrection. Paul's 'Gospel' is not Jesus'. Does this obtain generally? Q scholars for instance have found that in early Christianity several groups existed next to one another, each different from the others in many respects, for example gathering around a specific tradition: Q, Thomas, proto-orthodox Christians as indicated by Hurtado, a Pauline school, the Jerusalem community. The Pauline orientation is clear when one takes note of Paul's message, his language, the absence of quotations and other references to what Jesus had said. Hurtado interprets this period as the development of expressions of devotion to Jesus, probably including the Gospels as such.[20] This approach would be remarkable as tone and contents of the logia do not breathe that Christ devotion. The logia contain teachings and revelations, not typically devotion. These words deserve to be taken as such. The attitude of the disciples occasionally is even the contrary to devotion.

Thus historically in early Christianity the teachings shift to the second plane. In order to understand, says Hurtado (55), "the origin and development of Christ-devotion in Christian circles of the first two centuries, I contend that it is not necessary to make a specific case about what might have been Jesus' own aims or purposes." Does this imply that the developing Christianity took distance to the teachings proper? In favor of Paul for instance?

Hurtado's position is that there was a single dominant faith among the believers. Present-day views on early Christianity rather suppose a variety of Christian groups holding different sets of beliefs. In the logia we meet a close approximation of what Jesus said.

---

19 My explorations have not extended to a critical study of the texts of Q or Th, nor do I engage in the Q issue.
20 Hurtado, 2003: see the subtitle of the book, pages 3–4, and *passim*.

Why this long neglect of the importance of Q? After all, wasn't the Q hypothesis not launched as far back as 1838? The whole quest for Q had been seen as a technical issue in the first place. However, already Adolf von Harnack was triggered to the extent of composing an intriguing book, soon forgotten, *The Sayings of Jesus* as early as 1907 (Eng. ed. 1908) in order "to see how the teachings of Jesus sounded when divorced from a setting of miracle and myth."[21] It was the first time, says Mack, that a collection of sayings was published separate from its Gospel context. However, it took more than seventy years before interest was re-born. It now is accepted that at least part of the Gospel narratives of Mt and Lk are composed from an older tradition of sayings, or logia. The Q project has detected three layers in the history of composition. One feature may be mentioned here: like the complete Th, the first and oldest layer of Q is not eschatological.[22] It is important to note that one could suppose that in these sayings we find the oldest materials of Jesus. But even more important is that it indicates an original and authentic way of remembering Jesus, i.e. in his words, and that these were remembered independently from his acts of healing, exorcisms, and the like.[23] Reversely, by these new insights the credibility of Th is enhanced as being a parallel. Apart from its contents this Gospel initially did meet resistance if only because of its form that is foreign to the Gospels as they were known. Now things reverse: the Gospels as narratives retreat to the second stage. This is the very reason to start this wider project on the logia of the canonical Gospels. That is why I dare to take the logia apart and consider their contents and expressiveness independent from the narrative context.[24] This is the more so as I consider most of the logia as sacred text. What does that mean and imply?

* * *

Logia are sayings of Jesus with a special purport in the sense that they appear to convey his message. Therefore there are good reasons to take the logia as separate units / entities when studying NT texts. I propose three reasons. First, there is the sacred nature of the texts as they do represent the words of the master. Second, there is a widespread understanding that the logia represent the oldest

---

21 Mack 1993, 21. I have not been able to trace the original book in Dutch libraries although other Harnack books are available in abundance.
22 A counterview: "… the absence of apocalyptic eschatology in pre-canonical books such as the Gospel of Thomas was one of the reasons why these books never made it into the NT canon" (Vena, *Parousia*, 5). Yes indeed, that may be a consideration for not taking the canon as complete.
23 More about remembering in the section on sacred text below.
24 The narrative context is the creation of the evangelist. "Luke's freedom in formulating settings for his own editorial purposes means we cannot be sure that this attribution is original," referring in this case to Lk 17.20–21 (Nolland 1993, 851).

remembrance of Jesus' teachings. The third reason is the literary identity: a saying is a text different in nature from a narrative.

* * *

Logia as Sacred Text: The Message of Jesus

The Jesus logia in the NT typically represent a case of sacred texts. They represent as much as we can know of the words spoken by Jesus. Therefore, the key to the message of Jesus, the *euaggelion*, resides in these logia. They represent his message.

If Christianity is sincere to Jesus, the logia must be considered to be the essence of the NT.

Consequently NT criticism should focus more on the logia than on the Gospels in general, thus implying a different approach. Usually the logia are interpreted in the context in which they have been placed by the evangelist. Suppose they come from an older or at least an independent source, they merit to be considered also *per se*. The evangelists eventually have used these precious texts in a context perhaps completely different from the original one. In view of the differences in rendering some of the logia in the different Gospels, this dynamic seems probable in some cases at least.

Jesus has been viewed in so many different perspectives and images resulting from this variety. There is a tendency in Jesus research to reduce him to more human proportions in the line of an extreme modernism. Consequently the magnitude of the divine in purely human form tends to be lost. Jesus was the messenger of the time and of all times, the messiah not in worldly terms but in bringing the spiritual kingdom of God, a fresh attunement to the divine, bringing the universal—for divine—message, not only in terms of a christologically defined savior but also as a renewer of the spiritual divine human heritage. The grandness of Jesus needs restoring: he was a teacher and a revealer of the *mustêrion*.[25] A few years ago Nathan hit the point. He wondered if "we are not perhaps missing something when we engage in a merely scientific and historical analysis of a revelatory text."[26]

This book contributes to this new endeavor. The starting point is to recognize the logia as the central core of his message. The logia thus are seen as the words of the Master, as divinely given.[27] One of its aspects is that a sacred word when spoken emanates a 'value' *per se*. It stands for what it is, and for what

---

25 About the *mustêrion* see chapter 8.
26 Nathan 2007, 281.
27 Getty-Sullivan (2007) therefore proposes to distinguish methodologically Jesus texts (in her case: parables) from Gospel texts. However, she views the parables as vehicles of the evangelists' message, rather than Jesus'.

is behind it, provided the reader understands this inclusiveness. Religious literature abounds with testimonies about the power of words. Therefore, we need a subtle balance between taking texts literally *versus* implied multiple truths. On the one hand, I advocate to take the word and the logion literally: this is the 'Word' spoken. As the word represents a reality behind and beyond that word it implies that it is multi-layered, and therefore multi-interpretable. This concept implies that it does not suffice to define a logion either in this sense or in the other. It suggests a growing insight in the other dimensions of sense.

Another question is whether Jesus' words and acts were situation-defined or of a higher order? When speaking was it as it were God speaking, or was it man acting and reacting as a human being among humans? Or otherwise defined: was it a divine message or just wisdom *hic et nunc*? Here the issue of Modernity is at stake again.[28] My hypothesis, after studying the logia, is that they are mixed in character: inspired and sometimes revealed words, conveying a message beyond the ordinary, on the one hand, whilst, on the other hand, reflecting Jesus as a Jewish citizen. In this book the logia are treated accordingly.

> However, the logia should not be over-easily and "innocently" sanctified. Thus, Bovon (2006) cautions for the Gospels' principally theological impulse: be aware, he says, of the fallacy of absolute historical objectivity: a 'meta-historical dimension motivated by faith affirmation (3). Moreover, one should also be cautioned against the tendency to debase the Gospels as being 'just another story, not even e good one, yet exalted to the status of a true story' (Braun 2005).

The Logia as the Oldest Remembrance of Jesus

To what degree can the logia, or some of them, be taken as authentic?[29]

---

28 Meeks (2006) identifies "… four assumptions…in modernity that distort the Jesus Quest: historicizing literalism, a cognitive model of religion, pervasive individualism, and romanticism" (quoted by Carlson in *The Expository Times*); see Meeks 2006. Most of these are relevant to the logia of Jesus.

29 A word about the authenticity, whether a logion may be considered to contain words by Jesus. Apart from my hypothesis earlier in this chapter that logia claim authenticity by their nature, no discussion will be held about individual logia. Therefore, the whole issue of plausibility (Theissen 2002) will not be staged. The criterion of historical plausibility considers as authentic those texts that can be located within Jesus' Jewish context as well as allowing for the possible expansion of Jesus' effect on later Christianity. These criteria are external. My proposal is to consider its content per se, and ask if the logion may be understood as spiritual and/or as confirming his message: a criterion of spiritual plausibility, and one regarding his message, for example the type of Kingdom referred to in the text. However, these ideas are just suggestions to consider. They do not have the position of critiquing Theissen c.s. The quest in this book is not for authenticity but rather for detecting mysticism in his logia. The point we agree on is that a preset ideology cannot be prevented. Each researcher has a framework in which the explorations take place. To make this explicit

Alternatively to what extent have they been edited, re-edited, augmented? What was the bridge between the words spoken and the written text? James Dunn has introduced the key: remembrance.[30] The first volume of his masterly work on the Christian beginnings is titled *Jesus Remembered*.[31] Can we imagine how this remembering worked? The authentic words of the master, one must suppose, served as a treasure valuable above all: sacred words. People around Jesus, disciples and others, heard his voice, took in his words, got impressed and sometimes inspired. They kept the words as a sacred treasure in mind and heart, sometimes communicating with others about this intimate *mustêrion*, the very word Jesus used in order to indicate what was the nature of his teachings to the disciples.[32] They naturally wanted to remember, and to conserve this treasure with devotion and care, to keep the very words of the Master.[33] After the crucifixion, his words all of a sudden were the only thing left. The narratives of his life served as the context, but his living word continued to resound in the devotees' hearts where his words were conserved, transmitted orally first, and later also in written form. Remembering, and practising. Words may have served as directives for daily life: the words of prayer; words guiding one's words and acts; words used as a sort of mantra to meditate upon. Anyhow, they must have acted as a source of inspiration, and as a direct spiritual link to Jesus. To that end they were handed down from person to person, from community to community. Variations in text of course were unavoidable, but at the same time followers must have been particular about remembering these sacred words in a precise form.

---

and to remain true to one's fundamental ideas is a pre-condition. Finally, the tenor of this book is contrary to the criterion of plausibility of context. A pronouncement on the authenticity of a saying should rather take into account the qualities of mysticism and Messenger.

The argument of this section largely obtains to the parables too. Snodgrass (2008, 31): as to the authenticity of the parables "virtually everyone grants that they are the surest bedrock we have of the teaching."

30 James Dunn 2003.
31 Dunn has devoted much effort in critically assessing the authenticity of Gospel texts.
32 April DeConick (2005, 115) reminds us that this idea of precise remembering and recording belongs to the early Christian tradition. She refers to Clement of Alexandria (*Stromateis* I,1), who is "recording the speeches of his teacher Pantaenus in order to preserve the oral traditions which were fading and being forgotten. He states that the divine mysteries are communicated to the select 'few,' not the many, *through the power of speech*, not writing.... The mysteries are '*delivered mystically' from the 'mouth of the speaker*'" (emphasis added). These words illustrate and corroborate the specific character of sacred words.
33 James Dunn (*New Perspective on Jesus,* 2005) emphasizes "the faith impact he made on his disciples...expressed in the first disciples' earliest shared talks", rather than emphasizing the words and teachings by Jesus. By the way, this may well have happened. On various occasions the disciples show their incomprehension with the teachings. Example: the parable of the Sower (see chapter 8).

How reliable was the transmission? Do we not find variations in the text of a logion between individual Gospels? Variation in the narratives are well-known. What about the logia in the Synoptics? This issue has not been surveyed systematically. For the logia studied in this book variations do occur but are minor and they do not affect my assumption of respect and sanctity.

Intermezzo: The Oral Tradition[34]

It is common place that orality predominated in first-century Palestine. It is common place that orality played a major role in the early transmittance of the words of Jesus. However, it is only since the 1980s that the role of orality in the transmittance of Jesus' sayings (or other Gospel texts) came into focus. NT criticisms (source, form, redaction criticism) traditionally and naturally had searched writings, the only witnesses of the NT. Kelber initiated to focus attention to the relationships between orality, memory, and written texts. The key issue is what happened to the teachings of Jesus: spoken, memorized, transmitted, written.[35] The Q scholars, focusing on the origin of texts, played a role in breaking the ground. So did April DeConick (2005) analyzing the process of composition of Th. Dunn (2003a) brought into focus the role of remembrance in the process of transmitting the teachings of Jesus, resulting in the written Gospels. How does oral transmission operate?[36]

One of the major sources is Bailey who reports on the basis of personal empirical studies how knowledge is transmitted.[37] In common situations it is typically a group activity, mostly in a village community. In the case of the logia, different situations obtained: individual teaching, communal sessions, rituals, and the like. Bailey reports about such situations, that are very different as to the reliability of transmission: settings can be either formal or informal, text transmittance either controlled or uncontrolled. *Formal and controlled* is a condition

---

34 A survey of recent research on orality and the Gospels was performed by K. R. Iverson (Iverson 2009, 71–106). R. A. Horsley et al. (eds), *Performing the Gospel: Orality, Memory, and Mark*, Minneapolis: Fortress 2006 is a study of importance, though I am not in a position to include it in the present discussion. It is an achieved piece of work reflecting the new trends of viewing the transmission process: fluid rather than one-way; an extended process of re-editing in the oral phase. However, it pays no attention to the special position of the logia in the process.
35 The present state of the issue is summarized in *Jesus, the Voice, and the Text: Beyond the Oral and the Written Gospel*, edited by Tom Thatcher, published in 2008 circling around the contributions by Kelber.
36 Loubser (2007) joins in the flood of interest for orality and places it in the wider context of 'the media texture' of the NT. There is a complex convergence of orality, writing, and memory practices.
37 Kenneth E. Bailey, "Informal Controlled Oral Tradition and the Synoptic Gospels" 1991, 34–54. Based on his observations drawn from extended stays in Middle Eastern villages where he experienced oral transmitting processes life. Also "Middle Eastern Oral Tradition and the Synoptic Gospels", 1995, 563–67.

for remembering and reciting of sacred texts (nowadays like the Qur'an, says Bailey) where the entire memorized text is recited. One can easily imagine similar situations for the Jesus logia being recited, in communal readings and in ceremonies. It must be exact and precise. *Informal and controlled* is when a community is sitting in a circle and memorizes proverbs, poems, parables, stories, and historical accounts. Proverbs (logia) and poems may also be transmitted in exact and precise form. Divergences are corrected by interruption. This control is less strong with stories and so on. Traditional communities may keep a treasure of thousands of such proverbs orally memorized and recited at random. There is no flexibility. The control lies in the community, mostly delegated to an elder. The control is strict. The next level of flexibility refers to parables, stories, and accounts. Some liberty to improvise is granted, but control is still exercised. This dynamic is put into practice in the group by correcting the speaker. In all cases, however, the control is motivated by continuity: the preservation of identity. To be sure, all this constituted a living tradition and was witnessed and recorded by Bailey. Bultmann, in contrast, thinks that "What the sources offer us is first of all, the message of the early Christian community, which for the most part the Church freely attributed to Jesus."[38] If this refers to the narratives, I agree to a large extent. If it refers to the logia, it seems far out of sacred realities.

The logia clearly belong to the first category: transmission is under strict control as to their verbatim rendering: the holy word, relevant to the individual in the audience, transmitted by the elder. Acts like healing and exorcizing belong to the second category: they tell *about* Jesus, the logia *are* Jesus. Stories in their turn allowed for more variations. Kloppenborg finds that oral tradition is more constant: variability in the reproduction of sources is due more to scribal and rhetorical techniques than to oral tradition.[39]

Therefore, we may be pretty sure of the continuity and authority of the oral transmission of the Jesus logia, and sure of the smooth and gradual transition from oral to written.

However, when the various readings are studied, the number of variations is striking. Kloppenborg has analyzed all divergences and proposes explanations.[40]

What mattered in primitive Christian groupings like Q and Th was Jesus: his words and his acts. Consequently, "The words and deeds of Jesus are a holy word, comparable with that of the Old Testament and the handing down of this precious

---

38   R. Bultmann, *Jesus and the World*, Scribers, New York c.1921, 1958, 8, Quoted by Bailey, ibidem. See also Dunn, *Jesus Remembered*, 193–95.
39   Ibidem, 74, 80.
40   Kloppenborg (2007, 54) (also referring to Dunn) suggests that "a text of Q existed *alongside* oral performances of Q...." which would then interact and cause various readings. This may be a plausible scene but does not do justice to the peculiar case of the Jesus logia. Kloppenborg comes to this position referring to Pliny who finds that authors through public readings improve their texts step by step, draft by draft.

material is entrusted to special persons." These words were "memorized and recited as holy word."[41]

Similarly the Jesus Seminar differentiates between, in their terminology, aphorisms, parables (here taken together as sayings), pronouncement stories, other stories, and legends.[42] "There is a fundamental difference between the sayings of Jesus and stories about Jesus. The transmission of the sayings of Jesus was achieved by what was, in effect, a repetition of the original spoken event." "... there is intrinsically no difference between the original speaking of a saying and subsequent quotations of it," apart from questions of accuracy, etc. (9–10).

Dunn (239–45) deepens the discussion when he imagines how the disciples would remind one another 'remember, what did he say?' memorizing the impact of the sacred word, in a sacred presence. This process would develop into a sort of pre-canon of his words (241, n.275). At the same time he puts it into a different perspective when supposing that retelling again and again of a parable would eliminate the idea of an original. In his eyes, there is "the remembered Jesus, but not an original pure form" (241). Yes, that is what usually happens in everyday life and what may be the case for the stories and the image of Jesus in memory. Here, though, it is about sacred words: sanctity is involved, and it will have been respected.[43]

Besides, literacy in Jewish Palestine was on a low level. Orality, with its stated qualities, constituted the hub of transmission, says Kloppenborg.[44]

Remembrance, therefore, is the key concept when working with transmissions. The sayings were having their own specific history of transmission, different from other texts: they were remembered as units *per se*: holy words. Contrarily the stories *about* Jesus must have been memorized differently: informal and less controlled (in terms of Bailey). These narratives later developed into the Gospels when they were written, into which the logia then were incorporated. Logically, the sayings 'Gospels' continued to be kept alive parallel to the narratives,[45] well before they were integrated into the Gospels as we know them. Was there one

---

41   H. Riesenfeld, "The Gospel Tradition and Its Beginnings" 1970, quoted from Bailey, ibidem.
42   Robert Funk / The Jesus Seminar, *The Acts of Jesus*, 1998, 2–17.
43   As to the Gospels as such says Evans (2006, 54): "[T]he persistent trend in recent years is to see the Gospels as essentially reliable ...". As to the narratives inside the Gospels. my position is more critical (as expounded) and nourished by what Evans adds to this quotation: "..., especially when properly [?] understood", i.e., "to view the historical Jesus in terms much closer to Christianity's traditional understanding, that is, as the proclaimer of God's rule, as understanding himself as the Lord's anointed, and, indeed, as God's own son, destined to rule Israel." In my view this statement is colored. My review of the pertinent literature is much more nuanced. And it does not touch my argument for the logia *vs* the narratives.
44   Kloppenborg 2007, 55–56.
45   Dunn (2003c, 53 n. 4) considers it "extremely difficult to distinguish the two" [written, oral] i.c. in Q.

sayings collection or more of them? In view of the many logia in the Gospels that are not contained in either Q or Th, sets of logia may have been transmitted separately or in one or more sayings collections. We do not know, but it is easy to imagine how different groupings fostered their own favorite texts. There was no central authority to judge, let alone decide. There was no such thing as a canon.

The authors of the Gospels shaped their narratives in the perspective of on the one hand the situation they needed as a literary means, or in view of the intended audience,[46] and, on the other hand, in the perspective of cross and resurrection. That is more or less *communis opinio*. It is important to be aware that this was the crux that occupied their minds. The teachings of Jesus retreated to the background. Maybe some logia were left out? Or did some of these reappear in Th? Others may have been adapted to suit the narrative? Again others were incorporated in a context that turned their color changing their original meaning.[47]

Therefore, the understanding that logia have been transmitted from the very beginning in continuity is an enormous break-through, and in various respects. One of the far-reaching implications is the understanding that assigning a date to texts retreats backstage. After all, all written logia, like the narratives, must date back to an oral tradition that cannot be fixed in time. Their supposed authenticity may have guaranteed their continuity. It appears that sometimes this has not been appreciated sufficiently. If the transmission of the Jesus logia was comparatively authentic (as I am arguing) this might imply more. Various strands of oral transmission, apart from Q and Th, may have existed in parallel, each with its own selection from the rich array of logia, according to what was seen as crucial in the words of Jesus. In this way we find a different set of logia in Q as compared to that of Th. Partly overlapping and each with other logia peculiar to that tradition. Consequently it appears self-evident that other sets of logia may have been in circulation.[48] Could it be that one or more of these sets

---

46   A fine case in point is Crossan's analysis of a pericope in the extra-canonical Gospel of Secret Mark and the way Mk has employed elements from that passage in various places in his narrative (Crossan 1992, 76–83).

47   Against this thesis of gradual transmission—and a fortiori against the radical view of texts being constructed by proto-orthodox groupings—R. Bauckham formulates a radical counter-proposal: the Gospel texts originate from direct eyewitnesses (*Jesus and the Eyewitnesses*, 2006). Strong comments have been voiced (Schröter 2008 and Evans 2008, and by Dunn 2008). I will not engage in this high-level discourse. However, if the eyewitness hypothesis holds, it will favor my point of authenticity even more for the logia than for the Gospels.

48   It is sometimes suggested that some non-canonical words of Jesus may originate from the same authentic source as the canonical ones but were excluded in canonization. Should they not be recognized as such—without necessarily canonizing them? I join the many who consider canonization a matter of the past, of historical subjectivity, and the premeditated

have been incorporated in the Gospels in due time as sources for the non-Q logia? A multi-source hypothesis therefore. The observation developed above is one of my motivations to take the logia in the Synoptics apart.[49]

Saying versus Narrative

Narratives, therefore, tell the story about Jesus, and in doing so, the constituting facts and traditions attain context, and thereby may have an impact on the interpretation. The logia, on the other hand, contain the message: words of exceptional value, often with a deeper meaning than can be understood at face value. These are understood as sayings, as logia. They form distinct literary units, not necessarily united in a specific context. Function, expressiveness, and language are some features that suggest to view logia as a literary genre per se. Q is a proof in case, like Th is. Both present logia as an original authentic tradition. In the canonical Gospels, however, they appear as part of a larger text, and usually are interpreted as part of the narrative. Even so, there are good reasons to see them as a separate genre, the sayings genre.[50]

Narratives had a different role. Stories were told, the actions of Jesus remembered and retold in small gatherings, in early community celebrations. Narratives allow for limited variations, words from the mouth of Jesus much less as we have seen. Moreover, the Gospels were written each for its own circle of readers/hearers, in many respects for non-Christians rather than for the faithful.

Moreover, the redaction of the written narrative had to answer the requirements of current genres. It has often been argued and convincingly so, that the Graeco-Roman *bios* served as a model.[51] If that is the case, how

---

exertion of power: secular, confessional, theological. In this perspective one book in particular draws attention: Mayotte, *The Complete Jesus* 1997. It collects sayings from a rich array of 24 sources into 9 chapters on different subject matters.

49 Growing interest in the logia is testified by other publications consisting of poetical presentations of select sayings, like Crossan's *The essential Jesus: what Jesus really taught*, 1995 and *The lost Gospel*, 1996. Robert Miller (from the Jesus Seminar) (Miller, *The complete Gospels* 1994) has published a rich collection with the full text of all the Gospels, 22 in total: Narrative-, Sayings-, Infancy-, Fragmentary-, Jewish-Christian Gospels, and Orphan Sayings and stories. What is of concern here are the Sayings Gospels. Apart from Q and Th the Greek fragments of Thomas are included together with the Secret Book of James, the Dialogue of the Savior, and the Gospel of Mary.

50 Genre: "kind, sort, style, species, category", more specifically "a category of artistic composition...marked by a distinctive style, form, or content" (*Webster's*). "... used to designate larger literary entities, such as Gospel, epistle, apocalypse, historical writing, etc. Often used as a synonym of form. (Soulen 2001, 66 and 61–64).

51 Hurtado 2003, 259 says: the Gospels belong to the *bios* genre. Dennis MacDonald, in his *The Homeric Epics and the Gospel of Mark*, 2000, 3, concludes that "Mark wrote a prose epic modelled largely after the *Odyssey* and the ending of the *Iliad*," a fascinating and inescapable argument. But, so Macdonald, this is not an isolated case. It must be understood that Greek

convincing is the thesis that a more or less direct traditioning took place? The eyewitness hypothesis seems to retreat behind the horizon as to the Gospel texts. Finally, it has been recognized time and again that one needs to see the Gospel stories as the outcome of redactional history.[52] Few studies, however, recognize that a saying must be studied primarily without the context of the narrative. The contested Jesus Seminar does to some extent, and has inspired this study in some respects.

A challenging question remains. Which of the texts by Jesus are to be classified as a saying, as a logion? Methodologically this issue is left to further research. No specific definition is applied here. Typically they are condensed expressions of an important issue. For the specific issues discussed in this study, practically all pericopes with logia of Jesus, relevant to that issue, have been included. Moreover, in the case of the Kingdom of God sayings, parables have been included as they are indispensable to get insight in Jesus' Kingdom. Of course, practical considerations have guided me. As the book addresses some specific issues—Kingdom, *psuchê, pneuma, metanoia,* and the like, those logia have been selected that have a say in the respective fields.

De-contextualization

Consequently it is appropriate in principle to do a further step. The logia are viewed here as individual text units that later have been incorporated in a narrative. The question arises if possibly the saying has been adapted to the narrative. When analyzing a logion it is useful to analyse it as a saying per se, and to see it as independent from the narrative context. It, therefore, may be necessary to be de-contextualized. It goes without saying that this must be done conscientiously and with respect to the text, to the narrative as well as to the logion. This principle is applied in this study only intentionally. Nowhere the text of the logion has been changed on this ground. What has been done as a

---

culture had pervaded the Middle East, with literature as an important item. Educated classes grew up with Homer and other classics. Like other scholars he fights the claim of Norman Perrin "that the Gospel is *sui generis* 'the unique literary creation of early Christianity.'" (ibid., 204 n.4). Dunn (2003a, 185) agrees to some extent: "the overlap between Gospel and ancient biography remains substantial and significant." See also Macdonald 2006. Burridge (1992, 2004) after a minute analysis to prove the contrary concluded to the same already in 1992. He demonstrates that the Hellenistic influence was a living presence, already for about three centuries. The independence of the Christian tradition is underscored by the lack of such biographies of famous and other rabbis—thus my summary.

52 For example, "... the Gospel traditions passed through various stages and hands, and thus it is necessary to work through several layers of tradition if one wants to discern the historical kernel of a text, if any is to be found," Whitherington 1995, 250, referring to Raymond Brown, *The Death of the Messiah*, Doubleday, New York 1994.

principle is to read the logion irrespective of the narrative in which it appears. Logically its interpretation may vary vis-à-vis the usual one.

See the next section for further potentials.

> As an illustration here is an example that we will meet later is Lk 17.21. The crux is the logion that 'the Kingdom of God is inside you (pl.)'. The context in v.20 is a discussion with the Pharisees, a context that is complex and mystifying. The continuation in v.22ff invites to interpret the Kingdom as eschatological. Decontextualization in both cases has offered new perspectives for understanding.

Conclusions

Sacred texts differ from ordinary texts. As revealed texts, their perception needs an understanding on different levels of consciousness. They refer to the world of the spirit, beyond the physical and the psychological. Characteristically, multiple meaning is implied, like often in a poem. It may hint rather than express directly. The text may be in the form of a poem, or similar to a poem. It may appear as illogical on one level and reveal itself when the reader is in a different state of consciousness. In order to understand properly one may refer to texts by mystics. However, these texts often tell us about experience. Sacred texts bring a message from that state of consciousness. Is the exegete in a position to understand the text as it was given?

- *Logia contain the message of Jesus: sacred words, transmitting transcendent reality*
- *they may represent the oldest remembrance of Jesus*
- *as such they merit special attention apart from the gospel narratives*
- *it is proposed to distinguish the logia as a genre per se*
- *reasons are three: the sacred nature of what Jesus has said, the early oral handing down (followed by the same in written form), and the literary characteristic of a saying versus a narrative.*

Implications of Method for NT Criticism

What do the observations made so far mean to NT criticism?

- Recognition of the sayings as genre
- Decontextualization of the logia from the narrative context; or even de-editing
- Acceptance of the logia as sacred texts
- Sacred texts require a specific sensitivity in terms of an open mind and spirit
- Search for multilayer interpretation.

Let us have a closer look at the differences, in schematic form, between my proposals for NT criticism re sacred texts and 'normal' texts. Needless to say, the list and its wordings are simplifying and sometimes exaggerating formulations, both in general and in wordings.

Secular approaches to texts; narratives	Proposed approaches to sacred texts; logia
1 No differentiation between sacred and other texts; human words about human condition	1 Sacred texts reflect and translate transcendental reality; they contain 'charged' words about that reality
2 Words are the message; literal meaning	2 Words are shell of nut; meaning is content of nut
3 Narrative contains logia that in principle are not different from other text elements	3 Logia form well-defined separate elements of sacred nature
4 Text is a logical whole: one interpretation is valid Words are true	4 Multiple meanings on different levels of consciousness Words are indications of meaning
5 Logia are 'normal' wisdom in every-day language	5 Logia are words of the Master reflecting 'sacred' wisdom
6 Logia are part of other genres	6 Logia form a genre *per se*
7 Logia are part and parcel of the Gospel text	7 Logia texts hail from older 'De-editing' may be appropriate
8 Logia are reader-response directed: then and there in 1st c Palestine	8 Logia are reader-response directed: - at all times - at different levels of consciousness
9 Message of logia is addressed to particular situation	9 Logia contain universal message beyond time and place
10 Logia are unique sayings, culturally, religiously	10 As logia of the great religions share this universal message, comparative study is useful, also from outside Near and Middle Eastern religions[53]

---

[53] A recently published book (Sasson 2007), relevant to this issue, has been reviewed as an exemplary study: an experiment in comparative interreligious midrash (Frenschkowski 2009).

This scheme represents elements from this chapter, and presents a first suggestion to use when interpreting logia.

However, in practice things are not so simple. Let us have a look how it has worked out.

It turned out to be useful yet difficult to identify sacred texts from regular ones. Constructing relevant criteria is a task exceeding the format of this book. It has therefore been decided to consider all selected logia as sacred. (**1**)

Related is the question how to define what a logion is as compared to discourse and the like. Though in the first instance all words by Jesus qualify we need to be more specific. The word logion suggests a word or a short statement rather than, e.g., a discourse. Unfortunately no study is available that offers either a ready-made solution, or criteria to identify logia from other sorts of pronouncements. In this study a pragmatic approach has been chosen selecting those texts where Jesus is speaking in a concise way, particularly in a teaching mode, or in a clear call for understanding, for acting, or for remembering; also words that seem to come from a different 'world.' Consequently the selected text may be part of a longer discourse but is selected for its penetrating wording or meaning. Parables that are pertinent to the keywords will in principle be taken as a whole, but where applicable condensed. (**1**)

We have seen that words in sacred texts sometimes refer to a reality that lies outside the range of sensory perception, like the Kingdom of God in Lk 17.20–21. Or a logion transmits something sacred as a straight one-to-one translation will not do justice to the meaning behind the meaning of the logion. Sometimes another wording serves the purpose. The same goes for logia that reflect different levels of consciousness in the person speaking, or it may reflect a reality of different dimensions. Alternatively, when one understands words by Jesus as reflecting sacred wisdom, consequently on the side of the interpreter and translator, or of the reader in general a degree of wisdom is required. In principle this requirement cannot be met, as nobody will have the pretense of equalling Jesus' wisdom. Even, this idea should rule the interpretation. Being sacred wisdom the words have a different attunement and cannot be interpreted rationally or sensorially only.[54] (**1, 2, 3**)

---

54 The current requirements to sacred text do not suffice, if judged from this perspective. Shillington, in his challenging and appropriate textbook on *Reading the sacred text: an introduction to biblical studies* (2002, 20–25), suggests as exercise in 'knowing knowing' when assessing a sacred text to answer on four levels of consciousness: empirical, intellectual, rational, and responsible. What is missing dearly is the level of consciousness for the sacred, a spiritual level. "Sacred texture takes note of the divine in the text" (279), he suggests in line with my note. However, the divine does not limit itself to where it is mentioned explicitly. If one seeks to be spiritually conscious it is a matter of attitude, of approach.

The issue of the logia as a genre *per se* was discussed earlier. Summarizing, the motive of a logion is a more powerful and convincing expression, in a more concise form. The substance matter is of great or central relevance. (4)

Logia in principle have a heavier bearing in interpretation than narratives or other textual elements, as they may hail from an older and more stable and precise tradition than narratives. See the Gospel of Thomas and Q. They have priority therefore in interpretative value. (5)

Logia in the canonical Gospels appear in context, especially in narratives. It is conceivable that the text of the logion has been adapted to the context. In principle, if this is true, editing and/or de-contextualization would be appropriate. This issue has not been taken up in this book. If done, it would require caution, and adequate methods. (5)

Logia may in principle be understood as universal wisdom, to be compared for example with sayings from the messengers of other major religions. This idea offers a challenging perspective but has not been put in practice in this book. (6)

Another step in studying this *genre* might be to try and find out if the text of the logia as they appear in the Gospels could be a redacted form as compared to a hypothetical original form in the sayings Gospel. This concept would need studying the possibility of 'de-editing' the logia. In view of the now prevailing idea that the Gospels have been written for a more or less well-defined target group, it may look probable that the logia have been selected and edited while being included in the respective narratives of the Gospels. This may imply that also some 'revealed' or 'inspired' elements may have been redacted away in the course of the redaction of the Gospel text: a writer follows his vision of what he wants to convey. This leaves aside the issue that after the first copy had been made untold many of the sort followed in different lines of transmitting. In each copy the process of transcribing invited potential mistakes: copying errors: wrong spelling, omissions, additions, 'improvements,' misunderstanding of the text[55] and purposely corrupting a text for the sake of faith.[56] (7)

Reader-response critique may obtain when the Jesus logia are seen as reader-response directed. The logia evoke a response that is both timeless and of all times. Although their practical interpretation will vary from period to period, from culture to culture, from one level of consciousness of the reader to another, the underlying 'sacred' meaning, empowered in the very words of the logion, understood at the spiritual level of human consciousness will continue to evoke the same meaning and concomitant conduct.

If the spiritual nature of the logia is understood, and in case the divine origin (revelation) is taken into account, a challenging perspective is opening:

---

55 Ehrman 2005, 45–69.
56 Ehrman 1993.

the Jesus logia may contain universal messages beyond time and space. Compare 6 *supra*. (8)

A further step is included reaching beyond what is done in this book. It would be interesting when studying this *genre* to undertake a comparative study of sayings in sacred scriptures of other religions. This would widen the traditional comparative study of Near- and Mid-Eastern religions. Buddhism, e.g., has many traits in common with Christianity, also in its sacred texts (Borg). (9, 10)

Depending on one's particular view on spirituality and mysticism the elements listed above would appear 'reasonable' to be taken into consideration when studying sacred texts like the logia. This implies that these elements should be part of the methodology of exegesis. Consulting literature on Bible criticism it is hard to find clues for the proposed approach. For example, in the excellent introduction to Bible criticisms *To Each Its Own Meaning*[57] not more than a trace of the elements characteristic of and for sacred texts can be found. However, it seems so natural that these elements—or some of them—should play a role in understanding, interpreting, and translating this type of texts. Therefore they cannot be but part and parcel of a methodology with that end.

What is found missing in current methodology is a special *approach* to sacred texts, an approach based on the very nature of mysticism. More specifically, what is needed is adding some adequate perspective to existing criticisms rather than creating a new full-fledged one.

What do we learn from the argument up to here?

1. The Jesus logia, therefore, may be seen as a separate *genre* apart from the narrative in which they are embedded.

2. As sacred texts logia have a number of characteristics
   - are multi-layered in meaning
   - have universal significance
   - words are not just human but transcendent
   - words are charged
   - target group is universal (time, culture)

How do our findings relate with current approaches? Some of the characteristics can be found in current criticisms, but this scenario is never the case systematically or explicitly: no systematic word about sacred texts or poems, revelations of inspired texts as being a case different from normal texts.

There is one intriguing case: poststructuralist criticism (or: deconstructive criticism).[58] It is intriguing as, on the one hand, it answers quite a few of the

---

57 McKenzie, Haynes, *To each its own meaning*, 1999.
58 Beardsley, "Poststructuralist criticism," in: McKenzie, Haynes 1999, 253–67.

requirements formulated for sacred texts. On the other hand, in its present form it is not applicable as it claims to be "... highly critical of religion and theology, which are seen as false believing in the 'presence' of transcendent reality." In addition, it is said to be "the rejection of the attempt to find a privileged position 'above' the text, or above the world created by the text." It is "rather to lead readers to live without absolutes." Does this apply to sacred texts, to the logia? I submit that these are of a different nature. Yet, a series of pronouncements about this type of criticism appears congenial rather than opposed.

Poststructuralist criticism (or deconstructive criticism)[59] amazingly contains potentialities for spiritual criticism. Deconstruction as a method—or rather as an attitude toward the text—compared to other criticisms, is closest to the requirements of spiritual criticism.

To substantiate the positive potentialities I quote a few striking statements by Beardslee.[60] They serve to show the parallel with some essential characteristics in the proposed approaches scheme, like 'words are shell of nut, meaning is content of nut'; 'multiple meanings'; 'words are indications of meaning'; 'reader-response directed.' Here are a few striking quotations.

> "...discovering the incompleteness of the text and finding a fresh, if transient, insight made possible by the 'free play' of indeterminacy of the text"; "...its focus is on dismantling of existing patterns"(253); "...if we are to read any text fruitfully, we need to be aware of...its incompleteness, that is, the way in which the hearer or reader has to fill in the picture that is suggested by speech or writing...;" "...to deliver the interpreter from the repression of limits and traditions so that fresh interpretation may take place."(254) "Deconstruction...means dismantling a seeming coherence of the text and reading it in a way that resists 'closure'"(256). "...opening of a 'trace' of that which we cannot grasp" "What is required is a way of listening" (262). "...the text does not communicate a definitive or closed meaning." "The emphasis on...the plural meaning of texts...is intended to challenge reigning orthodoxies...." "...deconstruction has a very important role to play in biblical studies" (263). "One way of using deconstruction would be to deconstruct the 'public' or 'natural' patterns of religion and society and then affirm a 'confessional' or revealed pattern...." (264) "...promise for deconstruction as it is used as one tool and not the sole way of reading."(265.)

Thus, I find in deconstruction in this sense a useful approach as an attitude for current Bible criticism. It serves as a way to gain more insight. Important is to find a way of transcending the form, to rise above the positions formulated, and see the wider and deeper perspectives. This is an invitation to stretch the very essence of deconstruction to an application on sacred texts.

The spiritual dichotomy of this method is illustrated by another amazing fact. The philosophy of deconstruction bears resemblance to the negative

---

59 Beardslee 1999, 254–67.
60 "Poststructuralist criticism," in: McKenzie, Haynes 1999, 254–67.

mysticism of Pseudo-Dionysius, whom we met already in the chapter on mysticism, demonstrating its spiritual potentiality.

Many Gospel texts and especially Jesus *logia,* being sacred texts, need a new critical approach in finding meaning. In current methodology the sacred is not a focus. Apart from literal or symbolic meanings, sacred texts should be interpreted and understood as spiritual. Often they refer to mysticism which, as shown in chapter 2, is a strong current, a flow that is central to religion and to the history of Christianity, but neglected in Bible criticism.

ANNEX 1
Methodology Revisited

A few remarks in telegram style on some current criticisms, based on the book that provided us with a framework in the last section: McKenzie and Haynes, but the following interpretation is mine. Each criticism has been developed in a true and honest attitude toward the Bible texts. Even so, has the sacredness of especially the logia been accounted for? As shown above, this type of text requires a special approach in assessing the meaning. To that end some of the major Bible criticisms are summarily reviewed. It serves to see if the characteristics relating to sacred texts as formulated in the box may be relevant to these other methods of text analysis. The issue is in what way they could add to the current criticisms. The following proposals are preliminary suggestions for NT criticism, with a special eye on the logia. In the format of this book, we will not discuss in full the question whether or not these approaches do justice to the requirements from spirituality. Neither is any of the ideas put forward as operational.

In *source criticism* more attention may be given to the oral and verbal tradition of authoritative teachings, especially the sayings. The recognition of the unique place and position of Jesus' logia in early Christianity leads to a different attitude. 'Thus spoke the Master' as a basic approach. This implies separating the sources of a specific logion from sources of the Gospel pericope or narrative in which they appear. A larger role is to be attributed to Th and Q as collections of logia. These texts require the critic to study the logion per se.

In *form criticism,* apart from the observations on source criticism, more attention may be given to oral and verbal/literary tradition of authoritative teachings, esp. sayings. A more explicit recognition is needed of the logia as a genre, and that or how it was incorporated in the narrative of the canonical Gospels. Therefore a larger role is to be attributed to Th and Q as collections of logia. Comparisons may be made with other sacred sayings traditions in other cultures.[61] More adequate and more of this time is a comparison with sacred texts of other world religions, especially those with aphorisms. This approach may possibly meet with consequences for the recognition of logia as spiritual teachings for both everyday life and inner development. Thus, special attention to the universal meaning of Jesus' message, not only for first-century Palestine is necessary. This interpretation may shed new light on meaning of logia, particularly in terms of different layers of meaning that appeals to different levels of consciousness. Reader-response approaches may help to clear this issue, provided the spiritual approach is recognized. From a spiritual perspective, the following statement would not suffice: "... a text that was written by an author or authors who wrote with well-defined intentions in specific sets of sociohistorical circumstances." (Sweeney in McKenzie&Haynes, 83). Many of the sacred texts must be interpreted in a wider perspective.

Redaction criticism is more or less not applicable to logia as it focuses on text editing from different sources. While logia are separate text units, in principle they are independent of one another.

Even so, an important issue concerns the way in which original logia were edited in the Gospel narrative. How can these edited logia be de-edited, i.e., brought back to original form, undone from narrative compulsions. Maybe comparison with the logia of Th can be helpful.

Structural criticism admits that "biblical texts are religious texts that, in certain instances, emphasize that their goal is to transmit 'revealed' or 'inspired' knowledge" but it "does not prevent them from being instances of *human communication*" (emphasis in original). "Even though they are, for believers, 'Words of God', they remain human words." Sic: the words are human indeed but essentially (*origin*-ally) they convey a transcendent reality. Inspired or even revealed knowledge cannot adequately be transmitted in human words. A new perspective in this criticism may be added.

Reader-response criticism "... approaches biblical literature in terms of the values, attitudes, and response of readers. The reader, therefore, plays a role in the 'production' or 'creation' of meaning and significance. This…relativizes the conventional view that the meaning of the text is like the content of the nut, simply awaiting its extraction by the reader."[62] On the one hand, this assessment is true, yet the logia do form the nut. The trick is that the words of the logion are the shell, the contents being hidden within. What is required is enlightenment to open the shell and have access to the contents, i.e., to Truth. Sacred texts have the pretense of conveying truth irrespective of the

---

61 The history of religions method as developed in the nineteenth and early twentiethe compared biblical texts with other religious texts of the same period (D. Patte in McKenzie, Haynes 1999, 182).
62 E.V. McKnight, ibidem 230

reader/listener. At the same time, the attitude of the reader will determine whether or not [s]he may grasp the very significance of the text. Therefore interpretative meanings will be manifold. Referring to Gadamer: "But be aware: truth is larger than method." "Truth is no longer to be seen as decipherable by means of the right scientific method but now be seen as continually disclosing itself in our prejudices."[63]

For poststructuralist criticism (or deconstructive criticism) see above.

Conclusions

The last section of this chapter has asked whether or not current criticisms match the character of sacred texts, especially the Jesus logia in the Gospels. Current criticisms do not pay special attention to the characteristics of sacred texts. As to the logia, they do not receive particular attention. Some tentative characteristics of this type of texts are presented, but this section does not present specified methods for a 'spiritual criticism' nor does it advocate one. It proposes to enrich current criticisms with additional insights as how to address sacred texts. The thrust, therefore, rather is to try and develop an approach appropriate to the logia and other similar texts. Some suggestions are made, and some cases are presented focusing on some important terms. For each term a juxtaposition is made between a traditional approach and an alternative one. Further study and development is badly needed.

> *When love has carried us above all things…we receive in peace the Incomprehensible Light, enfolding us and penetrating us. What is this Light, if it be not a contemplation of the Infinite, and an intuition of Eternity? We behold that which we are, and we are that which we behold; because our being, without loving anything of its personality, is united with Divine Truth.*
>
> *Ruysbroeck*[64]

ANNEX 2
Greek and Aramaic

Two issues. One is the language in which the logia were spoken. The other one is about the original translation from Aramaic into Greek.

1. The mother tongue of Jesus was Aramaic, that is *communis opinio*.[65] What does that imply when studying the logia? Are we dealing indeed with the very words of Jesus when we use the only available text, i.e., the Greek? Here are a few considerations.

---

63 Nathan 2007, 297.
64 Quoted from Evelyn Underhill, *Mysticism*, vi.
65 Probably he knew Greek, as Nazareth was located on major trade routes connecting to the adjacent Greek-speaking communities. As a son of a carpenter, he was positioned in the

- Reconstruction of the supposed Aramaic text is useless if we want the *ipsissima verba*
- In view of the decades-long process of transmitting it is well possible that some texts had been translated and transmitted already well before the written Gospel
- The spirit of the logia must have been preserved in the process of transmitting even in Greek
    - because of the predilection for the exact sense of his words
    - because much of Palestine was bilingual
    - because of the check by and among bilingual adherents of Jesus
- The Greek text is the only available one
- The Syrian versions are translations from the Greek. The Syrian Orthodox Church however maintains that it is the original text of the Gospels (EEC).
- All serious NT research is based exclusively on the established Greek text (NA27).
- Reconstructing an Aramaic original from the Greek NT, based on known Aramaic equivalents is a laudable effort but cannot assure to bring back the authentic words.
    - Often this is done by tracing Semitisms in the words of Jesus, resulting in a new interpretation of that text. Casey (2007, Synopsis) does so for the Son of Man phrases, and finds that "Gospel translators deliberately translated in both literal and creative ways in order to produce a new Christological title [the Son of Man title]." His reviewer[66] continues that—in case the sayings in Greek do not represent a fairly literal rendering of Jesus' actual utterances—retranslating is rather useless.
- This reconstruction effort is part of the major current in present-day Jesus quests: retracing the Judaic and Jewish context of Jesus
- The language of Jesus in the logia employs current words (with their currently understood meanings). However, by his using these he charges them with new energy and meaning: he brought a new message in seemingly old wordings.
- Therefore, if we retranslate his Greek words into the underlying Aramaic in its then current usage, it may not convey what one is searching for.

2. The language in which the logia were transmitted.

Aramaic was the language Jesus used in most of his statements. In that form they were remembered and transmitted among people. What about the transition to Greek? Generally it is surmised that first was the Aramaic, and then at a point in time the Aramaic text was translated. However, it may have been otherwise.

First-century Palestine was a Hellenistic area where Judaism predominated, but Greek culture was present in many respects. It was bilingual to some extent. Studies differ in their conclusions. Stanley Porter (1994, 2006) presents

---

lower middle class: carpenters would function as small building and construction 'firms'. Maybe sometimes he did teach in Greek. To what extent the logia were handed down in Greek is unknown. Most authors think it was in Aramaic.

66 Paul Owen, review of Maurice Casey, *The solution of the 'Son of Man' problem*, RBL 2/9/2009.

convincing evidence of the widespread use of the Greek language among Jews in first-century Palestine whilst Chancey has come to other results.[67] Porter's argument is as follows. Contrary to current understanding, Greek was usual. Among overwhelming evidence to it, some are quite convincing. At Jewish burial sites, Greek inscriptions were frequent. At one specific site in western Galilee it mounted to 80%. Even in Jerusalem the number of epitaphs in Greek is approximately equal to those in Semitic languages (1994, 147). "If even rabbis and their families phrased their epitaphs in Greek, there is only one natural explanation of that phenomenon: Greek was the language of their daily life,"[68] or rather: 'was in many cases a second language'. In the 130s there is written evidence of the wide-spread use of Greek by common people: letters written by Jewish revolutionaries (fighting against the Greco-Roman suppression!): it was easier to find a scribe of Greek than of a Semitic language. Greek had a predominant role, is the conclusion of Porter. In lower Galilee Greek had a function in trade and therefore must have been current among many lower and certainly middle-class people. Is it a signal that two of Jesus' disciples had Greek names: Andrew and Philip? However, the contrary outcomes of Chaney, Bird, and Porter remain unsolved.

At the rate that the logia were transmitted in wider and wider circles, it was natural that bilingual individuals started to render them in Greek, or were helpful to assist, as the occasion demanded. The question when someone sat down to translate them is the wrong question. Gradually the logia were handed down in both Aramaic and Greek, I suppose, in an attitude of respect to the sanctity of the very words.

Therefore: the crucial point is not in which language the words were remembered and transmitted but by the attitude of respect and sanctity.

---

67 Chancey 2007. Bird (2006) in a discussion with Porter joins in the criticism.
68 Quoted by Porter 1994 from P.W. van der Horst, *Ancient Jewish epitaphs*, Kampen: Kok Pharos 1991, 24.

PART TWO
The Kingdom of God:
A Spiritual Interpretation

Introducing 'the Kingdom of God'

In the chapter on mysticism two characteristics were found to be essential to mysticism: presence and transformation. In this Part, we will investigate if these qualities are reflected in the logia of Jesus on the Kingdom of God, the *basileia tou theou*, a central focus of his Message.[1]

Important issues regarding the Kingdom have been, and continue to be, discussed in the scholarly literature. Does it refer to the Last Day (eschatology) or to a socio-political paradise to be established at the Second Coming of Jesus Christ? Or is it an inner reality inside the human being? Theology has found a difficulty in that the Gospels mention it frequently whilst Acts and the Epistles are reticent. Eschatological preferences have been influenced by texts in Revelation.

In the discourse on the Kingdom of God, one can easily discern that two topics hold an absolute top position: the 'when' issue, comprising not only the perspective on the eschaton but also the 'where': in heaven, in the historical Jesus, in Christ, among or even inside human beings; or spread out over the world? These questions cannot, of course, be answered without understanding the 'what' of the Kingdom, the *mustêrion* as Jesus calls it. Some logia speak about 'for whom' is the Kingdom, or about the 'how' to enter it. Answers to each of these questions are crucial for understanding. However, the central question is and remains: what does Jesus say to it?

Before tackling these crucial issues, chapter 4 will frame them in one of the current discourses: is it to be understood eschatologically? Is it a realm, an area? Or rather is it to be understood as a reign of social justice? Or the king ruling?[2] Or must it be seen as an inner reality? Indeed, how should one interpret what

---

†   Chapters 6 and 7 have been presented in an earlier version at the SBL Annual Meeting in Washington DC, 2006.

1   The Gospel of Matthew mostly speaks of the Kingdom of Heavens. "Since the Divine Name *YHWH* was uttered only once a year by the chief priest in the Holy of Holies, except for this very special usage it was a kind of 'taboo' term. So the 'Heavens' was used as a reverent round-about expression to avoid uttering or writing the Divine Name. Thus, 'the Kingdom of (the) Heavens' in Matthew is equivalent to 'the Kingdom of God' in the other Gospels," for example, Soesilo 2002, 239. Also Dunn 2003b, 384 n. 7. Throughout this book, therefore, the term 'Kingdom of God' is being used.

2   This discussion has triggered even more and rather vehement discussions. The distinction is one of form, not of contents. For example Ladd 1962, 230.

the concept of kingdom signifies? Chapter 5 addresses this question as a useful tool for understanding the *basileia tou theou* as a kingdom (rather than as reign, rule, or empire), as well as for its use as a biblical term for present-day culture.

Chapter 6 then proceeds to ask for the *when* of the Kingdom of God as reflected in the Jesus sayings. It is about the Kingdom's being now or rather in the future, or was it once only, during Jesus' lifetime on earth? If it will come in future at what time, right now or soon, or rather at the eschaton? Or is it here already?

The *where* (chapter 7) is about the here or elsewhere. Is the Kingdom of God this-worldly or rather in heaven? Whenever it may come (or in case it has come already), is it present here? Where is that presence located? Is it inside people (like Harnack maintained), or rather among individuals (as a spiritual power), or in society at large (as a unifying force of peace and love?)?

The crucial issue of course is the question of the *what* (chapter 8). Nowhere in the logia does one find clear concrete answers. A study of the parables on the Kingdom suggests an audacious interpretation, taking up the concept of *mustêrion*, a term Jesus uses various times related to the Kingdom. Generally it is rendered as secret or mystery. The following chapter 9 asks *whose* the Kingdom is. Jesus suggests the poor and people 'such as the children' as those whom Jesus mentions specifically. What is needed to enter the Kingdom.

To this end, all sayings by Jesus in the synoptic Gospels—and in the margin including Th and Jn—with this term and relevant for the inner-world dimension will be examined.[3] This endeavor promises to be quite audacious both quantitatively and qualitatively—qualitatively as the eschaton is considered crucial to Christianity by broad circles of Christians and scholars alike and quantitatively because over hundreds of years, and increasingly during the entire twentieth century, an overwhelming and enduring outpouring of views on the Kingdom has been flooding the professional world.

---

3   The Synoptics have 33 verses with *basileia* in Mt, 7 in Mk and 23 in Lk. Of these some are excluded from examination: those referring to the eschaton, e.g., where the Kingdom is placed in heaven at a future point in time, those referring to a worldly or historical kingdom, and those that do not define the Kingdom of God in terms of when, where, what, for whom, how.

Examined are: Mt 4.17,.23; 5.2, 10; 6.10; 7.21; 9.35; 10.7; 12.28; 13.11, 19, 24, 33, (38, 41, 43), 44, 45, 47, 52; 16.28; 18.1, 3, 4, 23; 19.23, 24; 20.1; 21.31; 22.2; 23.13; 25.1; Mk 1.15; 4.11, 26, 30; 9.1; 10.14, 15, 23, 24, 25; 12.34; Lk 4.43; 7.28; 8.1, 10; 9.2, 11, 27, 60, 62; 10.9, 11; 11.2, 20; 12.31, 32; 13.19, 20; 16.16; 17.20, 21; 18.16, 17, 24, 25; 21.31; Jn 3.3, 3.5; 18.36. All these have been examined, and except a few (repetition, indirect references to the Kingdom) have been used.

CHAPTER FOUR
The Kingdom of God[1]:
Eschaton, Polity, Inner Reality?

The Kingdom of God "is a silent, strong divine power in the heart"

It "comes to *individuals*, it enters into their *soul*, and they grasp it"

"The Kingdom of the holy God is in the individual's heart, *it is God himself with his strength*"

"It is the most important and indeed the deciding experience a human being can have, penetrating and controlling the complete sphere of his being"

"It grows surely and silently like a seed and it brings forth fruit"

"Its nature is a spiritual greatness, a force that sinks into one's inner being, and cannot be understood but from within"

"'It is not here or there, it is inside you (pl.)'"

Adolph von Harnack[2]

Introduction

These impressive statements about the inner dimension of the Kingdom of God testify the qualities of divine presence and the concomitant transformation of the whole human being. This characteristic was given by the great NT scholar of that time, Adolf von Harnack, during one of his famous 1899/1900 Berlin

---

1 Throughout this book 'Kingdom of God' is capitalized so as to emphasize the uniqueness of this kingdom. When this is not the case the word *kingdom* remains in lower case.
2 Harnack 1900, emphasis in the: original. Transl. E.: WvL.
 These statements have been selected from the full text..
 Here is the German original:
 "... es ist eine stille, mächtige Gotteskraft in den Herzen." 44
 "Das Reich Gottes kommt, indem es zu den *einzelnen* kommt, Einzug in ihre *Seele* hält, und sie es ergreifen." 45
 "... die Herrschaft des heiligen Gottes in den einzelnen Herzen, *es ist Gott selbst mit seiner Kraft*. 45
 "... dass es das Wichtigste, ja das Entscheidende ist was der Mensch erleben kann,..." 48
 "... so sicher und so still aufwächst wie ein Samenkorn und Frucht bringt." 48
 "Es hat die Natur einer geistigen Grösse, einer Macht, die in das Innere eingesenkt wir und nur von dem Inneren zu erfassen ist." 48
 "'Es ist nicht hier oder dort; es ist inwendig in euch.'" 48
 Harnack 1900

lectures.[3] He places this interpretation of the Kingdom of God next to its eschatological-apocalyptic aspect—the *eschaton* referring to the 'last' (what will happen at the end of times)[4], the *apocalyptic* referring to the same end of times but as a unique, immediate and sudden event, throwing everything upside down.[5]

What does Harnack say to this? "Die Predigt Jesu durchläuft alle Aussagen und Formen von der alttestamentlich gefärbten, prophetischen Ankündigung des Gerichtstages und der künftigen sichtbar eintretenden Gottesherrschaft bis zu dem Gedanken eines jetzt beginnenden, mit der Botschaft Jesu anhebenden innerlichen Kommens des Reiches." (Harnack 1900, 43). The here and now versus the there and then. In the statements quoted he brings to the fore the inner directed, more individual dimension, related to one's consciousness and its transformation by an overwhelming presence; the first part reveals the wider view on Jesus. Harnack continues and deplores that the disciples and early followers of Jesus did not hold to this side of the teaching but rather and one-sidedly interpreted Jesus' teaching as eschatological, placing it in the future and de-individualizing it.

Thus, Harnack respects both views, the eschatological and the inner Kingdom. This book accepts both as probably historical, but its motivation is to highlight the inner meaning.

The *Eschaton*?

Part II of the book addresses the issue of the inner teaching of the Kingdom of God. Before doing so, what is the scholarly consensus about the Kingdom of God? According to one recent interpretation "Jesus' kingdom of God means primarily the reign of God as king and the realm in which he reigns."[6] This is a good start. Obviously, however, this definition is more concrete and down-to-earth than the present approach.

When taking up the concept of the inner kingdom, it is necessary to frame the concept of this inner-worldly dimension within a concise overview of the three most important approaches of the Kingdom of God, interpreting it as other-worldly, this-worldly, and inner-worldly, respectively:

---

3   See also Dunn 2003b, 38 n 60
4   Eschatology, the study of 'last things', in a wide sense, refers to what will bring history and the world to a close, to the last judgment, the resurrection of the dead, the expected coming of the Kingdom of God, and to *parousia* (Jesus' second coming), the destructive perishing of this world, and the establishment of God's Kingdom and reign with Christ at God's right hand in heaven (Christopher Roland, in John Bowden, *Christianity: the Complete Guide*, Continuum, London 2005, 379–80).
5   For a wider treatment of these terms see, e.g., Dunn 2003a, 401.
6   Kanagaraj 2009, 25.

- as a new world at the end of times
  - will it be a real kingdom, as polity, as an institution? For example, will it be the fulfillment of the promise of the return of the Davidic kingdom under God's protection as opposed to the secular kingdoms of Caesar and the Herodians?
  - or is it the kingly rule at the eschaton when in an apocalypse all things will be made new, and the evil destroyed?
    : the eschatological dimension
        often in terms of the parousia, the Second Coming of Christ[7]
    :*'other-worldly'*

                                                                (Siglum: 'Bultmann')

- as a new world of justice to be established through social and cultural (r)evolution here and now
  - a metaphor for a social entity, a brotherhood where righteousness, justice, peace and order will rule and reign when the ethical message of Jesus, as lived by Jesus himself during his earthly life, will be followed and observed?
    : the contemporary social, political, and cultural dimension
    : *'this-worldly'*

                                                                (Siglum: 'Borg')

- as a divine spiritual entity, a *dunamis*, a strength, energy, a state of consciousness, *pneuma*, either on the individual level or at large
  - an inner kingdom developing in individuals
  - individuals, united heart to heart, soul to soul, where peace, happiness, light, good will, together with care, sympathy and love for one's neighbors are the driving forces inspired and guided by the Spirit

    : the spiritual dimension
    : *inner-worldly*

                                                                (Siglum: 'Pagels')

A Bit of History

After the early nineteenth century had paid very little attention to the Kingdom of God at all, Albrecht Ritschl was the first to take it up, the great theologian of the Kingdom of God in that century. His conception was this-worldly,

---

[7] The parousia is a post-Easter phenomenon, that gradually developed in some circles. It is closely related to Jewish messianic expectations. In 'our' logia the term does not figure, neither can we find Jesus announcing it in relation to the Kingdom unless eschatologically determined. Vena (2001) has written a well-argumented monograph on it. It is placed in the Jewish eschatology, Hellenistic culture, Roman politics, and doctrinal developments in some Christian communities (4). Due to the destruction of the temple some of the Christian communities in Palestine were unable to stay away from this apocalyptic mood" (259). Mark makes Jesus announce the coming of the Kingdom to counteracting the risen anxiety. Paul is the main determinant, announcing that the parousia is imminent.(257-58). The 1st c Christian apocalypticism, eschatology, and parousia are to be understood in historical and socio-cultural perspectives (271–72). There is definitely no call to the inner. Transformation is called for but is anthropological, sociological, and cosmological in character (159–60), not mystical. These logia do not figure as an object of study here.

monistic, and ethical in character (Lundström 1963, 3–9, esp. 6), the Kingdom really speaking as a sociological entity (ibidem 10). Although the pioneer, his influence was soon waning when two major figures entered the scene, Adolph von Harnack (preceded by Wilhelm Herrmann) and of course Albert Schweitzer (preceded by Johannes Weiss and others). Almost immediately after Harnack's lecture (1899/1900) the tide was turning, and in a most radical way. From then onwards the eschatological interpretation of the Kingdom of God became the dominant one, the *communis opinio* (Lundström, *passim*, esp. 27–103).

One of the forces at work has been Albert Schweitzer's eschatological and apocalyptic interpretation. He built on the work of the real pioneer, Johannes Weiss (1901). It was as an apocalyptic event in itself: Harnack's views disappeared virtually completely. Eschatology prevailed, apocalyptic elements appeared from behind the horizon. Jesus' teaching was placed on a radically new theater stage.

Half a century later Rudolf Bultmann continues the trend by underscoring the thesis that the kingdom is eschatological. As it is seen as the core of Jesus' message, the Gospel becomes other-worldly.

Rudolf Bultmann in his *Theologie des Neuen Testaments* (UTB 1948, 1984) considers the concept of the Kingdom of God (*Gottesherrschaft*[8]) to be the core concept (3), "der beherrschende Begriff der Verkündigung Jesu" … "Ihr unmittelbar bevorstehendes Hereinbrechen, das sich schon jetzt kund tut, verkündigt er." It is eschatological. It means that the reign and rule by God will put an end to the present world ("der bisherige Weltlauf"), destroying everything that is anti-divine and satanic "unter dem die Welt jetzt seufzt." All suffering will end, *das Heil* is coming to God's people waiting for the fulfillment of prophetic promises. Its coming is miraculous, it is a divine act, nothing human to it (3), Moreover, the Kingdom's coming is apocalyptic: "das Heil der Frommen…wird nicht in nationalem Wohlsein und Glanz, sondern in paradiesischer Herrlichkeit bestehen" (4). All this-wordliness is absent. The reign of Satan and his demons is past, "Jetzt ist die Zeit gekommen! Die Gottesherrschaft bricht herein! Das Ende ist da!" is Bultmann's paraphrase of Mk 1:15. He makes it referring to the Last Day, the judgment, the resurrection of the dead, the hell of fire, those justified will be imparted life (*zôê*) (5)—in my view an interpretation foreign to the spirit of the Gospel. Associations with gradual growth or human influences are rejected (6ff).[9] Interestingly, Bultmann

---

8   For rendering 'Kingdom' by *Herrschaft*, see chapter 5.
9   A different view is the following."In the 1940s and 1950s Bultmann became a controversial figure…for wanting to 'demythologize' the NT, interpreting (away) its mythological material, especially its futurist eschatology and apocalyptic language, in existentialist terms as well as for his historical scepticism…." See R. Morgan, 'New Testament, in 'Rogerson c. a.,*The Oxford Handbook of Biblical Studies,* 2006, 31.

THE KINGDOM OF GOD: *ESCHATON*, POLITY, INNER REALITY

does not pay any further attention to this issue in the remainder of this book, though he considers it to be central in the message of Jesus. The *Verkündigung Jesu* takes only 33 out of 600 pages (excl. annexes etc.). Obviously it is implied in the eschatology which is viewed as the dominant feature in Jesus' message, and therefore throughout the book. The fact that Paul fully neglects the concept of the Kingdom probably has its effect on Bultmann's argument. Jeremias is of the same opinion, summarizing that the 'Geheimnis der Königsherrschaft Gottes (Mk 4.11)' is "der Gewissheit der sich realisierenden Eschatologie. Die Stunde der Erfüllung ist da." (Jeremias 1952, 160). Bultmann's followings has maintained these basic insights and emphasizes them though mitigating it to the extent that is not wholly futuristic (Perrin 119, 159).

And More Recently

Only since the 'seventies new views have been presented, which turn the attention to actual issues of the present-day culture and society and to a returning interest in spirituality. One of these views is the realization of the kingdom in the dimension of the humane: following Jesus in his acts and words during his earthly life: realizing a brother- and sisterhood among men. Another is the realization of the kingdom in the inner life of the individual, but at the same time sharing and radiating out into the world. Resulting from the dominating trend of Modernity and other developments, the concept of the Kingdom itself lost much of its credibility.

Marcus Borg does both. The phrase 'the Kingdom of God' he considers as "perhaps the best shorthand summary of the message and passion [*sic*] of Jesus" (Borg 2003, 131). What the story of Jesus is most centrally about is the Kingdom of God, says Borg. See Mk 1:15, many parables and the Lord's prayer. He sees different aspects in the concept of the Kingdom (132): "Sometimes it points to the power of God active in Jesus' work as healer and exorcist [a]; sometimes it has a mystical meaning referring to the presence of God [b]. In other texts, it refers to a community [c], and it can refer to the kingdom at the end of history or beyond history, i.e., the eschatological or apocalyptic aspects [d]; 'Kingdom of God' also has a political meaning...." Out of these five aspects he prefers to interpret the concept as a process of social and political transformation resulting in "what life would be like on earth if God were king and the rulers of the earth were not." Here he seems to resume some central aspects of a movement active in the early twentieth century in Germany and around, and in the USA ('the Social Gospel'). This movement did not concern itself so much with exegesis, rather it would see in the teachings of Jesus advocating the Kingdom as an immediate, practical force operating in the present (Lundström, 17–26).

Borg, whilst not rejecting the apocalyptic and eschatological interpretation of the Kingdom of God explicitly, stresses its this-wordliness. Here lies the heart of justice (126–48). In *The God We Never Knew* (Borg 1997) he contrasts God's Kingdom to the kingdoms of Herod and of Caesar. "God as a king has not ordained a social order dominated by earthly kings and elites but wills an egalitarian and just social order that subverts all domination systems." "For Jesus, the Kingdom of God is both a social vision (and therefore future) and a present reality (whose power is already at work and which can be known in the present)" (166f.).

While first narrowing his treatment of the meaning of the Kingdom to this social political aspect, he complements it by a chapter in 'Born again' (Borg 2003, 103–23), preceding his treatment of the Kingdom. Here he discusses the other transformation that is at the heart of the Christian life, the spiritual-personal transformation. In order to work in this direction he advocates a dynamic Christian spirituality. Interestingly he broadens that to other religions: "This process of personal transformation—what we as Christians call being born again, dying and rising with Christ, life in the Spirit—is (…) central to the world's religions" (119). He continues to say that John's affirmation that Jesus is the way is a universal way, not an exclusive Christian one. "Jesus is the embodiment, the incarnation, of the path of transformation known in the religions that have stood the test of time (119).[10]

Aspects of this 'to be born again' relate to meaning [b] above: the mystical meaning of the Kingdom, referring to the presence of God, although Borg is not explicit about it. It is to his credit that he opens up the spiritual / mystical dimension of Jesus and his message. He even advocates the concept of pantheism: everything is in God. "God is not 'somewhere else' but 'right here'" (Borg 1997, 12). This is very close to the inner meaning of the Kingdom. Yet even to him, ultimately the Kingdom refers to an imminent eschatology (….).

Much earlier Robinson (1960, 161ff.) signals and substantiates that many of the *logia* on the KoG must be understood as relating to the *hic et nunc*: Jesus draws eschatology into the present.

Since the publication of the Gospel of Thomas the issue has sprung up if the Kingdom of God may refer to an inner reality, and where it would be located. The most striking logion is Th 3b: "Rather, the Kingdom is inside you and outside you", and: …New insights are developing leading to fresh discussions about Lk 17:21 (…because the Kingdom of God is among you"),[11] and other pericopes. Are we returning to Harnack's view? Harnack based his interpretation mainly on the parables, as I will do. In Th numerous *logia*

---

10 See for example Borg 1997 where sayings of Buddha and Jesus are shown to parallelize.
11 Most translations say 'among', or 'in the midst of'; some however prefer 'inside'. See chapter 7.

indicate in the same direction: the Kingdom of God has a personal meaning and it refers to spirituality and mysticism, an inner transformation. That is the picture Pagels paints for us.

Elaine Pagels has been in the frontlines searching for the meaning of Th for the history of Christianity as well as for Christianity today. As a historian she does not decide about what has been Jesus' proper view. Yet, throughout her work she has brought to the fore how much already early in Christianity views alternative to proto-orthodoxy have been neglected if not suppressed, views that represent aspects of mysticism and spirituality that are common to humankind (cf Borg, above). In some of her books we find valuable materials on, and her interpretation of, views by Thomas on the Kingdom of God. For Thomas the Kingdom of God is not to be thought of "in literary terms, as if it were a specific place" (*The Gnostic Gospels*[12]: 1981, 154), "it is not an other-worldly place or future event" (*Beyond Belief*[13] : 2003, 49) Instead, it is a state of self-discovery" (1981, 154). Alternatively, referring more explicitly to its spiritual dynamics, it "symbolizes a state of transformed consciousness", a process therefore. The idea that the Kingdom of God is an actual event expected in history is naïve, in the view of Th." (GG 155). Making a fine analysis she contrasts Thomas' views with both the Synoptics (esp. Mk) and Jn. She signals the controversy how to interpret and translate Lk 17:21 ('within' versus 'among' or 'in the midst of') and confronts the here and now of Th's Kingdom of God with the eschatological and apocalyptic views of esp. Mk 13.[14]

However, the other-worldly dimension, dominant in the first half of last century, has remained a powerful view ever since: Dunn and Wright, to mention only two prominent representatives, have reinterpreted the concept whilst keeping to its eschatological nature.[15] Dunn (2003) builds a well-considered argument though with no reference to a possible inner alternative. The other-worldly concept, therefore, has not been lost at all. Rather it has been revived in recent years. For Hurtado (2003) it is implied in his Christology. April DeConick, in her study on Th,[16] interprets it as eschatological whilst most others see it as referring to the inner world.[17] What she names 'The Kernel Gospel of Thomas' starts in her redaction with 'Speech One: Eschatological Urgency.'[18] Speech Two is called 'Eschatological Challenges.'[19] When studying

---

12   Elaine Pagels, *The Gnostic Gospels* 1981. Also idem, *The Gnostic Paul* 1992.
13   Elaine Pagels, *Beyond Belief* 2003.
14   Mk is ambivalent on whether the Kingdom is to be understood eschatologically or as present.
15   J. D. G. Dunn 2003a, 383–487, esp. 483ff. N. T. Wright, among other publications, in: Borg, Wright 1999, 31–52.
16   April DeConick, *Recovering the Original Gospel of Thomas* 2005, and idem, *The Original Gospel of Thomas in Translation* 2007.
17   DeConick 2005, 113–21 for example.
18   Logia 2, 4.2-3, 5, 6.2–3, 8, 9, 10, 11.1, 14.4, 15, 16.1–3.

the logia in these two 'speeches' one can hardly find a word in it that directly refers to the eschaton. I find it even difficult to interpret them as such. How come? I suggest that there are similarities: the nature of the inner Kingdom is expressed in words that refer to the beyond. This beyond, seen as an inner manifestation of the Kingdom of God, when seen from a completely different angle may manifest to mind as the eschaton. By way of example. Logion 5.1, classified by DeConick as an eschatological urgency, says, "Jesus said, 'Understand[20] what is in front of you, and what is hidden from you will be revealed to you'"[21]: the words are the same, different contents, the understanding is miles apart.

Toward the end of the twentieth century, we see Bultmann put back on stage by Prieur[22] in 1996: "Dass 'die Predigt Jesu vom Reiche Gottes' das Zentrum seiner Verkündigung und dass der begriff ,Reich Gottes' eschatologisch zu verstehen ist—diese Erkenntnis ist…Allgemeingut der theologischen Forschung geworden.' Diese Resümee Vielhauers hat bis heute Gültigkeit." On this point there is a clear *communis opinio*, says Bruce Chilton (1996, ix). Focant[23] (2009, 21) offers an eschatology permeated with a view on Mk as a Christology 'de type mystique'.

Some Further Instances of the Eschatological Model[24]

"… dass für Jesus die Herrschaft Gottes das eschatologische Heil bedeutet" …und ist [als solches] schon in der Gegenwart wirksam, "wenngleich die Vollendung noch aussteht" (Giesen 1995, 133).

"Jesus' great eschatological promise, the Kingdom of God" (Maloney 2004, 133).

"… 'the Kingdom of God' for Jesus was an alternative way of speaking of the age to come, of heaven, and of the way heaven impacts on earth" (Dunn 2003 (a), 36).

---

19   Logia 17, 20.2–4, 21.5, 21.10–11, 23.1, 24.2–3, 25, 26, 30– 36.
20   There is an original Greek version in an Oxyrhynchos papyrus (*POxy 654,27–31*). The first verb is *gnôthi*, the imperative of *gignôskô*, literally 'to know, related to the noun *gnosis*. Translations, therefore, with an equivalent to 'know' are preferable.
21   Comparison of various translations supports my point:
   • "Recognize what is before your eyes, and the mysteries will be revealed to you." (Pagels 2003, 227).
   • "Know what is in front of your face, and what is hidden from you will be disclosed to you" (Meyer, *The Gospel of Thomas* 1992).
   • "Erkenne, was vor deinem Angesicht ist, und das, was für dich verborgen ist, wird sich dir enthüllen" (Plisch 2007).
22   See also Alexander Prieur, 1996.
23   Focant, Camille, Une christologie de type 'mystique', 2009, 1–21.
24   Two fine overviews of the history of the interpretation of the Kingdom must be mentioned, both by Swedish scholars. One is Lundström 1963 covering the period from the end of the nineteenth century till 1960, the other by Aulén 1976.

"... The phrase 'enter the Kingdom of God' is...referring to the eschatological salvation, conceived as a realm of joy, abundance and life, and contrasted to an area of darkness, grief and death" (Kvalbein 2003, 222).

"The future coming of God's kingdom in power...centers on the glorification and authority of Jesus as God's Son," "Participation in the future kingdom..." (Rowe 2002, 160f).

"[Jesus was] announcing the Kingdom of God: not the simple revolutionary message of the hard-liners, but the doubly revolutionary message of a kingdom that would overturn all other agendas..." (N.T. Wright, in: Borg and Wright 1999, 51).

"Das Reich Gottes ist und bleibt für Christus das streng eschatologisch gedachte künftige Reich der End-Zeit, folgend auf die 'messianischen Wehen', folgend auf das göttliche Gericht" (Otto 1954, 127).

"The final Coming of the Son of Man will see the whole world gathered in communities of justice, for that is the eschatological horizon of human existence" (Maloney 2004, 136).

"... the teachers of the church unanimously described the kingdom of the Father as *regnum naturae* or *regnum potentiae*.... We are expanding this definition as *the dimension of the future*" (Moltmann 1981, 1993; italics in the original).

"The parable of the Sower is eschatological" (Snodgrass 2008, 176).

As appears in this short review eschatology remains a central item on the agenda.[25]

And here is a typical dilemma for eschatologists:

Bohlen (2008, 180) finds an inconsistency in two 'formulas' of Jesus: the Kingdom is future and yet one can enter into it. He seeks the solution in questioning the authenticity of the sayings with 'entering the Kingdom.

The entering issue as such will be discussed in chapter 9.

An Alternative View

C. H. Dodd and others have suggested a middle way. In the next chapter the issue will be discussed of the coming of the Kingdom. Will it come in the future, or is it present already? Dodd explains that the Kingdom in its fullness has to manifest in the future only. Yet it was present in the person of Jesus during his life on earth. Dodd has called this 'realized eschatology'[26], itself a *contradictio in terminis*: "to move the stress from the apocalyptic to that which is

---

25 See for example Nel 2002 who differentiates thus: "'n apoklipties-eskatologiese of eties-eskatologiese begrip."
26 C. H. Dodd, *The parables of the Kingdom*, 1936, 2

'realized' in Jesus' word and deed"[27]: the actual working of the kingdom, Jesus *is* the kingly reign that is effective by the Finger (or the Spirit) of God (Lk 11.20, Mt 12.28), and it is among you (Lk 17.21). Was it limited to the period of the earthly life of Jesus? Or did this reign continue after his death and resurrection? Prieur (11) says no: "...das Reich Gottes [sei] in Jesu 'erschienen', mit Jesu Weggang sei auch die Basileia in die Ferne gerückt, und erst bei Jesu Parusie trete sie wieder hervor...."

The Church, in its turn, states that the presence in Jesus during his lifetime continued in Church. The Church incorporates the presence of the Kingdom, i.e., in the institution of the early church communities and through the ages in the Church. In it the Kingdom is developing and growing, awaiting the eschaton. Indeed, Carmignac in his challenging work—the title tells the story—*Le mirage de l'eschatologie: Royauté, Règne eta Royaume de Dieu...sans eschatologie* (1979) supports the view that the Kingdom has arrived with Jesus, and it has continued in and as the Church unbrokenly. That is why there is no eschatology in the Synoptics, he says. It is a fine analysis of the absence of the eschaton in the Jesus logia. Schnackenburg proposes another view: it is not (only) in the Church but in the *Christusherrschaft* implying its effect in this world here and now and even more so in the whole of the cosmos, including the war against the demons and Satan. Another issue connected with the nature of Jesus' acts and words is whether he actually was the messiah as an important sign of the presence of the kingdom: did he claim so, was he recognized as such? According to Schnackenburg (1959, 79–88) Jesus was the messiah to be recognized in his words and deeds but in a hidden way (see also E. Sjöberg, *Der verborgene Menschensohn*, Lund 1955, 230, quoted by Schnackenburg, 80), words and deeds as the fulfillment of OT (messianic) prophecies. We have seen already that Jesus tells that the Kingdom of God has come 'to you' as he drives out demons by the finger of God (Lk 11.20). Schnackenburg explains it as a breaking through of God's eschatological dominion (*Herrschaft*) in the world, rather as a promise or a notion of the manifestation of his glory (*Herrlichkeit*) (85). Reference must be made also to, e.g., Moltmann 1980, *passim*, Perrin 1963 and 1976, *passim*. Frequently, therefore the Kingdom is understood as a concrete reality: Perrin (1976): God is to be experienced as king in the provision of 'daily bread,' in the experienced reality of the forgiveness of sins. Or, "a fully present and realized kingdom requires a present and reigning king"(Michaels 1987, 113), at the same time seeing Jesus as the apocalyptic prophet (117). Boring (1987, 131) "presume[s] apocalypticism as the primary context within which early Christianity's use of the term 'Kingdom of God' is to be understood. This interpretation may be valid, but certainly not for the early Q and the Th

---

27 Aulén 1976, 100.

peoples.[28] Michaels (1987, 113) wonders whether the kingdom in the Gospels is more theological than Christological. O'Toole (1987) is a typical case of such theological, i.e., confessional, interpretation.

Conclusions

This chapter has offered an overview of different concepts of the Kingdom of God. Three have been identified. For each of them a short look was thrown at the idea and on the literature on it.

The *other-worldly view* has been dominating the first half of the twentieth century and has continued to be important. The Kingdom is expected at the eschaton only, when it will create a radically new and other world. The role of Jesus was to announce it and make a call for repentance and belief. Dodd has mitigated this other-worldly view. The adherents of this view consider the Kingdom of God present on earth already, first in the person of Jesus during his lifetime (realized eschatology). However, it will fully manifest at the eschaton only. Thus, it is said the Kingdom has approached but has not yet manifested.

Under the impact of Modernity and the strong movement among NT scholars to bridge the gap between the figure of Christ and of Jesus the Jew, a *this-worldly view* developed. Jesus in this view emerges as a Palestinian Jewish peasant, as a sage, a healer. He is considered primarily as a human being preaching and struggling for a society based on justice, peace, and love. For some this ideal state will only come about through a social revolution.

The *inner-worldly view* finds few adherents only. The great initiator, as I found, was Harnack, quoted at the outset of this chapter. The idea of such an interpretation faded away and did not materialize until the Gospel of Thomas became better known, and its message was understood better. This view will be the guideline in the chapters to come.

---

28 Q remains ambivalent. Gregg (2006) analyses the final judgment sayings in Q. He offers a fine argument in favor of eschatology in respect to this selection of sayings. His analysis touches the Kingdom issue only sideways.

CHAPTER FIVE
What Is a Kingdom?
The Glory of the Kingdom Restored

The present-day concept of kingdom is different from traditional ones. The previous chapter has illustrated this understanding to some extent. Before embarking on an analysis of the Kingdom of God in the Jesus logia, it is appropriate to visualize the image of the ideal traditional kingdom. This chapter sketches what Jesus may have in mind when speaking of the Kingdom of God. It may serve as a device to look behind the words of the Gospels, to imagine about the *mustêrion* of the Kingdom.

Kingdom

What is a kingdom?[1] What is a Kingdom of God? Is it different? What can we imagine the Kingdom of God to be? What might it refer to in religious and spiritual texts like the Bible? What associations do we have of a kingdom in this age of democracy as well as of worldly autocracy? Some voices prefer to translate it in modern terms, like reign or rule, *Herrschaft*, *Reich*, *règne*, and the like. Marcus even introduces dominion (*sic*).[2] Do these terms convey the same associations as kingdom does? What would be the difference? One seems to be at a loss what the concept stands for: why this term?

Generally kingdom is taken in the political sense, as a polity.[3] What can we make of it in this age when most of the leading countries are republics and where democracy is the lead concept? Kingship is a foreign and strange entity, far apart from today's political reality. It feels outdated and consequently is marginalized from our sight. It does not belong to 'reality,' or so it seems.

---

1 Each time the terms 'kingdom' or 'king' are mentioned, it of course includes its feminine equivalent queen. 'Kingdom' *per se* does not imply masculinity. Why should it? It is the name of an institution. The Netherlands is a kingdom but the 'king' is a queen. If the term kingdom should be avoided for gender sensitiveness it is a conceptual fault. This sensitiveness is brutalizing abstract concepts like brotherhood and now kingdom or kingship.
2 *Webster's*: a supremacy in determining and directing the actions of others, and the exercise of such supremacy; also: the territory subject to a ruler.
3 E.g., Dunn 2003a, 388, 393ff.

Consequently Jesus' intent gets lost. Modernity takes its toll. At the same time kingdom and kingship are images preserved in the sub-consciousness of many, as a sort of fairy-tale, something wonderful, a mind-construction, an imagined ideal, valuable, yes, but out of date—delegated to the world of history as well as to fantasy—maybe lost forever?

Could we at least regain its meaning in terms of what the idea 'kingdom' did imply to contemporaries of Jesus? One only needs to imagine the horrors of the shadow kingdom of the Herods. Did it imply the dream of the Davidic kingdom coming true when the hated Roman rule would be thrown off? Did they think of the eschatological prospect of the apocalyptic coming of the Kingdom of God? Did they imagine a Presence of God or of the Spirit or a presence that 'reigns,' that *waltet*,[4] that works out. On the individual level it affects one's mind and heart, transforming it in order 'to see and to hear,'[5] and also as a consequence of such transformation that it may bring about such Presence. Maybe the strong eschatological and apocalyptic images in the NT (often borrowed from the OT), sometimes interpreted as mystical visions, are really symbolical for inner experiences, realized at a level of consciousness different from the level of consciousness fed by sensory perception. For example, "literary descriptions of visions in apocalyptic writings may originate in the actual practice of ecstasy" (*'ekstasis'*).[6] "The genre of apocalyptic must have originated in circles of ecstatic mystics who developed a literary corpus,"[7] in which gradually the ecstatic was overshadowed by the apocalyptic.

Some authors distinguish between kingdom and kingship, between reign and rule, or in French *royaume, royauté, règne*. Kingdom in the first place denotes a country ruled by a king. However, apart from this territorial aspect, it is also an institution (polity): kingdom versus republic. The powers and prerogatives implied in this form of statehood are vested in the king, in his *kingship*. They are expressed and executed in his *reign* or rule. It is clear that the Kingdom of God in the NT does not refer to a territorial unit. Though all current translations render it as 'kingdom', scholars therefore tend to refer to it as 'reign' or 'rule': how does God execute his powers? Mostly the images depict power, domination, victory, loftiness, in short: distance.

---

4 The German *walten* denotes a condition, but an active one that is working, and is effective. Like 'peace reigns here.' It is strong without any association with oppression and use of force. It is softer. It means it being at work. It refers to an enduring condition. It expresses presence. I purposely avoid 'reign' as it associates too closely to 'rule,' dominating, and so on.
5 Jesus differentiates between hearing and 'hearing' and between seeing and 'seeing.' See chapter 8.
6 Michael Stone (1974) quoted by Lietaert Peerbolte, "Paul's Rapture: 2 Corinthians 12.2–4 and the Language of the Mystics," in Flannery, *Experientia* 2008, 159.
7 Lietaert Peerbolte 2009, 159–60.

Kingship

Kingship has two aspects. One is that it stands for the power exerted over its subjects and manifested toward the enemy. This is the meaning one encounters in almost all literature on the Kingdom of God, inspired by such places as the Apocalypse, Mk 13 (although Mk 13 does not refer to the Kingdom with a single word), and others. For example, Dan Sindlinger in an internet posting[8] says, "I think 'sovereign rule of X', 'kingdom of X', and 'when X rules as King' all imply a government in which the king imposes his will on a nation, allowing the people little or no choice in determining the course of their lives." He adds, "this perception doesn't fit the Kingdom of God because God doesn't impose his will on us but allows us the freedom to determine the course of our lives. To avoid this misconception, I suggest describing the Kingdom of God as a community of people who freely choose to follow God's will/advice for a better life." That is fine also to me.

However, kingship implies more than dominating. It suggests royal qualities like glory, splendor, beauty, riches, radiance, magnetism.[9] In olden times it also implied light in an often dark environment. It exerted a wonderful attraction because of all that it stood for, everything that the people could only dream of. And it saw these dreams realized in the king, in their own revered (or beloved or 'feared'[10]) king. Thus a mental connection was formed that was felt as an emotional reality: he is *my* king, I belong to him in all his qualities, and he belongs to me. Through a psychological working a sort of identification was brought about, thereby imagining the same aspects in a way as their own, a sort of worldly 'mysticism.' This process in some way is comparable to the 'kings' of modern 'culture': the secular idols in sports, media, and music. These (royal) qualities reflect back in all its radiance on the 'subjects,' on the individual. It is like magnetism, an irresistible power to belong, to be part of, to be inside it. This process implies a concept of kingship that includes positive qualities towards his subjects. A positive kingship creates an atmosphere of safety, comfort, peace, and intimacy that come to define it as the Kingdom of God. "The kingship of God manifests in the blossoming of every soul."[11] He protects the citizens, he takes care of them, the country prospers, and he defends the kingdom against enemies and disasters. In brief, he guarantees safety and security. Also in the individual's life the king has positive qualities: he is dedicated to his subjects, he is like a father, a shepherd. Besides being this in his deeds, his appearance, his beauty, and his splendor radiate toward the subjects. Magnetism comes into play. They feel uplifted when seeing the king in his

---

8   Bible Translation Discussion List, February 23, 2007.
9   Cf. Chilton 1996, 40ff.
10 Fear in the sense of awe.
11 Khan 1989 XI, 23.

glory, especially if they may receive a glance. Touching the king's robe, his feet, or even his horse creates a reflection of that splendor and beauty in the heart and on the face of the person. Think of religious practices, like the kissing of an icon, touching the sacred image of revered saint. Receiving a hand or a present causes the soul to leap. The king is rich and beneficent and cares for his people. He surrounds himself with beauty, *is* beauty. Beauty has impact, it reflects on its spectators and thereby creates beauty. His presence makes one feel partaking in his qualities, one feels belonging to him. The effect is a feeling of belonging, of feeling 'at home' and safe.

Inner Strength

From this perspective there is a striking lack of understanding for these qualities of the kingdom in current interpretations of the concept. If the translation is present-day reader-focused, one might admit some good reasons for rendering it as reign or rule or in German as *Herrschaft* or *Reich*. However, then the quality of polity seems to dominate again. The concept is tarnished. What is missing dearly in the first place are the royal qualities mentioned. The use of words as reign and rule virtually exclude this association with glory, radiance, magnetism, and belonging, whilst kingship, and to some degree also kingdom, do suggest so.

In the OT / LXX we find numerous references to God as the King, and to the king in his relationship to God. For example a quote by Roberts from Isaiah states that "the king is equipped for his task by the 'spirit of Yahweh' which rests upon him."[12] Roberts further refers to the king and his ministers as human agents for Yahweh.[13] In the Near East it was usual that 'king' is the title of the godhead. In OT the king fights for "une situation de l'ordre et de bien-être, de shalom," says Coppens.[14] He continues by stating that in pre-exilic literature, it is specifically Isaiah who speaks about the majesty, the uniqueness, the transcendence of God. Only later, in the centuries before Christ, Yahweh as king is related to the return of the Davidic kingship.

What then is this power of the king that characterizes the kingship and thereby the kingdom? It is an inner strength as well as a potentiality. It radiates outward and defines the kingdom. In religious experience it makes itself felt sometimes when entering a church, a sanctuary: an atmosphere, an energy that cannot be measured but makes itself felt as an enveloping presence.

Therefore, the kingdom represents inner strength: *dunamis,* rather than just power: *exousia*. In quite a few cases where we find 'power' in the Gospel translations it stands for *dunamis*. However, *dunamis* indicates strength rather

---

12 Roberts 1983, 132.
13 Ibidem 134.
14 Coppens, *La royauté- le règne—le royaume de Dieu; cadre de relève apocalyptique*, 1979, 265–74

than power. In Dutch the English word 'power' translates as either *macht* or *kracht*, in German either *Macht / Herrschaft* or *Kraft*.[15] The latter means an inner power, referring to one's potentiality, to an energy one is having rather than what one exerts over another: inner directed rather than outer directed. It is more nuanced than the English equivalent strength. For BDAG *dunamis* in the first place is a potential, a potential for functioning in some way: power, might, strength, force, capability (sub 1), but also an ability to carry out (sub 2), and consequently a deed of power. It also refers to an "entity or being, whether human or transcendent, that functions in a remarkable manner: power as a personal transcendent spirit or heavenly agent/angel" (sub 5). It rather refers to *Kraft* and *Stärke* than to *Macht*. Think of the *dunamis* of the Holy Spirit, the *dunamis* that performs miracles, the strength that is living inside something (*die Kraft die in einer Sache innewohnt*)[16] Maybe *dunamis* is to be seen as an intrinsic power, *exousia* as exerted power?[17]

Such a kingdom implies a condition of offering protection, safety and security, adherence, and faith. It creates a potentiality for belonging, for feeling at home. Coming in contact with the king—seeing him, being seen by him, receiving a glance, a touch, prostrating—by itself implies a transfer of something of its qualities, of receiving something kingly. However, it reaches further: this *dunamis* radiates out as an energy field. His presence *waltet*.

It leads us to the parallel terminology for God as the father and as the shepherd. The qualities of father and shepherd fit into this interpretation of kingship. All denote the same: protection, love, a 'home feeling.' The King of the Kingdom of God is God—who at the same time is the father and the shepherd, the predominant nature and role of each being love, care, intimacy. Behind the metaphor of the Kingdom of God is hidden its implied power and strength, the power of love. In addition, the Kingdom of God is that of the good Father "der seine grenzenlose...Liebe den Menschen [schon jetzt] schenken möchte,"[18] belonging, being cared for, safety and security. He also is the shepherd who saves the sheep.[19] The shepherd's task typically is to function for the well-being of the sheep, to protect and guarantee safety and security, even if only for one single sheep.

---

15 In an earlier footnote the German verb *walten* was discussed. This word expresses the strong character without any association with oppression and use of force. It is softer. It means it being at work. Moreover, it refers to an enduring condition. It expresses presence.
16 WNT. See also TDNT II 299ff.
17 See for further supporting argument Johnson 1998, 6 sqq.
18 Giesen 1995, 133f.
19 Cf. the parable of the lost sheep (Lk 15:3–7). Also Jn 10. Dunn, Jesus and the Kingdom 2003b, 8 refers to Ezechiel 34: "Yahweh restoring and pasturing his sheep"; also David as shepherd.

Translations that discard the association with such royal qualities deprive the reader of an essential message of the Gospels.

Partaking

Let us come back to the term *kingdom*. Kingdom implies kingship but has as an extra strong suggestion that one can live in it, be part of, to participate in it.[20] Apart from its territorial aspect, it implies a sphere of influence as an effect of kingship. This sphere of influence is all-embracing and inclusive: it takes in all that is within its boundaries, all that wants to belong to the kingdom and associates with it. Interestingly, it relates to the present-day discussion about national identity in view of massive immigrations. Kingdom thus implies a sphere of influence, kingship and king, all of them. It is all-embracing.

We may move one step further. Entering the kingdom makes one partake of that sphere. One becomes conscious of another dimension and of another quality of one's existence. This is what Pagels tries to express in her analysis of Th: the Kingdom of God is a state of consciousness. Entering the Kingdom implies that one's consciousness is (being) transformed. Maybe that is what Jesus wanted to say also about becoming as a little child when he announced that the kingdom had arrived (Mk 1:15): *metanoeite*: change your *noos*, change your mind, and come to a different consciousness: trust in the good message that I am bringing.[21]

Maybe the Kingdom will then be experienced as both exalted and close, as grand as well as intimate, as radiant and fostering: all in one, and at the same time.

Conclusion

'Kingdom' has far wider implications than the issues of territoriality, of rule and reign, of domination and suppression. It carries with it suggestions of being cared for, protection, justice, safety, and belonging. Kingship in its glory radiates the positive qualities to all who want to receive and participate. It is *dunamis*, energy ('Kraft') rather than power. Kingdom thus is when these qualities reign. It is consciousness.

This chapter serves as a background to the understanding of the *mustêrion* of the Kingdom of God.

---

20 Inayat Khan (1989 VII, 45) quotes Mt 6.33 "Seek first the Kingdom of Heaven…and all things shall be added unto you", and continues " [it] is the silent life; the life inseparable, eternal, self-sufficient and all-powerful."
21 See chapter on *metanoia* as transformation. Also Borg 2003, 180.

CHAPTER SIX
The Kingdom in the Gospels: 'When'?

The Kingdom of God has approached
[i.e. and therefore present]
Mk 1.14–15

The Kingdom of God is within you
Lk 17.21

Introduction

To chapters 6 and 7: the 'when' and the 'where'

The two logia quoted in a concise form, here in an alternative proposed understanding, are a condensed summary of the mysticism of the Kingdom of God: its presence. It has approached and therefore arrived, i.e., present in time. Indeed, it is located within you, i.e., present in space.[1] How does this double announcement fit into the ongoing discourses around Jesus?

The Kingdom of God was a hot issue in the Jewish community in the intertestamental period. It was discussed widely. There were roughly three views. One was the view that the Kingdom would come at the eschaton: the end of the present world. Everything will be made new. Quite often it would take apocalyptic dimensions. A second way it was viewed was the re-establishment of the Davidic Kingdom, implying shaking off the Roman yoke, and chasing the hated satellite king. The third view contained a social and cultural revolution. There is some resemblance to the classification in chapter 4.

Jesus took actively part in this discussion, as we can see from the frequency of his pronouncements on it.[2] What position did he take? Furthermore, what

---

1 There is an intrinsic tension between the Kingdom as arrived and its supposed inner presence in the human being. Tradition teaches that the inner Kingdom and its presence presuppose the actual and historical appearance of Jesus.
   An alternative option is the following. Jesus, coming to renew the Message, wants to renew the promise of the presence of the Kingdom of God. As people had forgotten it—*vide* the eschatological expectation—Jesus announces it afresh. I propose to leave this issue open.
2 The term *basileia tou theou / tôn ouranôn* is found 63 times in the Synoptics of which 33 in Mt.

view do we, citizens of the twenty-first century, have on the Kingdom and on Jesus' position in it? In what have we been educated in Jesus' view on the Kingdom? Among Christians the doctrinal concept of the Kingdom of God generally is, and has been, an eschatological one. In the various churches' doctrines the Kingdom is taught as an eschatological event, associated with Jesus' suffering and resurrection, the Last Judgment and the Parousia, the Second Coming of the Lord Jesus Christ, conversion and forgiveness, the message of salvation.[3] It is other-worldly: there are no direct implications for one's earthly life. We find this idea reflected in the proto-orthodoxy of groupings in early Christianity. Traces are contained in the Synoptics. That is to say, according to this view the message of Jesus has been interpreted in a certain way by specific circles that gradually became dominant. This understanding is connected with how the early Church looked at the Kingdom of God and at the *eschaton*. Already at an early stage it shifted its attention from the core teachings of Jesus—the Kingdom of God, the Sermon on the Mount/Plain—to the Pauline doctrine of Suffering, the Cross, the Resurrection and, even more important, the Parousia. Implied in it is the *eschaton* and accompanying apocalyptic events. A clear indication of this shift is found in the Pauline Epistles: there is no reference at all to Jesus' Kingdom teachings. He hardly quotes Jesus' message in terms of his sayings. Paul's message rather than Jesus' teachings became *the* contents of the *kerygma* of the proto-orthodox church. An odd development as one of the core teachings by Jesus is the announcement (*kêrussein*, sic) of the arrival of the Kingdom of God, *hic et nunc*, and what that does imply.

The issue in this Part II is to find out how the sayings by Jesus about the Kingdom of God in the Synoptics (and, marginally, also in the Gospels of John and of Thomas) may refer to an inner state of consciousness, to the reality of the Kingdom.

The discussion will take off from two of the Jesus logia that are most discussed, and that at the same time are crucial in the discussion on the eschatology of Jesus versus the inner meaning: Mk 1.14-15 (the *when*) and Lk 17.20–21 (the *where*) They are most relevant for this issue as they focus on two essential issues:

- its time dimension: whether it is here already or that it is to come: the *when*:
  - this question was already discussed fiercely in Jesus' time: when will the Kingdom of God break through, when will it arrive? Or did it arrive already and therefore was present already? Added, of course, were the issues if its coming would be apocalyptic or otherwise, and if its coming was imminent or only at the 'Last Day.'
- its localization: whether it is inside or outside, the *where*:

---

[3] Recently worded in Hurtado's magnificent *Lord Jesus Christ*, 2003.

o and, strongly related to the former question: where is the Kingdom of God located, in heaven or here on earth, in the midst of people or within them? And where will it be after its coming?

By the way, as is visible in the formulations, it will turn out to be difficult to keep the two concepts ('when' and 'where') apart. However, as we will see, it is useful if not necessary to distinguish the one from the other.

Besides, an interesting issue is whether the Kingdom does fit in the dimensions of time and place, or that it lies beyond human conceptions like these? Does not God exceed all imagination and definition?

These two pericopes constitute a challenge to the eschatological interpretation of the Kingdom. The one says that the Kingdom has approached and therefore is (virtually?) present now. The other tells that the Kingdom is present locally, either 'among you,' or even 'within you.' Each of these revolutionary sayings is to be seen in the context of contemporary Judaism. Indeed, they are revolutionary for Christian views on the implicit doctrine of God being at a distance, "our Father in heaven."

The 'when' is discussed here, the 'where' in the next chapter.

When? Mk 1.14–15: The text

The Kingdom of God: is it now, or will it be in the future? Did the Kingdom arrive? Or is it approaching, even near? Or at hand? Or is it to be expected at the eschaton only? What are the answers for the time of Jesus? What can we derive from the Gospel texts?

There is a consensus that Mk 1.14–15 is the crucial text on this issue, not in the least as it represents one of the central concepts of Jesus' message at all (Dunn 2003(b), 383–87).[4] Part of the text, the call for announcing the message, with minor variations, recurs at other places in the Synoptics, up to ten times.[5] Schlosser, after a thorough investigation, concludes that the statement on the arrival of the Kingdom "c'est l'élément le plus solide du logion à un point de vue historique et remont probablement à Jesus même" (Schlosser 1979, 49). Carmignac (1979, 24) arrives at the same conclusion.

---

4 See further, and at random: Bultmann 1948/1984, 3 (quoted above), Borg 1999, 74; Perrin 1963, *passim*, Giesen 1995; Chilton 1996, ix, Jey J. Kanagaraj, 2009, 24–34, and many others. Also, Beavis 2004, 91.

5 Carmignac (1979, 26) enumerates: Mk: 1.15 par Mt 4.17; Q: Lk 9.2 and 10.9 with the joint parallel Mt 10.7; Lk 11.20 par Mt12.28; Mt: 3.2; Lk: 10.11, 21.31.

> Mk 1:14–15
> …Jesus came in Galilee, preaching the good news (or: Gospel) of God, and saying, "The time is fulfilled, and the kingdom of God has come near; repent and believe in the good news".
> NRSV
>
> …Jesus went into Galilee, proclaiming the good news of God. The time has come", he said. "The Kingdom of God is near; repent and believe the good news."
> NIV
>
> …êlthen ho Iêsous eis tên Galileian
> Kêrussôn to euaggelion tou theou
> Kai legôn hoti peplêrôtai ho kairos
> Kai êggiken hê basileia tou theou
> Metanoeite kai pisteuete en tôi euaggeliôi.
> NA27
>
> Here is an alternative translation which will be discussed below:
> …Jesus went into Galilee,
> proclaiming the (good) Message of God, and saying:
> the time is fulfilled / the moment is there[6], the Kingdom of God has arrived.
> Change your mind-and-heart
>   And put your trust in the message.
> Proposed
>
> And the Mt parallel:
> Mt 4.17
> From that time Jesus began to proclaim:
> Repent, for the kingdom of heaven is has come near"
> NRSV
>
> From that time on Jesus began to preach:
> Repent, for the kingdom of heaven is near"
> NIV
>
> Apo tote êrxato ho Iêsous kêrussein kai legein
> Metanoeite; êggiken gar hê basileia tôn ouranôn
> NA27
>
> Or alternatively:
> *From then on Jesus began to proclaim saying*
> *Change your mind-and-heart, for the Kingdom of heaven has arrived.*
> Proposed

---

6 *Erfüllt, vollkommen*, Blass etc., §341, n 3. It is sometimes suggested that *kairos* does not refer to time.

Let us get into this important text.

Unless noted differently translations are from the NRSV. The Greek text is NA27.

My own renderings are not translations that meet all normative forms and functions[7]. They intend to serve the purpose of tracing the so-called inherent meaning of the text, be it a term or a logion. Inherent in the context of this study it indicates the assumed basic, i.e. spiritual meaning: that is its specific *skopos*[8] : it serves study purposes, is directed to scholars and interested people, and relate to current translations on the basis of semantic and other studies and of spirituality.

Presentation of the major differences between NRSV / NIV/ the alternative proposals:

> **Proclaiming, (publicizing)** rather than **preaching**
>
> *Kêrussô* may have been in missionary use already before Mk was written and therefore could be translated as proclaiming or preaching.[9] It is not 'announcing' as it does not refer to news. Proclaiming need not have that connotation[10] if it fits with the the *êggiken*. See Intermezzo below
>
> **message (i.e., divine)** rather than **Gospel, or good news**
>
> *Euaggelion.* The traditional rendering in English carries with it non-original connotations. News is too much media oriented, and is actual at the moment only. In German it would be *Botschaft* that in English is message. Message[11] has a slight connotation of 'news' but its contents remain alive, it has a lasting tenor and an abiding purport. 'Message' renders the exceptional character: it is a message from God to the world, a divine message: the Message.

---

7   De Vries 2001 illustrates the variety of functions: liturgical, church, study, common language, secular literary-cultural, private, home functions (307).
8   De Vries 2001, 307: a *skopos* contains its functions, its audience, and its relationships with other translations.
9   Schlosser 1979, 41.
10 *Webster's,* sub 1a: make widely known (announce), 1b: clearly reveal, 2a: to declare solemnly / officially / formally.
11 'Good news' is the general understanding and is found in the dictionaries and comments. Strong's Exhaustive Concordance sub 2098, gives 'good message.' Consulting Liddell-Scott-Jones (via Pollux: Archimedes Project Dictionary Access). What is the meaning of *eu*? As an adverb *eu* in connection with knowledge or action stands for well, thoroughly, competently. As a prefix it qualifies the main body of the lemma (i.e., *aggelion*) in a great variation of meanings like abundance, prosperity, ease, fine-tuned to the headword. I suggest as an alternative to understand the *euaggelion* as the divine message in view of the context: Jesus proclaiming the Kingdom of God. This understanding may result in the translation by the Message, capitalized to indicate its divine character.

THE KINGDOM IN THE GOSPELS: 'WHEN'?

time is fulfilled, it *is* the moment	rather than	**time has come**

Peplêrotai. Schlosser (436, n 68) concludes that time here is clearly designated; to come is neutral and therefore not appropriate. Is *kairos* time? Or rather *the* very moment?[12]

has arrived / is present	rather than	**is near / is at hand**

Êggiken. See section Near or arrived.

transformation, change mind/ heart[13]	rather than	**repent**

Metanoia / metanoeô. Or: transform. *See chapter 11*

trust in, confide to	rather than	**believe**

Pisteuete. See Intermezzo below

Jesus proclaims the Kingdom of God as a reality! It has approached to the effect of being here. That is real breaking news! It is a new Message from God. For centuries people have been discussing its expectation. 'In the present age,' just preceding Jesus' coming out, the expectations had been growing in intensity. Hot discussions were conducted about the when, and about the form in which it would appear: a restored Kingdom of David? An apocalyptic event? A social revolution? Or simply the throwing out of the Roman reign and rule together with the hated Hasmonaeans. It is breaking news not only because of the fact itself. Rather it is a shocking proclamation as nothing of what had been expected, foreseen, and predicted was actually happening. Here is an impressive young figure telling that time is fulfilled, the moment is here, the Kingdom of God has approached, here and now. It must have sounded absolutely unbelievable. What was there in fact supporting the announcement? Any miracles, or other phenomena? Anything special to perceive? Therefore Jesus adds, in order to be able to see and hear: you have to transform, you have to understand that this *is* the new message, a good message. And you have to trust

---

12 Maloney (2004, 47) argues that k*airos* as opposed to c*hronos* does not necessarily indicate ordinary time (as does *chronos).* Kairos, in his view, rather indicates 'an opportune moment, a welcome time of possibility'. I agree. Focant is of the same opinion: "le *kairos* du moment decisif, de l'occasion favorable est traduit par 'bon moment'…, ce qui signale bien qu'il ne s'agit pas du temps au sens ordinaire (*chronos*)» (Focant, Camille, *L'Évangile selon Marc,* Cerf, Paris 2004).

   Maloney, though, interprets it eschatologically. Alternatively I suggest it rather refers to the crucial moment something great is happening, like the moment God's grace descends into one. Jey Kanagaraj (2009, 26), however, advocates the concrete time and fulfillment: the *peplêrôtai* "indicates 'the completion of a fixed period of time and at its completion a particular event will take place'(Cranfield)" and the *kairos* represents "the end of history and the end of the days on earth." Together they refer "to the eschatological time fixed by God to bring this kingdom into human history."

13 Part III will focus on the concept of transformation. In it, chapter 11 discusses *metanoia*.

it, to put your confidence in it, to confide in it (*pisteuete en*). And his personality radiated the same.

Another novelty is happening when Jesus pronounces this logion: the Kingdom is proclaimed as a reality, but there is not a word about repentance, like John the Baptist did as a warning, and Mt re-echoing. This issue will be further discussed in chapter 11.

Intermezzi

Kêrussôn

Generally it is understood as the proclaiming of news. That is how Mk 1.14 currently is read: time is fulfilled, announcing the almost-arrival of the kingdom as good news: it is all new and going to happen. *Kêrussô*, however, is also used for publicizing something that is already there but needs full attention, or proclaiming it: to clearly reveal, to give an unmistakable indication.[14] An example one finds in 2 Cor 4.15 or Ac 19.13, about proclaiming Jesus as Lord. Or when baptism is proclaimed by John the Baptist (Mk 1.4b): he calls people to be baptized, *hic et nunc*, so that their sins may be forgiven. Likewise Jesus does not announce the Kingdom of God as something to come about, rather it is publicized as something that is now made public.

How is this to be understood? In the audience of Jesus there is common knowledge that the Kingdom is *not* here but expected eagerly. But Mt reports that the Baptist had already been proclaiming that it had approached (*êggiken*) (Mk 1.4b, Mt 3.2), as a herald. Jesus echoes this proclamation repeating that it *had* approached and therefore was present now, adding the call to confide one to this incredible good message.

In the following chapters the self-evidence of the presence of the Kingdom will be highlighted by some central logia and parables. What makes the message of Jesus unique in the Palestine situation of the first century is that he shifts the horizon from the future to the timeless now: the moment (*kairos*) of God's presence. The tension between this message of his and the common understanding of the situation is treated subtly by using the verb *êggiken*: it has approached and is therefore present. See the section Near or arrived below.

Concluding, the announcement of the Kingdom is a proclamation of something that is here already but must be made known.

The Lord's Prayer: Your Kingdom Come
elthetô hê basileia sou

What about the Lord's Prayer? Does the phrase 'Your Kingdom come' (Mt 6.10, Lk 11.2) deny that the Kingdom is present? The suggestion is strong that it is not here but it may arrive. Chilton (1996, 66) advocates this position: "Prayer that the kingdom of God should come clearly marks out the kingdom as that which might encounter us in the future." ... "...the eschatological coordinate of the kingdom is evident and prominent." At the same time Chilton finds in the Lord's prayer "an assurance of the actual, present reality of the kingdom

---

14 *Webster's*: 'publicize: "to bring to the attention of the public"; proclaim: sub 1a "to declare openly, to assert openly"; sub 1b "to give an unmistakable indication of, clearly reveal; show."

[but only, *sic*] in heaven. It is announced as so near as effectively to have finished its movement toward us...." The eschaton being present, though in heaven? This petition, says Elmore (1987, 63), like the others in the Lord's prayer, is an exploration of fundamental possibilities for the experience of God as king in human life"

Another point is between brackets: is this a prayer for general use, or rather for private use? In Mt 5.1 the narrative teaches the disciples alone—and that is for the complete Sermon on the Mount. And the prayer itself is for private use (Mt 6.5–8): Jesus addressing the individual tells to pray in 'your room', with the door closed. No hint as to public use, which is even rejected, at least in the form described as current practice of the 'hypocrites.'

Elthetô, Come! Let us have a closer look. In the Greek text the imperative aorist mode is applied, a usual form for prayers (Blass 337, 4[15]): *elthetô* (come!), which cannot be translated as such in English where a vocative form of the substantive (the kingdom) would be needed. However, it transfers a strong suggestion of a necessity, a must. Because of this lack, in English the subjunctive is used, but that does not express the same. The imperative sounds more as an urgent call for something that is not here in order to materialize. The imperative in this context tells that there is an inner necessity that the Kingdom must come, i.e., to the person praying, being aware that it has arrived and therefore is present already. For the individual person praying it appears as a potential. It need not be something in the future dimension as an uncertainty, awaiting the eschaton. The mood of the prayer is that it is done in the present and on behalf of the present, in the here and now. And that it is done with an open heart, 'opening up one's heart,' and that thus the Kingdom as God's Presence may manifest. To put it in other words: the prayer impresses one that the coming is unavoidable, it 'must.' As it is a prayer, the inner attitude of the subject praying is essential: openness. The miracle of the *mustêrion* may then 'materialize.' As soon as one realizes, yes, the Kingdom *is* here, realities shift, 'prayer fulfilled,' provided one does it in the silent prayer of 'let my eyes be open to see it.'[16]

To sum up, it is found that the imperatives in the prayer may signalize actual potentialities inside to be realized now.

Pisteuete en tôi euaggelioî[17]

This phrase generally is rendered as 'believe in the Gospel / the good news,' or equivalents. NIV even says, 'believe the good news, where the *euaggelion* becomes the object of belief. The basic meaning of *pisteuein*, however, is to confide (in), to entrust (to), to put one's trust in (to), to have confidence, to confide oneself to.[18] I choose confide rather than believe, or have faith in order to avoid these religiously 'technical' terms.[19] It is an act. In the Synoptics it is

---

15 Blass 1990.
16 See chapter 8, Sower.
17 The observation in the paragraph to follow does not do justice to the theorizing on this concept and term. For example, systematic theology has analyzed the differences between *fides qua*, *fides quae* and *fiducia* (Kurtén 1994). I suspect that in order to capture glimpses of what Jesus teaches us (or wants to but cannot say) another path is more appropriate.
18 BDAG: sub 1: to consider something to be true and therefore worthy of one's trust (→ believe), 2 to entrust oneself to an entity in complete trust (→ believe in, trust), 3 entrust (*tini ti*), 4 to be confident about. Therefore, belief is a secondary meaning; the principal thing is trust, to entrust, to be confident. To confide is a rendering that does justice to the variety of meanings. Moreover: 'confide' etymologically refers to *fides*: believe, trust, credit[!].
19 The Dutch philosopher Otto Duintjer signals the same problem (Duintjer 2007, 34 n 2).

generally used absolutely, or with the dative, or with a preposition (*eis*, *epi*, and the unique *en* in Mk 1.15; it never stands with an accusative. The same one finds with the noun, *pistis*.[20] It never stands for a particular belief. Only once is it used institutionally (Mt 23.23). When Jesus uses the word he refers to a general attitude of confidence, of entrusting oneself. More frequent are the pericopes where it speaks of an attitude of confidence of the person healed or exorcised, or to the capability of the disciples to heal. Only once the word is qualified, i.e., confidence in God (*pistis theou*). In terms of the whole NT *pistis* and *pisteuô* are not typical for the Synoptics. The other books display a frequency many times higher than these Gospels do. The total frequency of the verb in the NT is 243, of the noun also 243. However, the noun is rare in the Gospels (24 out of 243), and does not occur in Jn. In contrast the verb is frequent in Jn and in the other NT books, but not in the Synoptics (34). Where Jesus employs *pistis* and *pisteuô* it invariably refers to confidence. Is this in contrast to the Epistles? The Pauline doctrines have put a heavy debt on this term with a retroactive effect on the understanding of the Synoptics. Bultmann seems to agree. In TDNT VI he renders the basic meaning of *pisteuô* in ancient Greek as 'to trust', 'to rely on'(177), also 'to believe' and in later (!) Greek also 'to confide in' (178). The term is used both in religious and in worldly context (179). Bultmann finds that "[f]rom a purely formal standpoint there is nothing very distinctive in the usage of the NT and early Chr. writings as compared with Gk. usage" (203). However, when shifting to the section 'General Christian usage,' Bultmann shifts to 'believe,' 'obey,' 'trust,' 'hope,' 'faithfulness' (205–8), meanings colored by NT theology. The section 'Specifically Christian usage' by Bultmann covers no less than 13 pages, mostly about Paul and other non-Gospel writings where meanings are distinctly different from the tone in the Gospels.

Why do I make a point out of this? In Christianity 'to believe,' 'a belief' coveys a static and doctrinal concept: when becoming a Christian one confesses 'a belief, to believe'. And this is confirmed from time to time. On the other hand, to have confidence or trust, to put one's trust in, to entrust oneself to, to confide oneself to something or someone is a more dynamic concept, involving mind, heart and soul. And 'faith' as a synonym for belief is often used to indicate a particular religion. Faith is a central issue to Christianity, says Bradley (2007, xiv). However, he continues, Mt refers to *gnosis* (knowledge) far more often than to faith. This may make one think of what knowledge means. Is *gnôsis* in Gnosticism by definition another knowledge than when it is used in the Synoptics?

My conclusion is that as to the Gospel writings it is safe to translate *pisteuô en* by 'to confide in' (Dutch: 'zich verlaten op'), 'to put one's trust / confidence in.'

For *euaggelion*, see the presentation above.

It is found that Jesus makes a call to confide oneself to the message, an act that is the first prerequisite to enter the Kingdom.

---

20   Confidence as a general attitude: Mk 4.40, Lk 8.25, 17.5-6, 18.8, 22.32. Confidence as an attitude (without explicating the object) regarding healing power, either to be healed: Mt 8.10, 9.2, 9.22, 9.29, 15.28, Mk 2.5, 5.34, 10.52, Lk 5.20, 7.9, 7.50, 8.48, 17.19, 18.42. Or to heal: Mt 17.20, 21.21. Only rarely in institutional sense: Mt 23.23. Only once: confidence 'in': Mk 11.22 (*theou*).

Near or Arrived?

What is the message Jesus is announcing? Indeed, the Kingdom *êggiken*, i.e., literally 'has approached.' What does that mean? In case something has approached it consequently has arrived, and therefore is present, though, at an undefined close distance. Generally it is understood as at hand, has come near, is near, all indicating a not-yet-presence.[21] However, *êggiken* as perfect tense suggests a completed action in the very present.

> One might ask, is this pericope indicating the time dimension, or is it spatial? Approaching may imply a spatial aspect, in the case of the Kingdom when one considers 'it' to be something placed somewhere. Schlosser (1979, 44) concludes for the time dimension. Elsewhere the locational meaning is clear, like in Mk 11.1 and 14.42. Also here the reference to a spatial nearness is distinct. But Mk suggests it to be in terms of time because of the preceding *peplêrôtai ho kairos*.[22] Rather than clock time one may think of 'the very moment' (see the earlier note). Or the incessant now, *the* moment.

This issue may be taken a step further, which gets us into some grammar.

> Does the word *êggiken* indicate a now or a not yet? A widespread interpretation says that "the Kingdom [is] yet *to come* but also *already present*" (Dunn 2003 (b), 405), a forced paradox it seems. Dunn recognizes that the perfect tense "here indicates an action already performed and resulting in a state or effect which continues into the present" (407). However, he finds that here it has the sense of "imminence rather than of presence" (408), an interpretation that is widespread among NT scholars, but is not necessarily consistent with this and other logia. Might it be motivated by theological interpretation? Also others have concluded that it is a perfect tense, and therefore indicates 'has come'. One of them is Ambrozic 1972, who also refers to Dodd (*The Parables of the Kingdom*, 1935) who already that early convincingly had shown the same.[23] However, after long-stretching discussions like these the issue remains on the

---

21 Prieur is rather hesitant (225f). On the one hand he concludes for a parallel text in Lk 10.9 and 11 that "...sonstigem ntl. Sprachgebrauch entsprechend, [wobei] das Nahegekommensein noch nicht das Angekommensein zu implizieren scheint" : *sic*, wvl. On the other hand, says Prieur, there are the healings, Lk 11.20 and 10.17f, all of these indicating the presence of the Kingdom. Consequently there is "kaum eine andere Interpretationsmöglichkeit, als das Nahegekommensein als angekommensein zu verstehen." To the latter of which I fully agree. But then Prieur withdraws again. The presence of the *basileia* 'must' relate to Jesus' presence or to the healings and exorcisms as works of the Basileia. Therefore the *eph'humas* in Lk 10.9 "gilt den geheilten Kranken" mentioned in v. 10.17a and 20a, scenes where Jesus was not present but where healing and exorcism was practised. *Sic*.
22 Referring to the note about *kairos* above.
23 See also in the *Festschrift* for Dunn: Kanagaraj, 2009, 26–28. Its conclusion is crystal clear: the perfect tense tells that it "has already arrived." However, he cannot understand how that can be true, and consequently wrestles with the presence versus the imminence. Illogically he wonders that the verb *êggiken* "speaks of a future that enters the presence while always

table. Too much is at stake because of the numerous interpretations of the Kingdom to manifest at the eschaton only. That is why most translations render: is near, is at hand. But the Greek for near is the adverb *eggus*. The case of *êggiken* is different. It is a verb (infinitive *eggizein*) and it is in the perfect tense. It means coming near, or approaching; even 'nahe sein oder kommen.'[24] *Êggiken* is the result of the approach: having approached means having arrived, and therefore being present. The perfectum is to be interpreted as a perfectum praesens also when the perfectum expresses a condition (Zustand). For example, *thnêiskô*: to die, *tethnêka*: I am dead. The present tense indicates the process, the perfectum the resulting situation (Blass etc. 1990, § 341)[25]. This is confirmed in Mt 2.20: "for those who were searching the child's life are dead (*tethnêkasin*, a perfect tense)

Hence it is to be rendered as has come near, has approached, implying to have arrived and even being present. It indicates a situation where exchange and dialogue are possible.

So Dunn is perfectly correct, and I repeat, when he concludes to the perfect tense "here indicates an action already performed and resulting in a state or effect which continues into the present" (407). As mentioned in a footnote, in the recent *Festschrift* for Dunn (2009) Jey J. Kanagaraj by and large comes to the same conclusion.

Let us see what other places with *eggus* or with forms of *eggizein* may offer as a clarification.

1   Lk 21:29b-31 is a case with the adverb *eggus* when Jesus speaks about the fig tree:
    Look at the fig tree and all the trees. When they sprout leaves you can see for yourselves and know that summer is already near (eggus)[26].

    What does it say? Trees sprouting leaves precede the arrival of summer, summer has not arrived, though obviously it is approaching. Though it is near, summer is not yet present: it is at the gates.[27]

---

remaining future": *sic*. He tries to solve the riddle by calling it an 'intrusive imminence' (Craig Keener), indicating presence and future, respectively, or rather by understanding it as "nearness in consequence of an arrival." His contribution to the discussion marks a shift from nearness to presence, although he cannot master the duality. This seeps through when not accepting the *entos humin* of Lk 17.20–21) as an internal presence.

24 Rienecker 1992.
25 Schlosser (1979, 54-57, 442-5 footnotes 135-167) in his well-documented and very complete study of the logia about the Kingdom denies this interpretation of the perfect tense. He suggests the other way round: the aorist renders the completion, the perfectum the all-but completion. He presents a number of arguments to this effect in the LXX and in the Epistles, which in some cases are more or less convincing: Dt 31.14 (can be either, Ez 12.23, Rm 13.12); in some others not quite: James 5.8. Yet, after due consideration, his conclusion is the following: "Bien que la philologie n'autorise guère à traduire *êggiken hê basileia tou theou* par "le Règne est là", le dit de Mc 1,15 est à placer sur la même ligne que les logia qui affirment la présence effective du Règne et ne vise pas la venue du Règne dans la plénitude ou *en dunamei*.
26 Mt (24.33) and Mk (13.29) explain the 'near': 'at the very gates' (*epi thurais*).

2   Mk 14:42 / Mt 26.46 (a case with a perfectum):
   Get up, let us be going. See, my betrayer is at hand (NRSV)
   Rise! Let us go! Here comes my betrayer! (NIV)
   Egeiresthe agômen; idou ho paradidous me êggiken[28] (pf) (NA27)
   My proposal: ...*See, my betrayer has arrived.*

   As compared to Lk 22.47 with an aorist:
   ...suddenly a crowd came...Judas...was leading (impf) them. He approached (*êggisen,* aor.) to Jesus to kiss him...but Jesus said to him...

Therefore:

   Judas is 'present' in Mk 14.42 par when coming to betray Jesus (*ênggiken,* perfectum) but in Lk 22.47 'is approaching' (*ênggisen,* aoristus) Jesus in order to kiss him, but before he can reach Jesus, Jesus stops him by addressing him.

   Here we find a clear case of this difference between the perfect and aorist tenses.

   My proposal:...*approached...but Jesus said.*

3   Lk 21:20 with a perfectum again:
   "When you see Jerusalem being surrounded by armies, then know that its desolation is here" (*eggiken,* pf)) (NIV near, or NRSV: has come near), meaning that on condition of the situation indicated (being surrounded etc.) the desolation is present.

   As to the aorist in the case of *eggizô* it would indicate approaching some place where one is within reach of it, after which something can be done. Here are a few cases. See also Lk 22.47 above.

4   Mt 21:1 par.: sending for the colt: 'When approaching (*êggisan,* aor.) Jerusalem...' NIV; NRSV: had come near.

5   Or sometimes it indicates an immediacy, e.g., in Mt 21:34: when time for harvest has come within reach (*êggisen,* aor.), one takes measures for collecting the fruit: 'When the harvest time approached...' NIV / had come, NRSV.

6   Lk 7:12: 'as he approached (*êggisen,* aor.) the gate of the town, a dead person was carried out': approaching, i.e., before being at the gate.

7   In Lk 15:25 about the elder son: 'when he came and approached the house (*êggisen,* aor.) he heard music...' etc., and called for a servant, obviously still at some distance.

8   Similarly Lk 18:40: Jesus ordered the blind man to be brought to him. When he (the man) came near (*eggisantos,* part. aor) Jesus asked him.... It indicates the process of coming within reach so close that they could speak to one another.

---

27 Immediately following this pericope Jesus tells the disciples (v. 31–32) "... you know that the Kingdom of God is near (*eggus estin*). Truly, I say to you, this generation will not pass away till all has taken place. Heaven and earth will pass away, but my words will not pass away." Thus: near, not present. I leave aside the incongruence between the Kingdom being near and being present.
28 Codices Sinaiticus and Ephraem have *êggisen* (aor.).

9   Lk 24:15: '... Jesus himself coming up (*eggisas*, part. aor.) walked along with them.' NIV. NRSV: came near and went with.

10 Mt 12:28 / Lk 11:20 says that "the Kingdom of God comes to (NIV: upon) you" (*ephthasen*, aor., in Hell. Greek 'come'[29]) on the condition that Jesus casts out demons, which he does. Logical conclusion: it comes upon you. Therefore, the Kingdom of God is near on the condition mentioned.

11 Lk 9.60 is another instance where the Kingdom clearly is in the here-and-now dimension: "Let the dead bury the dead, but as for you, go and proclaim the Kingdom of God," *dianggelô* meaning to make known far and wide (*weit und breit bekanntmachen*, WNT). It does no longer need to say that it has approached, or similar things. It practically implies the *hic et nunc*. Would it not be illogical for Jesus to insist that his disciples should make it known far and wide if it would not be present here already? Carmignac (1979, 57): "...s'il ne s'agissait pas d'une réalité déjà présente ou du moins imminente." Yet Carmignac, after a thorough study of the debate, conducted mainly in the 1920s and 1930s, concludes that the pros and cons of either solution are in balance. He takes the neutral way and leaves the issue open.

Some scholars make it a bit complicated, navigating anxiously between affirming the presence and at the same time stressing that it is not yet. Chilton (1996, 92), commenting on Lk 11.20 par interprets 'has come near' as something "which is so near that its approach has been completed, although it is not yet completely present," "the cusp between the process of arriving and arrival itself": (*sic*). What is challenging in his view is the statement that the *eschaton* is not primarily in time but rather as heaven touching the earth.

Though Ambrozic (1972) accepts that the Kingdom has come, yet it has to wait to become manifest. He, too, makes provisions. One: it is only "at the very moment of Jesus' proclamation of its approach; it is the proclamation that makes it present" (21). It is Jesus who by and in his presence represents the Kingdom and makes it a reality. Is the conclusion then that it is only where and when Jesus is present in person the Kingdom has arrived? For the time being then the Kingdom remains hidden "and is still waiting to become manifest and unfold all its *eschatological* powers" (24, 135) (*sic*, emphasis added). In the conclusion of his book, he formulates what is the common opinion among many: "... a kingdom yet to come which is, paradoxically, already present" (244) (Dodd's realized eschatology).

The Kingdom of God may therefore be understood as 'arrived', and therefore 'present' in the time dimension: it is not past, it is no future, it is *now*, its presence being the result of having approached.

The conclusion is clear: linguistically the *êggiken* cannot mean anything else than 'has approached (i.e., arrived) and, therefore, is present.

---

29 Zerwick, 1996.

Implied is the issue: if the Kingdom is present, why is it not perceived? In the 'where' chapter (chapter 7) we will find Jesus telling that one need not look neither here nor there, "it is inside you people." One needs to become conscious on a different level than that of the senses. Openness is needed, receptivity is required. It has to be interiorized. The power of the Spirit is underestimated greatly. Also in this sense the Kingdom seems to be both present and hidden, i.e., as a permanent potentiality. The duality is softened.

What do the Synoptics say more about the time dimension? At one place Jesus is quite definite about the *when*. In Mk 9.1 he assures the disciples that "there are some standing here who will not taste death before they see that the Kingdom of God has come with power" (or rather: 'in strength').[30] If we want to interpret this statement in terms of the eschaton, it implies that the kingdom will appear physically within a few decades at the maximum. We know it did not happen. So either Jesus was mistaken or he was not understood when he tried to make clear that the kingdom is of another dimension. And he makes clear that some of his disciples will realize that the Kingdom of God has come to them in strength, with an inner energy that consumes everything in its Light. Therefore, it cannot but indicate that the coming refers to a state of inner development in some of his disciples that Jesus foresees. One should refrain from the idea to know the essence of his message, the coming of the Kingdom on short term. It must have a different meaning: the inner kingdom.

Conclusions

A close analysis of the text of Mk 1.14–15 and its Matthean parallel prompts one of the following conclusion:

- the Kingdom of God has approached and therefore cannot be but present;
- the *euaggelion* stands for the divine Message, it is not a one-time news item, and its proclaiming refers to an enduring condition;
- the divine Message is the Kingdom of God
- 'time is fulfilled' does not refer to the time dimension but to 'the very moment'
- Jesus calls for confiding oneself to the Message;
- Kingdom is the essence of Jesus' Message and he calls people to confide themselves to it, rather than a call 'believe in the Gospel / the good news
- the Kingdom of God is present as a potentiality for the individual, and by implication for humanity at large.

The next chapters will clarify some of these statements.

---

30 Hatina (2005, 20, 34, passim) is one of the many who interpret this text as eschatological. The power referred to signifies a threat of judgment aimed at antagonists.

CHAPTER SEVEN

The Kingdom in the Gospels: 'Where'?

Godisnowhere[1]

Reading ancient manuscripts is an interpretative art. Spaces between words are not given. Great theological problems may hide in a phrase. In this chapter we will try and find out if God is 'now here', or far away, 'nowhere.'

The Scene

> *Let us try and imagine the scene behind what is reported in Lk 17.20–21. The pericope starts out of the blue with the Pharisees putting a catch to Jesus.*[2] *They ask when the Kingdom would come. Jesus intelligently does not answer the when. As it will turn out the when is an irrelevant issue. He rather reverses the question revealing the where. Then, we may imagine, how he turns around to other persons in the audience, maybe the disciples, in order to direct his answer to those who may understand. And his reply is the most shocking reply that can be imagined: the Kingdom of God is here already, 'in the midst of you,' or even, more precisely, 'inside you.' He introduces his radical statement by telling that the Kingdom is not a thing to be perceived; it does not come in the usual way: do not try to look around, do not look for signs that can be observed; it does not come with your careful observation. It is not here nor there. It is not relevant to expect that it will be exclaimed 'here it is,' or 'there.' It is the simple* idou *versus the expectant eager impatient observation suggested by* meta paratêrêseôs: *just look inside yourself! Mind you, it is just here, present at this moment! And what way of being present? The Kingdom of God is inside you! Jesus wants us to know that this promised Kingdom, so fiercely debated religiously as well as secularly for centuries already, is right here and now, not outside, not perceivable by the senses; no, it resides in the inner being of man. Is this concept of the Kingdom he is presenting the same as his disciples and others are expecting, or does he use common words but with an extra sense, maybe even a fresh new dimension?*

* * *

In order to understand the wording of the logion, three issues have to be addressed. The main one is about the 'where,' the phrase *entos humin*, as the 'location' of the Kingdom. Related is the issue of perceiving the Kingdom; key terms are *paratêrêsis* and *idou*. Finally the logion confronts the *erchetai* (comes) with the *estin* (is). Of these three the first one is crucial.

---

1   Credit to Bart D. Ehrman.
2   In Th 113 / OxyP 654.9–16 the question is attributed to the disciples. Nolland 1993, 851: "we cannot be sure that the attribution (to the Pharisees) is original."

THE KINGDOM IN THE GOSPELS: 'WHERE'?

> Lk 17.20–21
> Being asked by the Pharisees when the Kingdom of God was coming, Jesus answered them, "The Kingdom of God is not coming with signs to be observed; nor will they say, Lo, here it is! or 'There!' for behold, the Kingdom of God is in the midst of you."[3]   NRSV
>
> Once being asked by the Pharisees when the Kingdom of God would come, Jesus replied, "The Kingdom of God does not come with your careful observation, nor will people say, 'Here it is', or 'There it is', because the kingdom of God is within (or among) you."   NIV
>
> *Ouk erchetai hê basileia tou theou meta paratêrêseôs;*
> *oude erousin: idou hôde ê ekei;*[4]
> *idou gar hê basileia tou theou entos humin estin.*   NA27
>
> A proposed alternative interpretation:
> *The Kingdom of God does not come by careful scrutinizing observation,*
> *it will not be observable in terms of seeing,*
> *you cannot expect it to be here or there located,*
> *(do not trust that, according to the reading of D)*
> *for behold, the Kingdom of God is inside you.*
>
> The proposed corresponding translation:
> *The Kingdom of God does not come by close observation,*
> *One will not say: 'Look, it is here', or 'there',*
> *for behold, the Kingdom of God is inside you.*

---

3   Adding in a footnote "Or: within."
4   Codex Bezae (D) has an insertion here, *mê pisteusête*, do not believe so (NA27).

The Kingdom Is Inside[5]

This chapter is on the issue of where the Kingdom of God resides: the where. The clearest statement Jesus makes is this logion of Lk 17.20–21 that says that the Kingdom is 'inside you.' Other texts contain indirect additional indications of great significance. They are to be found in the parables on the Kingdom and will be further treated in chapter 8. Some hints were found when we discussed the 'when.' The other way round hints about the 'when' occur in the where discussions.

The way the logion is presented here represents a minority view, at best. The Kingdom is interpreted as a divine presence inside the human being: the interiority hypothesis. It will be checked in this chapter. This logion represents the most direct statement of the mysticism of Jesus in the Gospels, and as such is an important case in the argument of the book. Is this an accepted view? No, it is rare in NT studies and singular for the last century. The great exception is Harnack whom we met in chapter 4. Its exceptionality therefore requires a critical analysis of its various aspects. The issue is to find out about the validity of this point of view and of the concomitant rendering of the logion.

Its interpretation has had a long and varied history with engaging hot discussions. For at first sight it is in conflict with Church doctrines and theology, and with some other sayings attributed to Jesus. The Kingdom inside? Impossible! Many modern translations have followed that line by rendering the *entos* as in the midst of, or among.[6] Traditional translations throughout history, however, have been faithful to the Greek original. The early English King James (1611) and the Dutch Statenvertaling from 1637 are true to the text and have 'inside' and 'binnen ulieden,' respectively, like some other translations do.[7] The tradition reaches far back: the early Fathers did the same[8]. It has been a long tradition until Modernism got through. The turning point appears to be as late as about 1980. Modern exegetes generally prefer to translate 'among' but this meaning is elsewhere unknown.

Secular and patristic evidence has been adduced for an extension of the meaning.[9]

---

5 What is *entos*? BDAG: inside, within: first what is inside an object (Mt 23.26: *to entos tou potêriou*); a specific area inside something (Lk 17.21); it does not leave space for a psychological or spiritual understanding. Remarkably TDNT does not have *entos* as a lemma at all. Does this suggest that the hermeneutical weight is downplayed, in both reference books? Greek-English dictionaries give inside or within as the only meaning.
6 For example, ESV 2007, NAS 1977, NIRV, NJB 1985, NRS 1989, TNIV.
7 For example, ASV 1901, Derby 1884/90, Douay-Rheims 1899, Geneva Bible 1599, NIV 1984.
8 See Holmén 1996, 225–26.
9 Zerwick 1996, 251.

The logion proper 'is inside you' seems embedded in a short narrative where Jesus is in discussion with some Pharisees. The Pharisees' role however is only to frame the question in order to bring a logion consisting of a negative part ('it is not...'), followed by the positive statement ('it is'). The two parts belong together where the negative clarifies the positive. For how is it that the Kingdom is inside and nobody sees it? Regular observation obviously does not do, it seems.

This interpretation, now, has to be confronted with other insights.

First some technical remarks, followed by different views.

Observations

Some Textual Comments

Entos humin has a parallel in Pap.Oxyrh. 654.3 / Th 3: *...kai hê basileia tôn ouranôn entos humin esti k'aktos*: inside and outside, followed by the enigmatic *kai hostis an heauton gnôi tauten heurêsei....* and whoever may know himself will find it.[10] This addition in Th strengthens the inner meaning.

It has been suggested that *erchetai* may function as a future present: will come (Schlosser 1979, 95, n 67, 68, 69). These cases for the greater part are not convincing unless one takes the preconceived idea that the Kingdom of God is a future event. Rather the present tense suggests the contrary.

Conclusion: these observations do not lead to a text different from NA27.

Other Views

Lk 17.20–21 indeed has been embarrassing to translators and interpreters alike. *Grosso modo* five interpretations can be found.

- it is not here as it will arrive at the eschaton only[11];
- it is among / in the midst of 'you people'; in the strict historical sense it refers to those present in the situation described. This is the general view of the

---

10 Plisch 2007, 44–46. Also Koester, *Ancient Christian Gospels* 1990, 76).
11 This is a wide-spread view. A case in point is Nolland (1993) in his extensive commentary on Lk, here page 849-54. He presents different views. This one is motivated by interpreting the verses 20-21 in the context of the following passage vv 22–37 that has heavy overtones of eschatology. He interprets it as an anticipation of the future coming of the Kingdom, disregarding the present tense of the pericope.

Commentaries and reflected in translations since about 1980. For example, "the context with the Pharisees forbids the within you; rather it is in the midst of you"[12];

- or it may be interpreted as a timeless pronouncement, valid for any situation where Jesus is present, wherever his word and his work will touch people[13];

•more specifically, for both latter cases, it means that it is Jesus who stands for the Kingdom by his very presence (Dodd's realized eschatology);

- it is available to you, it is within your reach ("steht zu eurer Verfügung, ist in eurem Einflussbereich"[14]), (la Basileia est "à votre portée")[15] but one has to seek, to make efforts in order to enter; in your hands (ref. that for which one is responsible), in your power of choice (it lies with you), i.e., the Kingdom is yours if you choose it, if you will it[16];

- it is inside, à la Harnack (see chapter 4).

What does the literature contribute? There is more or less a *communis opinio* that 'inside' and the like is not the correct rendering. Here are some arguments.

- Perrin finds that the logion with 'within' contradicts other Jesus *logia*. This understanding of the Kingdom is "without parallel in the recorded teaching of Jesus".... "wholly foreign to the teaching of Jesus."[17] Obviously he wants to assert that it is in contradiction with the doctrine of the eschaton as a supposed central issue of Jesus' message. NT scholars by and large have interpreted this logion as confirming this doctrine.

- Rüstow[18] in a thorough and intelligent linguistic analysis concludes that the Kingdom is at hand; wait for it quietly, prepare yourself; it is a moral exercise, so that you can be accepted when it comes (216). His analysis rests on four conditions (197): philologically sound, matching with the entire Church tradition, make sense in the context, not contradicting the tenor of the Gospel teaching about the kingdom. No wonder he excludes the inside solution.

- For example, Zmijevski: On the one hand he says: "Vor allem kann man sich für diese (immanente) Deutung darauf berufen, dass die Betonung eines Erscheinens der Gottesherrschaft 'in der Verborgenheit des Menschenherzens' durchaus der Lehre und Vorstellung Jesu entspricht" [!] (p 373). However, on the other hand, he finds this cannot be true here as the saying cannot and should not be understood as 'spatially immanent' (räumlich-immanent) because it is a future statement. Thus, it must be in the future, as the Kingdom of God is not yet present and certainly not inside the

---

12 *A New Catholic Commentary*, Walton-on-Thames: Nelson 1981, 1013. Nolland (1993, 853) rejects it on the ground that it does not connect to the eschatologically interpreted vv 22–37.
13 Zmijevski 1972, 377.
14 Zmijevski 377, referring also to Roberts 1983, R. Schnackenburg 1963, A. Rüstow 1960, 377 n 83.
15 Schlosser 1979, 111f.
16 Zerwick 251–52.
17 Perrin 1963, 175f.
18 Rüstow 1960.

- Pharisees: a circle reasoning. He warns for this spatially immanent interpretation as it is close to a 'spiritualistische Verflüchtigung' [*sic*].
- Also Aulén finds that it "is one of the most contested and difficult texts on the Kingdom of God" (103): 'within you' is excluded by the great majority of scholars [i.e., in the 'sixties and early 'seventies], [and still is by many] as it is "having no correspondence with other utterances of Jesus, and representing a spiritualism which is totally alien to him" , a view that is contested in this book. He then speaks of "... the general rule that Jesus' words concerning the realization of the kingdom do not belong to the 'present' but to the 'coming era'" (103), a view that must be seen as one side of the coin only, referring to Harnack (chapter 4).
- Also Schlosser, turns his argument against the inner meaning. One cannot say, he argues that the Kingdom is 'inside you', unless it is conceived of as a purely spiritual, interior immanent entity. He continues: but this idea "n'est attestée ni dans le judaïsme ancien, ni dans les logia authentiques de Jésus, ni dans la tradition présynoptique, ni d'ailleurs dans la redaction lucanienne" (Schlosser 1979, 111).

However, other views deny such conclusions, and concur more or less with the thesis of the interiority of the Kingdom. Carmignac,[19] for example, recognizes the spiritual reality of the Kingdom: it is neither observable nor to be localized. But what he advocates is a spiritual variant of the so-called realized eschatology: "... Jésus considère ce Règne de Dieu comme une réalité dejà présente."

Even a 'breath' of mysticism is found in some rather isolated studies. Aulén signalizes Perrin who opens a new avenue of understanding: "the Kingdom is a matter of human experience." "... it is to be found wherever God is active decisively within the experience of an individual..." (p. 103f.).[20] Here reference is made to an experience within, a point central to mysticism. This offers a bridge between the 'eschatologists' and the 'entosists': the inner kingdom cannot be experienced but when God (or the *pneuma*) is active in the (inner) experience of the individual.

Another and recent contribution takes the divine presence as an issue. It differentiates between the presence of God with the human (accompagnement et assistance de Dieu), and the presence of God within the human: l'intériorité divine.[21] The NT texts selected for the interiority aspect stem mainly from the Pauline and Johannine books; Lk 17.20–21 does not play a significant role.

Another issue and of a different nature is whether this logion stands on itself in the text, or must be understood in the context of the following pericopes. Two points. One is the issue of decontextualization: the logion must be seen per se. When however the narrative is seen as the framework, the situation changes. Jesus, in the next pericopes, turns to what appears as eschatology (vv 22–37). Is

---

19　Carmignac 1979, 58–60.
20　Quoted from Perrin, *Rediscovering the teaching of Jesus* 1967, 74.
21　Siffer-Wiederhold, Nathalie, *La présence divine à l'individu d'après le Nouveau Testament*, Cerf, Paris 2005.

it part of the same logion, or has it been inserted here from another source? Scholars diverge in answering this issue. The wordings and the tone of the narrative change dramatically, suggesting a different source. Therefore, we conclude that the two passages, 20–21 and 22–37, probably do not belong together, neither as one argument, nor in terms of redaction.[22]

Inside, or in the Midst Of

The hermeneutical history of this pericope is long, creating hundreds of publications. For a century already the general line confirms Perrin as quoted. The main issue, of course, is the phrase *entos humin*. It needs further analysis. This has been made by Tom Holmén, in a thorough and well-documented article on the semantic restrictions of this pericope (Holmén 1996). He has shown unequivocally that the rendering of *entos* as within is the only viable translation. His thorough and well-documented article is showing the way. He has followed a fourfold route. Here are his conclusions.

- Philologically *entos humin* cannot but mean 'inside you.'
- Semantically he finds that the *humin*, the persons inside whom is the Kingdom, cannot refer to a specific group or person. It is inside 'everybody.'
- A thorough survey of the use of *entos humin* in Greek literature through the ages was conducted. Nowhere does it mean anything else than 'inside.'
- Finally he has checked how the early Fathers interpreted this passage. Invariably they have understood the phrase to mean 'inside you,' although in their conflict with Gnosticism it would have been logical for them to take the opportunity to render it as 'among' or equivalents.

Summing up: *entos humin* cannot but mean 'inside you.'

Here is a summary of the argument.

Holmén focuses on the *entos* as this word is crucial for the differences of interpretation of this pericope. It has been translated as 'in the midst of,'[23] 'in the possession of,'[24] and 'within.' He finds there is an almost *communis opinio* on the first rendering, 'in the midst of', "it is this explanation that clearly dominates at the moment" (205), which affirms my conclusion formulated earlier. In this rendering, Jesus is supposed to refer to his own appearance and his deeds as the

---

22 Zmijesvki, 333–42.
23 Frequently one finds also 'among,' which I assume is a synonym of 'in the midst of', in terms of Holmén's argument.
24 Holmén includes the following renderings: in the hands of, in the control of, im Einflussbereich, im Verfügungsbereich, im Wirkungsbereich, im Machtbereich, in the power of, within the reach of, and I add: à la portée.

identity of the Kingdom: Jesus himself *is* the Kingdom. Already since Weiss it is understood that (only) in this way the logion would fit the given context: how could the Kingdom possibly be located within the Pharisees?

Holmén approaches the issue in a number of ways. He investigates the use of 'in the midst of', first philologically. "'Within' is surely the most natural meaning of *entos* in Greek literature." Significantly he adds: "The philologists knowing nothing about the theological discussion would no doubt be surprised to hear about the meaning 'in the midst of'." In the LXX of the seven instances where *entos* occurs, five are used to designate inward parts; in the other two it simply means 'inside' (206–7).

Secondly Holmén makes a thorough examination of the semantic field of *entos humin* that we cannot possibly reproduce here (207–11) but may try to summarize. Who is the *humin*? His conclusion is that the translation by 'in the midst of' cannot hold. Elements of his argument are that the expression cannot imply that the 'you (pl.)' indicates a specific group with the exclusion of any others. This cannot possibly refer to the group mixed of disciples and Pharisees, nor to the Pharisees as such. Neither can it point to some individuals within the group addressed with the exclusion of others. He finds that it must encompass anyone both within and outside the persons present at that moment. What it does imply is that the 'thing' indicated must be inside and cannot be outside the individuals referred to. His conclusion therefore is that linguistically the *entos humin* cannot but mean 'inside you (pl.).'

Third, he examines the passages in Greek literature through the ages that have been used by scholars as proof of the 'in the midst of' translation. The range is from Herodotus to Symmachus' OT translation, via Xenophon, Plato, Josephus, Arrian, and Aquila's OT translation. His conclusion: "Among the passages quoted to prove that the preposition *entos* can also mean 'in the midst of' there is not one that is suited to the purpose" (211–23).

Fourth, Holmén analyzes "how the words *entos humin* in Luke 17.20–21 were actually understood by the earliest (Greek) interpreters of the saying," i.e., nine Early Fathers, from Irenaeus through Ambrosius. All of them do allude to Lk 17:20–21. What do they say? "... the Early Fathers knew no alternatives to the meaning 'within' of *entos* (225). Morever, "even prior to them, 'within' is the only sense in which *entos* has been comprehended in the saying." (226). He adds that this is the more remarkable as the 'in the midst' interpretation would have offered the Fathers a welcome argument against the heretics / Gnostics who of course advocate the inside meaning (223–25). His final conclusion (229): "I can but draw the conclusion that 'within' is the rendering of *entos* on which we ought to base our interpretation of Luke 17,20–21" (229).

The translation 'is inside you (pl.)', therefore, is fully justified.

Where Do We Stand?

From the reasoning so far, a *preliminary conclusion* springs forward. Current understanding rejects the interiority hypothesis, mostly implicitly. However, in the analysis conducted here, reasons for it holding ground have not been found. The phrase *entos humin* cannot but mean inside you. No counterlogic internal to this logion has been found. Literature objecting to it does not hold validity unless based on doctrines foreign to this logion. The interiority hypothesis confirms to the conclusion in the 'when' chapter: the Kingdom is actual, its coming is not eschatological.

Two issues have yet to be discussed: the when question and the perceptibility.

The 'When' Again: *estin*

Some scholars doubt about the present tense in this logion: the *erchetai* in 'the kingdom does not come' and the *estin* in 'is inside you,' and seek for a future use of the present tense.[25] The *erchetai* could be understood as a statement about the future, but it is more reasonable to understand it as a generality. Prophesying is not in order. Jesus is making clear that there is no point in discussing about coming: it *is*. This 'present' is insuperably expressed in the *estin* in the present tense. With the *estin* Jesus implicitly answers the when: there is no 'when': the Kingdom *is* inside you, stop looking here or there. With this reply, it is clear there is no coming of the Kingdom, and there is no somewhere. Thus the present-day relevance (as opposed to the eschaton) of the logion stands on firm ground.

Perceiving the Kingdom: *paratêrêsis*

What does this word *paratêrêsis* (including the verb), 'close observation,' signify?[26] It is about non-perceptibility. The Kingdom does not come by careful

---

25 Blass §323 offers quite a few cases where a future understanding is present. One of these is in prophesizing (sub 1).

26 KJ, ERV, ASV: with observation. TDNT VIII (Harald Riesenfeld), 148: in (classical) Greek: watching, lying in wait, inquisitive spying. No occurrence in LXX. In NT, Lk 17.20 is a *hapax*. My proposal: by careful scrutinizing observation. WNT (confirmed by Langenscheidt) renders it as 'Beobachtung' (observation). *Meta paratêrêseôs* is circumscribed in WNT as '... kommt nicht mit aüsseren Phänomenen, die Beobachtung (zuliessen). Langenscheidt offers an attractive simple solution: 'sichtbar', visible. BDAG renders it sub 1 as 'an act of watching or keeping an eye on something closely: observation, sub 2 'an act of following rules: observance'. For Lk 17.20: "... not coming with observation, i.e., in such a way that its rise [?] can be observed". Zerwick 1996, 251: "close observation , i.e., the

scrutinizing observation. One cannot say 'it is here' or 'there.' Obviously it is not visible. Yet Jesus says, 'for (!) (*gar*), behold, it is inside you.' It is not to be perceived physically, it is non-sensual. It is of a wholly different dimension. Thus, a different type of seeing is needed (*idou*, behold).[27] It is proposed here to view this Kingdom as an inner reality, a spiritual entity.

The next chapter will try and answer what the Kingdom is. It will be found to be a *mustêrion*. An analysis of some parables will underscore the conclusion that the Kingdom is inside the human being, as, for example:

- the seed in the soil
- the small mustard seed hiding its potential
- the treasure in the field
- the leaven in the dough
- the fine pearl among the many pearls.

Conclusions

As is evident from this assessment, there is no time dimension, the Kingdom simply *is*. This pericope, therefore, adds to and harmonizes with Mk 1.15's *when* saying: the Kingdom has arrived, it is no longer to be viewed as a future event, and it is to be found here, right inside those who listen to Jesus and his Message: the Kingdom has arrived, confide yourself to it: pure mysticism.

Thus, Jesus confronts his audience with an idea they may never have heard about—on a subject that was widely debated in Jewish society. Jesus supersedes the expressive images of an apocalyptic appearance of the Kingdom at the eschaton. He implicitly denies a return of the Davidic kingdom. And the expected Kingdom is not the revolutionary entrance into a paradisiacal society of justice, love, and social care (Borg[28]). What Jesus is telling refers to an inner knowledge that may have been known, probably hidden in some closed circles or in what is referred to in the Gospels as a secret (or: secrets), as *mustêrion*.[29]

Kingdom will not come with watching, or the Kingdom is not susceptible of observation." Nolland 1993, 850–51: "in a way that allows for advance observation."

Nolland (1993, 852) offers a diversity of interpretations, all of them with the limited view of seeing and observing in the rational physical way, interpreted in the socio-cultural environment of the time, where Jesus tries to open a different way of looking: the kingdom cannot be observed.

27 The *idou* is connected to the double meaning of hearing and seeing in many Jesus logia.
28 Borg, 2003, esp. 131–35. Also by Borg 2006, *Jesus: Uncovering the Life, Teachings, and Relevance of a Religious Revolutionary*, San Francisco 2006.
29 More about the *mustêrion* in the next chapter, on the parable of The Sower.

To return to Harnack: his statements have been confirmed: Jesus' message contains both dimensions: the here and now as well as the then and there: depending on the state of one's consciousness, it is to be experienced. Indeed, that is a gift that cannot be brought about. Again: the Kingdom of God permits us to deny the either/or, and to acknowledge the and/and. However, it requires us to accept the mystery of the beyond. In addition, it does imply the acceptance of the 'reality' that the 'hearing' and 'seeing' is to be experienced, as mystics through the ages have testified, including Paul.[30] Indeed, the implication is that the here and now may happen.

A side observation on 'near'

In regard to both aspects, the *where* and the *when*, a note on the meaning of 'near' may be useful.

What is the meaning of 'near' in the locational sense? Near implies a 'this' and a 'that'; the 'this' is near 'that', or it is not. There are two connotations of nearness in the relationship between 'this' and 'that':

One tells about 'this' not being in the same place where 'that' is, yet not far away: 'this' is just in the close vicinity of 'that', yet separateness is obvious.

the other stresses that 'this' is within the circle of 'that', ,is present, is among 'that': not as an identity but as a feeling of being together. It may even mean an intimate relationship between 'this' and 'that.'

Presence is stressed, sometimes even an intimate presence. For example, in LXX in some psalms (Ps 33:18, ψ 118:151, ψ 144:18) (Preisker in TDNT, II 330–32). See also Borg, 1997, e.g., 34–37. Borg (p. 91) beautifully expresses this idea when writing that Jesus must have experienced the Spirit—which in terms of Borg is synonymous to God— sometimes 'around' him, sometimes 'inside' him and sometimes 'on' him. In a special state of consciousness Jesus could experience the presence of the kingdom, and express it, calling people to transform so that they may see as well. What Jesus is teaching people, is calling them to this consciousness: the Kingdom of God, 'inside you people' and mind you: it has approached, it is present, if you are aware of it. Otherwise you may know it is near and at hand. Do not try and observe where it is, just open your inner eyes, look, and *see*. See also chapters in Part IV.

---

30 I refer specifically to the passages about the *psuchikoi* and the *pneumatikoi*, 1 Cor 2.14–16 and context. See Pagels, *The Gnostic Paul* 1992, 53–86.

CHAPTER EIGHT
The Kingdom of God in the Gospels: 'What' Is It?

Introduction

The conclusion reached in the two preceding chapters clearly establishes that the Kingdom of God is in the 'here' and in the 'now': it *is within*, with these two emphases. Now the question arises, *what* is it then that is within? Can one know it by perception? No, one does not, was the conclusion in chapter 7. It is, as it were, of another dimension, it even cannot be observed as it does not appear in terms of seeing or of other senses, we found. What does Jesus say to that? Does he explain what the Kingdom of God is? No! It is a shocking experience, but he does not define it. There is hardly a pericope where one will find clearly and unequivocally 'the Kingdom of God is this or that.' What Jesus does is providing indications to it. Significantly he says: 'the Kingdom of God is *like....*' Indeed, he does so when introducing many of the parables, parables that do not define the Kingdom but rather indicate a direction of understanding. Therefore, parables are a clue when one wants to grasp the essence of the Kingdom, it is these that raise a tip of the veil. However, what one finds in them is difficult to interpret as defining the Kingdom. When his disciples ask why he speaks in parables he speaks about the *mustêrion*. This term and concept will ask our attention first and then shift to the main body of information on the Kingdom, the parables.

This is what he says:

Mk 4.11[1] par[2]

"To you has been given (*dedotai*[3]) the secret [*mustêrion*] (or: mystery) of the Kingdom of God, but for those outside, everything comes in parables...."
NRSV

---

1   As part of Mk 4.1–20.
2   Mt 13.11 as part of Mt 13.1–23, and Lk 8.10 as part of 8.4–15.
3   Pf pass *didômi*. It has been given to the disciples: by whom? When? What exactly was the qualification of the thing given; what was the 'substance' of the *mustêrion*, if one may ask such a thing? Questions as these have been haunting exegetes, with no definite answer.

Humin dedotai to mustêrion tês basileias tôu theou; ekeinois de tois exô[4] en parabolais ta panta ginetai,...

Mk thus does not have '*gnônai*', to know (related to *gnosis*)

Mt 13.11: '...given to *know* the secrets (pl)' ... and 'but to them it is not given'.

Lk 8.10: '...given to *know* the secrets (pl)' ... 'but to others I speak in parables'.

It is well possible that these verses originate from either one oral source or from different oral traditions. The three minor variations allow for this assumption. However, theories abound with no consensus.[5]

The *mustêrion*

The *mustêrion*, i.e., of the Kingdom of God. Does the Kingdom contain the secret? Or is it so that the Kingdom itself is the *mustêrion*? The genitive does not offer clarity. Let us see.

This logion is one of the crucial ones. Why crucial if it is a *hapax* only? Several answers. It figures in all three Synoptics. It is presented as the key to the understanding of the parables, some of which Jesus considers as near explanations of the Kingdom of God (the Kingdom of God is like...). Indeed, the *mustêrion is* the Kingdom of God, let us take that for granted for the time being.[6] Finally, the understanding of the parables, and therefore of the *mustêrion*, is a privilege reserved for the disciples, dependent on the knowledge (*gnôsis*) given to them, a concept to be discussed below.

If it is crucial, is it authentic? There is a *communis opinio* that authenticity of whatever word of Jesus cannot be guaranteed. Even so, there are shades in what we can know. What is the situation here?

> The Jesus Seminar judges 'no'. But it does so for the complete pericope Mk 4.11–20. Why not take the logion quoted above *per se*? It is the only one with the *mustêrion*, maybe not the cake of the Seminar, it seems. Dunn (2003, 626; also 385) finds it well possible that these two verses may have roots in memories of Jesus' utterances. The pericope may betray 'recycling' in early communities, he says. Nolland (1989, 377–79) is of the same opinion.

Jesus speaks of the *mustêrion*, embedded in the Sower parable. What is this *mustêrion*? Kingdom apart, the text suggests that it is knowledge that transcends physical and mental reality. It is 'something on which silence must be kept.' It is experienced as well as experiential knowledge (*gnôsis*), not derived from logic

---

4 People inside are those to whom the *mustêrion* is made known, the others stand outside, a distinction sometimes interpreted as eso-teric and exo-teric. Josephus: *tois exôthen* (Dunn 2003a, 495 n. 27). Compare Lk 17.21 *entos*.
5 Kloppenborg, *Excavating* 2000, 35–36.
6 Focant 2009 interprets the *mustêrion* christologically.

and sensory perception (Lk 17.21–22), it is about divine Presence, as a hidden reality that transcends logic and escapes sensory perception. That is what Jesus may have conveyed (given, *dedotai*) to his disciples to know *gnônai, gnosis*).

A hapax

This is the only place where this term, *mustêrion*, occurs in the Gospels: it is a *hapax*. I will continue to keep to the Greek word, rather than fixing it as secret or mystery that might suggest specific meanings. And I prefer the Markan singular. How do the two terms relate: is the Kingdom itself the *mustêrion*? Or does it contain a *mustêrion*? I tend to interpret the phrase as indicating that the Kingdom itself is the *mustêrion*., including how to find it.

Terminology

What does it mean, this term *mustêrion*? The direct answer is: 'something on which silence must be kept', says Bornkamm[7] in an etymological analysis (ibidem 803): a basic meaning therefore. Its use in the classical world as rituals need not refer to Jesus' use of the term, he continues. Neither need it be seen as connected to initiation in a secret cult. It may refer to "the unmanifested...counsel of God, (God's) secret," awaiting "revelation to those for whom they are intended" (BDAG sub 1). Indeed, it is 'that which transcends normal understanding, transcendent/ultimate reality' (ibid. sub 2).[8] In Greek antiquity it was the word for the mysteries (Eleusis and others), which had an enormous significance in society that can hardly be underrated (Bornkamm 803–8). Its central command was silence. Why? "The true reason...is to be sought in the special sanctity of the actions...which establish a *metousia* [!] (participation, communion, Liddell Scott) with the deity" (808): a unification: mysticism. I do not want to infer that the *mustêrion* Jesus speaks of stands in any relation to the Greek mysteries. However, it is a sign of the universal nature of spirituality. Some refer the term to a Semitic background where it means 'the secret plan of God revealed to his people.'[9]

Interpretation

In Christianity it often is understood that the *mustêrion* refers to the fact of the coming of the Kingdom (Bornkamm 818), or rather that the *mustêrion* of the Kingdom is Jesus himself as Messiah (819). This interpretation goes back to Wrede.[10] Indeed, the sacrament is the key to it.[11] It has had a powerful impact and continues to do so. Dunn (2003, 495 n 24), contrarily, interprets the *mustêrion* eschatologically: "... reflects the characteristic apocalyptic sense of divine secrets now revealed by divine agency.[12] Commentaries on the *mustêrion* are rare and unclear or fail (Marcus, Gundry, Nolland).

---

7   TDNT IV 802–28 by G. Bornkamm.
8   "... le mystère est donné mais qu'il échappe à toute possession cognitive », says Focant (2009, 21). «...le don du mystère ne signifie pas la révélation d'un nouveau contenu de savoir » (ibid. 19).
9   Gundry 1994, 255 referring to R.E. Brown. Also Hooker 1991/1997, 127.
10 Wrede, *Das Massiasgeheimnis* 1901, taken from Focant 2009, 18.
11 In the early Latin church, *mustêrion* was translated as *sacramentum*. The term stood for the soldier's oath, a sort of initiation (Bornkamm 827).
12 See also *Commentary* 1981, 963.

However, a great many NT scholars, here in a quotation by Prieur, maintain that the pre-Easter kerygma of the *basileia* is to be found "...in den als Exorzismen verstandenen Heilungen...[darin] offenbart sich die Gottesherrschaft, die als Erfüllungsgeschehen Gegenstand der Basileiaverkündigung ist." Even so, is it appropriate to put the very words by Jesus on the Kingdom of God on the second plane, if not even lower, than his acts? It does not appear right to interpret the Jesus logia in the way Paul does, i.e., neglecting his message in favor of his own interpretation of his Pauline 'Gospel.' Here I find the impact of theology on, for example, the parables too strong.

If we take the understanding of the Kingdom by Harnack as a line of thought, the Kingdom signifies divine Presence as a hidden reality that transcends logic and escapes sensory perception. Therefore, it is 'something on which silence must be kept.' Speaking is not forbidden, but words do not touch reality: 'unworded words.' Silence is reality. In all traditions, so-called secret teachings have been kept and given only to those who could fathom them. The disciples are 'awakened' to a *mustêrion* that is beyond their comprehension; they need to receive understanding; rather than having matters explained to them, they need to arrive at an appropriate insight.[13]

The *mustêrion*, it is implied in the quoted text, should not and cannot be told about openly. Jesus communicates that the Kingdom of God *is* this *mustêrion*. The Gospels report that he did speak about it, but it was never done explicitly, as one can read in the parable texts (see below). Indeed, it was given to the disciples specifically, opening up the *mustêrion* when he explained the parable of the Sower (see the appropriate section below). This assessment is in sharp contrast to the crowd who receives it indirectly, that is in the form of parables. "I speak to them in parables, because seeing they do not see, and hearing they do not hear, nor do they understand"[14] (Mt 13.13).

To the disciples "has been given the *mustêrion* of the Kingdom." How then does it happen that time and again the disciples fall short of understanding Jesus? Mk is the most outspoken on the failure of the disciples. One of the striking cases is precisely the scene around the parable of the Sower.[15] In his narrative Mk has reported that Jesus has told the parable publicly (4.3–9). Afterward the disciples ask him 'concerning the parables.' Jesus then tells them that the *mustêrion* has been given to them (v. 10–11). Immediately he continues and asks the disciples: "Do you not understand this parable? How then will you

---

13 Focant (2009, 19) touches this interpretation in its essence: "[Les disciples] sont éveillés [!] à un mystère qui les dépasse [!] et qui requiert pour être accuelli moins de chercher des explications [!] que de parvenir à un entendement approprié' [!]. Otherwise Focant turns the issue of the *mustêrion* into a christological issue, and terms it 'mystical' (i.e., an inexplicable phenomenon, , in my view a wrong interpretation of mysticism).

14 *Suniêmi*, to put things together, to understand, related to insight. Lk 8.10 has the shorter version "so that seeing they may not see, and hearing they may not understand." Mk 4.12 has a variant in paralleling seeing / perceiving; moreover he adds at the end "lest they should turn (*epistrepsô*) again, and be forgiven."

15 Mt 13.3–13 par, continued in Mt 13.18–23.

understand all parables?" (v. 13) Here is a tension: to the disciples is given the *mustêrion* whilst at the same time they do not live up to this standard. However, what is Jesus' intention? If one is given something, it does not imply one is a good receiver: is the capacity to receive and understand developed? Obviously, the *mustêrion* whilst having been given has to be detected. Chapter 9 will be more specific on this issue. However, here we need to put on stage the issue of perceiving: another mode of hearing and seeing Jesus is proclaiming time and again.

Purposely parables are made hard to understand. That is also the clear object of the teller Jesus. His parables are put in seemingly plain words, yet hiding the *mustêrion*. At the same time, it is the parables themselves that contain the clue to understand, 'to put together' (*suniêmi*) the inner meaning of what really is the Kingdom of God, provided the gift can be received adequately.[16] Can the disciples put together (*suniêmi*) the inner meaning behind the outer one? Did Jesus give a clue himself? In Lk 17.20–21 Jesus tells that the Kingdom cannot be perceived physically. What then? Did Jesus suggest a way of inner perceiving? He did, as we find in some fifteen instances (including parallels) distributed over the Synoptics, and with variations. Clear indication: 'see!', 'hear!'[17]

Who has ears (to hear), hear![18]
Having eyes do you not see, and having ears do you not hear?[19]
Seeing they do not perceive, and hearing they do not hear[20]
Blessed are the eyes that see what you see[21]
… to see what you see but did not see it
and to hear what you hear but did not hear it[22]

All of these are said in association with a specific teaching by Jesus. When finishing, Jesus often does so with this adage. Most of these[23] are connected with the parable of the Sower. We find it in all three phases described in this parable: ending the presentation of the parable, ending the explanation of it, and in the pericope in between when he

---

16 Besides, do we, readers of the logia, do *we* understand? Do *I* understand, the I who is commenting here so self-consciously?
17 I refer to Bradley's in-depth study of 'seeing'. It breaks many set views whilst opening new grounds. He differentiates between the various terms, identifying the five different ways of seeing: the *id-*, *hora-*, *blep-*, *theô-*, and *ops-*forms. What a variety in types, and variations in depth (Bradley 2007, vii-xx). Moreover he connects seeing to knowing (*gnosis*) (49, 71).
18 Mt 11.15, 13.9, 13.43, Mk 4.9, 4.23, Lk 8.8, 14.35.
19 Mk 8.18.
20 Mt 13.13, Mk 4.12, Lk 8.10.
21 Mt 13.16, Lk 10.23.
22 Mt 13.17, Lk 10.24 (slightly different wordings).
23 Others: parable of the Tares (Mt 13.43), of the Salt (Lk 14.34); privately to the disciples (Lk 10.23 and 24); in connection with the Baptist (t 11.15).

gives the reason for speaking in parables. It is a call for understanding, applicable to all teaching, we may suppose.

"Ainsi le visible dit plus que le visible»[24]

Five logia, therefore, where Jesus continuously calls for what appears as a special way of seeing and hearing, for it is not like listening as apart from hearing (as some translations suggest[25]). No, he says 'he who has ears (to hear), hear!' Otherwise one belongs to the category of those who, though seeing, do not see and, though hearing, do not hear. Obviously, there is more to it than can be heard with 'normal' hearing or seeing.

Another perspective on the seeing arises when one sees the passage with the explanation together with the following verses as one whole. The text significantly continues with the well-known lamp pericope.[26] Paraphrased: a lamp just lit must stand high, implying that it may shine out. 'For what is hidden shall be made manifest and come to light.'

This 'seeing' and 'hearing,' and therefore 'understanding,' is of a different nature than what we usually consider the use of the senses involved. It, of course, does not refer to clairvoyance or other forms of extrasensory perception. It is related to mysticism, the search for connecting to the divine. One needs an understanding, a capacity to know, a putting together (*suniêmi*), a synthesis, on a different level of awareness, a higher consciousness (Borg, Pagels; see chapter 1), an attunement: to hear differently, 'deeper'; to see differently, deeper. Thus, again Jesus tries to make clear that it is more about how to access it; words are secondary. It is developing a 'feeling.' Logically, a secret is secret, a mystery is mystery: it cannot be told and it should not be told. One cannot go any further. The disciples attuned to the spirit of Jesus are those who potentially are in the position to understand: "blessed are your eyes for they see, and your ears for they hear"(Mt 13.16).

What are the implications of 'the teaching that the words of the teaching do not represent the teaching'? Earlier we found that sacred words like these may be multi-layered in meaning. To simplify: an inner meaning related to mysticism, and an outer one in the context of the cultural and religious environment. It thus implies utter care and restraint when trying to understand and explicate an inner teaching, the *mustêrion*.

Jesus tells that this inner teaching cannot be given but in parables.

---

24 Bovon 2003, 123, referring to Michel Serres, *Les cinq sens*, Paris 1985.
25 E.g. NRSV.
26 Mk 4.21–22, Lk 8.16–18; parallel Mt 5.15 in a different context.

The Sower Parable[27]

The Parable of the Sower[28] may help to understand what is at stake. Though it is not explicitly about the Kingdom of God implicitly it is.[29] Jesus himself indicates it is the clue to all parables, and thus to his teachings (Mk 4.13). Sowing is a natural image for the divine giving life.[30]

First Jesus teaches the parable to the crowd gathered at the shores of the lake, closing with the call, 'he who has ears, hear!'[31] Indeed, some time later when he is alone with his disciples and is asked about parables, he explains that the Kingdom of God is a *mustêrion*, a mystery, a secret.[32] What is the *mustêrion*? Maybe we can come closer by when reading the opening lines of the passage where Jesus explains the parable. These lines are a great teaching in itself. In each evangelist's story the same word is the pivot, in slightly different setting: the *word* is the seed the sower is seeding, a sacred word: *logos* rather than *rhêma*.

> The opening verses of the 'explanation'[33] are a great teaching by themselves: Each of the evangelists renders the word as the pivot of the parable yet each makes his own variation:
>
> | | |
> |---|---|
> | *When anyone hears the word of the Kingdom* | Mt 13.19 |
> | *The sower sows the word* | Mk 4.14 |
> | *The seed is the word of God* | Lk 8.11 |

---

27 This parable is generally called the Sower. Remarkably, the Sower is mentioned once only right at the beginning (Mt 13.3b and 4a). In the further text the seed / word is the actor (actively, passively). Is this a hint to understand it psycho-spiritually? Its origin often is traced back to the early Church (Nolland 1989, 383, and others), and therefore would not be a Jesus text. I find its authenticity defendable in the context of my interpretation of the Kingdom of God logia.

28 Mk 4.3–8 and 13–20 / Mt 13.3–8 and 18–23 / Lk 8.5–8 and 11–15.

29 Often this parable (and others) is interpreted as to imply (or refer to) eschatology, and its related exclusiveness of those believing *vs* those doomed, like Gundry 1994, 256 about seeing and hearing [sic], or Marcus 1999, 295–97 and more. Nolland (1989, 375) is of a different opinion. These eschatological views will not be incorporated in my argument as irrelevant to my alternative proposal. They of course remain valid as one of the current ones. To quote one of the 'eschatologists':

"The parable of the Sower is eschatological because it embodies the activity of God sowing his restored people through the preaching of Jesus. To suggest that the parable teaches how to manage despair or shows that in failure and everydayness lies the miracle of God's activity is to domesticate the parable...." (Snodgrass 2008, 176).

30 Nolland 1989, 375.

31 Imperative. Mostly translated as 'may hear'. The call refers to the capacity to listen to the 'inner' dimension

32 The sections with the explanation are sometimes thought to be later redactional work and therefore not Jesus' words, e.g. Hooker 1991, 129.

33 Mk 4.13–20, Mt 13.18–23, Lk 8.11–15.

The explanation Jesus gives tells how the word is received in the heart (Mt 13.19b, Lk 8.11b).[34] The heart thus represents the type of ground where the seed came down in.[35]

Herewith Jesus explains the *mustêrion*, tout court, as the word (*logos*): the word of the Kingdom, the word of God. The word, therefore, is the vehicle by which the Kingdom is conveyed, not to the mind but to the heart of the individual. The explanation emphasizes the importance of the attitude and the condition of the individual's heart in receiving the word (the seed).

The explanation of the parable is then continued by describing the types of heart, parallel to the types of soil of the original parable in terms of the type of soil and its ability to receive.[36] Suppose one interprets the types as stages in a person's psycho-spiritual development and 'cultivation' of the heart so as to serve as fertile soil?

- One situation described is when the *logos* is sown in the heart, but obviously not heard. When not 'understood' it will be snatched away by the evil (Satan, devil). (Mt 13.4, 20 par). The parable sketches how the seed falls on the path.
- Another situation is when one does hear the *logos* and one receives it with joy; but there is no root, it is a transitory: one believes for a while but then gives up (Lk 8.13). Mt and Mk explain further: it endures for a while but when affliction and persecution arise on account of the *logos*, one gives up[37]: the *logos* cannot take effect. (Mt 13.5–6, 20–21 par). The parable tells about rocky ground with insufficient depth of soil.
- In yet another situation one hears the *logos* also but the heart is full of cares of the world, of delight in riches, and of desire for other things (Mk, Lk adds: and for the pleasures of life), with the result that the *logos* is choked and, adds Luke, the fruit does not mature (Mt 13.7, 22 par). Here the parable talks about thorns that chokes the seedlings.
- However, there also is a situation when one's heart hears the *logos* and understands it. Then that person bears fruit, 30, 60, 100-fold. (Mt 13.8, 23 par). Lk (8.15) explains further: who, hearing the *logos*, holds it fast in a fitting and pure[38] heart, [....] he brings

---

34 The heart is not mentioned directly as the palace where the word is sown. However, in Mt 13.19 Jesus says "when anyone hears the word of the Kingdom and does not understand it" the phrase," and then continues "the evil one comes and snatches away what is sown in the heart," thus making clear the function of the heart as receptacle. Similarly Lk 8.12.
35 The quote from Isaiah (Mt 13.15) is illustrative of the hard soil and its relation to seeing and hearing: "for this people's heart has grown dull," illustrating the 'seeing they do not see, hearing they do not hear nor do they understand."
36 See also chapter 9, section on As a little child.
37 *Skandizetai*, 'stumble, fall away' are the current translations; Friberg's Dictionary: 'give up.'
38 'Honest and good' according to NRV2: *kalos kai agathos*. *Kalos k'agathos* is the classical expression for 'Ehrenmann', aristocrat (Langenscheidt), excellent, superb, noble, gentlemanlike (Muller).

Kalos according to WNT means in terms of 'Beschaffenheit' (condition): 2a brauchbar, gut, b sittlich gut. Lobenswert, (zum Heile) nützlich, c einwandfrei, tadellos, augezeichnet. I propose a combination of brauchbar and (zum Heile) nützlich: 'fitting', i.e. for the *logos* to be

forth fruit, with patience [!].[39] The parable speaks about good soil bringing forth grain in various large quantities.

The explanation given by Jesus himself, therefore, is that in order to understand the *mustêrion*, the 'word' must be taken to heart. The word is the key to understanding the parable.[40] Here it is the vehicle by which obviously something of the Kingdom is being conveyed. It is a 'word' that cannot be perceived but in and through the heart. It is of a different dimension than the spoken word. It is vibration of a special frequency, it is an attunement.[41] The secret then is that the Kingdom is given to the heart. For this, 'hearing' is a necessary prerequisite. If not, the word is taken away. This 'enlightened' way of perceiving leads to 'understanding, 'when elements are 'put together.' If the *logos* then is being held in a heart *kalos kai agathos* (see footnote above), a fitting and pure heart, i.e. a pure heart attuned to as well as fit to receive the word of God, the Kingdom can mature and produce fruit manifold, fruits sweet and nourishing, destined not for oneself but for others.

That is the *mustêrion*.

> On another occasion Jesus underscores the durability of his *logos*. In a discourse (Lk 21.29–33,[42] which includes the parable on the fig tree that blossoms, and which otherwise is rather eschaton-directed) he reminds the disciples that the Kingdom of God is near (*eggus estin*) (v. 31): "Heaven and earth will pass away, but my words (*hoi logoi mou*) will never ever (*ou mê*) pass away."[43] He does not talk about the effect of his *logos*, but of the *logos* itself that is durable to the extent that it will never be gone. That is the character of a divine Message. It is not the words remembered but the reality behind that is operational if conditions have been met, and grace is granted.

---

received and to grow and mature. WNT only refers to the *kalos* quality of the soil, the *gê* in Lk 8.15a, not to the other *kalos*, i.e. of the heart in v.15b.

Agathos, according to WNT, indicates that something is 1a 'tüchtig, brauchbar in outwardly sense, whilst inwardly 1b it denotes 'good', or 'pure'. TDNT stresses the meaning of excellent, fine, good connected to a thing or a person. I adopt the 'pure' from WNT. Summing up: 'a fitting and pure heart'.

39 Mk 4.13–20, Mt 13.18–23, Lk 8. 11–15.
40 If indeed the word is taken in the sense now attributed to it, the question arises if there may be a relation with the *Logos* of Jn 1.1-5.
41 Lietaert Peerbolte (2009,164-65) refers to 2 Cor 12.3-4: " 'and into paradise' where he heard unutterable words (*arrhêta rhêmata* [unwordable words, wvl]). Zerwick 1996: in-effable: "that a human is not permitted to utter". Hence these 'unutterables' are translated as secrets. This is another key to understand what 'secret' may mean. Peerbolte (166) again: *arrhêtos* was also used in certain Jewish literature as a characterization of heavenly glory [!]. He continues (167) that this term in Paul signifies a mystical experience.
42 Parallels in Mk 13.28–32, Mt 24.32–36.
43 Lk 21.33, Mk 13.31, Mt 24.35

Thus, the parable of the Sower is a call for psycho-spiritual transformation. In that process the first step is making the heart to hear. Then to soften the stony psyche, followed by learning to manage and master the effects on the heart of worldly conditions: worries, cares, desires: to take out the thorns that choke the heart. As a result, the individual is being prepared to receive the message purely.

Parables on the Kingdom of God

When one is searching for logia by Jesus on what is the Kingdom, in most cases one finds a parable.[44] They generally open with words as 'the Kingdom of God is like...' (e.g., Mt 13.31), or: 'it may be compared to ...' (e.g., Mt 13.24), or: 'it is as if...' (e.g., Mk 4.26). They offer an optimal opportunity to find out what Jesus may mean with the Kingdom of God. The parables discussed here are those where a direct reference is made to the Kingdom of God. Additionally the Sower was discussed *supra*. After that, pericopes will be surveyed where the nature of the Kingdom of God is described more directly, not in parables. The hypothesis of this analysis is that these parables do convey an inner meaning, as was demonstrated above using the words of Jesus.[45]

The presentation takes the form of a classification of characteristics: its motive or intent, its location, type of growth, how to find, its nature. I apologize for the summary rendering of the inferred sense of the parable.

First an explanation of the scheme adopted

> Example: the nature of the Kingdom is to grow: its *intent*, or motivation, for example, is to grow, and it is *intrinsic* to the seed to do so. The source of the growing power is *inside* the seed, nothing from outside is needed, except the good soil where it is offered

---

44 Stettler (2004, 471): *parabolê*, a didactic and enigmatic saying. Legion are the explanations and philosophies on the term, the concept, and the use. I take the parable on the Kingdom as it usually is identified as such.

45 Some of the pericopes, e.g., in the Gospel of Matthew, do show a dichotomy. Apart from the inner meaning they stand in the perspective of eschatology and focus on exclusion and punishment, particularly those that speak about darkness, weeping and gnawing of teeth (Centurion 8:11f, Net 13:47, Unmerciful servant 18:23ff, v. 35, Wedding banquet 22:13, Talents 25:30) and the one referring explicitly to the Last Day (25:31ff.). How does this relate to the inner meaning we just found in the above analysis? On the one hand, this is an illustration of Harnack's thesis that the Kingdom is both an inner reality and an apocalyptic and eschatological one. On the other hand, this dichotomy may be the result of redaction. For example, where Th has parallels the eschatological pericopes in the Mt parallel are failing in Th. Even in Mk, Lk and Jn the eschatological hints we find in Mt (weeping, gnawing of teeth, darkness) mostly do not occur. Later are there redactional additions? May we apply the rule of the *lectio brevior* to texts from different traditions too? It is significant that Th does not contain any reference to the Last Day, and so on. Some passages often are interpreted as eschatological whilst an inner meaning may be applicable (either / or, or both).

optimal conditions for growing and maturing. Its growth is *instinctive*: it works by itself, is in-born.

Another example: the Kingdom is like a treasure hidden in the field. Its kingdom quality is *intrinsic* but as it needs action to be realized its *intent* is potential: it lies waiting till it will be awakened to realize itself. It is *inside* the field that may signify the human being who keeps it hidden unknowingly, but it has to get out: it must be found. And in order to acquire it one needs to detach oneself from other 'possessions.'

This is what we find, in a shortened paraphrase:

The Kingdom is as the seed growing quietly by itself. The soil brings the plant about by itself, even the sower not knowing how, but the harvest is his.

Mk 4.26–29, no par.

- Its intent is intrinsic
- It is inside
- Its growth is instinctive
- The Kingdom is a silent treasure inside the human being, with its own peculiar growing power, by its very nature manifesting in due time only

The Kingdom is like a grain of mustard seed: it is the smallest of all the seeds but when blossoming it is the greatest of all shrubs and the birds of the air make nests in it.

Mt 13.31–32, Mk 4.30–32, Lk 13.18–19, Th

- Its intent is intrinsic
- It is inside
- Its growth is instinctive
- The Kingdom appears as the smallest of all seeds, sown as it is inside the human being. However, it grows by itself and it turns out to become great 'so that creatures from heaven will live there.' It represents the divine energy hidden as an inconspicuous element in the human soul.

The Kingdom is like leaven, small as it is, hidden in the larger quantity of flour[46] it serves to penetrate the dough to the effect that it raises the body of flour and makes it fit its purpose.

Mt 13.33, Lk 13.20–21

- Its intent is intrinsic
- It is inside
- Its growth is instinctive

---

46 The Jesus Seminar compares the fifty pounds of flour mentioned here to the same quantity that Sarah is instructed to use for her heavenly visitors, "a suitable quantity to celebrate an epiphany—a visible, though indirect, manifestation of God" (Funk 1993, 195): an appropriate symbol of the Presence of the Kingdom and its working.

- By it life in the world can be 'digested'
- The Kingdom of God seems as an inconspicuous small entity different from the human being in substance and quantity, but it serves to make the human being to fit its purpose: to be an embodiment of the Kingdom of God, the Holy Spirit, provided one allows the spirit / leaven to integrate with the dough and become one with it.

Note. Leaven was considered a symbol of corruption while "the lack of leaven stood for what was holy…a surprising reversal of the customary associations"[47]

The Kingdom is like a treasure hidden in a field; a man finds it and sells all that he possesses, and buys the field, and thereby acquires the treasure.

Mt 13.44, no par.

- Its intent is potential
- Action is needed to acquire it
- It is inside (the field is the person)
- It has to be found
- One needs to sacrifice all else
- The Kingdom of God is hidden in the field, i.e., inside the self. One needs to 'possess' it, i.e., to know the self, to manage it, to control it, in order to be able to access the treasure inside oneself; in order to be able to 'buy' the self one needs to give up all that is unessential in oneself.

The Kingdom is like[48] a merchant in search of fine pearls. Finding one pearl of great value he sells all that he has and buys this one.

Mt 13.45–46, no par.

- Its intent is potential
- It is outside the human being (or is it rather inside the self?)
- Action is needed to acquire it
- One needs to sacrifice all else
- While searching inside we may find something very precious and unique, worth giving up everything

The Kingdom may be compared to a king who practices forgiveness on debt but punishes the one who does not forgive on his turn,

Mt 18.23–35, no par.

- In the Kingdom of God debts are forgiven, and everyone is expected to do so that the light of the Kingdom breaks through

---

47 Ibid.
48 The wording here—like at more places—suggests that a subject (here: the merchant) represents the Kingdom. Rather it should read "The Kingdom is like the story about the merchant."

THE KINGDOM OF GOD IN THE GOSPELS: 'WHAT' IS IT? 137

The Kingdom is like a householder who pays his laborers an equal wage, independent of the hours worked, which arouses indignation. However, the wage was agreed upon.

Mt 20.1–16, no par.

- its intent is intrinsic, yet potential
- it is inside
- it is coming to life, either by itself or an actor is needed
- in the Kingdom a different dimension obtains

What one finds is that the Kingdom is inside the human being (sometimes indicated metaphorically). Its intent as a powerful force, therefore, is intrinsic: no outside help is required. This inside force when deployed manifests in growth that satisfies its intent. It is integral, nothing else is needed.

Summary and Conclusions

The Kingdom is a silent treasure inside one, with its own peculiar intrinsic growing power, by its very nature manifesting in due time only (seed). It appears as the smallest of all that is inside one but when grown, it turns out to become great 'so that creatures from heaven will live there' (mustard seed). It represents the divine energy hidden as an inconspicuous element in the human soul. It may be brought as it were inside oneself as an inconspicuous small entity different from one's self being incomparably bigger in substance and volume, but it serves to make the human being to fit its purpose: to be an embodiment of the Kingdom of God, the Holy Spirit, provided one allows the spirit to integrate with the dough and become one with it (leaven). Alternatively, in another image, it is hidden in the field of one's self. One needs to find it, and then 'possess' it by learning to know the self, to manage it, to control it, in order to be able to access the treasure inside oneself. In order to be able to 'buy' the self, one needs to give up all that is unessential in oneself (treasure). While searching inside we discover something so precious and unique that is really worth giving up everything (pearl). Even debts are forgiven, and everyone is expected to do so that the light of the Kingdom breaks through (the unforgiving servant): in the Kingdom a different dimension obtains (the householder).

What do the parables, therefore, convey as to the nature of the Kingdom of God?

On the one hand, we find a call to be active in order to find the Kingdom, or to acquire it. One has to renounce but with pleasure because one acquires the thing most wanted. On the other hand, there is a strong call to let it grow and mature by itself. Its energy is strong enough to break through all obstacles. It is growing by itself. From inconspicuous it becomes great. It is the essence of that by which we live; it is small but impregnates and raises our being. Its effect is silent but great. Its potentiality is great and powerful. It is unique, precious beyond comparison. Everything else is unessential. It is the spirit inside of man, it is a process of development; it is a silent power. It is something that works from inside, it is an inner process. In both cases, for searching actively and allowing natural growth an essential condition has to be fulfilled: the preparation of the heart. See the parable of the Sower.

Obviously, the 'what' of the Kingdom does not manifest by seeing and hearing. It remains a *mustêrion*, not accessible in terms of expectant eager impatient observation (Lk 17.22). At the same time, 'seeing' as well as 'hearing' are essential prerequisites. Jesus' explanation of the parable of the Sower lifts a tip of the veil. The message of the Kingdom is brought by the word. If the *logos* then is being held in a pure heart attuned to receive the word of God, the inner Presence can mature and produce fruit manifold, fruits sweet and nourishing, destined not for oneself but for others.

The parables through images convey a strong evocation of a divine Presence that may be sensed internally. The parables make a lively call for transformation either by actively searching or by peacefully creating the conditions necessary for experiencing the Presence.

CHAPTER NINE
The Kingdom of God in the Gospels: *'For Whom': Transformation*

Introduction

In the previous chapters it was found that the Kingdom resides in the human being, and therefore is for everybody. Nevertheless, it is hidden as a *mustêrion* and needs to be discovered and developed. In quite a few logia, one will find a call for transformation even as a requirement for transformation. For example, a great demand on the heart quality, as the last stage of the Sower parable has shown. In this chapter Jesus adds more information on the access to the Kingdom: For whom is the Kingdom of God? Is it for every human being, or for a selection of the human race, excluding some classes of people, or judging and punishing individuals? Apart from the approach through the eschaton, one cannot find Jesus outclassing individuals from the Kingdom of God, naturally as that sacred domain is found situated inside, in the heart.

This chapter first discusses at some length two crucial logia: the case of the little children (Mk 10.13–16 par), and the case of the 'poor in spirit' (Mt 5.3 par). Under the heading of transformation a subsequent section reviews also the other logia, where Jesus speaks about access to the Kingdom, both in terms of 'for whom' and by indicating the need for and the type of transformation. These logia are crucial because they present intriguing characteristics of people typically having access to the Kingdom, logia also that often are seen as essential to understanding the nature of the Kingdom.

As a Little Child, *hôs paidion* (see Box)

People are bringing little children,[1] even newborns (Lk 18.15) (*ta brephê*, WNT: embryo, infant), to Jesus. They do this in order for them to be touched (Mk,

---

1   *Paidion* to be distinguished from *pais*. *Pais* refers to a child, a boy, a youth below the age of puberty, or is used in a genealogical sense. It is also used for slave or servant, a situation of total dependency (BDAG). Cf Lk 2.42–43 when Jesus as a twelve-year-old boy visits the temple. A *paidion* is a newborn child, a baby, or sometimes in a wider sense, young child. (WNT)

Lk), or even that Jesus may place his hands on them and pray for them (Mt). His disciples want to prevent this by rebuking those who bring the children. Jesus gets indignant and answers the disciples: Let them come, for the Kingdom of God is theirs. More precisely, he is saying, not only is it theirs, the young children's, no, the Kingdom of God is of 'such as these.' Who are those who are like young children? 'Such ones' as to whom belongs the Kingdom? Or rather, whose is the Kingdom?

In discussing these three logia the following questions appear:

- 'belonging' to the Kingdom: the relationship between the 'such ones' and the Kingdom
- what is characteristic of a child?
- who are 'the such as children': what is it, becoming like a child?
- what is turning?
- what is receiving the Kingdom?
- what is entering the Kingdom?

Belonging

What is it that is happening here in the first logion (Mk 10.14 par) of these two crucial ones? It discusses the relationship between children (or rather the 'such ones'; see *infra*) and the Kingdom of God. Generally, it is translated as belonging: 'it *belongs* to them' (say NRSV and NIV), whilst the Greek has 'is theirs,' leaving open what is the relationship. 'Belonging' may easily be seen as possessing. Liebenberg[2] indeed classifies these logia under the heading of the kingdom as a possession, as he does with Mt 5.3 and Lk 6.20. I object to the idea that one can possess the Kingdom of God. More adequate is Bultmann's rendering of the *tôn toioutôn* as 'an der Gottesherrschaft teilbekommen,'[3] 'to become part of', more or less as a gift.[4] I have a strong preference for the literal and neutral 'is': 'for of such ones is the Kingdom of God.'

---

2   Liebenberg 462–66 affirms the concept of 'possessing' the Kingdom by the children.
3   Liebenberg 463, n. 93, quoting Bultmann 1957, 32.
4   Grammatically this is not correct: *tôn toioutôn* implies that the Kingdom is 'of such ones', while 'teilbekommen,' 'to become part of' suggests that one enters into it and then 'belongs to it,' the reverse of the text. See also the following discussion on the second logion.

Aphete ta paidia erchesthai pros me, mê kôluete auta *Tôn gar toioutôn estin hê basileia tou theou*	NA27
Let the children come to me, do not stop them, for it is to such as these that the Kingdom of God belongs	NRSV
Let the children come to me, do not hinder them, *for of such ones[5] is the Kingdom of God* Mk 10.14, Mt 19.14, Lk 18.16	Proposed
Amên legô humin *Hos an mê dexêtai tên basileian tou theou hôs paidion* *Ou mê eiselthêi eis autên*	NA27
Truly, I tell you whoever does not receive the Kingdom of God as a little child will never ever enter it[6] Mk 10.15, Lk 18.17	NRSV and proposed
Amên legô humin *Ean mê straphête kai genêsthe hôs ta paidia* *Ou mê eiselthête eis tên basileian tôn ouranôn*	NA27
Truly, I say to you, unless you change and become like children, you will never enter the Kingdom of heaven	NRSV
Truly, I say to you, *unless you be turned around[7] and become like children,* *you will never ever enter the Kingdom of God* Mt 18.3[8] [9]	Proposed

---

5 In German 'derartig', WNT. Generally this *toioutôn* is considered to be a *genetivus possessivus*, for example in Steyer 1992, 33B: 'belonging to', which may or may not refer to a possession. I propose a *genetivus attributivus* (ibidem, 33A), indicating that the terms belong together, forming a whole. I therefore render the phrase as 'of such ones is,' leaving open various interpretations.

6 The Greek text has *ou mê eiselthêi*, like in Mt 18.3 *ou mê eiselthête*. NRSV translates it in Mt as 'will never enter,' whilst in Mk and Lk as 'shall not.' I suppose the 'shall not' intends to lay the same stress as the 'will never.' The ever is added (by me, wvl) as a better rendering of *ou mê*.

7 *Straphête*, in the aorist subjunctive passive mode of *strephô*, to turn (around) (intrans.) (WNT), is to be rendered as to be turned around. See also the section on Turning.

8 The Mt parallel pericope is 18.3, located at a different place in the Mt narrative. It is included here and understood as the parallel pericope.

9 According to Jeremias (1952, 137) this has been transmitted independently. Later v.4 (with humbling') has been placed here.

What then is this relationship? Rather, in my view, it should be seen as an intimate and natural but unexpected relationship between the child and the Kingdom of God. *Unexpected*, because why should it be that it is the children whose the Kingdom is, a question that Jesus answers in Mk 10.15 par. *Natural*, because the nature of both is congruent; see the discussion *infra* about the similarity of the inborn nature of the child with the nature of the mustard seed, and others. *Intimate*, as this 'belonging' is an inner process as well as a reality. Belonging in another sense than possessing may be appropriate: 'to become attached to,' 'to be an attribute to' (*Webster's*[10]). If one wants to, the text would then run: 'for to such ones the Kingdom of God is an attribute,' if that does not sound too pretentious. I, for my part, prefer to keep to 'is.'

Therefore, however we read the text, a close and undeniable relationship between children and the Kingdom is established.

Characteristics

The next question is, what is it that is characteristic of a young child?[11] In current views positive aspects of the young child are rejected, sometimes on socio-historical grounds, sometimes based on anthropological suppositions. Let us see what opinions come to the fore.

> Nolland asks: "Is it openness, willingness to trust, freedom from hypocrisy or pretension, conscious weakness and readiness for dependence," and answers in the negative.[12] Fitzmyer registers the following qualities: "openness, sheer receptivity, freshness, lack of guilt or suspicion, their loving warmth, and their lack of claim to achievement," but rejecting this view immediately.[13] Grundman indicates another way: "to become a child again before God, i.e., to trust Him utterly, to expect everything from Him, and nothing from self."[14] Spitaler rejects what he calls "our western, contemporary perceptions of childhood, namely receptivity, humility, unselfconsciousness, modesty and dependence, a trusting attitude, innocence, simplicity, open-eyedness, curiosity, passivity, non-resistance, submission or helplessness." He finds qualities [or the position?] of children in that culture quite different, i.e., to become "society's 'last' (*sic*) (Mk 9.35)—before they are granted entrance to God's kingdom."[15] Another New Testament scholar, Geert van Oyen, supports most views of Spitaler in an excellent article where he states that the child in

---

10 *Webster's* adds to its meaning 'to be the property' also 'to become attached or bound (as to a person, group, or organization) by birth, allegiance, residence, or dependency' sub 3b, or sub 4: 'to be an attribute , part, adjunct, or function (of a person or a thing)—used with *to*').

11 In this paragraph I focus on the positive aspects of the child, conforming to my understanding of what Jesus wants to elucidate. It goes without saying that any child also possesses and produces negative characteristics of many sorts.

12 Nolland, 1993, 882.

13 Liebenberg 2001, 462, n 92, quoting from Fitzmyer (1985, 193).

14 W. Grundmann, TDNT VIII, 17.

15 Peter Spitaler, Welcoming a child 2009, 423–46.

that society was completely marginalized,[16] *un paria, un méprise*.[17] Jeremias rejects the idea of the child as being a reflection of the light of the Kingdom.[18] This idea to many is too spiritual but does offer an interesting scope on the passage.

Does this suffice? Do these views harmonize with the scene depicted in the Gospels and with the words of Jesus? Is the rejection of the positive aspects reasonable and sufficient?

I propose another view. In the first place, the lower position in society does not prevent one to love a child. Quality in the social hierarchy does not define qualities on mentality, morals, of love, of innocence. I refer to the perspective of how a young child is viewed by mothers and fathers, to the attitude of the public in general, by people seeing a young child, by spiritual people. These are reactions of endearment and tenderness, of love and a smile. That is an attitude adopted generally, it is of all times, even when the child is considered as a non-value in social traffic. The positive aspects mentioned by the critics quoted above belong to this attitude of appreciation of the individual child, particularly the young child, the age group Jesus refers to. I quote: openness, willingness to trust, freedom from hypocrisy or pretension, sheer receptivity, freshness, their loving warmth, receptivity, humility, unselfconsciousness, modesty and dependence, a trusting attitude, innocence, simplicity, open-eyedness, curiosity, passivity, non-resistance, submission or helplessness. It is all promise. It is inborn, good and bad both. The child has everything already in itself as a promise for growth. Isn't that what we found as characteristic of the Kingdom, in the parables of the mustard seed, and of the seed in the field? And the child does not worry about whether it will grow, and how: it is in a silent and full trust as its potentials are intrinsic and instinctive. That too is among our findings in the same parables. They stand for the more or less timeless characteristics typical of the young child, in the perspective of humaneness.

After all—and that is the main point if we want to trace what a child is and what 'such ones' are—Jesus makes his point quite clear. One, he uses the image of 'the child' as a reference to the Kingdom by showing the congruity between what he sees as 'the' child and the Kingdom of God. And two, only when becoming as a child can one receive the Kingdom of God—and enter it at the same time. As a child, what does that mean?

---

16 Geert van Oyen 2003, 177–93.
17 Schlosser 1979, 491.
18 Jerermias (1952, 136ff) rejects this exegesis. In general we do not find in commentaries much in this line.

'The Such Ones'

However, the issue is not what a child is. It is about 'the such ones.' Thus far we spoke about children. The logion, though, says that the Kingdom is of such ones like children. In the context of the logia under discussion it is clear that Jesus is speaking about adults, not about children. The image of the child is to put the reader on the track of the qualities required of 'whose is the Kingdom of God.' What is happening?

Jesus is addressing the disciples, correcting them for trying to keep the children away, but was he not correcting them beyond this? Some see this pericope as Jesus asking his disciples to emulate a child's behavior. However, it is not about behavior, let alone ethics. What is at stake is a mentality, or rather an inner nature that has to be developed, an inner culture. That is what Jesus calls upon. The disciples apparently do not understand the need for establishing the relationship between the children and Jesus as representing the Kingdom. He is teaching not only the relation between the Kingdom and the children, but rather what implications are involved when an individual is keen to enter the Kingdom. These pericopes are not just wisdom statements, deep philosophies of a rather absurd character ('become as children are'), or the like. Jesus is addressing his disciples, not just anybody, but his 'elite', those men whom he has chosen to follow him, i.e., on the Path of the Kingdom. Thus, we find he is teaching the disciples rather to belong to 'the such ones'.[19] What does that imply? One cannot escape the logic: the disciples are told that they should become like children, i.e. attaining the characteristics of children. Is that feasible? Psychology may say no. Common sense may ridicule it. Even so, this is the way of inner development, practiced in religions and cultures all over the world, in monasteries, in lay orders. Sufism is one of them. It implies training, concentration, meditation, contemplation; it implies the softening of the ego; it implies serving humanity; it aims at transforming the self in search of the Presence. This may bring about a transformation of the psyche, an ennobling of mind and heart. It may result in openness, receptivity, trust, freshness, being natural, and it may result in an 'innocence' in full wisdom, an innocence that reflects the Light of heaven, that echoes the divine Song. Here is a clear case of transformation in order to approach the Presence.

However, it need not refer to the disciples only. This is the potential of every soul. This call we find at the very beginning of Jesus' ministry (Mk 1.14–15), and repeated time and again: the moment is here: the Kingdom has arrived, transform, and entrust yourselves to this message: the Kingdom of God is inside you (Lk 17.21).

---

19   *Tôn toioutôn*: arthrously, i.e., with (definite) article. The article indicates it is not a general statement but refers to 'all' those who are as children.

Turning

What is this turning (*strephein*)?

* * *

At another time (Mt 18.1–5) the disciples ask Jesus "who is the greatest in the Kingdom of God?" This issue obviously occupies their minds more often. Typically Jesus reverts the question to the basic issue of entrance into the Kingdom, implying that the position inside it is secondary, if at all of any importance once you are part of that Kingdom. In answer he calls a child to him and puts it in the midst of them, saying *"Truly, I say to you, unless you change and become like children, you will never enter the Kingdom of heaven,"* adding 'to the point' *whoever humbles[20] himself like this child, he is the greatest in the Kingdom of heaven."* NRSV

* * *

He tells us, grown-ups, that we should become as these young children. That is what we found already. Now he is adding a proviso. There is a condition: change!, or rather 'be turned around' (*straphête*) (Mt 18.4) [21] and to become 'humble' (*tapeinos*), to be one's own natural self without any pretense.[22] Note that in my interpretation the active act of 'changing' (as rendered in NRSV) is replaced by the passive mentality of 'being turned around.' In order to become, we have to search for these same qualities that are in-born and constitute our real nature, the qualities of the Kingdom as we discovered them in the chapter on the 'what.'

Turning implies a change, or even transformation, of the direction of one's life, and the more so when it implies an adult to become like a child. In order to become 'one of the such' and to be able to receive the Kingdom something radical is needed. Jesus simply says: be turned around. The change required to

---

20 Rather 'will humble,' it is a futurum. According to Jeremias (1952, 137) v. 3 has been transmitted independently. Later v. 4 (with humbling') has been placed here.

21 WNT: *Strephô* in active form means to turn toward (hinwenden, zukehren). Here it is in the subjunctive aorist of the passive mode: *straphête*. It can be understood in a reflective meaning as to turn around (sich umwenden, sich zuwenden), or to change inwardly (sich innerlich umwandeln). I want to add: take it literally and in the passive mode: to be turned around, to be changed.

22 The characteristic indicated here is translated by NRSV as 'to humble oneself.' However, *tapeinoô* means to humble. A child cannot humble itself. What does it indicate? Rienecker, 1992: "der *tapeinos* gleicht dem Kinde darin, dass er in seinem Denken und Wollen auf das Kleine, Unscheinbare und in engen Grenzen Gefasste gerichtet ist, er wird nicht vom Machtwillen getrieben, sondern vollbringt im kleinen, ihm zugeteiltem Bereich den ihm aufgetragenem Dienst mit völliger Liebe; das trennt der Demut Jesu von aller asketischen Selbstentehrung" (47). I would suggest therefore: 'to be oneself without any pretense.'

become as a child is nothing less than to turn around. Or rather in the exact wording: to be turned around, i.e., in the passive mode. It is the receptivity of the child one has to learn and to adopt. *Unless you be turned around you will never enter the Kingdom of God.*

Receiving and Entering[23]

In Mk 10.15 par another condition is given before one may enter: receiving,[24] i.e., receiving the Kingdom like a child (*hôs paidion*). Zerwick interprets it 'as a child would receive it,' but this takes away the crux. I do not think rendering it as 'would receive it' is what the text wants to express. It is not about how a child would receive the Kingdom. Rather the logion is saying: become as a child, then receive it in the state you have become. How is that: receiving as a precondition to entering? It sounds as a "mind-boggling conundrum that one cannot enter the dominion of God unless one first receives it." (Marcus, 719). Yet Jesus is clear enough: what matters is first receiving the Kingdom, then entering, and therefore a puzzle: first 'receiving' the Kingdom implies that one thus is part of it; and then, after that, one 'enters' it.

Mt 18.3 puts it differently, as we have seen, by adding the 'being turned around.' This way of saying satisfies logics: turning, then becoming, and only then being allowed to enter. But logics sometimes divert one from an inner understanding. Or what if the present reader is invited so and is being turned around, and then tries to see it as Jesus puts it. In that line one may 'see' for the reality of the Kingdom behind the words about it, the Kingdom as a spiritual reality, as truth, as a phenomenon, where logics have to retreat for insight and understanding.

> Yet many scholars are at a loss with these pericopes. First, what does it mean 'to become as a young child', whose quality makes it to belong to the Kingdom of God? One of them tries to understand and puts it like this: "they must become like children whose duty it is to obey and be subject to others"[25] *Sic*, isn't this totally opposed to Jesus' attitude to these children at the scene described? Isn't this in total opposition to what we have found as characteristics of the Kingdom?

---

23 This section anticipates the chapter on *Metanoia* / Transformation.
24 Bohlen (2008) reviews the sayings with *eiserchesthaia eis tên basileian tou theou*: Mk 9.47; Mk 10.15 / Lk 18.17; Mk 10.23–25 / Mt 19.23–24 / Lk 18,24–25; Mt 5.20; 7.21; 18.3; 23.13; Jn 3.5. Generally these are indicated as entrance sayings (*Eingangssprüche*). He prefers to view them rigorously as admission sayings (*Einlassprüche*), narrowing down the concept inherent to 'entering'.Each of these sayings (except Mk 9.47) clearly refer to the spiritual Kingdom where admission rules contradict the essential quality of the Kingdom. If the Kingdom is not a spatial entity some question the concept of entering. In my view the image of spatiality is metaphoric and appealing.
25 Ambrozic 1972, *The Hidden Kingdom*, 246.

Spitaler, in a thorough and original analysis, puts this logion in another perspective. He understands it as "welcoming the kingdom of God as one welcomes a child"[26]. First he relates these pericopes with Mk 9.33-37 par, where receiving a child stands for receiving Jesus[27]. Here he sees how "Jesus embraces a child to demonstrate that he welcomes God's kingdom; his action does not reveal he is welcoming the kingdom in a child-like manner". That is fine. But it does not suffice. In my view, it is easy to welcome a young child; almost everyone likes it: the openness, the innocence, all qualities mentioned. Would that attitude be sufficient to welcome the Kingdom? What the logion tells is how much is required to acquire these qualities as characteristics of one's own in order to be in a position to receive the Kingdom of God.

Another interpretation is that these pericopes refer to the ongoing debate in the early church on baptism (J. Marcus, *Mark 8–16*, pp.714-715, *The Five Gospels*, pp.221, 370). 'Children' then would stand for initiates—which in itself is correct: to be in a position to become a disciple spiritually one must develop these qualities. But the baptism debate has not continued.

As to receiving and entering Van Oyen looks for the solution in terms of the Kingdom being divided in its manifestation: it has arrived but not yet in fullness. The most frequent interpretations he has found do tell that the receiving refers to the present, the entering refers to the future kingdom in its fulfillment. The author wonders if the two terms may be interpreted so differently; "... er zijn weinig uitspraken waarin het actuele doorwerken van het toekomstig perspectief in het heden zo nadrukkelijk aan de orde is,"[28] adding that in Mk the future thought of the Kingdom of God is affecting the present, because Jesus brings it to the people effectively.[29] In this the Kingdom is imagined as more or less feasible. Some, however, see the 'receiving' as a later addition in the early Church, meaning to accept the kerygma of the Kingdom of God.

And here again, the commentator cannot get free from the apocalyptic perspective, when interpreting the gesture of acceptance of the children (by taking them into his embrace, blessing them, and laying hands on them) as it "caps the sense of the apocalyptic advent that has permeated the narrative since the references to the dominion of God in 10.14-15" (p. 719).

Maybe the riddle is not so heavy. 'Receiving' may be seen here as an attitude of mind, a mentality. Receiving requires to be passive, 'actively passive', I would say. This is the nature of what has been found in chapter 8 on the Sower: the fertile soil, the hearing heart, the small seed. This mentality works like a magnet: the negative pole attracting the positive energy. It is the nature of the young

---

26 Peter Spitaler, "Welcoming a child as a metaphor for welcoming God's Kingdom: a close reading of Mark 10.13-16," *JSNT* 31,4 (2009), 423-46.
27 Spitaler translates *dechomai* by 'to welcome' rather than by the more precise 'to receive.' I definitely prefer the latter. Receiving someone stands for a more intense relationship than just welcoming someone. Besides, it is the first regular meaning of the Greek verb.
28 "There are but few logia where the future perspective is making itself felt in the present so pointedly" (author's translation).
29 Quotation from Gnilka 1989, 81.

child to be receptive, responsive.[30] The individual has to be turned around in order to achieve that state of consciousness. When this is happening the new mentality develops and matures, and the person may be open to perceive the Kingdom, not as entity that 'is here', or 'is there', it is not to be seen, neither can one hear it. Rather it is perceiving by 'hearing', 'seeing', an understanding maybe by the heart that has been found to be fitting and pure in order 'to hear' and therefore 'to receive' (see the Sower). This perception may be of such an intensity that one is overwhelmed by a presence. It is the Presence. And one is drawn into it, a glorious way of entering, yet intimate and silent. It is an inner process, a transformation by itself, something that happens. One is drawn into a state of consciousness that mystics describe as Presence, as being raised beyond the physical reality, beyond the mental and emotional states of being.

This I suggest as the condition in which these logia may be understood: this is the condition of the child, and of the *toioutoi* (Mk 10.14 par), this is the 'becoming' in Mt 18.3, and the 'receiving' *hôs paidion*. A condition that brings about an entry to the Kingdom of God. Though, in my understanding and feeling, this cannot be but a glimpse at the doorstep of that glorious Kingdom of the Spirit.

The phrase to be born *anôthen* is maybe a key to the door of understanding: entering the Kingdom requires to be born out of spirit, anew, from above

And it is also the result of a search for the Spirit, motivated by a condition of 'craving for the Spirit', being a *ptôchos tôi pneumati*, with the blissful effect that the Kingdom of God is 'yours.' But this is about our quest in the following pages.

* * *

Poor in Spirit, or Craving for the Spirit?

The Scene

Here Jesus, first in the Matthean version (4.25–5.2), sees the crowds that had been following him from far and wide: Galilee, the Decapolis, Jerusalem, from beyond the Jordan. Does he speak to them? No, surprisingly Jesus goes "up on the mountain, and when he sat down his disciples came to him. And he opened his mouth and taught them, saying…," and then follows the series of Beatitudes,

---

30 Adding to my argument *supra* I would suggest that a new-born child has developed 'a positive passivity' during the stay in the womb, an awareness of unity, a feeling of trust, a sense of peace, apart from the suggestions I made regarding the possible spheres of origin: light, clarity. Moreover, to welcome a child is much easier and requires less of a transformation than becoming like a child! But, of course, if one cannot see the spiritual positive qualities of the child, the logion is hanging in the air.

the first of which is the logion to be discussed (Mt 5.3), see Box. Striking to me, implicit in the report by the evangelist, is that the 'Sermon on the Mount' was not a public address but a private teaching to the disciples.[31] The teaching, therefore, has to be seen as inner teaching, coming close to the *mustêrion*. The same is the case with the 'Sermon on the Plane', the Lukan parallel. The scene preceding this sermon (Lk 6.17–20a) is similar to the Matthaean one, as just described: crowds following Jesus from 'everywhere', even from Tyre and Sidon, located in a Greek-speaking area. Luke adds: and the crowds trying "to touch him, for power came forth from him and healed them all." In Luke's version 'a great crowd of his disciples' is present too. Immediately following this Lk says: "And he lifted up his eyes on his disciples, and said...." So here again Jesus is speaking to the disciples, explicitly turning away from the crowds. And he addresses them as *hoi ptôchoi*, 'the poor' (Lk 6.20b). This is corroborated by the following words: *humetera estin hê basileia tou theou*: yours is the Kingdom of God, again against the background of the *mustêrion*. Does this imply the disciples are poor people, poor in a state of complete destitution?[32]

Then there is the enigma in the Matthean text which has been puzzling to innumerable scholars, apart from countless others, namely that it is the 'poor in spirit' whose is the Kingdom of God. Interpretations abound, trying to find a way of integrating the *tôi pneumati* in the generally accepted concept that this logion speaks about the materially poor: a moral teaching. Or is there another layer of understanding behind? Some include also some of the other logia of the Beatitudes as referring to the poor. Embarrassment has reigned in understanding the relation between the two terms *ptôchos* and *pneuma*. Could the *pneuma* be seen as related to the type of poverty? For the term and concept of *pneuma* see Part IV.

The box presents the texts followed by an alternative rendering, presented as a proposal.

---

31 Branden, *Satanic Conflict and the Plot of Matthew*, 2006).
    While Mt tells about the crowds following Jesus, it is the inward heart of the disciples which Jesus is seeking as those those who truly belong to the Kingdom of God (Branden 2006, 106–107).
32 TDNT VI 886, sub A I 3 "*ptôchos*, a mendicant, denotes the complete destitution which forces the poor to seek the help of others by begging (F. Hauck). For more, see below.

> *Makarioi hoi ptôchoi tôi pneumati*
> *hoti autôn estin hê basileia tôn ouranôn*   NA27
> Blessed are the poor in spirit
> for theirs is the kingdom of heaven   NRSV
> Blessed[33] are those craving for the Spirit
> for theirs is the Kingdom of God   proposed
> Mt 5.3
>
> *Makarioi hoi ptôchoi (tôi pneumati)*[34]
> *hoti humetera*[35] *estin hê basileia tou theou*   NA27
> Blessed are you who are poor   NRSV
> for yours is the kingdom of God
> Blessed are [you] who are craving (for the Spirit)   proposed
> for yours is the Kingdom of God
> Lk 6.20b
>
> Note for both Mt and Lk:
> Blessed: or: blissful
> Craving for[36]:   or in desperate (or: urgent) need of, begging for

---

33 Langenscheidt: *makar*: selig, (über)glücklich, reich, begütert. This last rendering brings an interesting tension with 'poor'!

34 S2, Θ Θ *f*.[13] 33 *al* it bo[pt] (NA26): these important witnesses have *tôi pneumati* added, as in Mt 5.3. This insertion is generally seen as a scribal harmonisation with Mt, but in view of the quality of these witnesses this version might well confirm the Matthean logion. The tradition may have considered the *ptôchoi* as implying the concept of spirituality.

35 W sy'; Mcion: these and somew other witnesses have *autôn* instead of *humetera*; *autôn* is a case of scribal harmonisation. The *humetera* personalises the *makarioi hoi ptôchoi* and identifies the disciples as such.

36 *Webster's*: in urgent need of gratification of …, desire to satisfy a vague inner need; longing, yearning.

And what about the Lukan version? In Luke 6.20 the words *tôi pneumati* are not included in the text of NA27. Yet they do appear in some important witnesses, as indicated in the footnote, *supra*). Reason enough to take these words seriously. We have seen that the Lukan context suggests strongly that the insertion may well be original.

> Margaret Hannan[37] states that "the first evangelist develops the motif of God's *basileia* as good news for the poor and marginalized," that is: worldly directed. She also finds that the Matthaean addition of *tôi pneumati* has led many scholars to see it "as a way of spiritualizing the Beatitudes so that they become a charter of ethical principles whose observance ensures entrance into God's eschatological *basileia*," which she rejects. Her solution reads "Blessed by the Spirit are the poor" (referring to a proposal by Michael Lattke). She finds it grammatically justified: the dative of *tôi pneumati* "is an instrumental dative which refers to the Divine Spirit through whom the action (blessing, or making happy) is effected." It will be hard to find places with a similar use. To my mind this solution is a forced one. Liebenberg, in his thorough and groundbreaking book,[38] rejects the *tôi pneumati* as being "a secondary 'spiritualization' of this aphorism," like the *humetera* in Lk 6.20b,[39] and thus recognizes the Matthean text. Liebenberg concludes that both renderings, in Mt and in Lk, originate from different (oral or written) traditions. The original is not to be traced with any historical plausibility (448–50).

Questions arise. First, what is the meaning of *ptôchos*? Second, what are the implications of this teaching being disciple-directed?

What is a *ptôchos*?

It is someone in need of something, craving for something essential that is missing and that one must acquire by asking for it: a mendicant.

> A *ptôchos*, both in the classical world and in the intertestamental period, is a mendicant: a mendicant[40] is not just a poor person, in comparison to the rich. A poor person is a *penês*[41] i.e. one who is poor but in a position to actually work and earn money[42]. The *ptôchos*, however, cannot earn his living. His poverty is of another magnitude. He has to go on search for what he desperately is in need of, what he is craving for, lest he will

---

37 Hannan, *The Nature and Demands of the Sovereign Rule of God in the Gospel of Matthew*, 2006, 46–52.
38 Liebenberg 2001.
39 "As a rule scholars regard the Lukan *humetera* to be secondary, accepting that the Matthean third person pronoun was more correct, e.g. ,Bultmann.
40 TDNT VI 886 sub A I 1, 2, 3 (Friedrich Hauck).
41 Liebenberg tells that Crossan acknowledges the same difference between *penês* and *ptôchos* but Liebenberg does not attach value to it. These are Greek terms. What would Jesus have said in Aramaic, is Liebenberg's point. He does not see synonyms in Aramaic for both Greek terms. (451, n 58).
42 TDNT VI 37–40.

perish. He is a mendicant, someone begging for his sustenance, looking for something necessitous to him, something that he necessarily cannot but seek, something he cannot live without. NRSV elsewhere (Gal 4.9) renders *ptôcha* (adj.) as mendicantly.

Being poor refers to the condition of the person, *ptôchos* rather suggests his role, his activity. a mendicant is active, being in search of something he is in need of. 'Poor in spirit' may therefore mean 'in need of the[43] Spirit'[44], craving for the divine, (desperately) seeking for the Spirit. The generally used way of rendering *hoi ptôchoi* as 'the poor' may therefore well be interpreted as meaning 'mendicants,' i.e., someone who desperately seeks to find what he needs to stay alive. That means of sustenance is presented here as 'the Spirit,' with a capitalized 's'[45] indicating that it does not refer to a general concept of spirit but to a definite spirit, the Spirit.

An interesting adstruction to the spiritual use of *ptôchos* is found in POxy 654,9–21 / Th 3. The logion explains that the Kingdom of God is both inside you, and outside you (Th 3.4). And it continues: "But if you do not know yourselves, then you will dwell in poverty, and you are poverty," in the partly reconstructed Greek: *[...ei de mê] gnô<es>the heautous, en [têi ptôcheiai este] kai humeis este hê ptô[cheia]*[46], where 'poverty' must be understood as the condition of desperately seeking for the essential. Here a spiritual interpretation cannot be avoided.

> When consulting the Book of Psalms one finds an interesting fact. Regularly *ptôchos* and *penês* occur together, forming one concept. "It is the regular expression in the Psalms for the attitude of him who prays to God."[47] For example,
>
> *Egô de ptôchos eimi kai penês; Kurios phrontiei mou.*
> *Boêthos mou kai huperaspistês mou su ei; o theos mou, mê chronisêis.*
> ψ39.18[48]
> Yet I am poor and needy, may the Lord think of me.
> You are my help and my deliverer, o my God, do not delay.
> Ps 40.17 NIV
>
> What does it teach? There is no reason why the Psalmist should be poor. On the contrary, he is a member of 'the great assembly' and therefore has a status (v.9,10). His

---

43 Note the arthrous use of spirit, which in all major English translations of this pericope is rendered anarthrously. See also chapter 15. Consulted were Darby, DouayRheims, ESV, GNV, KJV, NET, NIV, NRSV.
44 With dative we find it at only one other place, James 2:5: *tous ptôchous tôi kosmôi*, translated as 'poor in the eyes of the world' (NIV) (TDNT: the poor before the world). The context is opposing a person with gold rings and fine clothes to a poor person with dirty clothes.
45 The chapter on The Spirit will explain the why of the capital S.
46 Meyer, *The Gospel of Thomas*, 1992, and Plisch, *Thomasevangelium* 2007, 44.
47 TDNT 889 (E. Bammel).
48 DBG Stuttgart 1979.

call to the Lord is a query for mercy, love and truth (v.11), and a song of praise and supplication. And the closure is a cry for help and deliverance out of a deep-felt spiritual need that is experienced as a poverty compared to the Lord's being.

There are good reasons for the logion to be interpreted as referring to a craving for the spirit:

Blessed are those desperately seeking the Spirit, for theirs[49] is the Kingdom of God.
Or: Blessed are the mendicants for the Spirit....
Or: Blessed are those craving for the Spirit....
Or: Blessed are those in desperate need of the Spirit....[50]

Liebenberg prefers to interpret these logia in a limited context. But the range he takes is wider than the one presented above, and thereby confronting himself with his own adage to see the logia as more or less independent aphorisms, metaphors and parables— while admittedly defining the context as the case requires. One must be aware that once the narrative takes over the essence of the logion devaluates. The logion then becomes contextualized. It is one of the merits of the Gospel of Thomas (and of Q, for that matter): that the logia are presented in its own worth and quality in a total absence of a narrative that would define the meaning in various degrees. Now the logion, when taken *per se*, allows for a freer reception, insight, understanding and concomitant interpretation and translation. And one may hope to be close enough to the Spirit to realize what Jesus is telling, on what level of consciousness. In view of this I prefer not to go beyond the context discussed.

What about the eschatological dimension? It is rather superfluous to state "that there is nothing in this aphorism itself which makes it eschatological.[51] It is clear in itself.

What about this Logion as Disciple-Directed?

Generally the Beatitudes are interpreted as directed to a broad audience. It contains essential teachings of Jesus as elements of the future Kingdom of God, and the will of God to be done "on earth as it is in heaven" (Mt. 6.10). They form the basis of Christian morality and belief in God: take care of the poor, be meek, observe righteousness, be merciful, be pure in heart, make peace, don't be

---

49   Liebenberg groups this logion, together with some others, under the heading of 'the Kingdom as possession'. I prefer to interpret the 'theirs' as the 'poor' belonging to the Kingdom (spiritual) rather than that the Kingdom belongs to the 'poor' as a possession (material, political). His interpretation of these logia sticks to the traditional one that the poor are materially poor. But this is counterbalanced by the '*fact*' that they '*possess*' (emph, wvl) something of another (= higher) order (454–55). For further arguments see the previous section on The such as.
50   Or, to quote an other characterization: *"those who beg for (God's) Breath [pneuma] are blest"* Jack Kilmon, in a posting for e-group Bible Translation Discussion List of Feb 5, '05.
51   Liebenberg 455; emph. his. L. however extends the context to the pericope Lk 6.22 and further, which usually is considered eschatological.

anxious to be persecuted because of righteousness (Mt 5.3–10), and continued in much of both Sermons. Yet, as we have seen, Jesus addresses the disciples while turning his back to the crowds. The crowds had been following him, seeking healing and exorcizing (Mt 4.24–5.2, Lk 6.17–20a), and "who came to hear him" (Lk 7.17).

In the Lukan parallel it is even more explicit that Jesus is addressing his disciples, saying "Blessed are [*you*] who are poor, for *yours* is the Kingdom of God" (emphasis added). Does he address the disciples as poor men, or even as mendicants? Were his disciples poor, or mendicants? Nowhere do we find indications for that. No, they are addressed as being desirous. Desirous of what? Of the Kingdom. Therefore, also for the Lukan version we must conclude that the *ptôchos* is searching for *tôi pneumati*, whether or not the words *tôi pneumati* are included, like some manuscripts say.

> Above I referred additionally to the Beatitudes as the basis of Christian morality and trust in God. What if we take them as teachings to the disciples? In that case they might have a second layer of understanding. Here is a small selection, as a suggestion for further research. The first line indicates summarily the established understanding; thereafter I suggest an alternative understanding.
>
> take care of the poor (Mt 5.3), see *supra*
> - for the 'poor in spirit' we found an alternative understanding, being in urgent need of the Spirit, implying a spiritual search and a recognition of what / who is the Spirit in its relation to the *psuchê*
>
> be meek (Mt 5.5)
> - *praus* in secular Greek means 'mild, gentle, friendly, pleasant as opposed to rough, hard and violent'[52]. Also: not being overly impressed by a sense of one's self-importance (BDAG). It refers to 'the quiet and friendly composure which does not become embittered or angry at what is unpleasant, whether in the form of people or fate'. In the Gospels we find a similar meaning when Jesus speaks of himself as gentle next to humble, resigned, modest, unassuming: "take my yoke upon you, and learn [!] from me; for I am gentle and modest of heart, and you will find rest in your *psuchê*. For my yoke is easy , and my burden is light (Mt 11.29). In that way one may inherit the earth. This is a paramount example of teaching and learning in a psycho-spiritual way. And it does not refer to weakness. This is an active attitude and deliberate acceptance, not just a passive submission.... Greatness of soul is demonstrated by this superior acceptance.... The sage is tranquil in relation to the acquisition of external goods and honours." And *Langenscheidt* 1993: "sanft, zahm, milde, freundlich, gnädig, gelassen, ruhig."
>
> be pure in heart (Mt 5.8)

---

52 TDNT VI, sub A 1 (F. Hauck, S. Schulz).

- the pure in heart (*katharoi têi kardiai*) will see God (*ton theon opsontai*). Remember the passage in The Sower where in the last stage, the successful sowing of the logos is in the hearing heart where it results in bearing fruit. The condition is 'hearing' and 'seeing'. The secret then is that the Kingdom is given to the heart. For this, 'hearing' is a necessary prerequisite. If not, the word is taken away. This 'enlightened' way of perceiving leads to 'understanding', when elements are 'put together'. If the logos then is being held in a heart *kalos kai agathos*, a fitting and pure heart, i.e. a pure heart attuned to as well as fit to receive the word of God, the Kingdom can mature and produce fruit manifold, fruits sweet and nourishing, destined not for oneself but for others." [53]

This argument in itself does not exclude the usually adopted meaning. As said earlier, the Jesus logia per se are to be seen as implying multi-layer understanding. See also Liebenberg 2001.

In the Beatitudes Jesus teaches the path of transformation, both for inner life and for daily life. It is a sorry case that the Beatitudes and so many other high ideals about life, the psyche, morals, etc. have so often been connected exclusively to the Kingdom of God as a future event. Thereby interpreters have neglected the directness of Jesus' teachings relevant as they were to the disciples for direct practice and as teachings for inner development. And they continue to do so for our daily life and development. Each religion has its inner schools, mostly alive, sometimes hidden, sometimes forgotten and derelict. Many of Jesus' teachings are an assignment to search for the Kingdom, discover the beauty of it, thus transforming the self in order to enter it, and to be blessed by its Presence.

Transformation

In the preceding chapters we have found that the Kingdom is present, it is given to one, one can enter it, it enters into one. And, as I understand it, it is crystal clear that according to Jesus the Kingdom is for everybody, not for a predefined sect or class of people. Yet, these texts tell that in order to receive the Kingdom, or to enter into it, or to perceive it, requirements have to be met. This was clear already in the cases of the 'poor in spirit' and of the 'such as' above. Conditions as these are implied in any major decision for change, be it to cross a boundary, to open a door, to initiate a new enterprise—a new attitude is required, an openness to the unknown, a strength to meet the unexpected: a longing, a willingness, an attitude, all geared to the requirements and the qualities, in this case regarding the Kingdom. In other words: transformation, in order to become.

---

53 See explanation in chapter 8.

How does such transformation come about? In some texts we are told it requires responsiveness and receptivity through opening up: the royal way. Other texts tell that positive actions are required, and that one has to work for it in order to be prepared, to be ready, to develop an inner stability. Generally what we have found in the texts analyzed is that the Kingdom seems quite near, almost present already—whilst at the same time it appears as far away. Thus the issue is how to come into contact with that Kingdom, with that specific state of consciousness inside, and become aware of a presence that manifests to oneself as being at home in the 'palace.' It is the testimony of spiritual people and mystics: it occurs, it is happening. The Presence is a present, a sacred present, undeserved yet bestowed upon those who are open, who are receptive to the Spirit, to holy spirit. Isn't it wonderful that this blessing is awaiting one, anytime, anywhere? Crucial in this process is to come in touch with that *dunamis*, that energy that is the Kingdom.

Aspects of this transformation have become familiar in this chapter so far and in the chapter on the 'what.' A wide range of concepts have passed the attention: turning, receptivity versus action, seeking, craving, be prepared, attunement of mind and heart, purification of the heart, 'seeing' and 'hearing,' growing, maturing, discovering the self, working in the vineyard: a number of interrelated qualities, attitudes and actions. Part III will offer further insights in the concept of transformation.

Here follows a summary of the pericopes analyzed, with an indication of the transformation required.

> Jesus announces the Kingdom as having arrived. He does so to wide circles, traveling around, visiting towns and villages, all around Galilee, attracting crowds even from outside Galilee, and sending his disciples on mission to do the same
> Mk 1.14–15 and *passim*
> : *the Kingdom is for everyone*
> : *transformation is needed (*metanoia*)*
>
> The Kingdom is inside the human being
> Lk 17:20–21
> : *the Kingdom is inborn in everyone*
> : *discovering it is the golden life's query*
>
> It is for those who are 'poor in spirit,'
> i.e. for those who are craving for the Spirit,
> who are in need of the Spirit.
> Mt 5.3 / Lk 6.20
> : *the Kingdom is for those who are desperately seeking the Spirit*
>
> It is for those who have suffered for the sake of 'righteousness',
> who have been 'persecuted' for its sake,

who bear its wounds[54]
Mt 5.10
: the Kingdom is for those who have stood for righteousness
: transformation (metanoia) of mind and heart is a condition sine qua non

The Kingdom of God is for those practising and teaching God's commands—who are called great in the Kingdom of God—even those who break the least of these commandments though they will be called least in the Kingdom
Mt 5.19
: these wordings imply that it is for everybody
: see Mk 7.21

Seek first the Kingdom and all that one needs will be given[55]
Mt 6.33, Lk 12.31
and Luke adds:
It is your Father's good pleasure to give you the Kingdom
Lk 12.32
: although the Kingdom of God is here, seeking it is required; then it will bring all that you need, even the Kingdom as such will be given.
Here is the astonishing double logion by Jesus:
all things will be given
 and moreover the Kingdom itself will be ours,
and God does so with pleasure

It is for those who do the will of the Father;
they will enter the Kingdom of God
Mt 7.21
: the Kingdom is the world of who do the will of God
: when having 'sensed' the Kingdom: attunement

The Matthean parables in Mt 13 contain a wealth of suggestions for connecting to the Kingdom of God:

> In order to actually enter into the Kingdom, or to receive it, one needs to grow and mature. Required is good soil (Mustard seed, Mt 13:31, the Sower), care and knowledge (Yeast Mt 13:33). It teaches that although the seed of the Kingdom appears as small, almost insignificant, when treated adequately develops to something unexpected and great. Although it looks static the Kingdom essentially is a dynamic entity.
> : growing, maturing
> : preparing the heart as 'good soil': a hearing heart, a pure heart

---

54 Zerwick 1996, 10.
55 Inayat Khan (1989 VII, 45) quotes Mt 6.33 "Seek first the Kingdom of Heaven…and all things shall be added unto you," and continues" [it] is the silent life; the life inseparable, eternal, self-sufficient and all-powerful."

Another required quality is to be open to Jesus and his message as contained in his logia, and to hear the *logos* of his message and understand it. Then one has prepared the right soil and may receive 'the seed' and produce a rich crop (Sower, Mt 13:24).
: *'hearing' by preparing the heart*

In order to know the secrets of the Kingdom (i.e., what it is and how to 'enter' it) 'hearing' and 'seeing' is required, and making one's heart as fertile soil (Mt 13:11–17).
: *'hearing' and 'seeing'*

Although the Kingdom of God is here, searching it is required and then it will bring all that you need (Mt 6:33, also Pearl and Treasure). These two parables also teach the need of discrimination (great vs small) and of determination (selling all that one possesses: making room in one's heart) (Mt 13:44–45).
: *searching with discrimination and determination*

The Kingdom of God will be given to people who will produce its fruit
Mt 21.43
The Kingdom is given rather than acquired or merited.
: *It will be given to those who will grow and mature to the extent of producing the fruit of the Kingdom*
: *through transformation: Presence*

The invitations for the Wedding Banquet, the Kingdom of God, are sent around successively; clearly everyone is welcome. Most of the guests however refuse to celebrate. Obviously they are not geared to the feast of the Kingdom: their interest lies in worldly affairs. Others like it and come. However, if not prepared for the Kingdom (not wearing wedding clothes) such ones are rejected
Mt 22:1–14, Lk 14.15–24).[56]
: *everyone is invited to the celebration of the Kingdom:*
does one recognize to what one is invited?
: *is one prepared?*

The parable about the Ten virgins tells about guests (virgins, *parthenoi*) who were invited to meet the bridegroom. There is a lot of expectancy, the virgins are required to have lamps that will be lighted: the bridegroom stands for Light. However, when he appears some of the virgins do not have oil anymore, they have spent it prematurely, and consequently they are refused.
Mt 25.1–13
: *everyone invited*
: *be prepared*

The pericope about the rich men (*chrêmata echontes*: 'men of capital'[57] (Mk 10.23–24, Mt 19.23–24, Lk 18.24–25) teaches an attitude in life where "not money itself but

---

56 Mt and to some extent Lk end the parable indicating the eschaton, and in the case of Mt, a Christological interpretation. The text would have been redacted strongly. See *The Five Gospels*, 235. The Lk version is deemed probably authentic.
57 TDNT IX 480 (Bo Reicke)

personal dependence on it and all unworthy use of it are rejected"[58]. This comes close to a different reading in some important witnesses saying how hard it is for those who trust in riches to enter the Kingdom of God (Mk10.24).[59] We offer yet another alternative. The Greek *chrêma* also stands for (German) Ding, Sache, Stück, Ereignis, Unternehmen (Langenscheidt). This might help to interpret the logion as about someone whose mind is occupied with worldly things, money, business, affairs, whose psyche is voluminous like a camel wanting to pass through the eye of a needle. It teaches that a person has to transform: his ego has to become so small as to be able to pass the eye of the needle. In this explanation it is connected with the parable of the Sower: preparing the heart
: *prepare the ego (mind, heart) so that is may pass the eye of the needle*

The essential thing is whether or not one is prepared to work in the vineyard, it is the attitude that counts (Laborers in the vineyard Mt 20:1–16). The vineyard is the garden of God, one's soul.

And, finally, taking up again the 'such as' pericopes:

Truly I say to you, whoever does not receive the Kingdom of God like a child shall not enter it
Mk 10.15, Lk 18.17
: *anybody may enter the Kingdom of God, provided one has received it being like a child*
: *becoming innocent, pure, reflecting the heavenly spheres*
: *finding again one's natural quality of the little child—obviously one's very nature by birth—*

And:
Unless you be turned around (*strephô*) and become like children, you will never enter the Kingdom of God
Mt 18.3

And:
Of such ones (*toioutoi*) is the Kingdom of God
Mt 19.14, Mk 10.14, Lk 18.16
: *'turning', or precisely: 'to be turned around' is an essential step to become like a child, implying a complete change of mind and heart, a purification*
: *having a receptive attitude*
Receive the Kingdom of God like a child
Mk 10.15 par

Therefore, it is about *discovering* one's pneumatic nature, the light in oneself, its peace and glory.

How does this transformation come about? We have referred to two opposing ways: by working on oneself, and/or by opening up, one becomes receptive and responsive. The latter one is the royal way: acquiring the quality of

---

58 Ibid.
59 See also Authorized Version (KJ) 1611, Cath. version of RSV 1965, ERV 1881, ASV 1901.

receiving. One needs to develop an inner stability to be able to receive, to be open, to be ready, to be prepared: "Anyone who will not receive the Kingdom of God like a little child will never enter it" (Mk. Lk). It is the testimony of spiritual people and mystics: it occurs, it is happening, the Presence is a present, a sacred present, undeserved yet bestowed upon those who are open, who are receptive to the Spirit, to holy Spirit. Isn't it wonderful that this blessing is awaiting us, anytime, anywhere?

In the text first referred to above (Mt 18) there is also action by the childlike person himself. This action is to turn and become as the children. See above. Jesus adds as a special qualification to become greatest in the Kingdom of God is to 'humble oneself'. Referring to Part III on Transformation, this may be interpreted platonically as to control the restive horse or to 'humble one's psyche'.

Summing up, what is required is transformation of mind and heart, of one's life conduct, purifying the heart, a receptive attitude, permitting one's nature to grow and mature, being prepared for change and a willingness to transform:

> *The Kingdom is announced to* everyone, *is* inborn *in everyone, yet requires transformation.*
>
> Receiving *the word of God in good soil*
> *requires a purified heart.*
>
> *It is for those who are craving for the* Spirit
> *and for those who have stood for righteousness.*
>
> *The Kingdom is* given *rather than acquired or merited.*
> *It will be given to those who will* grow and mature.
>
> *Everyone is* invited *to the celebration of the Kingdom*
> *Provided one is prepared.*
>
> Seeking *it is required;*
> *then it will bring all that you need,*
> *even the Kingdom as such will be given.*
>
> *The Kingdom is* entered *by those who do the will of God*
> *it is for everybody* practising *God's commands.*
>
> *Anybody may enter the Kingdom of God, but one must receive it* being as a child
> *:it belongs to anybody who has become like a child.*
> 'Turning' *(or being turned) is an essential step to become like a child, implying a complete change of mind and heart, a purification.*

Conclusions

What is needed in order to connect to the Kingdom of God?

The Kingdom of God is for everyone, indeed it belongs to one by birth, yet Jesus suggests quite a few conditions, or rather incentives that help to produce the right conditions, for perceiving, discovering and receiving the Kingdom, e.g. by causing a transformation of mind and heart, to induce a different level of consciousness.

The Kingdom of God is for those seeking the Kingdom, by turning inside,[60] by becoming like an innocent and pure child, and everything will be given, even the Kingdom itself will be ours.

One needs to understand that the Kingdom may come only after growing and maturing. The first condition being to prepare the heart like good soil, so that the seed is welcome and can deploy its qualities, and provide a harvest (10, 60, 100 times). Then it will turn out that what seemed small becomes great. And: does one understand that the Kingdom may appear as something foreign (the leaven in the dough), but is a necessary requirement, like the spirit in one, in order that one's being becomes as it should be (the bread)? The Kingdom can be ours only when one desperately seeks for the Spirit, like a mendicant who is in utter need of material things. Are we able to 'hear' and 'see' in a way essentially different from what we are accustomed to, in order to 'understand'? Are we prepared to renounce everything we possess when we find the treasure, realizing this is the thing we have been looking for, something essential to our being? And can one discriminate the essential from what one thinks one is in need of? What does one understand by 'to be born again'? Or maybe to be born from above 'on high'? Does one understand the real nature of the young child, and is one prepared to acquire these qualities? Unless one does, one cannot enter the Kingdom.

---

60 In a mystical paraphrase: "… in seeking the Kingdom of God we seek the center of all, both within and without" Khan 1989 VIII, 116.

Concluding Part Two
The Kingdom of God: A Spiritual Interpretation

Let us recall the statements by *Harnack* that may be traced back to logia by Jesus. From the analysis of the relevant texts we may conclude that they have been confirmed:

> *The Kingdom of God is a silent, strong, divine power in the heart. It comes to individuals, it enters into their souls. It grows surely and silently like a seed and it brings forth fruit. It is the most important and indeed the deciding experience a human being can have, penetrating and controlling the complete sphere of his being. It is a force that sinks into one's inner being, and cannot be understood but from within.*

This understanding by Harnack of the inner dimension of the Kingdom of God has been substantiated in this Part II by the analysis of the pericopes on the subject in the Synoptics. The other dimension, the eschatological / apocalyptic, has remained outside the scope of this book. I agree with Harnack that both dimensions are understood to co-exist in Jesus' teachings. Bultmann's eschatological thesis of the Kingdom, as well as the contemporary vision of Dunn, has been found clearly one-sided.

The inner dimension has been confirmed. Essential for it is a spiritual understanding of the texts in terms of transformation, of consciousness, of allowing the divine to manifest in the world and in human beings.

The mystical meaning of the Kingdom referring to the presence of God has been found in the texts analyzed.

As a result it is clear that many logia substantiate that the Kingdom has arrived and therefore is virtually present. Virtually, because of conditions to be fulfilled for the Kingdom to become part of human consciousness. It has arrived but this does not automatically imply entry into it. Transformation is necessary. The call to enter the Kingdom is a *general* message to each and everyone. Therefore it is a call to the *individual*: the Kingdom is here, it is even inside you, yet you need to enter it, i.e. to clear your mind (*metanoia*) and transform. The logion that the Kingdom of God is inside has been substantiated and found confirmed in the wider context of the Kingdom. In the chapter on what the Kingdom is the silent, strong, implicit nature of the Kingdom of God has been found: an enormously strong growth potential. In the chapter 'for whom' the

THE KINGDOM OF GOD: A SPIRITUAL INTERPRETATION

natural implicit growth and development potential was found again. At the same time it becomes clear that the implicit nature of the Kingdom is a potential but needs development and growth, for which numerous conditions have been found. These were further accentuated in the section on transformation.

Now that we have finished the examination of the Jesus logia and some other pericopes from the Gospels it is time to return to the hypothesis worded at the outset of this chapter.

> Do the Jesus logia display an inner dimension, apart from the also present eschatological dimension?

This question must be answered in the affirmative: the texts analyzed in many instances allow an inner interpretation, often divergent from the usual interpretations, sometimes in the usual translation, sometimes in a different rendering. In some cases this inner interpretation stands next to the current one (or ones), in other cases it might be the better one.
This leads to a further hypothesis:

> Does the recognition of the alternative meaning of quite a few pericopes require a review of the eschaton as the (or a) leading interpretation of Jesus' message?

This hypothesis has not been tested systematically. Yet I pretend to have brought to the fore enough instances where it may be questioned whether or not, or to what extent, Jesus was an eschatologist. In the NT critique of the past few decades I have found many instances where pericopes with the eschaton have been questioned on the issue of whether or not probably

- they represented authentic words by Jesus
- or that they have originated in an oral or written proto-version
- or that the wordings may refer to a redaction by the evangelist
  - either because of his particular use of the sources
  - or because of the impact of the early proto-orthodox church
  - or reflecting the beliefs, convictions and traditions of a particular Christian community

Answers could lead to the further hypothesis that the inner meaning of these texts may refer to a more original interpretation. Anyhow, the inner dimension has been confirmed throughout the discussion of the Kingdom of God.

Grosso modo the contents of this Part may be summarized as effective illustrations of the two characteristics of mysticism: Presence and Transformation:

- Presence of the Kingdom of God inside the human being.
- Transformation of the self, both as a natural implicit nature of humans, and as a condition to become fully human, i.e., to develop one's spiritual potential.

At the end of the discussions in this chapter on aspects of the Kingdom of God, what has been reached? My pretense is not that I have found *the* new and valid re-interpretation of the logia discussed in this chapter. What I do hope is the following. Resuming the spiritual interpretation of the Kingdom of God as an inner reality, and trying to see its consequences, the plausibility of some alternative presentations open new avenues of understanding the Message of Jesus, that are worth further exploration, be it in understanding, in interpretation, in translation.

Summarizing

Part II has tried to find out what the Jesus logia tell about the Kingdom of God and its mysticism, as exemplified by the elements of Presence and Transformation. Simple questions have guided the reader through the intricate field, first asking about its when and where. This has led to the central questions what the Kingdom really is, and for whom it is destined. Finally the issue was looked at in what way one may establish a link with it. What can be concluded?

A word in advance: what *is* a kingdom? Some associate it with domination, with autocracy, with dependency. Here the kingdom is understood completely otherwise, by interpreting it in a long tradition as idea, as an ideal. It offers safety, it is as a haven, one feels secure and at home. The kingdom is exalted, glorious and full of grandeur and beauty. And it reflects on the subjects, like nowadays idols do, whether in sports, in pop music, or as a tv star. That is what *mutatis mutandis* the concept of the Kingdom of God conveys.

What is it? Taking together all that is said about it what does one find? Very little and yet a whole cosmos. The only single 'definition' Jesus offers is: the Kingdom of God is a *mustêrion*, and it is something that can not be spoken. End of the story? The key is given: 'who has ears, hear!, who has eyes, see!' Why? It is of another dimension. 'The Kingdom of God is inside you.' And Th adds, 'and it is spread out upon the earth.' It withdraws from precise observation, 'one cannot say, it is here, or it is there.'

The parable of the Sower lifts something of the veil of the mystery. It tells about the seed as it falls on different soils. It falls on the path and is taken away; it falls on shallow soil, and the plant withers away; or it falls among thorns and is choked. Or it may be received by good soil, and it brings a rich harvest. What does it mean? Even the disciples are confused, although it is they who should understand, for to them—to those who can 'hear' and 'see,' who are receptive—it is given to know the *mustêrion*. The seed is the word of God, the *logos*, the soil is the heart. What is happening? Often the word is not even heard, and thus gets lost. Or the word is received with joy but there is no depth. Some hear the word but it is choked in the worries of life, in the delight for riches, in the desire for other things: it cannot take effect. But when the heart is fitting and pure the word is held fast, and it brings forth fruit in abundance.

It is like the leaven that raises the dough. It is like the mustard seed, the smallest of smallest with its inborn enormous potency. It is like the treasure hidden in the field of one's being, like the one unique pearl in the heart. It is to save the oil in order to be illuminated. It is like wearing the festive garment in order to celebrate at the wedding banquet.

Time and again what Jesus tells about the Kingdom it refers to something that is inside one, it is intrinsic to its nature, and its growth is instinctive.

What is the lesson? It is about Presence and it is about Transformation, the two signs of mysticism. All this is about a presence, a divine presence, that is inborn. But it is hidden. Do not put it under a bushel, but let it shine out. And it is about the transformation of the self. On the one hand it is required as a precondition in order to become aware of this presence. And on the other hand it happens by itself, as a grace effected by the presence.

Jesus teaches about the divine presence in the heart, and about the need to transform. One call for transformation is when Jesus asks one 'to become such as a child': sheer receptivity, openness, willingness to trust, freshness, loving warmth, humility, unselfconsciousness, non-resistance, to name a few, 'for theirs is the Kingdom'. Another such call is 'to crave for the Spirit' ('poor in spirit,' as is mostly said), to be like mendicants going out to obtain what is essential for one's subsistence, 'for theirs is the Kingdom.' To become the leaven in the heart, to be conscious of the mustard-like seed potential, to exhume the treasure in the personality, to detect the unique pearl in the heart.

Is this the Kingdom of the Gospels? In the Christian tradition mostly it is seen as other-wordly, referring to the eschaton. Some interpret it this-worldly: an ideal social state to be established, hopefully in some here and now. Rarely it is seen as inner-wordly, referring to being in a different state of consciousness, mysticism maybe. Both the Church and academia have left this solution aside. Christian mysticism on the other hand has fostered it dearly, less in terms of the Kingdom than as presence of the divine and transformation of the self, as we found in chapter 2.

How come that the proclamation of Jesus was understood so differently? In the Gospel narratives it is interpreted as good news rather than as a lasting and universal message. And it is understood as an undetermined future event. Whilst Jesus proclaimed that the Kingdom had approached. We have seen that this implies that it therefore was present. However, generally the Kingdom was understood to be concrete and therefore perceptible physically. Consequently it was obvious understood either as a future promise or as present in the person of Jesus.

Historically, in the first century, the Kingdom of God was a hot topic, widely and fiercely discussed. Will the Kingdom of David be re-established, with its glory and righteousness? No, others were saying, that Kingdom is not of this world. It will come in a flash, at the end of times, at the eschaton, when the powers of the world will be destroyed and God's reign established. Others may have expected a social revolution where peace and righteousness would reign, the colonial power of Rome erased.

And then Jesus steps forward, proclaiming that the Kingdom of God has approached. And Jesus adds to his proclamation: confide yourself to my message, a message seemingly out of order as it does not fit into any of the expectations. Or it should be that it will appear like in an apocalypse. Some may have thought so. A few only did 'hear' or 'see'. Anyhow, neither of these kingdoms did appear, neither during his lifetime, nor afterwards. What to do with this message of the coming Kingdom? History made it even worse: the temple destroyed, Jewish identity harmed. Proto-orthodox groupings started to re-interpret the expected coming, even within the lifetime of some of the disciples as Jesus predicted, as an eschatological one: Christ would return, the *parousia*, as the mighty King, God's reign destroying enemies and the evil. The inner interpretation of the message retreated further and further in the background, supported in some inner circles, witnesses of which are found in th early layers of Q and of Th. But it cannot be denied when studying the logia. That is what happened in this Part II.

PART THREE
Transformation: The Psyche

Introduction

This Part takes up the issue of transformation and focuses on the concept of the self, the psyche. Transformation was found to be one of the key concepts of mysticism (chapter 2). In Part II transformation emerged as an essential element of the Kingdom of God: the call to transform (*metanoeite*), the call to become 'such as the child', to seek for the Kingdom like a mendicant, to be aware of a presence. This Part will take the issue of transformation as its focus. Largely it consists of some semantic analyses of the terms *psuchê* and *metanoia* from a psycho-spiritual view. What is this transformation? What is changing? Obviously the self is involved. What is that self? In the Greek text of the Synoptics that term is an important one, the *psuchê*. Is that the psyche? As an element of the human being that is non-physical and non-spiritual[1], often called soul, or self, or a compound of mind and heart? No, mostly *psuchê* is not understood as such, but rendered as life. Chapter 10 will dive into this issue: how is the term understood. Mostly the NT is considered not to differentiate between elements in the human being, like the psyche. Neither does one acknowledge spirit (*pneuma*) and body (*sôma*, or its sort of equivalent: *sarx*, flesh) as recognizable elements: there is no trichotomy. Moreover, *psuchê* is mostly understood as deriving from the Hebrew *nephesh*, which in many cases stands for life. All three elements figure in the Gospels but the question of a trichotomy of body, psyche and spirit remains open, if discussed at all. But what matters is whether this 'psyche', conceived as self, soul, or mind-and-heart, is to be found in the Gospels? Is that maybe the term *psuchê*? Then we will jump to chapters 12 and 13 where the use of *psuchê* will be explored in some important logia: saving or losing the *psuchê*, laying down one's *psuchê*.

If transformation is an issue, does one find the *psuchê* as something static, or is it referred to as an element of change? In order to get a grasp of the concept of transformation, the second chapter of Part III, chapter 11, will be devoted to that concept. Here again, this concept will not easily be traced in English translations of the Gospels. Yet there is a Greek term for it, *metanoia*. It is not frequent but it carries much weight, as we will see. *Metanoia / metanoeô* has been touched already earlier in this study, in the Kingdom of God chapters. There we

---

The first draft of some parts have been read at the SBL Annual Meeting, Nashville 2000.
1   The human being as it appears forms one whole, one functioning organism, in which the body, the mind, the heart and the spirit form the 'elements' of this complete being. Mind and heart together function as the psyche.

found that it usually is rendered as repentance and the like. Here, alternatively it is understood as transformation, as transformation of the self. The analysis of the Kingdom of God has opened the vision that divine spirit has to do with the dynamics of the self. It was found that transformation is needed. What does that imply? We have seen that the very first sentence of Jesus on the Kingdom requires his audience to change: *metanoeite*! Why? That same sentence explains that it is because the Kingdom had arrived: a reason in the time dimension. John the Baptist, however, in his announcement of the Kingdom had given another reason by adding: for the forgiveness of sins. This implies that the Kingdom is presented as a condition rather than as a consequence. Jesus, in his announcement, on the contrary tells that this call to transform is presented as a consequence of the arrival, not as a condition to. Ever since, the two terms, *metanoia* and sinning have been associated as twins: the one supposes the other. *Metanoia* then became associated with the concept of penitence and conversion, suggesting that otherwise the Kingdom remain closed. But to Jesus sin was not an issue, the centrality of that issue being another misunderstanding in my view. What then is this *metanoia*? It has to do with transformation. Transformation of what? It refers to a change of mentality. This issue will be discussed in the next chapter, chapter 11. It is placed here rather than after the chapters on the *psuchê* because of its tie with the Part on the Kingdom of God. All pericopes with the double term *metanoia / metanoein* will be analyzed in context, literature studied, resulting in a concept of transformation that is goal-oriented, from a positive view of the human psyche. But what is the psyche?

The concept of psyche will be the object of the further chapters in Part III. It is essential for our understanding of transformation, and it is important as it allows for a new perspective on the anthropology of Jesus. The term will be central in the rest of this Part. It will be explored if it could be understood as self, or psyche, or mind-and-heart, rather than in the traditional sense, where it is understood as life. Consequently the major pericopes with this term are explored. Is it correct and authentic that Jesus would require his followers to lose life in order to save it (Mk 8.35 par)? Or does it refer to a psycho-spiritual process of transformation? And what about laying down one's life out of love for one another, as Jesus is understood to require of his closest disciples (Jn 13 and 15). And what about the good shepherd laying down his life for the sheep (Jn 10)? In both cases it hinges on the phrase *psuchên tithêmi*, usually understood as laying down one's life. What about analyzing this phrase more closely and exploring a more literal rendering as dedicating one's self?

In conducting this exploration the field studied widens from terms to concepts, from isolated pericopes to a semantic study, from concepts to a wondering about the message of Jesus. Here the question arises of what the anthropology of Jesus is like. Is it feasible, in line with the findings on the

INTRODUCTION

Kingdom of God, to understand it as a positive approach to the human being where the psyche is seen as an element that can be addressed in order to serve the spirit?

And, do the concepts of presence and transformation, central in this work, play a role in this anthropology? What does this Part contribute to finding mysticism in the Gospels?

CHAPTER TEN

Transformation of the Self:
What Is the Self, the *Psuchê*?

Introduction
Does *psuchê* Signify 'Life'

The Introduction just presented implies a challenge: is it correct linguistically as well as plausible to render *psuchê* by self, soul, psyche, mind-and-heart, or the like? This challenge is taken up here.

Does Jesus speak about the psyche? In Gospel translations one will not find the term. Yet the Gospels contain important words by Jesus on the self and its transformation. Here are three samples where *psuchê* is the central term.

> For whoever wants to save his *psuchê* will lose it, but whoever loses his *psuchê* (.....[1]) will save it.
> Mk 8:35 par, also Mt 10:39[2]
> Greater love has no one than this: that he ' lay down'[3] his *psuchê* for his friends.
> J 15:13
> The good shepherd 'lays down' his *psuchê* for the sheep
> Jn 10.1

But is it about the *psuchê*? Most principal Bible translations render it as 'life'.

> For whoever wants to save his life will lose it, but whoever loses his life (.....) will save it.
> Greater love has no one than this: that he lay down his life for his friends.
> The good shepherd lays down his life for the sheep.

Sounds quite different. When diving into the documentation one finds that this Greek term is thought of as rendering the Hebrew / Aramaic *nephesh*. That is

---

This paper is a revised and extended version of parts of my paper for the SBL International Meeting, Cambridge, UK, 2003.
1 The passage between brackets says *for me and for the gospel*. It will be discussed later.
2 The translations referred to in this chapter generally are from the New International Version 1984 (NIV). Others mentioned are New American Standard Version 1978 (NSAV), Jesus Seminar (Miller: The Complete Gospels, Harper 1994 (JS), and Lamsa's translations from the Peshitta (Harper 1933/1968) (Peshitta).
3 Greek : *tithêmi*, 'to put'. This will be discussed later.

how the Septuagint (LXX) renders it in many instances. Yet, *nephesh* is a word with a great variety of meanings. It has a rich history though over the whole period of OT writing is seems to be rather constant. Is this a sound basis for translating *psuchê* in the Gospels in the same way?

In major translations the rendering by 'life' preponderates, except where the word occurs together with body, or spirit, or heart, etc. when it is given as soul It seems there is a preference for 'life' unless the context requires a different view.[4]

This book proposes another translation[5], viz. by psyche or self or soul; sometimes mind-and-heart.[6] The same pericopes then sound as follows:

> For whoever wants to save his self will lose it, but whoever loses his self (for me and for the gospel) will save it.
> Greater love has no one than this: that he dedicates his self for his friends.
> The good shepherd dedicates his self to the sheep.

What is the reasoning leading to my dissident rendering? It is a matter of translation, but even more of interpretation. It is both linguistics and understanding, it is the contents that speaks, it is the concept behind the term. Therefore, the issue is what does *psuchê* signify: life or soul etc.?

Analysis

What do the Dictionaries Contribute?

TDNT displays a great variety of what *psuchê* stands for.[7] Yet it concludes *im grossen und ganzen* for the unitary meaning: it is the whole life of the individual

---

4 A short review. I have checked NIV, NASV, JS and the Peshitta. The Greek word *psuchê* occurs in 34 places in 18 of which all four translations give 'life' plus 5 places where one to three give 'life.' Conversely, in 5 places all translate with 'soul' plus 11 where one to three do so. Interestingly, in these latter places *psuchê* invariably is mentioned together with other parts of the human being: 'body' (Mt 10:28); spirit (Lk 1:46); or in the combination of 'heart,' 'soul,' 'mind,' (strength) Mt 22:37 par). So it seems. E.g. because in the same pericope 'life' appears already with a different term.
5 These proposed renderings intend to convey an interpretation, not a final translation.
6 When reviewing my initial research for *psuchê* I found my earlier suggestions for another rendering confirmed, in almost the same line of thought and interpretation (Adams 2005, 283–85), an exceptional experience as the reader will learn from the analysis of the meaning of the term.
7 E. Schweizer in TDNT (IX 608–3|) offers a wide view on the concept in 56 pages. Eleven pages (637–47) cover the Gospel (and Acts) texts. He classifies the different meanings of the term in these books as follows:
   1. as natural physical life, incl. the giving of life, and seeking, killing and saving life
   2. as a term for the whole human being, also denoting the individual ego
       Comment: *In the items 1 and 2 we are on the same line as Dautzenberg (see* infra): *life*

in its different aspects. *Psuchê* in TDNT therefore would not primarily refer to the *psuchê*.

Yet it also explicitly recognizes *psuchê* "as the place of feeling" and "as true life in distinction from purely physical life."[8] The concept seems to expand into a dichotomy, and allows for a wider interpretation.

WNT/BDAG interprets *psuchê* largely in the same way as TDNT does. It too suggests a strong relationship with *nephesh*. It therefore allows the *psuchê* to be understood, not only as seat and bearer of earthly life itself, but rather as seat and bearer of desires, of emotions; as bearer of 'überirdisches' life. By the way it may also function as a personal pronoun. Besides, it says, metanomically it may mean the living being itself.

The dictionaries, therefore, in principle support the traditional renderings—*psuchê* understood as *nephesh* stands for life—, yet do not exclude an understanding as proposed : *psuchê* as 'soul', etc.

Literature[9]

Among the great number of authors who have published about one or more of the pericopes by Jesus with *psuchê* the main author is Dautzenberg, whose principal book covers all cases with *psuchê* in the logia. Apart from some later publications of his he has written *the* standard work on *psuchê* in the Jesus logia

---

> including physical life. Classifies also texts like the one about the good shepherd who lays down his life (Jn 10). Also referring to seeking and saving life: Mk 8.35 par; it is the whole being.
> 3. as the place of feeling: the person as influenced by others; as he experiences joy, sorrow and love; in the sense of heart
>   Comment: an aspect well distinct from physical life as such: a conceptual difference between body and the seat of emotions (and even of faith, he adds)
> 4. as true life in distinction from purely physical life
>   Comment: under 3 and 4 the concept seems to expand into a dichotomy, though he does not acknowledge so.
> 5. life as the supreme good.
> 6. in contrast to the body.
> 7. the *psuchê* after death.
>   Comment: under 6 and 7 the dichotomy becomes unavoidable.
>
> Yet this classification is supposed to reflect the concept of *psuchê* as defined by Dautzenberg (1966) which is the *communis opinio*. Schweizer sticks to the interpretation that the *psuchê* intrinsically belongs to the corporeality of the human being. Yet I note some openings in his argument enabling my view as an alternative. *Psuchê* and body belong together, form one whole, he says. This seems a contradiction when he wonders about "the life with God which takes shape in, e.g., prayer, praise and obedience, and which fashions a union with God that does not come to an end with physical life" (p. 640) suggesting that the *psuchê* is an element that functions *per se*.

8   See under 3 and 4 of the previous footnote.
9   See also Annex 2.

in the Gospels.[10] Though published as far back as 1966 it remains authoritative: it continues to stand out as a work of the first rank, a thorough pioneer treatment of the term *psuchê*. And it is an equally thorough analysis of all logia with this term. He interprets *psuchê* in the Gospel texts in line with the OT *nephesh* concept. His analysis is thorough and convincing within the framework adopted. However, he does not discuss the possibility that the Jesus *logia* may be seen in a different frame of reference, distinct though not completely separate from either the Hebrew *nephesh* concept or the Greek postclassical *psuchê* concept.

When looking at the Gospel passages quoted above it does not really convince that this is the only valid hypothesis. Even as to the OT use what strikes is the plurality of the meanings of *nephesh* there. Would an interpretation of *psuchê* as an identifiable part of the human being yet inseparable from its other parts as I do here, be viable? Dautzenberg's work on each of the Gospel texts with *psuchê* is impressive but certainly not convincing as the single valid interpretation of these sacred words.

He argues, at first sight quite convincingly, that *psuchê* in the logia stands for life, representing the Hebrew *nephesh*. Here is an abstract of his findings.

> In the first place Dautzenberg has dived into the concept of *nephesh* and into the argument why *psuchê* must be understood as its Greek equivalent in the Gospels. *Nephesh* stands for the unity of the human being: body and soul are not two distinct elements. These are inseparable units where even the terminology may be interchangeable: body may stand for soul, and reversely.[11] Within this concept of the whole man the central idea is that *nephesh* stands for life, the life of the individual, in its totality, taken quite physically. It therefore also signifies the life power, its energy, also its emotions and will.[12] Finding that the LXX fairly consistently translates *nephesh* by *psuchê*, Dautzenberg takes a daring step forward concluding that it is justified to render *psuchê* in the Gospels by life. For it must be understood, he says, that the evangelists were part and parcel of late Judaism, of its culture, of its language. The language of the Gospels cannot be interpreted otherwise.

There is, however, a moment in his argument that draws attention. When 'scanning' the term *psuchê* throughout the LXX it turns out that it also stands for a wide range of meanings instead of just this single 'life.' This implies widening (but also to some extent denying) the equation *psuchê* = *nephesh*. *Psuchê* obviously is richer and in a sense more precise, adopting aspects of e.g. thinking, will, heart, consciousness.

---

10   Dautzenberg, G., *Sein Leben bewahren:* psuchê *in den Herrenworten der Evangelien*, München 1966. Moreover, in his 1984 article he has widened his analysis to the OT.
11   Ibid., 16f, 27–30.
12   Ibid., 18–25.

> Though *nephesh* in the LXX normally is rendered by *psuchê* this latter term adopts also other meanings than life, like heart; it is associated with "vorausschauendes Planen, Denken, Bewusstsein, Erinnerung, geformter Wille, personaler Mut, Charakter" (Dautzenberg 1966, 42). For each of these terms he refers to the relative places throughout the OT: Chronicals 1 and 2, Proverbs, Isaiah; also Deuteronomy, Iob.
>
> After having reached this conclusion Dautzenberg turns around. He finds that *nephesh* or *psuchê* in other scriptures of Palestine Judaism again signify life as a whole (Sirach, Judith, Tobias, 1 Maccabees, Qumran). This he says is the basis of the use of the term *psuchê* by the evangelists: although the image of man and God is shifting, it is hardly possible that this would reflect in the Gospel language (43-48). He binds the use in the Gospels with the 'jüdischen Sprachhintergrund' choosing 'life' as the appropriate rendering (51). All in all, the equation *nephesh* = *psuchê* is not consistent.

Nephesh apart, *psuchê* in the LXX in 25 instances is a translation of the Hebrew word for heart: another proof that *psuchê* is not the same as *nephesh* ! Lys 1966 (214–16) offers the following cases: "the heart is troubled"; "the heart' as the center whence decisions come"; "the oath is made with 'all their heart'"; 'despising somebody in one's heart'; the heart as the center of affectivity, feelings, or love; as "the source for desires"; "the decisive center which is planning a bad behavior and the whole potentiality which may be in communion or in opposition"; "the heart is timid"; "the heart melts"; "the merry-of-heart sigh." *Psuchê* obviously was also understood as meaning 'heart'. Though, of course, the *psuchê* is part and parcel of the *nephesh* it is considered as acting as an entity.[13]

The equation *psuchê* = *nephesh* has been defended strongly, almost strained. If my argument be valid the equation appears undermined, thus making room for other interpretations.

Greek Words for 'Life': *bios* and *zôê*

The next question is the reverse: how does the Greek render the concept 'life.' The terms that may be relevant are *bios* and *zôê*. Let us check whether the meaning of these two terms is different from that of *psuchê*.[14]

Bios is used quite differently from *psuchê*. Generally it indicates life, and the means of subsistence, or resources needed to maintain life. It also stands for life conduct, character.[15]

---

[13] Lys 1958 provides a few more interesting instances in the LXX where the *psuchê* obviously is considered to be separate from the body. Gen. 35:18 describes how her soul went away when Rachel died (*aphienai tên psuchên*) (NIV freely translates: she breathed her last: *sic*) (224). And there is another instance (Iob 7:5 in a variant reading) (208): *"Thou wilt separate my soul from my spirit, and my soul from my body"*. This even may refer to a trichotomy of body, soul and spirit.

[14] TDNT II 832-872, esp. 861–72 (concerning NT) (both *bios* and *zôê*, etc.) and CNTG 283 (*bios*), 771-779 (*zôê*, etc.).

Greek has an other and less ambiguous term for 'life': *zôê* (verb *zaô, zô*). In the NT, Bultmann writes in TDNT, it "is first used of the natural life of man. Its opposite and end are to be found in natural death,"[16] but it can also be interpreted as the supernatural life, belonging to God and Christ (WNT), which can be imparted to man.[17] So in its primary meaning it refers mainly to physical life, or as a metaphor for it (unless qualified differently). But it may qualify as spiritual life, or everlasting life, mostly by adding an appropriate adjective.[18] Zôê thus is the normal term for life.

It is not plausible, therefore, that *psuchê* should be seen as a term for physical life, as a synonym of *zôê*.

> Moreover, there are some more indications in the Gospel texts which must make one the more cautious to translate *psuchê* with 'life'. There are a few pericopes where we find

---

15 BDAG *bios*. The term *bios* occurs 6 times in the Gospels, mostly in Luke (Mk 12:44, Lk 8:14, 8:43, 15:12, 15:30, 21:4) It is hardly used as 'life'. Except in one case it just means the means of living, property. In itself *bios* also means the individual life, life conduct, character (TDNT II 835–56). In classical Greek it also was used for biography.

16 Bultmann gives a footnote and refers to the OT use of *psuchê*, adding that this is as a synonym of zôê in the NT, mentioning specific places (TDNT II 861, n 241, 242). Sic.

17 WNT, *zôê* sub 2.

18 As a verb (*zaô, zô*) it occurs 35 times and as a substantive (*zôê*) 52 times in the Gospels. John has it more frequently: 17 and 36 times, respectively.18 How is it used? Some typical cases in the synoptic Gospels: 'Man does not live on bread alone'; life as opposed to death; 'the living God'; 'living water'; 'to live with someone'; 'living wildly'; 'small is the gate...that leads to life'; 'to enter life'; 'eternal life'. So in its primary meaning it refers mainly to physical life, or as a metaphor for it (unless qualified differently). But it may qualify as spiritual life, or everlasting life, mostly by adding an appropriate adjective.

In John the term *zôê* (etc.) is quite frequent. It is used predominantly in a spiritual, mystical sense. However, whenever this is the case, again this is specified by adding spiritual qualifications like 'eternal', 'everlasting', or by the context (life of God, of the Spirit, etc.). In fact, the concept of physical life is transferred metaphorically to spiritual life. This indicates that the term *per se* does not necessarily imply a spiritual or religious concept. We conclude that the usual meaning of *zôê* is physical and stands opposed to death (cf the dying son of the official in Capernaum who 'is living' (*zêi*) after Jesus' healing, John 4:50).

Bultmann, in TDNT II, confirms this for both the classical and Hellenistic usage, and as the basic concept in the NT. He says that in classical Greek "*zôê* belongs to the world (...), it does not belong to the other world in the religious sense" (837), It "denotes in Greek the physical vitality of organic beings, animals, men and also plants" (832). In Hellenistic usage (837-843) the main meaning remains as in classical times, except with the Gnostics. In LXX (*ibidem* 851-4, by Bertram) it has maintained the ancient meaning of 'life by which we live'; "it is only in the hagiographa and apocrypha that the word really becomes a moral and religious term", "it always has a purely quantitative sense".

psuchê and *zôê* together or close to one another. In Lk 17:33: "whoever loses his *psuchê* will make it alive (*zoogoneô*)": making life alive? Absurd![19]

Or the places where it is difficult or even inconsistent to translate *psuchê* with 'life'. E.g. Jn 12:25 says, "the one who loves his *psuchê* will lose it while the man who hates his *psuchê* in this world will keep it (or rather: protect it [*phulaxei*]) for eternal life (...)." Or in Mk 8:35-37 where some translations (e.g. NIV) render *psuchê* as 'soul' (v.36-37) whilst one verse earlier (v.35) they translate the same *psuchê* as 'life'[20], although obviously in Greek it is the very same word in the same argument.[21]

Our conclusion then is that it is not self-evident that *psuchê* must be translated as 'life' as the NT Greek has one or two other terms for that concept. This much for linguistics.

Greek-Hellenistic Influences

There is a further item in Dautzenberg's analysis that drew my attention. It tells about the influence of Greek-Hellenistic culture, which, during the three centuries preceding Jesus' life, and continuing throughout the first century CE, had been actively present in Palestine, and continued to do so. It exerted an increasing impact on life and language in Judaism, though it remained secondary. Under that influence dualistic concepts in anthropology took over in Judaism.

> Although Dautzenberg finally rejects dualism and sticks to the equation *psuchê* = *nephesh*, he does signalize how Greek concepts of *psuchê* naturally penetrated into the Greek speaking Judaism. There are texts (I referred to them in one of the preceding paragraphs) in the LXX where "der griechische Begriff der Bewusstseins- und Denkseele zu seinem Recht gekommen ist, [...] Symptome für die allmähliche Aufnahme griechischer Psychologie ins griechisch sprechende Judentum" (Dautzenberg 1966, 42) Even the dichotomy of body and soul is clearly represented, he says. He continues that this is the case in for example *Wisdom of Solomon*[22], and likewise in other books of the Hellenistic-Jewish literature. In this period often the soul is seen as of a higher order: the *psuchê* is the active, conscious and willing element in the person, the carrier of all psychological and spiritual function, 'das Gemüt', the character (ibidem 42f). Hillel (a contemporary rabbi) is told to have said "Ist denn die arme Seele kein Gast im Leibe?

---

19 Some major translations have a problem with this phrase. NIV and RSV say: "whoever loses his life will preserve it", although obviously the latter is quite different from making alive! NSAV: "those who lose their life will keep it", also a clear case of embarrassment.
20 Chapter 13 will discuss this pericope extensively.
21 Outside the Gospels 1 Jn 3.14 uses the term *zôê*, passing from life (*zôê*) to death. Two verses later (v. 16) there is a matter of laying down one's life (NIV) but here it is *psuchê*, an obvious inconsistency in the translation.
22 E.g. ,1.4, 8.19f, 9.15 where even a trichotomy is suggested with Wisdom as the spirit.

Heute ist sie (noch) hier, morgen (aber) ist sie bereits nicht (mehr) da".[23] Therefore, in the time of Jesus the term *psuchê* carried very different meanings.

Dautzenberg does not make clear how he harmonizes this argument with his decision that *psuchê* must be understood as *nephesh*, life.

Also other authors testify that dualism is current in contemporary Judaism as it "may be detected in some intertestamental writings" and is also present in "the Essene view of death as the separation of body and soul", and "Greek ideas were in wide circulation during the NT period" (Osei-Bonsu 1987, 589). This author contributes to this showing that this position exposes incongruences. His point is Mt 10.28 (and other places outside the Gospels) where body and soul clearly are contrasting entities: man can kill the body but not the *psuchê*. "*Psuchê* here is not the breath of life, since it survives death and can live in Hades and be punished by God. *Psychê* and *sôma* seem to be used anthropologically, i.e. they refer to the two component parts of man" (572f.).

Life after death came to be accepted. Internal dynamics of Hebrew and Aramaic on the one hand, and a prevailing influence of Hellenistic culture, brought about a break in the static situation where the Hebrew language had remained in for many centuries. Even in later texts of the LXX the idea of the individual becomes stronger and "the idea of potentiality *in* the being becomes more important than the potentiality *of* the being" (Lys 1966, 182). The aspects of the individual become more independent. *Nephesh* is "the center of the personal decision and freedom of being" (ibidem, 195f), "the center of longings and the source of desires" (204). Sometimes *nephesh* stands for heart (ibidem). In later times the *psuchê* "als das Eigentliche des Menschen" personally continues to live after death.[24]

It makes one think that this fact is often forgotten in the Christian anthropology when the doctrine of the resurrection is opposed to the idea of the self as a unit. "... all[25] eschew the Platonic self in favor of an apocalyptic resurrection body"[26]. Why should one not recognize another idea of self, as developed in this chapter? It is well-known, for example, how much for example the Gospel of John is rooted in both Greek and Jewish culture.[27]

The issue is whether the term *psuchê* in the Gospels can be fully explained against the background of its use in the LXX. Most scholars do, and therefore see it as an equivalent to *nephesh*, in the sense of life. But it does not do to explain the use of *psuchê* from its LXX use. The analysis just made indicates that the foundation of this argument is less firm. Anthropology in contemporary Judaism had developed in the direction of the Hellenistic dualism—though

---

23 Dautzenberg 1966, 46.
24 Füglister 140. He refers to Philo, Josephus, several apocryphal books and rabbis.
25 The 'all' include the New Testament and especially Paul, but also Justin, Athenagoras, and Tertullian.
26 Segal 2008, 19.
27 E.g. Lys 1958, 182–83, 195–96, 204, Schmid 1962, 116, Osei-Bonsu 1987, 589, Füglister 1980, 140. Neyrey 2001.

retaining its own character—in the sense that the soul gained a greater independence from the body.[28]

I summarize my two points of comment on the linguistic level. One is that this understanding of the meaning of *psuchê* in the logia is at variance with the variations in meaning Dautzenberg signalizes throughout the OT. Two, the dynamics in the development of the Hebrew/Aramaic language under the influence of Hellenistic culture undermine the understanding of *psuchê* in the Gospels. One is the use of the term in the LXX and second the penetration of Greek concepts, even into Hebrew / Aramaic, and appearing then in the LXX.

When we take these observations into consideration the all too easy understanding of *psuchê* as 'life' does not do. No other conclusion can be deducted from these two 'new' insights than: *psuchê* also stands for 'soul'.

Notwithstanding this, many English Bibles (and of other languages, for that matter) have not taken recognition of this fact. They stick to the trodden path, to render *psuchê* as 'life' in crucial texts of the Gospels, like the samples given. Worse even, the main scholar in the field of the logia with *psuchê*, Dautzenberg, though signalizing this development as well as the variety of meanings throughout the OT, has stuck to the traditional rendering of 'life'.

Another Paradigm?

An important question arises. Could it be that there is an extra-linguistic element at play? Why is there so much argument around the meaning of *psuchê*? What is the concept functioning behind the term?

There is a striking point. Remember the rendering of *psuchê* by life as we found it in the pericopes quoted in the beginning of this chapter (Jn 10 and 15, Mk 8.35par): laying down one's life, saving or losing life) implies a reference to the prospect of Jesus' death, resurrection and his saving work, be it explicit or implicit. That is how commentaries explicitly understand these pericopes. I will go into details of that matter later. How does this rendering relate to doctrines of the Church, to the theology of salvation and penitence? Legion are the statements in commentaries and other literature that attest this scenario. It stands in a long history of interpretation and translation.

Distinct from this interpretation is my proposal. Quite contrarily it understands these and other pericopes in the framework of psychology and spirituality, a psycho-spiritual view, with reference to mysticism. In this discrepancy, therefore, we find a clear instance of clashing paradigms: the classical clash between doctrinal religion and spiritual mysticism, sometimes in history between Church and mysticism. Religious culture of today—with

---

28 Schmidt 1962, 116. In general Schmidt rejects the dualism of *nephesh* although the *psuchê* aspect is present (113f).

TRANSFORMATION OF THE SELF: WHAT IS THE SELF, THE *PSUCHÊ*?

dwindling church visits in many communities, private forms of believing, the rise of spirituality (both in pure appearances and in deviant derivatives)—seems to reject doctrines when dogmatic and institutionalized. In the present argument that I am proposing, it comes down to the contrast between the traditional concept of *nephesh* and hence of *psuchê* (as ultimately related to Christology), and the new concept of *psuchê* as one finds it in the logia in its sense of one's *psuchê* as an aspect of the whole being that can be managed, at least that is what will be argued in the following chapters of Part III, with reference to the conepts of presence and transformation as signs of mysticism.

> Dautzenberg's confessional motivation and breeding ground are clear and sincere, throughout his book, and fit it into the paradigm of classical doctrinal theology. In it the *euaggelion* of Jesus circles around his savior work culminating in passion, crucifixion and resurrection, a saving sacrifice washing away the sins of mankind for those believing in Christ. As we have seen, there are some logia with *psuchê* that are considered indicative of this doctrine. One is where Jesus pictures himself as the good shepherd laying down his life for the sheep. Another where he asks the same of his disciples that out of love for one another they will lay down their lives. At an other occasion he tells his disciples that in order to gain life one has to lose it, in order to save life one has to destroy it, for the sake of Jesus and the good news.
>
> I have continued to be wondering if this word 'life' could be the correct rendering of *nephesh*. If it is, the consequences are dire. Imagine what will be the fate of the sheep when the shepherd dies? Why dying willingly out of love for one another? Who then will spread the message? Is there compulsive need indeed to give such a great priority to this one single meaning? What happens when one takes a look from common sense? Traditional renderings show gaps in the consistency of the concept. See chapters 12 and 13.

In this chapter the two compulsive agents for rendering *psuchê* as life, linguistics and theology, have been loosened. On the one hand the traditional paradigmatic view of the contents and role of the *euanggelion* has been placed in a new light. On the other hand it is seen that the language of Jesus and his message may be interpreted as a renewal of a wide range of concepts and views. A word used by Jesus may seemingly fit in the tradition of the Hebrew and Aramaic languages but in its fresh energy and in the new dimension of the psycho-spiritual message of Jesus it stands open for new perspectives for human development. The good shepherd devotes his self, his *psuchê*, to the sheep, he dedicates himself with heart and soul. One does so for one another, out of love and sympathy. It is about one's self or soul or *psuchê* that one is in a situation where one may lose it or gain it.

One point more. Jesus and his language may not at first glance be understood in terms of the then current meanings of words, let alone they would be fixed by these. The charismatic and revolutionary figure Jesus was uses well-known forms charging them with new life and meaning: new wine in old sacks. This is the case with *psuchê*. When interpreting it one needs to account for the context. Dautzenberg and others fall into the trap of taking doctrine as the context instead of seeing *psuchê* in terms of spirituality. Inspired sacred words must be placed in the context of spirituality rather than in the context of doctrine: they have a dynamics of its own. The *psuchê* is an element in the human being to be distinguished but not set apart from the body. The human being is a complete whole, body, *psuchê* and, with reservations, spirit.

Conclusions

The analysis made shows that the traditional translation of *psuchê* by 'life' or 'I' (including equivalents) may be questioned. Yet there is an almost-consensus among NT scholars to the contrary. In my view an interpretation of *psuchê* as one aspect of the human being next to body and spirit stands to reason. It cannot easily be refuted as an alternative possibility. An alternative translation would be 'mind-and-heart' (spelled in this way to indicate that it is one concept considered as a singular for the accompanying verb); occasionally the translation by 'the self' is justified if it is clear that on that place 'self' stands for '*psuchê*'. Technically it may well be translated by '*psuchê*' in general. But for a current translation 'mind-and-heart' or 'self'—depending on the context—is to be preferred. This argument relates to and supports the hypothesis of the trichotomy of body, *psuchê* and spirit.

A second and more important result is that we have discovered a few different views on some crucial Jesus *logia*. Some of the *logia* appear not necessarily to point to passion, crucifixion and resurrection. Rather they address issues of life here and now. They view human life from a spiritual point of view. The teachings by Jesus are clearly related to everyday life.

Thus this book opens up a new and alternative approach to some of the Jesus *logia*.

The third result is that we may view quite a few *logia* in the Gospels as marking a transformational spiritual psychology. This will be explored in the following chapters. Chapter 11 presents *metanoia* as referring to transformation rather than signifying repentance. Chapter 12 will argue that the phrase 'saving or losing one's *psuchê*' is more plausible than 'losing one's life. Handling the *psuchê* means to get access to one's real being. That conclusion will be corroborated by a similar interpretation of the good shepherd pericope and of other Johannine passages (chapter 13). Quite a number of pericopes illustrate the multifariousness of the term, Yet mostly it stands for one aspect of the human being rather than indicating the sum total (chapter 14).

ANNEX 3
Classification of the Occurrences of *psuchê* in the Gospels

The term *psuchê* occurs:
48 times in the Gospels in 30 different passages, i.e.
16 times in 10 passages in Mt: 2:20, 6:25, 10:28, 10:39, 11:29, 12:18, 16:25-26, 20:28, 22:37, 26:38,
8 times in 5 passages in Mk: 3:4, 8:35-37, 10:45, 12:30, 14:34,
14 times in 9 passages in Lk: 1:46, 2:35, 6:9, 9:24, 10:27, 12:19-23, 14:26, 17:33, 21:19,
10 times in 6 passages in J 10:11-18, 10:24, 12:25, 12.27, 13:37-38, 15:13.
When parallels between and among the Gospels are clubbed together the number of passages remaining is 21.

In some cases *psuchê* undoubtedly stands for physical life, or for the life of an individual as a whole. But there are numerous instances where current translations present 'life' where another word is also possible or even better, depending, of course, on one's interpretation of the text. This section classifies all 21 passages according to my understanding what appears to be the meaning-in-context.

- One text (with parallels and variations) concerns finding and losing the psuchê (*sôizô / philô / ktaomai / heuriskô / phulassô / zêteô / peripoieomai / zôogoneô* versus *apollumi / zêmoô / miseô*).
  Mk 8:34-37 par (Mt 10:39, 16:25, Lk 9:24, J 12:25). Cf *et* Lk 17:33 (cf 14:26; see under d), 21:19)
  See chapter 13

- Related are the texts about killing or saving) the *psuchê* or piercing it (*sôizô* versus *apokteinô / apollumi / dierchomai*
  Mk 3:4 par (Lk 6:9), Lk 2:35
  See chapter 14

- Another case is formed by the texts about 'to dedicate one's *psuchê*, to give one's self (*tên psuchên tithêmi / tên psuchên didômi lutron*)
  Mk 10:45 par (Mt 20:28), J 10:11, 15, 17-18, 13:37-38, 15:13
  See chapter 12

- Then another group of texts is found on emotional aspects of the *psyche*
  Mt 11:29-30: to find rest for the *psuchê* (*heuriskô anapausin tias psuchais humôn*)
  Mt Mt 26:38 par: the *psuchê* is grieving (*perilupos estin hê psuchê mou*)
  Lk 14:26: to hate one's *psuchê* (*miseô*)
  J 10:24 to keep in suspense (*airô*)
  J 12:27 to be troubled (*tarassô*)
  See chapter 14

- a poetical expression is suggesting rather than defining
  Mt 22:37 parr (Mk 12:30, Lk 10:27): all your heart, soul, mind, strength (*kardia, psuchê, dianoia, ischus*)
  We will not include this text as it is a quotation from OT.

- Again a group of texts is presenting psuchê as related to body and/or spirit, or as physical life

Mt 2:20 (physical life), 6:25 / Lk 12.22 (*psuchê* more than food), 10:28 (killing the *psuchê*), 12:17-18* (*psuchê* is pleased), Lk 1:46-47* (*psuchê* magnifies), 12:19-23 (speaking to the *psuchê*, (*psuchê* required)

The two with an * will not be included in the argument as again being quotations from OT.

ANNEX 4
Some Literature Reviewed

Here is a review of five major contributors on the issue of *psuchê*: Schmid 1962, Dautzenberg 1966, 1984, Lys 1966, Füglister 1980, and Osei-Bonsu 1987.

Dautzenberg (1966) has dedicated his doctoral thesis (1964) to this issue looking into the words of the Lord in the Gospels, summarizing previous authors (including Schmid 1962), and breaking fresh ground. In 1984 he has taken up the subject again in the wider context of the Bible. Some others have followed: Füglister 1980 (discussing it together with *pneuma*), and Osei-Bonsu 1987 (discussing it together with *pneuma, sôma, sarx*). Besides, Lys 1966 writes about the *psuchê* in LXX. Of course, quite some attention has been given to the *psuchê* concept in the Pauline letters in the pair *psuchikos / pneumatikos* (Pagels 1975, Pearson 1973 and others). This however is beyond the scope of this paper. The same obtains for the frequent comments in publications covering wider fields.

Lys (1966) reviews how *nephesh* was translated into Greek in the LXX, and what other antecedents in the Hebrew Bible were translated as *psuchê*. His work is in the same line as Dautzenberg. A few points in Lys' work of interest to our argument are the following. The LXX translation, broadly speaking, has used *psuchê* consistently for *nephesh* (680 out of 754 times) (186). In the earliest OT texts *nephesh* has several meanings: "life; what lives and dies; the affections, i.e. need and appetite, desire and pleasure, the feelings; several localizations ('interior', liver, blood, breath); the animate and living being (even the animal), and then the Self, I"(182). The idea of 'potentiality' is central. But in the later texts of the LXX the idea of the individual becomes stronger. "... the idea of potentiality *in* the being becomes more important than the potentiality *of* the being" (l.c.). And, "... the soul is nothing but the animation of the body" (183). This means that in pre-Christian times the meaning of *psuchê / nephesh* had moved closer to the interpretation we have suggested. See also below. Also at other places Lys underlines that *nephesh* includes the connotation of 'longings, either physical or moral'; it is 'the center of the personal decision and freedom of being' (195, 196), 'the center of longings and the source of desires' (p.204). In some alternate readings we find 'heart' for 'soul' (l.c.) (!, WvL).

Lys then proceeds with the analysis of the places where LXX has *psuchê*, not as an equivalent for *nephesh* but for other terms, and reversely where *nephesh* was not translated by *psuchê*.

The latter case shows in about half the cases that *nephesh* is given in Greek as 'being, self, or the personal or reflexive pronoun' (199). This appears to be a strong motive to not lightly interpret *psuchê* in the NT as *nephesh*. Obviously, *psuchê* was not considered to be a full equivalent to *nephesh*.

The former case presents 25 instances where the Hebrew word for heart is translated as *psuchê*: another proof that *psuchê* is not the same as *nepehesh*! a few extracts

(214–16): "the heart is troubled"; "the heart' as the center whence decisions come"; "the oath is made with 'all their heart'"; 'despising somebody in one's heart'; the heart as the center of affectivity, feelings, or love; as "the source for desires"; "the decisive center which is planning a bad behavior and the whole potentiality which may be in communion or in opposition"; "the heart is timid"; "the heart melts"; "the merry-of-heart sigh." We interpret this as a support to our interpretation that it is doubtful whether *psuchê* may be considered to be an equivalemt to *nephesh* as 'life'. *Psuchê* obviously could be understood as meaning 'heart' by the LXX translation.

Notwithstanding this Lys concludes in general that *psuchê* for the LXX translators had more a Hebrew than a Greek content, i.e., the *psuchê* (soul) is inseparably part and parcel of the individual. I find it striking, though, that the *psuchê* is considered acting as an entity. Yes, it is inseparable—at least here on earth, I would add—but yet can be distinguished clearly as it is quite different from body and spirit both.

Lys continues that, of course, the *psuchê* (soul) is not a divine element, a representative of the good and sacred. I agree with this conclusion, but it cannot function as an argument against my hypothesis. What he is arguing against is against *psuchê* or soul in the sense of spirit, *pneuma*. His characteristic of soul, however, fits well with the concept of *psuchê* as defined in this paper. This *psuchê* (soul) is not opposite to body, but another component of the human being, different from but functioning in an integrated manner with the body.

There are, moreover, at least a few interesting instances in the LXX where the *psuchê* obviously is considered to be separate from the body. Gen. 35:18 describes how her soul went away when Rachel died (*aphienai tên psuchên*) (NIV freely translates: she breathed her last: *sic*) (p. 224). And there is another instance (Job 7:5 in a variant reading) (208): *"Thou wilt separate my soul from my spirit, and my soul from my body"*, a text which fits excellently in my argument and even with the hypothesis of the trichotomy.

Schmid (1962) is another one who rejects the dualism soul/body in the sense that the Gospels could not understand the body "niemals als das Gefängnis oder Grab der Seele und die Verbindung der beiden als eine widernatürliche und als ein Unglück der Seele" (p. 113). "*Nephesh* aber bedeutet einmal das Leben, die Vitalität, und zwar nicht nur das 'animalische', niedere Leben, sondern auch das höhere, das sogenannte geistige, *zu dem das Wollen, Denken und die Affekte gehören* (emphasis added), und zwar das mit dem Körper verbundene Leben" (114). No problem! Therefore it can also mean the individual person, *or his psyche-part*. This may be related to Gen 2:7: God has breathed his spirit into man by which he became a *living* soul (emphasis added). This indicates that the *psuchê* is becoming alive only when the spirit is added. Schmid continues that in Palestine in later periods the OT anthropology developed in the direction of the Hellenistic dualism in the sense that the soul gained a greater independence from the body (116), which tends toward the time of Jesus and the writing of the Gospels! This confirms Lys above.

Schmid obviously views the NT use of *psuchê* as a continuity of the OT usage. Yet he too indicates contrary developments in later Judaism, a period relevant to the issue discussed here, developments which support our hypothesis.

Osei-Bonsu (1987) is practically the one single author who supports dualism in NT and is of the opinion that the *psuchê* concept relates to Greek sources.

Apart from the dualism *sôma, sarx—pneuma* he shows how the Gospels contrast *sôma* and *sarx* to *psuchê*, i.e., Mt 10:28 with par Lk 12:4–5 (although Lk does not have *psuchê*, the author thinks it is implied) (572–73). Other instances are found in Acta, Hebr, 1Thess. Implied contrasts are found in 2 Cor (581–83, 585). Mt 10:28 says that man can kill the body but not the *psuchê*. But God can, i.e. in Geenna. "*Psuchê* here is not the breath of life, since it survives death and can live in Hades and be punished by God. *Psyche and soma seem to be used anthropologically, i.e. they refer to the two component parts of man*" (p. 573; emphasis added). Luke omits the *psuchê* but it is argued on several grounds that Mt is the original formulation. One could also argue that the entity which will be thrown in Geenna is the *psuchê* and not the body. The text is not explicit about either version.

Osei-Bonsu presents a second argument which, I feel, is important. Most scholars do not believe in anthropological dualism in NT as this would be unhistorical in the Jewish context. The NT would not reflect Greek thinking. This author, however, argues that such a dualism was current in contemporary Judaism as it "may be detected in some intertestamental writings" and is also present in "the Essene view of death as the separation of body and soul" (589). Moreover, "Greek ideas were in wide circulation during the NT period" (l.c.). Cf Schmid and partly Lys as discussed above. This we feel as a strong, be it rather isolated, support for our argument.

Some support we find in Füglister (1980) too. Yes, he argues that biblical anthropology is monistic and not dualistic (145). Yet he implicitly supports the previous author stating that in late OT times according to Philo, Josephus, several apocryphical books and rabbis the *psuchê* "als das Eigentliche des Menschen" personally continues to live after physical death (140). In his analysis of the relevant NT texts, however, he is not consistent to this finding.

Overlooking this short review of relevant literature the conclusion is that largely there is a scholarly consensus although it shows some rifts. The present consensus roughly is that the *psuchê* concept is to be interpreted in OT terms, as *nephesh*, that the *psuchê* is not a separate entity and does not continue to live after death. But we have found convincing facts that necessitate to formulate an at least alternative interpretation. This challenge we have taken up in this chapter.

CHAPTER ELEVEN
Metanoia as Transformation

Introduction: Mk 1.15 par

Jesus announces the arrival of the Kingdom of God, calling to transform heart-and-soul (meta-noia) and to put one's trust in the (good) Message. What is this transformation? Currently it is being rendered as repentance or conversion. Or did Jesus rather call for an inner transformation, closely associated with the transformation required for the Kingdom? When speaking about 'sin' he speaks in terms of missing the target, 'not making it,' being more or less an outcast. Metanoia is suggested as a remedy: transformation of one's life's attitude.

This hypothesis is tested through an analysis of the terms metanoia, hamartanô *and* aphiêmi. *How is it that at the same time in some logia the tone is different, pointing to the eschaton?*

Transformation is one of the key concepts of mysticism (chapter 2). Is this concept reflected in *metanoia*? What does Jesus say to it?

Here are the texts from Mk 1.14–15 and Mt 4.17 in my alternative proposal. For further details of this logion, see chapter 6.

> *The time is fulfilled / the moment is there,[1] the Kingdom of God has arrived.*
> *Change your mind and heart[2]*
> *And put your trust in the message.*
>
> *From then on Jesus began to proclaim saying*
> *Change your mind-and-heart, for the Kingdom of heaven has arrived.*

N.B. NRSV has 'repent' for 'change your mind,' *metanoeô*. For other terms see chapter 6.

Thus Jesus proclaims the presence of the Kingdom of God: its approach is complete. He calls for transformation, a change of one's life's attitude, of mind-and-heart, one's conduct. See the Sermon on the Mount / Plain. Usually, however, it is rendered as repentance, in connection with sin, penitence, and

---

A draft of the first version was read at the SBL International Meeting at Cambridge 2003.
1   *Erfüllt, vollkommen*, Blass etc., §341, n. 3. It is sometimes suggested that *kairos* does not refer to time. See chapter 6.
2   In *The Lost Gospel*, 1996, the editors, Borg among them, propose 'change of heart.'

forgiving. This understanding of *metanoia* is in line with the confessional and doctrinal interpretations. The transformation goes hand in hand with the call to confide oneself to the *euaggelion*, the Message. That message is contained in the presence of the Kingdom.

What else do the Gospels report about *metanoia*? The term is infrequent in the Synoptics, and is absent from Jn. The analysis is limited to the words of Jesus, where it occurs in ten pericopes only. Its appearance is varied and confusing:

- One set of logia that will be central in this chapter traditionally representing a call to 'repent' at the announcement of the Kingdom of God (Mk 1.15, Mt 4.17, and some related pericopes), often interpreted as eschatological.

- Two sets of logia exhibit eschatological flavors: menace and judgment, requiring repentance for bad performance, in the traditional Jewish sense (Lk 10.13 / Mt 11.20–21; Lk 11.32 / Mt 12.41). Also Lk 13.3,5.

- Two logia Lk 5.32 and Lk 15.7, repeated in v.10, relate sin and repentance

- Lk 17.3–4 presents 'sin' and 'repentance' in a day-to-day setting of the disciples acting and reacting among themselves.

- One pericope will be presented summarily but lies outside the scope of analysis: Lk 24.47 is a post-Easter logion.

A few remarks. Mt 4.17 makes clear that the call *metanoeite* is made just *because* the Kingdom has arrived rather than the often inferred reversed logic: to 'repent' in order for the kingdom to arrive. From the discussions about the Kingdom in Part II it has become clear that a change, *metanoia*, is necessary in order to receive it. There is no mention about 'sinning'. Lk 5.32, however, reports Jesus saying that he has not come to call the righteous for *metanoia* but the 'sinners'; a critical note will be given later. Later on we will try and find out what these individuals are, what 'sin' is. The sinner again is mentioned (Lk 15.7, 10) when Jesus tells that there will be more joy in heaven over one sinner who practises *metanoia* than over 99 righteous people who don't need such. Finally *metanoia* is discussed with the disciples (Lk 17.3, 4). Jesus teaches them to rebuke another disciple who 'sins', but if there is *metanoia*, one must forgive. Apart from these cases, in two instances (Mt 11.20–21, par Lk 10.13, and Mt 12.41–42, Lk 11.32) Jesus takes up the traditional Jewish concept of *metanoia* referring to 'sitting in sackcloth and ashes'. Several comments consider these verses as redactional additions.

This chapter, then, will focus on what this metanoia *may refer to, and on related problems like sin and forgiving. Repentance and sin are often seen as a pair, the one belongs to the other, in Church doctrine and elsewhere. Therefore it is often translated in terms of the eschaton. Does the Greek noun* metanoia *and its verb* metanoeô *convey the sense of repentance? Does the Greek* hamartêma *convey the sense of sin? This will be explored critically, followed by a critical analysis of the relevant logia.*

METANOIA AS TRANSFORMATION

Each of these pericopes will be explored. To begin with the logion that is central to Jesus' message. At the end of the chapter the other logia will be treated. Following it are some elaborations on what is *metanoia*, and what is sin and forgiving.

The next section reviews the various translations, followed by an analysis of the term repentance, and what it represents. John the Baptist and Jesus both speak about *metanoia* in a similar phrase. This gives rise to ask whether the two sayings betray a continuity or rather a discontinuity. The related concepts of sin and forgiving will be analyzed. Finally each of the pericopes with the term *metanoia* will be discussed shortly.

Terms and Concepts[3]

What about the variation in interpretation used e.g. in the quotations above? What concept does the Greek term stand for? What is the call by Jesus about? Does it refer to the later interpretation as repentance? Is it an action or a *Geistesgesinnung*? Does it refer to rituals and procedures? What is its implication for daily life: morally, spiritually, ritualistically? In the course of our argument it will become clear that *metanoia* / *metanoeô* may be understood quite differently. This section will have a triple look at the term: first, at how *metanoia* has been rendered in different translations of the Gospel texts under review; then, as 'repentance' turns out to be the standard English translation, what does this term imply?; finally I will try to find out what the Greek words *metanoeô* / *metanoia* convey.

Back to the basics of the Greek terms *metanoeô*, *metanoia*[4],[5]

---

[3] *Metanoia* / *metanoeô* has different synonyms. Among these *metamelomai* is close to but different from *metanoeô*. It occurs three times only in the Gospels, and only in Mt. NIV translates 'changed his mind' (21:29), 'repent' (21:32) and 'seized with remorse' (27:3). Michel in TDNT IV, 626-629: in classical Greek it means 'to experience remorse' while *metanoia* means a change of heart either generally or in respect of a specific sin. In the quoted instances *metamelomai* refers to a change of decision on a secular matter (21:29), to the not repenting of the high-priests and elders in the case of John the Baptist (21:32), and to the remorse of Judas (27:3). It will not be discussed as it does not affect our argument.

[4] The relationship of *metanoia* with the Hebrew / Aramaic equivalents is widely discussed, especially for the LXX. However, for the argument in this chapter it is not essential. This obtains the more while the Hebrew / Aramaic terms vary over time. Moreover, the LXX is not consistent in its translations from *shub* (and derivatives) and *nacham* into *metanoein*, *metamelesthai*, *parakaleisthai*, *(ana)pauesthai*, and a few others. See A.W. Argyle, "God's repentance and the LXX", *The Expository Times* 75 s (1964) 367. See also Nave 2002, 111-18, and the extensive discussion by Bryant J. Williams III (see next Note)

[5] Bryant J. Williams III, *Repentance*, attachment to his posting in Bible Translation e-group, April 9, 2008 discusses two parallel terms *epistrephô* and *metamelomai*. *Epistrephô* is used both

190   PART THREE: TRANSFORMATION: THE PSYCHE

The term *metanoia/ metanoeô*, according to Behm in the TDNT, is composed of the prefix *meta* and a form of *-nous / -noeo*. *Meta* is generally interpreted as indicating a change, but may indicate a 'later'. *Nous* refers, among others, to mind or mentality[6]. *Metanoeô / metanoia* bears three meanings: later knowledge, change of mind (feelings, will, thought), and sometimes connected with regret or remorse.[7] BDAG renders the verb first as changing one's mind, then as feeling remorse, repenting, being converted; the noun is rendering the same, including turning about, but its primary classical meaning is given as 'a change of mind'.

What does this imply for the NT? According to Behm, "the only possible meanings are 'to change one's mind', 'change of mind', or 'to convert', 'conversion' ", apart from Lk 17.3 and 2C 7.9f. But then he turns around, saying, "the terms have a religious and ethical significance along the lines of the OT and Jewish concept of conversion…for which there is no analogy in secular Greek. Hence the only apposite renderings are 'to convert' and 'conversion' ".[8] *Sic*.

I will come back to this discussion somewhat later in this chapter.

Translations[9]

The major English-language translations of Mk 1.15 exhibit a maximum of consensus: each and every Bible that I have checked agrees to 'to repent'.[10] What does 'repent' signify? How firm is that rendering compared to translations in some other languages? Some give other shades, or even render radical divergencies. Three types predominate, in English equivalents: conversion; turning around, change of behavior; doing penance, having remorse, to review, return to God.[11]

---

    in the LXX and in the NT "primarily for descriptions of a concrete physical turning or changing of direction" (3.3). *Metamelomai* is infrequent in the NT and refers to practical situations.

6   TDNT IV, 1006, n.179: Clemens Alexandrinus defines the word in purely Greek terms (as opposed to Christian use) [!]. On p. 978 n.5 this Clemens is referred to as defining *metanoia* as *bradeia…gnosis*, "knowledge which only comes later" (Stromata II 26.5). Also 1 Clemens (IV 143) tells that the etymology of this word is composed of *meta* and a form of *noêo*: *meta tauta noêsantes*. These definitions refer to the 'first' meaning according to Behm in TDNT 976, 978. However, the primary meaning is change of mind (l.c.).

7   Behm in TDNT IV 976f. and 978, respectively.

8   Behm, ibid. 999.

9   All information unless indicated differently is from BibleWorks 8.

10 ASV 1901, Darby 1894/90, Douay Rheims, American 1899, ESV 2007, KJV 1611/1769, NAS 1995, NET, NJB, NIV 1984, NRSV 1989.

11 Most Dutch translations render it by 'bekeren', which is an equivalent to the English conversion, used either as a one-time moral act of a confessed Christian or as the decision to become a Christian: changing faith. It implies leaving the wrong thing in order to do the right thing. The three principal Scandinavian languages do the same: omvende (D, N), omvända (Sw). In German, however, the traditional and Lutheran versions render 'Busse', laying stress on remorse and penitence; more modern German Bibles say 'kehrt um': to turn

What does the Latin say? This is relevant as Latin has been a major agent in making Western Christianity what it is. The terminology is telling. It is either *paenitentia* (remorse) or, and that is significant, the Middle and Late Latin equivalent *poenitentia*: penitence—that contains the association with *poena*: atonement, penalty. The transition from *paenitentia* to *poenitentia* is telling indeed.

> Matzkow[12] confirms that the Romans did not have appropriate words to render *metanoia* (Matzkow 1933, 29). More interesting is his making the find, on the basis of studying the Old Latin codices, that the Romans in some way thought that paeniteo had to do with *poena*, and therefore changed *paeniteo* in *poeniteo*.[13] This issue will be taken up again in a later section when discussing Tertullian and Lactantius.

Indications for this transition are found in the versions of the Vulgate: like the Nova Vulgata (NOV, Nestle-Aland 27) and the Latin Vulgata (VUL) giving *paenitentia*, while the Clementina (1598, VUC) renders *poenitentia*.

Summarizing, the dominant translation is repentance and its equivalents, more or less like *paenitentia*. The Lutheran and some other translations tend to the Latin *poenitentia*: atonement, penalty. The third rendering we find is conversion, indicating moral change, or also: becoming a Christian (conversion). Also in literature these interpretations abound.[14]

Is *metanoia* Repentance?

Now then, what does repentance mean?

> The *Webster's* defines repentance as "contrition for one's sins together with the dedication of oneself to the abandonment of unworthy purposes and values and to the amendment of one's life". To repent is "to turn from sin out of penitence for past wrongdoings". Also to feel regret or contrition for something, to change one's mind

---

around.11 In French three versions appear: 'convertir' (Traduction oecuménique), 'repentir' (Nouv. Éd. Genève 1979, Louis Segond 1910), and 'changer de comportement' (behavior) (BFC). In all but one Spanish versions (and also as to the Portuguese equivalent) the rendering is : 'arrepentirse': 'to repent', remorse. In Italian it is either 'convertire (IEP NVB 1995)' or 'ravvedere' (Diodati 1991, NRV 1994) 'to review': to have remorse, to see you have been wrong. The New Greek retains '*metanoia*' (MET 2004, MGK). In Russian the generally applied translation is remorse and penitence: 'pokaytes' (RSO, RST) with the exception of CRV saying Обратитесь к Богу, 'Obratites' k Bogu': (re)turn to God).

12   Walter Matzkow, *De vocabulis quibusdam italae et vulgatae christianis quaestiones lexicographicae*, Berlin 1933, 29–33 (on *metanoia, metanoein* etc.)

13   Ibid.: "Sed populus Romanus verbum *paenitendi* aliquo modo ad vocem *poenae* pertinere ratus mutavit in verbum *poenitendi* ...."

14   My search has not covered this literature systematically. As exception I mention Getty-Sullivan (2007) who proposes 'mind and hearts,' though she keeps to the eschatological meaning.

about something, to feel sorrow or regret, be dissatisfied, to feel repentance. a repentant is a 'penitent.'

Thus two mental aspects may be discerned, both in the field of morals: the 'negative' attitude by looking back to what went wrong, and much less the 'positive' attitude by looking forward for a better conduct. The negative has often predominated in Christianity[15], as the positive step first supposedly requires remorse and regret. And that is what usually was getting most of the attention. The process often stands under pressure because of the moral load of sinning.

Traditionally repentance is explained in four aspects, or steps:

- as the awareness that one has been wrong in attitude and/or in one's life's conduct (in both thought and action);
- as a decision to do it differently;
- as an act of penance,
- and as an actual complete change of one's mentality as well as of one's way of life.

In short: turning around, condemning one's past, undergoing punishment for past sins, and beginning anew.

This is accentuated in the Roman-Catholic Church by the so-called five sacraments comprised under the Sacrament of Penance and Reconciliation, as formulated by the current Catechism[16]:

> Among the sacraments of the RC Church is the sacrament of penance, "consisting of three actions of the penitent and the priest's absolution. The penitent's acts are repentance, confession or disclosure of sins to the priest, and the intention to make reparation and do works of reparation."[17] · This sacrament implies the following sacraments: of conversion, of Penance, of confession, of forgiveness, of Reconciliation (capital letters in the, original).[18]

---

15   And is threatening also today. Ratzinger (1972) warns against a light-hearted interpretation, making the Good News world-oriented. By this Christianity is given a fresh competition motive but will result in a fundamental loss. Essential is *Busse* and *Beichte* (penitence and confession) provided it is joined to *Bekehrung*. This is a transformation (!) concerning the whole and complete person, and his life conduct. If interpreted in catechismic terms, of Church doctrine and rules and regulations, Ratzinger does not conform to the meaning of the logia as we will come to view them. If interpreted spiritually in terms of pure mysticism. I think he may be right in principle. The risk remains that *metanoia* and the complex of concepts around it will continue to be interpreted primarily as a moral concept. Sure, the moral dimension is there but is valid only in the perspective of spirituality.
16   *Catechism of the Catholic Church* 1999.
17   Ibidem, 1491 / p .335.
18   Ibidem, 1423, 1424 / p. 320.

As to terminology, three related terms derive from the basic Latin *paena* or in Middle and Late Latin *poena*: penance, penitence and repentance. What do they mean? Penance, according to the *Webster's*, is "an act of self-abasement, mortification or devotion, either voluntarily performed (...) or imposed as a punishment for sin". Penitence (*paenitentia / poenitentia*, LL, ML): "a state of mind of one who acknowledges and deeply regrets his wrongs and is determined to amend," a position with some positive outlook, it appears. This term does not occur in the Catechism. Even to repent derives from the same origin via the French *re-pentir* from Latin *paenitere*, or *poenitere*), related to Latin *poena*: penalty, punishment, and bear that connotation. Repentance was defined earlier; see above.

From the definitions from the *Webster's* as well as from the wordings in the Catechism it is clear that repentance is associated to a considerable degree with the concepts of sin, penance and even punishment. These words are derived from the Greek *metanoia*. Are they adequate renderings? No, they do not. The answer is closely related to what we have been discussing about *paenitentia / poenitentia* a bit earlier. Let us turn to an early Christian analysis by Lactantius (ca 250-ca 325) and Tertullian (fl 200).

Remarkably both Tertullian and Lactantius are of the opinion that the Latin does not render the concept *metanoia* adequately[19]: Tertullian deems *paenitentia* inadequate, saying "in Graeco sono paenitentiae nomen non ex delicti confessione, sed ex animi demutatione compositum est"[20]. In his opinion *metanoia* represents the positive aspect, as I called it, as opposed to the Latin *paenitentia*. The Latin possesses another word for *metanoia*, *resipiscientia* (verb: *resipisco*): "a translation of *metanoia*, a change of mind, reformation, repentance"[21]. However, Lactantius is even less sure about its adequacy. He says, "(...) Graeci melius et significantius μετάνοιαν dicunt quam nos Latine possumus resipiscientiam dicere" (Lactantius, *Divinae Institutiones* VI 24,6); Lactantius uses *resipiscientia* explaining "quem (...) facti sui paenitet, errorem suum pristinum intelligit" (ibid.). The Greek word is better and clearer, he says. An interesting and enlightening discussion!

Significantly, the Latin term *resipiscientia* has not survived: the concept of punishment in 'penitence' and 'repentance' has been stronger, although *resipiscientia* obviously is a better rendering of *metanoia*: self-consideration (J. Behm in TDNT), change of mind, reformation, self-consideration.[22] Yet both Church Fathers agree that it does not render

---

19 Behm, in his article on *metanoia* in TDNT (IV 978 n.7).
20 Tertullianus, *Adversum Marcionem* II 24, quoted in Behm in TDNT IV, l.c.
21 C.T. Lewis, Ch. Short, *A Latin Dictionary, Founded on Andrew's edition of Freund's Latin dictionary*, Oxford 1879. Notre Dame's internet Latin Dictionary and Grammar Aid says, "to recover one's senses; to become rational again,' which makes it even less confessionally tinted. In Dutch the verb is rendered as 'weer verstandig worden,' weer tot bewustzijn komen / tot zichzelf komen.'
22 Sic. Lewis and Short, *Latin Dictionary*, Oxford 1962.

the Greek *metanoia* properly. For our purpose it suffices that with 'change of mind' and 'reformation' *resipiscientia* is close to our preferred 'transformation'[23]

The positive side of the concept *metanoia*, therefore, has suffered from the Latin translation *paenitentia / poenitentia*. Some even deplore the use of repentance as it suggests 'groaning and lamenting over one's past sins', says Dircksen,[24] here in a quotation of M. Arnold. He rejects 'repentance' as translation; it was a Protestant innovation and maintains: in Jesus' conception of *metanoia* the bewailing of sins was a small part; the main part was far more active and fruitful (ibid.). Arnold would even prefer 'the bald phrase of change of mind': it is a change of the inner man. This is a conclusion that I would readily adopt. As a matter of fact, Behm,[25] having searched the Greek classical literature, as well as the koine, concludes that *metanoia / metanoeô* do not refer in any way to the way Christianity sees the term, both in the OT and in the NT: "Whether linguistically or materially, one searches the Greek world in vain for the origin of the NT understanding of *metanoeô* and *metanoia*. Had this (mis)understanding been imported into the term by the Church or early Christian communities? In retrospect and in my view, it is amazing that this misleading interpretation and translation has largely escaped the attention of both Church and academia, thus keeping to a confessional sense of *metanoia*.

Anyhow, linguistically the term *metanoia* refers to a wide range of meanings. Jesus' call *metanoeite* may be seen as "an emotional appeal: 'Feel sorry', or as the stirring of the whole consciousness: 'Change your mind', or as a demand for acts of expiation for wrongs committed: 'Do penance,' or as a summons to a radical change in the relation of God to man and man to God: 'Convert,' 'be converted.' According to these various interpretations there will be radically

---

23 The proposed translation of *metanoia* as 'transformation' could be criticized, as it would be the translation of *metamorphosis*. However, Behm (TDNT IV 758–59) suggests that *metamorphousthai* (Mt 17:2, Mk 9:2) refers to physical change (garments; also countenance in Mt and also par Lk 9:29). *Metanoia* then may refer to a change of the *nous*. However, Paul uses *metamorphousthai* in relation to a renewal of the *nous*. But close reading places the passage in the context of offering the body as a sacrifice so as not to conform to the world but rather to be transformed by the renewing of the mind (R 12:1–2 NIV). In 2C 3:18 the verb is related to *eikon*, a concept with physical associations. Of course, etymologically *metamorphosis* means change of form, whilst *metanoia* means change of *nous*. *Nous* may best be translated as 'mind', especially in the sense of 'attitude,' 'way of thinking,' the 'sum total of the whole mental and moral state of being' (Bauer 3; German: *Gesinnung*), mentality. Commentators on the NT use of *metanoia* invariably indicate that it does not refer to cases but to one's whole attitude and life conduct, not a change in one's mind but rather a transformation of the mind. Summing up: 'transformation' appears to provide a basic sense of the word *metanoia*.
24 Dircksen 1932, 224.
25 TDNT, ibid., 980.

different understandings of the message of Jesus.[26] And I would add: as a call to one's inner being to transform the psyche and one's consciousness and to become aware of the spirit, outside as well as inside.

What is conversion? *Webster's:* "change from one belief, views, course, party or principle to another." Therefore, in terms of today's language 'conversion' does not refer to anything like repentance, remorse, or whatever moral aspect. Also the Dutch equivalent 'bekeren' refers more to changing one's religion. The Scandinavian equivalent does so but is used for meaning repentance.

Concluding, it is quite unsure on linguistic grounds whether the idea of a specific Christian (orthodox) meaning can be maintained, even for primitive Christianity. For the Post-Apostolic fathers, apart from *metanoia* as 'Christian conversion', it was an ordinary word: 'to come to be of another mind,' 'change of mind.'[27] How standard its meaning was is revealed when seeing that it even could mean 'to renounce Christianity,' i.e. in some martyrologies.[28]

Nave, in his leading work on repentance in Lk-Acts,[29] comes to a different conclusion altogether: "Clearly the meaning of *metanoeô* and *metanoia*—and therefore the meaning of repentance [!, wvl]—in Luke-Acts is essentially the same as that found in Graeco-Roman, Jewish, and early Christian literature." This is remarkable for two reasons. One is that he understands repentance as the complete four stage process (as given above); terminologically this does not seem to work out. Another reason is what I see as an incongruity with his view (see below) that its place is in the Hellenistic culture of that time. The third reason is that he understands the Lukan concept of repentance as uniquely Christian. This is mentioned also by Merklein who sees the Lukan *metanoia* as" den ethischen Gesinnungswandel als Vorbedingung für die Vergebung, die wiederum Voraussetzung für den Heilsempfang ist (Merklein 1981, 40). Here, like with most authors, *metanoia* is interpreted as moral concept, logical because of its long history—mistaken indeed in my view. This seems a right point to recall again one of the principles underlying this study. All divergent outcomes are to be seen as alternatives to the current understandings.

In Nave's view the concept and therewith the emerging Christianity is to be placed in the Hellenistic culture of that time, rather than to be interpreted as a renewal of Jewish concepts only. On the other hand, *metanoia* not to be

---

26 Ibid., 1000.
27 Ibid., 1006f, n. 179, 180, referring to the *Shepherd of Hermes* (Visiones 3.7.3, Mandata 11.4, 4.2.2).
28 Ibid., 1007, in the *Martyrium Polycarpi* and onwards, mainly as a legal technical term.
29 Guy D. Nave, *The Role and Function of Repentance in Luke-Acts,* 2002. Also by the same author "'Repent, for the Kingdom of God is at hand': repentance in the Synoptic Gospels," 2006.

understood in the sense of the understanding by later early non- or even anti-Jewish Christian writers, more or less Hellenistic authors. Illustrating this, Nave refers to Origen, Clement of Alexandria and the author of the *Shepherd of Hermes* whose writings are filled with the concept "which reflect the beginnings of the development of a Christian theology of repentance (i.e., Penance) as well as a penitential discipline in the Church" (Nave…,120). Their interpretation of 'repentance' "cannot and should not be used to determine Jewish/Gentile-Christian attitudes regarding repentance during the first century C.E." (p. 120). This implies that we should view the concept of repentance largely free from later Church interpretations. So far I can agree with Nave. However, in order to do that an analysis of the Jesus logia is required. But Nave's interpretation of *metanoia* takes another direction. His body of analysis is the narrative of Lk-Acts, with much attention to Acts. He even does not take a separate look at the logia as an identifiable signifying entity within the narrative. Instead, he identifies a strong line from John Baptist through Jesus to the apostles.[30] Yes, indeed, in Lk the Baptist plays a large role. By recognizing this role the perspective changes indeed. *Metanoia* then gets a clear connection with sin and forgiveness. The Baptist is "preaching a baptism of repentance for the forgiveness of sins" (Lk 3.3b). Is Jesus to be placed in a line of continuity with the Baptist? Is his *metanoia* the same? My thesis in this book is that Jesus takes a unique position in bringing the message of the Kingdom as a spiritual inner reality for which transformation of the psyche is a necessity. This has been amply illustrated in Part II. The difference between Jesus' *metanoeite* and the Baptist's is clear: the latter connects it with sin and forgiveness, Jesus does not. Let us have a closer look at the issue of continuity.

Continuity

Without any doubt there is an overriding continuity of Jewish religion and culture in what Jesus says and does. How could it be otherwise. Yet though using current terminology his words carry a new meaning. His message in many respects is a new message, a radical renewal. His teachings of the Kingdom are a clear break. The Kingdom is not eschatological, it is not a re-establishment of the Davidic kingdom, it is not an ideal social moral society. It is a spiritual inner reality for which transformation of the psyche is necessary indeed[31]: the ideal moral society may follow as a consequence, not the other way round. Let us take a view on the *metanoia* call messages of Jesus and the Baptist, respectively.

---

30 See also Čabraja 1985, 235 sub 3.
31 "But Jesus also is the source of a new life that renews the individual from within" (Richards 1991), 570.S

John in Mk 1.4	Jesus in Mk 1.14–15
to be baptized	.....
for metanoia	metanoeite
for forgiveness	....
of sins	....
.....	the completed approach of the Kingdom of God
.....	while trusting / believing
....	in his message / in the Gospel

A remarkable presentation: the overlap is minimal. No word here by Jesus about sin or forgiveness, no word about baptism,[32] concepts that soon were to become dear to the Church, but not grounded in these Jesus logia. But it is a clear call for *metanoia* in relation to the arrival of the Kingdom of God, to the good message and to believing the same.

The Church's interpretation may seem to find a foothold in Mk's narrative where there is another and earlier call for *metanoia*. Jesus when calling for *metanoia* seems to re-echo a similar call by John the Baptist, his forerunner. The similarity has often been stressed, for example in their supposed eschatology.[33] But what did John say in fact? Mk 1.4 reports John "preaching a baptism of repentance for the forgiveness of sins." Is Jesus' call a re-echo? No, not at all! Jesus' call is about *metanoia*, confiding and the Message, John's about baptism, *metanoia*, sin and forgiveness. Comparing the two calls the only correspondence is *metanoia*. No word by Jesus about sin or forgiveness, no word about baptism.[34] But there is a clear call by both for *metanoia*. Are they calling for the same whilst the other elements in the mouth of the two differ radically? I will have to answer that question in this chapter.

Therefore, rather than a continuity, I see a clear contrast where Jesus in his pronouncement—which seemingly points in the same direction as John's (*metanoeite!*)—does not refer with even a single word to sin and forgiveness, a contrast mostly neglected.[35] For example, in Mt 3.2 the Baptist says 'Repent,' followed by vs.6 'confessing their sins.' This stands in stark contrast to Jesus' pronouncement in 4.17, "Repent for the kingdom of heaven has approached". Or in Mk 1.4 where John is "preaching a baptism of repentance for the

---

32 Chapter 16 will discuss the baptism scenes. See also Merklein 1981, 31 who stresses the point that the Baptist's call is typically the Baptist's.
33 See, e.g., Ferguson 1990, lemma Repentance, 780.
34 However, in Mt 3.2 John Baptist is reported indeed to say "Repent, for the kingdom of heaven is at hand", the exact verbatim wording by Jesus in his call (Mt 4.17). Neither Mark nor Luke in the parallels to Mt 3.2 have the announcement of the Kingdom. It appears this is a redactional appendant by Matthew in order to harmonize the words of the Baptist with Jesus.'
For Mt 4.17 some witnesses omit the *metanoeite*: k, sy^{sc} ; Eus.
35 Unlike Crossley 2004, 138.

forgiveness of sins," as contrasted with v.1.15: "Repent, and believe in the good news." (NRSV) Jesus wants to make clear that his message of *metanoia* is different: it refers to an inner change, a transformation of mind, heart and soul, a change brought about by the spirit. Baptism from then onwards is supposed to be an immersing in holy spirit.[36] That is what John himself says about Jesus; it is a break in the continuity from Judaism to Christianity.

> Let us have a further look at the issue of continuity. Did Jesus adopt the traditional rituals of repentance, as a 'righteous' Jew and rabbi would do? Hägerland has made an interesting analysis of the Gospel texts in this respect.[37] He finds that "the historical Jesus took a controversial view on repentance. While sharing the common belief that moral improvement was necessary for sinners, he did not require the traditional rites included in the concept of repentance to be carried out." ... "as these specific rites were incompatible with his message". Among these were public confession of sin, formulaic penitential prayer, fasting, and other bodily penitence. He refers to the story about King Ahab who "rends his clothes, mourns and fasts in sackcloth" (187, 172). Half a century earlier Margarete Hoffer already rejected the idea that *metanoia* should be understood in the sense of the rabbinic *Bussleistung*.[38] Hägerland makes clear that the Lord's prayer clearly sets Jesus' ideas about repentance apart, on two sides. Jesus rejects implicitly the traditional 1st c Jewish rituals[39], while on the other hand not lending any support to "the tendency of the early Church to view God's forgiveness as christologically or sacramentally grounded"[!] (180, also n 53). Reading the logia Hägerland finds that "Jesus thought it sufficient for the sinners to associate with him, and almost certainly to heed his moral preaching" (187), or in my words, to experience his presence, absorb his spirit, and therefore be prepared to transform and act accordingly. In this process the phase of regret and remorse retreats to the background, due to the light that shines on the path ahead. As to fasting Mk is quite explicit that Jesus and his disciples did not fast, contrary to the Baptist and the Pharisees. When questioned Jesus is clear that his presence has a far greater effect in 'repentance' than fasting: how could one fast when being a guest at the wedding banquet? It also refers to the joy of turning to the 'light' rather than being in the dark. The text of 2.20 ("on that day they will fast") "should be taken as a post-Easter addition to the historical core tradition of 2.19" (182f.). Some exegetes reject the continuity hypothesis even more radically. So Merklein,[40] who finds that nowhere the authentic Jesus logia make a call to turn around to the Torah, neither "bemüht Jesus die heilsgeschichtliche Vergangenheit Israels als Berufungsinstanz" (42). So far, so good. Then, however, Merklein takes a different path. His interpretation of Jesus' call for *metanoia* is radically eschatological. His further interpretation is purely classical theology. Both he and I interpret the message of Jesus as unique but in a rather

---

36 See chapter on *pneuma*.
37 Hägerland 2006, 166–87.
38 Hoffer, *Metanoia*. From review in *Theologische Literaturzeitung* 1950, 10, 625f.: "Doch nicht an das rabbinische Verständnis dieses Begriffes knüpft das NT an, sondern an die prophetische Predigt. Nirgens im NT wird *metanoia* im Sinne der rabbinischen *Teschuba* als eigene ‚Bussleistung' des Menschen verstanden .... "
39 Hägerland (2006, 170): "There is the petition for forgiveness in the Lord's Prayer, but it does not conform to the standards of first-century Jewish penitential prayers ..."
40 H. Merklein 1981, 29–46.

opposite sense. My argument is that Jesus took a path different from traditional Jewish understanding and the dominant eschatology.

What about the pericopes with *metanoia* in combination with the mentioning of rituals? ("sackcloth and ashes," Lk 10.13 / Mt 11.20–21), or implying them (Lk 11.32 / Mt 12.41–42)? Here Jesus refers to repenting in Jewish historical traditions. Čabraja[41], on he contrary, sees these pericopes as directly menacing warnings for the impending Judgment, and therefore a call to repentance. I think that Jesus here adapts himself to the Jewish tradition, different from his particular terminology elsewhere. I will discuss these cases in the section on the individual pericopes.

What about the aspects of regret and remorse, seemingly so intimately and inextricably connected with repentance?[42] Two remarks. In the first place we have seen that this connection with regret and remorse is not that strong. Remember how both Lactantius and Tertullian rebel against this strong relationship with *metanoia* which they do not see. The TDNT as well as the analysis by Nave[43] argue that *metanoia* does not necessarily imply much more than just change of mind, particularly change in life conduct, though with at least a touch of a change to the good compared with the present or past; with the possibility of this process to merge into regret or even remorse. Of course Nave and others make clear that apart from the logia *per se* the Lk-Acts narrative finally and essentially focus on the call by Jesus to follow him by transforming one's life's goal and conduct.

The second remark focuses on the positive side of change: not looking back at the wrong but looking forward to a positively rated future. In the first century BCE "changing one's mind [*metanoia*] was often a sign of wisdom and a cause for praise", not only of remorse (Nave p. 46).

Let us try and imagine the situation described in Mk 1.14–15 and Mt 4.17. The audience has gathered in great numbers, having heard of this charismatic rabbi, healer and bringer of what he calls the good message. He tells that the great expectation of the nation is on the verge of being fulfilled, yea, as a matter of fact this man, Jesus, is telling that the expected eschatological Kingdom of God has approached, and therefore is hic et nunc. Does this really mean it is here and not far away in heaven? That it is now and not in the apocalyptic future? His whole being appears to radiate his message. He calls for metanoia, but does not ask to regret, nor does he talk about remorse, let alone about penitence or even penance; no fasting nor sackcloth and ashes, nothing of the well-known Jewish rituals imposed

---

41 Ilija Čabraja 1985, 235.
42 Merklein (1981, 29) refers *metanoia* to the tradition of the OT and Judaism (incorporated in *šûb*) "das allgemein eine Abkehr vom Bisherigen und eine Rückkehr zum Ausgangspunkt beinhaltet."
43 For example 221f.

> upon the penitent. His listeners, spell-bound by Jesus' inspired talk—should we not imagine that Jesus did not leave it at those few words?[44]—get inspired, receiving an inner energy which seems to transform the psyche, involving thinking and feeling, doing and being. In the light of the realization that the Kingdom of God has arrived, or at least is at hand, the audience of Jesus cannot but be impressed by the implication that it is called to radically change in order to be ready either to enter the Kingdom, or that it may enter them: a positive change not necessarily implying concentration on past wrongs, let alone sin, let alone the implied need for penitence or penance. No, in the perspective of such reality and in the presence of Jesus a positive energy starts flowing, pushing aside the past, negative thoughts and feelings, acts and life conduct.

A personal imagination thus, inspired by the scene evoked by the Markan logion, the personality of Jesus, his words and his acts. This argument is clear as to Mk 1.15 par. What about other pericopes, e.g., those with an eschatological flavor? This will be explored further below.

Change, Conversion, Transformation

Is change the correct term for this process or occurrence? In the case of Mk 1.14f / Mt 4.12 the call for change is for a radical change, either a momentary one or along a process, either short or prolonged. What is the object of change? It is the mind, one's outlook (inclination, disposition, German *Gesinnung*, Dutch *gezindheid*), and in its effect on one's life conduct. Is there any relationship with the spirit? Anyhow, it is about the psyche: thinking and feeling, mind and heart. The logia and the related Gospel texts make quite clear that this change is not just change. The call is for a change that is enduring, and affecting one's environment. Should we not call such a radical change transformation? Let us try and see—here and further in this chapter—if 'transformation' is a, if not *the*, appropriate translation of *metanoia*. This is in line with Borg (1997) (see chapter 4) too. It refers to the totality of the psyche.

> Indeed—and this is in advance of chapters 13 and 14—in terms of a psychological process as well as that of spiritual development, turning, and specifically toward the light implies a transformation of the psyche, which in turn naturally involves repentance. However, here repentance has lost its heaviness, its character of being imposed: instead of 'first pay your penalty, only then you will be released', it directs the self to the awareness of the Kingdom of God, which brings light and a state of forgiving and being forgiven (see Part II).

---

44 I refer to the great number of pericopes where the Gospel author simply states that Jesus was teaching, often without any qualification.

What is transformation? Gavender has written an important study on conversion.[45] What is it, also in view of its role in modern religious situations? Is it relevant to *metanoia*?[46]

She focuses on conversion types and conversion cases, the latter in Acts and Epistles. Her typology is a typology of change in terms of the original state of being versus the resultant state of being. She distinguishes three types of change (p. 8-12) within the semantic field of conversion. As we shall see its use for *metanoia* is appropriate. Her typology refers to whether or not the past is cut off by the change, and if not how do they relate? The cells of her typology are alternation, conversion and transformation.

The author describes them as follows, summarized in pages 12–14 and 147–49:

- *Alternation* is "when change grows out of an individual's past behavior"; the past is not rejected and may continue to play a role, but in a (very) different role
  - See the case of the Ethiopian eunuch (Acts 8.26–40) and that of Cornelius (Acts 10.1–9)
- *Conversion* (in fact she calls it : 'pendulum conversion') is "rejection of past convictions and affiliations for an affirmed present and future", "a new commitment and identity": a concept close to traditional repentance
  - See Paul's first conversion (Acts 9). Also the 'to be born from above' or 'anew' in John and 1 Peter, a clear dichotomy between past and present, this reality versus that one: dualism
- *Transformation* is when "a new way of perception forces the radical re-interpretation of the past. (...) the past is (...) reconstructed as part of a new understanding of God and world", "a radical change (...), an altered perception re-interprets both present and past." It is a paradigm change: everything appears in a new light, or rather the former situation appears as a scenery in darkness, or chaos, whilst the new situation is clear, full of light, and with an obviously logical structure
  - See Paul's transformation as referred to by himself Gal 1.11–12 and Philippians 3. Cf *et* R 9.1–5.

To which of these three types *metanoia* belongs?

Metanoia as Transformation

The concept of *metanoia* as understood in this chapter does not match completely to any type of Gavender, but is close to 'transformation.' Superficially it is 'conversion' in the sense of rejecting the past and affirming a

---

45 Gaventa, *From darkness to Light*, Fortress, Philadelphia 1986.
46 "Although a distinction is often drawn between 'to repent' (*metanoein*) and 'to convert' (*epistrephein*) in Luke as elsewhere, the two terms are virtually interchangeable." *Epistrephein* used metaphorically, however, occurs only sparingly in the Gospels, e.g., where Jesus says that those to whom has been given the secret of the kingdom of God, they will see, hear and understand "and turn, and I will heal them" (Mk 4:10–12, par Mt 13:11-15 in a quotation from Isaiah), a major change indeed.

new future life's conduct, often implying some sort of penance to be done. Facing this, *metanoia* in my interpretation does the contrary: the past is not totally rejected.

Therefore the traditional Bible translations, understanding it as 'conversion render it as repentance (or even stronger as *Busse*), as a strong negative feeling—one has been wrong but that now one wants to be different. This awareness may cause a change, sometimes in the form of conversion. This implies that the change comes about through regret and remorse, a looking back and down. The psychological consequence is that the negative tends to prevail. Focusing on the darkness blinds one to the light.

> Metanoia *in my view requires the contrary: looking upward, focusing on the positive': transformation Gavender-style, but less defining, more natural and spiritual. Such a real change or transformation, is caused by light, by a bright perspective that turns one away from the gloomy and heavy-weight past, completely fascinated as one is by the new perspective where everything is renewed. It is the awareness of the presence of the kingdom of God. The past is viewed from a new point of view by which all that one has done 'wrong' appears in a new light. There is a natural state of forgiving and being forgiven. One may smile at what has been done before unwittingly of the reality that has appeared by now*[47]. *In other words: a less Pauline-coloured view.*[48]

> *Rather it refers to the experiences of the mystics across cultures, throughout time (Borg). When one's mind is transformed, thoughts, feelings and deeds will naturally be transformed through this light that sheds a new light on all the past. The past looks different and although one sees things as they were, it is like another scenery. Like a landscape that transforms when the mist dissolves, the miserable rain stops, the dark clouds vanish and the bright sunshine transforms every single element into almost its opposite. One's whole life's perspective is changed; one's life's conduct becomes completely different caused by a different level of consciousness. It is a sort of inner lifting that affects both body and psyche. In that light sorrow may transform into peace, fear into caution, humor into happiness, anger into ardor.*[49]

All that one has done is viewed in a different light now. Transforming therefore is what masters and mystics have been calling for through the ages, among cultures. Transformation implies working on one's psyche, mind and heart and at the same time be open to inspiration and grace from God.

Metanoia then is not eschatological, but *hic et nunc*. Traditional authors do not agree, of course. See Ambrozic 244, Merklin 42, 44; Michiels 75: "dans les évangiles synoptiques la *metanoia* est une notion manifestement

---

47 See also Borg 1997, 34–44.
48 Or Maly (1979) who in analyzing the Hebrew Bible condemns as it were the human being to sin and its dire consequences.
49 Khan 1989–1990, vol. V, 234. Also Van Lohuizen 1996.

eschatologique», and so many others. Also Nave (p. 30) maintains, "In Luke-Acts salvation and repentance work hand in hand." On the other hand, when penitence and *Busse* are implied, *metanoia* of necessity must be very much present-worldly.

I therefore propose transformation of the psyche as an adequate alternative rendering of *metanoia*.

This results into an alternative rendering of Mk 1.14–15, offered as a proposal. Added are the NRSV and the Greek text again of Mk 1.14b-15:

> *Kêrussôn to euaggelion tou theou kai legôn hoti peplêrôtai ho kairos kai êggiken hê basilea tou theou; metanoeite kai pisteuete en tôi euaggeliôi*
>
> Proclaiming the good news of God, and saying, "The time is fulfilled, and the kingdom of God has come near; repent, and believe in the good news." NRSV
>
> *Announcing the (good) Message of God, and saying "The moment is there, and the Kingdom of God has approached [and thus present]; transform [heart and soul], and confide to the Message."* Proposed

Now what is it that one transforms to? What is the ideal one detects? What is the motivating strength and propelling *dunamis* that enables the transforming process? This should be found in Jesus' teachings as a counterpart to the call *Metanoeite!*, as the goal to live up to, as an instrument for change. Is it not going without saying to turn to the Beatitudes? Here Jesus offers the motivating ideal. Here we find ways as for what to 'repent', how to do it, as well as the goal we hope to attain, maybe by grace of the spirit only.

Then the audacious question rises: what is it to be in a transformed state of consciousness, of being?[50] The Beatitudes' central quality is to be *makarios*, mostly rendered as blessed. What is *makarios*? It is blessed and blissful, a state of happiness beyond the usual, an enduring state of 'equiminded' happiness and deep-felt joy. In traditional terms, Hauck (TDNT IV 367) explains: "the distinctive religious joy which accrues to man from his share in the salvation of the kingdom of God," where I interpret salvation as the enduring Presence, as a elevated state of consciousness. Reference is made by Hauck to the change in mind (!) : "men whose mind corresponds in content to the higher law of the kingdom of God."

And how to reach to that blissful state of consciousness? The Beatitudes offer some specified roads to travel upon. One of them requires that one craves for the spirit[51] (v. 3). An other one teaches us to become 'gentle[52] (v. 5). Hungering

---

50   See further in chapter 8 and 9.
51   Poor is to be understood as a mendicant, i.c. for spirit. See chapter 9.
52   See page 155.

and thirsting for righteousness is another way to travel upon (v. 6). Becoming merciful (v. 7), pure in heart (v. 8), a builder of peace (v. 9): each of these wonderful qualities constitute an agent of transformation once it has been discovered as an ideal outside as well as a hidden quality inside. But only on the condition that it is put into motion on the psychological level: a psycho-spiritual process. Each and every one of these qualities can function both as a motivating force and as a goal to attain, in a mutual play of exchange.

Does this rendering of *metanoia* apply to the other pericopes as well? Before answering this question an analysis is needed of the Greek words for sin and forgiveness.

* * *

Sin and Forgiveness

In the Christian Church tradition *metanoia* as repentance is closely tied with sin and forgiveness. Is this Jesus-like? We find it in the call of the Baptist, which contains all four terms: baptism for the forgiving of sins through *metanoia*. What do we find in the logia on this issue? Nowhere does Jesus interconnect these three terms. This is confirmed by e.g. Merklein (1981, 30), rejected, e.g., by Dircksen (1932, 207). So, as to Jesus we can dissociate baptism with sin, forgiveness and *metanoia*. In the Baptist sin and forgiveness appear interrelated.

> The three terms *hamartanô* (to sin) and *hamartêma* and *hamartia* (both: sin) are quite frequent in the NT (43, 4, 173 times, respectively), often connecting sin with forgiveness (*aphiêmi, aphesis*). The Synoptics have sin / to sin 7, 2, 26 times respectively, of which quite a few in the logia. However, nowhere in the Synoptics a link is laid to *metanoia* nor to anything like original sin, penitence or whatsoever. What we find several times are references to inter-human contacts (Lk 17.3–4 / Mt 18.15–18, 21–22) or about the prodigal son (Lk 15.10, 21). Quite often we find cases where a person is healed and Jesus suggestively tells him/her not to sin again. Is this a sign that illness is a punishment for having sinned? On quite a different level are the pericopes about blaspheming against the Holy Spirit (Mt: the Spirit). This will not be forgiven as it is an eternal sin, contrary to all other blasphemies and sins (Mk 3.28–30 / Mt 12.31–33 / Lk 12.10).

Pra-us. TDNT VI (F.Hauck / S.Schultz) a] in Mt 5.5: low, weak (649), b] for 'secular' Greek (645) quite different qualities ar given of persons: mild, friendly, gentle, pleasant (as opposed to hard, rough, violent). As an adjective *pra-us* it indicates "a quiet and friendly composure which does not become embittered or angry at what is unpleasant…. This is an active attitude and deliberate acceptance, not just a passive submission…. Greatness of soul is demonstrated by this superior acceptance…. The sage is tranquil in relation to the acquisition of external goods and honours." And *Langenscheidt* 1993: "sanft, zahm, milde, freundlich, gnädig, gelassen, ruhig."

Remarkable is that Jesus does not give any indication of what he considers to be 'sin,' or 'sinning.' The solution must be that no deed or word in itself is a sin. What makes an action 'sin' is when the action has not reached its target.

TDNT and BDAG give revealing results for these terms. Neither in classical Greek nor in LXX 'sin' needs not refer to the religious domain. The verb means 'not to hit', 'to miss', 'to err', 'to fall short' morally, 'to do wrong'; it refers to an intellectual shortcoming. The *sophos* is the opposite to the sinner (TDNT I, 293), a remarkable and illuminating statement. *Hamartema* is a fault (*Verfehlung*), like similarly *hamartia*. In the NT it is said to stand for "offense against God with a stress on guilt". Is that what the term says? A *hamartolos* is 'someone who misses something, someone inferior, either intellectually or morally', someone who 'has not made it' (TDNT I, 317). The basic thought is 'not hitting', 'missing'. A shortcoming is a condition or fact of failing to reach an expected or required standard of character or performance; it is a defect, an imperfection (*Webster's*). It may be called an inadequacy. As to what a sinner is in the Gospels one could wonder if there is a parallel with today's deprived, downtrodden, underclass people, or with those who have not 'made it'. This may be corroborated by the fact that sinners and collectors are mentioned together (e.g., Lk 15.1, Mt 9:11). 'Sinners' form a category, both in the abstract and identifiably in society. Collectors, for example, belong to the despised, a sort of lower class, ceremonially unclean, hence considered close to the 'sinners' (BGAD 999). Those are the sort of people Jesus cared for, in contrast. Sinning is a personal act; being a collector is belonging to a class of people.

And what about 'forgiving'? In Greek usage it means to release, to let go, to let be (TDNT I 509). It may also mean concepts like to pardon, send off, let alone, remit, forgive, to become free of; also secularly regarding errors, trespasses and offenses; also, in legal use, 'to release someone from a legal relation'. In EWNT I 435–41 (H. Leroy): *aphiêmi*: fortlassen, verlassen, gewähren lassen, erlassen, vergeben, überlassen, gestatten; *aphesis*: Freilassung, Befreiung, Vergebung. It is remarkable when moving to the NT that nobody seems to explain why then the 'official' translation shifts exclusively to forgiveness, leaving alone the many nuanced meanings given earlier. The rendering as forgiveness is alright but one should be aware that it is not a technical or theologically defined term, but a free-moving word from everyday language. We have seen with 'sin' that the use in the Synoptics does not refer primarily to heavy sins. Yet, in quite a few cases parallel words for both concepts is preferable. We will try and see in the next section what this would work out.

Therefore, the association of *metanoia* with sin and its forgiving is not intrinsically justified when analyzing. the *logia* and the Synoptics. This is acknowledged authoritatively by Grundmann. He signalizes in TDNT, "In the Synoptic Gospels it is striking how slight is the role of terms for sin as compared with their application in other parts of the NT" (I 302). Even: "Jesus does not speak of sin," "there are no pronouncements of Jesus on sin as such." "He gave His disciples no doctrine of sin, nor did He engage in profound speculations concerning it" (I 303, 329). Therefore, I conclude that the current association between *metanoia* and sins and their forgiving is *an* interpretation, which plausibly does not originate from Jesus. Looking at the logia tradition the impression of love and a positive faith in the 'good' essence of human nature is predominant: 'good' in the sense of the readiness—or even hidden desire—to answer the call to turn to the light. In the Q sayings the word for sin is missing, except in Lk 17:3-4 where it refers to human shortcomings, as is the word sinner (*hamartôlos*).[53] Even in the logia outside Q the positive attitude in the *metanoia* pericopes is predominant: *metanoia* in view of the kingdom (God's reign) (Mt 4:17), because of the 'good message' (Mk 1:15), the opening given to the 'sinners' (Lk 5:32, 15:7, 10). The character of sin is softened in Lk 17:3, 4 when referring to the normal inter-human relationships (brother to brother).

Shouldn't we understand the Greek for 'sin' in a lighter way than theology does: as shortcoming, as falling short, as failing to reach the goal, not hitting the target, falling short of the ideal or task or standard of values. Compare the parable of the fig tree: the gardener pleads for a renewed chance for the tree bearing fruit next year. The good message is opening new possibilities.

Forgiving, then, implies that we are not necessarily taken to task about it. That our shortcomings are dismissed, that we ourselves may 'let go' what went wrong, trying again for the better, using new opportunities. Moreover, in the Synoptics the call is for *metanoia* in view of the imminence of better times: the reign of God, the good message, rather than a call for *metanoia* for the forgiving of sins.

Then how do we deal with the frequently occurring combination of 'sinners' and tax collectors'? Above we interpreted sinners not as 'sinners' (breaking the law) but as all individuals who have missed the mark, for example socially. The context of 'sinners and collectors' refers to stated categories in the population that are considered to deviate from the path of God, i.e., from the 'divine law' and its institutions. Therefore a sinner in this context is a person who is sinning structurally and therefore to be rejected principally. This is exactly the position that Jesus emphasizes: each individual is a personality not necessarily bad, even if he has a job with a bad general image, but rather each with an inherent scope for betterment. That is what Jesus addresses.[54] In Luke humans are not bad by nature: one is *corrigendus* rather than *salvandus* (Taeger, p. 225). Jesus uses the terminology of his culture and his people, yet rising beyond and opening new perspectives, offering new scope for the oppressed and downtrodden. His terminology is the current one but by his widening the scope of it and by his personality he makes clear that the path of God is an expanded path, not one of institutions. He makes this obvious by joining sinners and tax collectors even in meals. He has not come to call the righteous—those who are

---

53   Except in Q/Lk 7.34 but this is not said in the mouth of Jesus.
54   Carey (2009, chapter 1) points out that people are sometimes labelled as sinful simply because society identifies them as such. *When Jesus forgives sin he does not require repentance* (italics added).

on the path of God: these are with Jesus already if they are sincerely righteous—but to call those who have missed the target, who have fallen short of the ideal. Inner reality need not correspond to the outer rules and regulations of law and custom. The call of the mystic may go right into the heart even of he worst sinner and produce a total transformation.

The Other Logia

The argument in this chapter has been presenting an alternative sense to the key words *metanoia, hamartêma, aphiêmi*. It was convincing for the central logion, Mk 1.14-15 par. How does it hold for the other pericopes?[55]

> Note
>
> In some of these pericopes, and only these (Lk 5.32, 15.7,10, 17.3–4), one finds *metanoia* combined with sin and forgiveness. This low frequency is a remarkable fact in view of Church tradition where repentance, sin and forgiving are closely tied together, and form an important part of orthodox Christian life and doctrine. One would expect Jesus to expand on the topic. But apparently he does not. Of the three Lk 17:3–4 even does not refer to what we tend to see as sin. On the contrary, Jesus refers to daily conduct where Jesus admonishes his disciples how to deal with one another: it is anthropological rather than theological (see also Merklein…, 40). This passage will be discussed later.

Lk 5.32

The main body of the text does not have *metanoia*: "I have come to call not the righteous but the sinners…." (NRSV). It is a text common to all Synoptics, it is only Lk who adds "…to repentance" (*eis metanoian*). It may safely be taken that this addition is redactional,[56] and therefore not authentic: otherwise one or two other evangelists would have included it either. For this reason this pericope is not analysed further. Yet I venture a proposal for an alternative rendering:

> \>\> *I have come to call (for transformation) not the righteous but those who have not made it / the underdog.* \<\<

> Jesus by joining Levi in his home and eating with him offers Levi the unique opportunity to open his eyes and experience the great change brought about by the very presence of Jesus, the transformation of mind and heart, of his life conduct. As Marcus puts it about Jesus' presence," In that new situation holiness rather than sin turns out to be contagious" (I ,231), referring to the anxiety of Pharisees to be in contact with 'sinners.'

---

55 Lk 24.47 is left out of the review as it is a post-Easter logion.
56 "The present structure is clearly a literary one, Luke's own, but based extensively on the Markan construction. The source is entirely Markan." (Nolland 1989, 242).

Lk 13.3, 5

The logion refers to two occasions—otherwise unknown—when many Galileans suffered death. Jesus then tells his audience that unless you people *metanoête* you will all *apoleisthe*. NRSV says in both v. 3 and v. 5, ".... Unless you *repent*, you will all *perish* as they did". Is this what Jesus wants to tell? The text of the pericope implies that it was commonly understood that the Galileans perished because of their sinning. Jesus, however, rejects this idea: they are no more sinners than all of you, that's not the reason. Then, in a play of words, he turns around, saying, "... unless you *transform*, you will all *lose* out." He uses the alternative sense of *metanoeô* and the alternative sense of *apollumi*.[57]

> This appears to threaten the audience 'to repent': otherwise they will 'perish' as well. *Apollumi* suggests death or destruction. However, as we will see in chapter 13 on the *psuchê*, it may also mean to lose. It may refer to what mystics have called the false ego that has to be 'destroyed'. Or rather: to transform the false ego into the real one, the being that was created in God's image. If this does not happen one's soul is 'lost'. On the other hand, a connection between sin and calamity was a firm background of Jewish thought (Nolland 1993, 718). Jesus suggests this connection in order to get people moving.

>>unless you transform, you will all lose out<<

The logion is followed by the parable of the fig tree (Lk 13.6-9), which is barren yet gets the opportunity of flowering by holding out.[58] It appears that taking the verses 3 and 5 per se is justified: "... more originally the material probably lacked narrative setting and is to be seen as teaching by Jesus...."[59]

> What more does the parable of the fig tree teach? What does the fig tree stand for? And the gardener? And the owner? Optionally we could see the tree as representing an individual, as a complete being of body, mind and soul. The gardener is the element inside man who wills, steers, guides and decides; it is related to one's consciousness / conscience, one's psyche (mind, will, heart). The garden or vineyard (!) stands for the Kingdom of God, the owner obviously being God himself, or his representative, Jesus. Thus the whole passage 13.1-9 is as a personal teaching whilst at the same time it addresses humanity.
>
> This interpretation is offered for critical review, not as an absolute outcome of thorough research. It does not do justice to all respected scholars who have worked many other plausible solutions.

Lk 15.7, 10

> Again, two logia with a similar content appear at the closure of two different sort of parables, in the Lukan narrative closely associated. "... there will be more joy in heaven

---

57   See chapter 13.
58   The parallels in Mt 21.19 and Mk 11.12-14 tell a different story.
59   John Nolland 1993, 716f. My interpretation, of course, is not Nolland's.

over one sinner who repents than over ninety-nine righteous persons who need no repentance" (v. 7), and "... there is joy in the presence of the angels of God over one sinner who repents" (v. 10). The narrative context is the Pharisees' grumbling about Jesus' association with 'sinners.'

The story is about a lost sheep that is recovered and about a lost coin that is found again. The morale is the heavenly joy over the repentance of a sinner.[60] I find the connection illogical. What then? On the one hand I take the narrative part as authentic. They rather evoke the meaning of some Kingdom logia[61]: seek the lost object, one does not know where to find. The search for it overrules all other pursuits. It stands for the inner treasure. Finding it evokes immeasurable joy. The object lost was a minor thing, yet the joy of returning overriding. On the other hand the closing logia, the morale, looks redactional. The solution obviously lies in the translation of repentance and of sinner. The sinner is the one who has lost something essential. Repentance is the great change of making the effort of going and finding. a *hamartolos* is someone who has missed the target, i.e. who has lost what he wanted to achieve. *Metanoia* is the great change brought about by effort, changing the situation and bringing about the restoration of the loss. This transformation is the great joy. The return from darkness to light.

>>*There will be more joy [in heaven[62]] over one person who has fallen short but who changes his mind-and-heart than over ninety-nine righteous persons who need not change*>>

Lk 17.3-4

In this pericope Jesus draws the concept of sin right into daily life. Jesus speaks to the disciples: "If your brother sins (*hamartêi*), rebuke (*epitimêson*) him, and if he repents (*metanoêsei*), forgive (*aphes*) him" (NRSV). And he continues that even if this happens seven times, forgive him seven times.

Here, a *hapax*, sin, repentance and forgiveness appear together in a concise way. And in a refreshing situation: without any trace of the eschaton, without pending Judgment, without threats of punishment, just an everyday situation among the disciples. Jesus admonishes them to be fair to one another, and to other 'brothers'. Should we not then tone down the translated terminology as well? If sinning just means missing the mark, then repentance should turn to

---

60 Funk 1993 finds the two parables authentic and haling from the oral tradition whilst the morale logia would be redactional.
61 Th 107 has a text close to the Lk text, It indeed refers this logion to the Kingdom: "The Kingdom is like a shepherd who had a hundred sheep, etc.
62 I put 'heaven' in brackets referring to Mt 18.13: "... he rejoices over it ...": no mentioning of heavenly joy.

change, or here even just 'sorry'. And forgiving turns into let go or, indeed, 'forgiving.'

Here 'sin' clearly is of a different nature, it is more in the sense I advocate: falling short. Repenting is more like, saying sorry, or if it is some grave thing: changing one's mind, transforming. Forgiving more like let go. Rebuking (*epitimaô*, LS II 2) rather means just to blame, reprove, find fault with. Hence:

>> If your brother misses the mark, blame him
And if he says sorry, let it go<<

Lk 10.13 /Mt 11:20-21 and Lk 11.32 / Mt 12:41-42

The tone of these pericopes and their content stand in stark contrast to Mk 1.14-15 and many others. These pericopes strongly suggest to belong to the eschatological logia tradition. Apart from that, the authenticity may be questioned.

> The Jesus Seminar[63] suggests that condemnation is not in line with other sayings by Jesus, and therefore these pericopes may have been influenced by later Christian prophets (181). There is consensus this pericope 10.13 to be part of Q, which suggests an early origin. However, Mack[64] as well as Kloppenborg[65] classify it under a second and later version and 11.32 even to a later, third redaction layer (Kloppenborg 138). Kloppenborg sees 10.13-15 as "editorial intrusions". On the other side Merklein considers both Lk 10.13 and 11.20 etc as authentic.

Being eschatological they are not spelled out here: I propose neither an alternative understanding nor an alternative translation. Only a few side remarks.

In Lk 10.13 par Jesus reproaches two towns that had not responded to 'the deeds of power (NRSV)[66] (*dunameis*, pl.) done in you', and he refers to the Kingdom of God having approached and being present therefore. Yet, what is *dunamis*?[67] Elsewhere we have found it suggests something like spirit. Is it the spirit of the Kingdom that has been done in them? Obviously the population of these towns had not taken it. This passage might be ascribed to the inner tradition (with *metanoia* as transformation of mind-and-heart, of one's life style), were it not encapsulated with eschatological exclamations: "*ouai!*" (woe), and Jesus adds that it would have suited them "to have repented...sitting in

---

63 Funk 1993.
64 Mack 1993.
65 Kloppenborg Verbin, *Excavating Q*, 2000.
66 NIV: the miracles, Nolland 1993: idem.
67 BDAG: indicates 'a potential, [and therefore often rendered as power, WvL]), an ability to carry out, a capacity. Is often related to the doing of miracles. Any relationship to spirit?

sackcloth and ashes"[68]. In this context *metanoia* means repentance, clearly in the Jewish tradition of repentance including penitence. Lk 11.32 par stands in the same line. Jesus addresses an assembled crowd as 'an evil generation'; at judgment it will be condemned: the people of Nineveh did repent when Jonah gave a sign, this generation does not repent even with the Son of Man present as the sign.[69]

The proposed interpretation of the key terms *metanoia/metanoein*, *hamartanô* and *aphiêmi* has been confirmed for the 'other' logia as well.

Conclusions

The perspectives adopted in this paper have resulted in some interesting outcomes.

The focus on the Jesus *logia* gives a fresh look at the concept of *metanoia*. The general understanding of *metanoia* as related to sin, of *metanoein* as related to sinning has been undermined. Mostly it is considered a concept in the field of repentance and penitence, rather heavily charged with theological concepts. There is even a tone of the eschaton discernable.

The hypothesis that the concept rather is to be understood psychologically and interpreted spiritually has found firm grounds in the logia with the terms. Consequently a refreshed look has emerged where *metanoia* appears as a positive concept, an invitation to change of mind-and-heart, a transformation of the psyche.

Application of this alternative terminology has produced interesting and challenging outcomes in terms of alternative translations. New perspectives for understanding the message of Jesus have emerged.

Transformation is a process including both aspects: looking back in regret but taking up the challenge of changing one's mentality, looking happily into the new bright future. It focuses on the *hic et nunc* rather than referring to eschatology.

Overviewing the totality of what Jesus said about the semantic field we have explored, it is striking how small is the attention Jesus gave to the topic. So scant is the number of sayings, so few his wordings. If compared to what theology has inflated it into, to what the Church has taught people—these are a few words. These scant words, however, need to be taken to heart: it is the inner transformation, opening up to the message, to be receptive to the words of Jesus.

It is in this understanding the *metanoia* relates to mysticism.

---

68 Nolland 1993, 556.
69 The traditional interpretation of not recognizing the Kingdom as represented by Jesus is a bit far sought. For the same tradition supposes these works to refer to his healings.

>>*The time is fulfilled,
and the Kingdom of God has approached [and thus present];
transform [heart and soul],
and trust in the Message*<<

>>*Unless you transform, you will all lose out*<<

>>*There will be more joy over one person
who has fallen short but who changes his mind-and-heart
than over ninety-nine righteous persons who need not change*>>

>> *If your brother misses the mark, blame him
and if he says sorry, let it go*<<

Chapter Twelve
Laying Down One's Life? 'The Good Shepherd' and Other Pericopes in John: *"tên psuchên tithêmi"*

Introduction[1]

The author of the Gospel of John in 15.12–17 reports about the teaching by Jesus on love and the ensuing discussion with Peter: the love of the Father for Jesus, the love of Jesus for the disciples, the love among the disciples for one another, the love of the disciples for Jesus:

> My command is this: Love each other as I have loved you. (12) Greater love has no one than this, that he lay down his life for his friends" (*hina tis tên psuchên autou thêi huper tôn philôn autou*) (13) You are my friends if you do what I command. (14) (…)…. I have called you friends, (15a) (…), and appointed you to go and bear fruit, fruit that will last (16b) (…) This is my command: Love each other. (17)

And a little earlier in the narrative, Jesus had said (John 13:34–38):

> A new command I give you: Love one another. I have loved you, so you must love one another. By this all men will know that you are my disciples, if you love one another. (34) By this all men will know that you are my disciples, if you love one another. (35) (…) Peter asked: Lord, why can't I follow you now? I will lay down my life for you. (37) Then Jesus answered: Will you really lay down your life for me? I tell you the truth: before the rooster crows, you will disown me three times! (38)

The author of 1 John says similar things in his letter on love (1 John 3.11–17):

This is a revised version of a paper read at SBL International Meeting, Cambridge, UK, 2003.

1   Throughout this paper all references and quotations in Greek will refer to Aland, Kurt, Black, Matthew, Martini, Carlo M., Metzger, Bruce M., and Wikgren, Allen, *The Greek New Testament*. Bibelgesellschaft Stuttgart) 1983 (Logos Bible Software 2.1D).

Throughout this paper the NIV translation is used, unless mentioned otherwise: *The Holy Bible, New International Version*, Int. Bible Soc., East Brunswick, NJ 1984 and/or *The New International Version*, Zondervan Publishing House, Grand Rapids, MI 1984 (Logo Bible Software 2.1d). By way of comparison reference is sometimes made to Darby 1890, ASV 1901, KJ 1769, NCV 1991, NLT 1996, NRSV 1989.

> (...) we should love one another. (11b) (...) We know that we have passed from death to life, because we love our brothers. Anyone who does not love remains in death. (14) (...) This is how we know what love is: Jesus Christ laid down his life for us. And we ought to lay down our lives for our brothers. (16) If anyone has material possessions and sees his brother in need but has no pity on him, how can the love of God be in him? (17)

In the Good Shepherd pericopes (John 10.11–18) we find similar texts:

> I am the good shepherd. The good shepherd lays down his life for the sheep.(11) (...) The reason my Father loves me is that I lay down my life—only to take it up again.(17) No one takes it from me, but I lay it down of my own accord. I have authority to lay it down and authority to take it up again. This command I received from my Father.(18)

Jesus speaks about love to one another, about love to one's friends, and about dedication to the ones dependent on you. The highest mode to show this love and dedication: what is it? Can one imagine this is by laying down one's life? Or could the phrase bear a different meaning?

The terminology used is *tithêmi tên psuchên autou huper tinos*.[2] Literally it means something like 'putting one's *psuchê* for somebody.' What does it mean at other places? Unfortunately there are no other NT pericopes with this phrase: it is unique to these pericopes (Maurer, TDNT VIII, 155). Most current translations exhibit a *communis opinio*: invariably the phrase is rendered as presented above: laying down one's life, i.e., willingly giving one's life, dying willingly. Theology takes these pericopes as alluding to Jesus' death and preluding martyrdom.

In close reading one finds contradictions and improbabilities. Would it not be more reasonable for the shepherd to stay alive and devote himself to the sheep wholeheartedly and in dedication?[3] And when the disciples are loving one another, should they not rather take care of one another in view of the mission Jesus has entrusted them with? How can they go and bear fruit (*kerygma*)—fruit that will last (v. 16b)—if they should die? And how would someone with material possessions take pity of his brother in need by laying down his life? And when Peter says he wants 'to offer his life,' Jesus only answers that Peter will disown him, nothing more, nothing less.

Supreme love. I rather suggest that this *psuchên tithêmi* is nothing but to give one's heart and soul, to offer it, to dedicate it whole-heartedly, to put one's

---

2 Some important mss (P45, S*, D and others) have δίδωμι (*didômi*) instead of τίθημι. Kowalski and other authors prefer the latter version, which is the Nestlé-NA27's. Kowalski argues that *tithêmi* fits better as it contains the unique Johannine phrase 'to lay down one's life.' For our argument the issue is of no importance.
3 Lightfoot (1956, 206) is one of the rare authors who wonder about the shepherd's laying down his life: "... it is not the duty of every shepherd to give his life on behalf of his charge".

full will, to take a direction in life, to dedicate one's life on behalf of someone. Mystics have often referred to the experience that by giving one's self one gains the spirit, or Self in some traditions: by whole-heartedly focusing completely and single-mindedly on 'the other one,' or 'the other One,' one's self may be transformed. This is what in my view the pericopes on *psuchên tithêmi* are transmitting to the reader. And we will come to the same conclusion in the other case, saving or losing. See the following chapter.

Finally, in view of this argument it is striking that throughout the literature on the subject not a single author has been found who discusses in principle this translation of the phrase,[4] let alone questioning this understanding. Even both Dautzenberg and Simonis ignore the issue.

In chapter 10 it was learnt that *psuchê* should be viewed as self, psyche or mind-and-heart rather than as life. It was suggested that this has implications for several logia, like the ones at order here. So the issue is to trace the meaning of the phrase *tên psuchên tithêmi* as a whole, as well as of the two constituent terms *psyche* and *tithêmi* in the context of the respective logia. The current interpretation—relating it with crucifixion[5] and resurrection—will be ignored initially and then challenged. We will see that the meaning 'laying down one's life' is not unambiguous. An alternative meaning will be proposed, 'to dedicate [or: devote] one's self (or oneself). This will result in a phrase like Jesus asking his disciples to love one another by dedicating heart and soul to one another. And that Peter says that he will dedicate himself with heart and soul to Jesus. And that the shepherd dedicates his self to the sheep. Then this result will be checked in the context of the pericopes (including a look at the related terms *lambanô, airô, exousia, entolê*).[6]

On the basis of the findings an alternative interpretation and translation will be proposed for the pericopes under review, as an alternative to the current one. In this exercise I will leave the theological and other implications aside. The results are to be seen as a possible alternative rather than as a substitution, and

---

4   Even the great works on the Shepherd Discourse do not question the current interpretation nor do they go into the why of the current translation of the phrase. E.g., Simonis 1967, Beutler c.a. 1991, Kowalski 1996. I could not lay hands on Kiefer 1967 and Tragan 1980. From Kowalski's treating these authors I guess they share the attitude of the others on this matter. Kowalski, who gives a full account of the literature on the shepherd pericope, does not refer to any author questioning the issue brought up in this paper (5–27). Nor is the issue mentioned as one of the open issues (27–31). Neither do commentaries like Lightfoot 1956 or Barrett 1978 question this interpretation.
5   To give just one instance of the self-evident relation: Barrett 1978, 374.
6   Elsewhere in the Gospels we find pericopes also referring to life: saving or losing or finding or loving it, hating and keeping it. Chapter 13 will argue that also here a translation as self or psyche has to be taken into account as an alternative to be considered. See Mk 8.35–37, Mt 16.24–26, Lk 9.24–25, Jn 12.25.

are presented for discussion. The point is to check the feasibility of this proposal is an alternative, not necessarily as the best one. The underlying philosophy is that spiritual texts have different meanings at the same time.

What Is the Meaning of *psuchê* and *tithêmi*?

The expression *tên psuchên tithêmi* is a rarity in the NT. In the canonical Gospels we find the phrase *psuchên tithêmi* almost exclusively in John, in three pericopes: 10.11–18, 13.37–38, and 15.13, besides one instance in the Epistles, in 1 J 3.16. In the synoptic Gospels only Mark 10.43–45 (par Mt 20.28) has a similar yet different phrase: *didômi tên psuchên*, to give one's *psuchê*. We find the phrase a few times in LXX as well. References will be given below.

In this section the two constituent terms will be examined. For *psuchê* a short summary will suffice, referring to the previous chapter.

Psuchê[7]

Let us summarize the main line of the earlier chapter 10. NIV—as do most translations—mostly renders it as 'life' throughout the Gospels. However, in some cases it is translated as 'soul': as opposed to body (Mt 10:28), finding rest for one's soul (Mt 11:29), Jesus' soul is overwhelmed with sorrow (Mt 26:38 par), to forfeit one's soul (Mk 8:36), soul pierced by a sword (Lk 2:35). So it is not out of the way to render it by 'psyche' or an equivalent: there is no necessity to translate it by 'life.' Laurin [!] (1961, 132–33) shows how the NT sometimes presents *psyche* as a recognizable part of the human being, and not as the total being, or as life.

> This book does not have an a priori as to a separate identity of the psyche, a dichotomy between the body and the psyche, like in Greek culture, esp. Platonism.[8] Yet even when accepting the unity of body and psyche (and spirit?) in the human being, these aspects may be identified separately and discussed as such. We distinguish these three aspects. One is the non-physical mental and emotional side, called the psyche (*psuchê*), the aspect of mind and heart, of thinking and feeling, or soul. Another the physical side, the body (*sôma*) or flesh (*sarx*). And the third the spiritual side, the spirit (*pneuma*), sometimes seen as part of human nature, sometimes outside it, often considered divine

---

[7] There is a fairly extensive literature on *psuchê*. Under References some of the titles are to be found, like Aland 1998, Blanc 1996, Boyd 2000, Claus 1981, Dörrie 1984, Dussaud 1945, Füglister 1980, Kremer 1984, Kuhn 1952/53, Laurin 1961, Lys 1966, Osei-Bonsu 1987, Scharbert 1872, Schmid 1962. See chapter 10. In this chapter our focus is on the phrase *psuchên tithêmi* about which the literature is scant.

[8] Bible scholars are hesitant to translate *nephesh* by 'soul' as it might be confused with the Platonic soul: the immortal and divine part of man, the self as a center or microcosm of his whole being (Claus 1981).

or sacred. Thus the psyche is conceived as the non-material (non-physical) as well as the non-spiritual aspect of the human being. It may also be rendered by 'self,' 'soul,' 'mind,' 'psyche,' or 'heart and soul' ('to put one's heart and soul into something') as its more colloquial equivalent.

The conclusion is that an alternative rendering of *psuchê* is permitted, depending on the context.

Tithêmi

Let us have a look at *tithêmi* then, both *per se* and together with *psuchê*. Maurer in TDNT VIII 152–57 finds different meanings but not 'laying down (sc. one's life)', except in these specific pericopes, he says. Is there compelling reason then to maintain this specific translation here? In local sense *tithêmi* means 'to put', etc., Maurer says. In classical Greek *tithêmi*, in the metaphorical or transferred sense, refers to positive things like 'to establish', 'to bring to a specific state', 'to bring about', 'to institute', 'to make' (152), meanings which are close to my interpretation. Maurer submits that neither in profane Greek nor elsewhere in the NT does this verb convey anything like 'to lay down (one's life).'

Tên psuchên tithêmi

Notwithstanding these findings Maurer in TDNT finally does opt for 'laying down one's life' for the phrase *tên psuchên tithêmi*, but he does exhibit his hesitations: "The Greek-Hellenistic parallels, which use *tithêmi* all denote taking a risk rather than full sacrifice of life" (155). Apart from these direct parallels, Maurer summarizes that nowhere else is there any reference from which to derive that, in combination with *psuchê*, this phrase could mean anything like 'laying down one's life', 'sacrificing', 'giving something', neither in profane Greek nor anywhere else in the NT (where the verb itself occurs no less than 101 times).

Nevertheless, when Maurer discusses the John texts, not being able to refer to any parallel for his interpretation, he maintains: "Yet the emphasis in all these verses is on the actual sacrifice of life, ... to depart, to give or to offer up one's life. John thus adopts the form of the Greek phrase *tithêmi tên psuchên* but gives it a new sense...." (156) [*Sic*]. The Greek, he admits, uses other terms for the actual sacrifice of life: *ekpneô, aphiêmi, proballô, proteinô* (155). There is no text found from which to ascertain that 'laying down' would be the correct translation. Interestingly nowhere in literature is the challenge named, let alone taken up, i.e. to critically view the meaning of *tithêmi* in the given context.

What is it that Jesus Wants to Communicate?

Let us return to the current translation in John 10, 13 and 15. What are the implications of the shepherd laying down his life? Should it not be a disaster indeed if the shepherd would seriously risk and sacrifice his life and cončsequently die? Would he not rather direct his thinking and feeling, his whole psyche, his actions, to the well-being of his flock. Yes indeed, he does devote his life to the flock. Here life is used not as an antithesis to death but rather as an intention, the motivation of one's life here in the world, or more deeply: one's whole-hearted devotion to a higher purpose. That is what the shepherd does, that is what Jesus does to mankind. That is the implicit call to humanity.

As to Jn 13 and 15, is it not a call to love life in order to care for one's fellow-beings? The words of Jesus form a flow of love to his disciples, calling for the same flow from each disciple to each other, love as an obvious sign of being a disciple of Jesus.

The context of the phrases in Jn 13 and 15 is clear: Jesus addresses his disciples preparing them for their task in the Message: love, dedication, friendship.

For J 13:37–38:

Peter asked, "Lord, why can't I follow you now? I will dedicate my self to you."

Then Jesus answered, "Will you really dedicate your self to me? I tell you the truth, before the rooster crows, you will disown me three times!

For J 15:13:

Greater love has no one than this, that he dedicates his self to his friends (or: beloved ones).

In J 15:13 Jesus in his great speech says, "Greater love has no one than this, that he dedicates his mind and heart, his whole self to his friends". In v.12 Jesus had just told his disciples to love each other as he had loved them. It does not appear reasonable that this would mean that he requires someone to die for his friends, as a rule of life. It would not be a good advice too in view of the good Message to be spread by these very disciples.

There is another pericope related to this one, in 1 J 3. It has to be viewed in context. It is preceded by a long text on the importance of love, especially about love among one another ("We should love one another" [v. 11b], "we love our brothers" [v. 14a]). Would the author in v. 16b really argue that the addressed community is required to give their physical lives for one another? Why should that be? What use would this have? It stands in contrast, or even contradiction, to the immediately following v. 17, "If anyone has material possessions and sees his brother in need but has no pity on him, how can the love of God be in him?" It refers to life, to daily life, and not to death. The sequence appears as illogical unless 16b is read as 'dedicating one's self.'

The 'Good Shepherd'

As to Jn 10 a closer look at the text is necessary. Does the interpretation of *psuchên tithêmi* hold when it is placed in the wider logion context? Here are the relevant phrases for our study of *psuchê*, in NIV translation.[9]

For Jn 10

"I am the gate; whoever enters through me will be saved (*sôizô*)" (v. 9).

"… I have come that they may have life (*zôê*), and have it to the full" (v. 10.b).

"I am the good shepherd. The good shepherd lays down his life (*psuchê*!) for the sheep" (v. 11).

"I am the good shepherd (v. 14)…and I lay down my life (*psuchê*!) for the sheep" (v. 15b).

"The reason my Father loves me is that I lay down my life (*psuchê*!)—only to take it up (*lambanô*) again" (v. 17).

"No one takes it (*airô*) from me, but I lay it down of my own accord (*ap'emautou*) (v. 18a).

"I have authority (*exousia*) to lay it down and authority to take it up again (v. 18b).

"This command (*entolê*) I have received (*lambanô*) from my Father" (v. 18c).

What does Jesus communicate? The so-called Good Shepherd 'narrative' is really speaking an extended logion, like others in Jn also. We, therefore, may take it as it is, leaving out the context.

What does it stand for? Here is an annotated alternative rendering:

I am the gate; whoever enters through me will be saved. This saving implies that through Jesus one will be transformed, be in spirit, enter the Kingdom, transform from *psuchikos* into *pneumatikos*: one's spirit gets the upper hand over the psyche.

I have come that they may have Life and have it to the full. Zôê, in the words of Jesus, refers to everlasting life, without limits, continuous: the life of the Kingdom of God, of the Spirit, which will envelop one.[10]

I am the devoted shepherd. The devoted shepherd dedicates his self heart and soul to the sheep, in other words he devotes his psyche, he does so with heart and soul, wholeheartedly. Jesus makes clear he is the one through whom one is saved toward everlasting life, the Kingdom of God, the Spirit, i.e. having Life and to the full. This is so while

---

9   The remaining verses are not central to the understanding of *psuchê*, and to some degree to the intent of the logion. Large parts of Jn 10.1–21 do not contribute to the essential message that is visible in the pericopes analyzed.
10 See also Jn 6.63a,b.

Jesus takes care, by dedicating himself to his followers. He dedicates his self, purifying it by selfless care, and thus regaining it renewed.

There is empathy, there is sympathy, a caring atmosphere, full of love. That is why God loves the shepherd: *the reason why my Father loves me is that I dedicate my self, so that I may receive it again,*[11] i.e., transformed. This implies that one receives back in return one's (transformed) psyche (or: self, or: mind and heart), i.e., I give myself and I get it back transformed. This is the spiritual process: giving all that one has implies receiving a gift greater than what one has offered. Or, if Delling (TDNT IV, 5) is to be followed: I dedicate my mind and heart in order to control it again and again, i.e. more on the level of the psyche itself.

Nobody upsets me, nothing disturbs me, I keep my attunement but I dedicate my self on my own initiative knowing my Father's will. I have the capacity to dedicate my self and I have the capacity to regain it. That assignment I received from my Father.

Summary

Here is my alternative proposal for Jn 10.9a, 10b, 11, 14a, 15b, 17, 18

I am the gate; whoever enters through me will be saved.

I have come that they may have Life and have it to the full.

I am the devoted shepherd. The devoted shepherd dedicates his self / heart and soul to the sheep.

I am the devoted shepherd, I dedicate my self to the sheep.

The reason why my Father loves me is that I dedicate my self / heart and soul, so that I may receive it again.

Nobody upsets me, but I dedicate my self on my own initiative. I have the capacity to dedicate my self / heart and soul and I have the capacity to regain it. That assignment I received from my Father.

My proposal is based on a semantic analysis and leads to fascinating results. I do not enter into a discussion with the persistent literature on the Good Shepherd pericope, invariably considered a sort of narrative[12] and mostly seen as a metaphor for the Savior[13]; Dautzenberg and the Dutch cardinal Simonis are noteworthy representatives. Generally the pericope of Jn 10.1–21 is taken as a whole, sometimes (Lewis) in an even wider context including 9.39–41 about

---

11   *Palin* according to the Bauer/Aland has the following principal meanings: 1 back; 2 again (return to a previous activity); 3 again, once more, anew; 4 furthermore, thereupon (connecting things that are similar); on the other hand, in turn.

12   Lewis particularly takes the pericope 9.39–10.21 as a whole, taking it as a literal unit.

13   Some of the relevant titles (alphabetically ordered): Bailey 1993, Dautzenberg 1966, Kiefer 1967, Kowalski 1996, Lewis 2008, Neyrey 2001, Rêgopulos 1989, Sabbe 1991, Schenke 1996, Simonis 1967, Thiagarajah 2001, Tragan 1980, Turner 1991.

judgment. Neither of them takes account of the term *psuchê*, taking for granted that it means life.

Comments

Psuchê and *zôê* (v. 10b, 11)

The English translation creates confusion by rendering two different Greek words (*zôê*, *psuchê*) by one English (life) in two consecutive sentences: Jesus has come to give life (*zôê*) to his followers / people (the sheep) whilst laying down his life (*psuchê*) for the same ones.

My proposal: he gives life being the door because by entering through that door one is saved. He does so by dedicating his self, i.e. with 'heart and soul' to the sheep.

To take: v. 17 and 18a. In two consecutive sentences the same verb 'to take' occurs, first as 'to take it up', the other as 'to take from'. In Greek two different verbs are used *lambanô* and *airô*.

And take it up again (v. 17, 18b)

The *psuchên tithêmi* in v. 17 is immediately followed by another phrase: *palin lambanô tên psuchên*: 'only to take it up again,' generally interpreted in the light of crucifixion and resurrection: laying down one's life and retaking it, respectively.

What would this phrase indicate in the alternative proposed?

Lambano occurs in two different combinations in this pericope: with *psuchê* and with *entolê* (v. 18b and 18c). *Lambano* has two main meanings: 'to take' and 'to receive.'[14] The second, he says, is dominant esp. in theologically significant verses, "to some extent in marked contrast to G(ree)k religion and to Judaism". We find it in v.18c: *tauten tên entolên elabon para toû patros mou*: 'that assignment (rather than 'command') I received from my Father.'

This supports an alternative interpretation: to dedicate one's mind and heart (to the sheep) (sc. in the name of God) and to receive back in return one's psyche (one's mind and heart), transformed and purified, as a gift from God: to give one's self and to receive 'it' again: the self that is given is the 'limited' (or 'natural' or 'unreal') self, whilst the self that is received again is the spiritual or 'real' self: in Pauline terms the former is *psuchikos* and the latter *pneumatikos*, the 'mind-self' and the 'spirit-self' (apart from the 'body-self' (*soma, sarx*). In that interpretation it would run as follows, 'I give my self and I get it back transformed, i.e. in a refreshed, renewed, purified form. By devoting oneself with heart and soul one forgets one's ego and receives energy, one feels revivified.

---

14 Delling in TDNT IV, 5 sqq. Delling (p.6) offers a further scope. He gives as a frequent meaning of *lambanô* also 'to kill'. This might suggest another psycho-spiritual interpretation: to kill the psyche is to subordinate it to the spirit, to take it in hands. I.e., a mystical process in the sense of inner purification. So then it would translate as: 'I dedicate my mind and heart in order to kill it, i.e. to control it again and again' (*palin*),14 i.e., by one's spirit. This is in line with some types of spirituality where mortification of either body or mind, or of both, is advocated.

This much for v. 17.

In v.18b the phrase returns in a slightly different form: *exousian echô theinai autên, kai exousian echô palin labein autên*, generally translated like 'I have authority to lay it down and authority to take it up again'. We see that the noun *exousia* is translated as 'authority'. Förster (TDNT II, 562–63), however, gives for the ordinary Greek usage two meanings: 'ability to perform an action' (though not as an intrinsic ability, he adds) next to 'the right to do something....' Thus both 'ability' and 'power' appear as possible translations, and are in place here. One might also say 'capacity'; this is a good alternative. So we may consider the rendering of this pericope as 'I have the capacity (power) to dedicate my self and I have the capacity (power) to regain it. Barrett (1978, 377) makes it even simpler: "*exousian echô* in John means little more than *possum* (I can)", and therefore should not be given too much meaning That assignment (*entolê*) (rather than 'command' or 'authority') I, Jesus, have received from my Father (v. 18c).

The verb *airô*

Then one more thing in relation to *lambanô*. In v.18a another verb occurs in combination with *psuchê*: *airô*: *oudeis airei autên ap'emou*) (NIV: no one takes it from me). The primary meaning of *airô* is 'to take up' or 'to take away' (whether or not with *apo*). So both verbs generally are translated with 'to take', in one or the other form. However, the same *airô*, though in a different context, returns in the same chapter only a few verses later (10:24: "The Jews gathered around him, saying, 'How long will you keep us in suspense? If you are the Christ, tell us plainly'"). In Greek: *heôs pote tên psuchên hêmôn aireis?*). Literally it is 'to take someone's psyche', 'to occupy someone's mind'. In NIV it is taken in the sense of, 'How long will you upset our minds? if you are the Christ, tell us plainly.' I therefore prefer to interpret v.18a rather differently but closer to the Greek, as follows: 'Nobody upsets my psyche ('takes my psyche from me'), i.e., I do not allow that others control my thoughts and feelings so that I lose control over myself but by my own will I dedicate myself with heart and soul'.

The 'good' shepherd

What does the adjective *kalos* convey? The shepherd is described here as someone who does all and everything for his flock. So he is skilful, excellent, noble, totally dedicated[15], rather than (morally) good: *kalos* rather than *agathos* (good, fine moral character [Swanson, *Dictionary*]). This is important and corroborates our interpretation of these pericopes. My proposal is 'devoted' as it refers to all these qualities.

The word *palin*

is here not Bauer/Aland's "2 *again, once more, anew*" but rather its "1 *back*—a. w. verbs of going, sending, turning, calling etc." or "b. in phrases that denote a falling back into a previous state or a return to a previous activity." Here it contrasts the dedicating on

---

15 Cf. Bauer/Aland for *kalos*: "unobjectionable, blameless, excellent" (*kalos*,3c). Neyrey (2001) too rejects 'good', as the opposite of *kalos* is evil, *ponêros*). *Kalos*, according to Neyrey, is to be understood in terms of the cultural value of honor and shame, to be translated as 'noble.' Neyrey puts it into the context of the noble death, which of course is not a necessary corollary. The deeds of the shepherd are noble in that he dedicates his heart and soul to the sheep. Yet we propose 'devoted' as it combines the excellent of Bauer/Aland with the noble of Neyrey.

the one hand and the regaining or receiving back on the other hand. The prefix 're-' could be a correct rendering.

The word *hina*

NIV is rather free in rendering it as 'only to take it up again'. NRSV takes it as final: 'in order to. I propose 'so that' expressing an explicit natural relationship. Giving implies receiving. Bauer/Aland does not refer to this pericope in this lemma. Sub I it says: "in final sense to denote purpose, aim, or goal *in order that, that.*" It denotes an intentional relationship between the dedicating and the regaining rather than a causal one. In Hellenistic Greek the sense of purpose is weakened (Barrett 1978, 377).

'Self'

is to be understood as the *psuchê*: psyche, mind and heart, heart and soul. It refers to the 'lower' self as opposed to the 'real' self, which is given in grace through spiritual illumination, *metanoia*, baptism, rendering one's self (oneself) to Christ. In other words: by dedicating one's mind and heart one is no more focused on the self but rather using it as an instrument. Therefore it is sometimes said that one loses it, or annihilates it— only to find it, save it, receive it back purer, in a transformed state.

In J 10:18 this difference is suggested rather than explicated: in v.18a Jesus states that he dedicates his psyche; through this full dedication with heart and soul in v.18b he receives back, or regains, his self from God in a transformed form.

Conclusion: To Dedicate

The scope of this chapter has been twofold, one, to check the meanings of *psuchên tithêmi*, both *per se* and in the given contexts of the pericopes under scrutiny. The second objective has been to propose an alternative translation and to test whether the concomitant interpretation of the text may hold in terms of common sense in the wider context.

What can we conclude? Linguistically there is no need to translate this phrase as tradition has it. Neither could we find any decisive objection to our proposal. There is no single passage where *psuchên tithêmi* must by necessity be translated as 'to give (or: to lay down) one's life'. Rather it appears far more reasonable to interpret the phrase as dedicating one's self (or: one's psyche), giving oneself with heart and soul (or: wholeheartedly) to something or somebody. The shepherd does not die but rather dedicates his self with heart and soul to the sheep. In the other pericopes Peter intends to do everything for Jesus, and Jesus calls for mutual friendship among his disciples like God loves him, that they may dedicate their psyches to one another in love.

Therefore, our hypotheses have held out. It is here offered for discussion.

Chapter Thirteen
To Lose One's *psuchê*, or to Save It?

For whoever wants to save his psuchê
will lose it
But whoever loses his psuchê *(...)*
will save it
                Mk 8:35 NIV

Hos gar ean thelêi tên puchên autou sôsai
apolesei autên
hos d'an apolesei tên psuchên autou (...) sôsei autên
                Mk 8.35

* * *

Chapter 10 has provided the insight that psuchê does not necessarily stands for 'life'. Chapter 12 has illustrated this with two cases in Jn, both with the phrase tên psuchên tithêmi: *the devoted shepherd does not lay down his life on behalf of the sheep but dedicates his self to them. The disciples do not out of love lay down their lives for one another but out of love they rather dedicate their selves to one another. This interpretation opens a new vista on these logia that are so significant in Christian doctrines.*

This chapter continues the search for the meaning of psuchê *in studying the phrase to save or to lose the* psuchê. *Again we find that the major English Bibles render it as saving or losing one's life. Here the alternative will be explored to translate it as saving or losing the self. Does Jesus require his disciples to die, or rather to surrender to a process of losing one's self in order to gain the Self?*

What do the logia in this chapter contribute to the concept of transformation as a sign of mysticism?

Logia about Saving or Losing the *psuchê*

This text is maybe the strongest single case where Jesus calls for transformation, a specific one. He does so in the form of a typical paradox, in a stimulating and stirring way: what you keep you lose, what you lose you keep. Two issues I want to discuss. First, what is the tenor of the saying: does it refer to death and eschatology, as is it conceived psycho-spiritually: referring to transformation of the psyche here and now? What is it that be saved or lost: life, psyche, self? The second issue asks what is that transformation of losing and saving?

Logia about Saving or Losing Life	
Italics where the wording differs from Mk 8.35	
English text from Synopsis *(RSV)*	
Mk 8.35	
For whoever would save his life, will lose it	And whoever loses his life (…), will save it.
Mt 16.25	
For whoever would save his life, will lose it	And whoever loses his life (…), will *find* it.
Lk 9.24	
For whoever would save his life, will lose it	And whoever loses his life (…), he will save it.
Jn 12.25	
He who *loves* his life, loses it *world*	and he who *hates* his life in this (…), will *keep* it *for eternal life*
And also:	
Lk 17.33	
Whoever *seeks to gain* his life, will lose it	and he who *hates* his life (…) will *find* it
Mt 10.39	
He who *finds* his life, will lose it	and he who loses his life (…), will *find* it
Notes		
RSV	Greek	alternative
To save	*sôizô*	[or preserve from danger; has connotation of obtaining salvation]
To lose	*apollumi, apolluô*	[rather: destroy, ruin; lose out]
To find	*heuriskô*	
To love	*phileô*	
To hate	*miseô*	[have strong aversion, disfavor → disregard]
To keep	*phulassô*	[to preserve]
Eternal life	*zôê aionios*	[everlasting, 'timeless'[1]]
To seek	*zêteô*	
To gain	*peripoieomai*	[rather: acquire, preserve]
Life[2]	*psuchê*	[rather: self, soul, psyche, mind-and-heart] [partly: wvl]
(…)	for my [Jesus'] sake; Mk adds: and the Gospel's	

---

[1] : 'a very long time, endless, not being subject to time ': I. Ramelli, D. Konstan, *Terms for eternity: aiônios and aïdios in classical and Christian texts*, Piscataway, NJ: Gorgias 2007.

[2] Translators almost invariably have rendered *psuchê* by 'life' (e.g., NIV, NRSV, NKJ, JS). There is also good news. A recent Dutch translation does render 'soul' (*ziel*) (or 'body-and-soul', *lijf-en-ziel*) in all these cases (P. Oussoren (transl.), *De Naardense Bijbel*, Skandalon, Vught 2004.

It is an important saying as we find it in all canonical Gospels, and great theological value is attached to it![3] The parallel versions derive from different sources. Some on the basis of Mk (Mk 8:35, Mt 16:25, Lk 9:24), others derived from Q (Lk 17:33, Mt 10:39); Jn 12:25 seems to rely on an independent source. Taken together it is found in six versions from three independent sources.[4] An overview of the logia is found on the opposite page with some notes.

Characteristic is the unison in wordings of the concept saving/losing. Even when the terminology varies, the structure remains in unison: if A then B, and if B then A: the second part retains the words (if not the words, still the concepts) but in reversal. All logia deriving from Mk are identical, even in the reversal (saving/losing, losing/saving[5]: a sign of a strong tradition: the words of Jesus are kept conscientiously, we may take. Jn is close: loving/losing, but the reversal chooses other terms: hating/keeping for everlasting life. The Mt text from Q still keeps close: finding/losing, losing/finding (Mt), the Lk one varies considerably: seeking to gain/losing, and in the reversal hating/finding.

What now is the object of these verbs? It is the *psuchê*, but what does it signify? Major English Bibles say 'life.' It represents an interpretation in terms of passion, death, resurrection, and of eschatology and martyrology. What happens when the solution we found in the previous chapters is applied? *Psuchê* as self, psyche, or mind-and-heart, rather than life? But how does that solution relate to the broader context? Let us first look at the alternative wording. What about when instead of saving and losing life, it is the self that is saved or lost? Is it not reasonable to talk about handling the self rather than being subjected to a play of life and death? Let us see what would result. Then the logion could say: who loves the self will lose it, but who disregards the self, will keep it for everlasting life. Or: when one seeks to preserve the self one will lose it, but when one disregards it one will find it. To find your self is losing it, losing the self one will find it. But what is that self? How can one find it when it is lost? It is a saying full of riddles. One feels to be played around, hide-and-seek? Or is it a word play?

On the contrary, here we find a unique instance where the double meaning of the self is presented as a riddle, yet as clear as crystal, a sort of *haiku*. I'll come back to it shortly. For the moment take a serious look at the alternative.

---

3 As outlined in e.g. Lê-Minh-Thông J., « Aimer sa vie' et 'haïr sa vie' (Jn 12,25) dams la Quatrième Évangile», *Revue Biblique* 115,2 2008.
4 Funk, *The Five Gospels* 1993, 79.
5 Except Mt 16.25 where in the reversal we find 'find' for 'save.'

* * *

The same logia, with 'self' instead of 'life'

With apologies for the non-inclusive gender use

Mk 8.35 par
For whoever would save his self, will lose it   And whoever loses his self (…[6]),
                                                                      will save / find it.

Jn 12.25
He who loves his self, loses it   and he who disregards his self in
                                                                      this world (…), will keep/
                                                                      preserve it for everlasting life[7]

Lk 17.33
Whoever seeks to preserve his self, will lose it   and he who disregards his self
                                                                      (…) will find it

Mt 10.39
He who finds his self, will lose it   and he who loses his self (…),
                                                                      will find it.

* * *

The Immediate Context

Let us look at the Markan text first. The rendering by 'self' fits well also in the preceding pericope (Mk 8.34b) where individuals[8] are addressed:

> If anyone would adhere[9] to me, he must[10] deny[11] himself and take up his cross and follow me.
>
> *Ei tis thelei opisô mou akolouthein, aparnêsasthô heauton kai aratô ton stauron autou kai akoloutheitô moi.*

---

6   Mt, Lk: 'for my sake'. Mk: 'for the sake of the good message'; some witnesses have 'for my sake' added.
7   In this pericope we find both *psuche* and *zôê*. Mostly both are rendered as 'life.' This, however, appears rather contradictory. It is better to translate each term differently, here as 'self' and 'life,' respectively. Eternal life is conceived as other-worldly generally but we would rather interpret it as co-existing with worldly life. This is the connection with *aiônios*. Therefore we take the Greek *eis* as meaning 'in' (cf the earlier note on this item).
8   Mk: the multitude with his disciples. Mt: his disciples. Lk: to all.
9   Aland, *Synopsis*: come after. Some authoritative witnesses have *elthein*, coming after, following.
10 Ibid.: let him.
11 BDAG sub 1: also: to refuse to recognize / acknowledge.

Also here it is the self that is addressed: denying oneself, taking up one's cross, adhering to Jesus and following him.[12] The denying oneself is logically taken up in the losing the self which implies saving the self in v. 35:

> For whoever would save his self, will lose it, and whoever loses his self (…), will save it.
>
> *Hos gar ean thelêi tên psuchên autou sôsai apolesei autên; hos d'an apolesei tên psuchên autou (…) sôsei autên*

In this rendering the two verses are consistent with one another. The following verses (v. 36–37) add to it and confirm the flow of the argument:

> For what does it benefit[13] a man to acquire[14] the whole world and suffer the loss[15] of his self[16]?
>
> For what can a man give in exchange[17] for his self[18]?
>
> *Ti gar ôphelei anthrôpon kerdêsai ton kosmon holon kai zêmiothênai tên psuchên autou?*
>
> *Ti gar doi anthrôpos antallagma tês psuchês autou?*

These three pericopes appear as a flowing argument. It is one logion, with the saving/losing saying as the kernel. What does it say? Let me try and reword it:

> *As an adherent of Jesus one has to recognize in oneself the self, recognizing that one is not oneself. Then one rather takes up his cross (another sign of denial of that self[19]), and follows Jesus, out of devotion. What does that mean? It implies losing one's self and thereby saving one's self[20]. It is transformation. If one adheres to the world acquiring all that is of the world the consequence is that one will lose the self.*

---

12 Does following Jesus and taking up one's cross signify one has to follow Jesus on the way of martyrdom? Or of asceticism, denying the world? Or is the cross a symbol of crucifying the one self in order to save the other self?
13 BDAG *ôpheleô* sub 1: help, aid, benefit, be of use.
14 BDAG. I prefer acquire over gain.
15 BDAG *zêmioô* sub 1: to experience the loss of something, with implication of undergoing hardship or suffering: suffer damage/loss, forfeit.
16 NIV here and in the following sentence has soul instead of life for *psuchê*, A remarkable inconsistency that mars the logic of the logion.
17 Liddell Scott; Aland, *Synopsis*: in return.
18 NIV has soul here instead of life as in v. 35. *Sic.*
19 Funk (1993, 79) denies this interpretation. "There is no evidence that the cross served as a symbol of radical self-denial outside the crucifixion of Jesus or prior to that event."
20 Saving has a connotation of salvation, in the framework of the doctrine of salvation. Here it has the sense of expanding the self, expanding the consciousness of self to a wider and deeper level.

> *What would that result into? Nothing is as valuable as that (real) self, it cannot be exchanged for whatever in the world.*

All this sounds revolutionary as well as strange. What is that self that one loses and the self that one saves, or finds, or acquires, a *double entendre*? Something similar as the false ego and the real ego? Here is a attempt of interpretation.

Psycho-Spiritual Transformation

What these pericopes—forming one single logion—convey is a call for transformation, one of the signifiers of mysticism. Transformation as a process was referred to in the chapter on *metanoia*. It resurfaced in the previous chapter, where the phrase *psuchên tithêmi* was understood as a transformation of the self. In supreme love (Jn 15) as well as in devotion ('adhere to me', in this logion) there is nothing but to give one's heart and soul, one's self. Mystics have often referred to the experience that by giving one's self (*losing the self*) one gains what in some traditions is referred to as the Self (*saving the self*). By whole-heartedly focusing completely and single-mindedly on 'the other one', or 'the other One'. one's self may be transformed, from self to Self. In the Shepherd pericopes, it is told that by dedicating one's self one may receive it back transformed. This is the spiritual process: giving all that one has implies receiving a gift greater than what one has offered. It is an aspect of mysticism.

> Moreover it helps out to solve some inconsistencies and riddles of the traditional text. One is the confusion over *psuchê* in Mk 8.35 versus 8.36 NIV. In v. 35 *psuchê* is rendered as 'life', whilst in the immediately following verse it is translated as soul. The proposed text speaks of 'self' in all cases.

Thus the traditional meaning of *psuchê* is challenged. It is a daring enterprise as it questions truths that have stood the ages, some twenty to be precise.

Some further problems have to be looked at. *Psuchê* apart, the proposed text contains some alternative wordings that support the proposal but differ from the current understanding. Or the wording is the same but the implied understanding differs. This is the case with the saving/losing terminology. If *psuchê* stands for life, losing or saving seems to be a clear case, at least at first sight, if understood as part of doctrines. But if it stands for 'self', what does it mean? Above I have proposed my understanding. But how does that work out in the terminology of this logion?

> *Apollumi* is generally translated as 'to lose,' *sôizô* as 'to save'. Some of the Gospels have other terms.

Its first meaning[21] is not 'to lose', but to ruin or destroy.[22] There is a parallel in Buddhism. Buddhists would say 'to annihilate,' referring to *nirvana*, the 'nothing,' heaven or God, in terms of negative theology. See also the great mystic John of the Cross. The 'nothing' is experienced as the 'all'. So *apollumi* has two sides: a negative and a positive one. It is a play on words indicating a profound mystery. 'To annihilate' is a term used more often in spiritual texts, like Sufism. Surprisingly it often bears a positive connotation: to transform the unreal self into the real self. See the phoenix metaphor. Or the transformation of the caterpillar into the butterfly.

Returning to the meaning of 'to lose', we have seen in Mk 8.35 par that in the first part of each pair of *logia* it has a negative meaning, in the second part a positive. To lose something on the one hand means to be absolutely deprived and on the other hand absolutely happy to have found a new perspective, even a new reality by getting rid of something unwanted or superfluous. Related to *psuchê*, it suggests that if we lose our self in God, instead of keeping it and identifying with it, we will find the new self. A loss turns into gain. Often in mysticism this is described as a process, a process of transformation, i.e. of the self, the *psuchê*. Therefore the translation 'to lose' is supported.

In John (12.25), the more mystic Gospel, the process is described as follows. 'Loving one's self' means to lose, ruin, or destroy the true self. Or, in other terms to lose control over it. The self becomes master over rather than being an instrument of. But, on the other hand, if it is viewed as the 'false' self, and it is hated one will watch over it (*phulassô*) towards unlimited / eternal life (see the note on *aiônios* elsewhere), then one has mastered the self.[23]

Sôizô is the other central term, generally rendered as to save.[24] It is used consistently together with 'to want': who would want to save.[25] The Mt parallel uses it in the first line but substitutes it in the second line by 'to find', which is so in Mt 10 too. The common denominator is identifying with the *psuchê*, and holding it. The same is suggested in Lk 17 by *peripoieô* with its synonym meanings to acquire, obtain, gain for oneself.[26] If one gains the *psuchê* for oneself, one loses it. But if one loses the self, one

---

21 BDAG 1 to cause or experience destruction: *ruin, destroy / perish, be ruined* (mid); 2 to fail to obtain what one expects or anticipates: *lose out on, lose;* 3 to lose something that one already has or be separated from a normal connection: *lose, be lost*;
22 Here is another reason to not easily associate *apollumi* with dying or killing. In Mk 12:1–9 the tenants kill (*apokteinô*) somebody, one after the other, but the owner will come and ruin (*apollumi*) the tenants. NIV, however, translates both with killing.
23 See also Bradley 2007, 61.
24 BDAG *sôizô* preserve / rescue / save from danger: from death (1a), from disease (1c), keep/preserve in good condition (1d); from eternal death (2), (pass.) be saved, attain salvation (2b).
25 Generally the *thelêi* is taken 'as a simple condition' (Zerwick, for all three parallels), and thus neglected in major translations, rendering only the conjunctive, 'would save.' (*Sic*).
26 WNT, sub 2. The meaning sub 1 is the usual one but is poorly attested. Though it conforms better to the traditional interpretation of these pericopes, the *to gain for oneself* supports the meaning I propose. Bauer attests a wider support to it than there is to the first meaning.

gives life to it, literally giving birth to it.[27] The inspiring *zôogoneô*, giving life to, is 'robbed of its life' by the usual *to keep* (NRSV), *to preserve* (NIV, NKJ). 'To make alive' is very different from 'to preserve life', which we therefore reject. For John see above.

Lk 17:33 gives an interesting variant for *sôizô*. "Whoever tries to acquire (*peripoievô*) (WNT: "sich erwerben, sich gewinnen") his soul, will destroy / lose it, and whoever annihilates / loses it, will make it alive." Most translations (NIV, NSAV, P, JS) give 'preserve' for 'making alive.' But the Greek indeed says *zôogoneô*! Here is a clear case that *psuchê* cannot mean 'life' in the context of Mk 8:35 par: how can one lose one's life and then make it alive? Maybe a mystic could get along with the saying. This logion is very clear and strong: the psyche (self, soul) becomes alive when it is lost, 'annihilated'. But when one wants to acquire it, one will lose it by the very act of identifying with it.

Miseô, 'to hate', may be understood as a Semitism, says Barrett (1978,. 424). He compares it to Gen. 29:31, 33 and Deut. 21:15 where NIV translates as 'not being loved'. Barrett interprets it that the person "regards his life [his self, wvl] [*psuchê*] as of second desirability and importance." It is about disregarding the self rather than hating it: denying as not acknowledging what the self is.

The Wider Context

The logion as defined (Mk 8.34-37) is part of the narrative of Mark.[28] It is connected to the Gospel text as a whole and to particular parts, and especially to the pericopes preceding and following it.

Yet in the view of this work this is of less importance. For indeed the philosophy here is that the logia are 'separate' units belonging to specific traditions that 'happen' to be included in the particular Gospel narrative, written for a particular audience and with an implicit purpose or motivation. Yet it is useful to pay some attention to the wider context. For this logion, what precedes in chapter 8 is the feeding of the four thousand, the healing of a blind man, Peter's confession of Christ, Jesus predicts his death followed by his conflict with Peter. What follows immediately on our logion is the pericope about the son of man being ashamed, and then telling about the Kingdom of God.[29] Mt's narrative is similar, as is Lk's. Each of the narratives thus offers a rather heterogeneous lot of events. It is clear that the logion about saving and

---

27 See BDAG sub 1 to cause to be alive, *give life to, make alive* , 2 *keep* or *preserve alive*. Cf Jesus telling Nicodemus that one has to be reborn (or: born from above, *anôthen*) to see the kingdom of God (Jn 3:3).

28 As to Mt the conclusion is the same. Chapter 16 starts with the demand for signs, followed by the yeast of the Pharisees etc passage, and by Peter's confession of Christ.

29 Mk 9.1: "... Truly I say to you, there are some standing here who will not taste death before they see that the Kingdom of God has come with power." A possible relationship with Mk 8.35 is imaginable in the sense that if 'some standing here' would 'save their selves by losing their selves' they might be able 'to see' beyond seeing and perceive the Kingdom of God having come in its full strength.

losing, occurring in each of the Synoptics needs not and must not be seen in this wider context.[30] However, one could counter, this logion occurs in each of the Synoptics, specifically in about the same context in each of them. Should this not be seen as this logion being part and parcel of the respective narratives? No, to the contrary, just because the logion recurs in all these Gospels, it must be considered a text in a tradition independent of the narratives. Moreover, this logion is so expressive and so authoritative that it is speaking for itself. The context rather diminishes its power. The narratives create a context of Christology and miracle working, in which the clearly inner meaning of the logion disappears more or less.

Conclusions

The search for what *psuchê* may stand for in the logia of Jesus has continued in this chapter. The outcomes of the argument developed in chapters 10 and 12 have been confirmed and corroborated: *psuchê* is not life but self or psyche. That is the result of a minute exploration of the semantic context in the logion of Mk 8.34–37.

This logion communicates that it is essential to become aware of one's identity. It implies losing the 'self' and thereby saving the 'Self,' in a notable similarity to what we found in chapter 12: to dedicate the self (*puchên tithêmi*). It is transformation. If one adheres to the world acquiring all that is of the world the consequence is that one will lose the self. What would that result into? Nothing is as valuable as that (real) self, it cannot be exchanged for whatever in the world. And in it is a touch of divine presence.

---

30 Some take for example Mk 8.38b (about this adulterous and sinful generation and about the son of man coming in the glory of his Father with the holy angels) as a sign of an assumed eschatological meaning of Mk 8.34–37.

Chapter Fourteen

The Multifariousness of *psuchê*: The Other Pericopes[1]

Thus far logia have been discussed where *psuchê* is to be understood as self, or equivalents.

Is that the only meaning in the Gospels? It is appropriate to look at the other pericopes with this term in the Gospels. They fall under two headings: emotional and physical.

Emotional aspects of psuchê

... you will find rest for your souls[2]	Mt 11.29b
My soul is overwhelmed with sorrow to the point of death[3]	Mt 26.38 (par Mk 14.34)
... (to) hate one's own life	Lk 14.26
How long will you keep us in suspense?	Jn 10.24
Now my heart is troubled[4]	Jn 12.27

Alternate suggested translation:

... *you will find rest for your psyche (mind-and-heart)*	Mt 11.29
My psyche (mind-and-heart) is grieving until death	Mt 26.38 (par Mk 14.34)
... *(to) disregard one's psyche (mind-and-heart)*	Lk 14.26
How long will you upset our psyche (minds)?	Jn 10.24
Now my psyche (mind and heart) is troubled	Jn 12.27

Note: the English texts are NIV

---

1 Please refer to chapter 10, Annex 1 for the framework..
2 Funk 1993: *your lives will find repose.*
3 Ibid.: *I'm so sad I could die.*
4 Ibid.: *My life is in turmoil.*

Here is a number of places where *psuchê* clearly is not biological life and where translating with a term referring to the complete self would create confusion. Neither is it necessary to suppose that *psuchê* refers here to the whole being. Most translations therefore do translate with terms like 'heart' or 'soul'. Which, by the way, makes clear that there is no implicit necessity for rendering it as life.

These texts thus clearly refer to the psychological aspect of one's being: mind and heart, or one's self on the psychological level. Other aspects are the body and the spirit. All three are integral parts of the complete human being, is my contention: if one of these is missing one cannot live in this world.

Let us have a closer look at each of them with the proposed rendering and the Greek text.

Mt 11:29b: ... you will find rest for your *souls* → for your souls (alt.)
kai heurêsete anapausin tais psuchais humôn[5]

NIV and most others translate *psuchê* here as 'soul' (Funk: 'life'). This is about the same as our suggested 'mind and heart'. Obviously it is not the same as one's complete self. E.g., 'one's mind and heart finding rest' does not mean that one cannot be physically active at the same time.

So here we find a support in NIV for the argument that *psuchê* is not 'life'.

Proposal: soul, psyche, mind-and-heart.

Lk 14:26: If anyone does not hate his *psuchê* he cannot be my disciple → disregard

Ei de tis erchetai pros me kai ou misei...tên psuchên autou

This term to hate was discussed in chapter13. It was proposed to render it by 'to de-identify', 'to disregard'. Also here it refers to the same: disregarding the psyche. Jesus says that if one does not disregard one's psyche, one cannot follow him. What does it mean? It is putting Jesus first, one's ideal, the spirit, and as a consequence of (or rather as a condition to) it one needs to disregard one's psyche. Spirit to prevail over mind. It is something relative to one's relation in discipleship. It is not 'hating' one's life (*vs* death) but one's psyche (self), as opposed to one's spirit. By de-identifying with this psyche (self), with one's mind and emotions one can be a true disciple. These will otherwise block the spiritual development (i.e. following Jesus). By standing firm and enduring all the hardship one will really own one's psyche (soul).

Passages like J 12:25 (which were discussed in chapter 13 too) say the same: if you love your self (your mental identity) pushing aside your Self (your spiritual identity), you will lose (or even 'destroy') the Self; by disregarding the

---

5 A semi-quotation from Jeremiah 6.16 where LXX has *hagnismon* (purification) instead of *anapausis* (Mt).

self, you will guard the Self in this world for everlasting life. *Psuchên heautou*, therefore, in this Lk text is best rendered as 'his own self', 'his very soul'. Most translators, however, say 'his own life'. If this is understood as one's way of life I would agree more or less but probably it will be understood as life *vs* death. WNT gives 'himself'; this seems close to our rendering but suggests the complete person rather than the aspect of the psyche.

Proposal: to disregard the self, to de-identify.

> John 10:24 ... The Jews gathered around him, saying: "How long will you keep us in suspense?"
>
> *... heôs pote tên psuchên hêmôn haireis?*

We propose an alternative translation. *"How long will you upset our psyche?"*, or: *"... our minds and hearts?"* The traditional rendering 'keeping someone in suspense' obviously agrees that here *psuchê* is meant on the level of the mind and heart. As discussed in the previous chapter we prefer 'to upset the mind': *airô* means 'to take away', i.e. the psyche is no more in one's control: the psyche is raised, or aroused. For further corroboration, see also the section on *airô* in chapter 12.

> Mk 14:34 / Mt 26:38 My soul is overwhelmed with sorrow to the point of death
> *Perilupos estin hê psuchê mou heôs thanatou*
>
> J 12:27 Jesus predicting his death: Now my heart is troubled
> *Hê psuchê mou tetaraktai*

Jesus states that his mind and heart is grieving[6]. At the same time, as I understand it, he is fully aware of his spirit which is above his emotions: in his deeper consciousness his spirit is one with the Father's. How can it be otherwise? NIV translates justly 'soul' (Mt, Mk), 'heart' (Jn), as do most others. Only JS says 'I', 'my life', which creates the confusion of one aspect of one's being *versus* one's complete being. Remarkably, NIV differentiates *psuchê* into soul in one logion, and heart in another. It is rightly understood that the term refers to aspects of the human.

Our proposal:

My heart is deeply sad to death, or:
My mind-and-heart is grieving until death   Mt 26:38, Mk 14:3

Now my heart is troubled   J 12:27

---

6 This NIV version is rather dramatic, NRSV 'deeply grieved'. BDAG: very sad, deeply grieved, very unhappy. NRSV gives 'sad' for the rich ruler in Lk 18.23.

This section has presented the cases where the *psuchê* assumes emotional characterisitcs. Thus it clearly supports our hypothesis about the *psuchê* as an entity *per se* within the completeness of the human being. Here translations as mind-and-heart, heart, psyche, self are adequate.

Physical Aspects

In this section we will look at the passages in the Gospels where the authors of the Gospels differentiate clearly between the aspects of body, psyche and spirit. Or where it is absolutely clear that *psuchê* stands for physical life.

There is one sole instance where *psuchê* undubiously stands for physical life.

> Mt 2:20: ... for those who were trying to take the child's life are dead
> ... *tethnêkasin gar hoi zêtountes tên psuchên tou paidiou*

referring to the child slaughter by Herodes when the family had fled to Egypt. But this meaning need not be conceptual. I submit this is a *pars pro toto* case, *psuchê* for the whole being.

And at one place it seems rather probable; this is the parable of the rich man (Lk 12:19ff). We will discuss it below.

* * *

As we have seen there are plenty of places where *psuchê* is a term for a different concept. Some pericopes indeed differentiate between *psuchê* and body.

> Mt 6:25: Do not worry about your life, what you will eat or drink; or about your body, what you will wear. Is not life more important than food, and the body more important than clothes?
>
> *Mê merimnate têi psuchêi...mêde tôi somati.... ouchi hê psuchê pleion estin tês trophês kai to soma tou endumatos?*
>
> *Proposal*: Do not worry for your psyche what you will eat or drink nor for your body what you will wear. Is the psyche not more than the food and the body than the clothes?

The logic of the saying is rather loose and lacks strict logic: both eating and drinking is for the body rather than for the psyche, as is clothing. Yet Matthew does give different terms. Most translations say 'life' for *psuchê*. Yet this is no more convincing than the alternative. Of course, not only the psyche will feel when there is no food or drinking, and not only the body will feel when there are no clothes. The juxtaposition of body and *psuchê* is poetical rather than definitional. Does the poetical character suggest the juxtaposition of two terms as synonyms, or as different concepts? This must remain open.

Anyhow, *merimnaô* c.dat.—it seems to me—means 'to worry for' rather than 'to worry about'. The latter is mostly rendered in a different way: with *peri* (e.g. Lk 12:26) or c.acc. (e.g. Phil 4:6). With accusative it also means to take care of, to care for. *Merimnaô*: 'sich Sorgen machen wegen' [7], 'sorgen, die das Gemüt gleichsam spaltende hin- u. herzerrende Erwägung der Möglichkeiten, insbes. der schlimmen Möglichkeiten' (Rienecker 15). In this passage the object of worry clearly is 'what to eat etc' whilst the soul is mentioned as the object to suffer or to benefit.

By the way, in the last sentence the correct translation is not 'more important' but just 'more'.
Cf et Lk 12:19-23. See also *infra*.

* * *

Here is another one (with parallel):

Mt 10:28: Do not be afraid of those who kill the body but cannot kill the soul. Rather, be afraid of the One who can destroy both soul and body in hell

Kai mê phobeisthe tôn apokteinontônto sôma, tên de psuchên mê dunamenôn apokteinai; phobeisthe de mallon ton dunamenon kai psuchên kai soma apolesai en geennêi

Proposal: Do not be afraid of those who kill the body but are not in a position to kill the psyche. Rather hold in awe the One who can make both the psyche and the body get lost in Geenna

And the parallel. Contrary to the Mt text the word *psuchê* does not figure: this element remains unnamed:

Lk 12.4-5: I tell you, my friends, do not be afraid of those who kill the body and after that can do no more. But I will show you whom you should fear: Fear him who, after the killing of the body, has power to throw you in into hell. Yes, I tell you, fear him.

Mê phobêthête apo tôn apokteinontôn to soma kai meta tauta mê echontôn perissoteron ti poiêsai.

Hupodeixô de humin tina phobêthête: phobêthête ton meta to apokteinai echonta exousian enbalein eis tên geenna. Kai legô humin, touto phobêthête.

Proposal:
I tell you, my friends, do not be afraid of those who kill the body and after that can do no more. But I will show you whom you should fear: Hold him in awe who, after killing the body, has power to throw you in hell. Yes, I tell you, hold him in awe.

Lk 12:4-5

NOTE.
Note the difference in Mt between the first *phobeô apo* c.gen. and the second without *apo* but c.acc. Is there a linguistic difference in meaning? I cannot find it, neither in TDNT nor in WNT nor in Muller. I wonder whether the difference between the two

---

7 Steyer 1992, 34

forms can be translated in the former case as 'to be afraid of' whilst in the latter case it refers to 'to hold someone in awe'.

Here is a clear differentiation between 'body' and 'mind and heart'. Here it can well be translated as 'self' in the sense of psyche. It is impossible here to translate *psuchê* with 'life': body and life do not relate in the way meant here. Indeed each translation used gives 'soul' here.

Obviously someone here on earth can kill my body but cannot kill my *psuchê*: the *psuchê* does not die together with the body. This would imply that the *psuchê* survives the death of the body. However, in the hereafter also the soul will die, or rather be lost [!] (: *apollumi*). This is in line with those philosophies which teach that the immortal part of the human being is the spirit, not the psyche (soul). The Geenna[8] is the place of the purifying fire where the psyche is transformed or dissolved[9]. The text mentions that both body and *psuchê* will get lost. But isn't the concept of the body in Geenna a contradiction: the body stays on earth, the *psuchê* lives on until it gets lost in the hereafter. In my view the spirit continues to live after the loss of the *psuchê*. I wonder whether either the term body in relation to Geenna or the mentioning of Geenna in relation to the body are additions. Or is it a poetical expression?

Let us look at the Lk parallel (text see above). In the context and in terms of everyday language (Jesus, in the Lk version, is talking to many thousands) it would mean that the body here is killed by human beings and then whatever remains after death is thrown into hell. The Lk parallel is simpler and does not mention the *psuchê*. It even does not specify in v.5 what is killed and what is thrown. If this text might be considered to be the original one, the perplexity would be solved: we are free to interpret that the body is killed here on earth, the soul is sent to Geenna.

Recent research says both the Mt and the Lk texts have been derived from Q (QS 36)[10]. Mack 1993 considers the single sentence *Don't be afraid of those who can kill the body but can't kill the soul* to be the first Q version.[11] The sentence with body and soul in Geenna would be a later addition. The passage in Mt is part of a speech by Jesus to his disciples in which (contrary to the Lk

---

8   Other places with Geenna: Mt 5:22,29-30, 10:28, 18:9, 23:15, 33, Mk 9:43,45,47, Lk 12:5. Geenna is very different from Hades; for Hades see: Mt 11:23, 16:18, Lk 10:15, AG 2:24v.l., 2:31v.l., 27:31, 1C 15:55v.l.
9   Such purification and/or cleansing are suggested by Clement of Alexandria and Origen because eternal condemnation is excluded, punishing being remedial, though in both their writings they express some reservations. Purification or purgation was through fire. Fire, or light? *Webster's* sub 3a: "moral or spiritual purification, b: the first stage in a mystic's progress to perfection.
10 Funk 1993, 172
11 Mack1993, 77, 93

text) he obviously refers to hidden teachings which in time will be understood (v 26,27: *There is nothing concealed that will not be disclosed, or hidden that will not be known*). In the same way he makes clear that they should be aware that they are more than body and that there is a part of their being which is beyond death and destruction (Geenna) although he makes sure that even that part (the *psuchê*) will be lost later on (leaving the spirit alive!, although this is not mentioned as such). Thus he consoles the disciples after having them confronted with all the hardships he predicts them (v 21-23).

Besides, it is not clear who is the one who can throw into and kill in Geenna: is it God or Satan? The text does not specify: it simply uses the pronoun *ton*. Interestingly many translations do not use a capital letter to indicate the one who will make the psyche get lost in Geenna. I would agree with those who do, implying it is God who does, of course.

* * *

One text remains to be discussed. It is Luke's story of the rich man (Lk 12:19-23) which precedes Luke's version of Mt 6 as discussed above (concerning worrying about the self).

> *And I will say to myself* (psuchê), *"You* (psuchê) *have plenty of good things ... "*
>
> *"(God speaking:)... This very night your life* (psuchê) *will be demanded from you. Then who will get what you have prepared for yourself?"*
>
> *"This is how it will be with anyone who stores up things for himself but is not rich toward God."*
>
> Lk 12:19,20,21 (part)   (NIV)

As an alternative we present:

> *And I will say to my psyche (self), "Psyche (self), you have plenty of good things ... "*
>
> *"This very night they will demand your psyche (self) from you. Then what you have prepared for yourself, whose will it be?"*
>
> *"Thus it is with the one who stores treasures for himself not being rich toward God."*

The text is interesting as it shows the psyche clearly as an entity one can address. Some translators view it as a *pars pro toto* and treat it just as a personal pronoun. But I think here the man speaks with his psyche. Thus the psyche is taken as a separate entity that is addressed by the I: therefore here logically the psyche and the I are not the same entities, as the one addresses the other.

I agree with the general interpretation that the man will die. However, alternative interpretations are left open because of the term *psuchê* being used rather than *zôê*. The central meaning of *apaiteô* is 'to demand' (or more specific 'to demand back', i.e. what has been stolen, or 'to call in debts'. Earthly possessions do not really belong to one. When the psyche departs the possessions remain on the earth. This may make one aware any moment, that all the possessions do not really belong to oneself: they may be demanded back anytime. The story's wisdom tells us that the *psuchê* is an entity on itself not dependent on earthly treasures, on food, drink and clothes. It is being rich in (or toward: *eis*) God.

By the way, interestingly the Greek has the verb in the third person plural. NIV translates in the passive form. This suggests that it is God who is demanding. But this is not necessarily implied in the wording of the text. God speaks and says "...This very night they will demand your psyche from you ...". In Dutch the 3rd person plural is a general indication, equivalent to the German 'man' (Dutch 'men'). In English one may use the passive form. Why should God say it so indirectly? One could wonder whether it hints at various people wanting something from the psyche of this man. When one has not found one's true identity one feels torn apart, and one does not know anymore whose are the things which one has prepared.

There may be another interpretation, however. The man has to account for how he views life and his self in the perspective of the spirit and of eternity. He has to give account to himself: what do temporary things mean to him and whose are they: he does not really possess them!, a person's real possessions are in the spirit. Even food and clothes are not essential. This is explained further in the next verses (v.22ff): do not worry about eating, drinking and clothing (cf the beginning of this section). In that way the phrase may also considered metaphorically to stand for the seeming riches accumulated in mind and heart for which one may have to account at any time ('this night'). When one's psyche is being demanded it means that one should dedicate one's mind-and-heart, i.c. to God.

* * *

I want to add a comment on two passages which formally are beyond the scope of this paper as they are quotations from the OT. Yet they are too important to be left out, all the more as it forms a bridge to Part IV. They expand our argument on the *psuchê* to that of the spirit, the *pneuma*, the subject matter of the last Part.

> *Here is my servant* (ho pais mou) *whom I have chosen, the one I love, in whom I*
> (hê psuchê mou) *delight;*
> *I will put my Spirit on him* Mt 12:18 NIV
>
> *My soul* (psuchê mou) *glorifies the Lord*
> *and my spirit* (to pneuma mou) *rejoices in God my Savior* Lk 1:46-47 NIV

These texts obviously underline the hypothesis that different aspects of the human being are being recognized, not only soul but also spirit. This 'Magnificat' text in Lk makes clear also that the soul is different from God whilst it is about *her* spirit. Also in the Mt text the function of heart (rendered as 'psyche' here) and spirit are different. It is not just two terms for one entity. NIV obscures the entity of the soul by translating *psuchê* as a personal pronoun.

Conclusions

This chapter is more or less an annex, covering the remaining pericopes with *psuchê*. The findings corroborate the outcomes of the previous chapters: there is quite some contextual evidence that *psuchê* is to be considered as a special entity in the human being. Current translations as life (in many instances crucial in Christian understanding) had been challenged in chapters 12 and 13. In the pericopes treated in this chapter a few more cases with 'life' were found and could easily be re-interpreted with psyche (or equivalents) into sensible phrases. In some cases it is clear that life is a correct rendering when it clearly refers to physical life as opposed to death. What are the other translations of the term found in NIV in the Gospels? In quite a few cases a rendering by 'soul' was found. At some places it was understood as a personal pronoun. For all pericopes under review in this chapter I have tried to keep respect for *psuchê* as a significant term. In most cases an alternative rendering resulted. Consistency has been applied where plausible.

Concluding Part Three
Transformation: The psyche

We have seen again how necessary it is to scrutinize words on their meaning, and to see what spirituality is hidden in them, rather than assume unaware as correct, logic and natural what traditionally is understood. This is the more so with some keywords that carry special weight. In the course of time they acquired specific meanings, for example due to the developing theology, or to specific meanings in early Christian communities, and to the gradual development of doctrines in Church. When researching these terms it sometimes is useful to strip them—for the time being—from their acquired sense, and try to discover with a fresh eye and an open mind if there may be any other meanings that may be more basic, or more authentic, or even just plausible alternatives. Essential in such endeavor is the awareness that a word by Jesus and the logia in which they occur will of necessity be understood within the framework of the student and of the translator. All research is done from a 'preconceived' set of ideas that guides the research. It is the task of the researcher to make this explicit, and then to try and get in an impartial way to 'truth'. In the case of this present exploration of the Message of Jesus the 'bias' is spirituality and mysticism. The check on this bias is prudence and carefulness, coupled with a basic scholarly scrupulosity, as far as mine may reach.

This Part has concentrated on two word groups in particular, one being *metanoia / metanoein, hamartia, aphiêmi* and the other *psuchê*, and their underlying understandings: what are the concepts. From studying these words as specific terms, concepts have been discovered revealing the transformational energy of the message of Jesus. It is found that *metanoia* alternatively may not refer to repentance, penitence etc, but rather to transformation of the mind, leading to a different attitude against life, a new philosophy of life. For example, the term 'sin' does not cover the meaning of *hamartia*. *Aphiêmi* is found to imply not so much an act from above to below as rather that the burden is taken from one's shoulders. 'Sinning' (*hamartanô*) rather refers to an activity where one is missing the target, and needs to be corrected. *Metanoia* moreover is not seen as a unique act of transformation, at one specific moment in time, but rather as multiple stages on the path of spirituality, or a gradual development.

Then, what is it that changes and transforms, and consequently is changed and transformed? The second term studied is *psuchê*. It appears in some crucial passages when Jesus is teaching. He tells his audience to dedicate the *psuchê*, their selves, their minds-and-hearts, their 'psyches' to the Message. How? By loving one another. By dedicating one's self to the other. Jesus sets the example of the devoted shepherd who dedicates his self to the ones dependent on him, to those whom he leads on the path of life. The traditional rendering—laying down one's life—is not the single correct one, even not the most natural and logical understanding: how can one continue to serve the other when one lays down one's life? Elsewhere Jesus tells his disciples an essential truth of the spiritual path regarding the *psuchê*: to 'save' the self implies 'losing' it. However, 'losing' the self leads to 'saving' the self. It is a matter of what one is conscious of, of what one identifies with. It is about what *is* the self, differentiating between the self and the Self. Elsewhere it may be called the difference between the psyche and the spirit, *psuchê* and *pneuma*. When one identifies with the psyche, with one's thinking and emotions, with one's self, there is no place for the *pneuma*, for the Self, and it is 'lost' whilst the self is 'saved'. Conversely, when one lives in the spirit the self is 'saved' as Self; implying that one does no more identify with the psyche, one is no longer in the hands of the 'self'.

The outcome of this exploration is an alternative to the eschatological interpretation. It is not that Jesus lays down his life for humanity, it is not a requirement to lose one's life, referring to martyrdom or final judgment.

The outcomes of the chapters on Transformation support, corroborate and deepen the conclusions of Part II, on the Kingdom of God.

A new view on the anthropology of Jesus is forming. The individual is set on the spiritual path, transforming the self, ascending to an awareness of the spirit, of the Kingdom inside.

In this way new concepts behind terms are found, a new riches of spirituality. Conversion or penitence become a field of transformation, sin becomes a missed opportunity, forgiveness a letting loose, the *psuchê* gets a new content as the self, mind-and-heart, the soul, the psyche: the non-spiritual and non-physical elements of the wholeness of the human being. The next Part will take up the spiritual aspects concentrating on what *pneuma* is, with a wink to the question: spirit, human or divine?

PART FOUR
Explorations in the Field of *Pneuma*, Spirit

Introduction

> *I believe that the concept of 'spirit' originally and best refers not to a distinct hypostasis either beside God or within the Godhead, mediating between God and the world, but to God's own personal presence and activity in the world.*[1]

Part Four will make an expedition into the field of *pneuma*, or spirit. Its purpose is to conduct some explorations in what the Gospels have to say about it. It does not have the pretense of covering the field but rather to present four *capita selecta*. Its content is closely linked to other Parts of the book. The Kingdom of God was found to be a spiritual realm, in which to enter, to live and have one's being, and that enters into one: a presence divine, a sacred transformation. Part III offered insight into the phenomenon of transformation of the psyche. These in turn are closely linked to what will be found in the next chapters: the indwelling of spirit, the power of the spirit inside oneself, the presence of the spirit generating rapture and ecstasy. The process of *metanoein* was found to point in the same direction: changes in the self induced by spirit. In the chapters on the psyche it was shown how much the need to dedicate one's self and the power to turn the self into Self is motivated, inspired, empowered by spirit.

> *What is this spirit? When Christians think of 'spirit' the principal association often is with the Holy Spirit, with the Counselor, with the Trinity. But what about Jesus immersing individuals in holy spirit? Or driving out spirits being in God's Spirit? Rejoicing in the holy spirit? Handing over his spirit? Also with other persons: Mary being pregnant out of holy spirit, Zachariah and Elizabeth filled with holy spirit, David speaking while being in spirit, the child growing up strong in spirit. And what about being born out of spirit, praying being in spirit, God is spirit? All these questions reflecting statements in the Gospels that will be explored. And, could ecstasy have to do with an indwelling spirit expressing itself? What do the words on the cross purport spiritually?*
>
> *All these questions will be highlighted in this Part, based on grammar and the Greek text interpreted from a new perspective.*
>
> *Does this shed a new light on the gospels as spiritual texts? Or even, do the findings support an anthropology where 'spirit' is a part of the human being?*

---

1   M.E. Lodahl, *Shekinah / Spirit: Divine Presence in Jewish and Christian Religion* (1992, 41).

Some introductory and explorative words will be said in the first chapter of this Part, chapter 15. In the Gospels *pneuma* or spirit appears frequently, but in different forms: as spirit and as the spirit, as holy spirit and as the holy spirit, small differences of just one word, but full of bearing. This issue will be discussed in that same first chapter, leading to a closer understanding of *pneuma*. Connected to these discoveries chapter 16 will take a closer look at and explore the challenging expression *en pneumati* in the canonical Gospels, mostly rendered as 'by the spirit.' Is spirit indwelling, or does one dwell in spirit? Whom does it refer to, then? Or is it something alien to the human being?

What follows as chapter 17 is an essay addressing the words of Jesus on the cross in the Gospels, and the role of *pneuma* therein. What do these words reflect? What is the atmosphere of the passion narratives? The closing chapter of this Part, chapter 18, is an excursion to be made to *ekstasis*, both as term and as concept. Is ecstasy a phenomenon of spirituality, or an abnormal state of the psyche? A crucial passage is Mk 16.8 where the women 'flee' from the memorial. Part Four will close with an evaluation and some conclusions.

In some aspects this Part is different from the previous ones. Until now the focus was on the Jesus logia. But apart from Jn, the Gospels are scarce in reporting words by Jesus on the topic of spirit. Yet what the Gospels do report about *pneuma*, even if not as logia, is important from the point of view of some topics discussed in the previous Parts.

What was found foremost is the concept of Presence. We will find relationships chiefly with the Kingdom of God sayings, especially about the indwelling of the divine. It will help highlight what was said about the *psuchê* and the related view on anthropology.

Note

This Part, being a set of capita selecta, intentionally disregards the voluminous literature on the word group *pneuma* as a whole. TDNT alone provides 132 pages of in-depth information on the topic, of which a greater part on the Gospels. BDAG offers 11 columns alike. I apologize for not placing my contributions in chapters 15 and 17 in the perspective of the accumulated knowledge on the whole field. However, this would require another book. The outcome of this study is presented as an additional perspective on aspects of what the Gospels tell us about *pneuma*.

A special note on *pneuma* as breath. In this work the Greek term has been translated as spirit more or less consistently. Another translation is breath. I have neglected the option that spirit and breath may not be far apart. TDNT offers an useful history of the connection. In religion, and even more so in mysticism, spirit and breath are often seen as closely connected, even mutually implied. The reader will find quite a few instances throughout this book, ranging from Gen 2.7 to Jn 3.3-8. A direct connection is found in some OT texts (see page 266), and in chapter 17.

Chapter Fifteen
The Concept of *pneuma* in the Gospels and Its Forms

An expedition into the field of pneuma, spirit. But why is an expedition needed? Why make explorations in a field so well known by so many earlier expeditions? The call to go and explore came to my ears when I found out that small grammatical differences may have a bearing far wider and fundamental than one would suspect.

Isn't it a contradiction that a concept like spirit should need an analysis 'on the ground' rather than a lofty poetical treatment, close to wordless music? Only hesitatingly I decided to include that analysis in this book that tries to turn the attention of NT critics and theologians to a spiritual perspective of the Gospels and the Jesus logia. Surprisingly we will discover that precisely this grammatical precision work will disclose new perspectives and open new layers of understanding what the Gospels teach about spirit.

There is one more reason to do so. Evidently most treatises on pneuma interpret the term in the light of later pneumatology and Christology: 'spirit' must refer to the Holy Spirit[1]. *My analysis will uncover varieties of 'spirit'.*

'The Spirit' or 'Spirit':
Pneuma (hagion) / to pneuma [to] (hagion)

When analysing the occurrences of *pneuma* in the Gospels we find different forms in which it appears. The texts speak about the holy spirit (*to pneuma [to] hagion*), of course, but surprisingly also about holy spirit (*pneuma hagion*) without the definite article. It appears 11 times with the (definite) article (the so-called arthrous use) but even 15 times without (anarthrous). What does this

---

The basics of this chapter and the next one have been read at the SBL Annual Meeting, Nashville, TN, 2000, Bible Translation Section.

[1] Franz Dünzl, *Pneuma: Funktionen dses theologischen Begriffs in frühchristliecher Literatur* 2000. The work does not even leave the slightest doubt if spirit might refer to something else than the Holy Spirit, throughout this grand work. Ju Hur, *A dynamic reading of the Holy Spirit in Luke-Acts* 2001 views the Holy Spirit as a character in the Lk-Acts narrative, functioning in its plot [sic], 181–278.

different expression, with and without the article, imply? Is the difference relevant? Is holy spirit different from spirit? Is the spirit different from the holy spirit? Is the difference relevant?

Most translations and critics do not take notice of these differences. Even in thorough and fine analyses where each and every word is put under the microscope, this is missing.[2] Not a word is spent on whether or not the article matters, neither in substance nor grammatically. No discussion whether spirit and holy spirit refer to the same entities, or that they are different. See also the chapter on *en pneumati* for a further discussion.

Intermezzo: Does the article matter?

The issue is whether the use of the article is relevant as to content: the arthrous issue: if a noun is with the article it is called an arthrous use, if not it is anarthrous. In Greek there is only one article, the definite article. Thus *pneuma* without article may stand both for 'a sprit' and for 'spirit'.

Let us first check with *the grammar*. Blass/Debrunner 1990 (German language 17th edition) gives detailed information for all relevant cases (§§ 249 through 276). Specific rules are given in § 257 for *pneuma*, together with *thanatos* (death) and *patêr* (father). To sum up, the article does matter: *pneuma* with article refers to an entity "gewissermassen als Person", e.g. *to hagion pneuma*. Without, "als göttlicher in den Mensch einziehenden Geist" (as divine spirit entering into a human being) (§ 257.2).[3]

> Another grammar[4] takes the opposite stand saying that the article is left out in koine Greek "bei manchen Abstrakta, die als besonders bedeutsam empfunden" (Steyer 37G). In these cases the article is supposed and translations therefore have to be arthrous. What does 'exceptionally significant' mean? This is important. From his example ('das Heil ererben') we may understand that it suggests meaning 'theologically very important', referring to concepts like salvation or spirit, which theologically have got a specific meaning, but which in another context are more or less indefinite. Obviously the same argument is often practised for *pneuma*. In many cases this is the reason why *pneuma* is translated with 'the spirit', referring to the (Holy) Spirit, later personified as a Person of the Trinity. As we have seen above, Blass' rules infer that the (definite) Jewish or Christian God or Lord is

---

2   E.g., Makambu 2007, 12. He points out that *pneuma* appears both arthrously and anarthrously (Jn 1.33, 14.26 [mistakenly given as 16.26] , 20.22) yet no attaching any sense to the difference. Also Hur, Dünzl.
3   The 13th edition § 254 formulates as follows: "Der Artikel steht, wennn der bestimmte jüdische oder christliche Gott oder ‚Herr' gemeint ist (nicht ein Wesen göttlicher Natur' oder ein ‚Herr')."
4   Steyer 1992.

arthrous, but that "ein Wesen göttlicher Natur oder ein Herr" is anarthrous.[5] The latter is the case with quite a few times when the anarthrous *pneuma* or even *hagion pneuma* nevertheless is translated with the definite article. So it seems that the rule is based on a false argument: because theology has attached specific importance to that specific concept, it *must* be translated arthrously.

Thus, the usage of the article does matter. The anarthrous Greek should be translated anarthrously in English (and 'any' other language), the arthrous Greek arthrously in English. Therefore, *pneuma* is spirit, *to pneuma* is the spirit.

Blass/Debrunner, however, makes a proviso for cases with a preposition, like *en pneumati* (a case of quite some importance; see next chapter). In such a case the article is left out (§ 257, n.4; also Steyer II 37K). Is this so? Here a critical note on this rule is required. Obviously the rule is not general, for exceptions are found with the phrase *en pneumati* (see next chapter!) in Mk 12.36, Lk 2.27, Lk 4.1 and Lk 10.21 (in some witnesses): all these pericopes have *en tôi pneumati*, arthrous use. The rule, moreover, is in conflict with § 257.2, which says for *pneuma*: sometimes it occurs with, and sometimes without the article, both with and without *hagion*, holy.

To sum up, grammatically the presence or absence of the article is relevant as to the contents: spirit is different from the spirit; holy spirit is different from the holy spirit.

This conclusion from Blass/Debrunner is supported by Schwarz who for '(the) holy spirit' made an analysis.[6] Swartz states that the presence or absence of the article with *pneuma* is neither accidental nor arbitrary. The anarthrous usage is the default usage throughout the NT. He consistently and convincingly demonstrates that invariably this phrase indicates a holy spirit as God-given power (!) (137, *passim*). TDNT[7] supports this view implicitly referring to the Matthaean and Markan sense of *pneuma* in the OT sense of the power of God (136). *Mutatis mutandis* his conclusion is valid even for *pneuma* without *hagion*.[8] On the other hand, he contradicts himself, saying "The presence of the article...signifies a definite and

---

5 See also the interesting discussion in the Johannine Literature e-group on the difference between *theos* and *ho theos* which took place summer / fall 2000. In December 2009 and February 2010 the topic was discussed in the Bibexegesis e-group.
6 Steve Swarz, "The Holy Spirit: Person and Power: the Greek Article and *Pneuma*," *Bible Translator* 44.1 (1993), 124–38.
7 Friedrich in TDNT VI 404.
8 Closing his article Swartz looks back at 500 years of English bible translation history: "… it is to be wondered if at least some of the current wrangling over the Holy Spirit and the charismata might have been avoided if the English translations had reflected on occasion some of the nuances of the article with *pneuma*." (137).

theological reference to the Holy Spirit as perceived as Person." (Swartz 136) This obviously is a theological interpretation, that is, viewed from the perspective of the Trinity, this notion being a later interpretation of the concept notion of the holy spirit in the Gospels. To me it is safer to conclude that 'the holy spirit' refers to God's spirit as *dunamis*, a definite entity. As a matter of fact, the (mis)understanding of the anarthrous *pneuma hagion* often is driven with the view to demonstrate the doctrine of the personhood of the Holy Spirit on the basis of grammatical considerations in the Greek text.[9]

From this analysis in the Intermezzo, it now may be concluded that the use of the article in Greek conveys a clear sense: with the article (arthrous) it refers to something definite, without (anarthrous) to something indefinite. This has a direct bearing on what is said about *pneuma* in the Gospels. *Pneuma* is spirit (or a spirit), *to pneuma* is the spirit, *hagion peneuma* is holy spirit (or a holy spirit), *to hagion pneuma / to pneuma to hagion* is the holy spirit. In the further analysis the options for *a* (holy) spirit (indefinite) are excluded.[10] This would not obtain in case the evil spirits would be included. This is not the case.

The Literature

Now what does literature contribute to this issue? Is the issue paid attention to? No, it is not. No author (as far as I could get hold of) raises the question if an anarthrous *pneuma* differs from an arthrous one as to substance, with one exception. Although Flowers and Francis do, they play the issue down to the simple conclusion: with the article it indicates the Holy Spirit, without it does not', whilst the issue is more complicated. For an inventory see the extensive note[11], also for some nuances.

---

9 A clear instance was found in the B-Greek Group discussion on '*Pneuma hagion* as a proper name?' in May 14, 2010.
10 Here an inconsistency crops up. The evil spirits appear as definite entities, i.e. with the article. In case *a* spirit is indicated, in Greek it will be anarthrous, in English with the indefinite article. Why this does not obtain to spirits not belonging to the evil category? Are these entities or of another category?
11 Bennema 2003, on the Gospel of John, does not pay attention to the issue: no differentiation between '(holy) spirit' with or without article.
 • Comfort 1984 does not address the article issue.
 • Crump 1954 does not make a point of the use of the article as such. Neither does he see any consequences as to the substance. In one part of his work, however, he does review the different opinions re the holy spirit before the baptism of Jesus as to the article use. Several authors, he says, mention the absence of the article. These conclude that *pneuma hagion* refers to OT use, e.g., 'a special energy' (Lagrange 1921), 'a divine power or force' (Lebreton 1927), 'impersonal', like in OT (Plummer 1910). This distinction,

Swartz 1993 is the exception. His publication is about holy spirit only. He shows convincingly that the anarthrous use is to be rendered in English as holy spirit, different from the arthrous the Holy Spirit. He makes a proviso though, warning against an all too easy theological conclusion from a purely grammatical argument, particularly like the presence or absence of the article. He refers to Moule (1968, 111–12) who also cautions against an easy interpretation of the occurrence or absence of the article in Greek (Swartz 126). That is correct, of course. Yet I uphold my argument as an alternative to be considered. I from my side warn against an all too easy assumption that the article does not matter so that any anarthrous use does not convey a sense in itself. For example, it is questionable whether in any of these anarthrous instances of holy spirit the Holy Spirit as a Person is referred to. Though Mk 12:36 has the article, the parallel Mt 22:43 does not. Would Simeon really have the Holy Spirit upon him (Lk 3:25)? would the Holy Spirit act with him (v.26, 27)? Lk 10:21 tells Jesus rejoiced being in the Holy Spirit, or according to some witnesses 'by the Holy Spirit', whilst others say 'by spirit', and again others 'in the spirit', variants that impede an easy interpretation of this as the Holy Spirit.

The conclusion of this inquiry is that as a principle parallel translation is certainly applicable: the Greek article is retained in English, as does its absence. Therefore, the distinction between spirit and the spirit is genuine, as well as between holy spirit and the holy spirit.

English

In practice English Gospel versions, like many other language renderings, ignore the issue of the article use completely: a majority translates the anarthrous cases

---

however, does not have any relevance for the Christian concept of pneuma, I must conclude. Also in the later treatments of *pneuma* the article is not an issue to Crump.
- Flowers 1953: if referring to the Third Person it is arthrous, otherwise anarthrous. Therefore, the distinction is relevant but does not conclude about the meaning of spirit without the article.
- Francis 1985, idem.
- Kraus (2000, 262–72) does not discuss the (an)arthrous issue but underlines the importance of the article for our understanding of the thought and theology of the NT writers.
- Levinsohn 1993 protests against Swartz's argument in a highly technical analysis. His point is that the noun is anarthrous when salient or highlighted and when it is not the subject. His argument is not as powerful as Swartz's, and does not work out for many instances. See the chapter *en pneumati*.
- Makambu 2005 signalizes anarthrous cases from arthous ones, e.g. in Jn 3.3-8, but does not attach sense to it, notwithstanding the meticulous nigging analysis and the obvious differences (141–48).
- Mowery 1986 analyzes all articular phrases with the holy spirit, leaving unattended the ones with *pneuma hagion*. Therefore it does not discuss the (an)arthrous issue we are addressing.
- Mundhenk 1997 discusses how to translate 'holy spirit' in languages like Papua, but does not deem it worthy to go into the anarthrous issue.

into English with the definite article. Thus the sense of the text is altered. When reading the Gospels in English one is given the idea that the only thing is *the* holy spirit, and *the* spirit.

Should it not be reasonable to at least explore whether 'holy spirit' may convey a meaning different from what the term 'the holy spirit' is telling? What is the implication of the lack of the definite article, in the first place grammatically? And what about its meaning in terms of content? What is the implication of spirit being indefinite? Or holy spirit being indefinite? What do the pericopes with 'holy spirit' and 'spirit' (without the article) convey as meaning? Do they have sense? In the Intermezzo this issue has been addressed. Now what are the implications?

Is 'Spirit' a Feasible Translation of the Anarthrous *pneuma*?

Here is an overview of the passages with 'spirit' or 'holy spirit' without the (definite) article (anarthrous). When read without prejudice, unconditioned by the usual rendering, trying to forget for a while the context, does one find a sensible text? This functions as a test case if the anarthrous rendering makes sense, what is it that the words are saying. Let us have a look. The list is complete.

> The translation used basically is NIV, but rendered anarthrously. Sometimes I give an alternative rendering. I have been particular in translating the preposition as close to the basic meaning as possible, for exmple *en* I take as 'in' rather than what often is done, as an instrumentalis.
>
> Note. In this presentation capitalization of '(holy) spirit' is avoided; this is done without prejudice.

First, texts from Mt and Lk before the baptism of Jesus:

- Mary is pregnant out of (*ek*) holy spirit (Mt 1.18)
- Joseph is told by the angel that Mary conceived out of (*ek*) holy spirit (Mt 1.20)
- Zachariah is told that he will be filled with (gen.) holy spirit [12] (Lk 1.15)
- Zachariah indeed is filled with (gen.) holy spirit (Lk 1.67)
- Mary is foretold that holy spirit will come upon (*epi*) her (Lk 1.35)
- Elizbeth filled with (gen.) holy spirit (Lk 1.41)
- John the Baptist going in (*en*)[13] spirit and power of Elijah Lk 1.17x)
- And the child grew and became strong in (dat.) spirit (Lk 1.80)

---

12 Zerwick 1996: without article rather 'with divine inspiration', which renders it in the same spirit as I do.
13 Ibid.: equipped with.

- Holy spirit was upon (*epi*) Simeon (Lk 2.25)

About baptism:

- John the Baptist foretells that Jesus will immerse in (*en*) holy spirit (and fire, Mt and Lk). All four canonical Gospels report this remarkably consistently: Mt 3.11, Mk 1.8, Lk 3.16, Jn 1.33. Further argument is given in the section on *en pneumati*.

Gospel of John. In the Jn texts, in the anarthrous version, only 'spirit' occurs, not 'holy spirit':

- ... unless he is born out of (*ek*) water and spirit nobody can enter the Kingdom of God (Jn 3.5)
- What is created out of flesh is flesh, and what is created out of the spirit is Spirit (Jn 3.6)[14]
- ... praying to the Father in (*en*) spirit and truth (Jn 4.23)
- God is spirit[15] and his worshipers must worship in spirit[16] and truth (Jn 4.24)

---

14 Here and in 6.63 the text speaks about both 'the spirit' and 'spirit', obviously making clear that the two represent different concepts: a definite one and a more or less indefinite one. Jn 6.63 is another case where spirit with and without article occur together in one verse: 'the Spirit is the life-making one' (*to pneuma estin to zôiopoioun*), contrasted to the flesh (a), and 'the words spoken by Jesus to the disciples are spirit and life' (*ta rhêmata...pneuma estin kai zôê estin* (b).

15 *Pneuma theos*: rather: spirit is God. A short excursion. Is spirit God? Or is God spirit? *Pneuma ho theos*, says Jn 4.24. God is spirit, say most translations. These translations are correct: no article in Greek, therefore no article in English. In 'God is spirit', however, two differences between Greek and English appear. First about the reversal of the word order, which grammatically is possible. But could it also be understood the other way round, i.e. as is written? Second, the adding of the verb, which grammatically is possible either. But the missing of the verb might imply the suggestion that spirit is God and at the same time God is spirit: both options included. An upgrade for spirit, resulting in writing it as *nomen sacrum*! To be rendered here as Spirit.

Comfort 1984 addresses the issue of *nomen sacrum* in the mss in order to determine whether *pneuma* refers to the divine spirit or to the human one. Unfortunately he does not include the issue of the article use: is there a parallel between *nomem sacrum* and the arthrous usage? In almost all papyri *pneuma* is considered a *nomen sacrum*, i.e. abbreviated. Only five (p11, 13, 46, 66, 75) have both versions, abbreviated and written out. As to the Gospels, only Lk 10.20 (in p75) (referring to an evil spirit) and Jn 3.6 (p66) and Jn 3.8 (p66*) have *pneuma* written out. Jn 3.6 has 'that which is born of the Spirit (abbreviated) is spirit (written out)'. In Jn 3.8 the same copyist first wrote out *pneuma* as indicating 'wind', but then corrected it into the abbreviated version: Spirit [!], so Comfort. What I want to stress is that in these mss all *pneuma* was considered *nomen sacrum*. Yet it is current practice to render it as 'wind' in Jn 3.8a.

Swartz (1993, 128) suggests that the arthrous *ho theos* is God whilst the anarthrous *theos* is 'deity': the Word was with God and the Word was deity [or divine?].

16 Makambu 2005 (190–97) argues that this 'in spirit' does not refer to human spirit but rather "l'oeuvre merveilleuse de Dieu à l'homme, laquelle devient manifeste dans la Révélation" [sic] (Makambu follows Bultmann).

- (The spirit is what is giving life, the flesh serves nothing[17] (Mk 14.38 par)
- the words that I have spoken to you are spirit and are life. (Jn 6.63)

Remaining texts from the Gospels of Luke[18] and Matthew:

- Jesus full of (gen.) holy spirit (Lk 4.1a)
- Spirit of the Lord is upon (*epi*) me (Lk 4.18) (quotation from Isa 61.1)
- … how much more the Father will give from heaven holy spirit to those who ask for it Lk 11.13)
- If I drive out demons being in divine[19] spirit, then the Kingdom of God has come upon (*epi*) you (Mt 12.28)
- David speaking in spirit (Mt 22.43), i.e., while being in spirit

The conclusion is that an anarthrous translation is feasible because sensible. But what does 'spirit' mean?

A side note

What does Acts say about the Holy Spirit at Pentecost? Remarkably what happened was that all were filled with holy spirit: *eplêsthêsan pneumatos hagiou* (2.4). It is remarkable because traditionally it is translated as the Holy Spirit marking its promised outpouring.

And: Jesus had instructed the apostles through (*dia*) holy spirit (1.2)

What is 'Spirit'?

Contrary to the traditional interpretation,[20] spirit / *pneuma* in its indefinite form emerges as a concept of its own; a new 'entity' becomes 'visible': holy spirit, that obviously is not the Holy Spirit, let alone as a Person of the Trinity; spirit, that is different from the spirit (either as a synonym of the holy spirit, or as a quality of an individual). Then another dimension opens, like 'how much more will the heavenly Father give holy spirit' (Lk 11.13). See also the above cases.

What is that so-called concept of its own? In order to grasp the words in their spiritual value reading them as *lectio divina* is required. What emerges then is a sense of Presence, of an entity that is open to be experienced, yet incomprehensible, accessible to (and by) a consciousness that is open to a perception other than by the senses and reason only.

---

17 Makambu (220) makes a sharp divide between *sarx* and *pneuma*: 'l'éphémère réalité terrestre' *versus* 'l'éternelle réalité divine' whilst in my interpretation the spiritual reality of the human being is contrasted to his physical condition, both dimensions fusing into one being.
18 Not included are Lk 24.37 and 24.39 where *pneuma* is spirit as a ghost.
19 *En pneumati theou*: with an implied *ôn*: being in. The noun *theos* without the article is indefinite and is therefore rendered as an adjective, 'divine.'
20 E.g., Crump 1954: *the* Spirit is upon him (Lk 4.18), by *the* Spirit of God (Mt 12.28), how much more will the heavenly Father give *the* Holy Spirit (Lk 11.13).

Barret, in his commentary on the phrase God is Spirit[21], quotes Bornkamm on this issue as saying "God is Spirit! That means, once and for all: He is there, present, he is waiting for us; indeed he is not only waiting, he has run towards us with open arms, as the father ran to meet the prodigal son" (239), a remarkable substantiation of the supposed presence of God, here and now. However, is this so definite, so personal? Crump (1954 *passim*) admits that 'spirit' is used in various situations. This implies on the one hand the trinitarian use, and on the other the OT use. But he draws a sharp line between the use before Jesus' baptism and after: then it is the Holy Spirit.

> Some authors conclude that *pneuma hagion* refers to OT use: it refers to 'a special energy' and therefore is anarthrous (Lagrange 1921, quoted by Crump 1955, 26f), or to 'a divine power or force' (Lebreton 1927), or it is 'impersonal', like in OT (Plummer 1910). Makambu 2005 differentiates between the a-personal *pneuma* in the Synoptics and in part of Jn on the one hand and the person-spirit as Paraclete (27).

But is there no other? When reading the passages quoted above with the anarthrous spirit, the impression gains ground that spirit is a divine element residing in the human being immanently, and at the same time coming upon one transcendently.

Spirit, therefore, cannot be defined, and certainly not in the indefinite form of the anarthrous use. If it should be defined, it must be done indirectly: it is not definite in any sense. It escapes rationality, it is neither visible nor audible, it cannot be perceived by any of the senses: rather there is another dimension to it. Therefore, in sacred books and in mysticism it is presented as 'real', even as a Reality that can be perceived. 'If you have ears, hear!' 'If you have eyes, see!'[22]

> It is an expedition into the field of *pneuma*, it was said above. Field here indicates that *pneuma* is not just a word but rather represents a field. But there is more to that term. Field is also used in concepts like magnetic field, where an active power exists all over. If I understand rightly, in physics a field is a physical quantity associated to each point of spacetime. It may be thought of as extending throughout the whole of space. In association, spirit may be conceptualized as being present all-over, non-localized, yet as real as anything, operating, inconceivably conceivable.

Back to the texts: The anarthrous use of *pneuma hagion* is frequent in Luke, whilst that of *pneuma* is found mainly in John. The frequency of these terms is low in Mark and Matthew. In John we find a particularity. In two pericopes both occur, the arthrous 'the spirit' and the anarthrous 'spirit' (Jn 3.6, 6.63). 'What is created out of the Spirit is spirit', 'The Spirit is giving life; my words to you are spirit'. The Spirit obviously is God's which creates and gives life. What

---

21 Barrett 1978, 239.
22 Chapter 8, The Sower.

is created by the Spirit is spirit, the words spoken by Jesus are spirit. This 'spirit' is living, is an energy (power in the sense of 'kracht'), it is *dunamis*. It is an entity that is present, it is an activity of the Spirit, and at the same time a result of its activity. Therefore, spirit is a condition of the spirit, and spirit is a condition of Spirit.

This issue is discussed in more detail in the next chapter on *en pneumati*, being in spirit.

What Do These Four Forms Imply: pneuma, to pneuma, to pneuma (to) hagion, pneuma hagion: an improvisation

After finding out more or less the meaning of 'spirit,', what is the notion at the back of the four forms in which *pneuma* appears in the Gospels?

Pneuma, we have seen already, appears in four distinctive forms: *pneuma, to pneuma, to pneuma to hagion, pneuma hagion*: spirit, the spirit, the holy spirit, holy spirit. Two forms without and two with *hagion*. Two forms with the definite article ('arthrous'), two without ('anarthrous').

From the contexts in the Gospels, as a hypothesis, I derive a preliminary interpretation that partly has been discussed above already. Here it is schematized. Note, all words used are tentative indications of the reality behind.

1. 'the holy spirit' is located outside the human being but may come to it, or upon it; one may therefore be conscious of it and even be in it; is 'divine in nature'; 'definite'; generally not perceptible by the senses, but exceptionally it is; cf Pentecost. Its meaning is close to the Kingdom of God. It will be written with capitals in this book. It is not necessarily identical with the Holy Spirit in the Trinity, a concept developed theologically centuries later.

2. 'the spirit':
   a. is sometimes synonymous with the Holy Spirit; definite; it will be written with capital S in this book; it may refer either to an individual (divine) entity outside oneself, or rather to a prevailing presence that one can take part in.
   b. sometimes however it denotes the spirit inside a human being[23]; it is definite; yet not perceptible due to its spirit-state, it stands opposite to *sarx*, flesh (or body); it is not the p*suchê* which stands for mind and heart.[24]

---

23 *Pneuma* als "natürliche Ausstattung" as a possibility (Dünzl 2000, 276) that is also denied because *pneuma* is a gift, a grace, e.g., at baptism. Generally it is considered not to belong to human nature. Others refer to Gen 2.7 where God breathed spirit upon Adam. This is countered by those who say, this is *pnoê* (breath), not *pneuma* (spirit).(Dünzl 295). Also BDAG sub 3: 'as a part of human personality'.

24 Often *pneuma* and *psuchê* are equated as meaning life (e.g., Makambu 271; not so: Dünzl *passim*. Crump (1954, 38) interprets spirit as the human soul, i.e. of Jesus: troubled in spirit (Jn 13.21), representing the intellect (sic, wvl): Jesus knew in spirit (Mk 2.8), of the will (*sic*,

3 'holy spirit' denotes an entity not well-defined, generally outside the human being, which sometimes manifests. The closest feasible description is as the *mustêrion* of the Kingdom of God

4 'spirit' denotes an entity not well-defined, maybe inside, maybe outside the human being, generally not perceptible by the senses.

The entities sub 3 and 4 have been covered approximatingly in my text above. Here 'the spirit' as meant sub 1 and 2b will be discussed.

What is 'the Spirit'?

To pneuma (hagion) is found in two different contexts. As specified in the display it is found either as the holy spirit (part of group 1) or as the spirit (group2).

The holy spirit as term is found in the following contexts, clearly referring either to a personal form or as the divine power:

- The Holy Spirit descending on Jesus at his immersal (baptism)
- The Holy Spirit relating to one personally
    - I will put my Spirit on him (Mt 12.18) (though the term holy is lacking I suppose it is understood)
    - The Holy Spirit speaking through you (Mk 13.11, Lk 12.12)
- Blaspheming the Holy Spirit (Mk 3.29, Lk 12.10)

There is one pericope where the Spirit appears as a divine entity

- Jesus was sent out by the Spirit into the desert[25]
    - *Referring also to the parallels it is the Spirit acting on Jesus*

In what context *the spirit* is mostly mentioned?

- The spirit is willing, but the flesh is weak (Mk 14.38, Mt 26.41)
    - *Obviously referring to the spirit and the flesh as his own, or rather as a generl statement on human nature*
- Jesus knew by his (*autou*) spirit (dat.) what they in their hearts were thinking (Mk 2.8)
    - *Obviously his own*
- Jesus renders his spirit (Mt 27.50, Lk 23.46, Jn 19.30)
    - *Oviously his own*

---

wvl): the spirit is willing (Mt 26.41). Crump neglects the article that precedes 'spirit' in all these cases, sometimes with *autou* added (Mk 2.8).

25 Mt 4.1: Jesus was led by the Spirit into the desert; Lk 4.1–2 Jesus, full of holy spirit, returned from the Jordan, and being in the Spirit was led in the desert. See also next chapter.

- Jesus returned to Galilee in the power of the (*tou*, gen.) spirit (Lk 4.14)
  Meaning either his spirit or the Spirit
- Simeon went to the temple being in the (*en tôi*) spirit (Lk 2.27)
  Idem
- My spirit rejoices in (*epi*) God (Lk 1.47)
  o *Mary speaking*

And one instance where it is clear that the spirit is inside a person:

- Her spirit (*to pneuma autês*) returned (daughter of Jairus) (Lk 8.55)
  i.e., she returned from death when her spirit had departed, and it came back to the effect that she was alive again (*pneuma*, not *psuchê* for 'life')

This is the category (sub 2b) where the spirit is interpreted as an entity inside the human being.

A spirit being inside one is not an idea foreign to the Gospels. Numerous are the pericopes where an evil spirit is depicted as dwelling inside the human being. In imaginative terms such a spirit is given form as a definite entity. Why not conceive of the same, maybe even as a divine entity inside? Therefore, the concept of the spirit indwelling is logical.

The following cases do not have the personal pronoun. The meaning is dichotomous in the sense that it either refers to the individual's spirit, or to 'the' (a definite) spirit outside; as I do not find clear references in the Gospels as to the nature of this 'the spirit', I will try and see what an interpretation as an individual's spirit may work out, rendering *to pneuma* as his spirit.

Note. The function of the article is to point out an object. Its use with a word makes the word stand out distinctly: the object is definite.[26]

- Jesus gave up the (*to*) spirit Mt 27.50
  which was his
- Jesus hands over the (*to*) spirit (Jn 19.30) [27]
  which was his

In some of these texts the subject is Jesus (Mk 2.8, Lk 4.14, Mk 14.38 par), also in the pericopes referring to his death (Mt 27.50, Lk 23.46, Jn 19.30). Other subjects are Simeon (Lk 2.27) and Mary (Lk 1.47). Apart from these three

---

26 Swartz 127 referring to H. E. Dana and J. R. Mantley, *A Greek Grammar of the Greek New Testament*, Toronto 1955 (137–51).
27 Karel Hanhart (e-discussion group Kata Markon 24 Nov 2000): *ekpneô* refers to Jesus breathing out the spirit (Mk 15.37) (that he had received at baptism). He refers to Bas van Iersel who remarked that this *ekpneô* is rarely used as a euphemism for dying. This implies that the word suggests a relation with *pneuma*.

figures, the pericope about the return to life of Jairus' daughter (Lk 8.55) at least suggests that all people have a spirit that is life-giving.

Therefore, 'the spirit' in many cases obviously refers to an aspect of the human being.

> If we take the pericopes with '(holy) spirit' together with those with 'the spirit' (in the sense of '2b') the idea arises that the two are not so far apart as the difference between definite and indefinite suggests. Would not the nature of the spirit inside be very close in nature to spirit as Presence? The only difference being that 'the spirit' is limited to the individual and thus defined.

Conclusion

> *Before going to the conclusions a note of caution must be made. Christian exegetes and critics tend to read 'the holy spirit' even when the Greek says 'holy spirit': the Holy Spirit doctrinally is a very important item, interpreted as one of the Persons of the Trinity, as developed much later in Church. 'Neutral' or secular colleagues tend to negate the difference as the issue to them is non-existent, and the concept behind the term is underrated.[28] I have taken a different stand. The texts in the Gospels clearly refer to* pneuma *as a divine element; this has to be respected by trying from the inside of the term to understand (*suniêmi*); I have tried to do so. Moreover, I have made clear from the very beginning that things divine cannot be expressed in words and logics. The reality of* pneuma hagion *exceeds what we can explain about it. Spirit resists being described, defined, classified.*

> *Here is a penetrating quotation from Martin Buber discussing whether* ruah *means wind or rather spirit: "... ruach nicht eins von beiden, sondern unzerspalten beides in einem: jenes von Gott ausgehende brausende Urwehen, das in 'Wind' eine naturhafte, im 'Geist' eine seelenhafte Gestalt annimmt". K.L. Schmidt[29], who presents the quotation, adds Buber's rendering for Jn 3.8: "der Geist geistet wo er will," a wonderful way opening new insights.*

The articular differences as to 'spirit' and 'holy spirit' have been a neglected issue. Is spirit the same as 'the spirit'? And likewise, is 'holy spirit' the same as 'the holy spirit'? Analysis of these terms in the Gospels permits, if not justifies, the conclusion that these differences of form may imply differences of contents. Apart from the Holy Spirit—later interpreted in terms of the Trinity—what is emerging? The indefinite versions of both spirit and holy spirit may be indicating a sense of Presence, an entity that is open to be experienced, yet incomprehensible, accessible to (and by) a consciousness that is open to a

---

28 By way of example, Benjamin 1976, 38 does not differentiate between holy spirit and spirit whilst also neglecting the arthrous issue: all is focused on understanding it as the Holy Spirit.
29 K. L. Schmidt, "Pneuma, Wind, Geist," *Theologische Zeitung* 4.5 (1948), 398.

perception other than by the senses and reason only. The most accessible approach of what holy spirit may imply is when John Baptist tells about how Jesus will 'baptize': he will immerse in holy spirit. That is the very activity Jesus deployed: healing, exorcizing, inspiring, teaching, being present to all those coming for blessing. Holy Spirit apart, we find phrases like to be born out of spirit, God is spirit, spirit will be given when asked for, spirit of the Lord is upon me, David being in spirit. In Part II it was found that the Kingdom of God represents a Presence both within and 'spread out'. Would spirit not refer to that entity? Should we not realize that this entity may be active in our present society and in people here and now? So much for 'spirit.'

'The spirit' sometimes is synonymous with the Holy Spirit, but otherwise indicates something the human (or some humans?) is having, like the spirit that returns to the daughter of Jairus when healed. Is the spirit an entity within us, the breath God breathed unto Adam? Or the spirit that Jesus commits in God's hands. Or Mary's spirit rejoicing.

These conclusions serve as a background to the further chapters in Part IV.

* * *

Excursus: The Issue of the Spirit Inside

The issue of spirit being inside leads to the question of divine presence. Earlier in the book it was found that the Kingdom of God is an entity residing both within and 'spread out.' This idea leads to the question of the interrelatedness of God and the individual, to the issue of the presence of God in the human, specifically in the NT or the Gospels. This issue has been covered in scholarly work only seldom. Fairly recently, however, Nathalie Siffer-Wiederhold's [Siffer] excellent doctoral dissertation was published, *La présence divine à l'individu d'après le Nouveau Testament*[30]. The concept 'presence' as to the individuals is found in the NT in two forms, she says: one is presence *with*, the other presence *in*: 'Dieu est avec…' (*meta*) ('accompagnement'), and 'Dieu est en…' (*en*): 'l'intériorité divine'. Both are relevant to our quest: presence inside, presence all-around. She demonstrates that the concept of the divine presence (God, Jesus, the Holy Spirit) inside the human individual as well as with him/her is presented as a fact in NT writings, mainly in Jn and the Epistles. As a fact: she shows that the NT texts establish this in clear terminology. The contrast between immanence and transcendence is shown as a coexistence: God as the completely Other, God as present inside the individual. I think this is remarkable in view of Christian doctrines that do not allow God and the human

---

30 Nathalie Siffer-Wiederhold, *La présence divine à l'individu d'après le Nouveau Testament*, Cerf, Paris 2005.

to come so close. Although she herself may not agree, I find it to be a great achievement in terms of mysticism in the NT. Her approach rather is in terms of the believer and the savior.

> The concept of her book is wide-reaching, yet her range of the texts studied lacks comprehensiveness. She makes a formal decision to only include the Johannine and the Pauline corpora. Consequently she does not try and find indications of presence in the other Gospels, let alone in Th. Therefore the concept of the Kingdom of God remains out of scope. Neither does she take account of other texts with *pneuma*, and particularly with *en pneumati*, the latter to be discussed in the next chapter.
>
> Her conclusion is—see her title!—that many texts indicate that divine presence is inside the individual. Critics of her work argue that this presence in the individual should be questioned: these texts, they say, are very specific and refer to 'Christians', rather than to individuals in general.

However, could we get an image of what divine immanence means? Listening to such great diversity of voices, reading arguments, consulting the human potential of rising and widening one's consciousness, the great question remains: if God is inside, where does he reside? And if God is incomprehensible, unperceivable, surpassing everything in vastness, beyond sensory perception, beyond..., how can he be with one, or even inside one, and in which / what appearance? A metaphor tells about the drop of water. Analyzing the nature of water, it exclaims 'so I am the ocean!' But where is its vastness, its embracing, its power? Only when becoming ocean in its consciousness, only when annihilating the drop-awareness it becomes ocean (rather than the ocean!), yet not losing anything of itself. The only items lost is the consciousness of limitation, of smallness. The drop then realizes it is part of the ocean, it *is* ocean. Yet it is not *the* ocean. That's the difference. That is the difference between God and spirit, Spirit apart. The drop has become ocean with all its potentials. One then may be able to grasp that the presence of God inside the individual extends limitless, beyond time and space, and therefore both being in spirit and spirit being inside represents a single reality beyond reason. This is the solution to the contradiction of entering the Kingdom versus the Kingdom entering the individual. Spirit is vibrations manifested: on one level perceptible by the senses, on another level perceptible non-sensorially. In the former case perceptible is understood as light, as sound, as touch, and so on, whereas in the latter case understood as invisible light, as inaudible sound, as intangible touch.

Chapter Sixteen

Being in Spirit:
A Case Study on the Pericopes in the Synoptic Gospels with *'en pneumati'*

Introduction

Did John the Baptist tell that Jesus would 'baptize with the Holy Spirit'? Or did he rather baptize in holy spirit: 'immersing in holy spirit'?

Does Jesus drive out spirits 'by the Spirit of God', or rather 'being in God's Spirit'?

Is it conceivable that answers to these and other questions depend on the grammatical use of the article: holy spirit or the Holy Spirit? Or on how a single preposition is being translated: en *as 'in' or 'with'? Or by taking a literal translation rather than one formed in the traditions of the Church: baptizing or immersing? In the previous chapter it became clear that such situations may occur. Consequently even theological relevant meanings may depend on seemingly minor details.*

One of these questions—involving the differences between holy spirit and the Holy Spirit and spirit and the spirit—have already come up in the previous chapter. Here however a closer look will be given, as a test of my suppositions.

Another characteristic of this chapter is its limited focus. Essentially the only topic addressed will be the expression en pneumati *in its occurrences in the gospels and elsewhere in the NT.*

This chapter is the elaboration of one aspect of 'spirit' as treated in chapter 15, the phrase *en pneumati*, (being) in spirit. It emphasizes the argument of this Part that spirit is not apart from the human.

It is a rather technical treatise, but with challenging outcomes. Readers following the general argument of the book may skip the main body of the text and jump to the conclusions.

The study presented here stands on itself. Hence some repetitions from previous chapters seem to be unavoidable.

Note: as told in the caption this chapter discusses the phrase *en pneumati* in the Synoptics only, save where indicated differently.

And, all passages (pericopes) referring to bad and impure spirits are left out of the presentation[1].

Being in Spirit: *en pneumati*; the Gospels

This is a central concept in spirituality and mysticism: being conscious of one's spirit, of the divine, of Presence. It is about a state of consciousness that is beyond the normal state of awareness yet not separate from it. "[Simeon] being in the Spirit went into the temple courts" (Lk 2.27). Yet 'being in (the) spirit' is not found in current translations though in the Greek text it is testified quite a few times.

Therefore, what is the meaning of the concept *en pneumati*, literally 'in spirit', as presented in the 11 pericopes in which it occurs in the synoptic Gospels of the NT?

Two issues come to the fore. One is the preposition *en* and its diverse renderings in English translations. The other one is the use of the article, building on what was said on it in the previous chapter. These are two apparently minor things that in my interpretation have an enormous bearing.

First a few words about the *en* issue. Of all 11 pericopes with *en* in Greek only one is rendered as 'in' in NIV. In the other 10 cases the *en* is translated differently and mostly understood as an instrumentalis. Consequently the sense is seen not as 'in spirit' but 'by/with/through spirit'. a completely different sense, certainly in view of what we have found in the previous chapter.

Similar results are found when considering the other issue, the article use[2]. Of the 11 cases the Greek has seven pericopes without the (definite) article. Amazingly the English rendering in the NIV and NSV versions negates these seven cases and translates all of these with the definite article. In view of the insights gained in the previous chapter the two versions, Greek and English, seem to represent two different worlds: the Greek referring in most cases to an indefinite spirit, the English talking about the spirit as something definite. This is the more important when the adjective *hagion* (holy) is included in the concept: holy spirit or *the* Holy Spirit! Does *en pneumati hagiôi* (in holy spirit) refer to an indefinite holy spirit? Or, by adding the definite article, to the Third Person of the Trinity, the Holy Spirit? On the other hand it is interesting to see how the so-called anarthrous use (i.e., without the definite article) suggests divine spirit (or holy spirit) to be present. Thus, a seemingly inconspicuous

---

1   Invariably these spirits are qualified by adding adjectives like *akarthaton, ponêron*. Significantly such spirit generally appears with the article unless it is not yet identified, or referred to in general.
2   About the technicalities see the relevant section in the previous chapter.

detail carries with it theological weight. How has this issue been treated in the professional literature? Consulting the scholarly literature over the last many decades one finds that hardly an author has analyzed this issue *per se*. In general one sees that the concept of spirit in the Gospels is interpreted from the concept of Holy Spirit as it developed in Church in later periods. Consequently this will have colored the translations and interpretations of these Gospel texts. Most studies addressing Holy Spirit are of Christian origin where it is believed that the Holy Spirit is the Third Person of the Divine Trinity who manifested for the first time in Jesus from his baptism, who was sent on the first Pentecost and who is accessible for those believing in Jesus Christ.

Even so, the concept was not new at all in the time the Gospels were written. The Hebrew Bible and its Greek translation, the LXX, frequently mention (the) spirit being with / in / upon a (or the) human being, as we will see later. Christian authors tend, however, to distinguish sharply between the Christian concept of the spirit and the non-Christian. This paper does not take this Christian a priori but rather tries to trace what meaning of 'spirit' emerges when we take the concept at face value—which suggests that (the) (holy) spirit (of God) may be with, upon or in the human being.

> *This chapter therefore proposes as a hypothesis that the pericopes with* en pneumati *indicate that a person can be 'in spirit' in terms of a condition of his/her consciousness and as an inner experience of reality. Conversely one can experience 'spirit' inside oneself as an inner reality. Therefore* en pneumati *may be rendered as '(being) in spirit'. This is preferred above renderings like 'by spirit', 'through spirit', 'with spirit', and so on.*

Consequently, four questions will be addressed:

(1) how to translate *en* in these pericopes?
(2) whether, if by way of exercise it be translated as *in*, it results in a sound text;
(3) how to translate the (an)arthrous (i.e., with/without the [definite] article) use of 'spirit'?
(4) to what view does the variant translation lead us?

What do the texts say? Here it must suffice to render the essential phrases only. For a wider one is referred to the Annex. Three versions of each pericope in the Synoptics with *en pneumati* are given: the NIV rendering, the Greek text, and my proposal.

The texts form an impressive witness to the nature of *pneuma* as referring to a state of raised consciousness.

Texts with *en pneumati*[3]

Immersion or Baptism

> I baptize you with water.... He will baptize you with the Holy Spirit and with fire
> *Egô men humas baptizô en hudati.... Autos humas baptisei en pneumati hagiôi kai puri*
> **I immerse you in water.... He will immerse you in holy spirit and fire**[4].
> Mt 3:11

> I baptize you with (in) water, but he will baptize you with the Holy Spirit
> *Egô ebaptisa humas hudati, autos de baptisei humas en pneumati hagiôi*
> **I immerse you in water, but he will immerse you in holy spirit.**
> Mk 1:8

> I baptize you with water.... He will baptize you with the Holy Spirit and with fire
> *Egô men hudati baptizô humas.... Autos humas baptisei en pneumati hagiôi kai puri*
> **I immerse you with water.... He will immerse you in holy spirit and fire.**
> Lk 3:16

> ...who sent me to baptize with water...he who will baptize with the Holy Spirit
> *...all'ho pempsas me baptizein en hudati...houtos estin ho baptizôn en pneumati hagiôi*
> **...who sent me to immerse in water...he is the one immersing in holy spirit.**
> Jn 1:33

Evaluation of the baptism pericopes Immersing rather than baptizing

> Notes
>
> *Baptizô*: WNT: *dip, immerse, ... wash* (in non-Christian lit. also 'plunge, sink, drench, overwhelm'; fig. 'soak')., in our lit. only in ritual sense.[5]
>
> Immersing is done *in* water rather than *with* water. This is clear in John's baptism that takes place in the Jordan river.
>
> 'Immersing in holy spirit' is expressive of a presence all around in which one *is*.
>
> 'In fire' is specific for Mt and for Lk in the baptism pericopes and underlines the sanctity of this announced 'baptism'; it is related to fire as purifying. Theologically it is considered to refer to the eschaton.[6] However: "In almost all OT theophanies it appears

---

3   Annex 3 offers a complete analysis of each of the pericopes.
4   Immersing in fire: mostly thought to refer to apocalyptics, in another view stands for the purifying effect of fire or light.
5   Ferguson (2009, 53–54) refers to metaphorical usage in classical Greek where it may mean 'being overwhelmed,' or more generally: "something exercises a controlling influence that brings about a change of condition."
6   TDNT VI (F. Lang): "The reference in the Synoptics is always to eschatological judgment" (sub D II 1). And: "In the Messianic preaching of John the Baptist the final judgment is portrayed already as a baptism of fire" (sub D III ('Theological use')', 2 ('Fire as a means of divine judgment), b, (a).

as representing the unapproachable sanctity and overpowering glory of Yahweh", cf the burning bush (Ex 3.2), and: "Fire is a means whereby God reveals His presence [!], and it represents the mystery of the Glory of Yahweh...." (Ex 24.17).[7] Old traditions hold fire to be purifying; fire is a most refined element connected with deity and spirit.[8] An excellent exposition on baptizing in fire is given by Dunn[9]

Traditionally the NT translations render 'baptism with the Holy Spirit.' Close reading reveals that the Greek says 'in holy spirit.'[10] Moreover, I prefer to translate as immersing, avoiding the confessional non-contemporary term baptizing. Reviewing the 'baptism' pericopes, the proposal—to immerse in holy spirit—appears as an at least feasible alternative. From our critical evaluation of the announcement by John the Baptist what Jesus will do a picture emerges that is completely different from what the current translations transmit. The traditional image of baptism with water is replaced here by an image of Jesus immersing people in encompassing holy spirit and purifying 'fire,' as announced by the Baptist.[11] From the analysis of the Kingdom of God, we have learned what this immersing in spirit may mean: entering into the Kingdom, the Kingdom entering into one. As is known from the Gospels Jesus did not 'baptize' during his ministry, neither in nor with water. What he did do was

---

7   Both quotations, TDNT VI, C, I (Fire in the OT) 4 (Fire in relation to God), a (Fire in theophany).
8   TDNT VI, A III (Fire in religion), 1 and 3.
9   Dunn 2003a, 366–69. Also Ferguson 2009, 90–91.
10 Dunn (2003a, 366–69) to my knowledge is the first one to publish the translation as 'in (Holy) Spirit and fire. I had found this translation independently already when preparing my SBL paper for the Bible Translation Section 2000. Dunn, however, does not take the consequences of the anarthrous use, as far as I can see. Moreover, he continues to interpret it in an eschatological perspective. For example also in Mt 12.28 / Lk 11.20 (discussed in Part II) about the Finger (or the Spirit) of God which implies "a plenitude of the (eschatological) Spirit" (459).
11 Most authors do not explain their preference for the instrumental use. For Bennema 2003, however, spirit baptism refers to revelation and cleansing [I would prefer 'purifying' in order to prevent association with rituals], in which "the Spirit would be instrumental" (40). He considers "*baptizein en pneumati hagôi* as a metaphor for *the Messiah's ongoing revelation of God and the cleansing of Israel* [sic] *by means of the Spirit*, effecting both salvation and judgement ..." (55) (italics in the original). Therefore, Bennema interprets 'spirit baptism' not in terms of an individual being immersed in holy spirit, thus detaching it from its meaning as formulated by the Baptist. Finally he understands it as "Jesus' programme of cleansing people through revelation by means of Spirit" (60), the revelation culminating on the cross (52). Thus for Bennema it "is not the mode of *baptizô*, but the purpose for which the rite is performed" (38). A more recent interpretation by Dunn is found in Dunn 2003a, 366–69.

My proposal is closer to Dunn's who sees this spirit baptism as Jesus initiating others into the new age / Kingdom (as worded by Bennema 56). He refers to J.D.G. Dunn, *Baptism in the Holy Spirit*, Philadelphia 1970.

immersing in holy spirit.[12] He did so when healing, when exorcizing, and 'simply' through, by, and in his holy presence and radiance. People thronging around him just to touch him, even only his garments (expressed in objectifying terms, "exercising a controlling influence that brings about a change of condition," Ferguson 2009, 54).

A change of the usual scene of baptism emerges when one just scrutinizes the text on prepositions and articles and when one tries to view the text independent of church traditions.[13]

Being in Spirit, Spirit Being Inside

Here the remaining pericopes in the Gospels with *en pneumati* are presented

> But if I drive out demons by the Spirit of God
> *Ei de en pneumati theou egô ekballô ta daimonia*
> **But if I drive out the demons (being) in God's spirit....**
> Mt 12:28

> How is it then that David, speaking by the Spirit, calls him 'Lord'? For he says...
> *Pôs oun Dauid en pneumati kalei auton kurion legôn...*
> **How is it then that David (being) in spirit calls him 'Lord'? For he says...**
> Mt 22:43

> David himself speaking by the Holy Spirit...
> *Autos Dauid eipen en tôi pneumati tôi hagiôi...*
> **David himself (being) in the Holy Spirit declared: ...**
> Mk 12:36

> And he [John the Baptist] will go on before the Lord, in the spirit and power of Elijah
> *Kao autos proseleusetai enôpion autou en pneumati kai dunamei Êliou*

---

12 I have found one author indicating that baptizing is to be understood as immersing: "immergés dans une vie spirituelle renouvelée" distancing Jesus from John the Baptist (Makambu 2007, 110). Yet even he mixes up holy spirit with the Holy Spirit (103ff).

13 Ferguson (2009) has written a thorough treatise of baptism in the first centuries. He produces (38-59) a fine analysis of the term *baptizô* confirming my interpretation as 'immerse'. The Baptist's prediction of immersing in holy spirit is not carried further into Christian baptism issues, as far as I could trace. Neither does he pick up the article issue in the statements by the Baptist 89-95): he translates correctly as Holy Spirit (not: the Holy Spirit) but does not ask for the difference. The issue of the meaning of *en* is treated extensively in the same section but without asking what 'in holy spirit' would imply as different form 'with'. Ostensibly the issue is not seen as such because baptism is conceived as receiving the Holy Spirit "as Jesus' reception of the Spirit was described as an anointing" (198). Viewed thus the 'with' is more at hand than 'in.'

And he [John the Baptist] will go on before the Lord, in spirit and power (energy) of Elijah,
Lk 1:17

Moved by the Spirit, he went into the temple courts
Kai êlthen en tôi pneumati eis to hieron
Being in the Spirit he went into the temple courts
Lk 2:27

Jesus, full of the Holy Spirit, returned from the Jordan
and was led by the spirit in the desert...
*Iêsous de plêrês pneumatos hagiou hupestrepsen apo tou Iordanou
kai êgeto en tôi pneumati en têi erêmôi...*
**Jesus, full of holy spirit, returned from the Jordan
and (being) in the Spirit was led in the desert...**
Lk 4:1

At that time Jesus, full of joy through the Holy Spirit, said
En autêi têi hôrai êgalliasato [en] tôi pneumati tôi hagiôi, kai eipen....
At that time Jesus was full of joy (being) in the Holy Spirit, and said....
Lk 10:21

Discussion

This rendering by 'in'—in spirit, in the spirit, being in spirit, being in the spirit—appears to offer a sensible and even plausible alternative to the common interpretation as an instrumentalis: 'by'(5 times), 'with' (4), 'in' (1) (sic), and 'through'(1), unless theology takes the lead. Right on that point the reluctance may reside in recognizing 'in spirit' as 'in spirit'. Seeing the results above, the proposed rendering changes the sceneries completely: being baptized turns out to be enveloped and purified in holy spirit; when driving out demons Jesus is in spirit rather than being prompted by it from outside; Jesus was in the spirit when being led in the desert; he returned to Galilee being in the power of the spirit rather than being guided from outside. Spirit is not outside but rather within. David was speaking in spirit (or even in the holy spirit) rather than being prompted from outside; one can be full of holy spirit. This suggests that apart from being in spirit, spirit may be inside one. This proposal is rather radical. It must be seen as an alternative—not less, not more—to be taken into account seriously. This is an exercise rather than being definite, let alone to be the truth. It is necessary therefore to get into a few checks.

BEING IN SPIRIT: A CASE STUDY

To begin, is there is an inherent relationship between (the) spirit and the human being, either (the) spirit dwelling inside a human being or the human being in (the) spirit?

The other issue to be addressed is whether or not the (an) arthrous reference to the spirit (i.e., with/without article) is relevant to the meaning of a text.

First we will look at two major dictionaries (on the former issue) and then review some general literature (on both issues).

The dictionaries: TDNT, WNT/BDAG

The TDNT and the WNT/BDAG offer a concise overview.

Note: The NT texts referred to appear in the footnotes, generally in the NIV translation. *The italics are mine (in the text below as emphasis, in the footnotes to highlight the words with 'spirit'*; a variant translation is presented in [ ]).

TDNT (author: A. Oepke)[14]

In a special lemma, *En* with *pneuma*, the TDNT argues that "[t]he thought of *the Spirit in man* is local. Like evil spirits…the Spirit of God dwells in man (cf. Num. 27:18[15]; Jn. 14:17[16]; R 8.9[17], 1 Cor. 3:16[18], 6.19[19])"[20]. "The converse, that *man is in the Spirit* (Mt. 22:43[21]; Rom. 8:9[22]; Rev. 21:10[23]; 1 Cor. 12:3[24]; Eph. 6:18[25]) is also based on a spatial sense…. [It] approximates to the idea of a state". "…the Spirit may easily be identified

---

14   TDNT II *en* B 2.
15   So the LORD said to Moses, "Take Joshua son of Nun, a man *in whom is the spirit* [who has spirit in him], and lay your hand on him.
16   The Spirit of truth. The world cannot accept him, because it neither sees him nor knows him. But you know him, for *he lives* (oikei') *with you and will be in you.*
17   You are controlled…by the Spirit, if the Spirit of God lives in you.
18   Don't you know that you yourselves are God's temple and that *God's Spirit lives in you*?
19   Do you not know that your body is a temple of the Holy Spirit, who is in you, whom you have received from God?
20   To these references I add Ps 51.11 "Do not cast from me your presence or take your Holy Spirit from me" (NIV); ψ 50.13 *to pneuma to hagion sou* (LXX).
21   He said to them, "How is it then that David, speaking *by the Spirit*, calls him 'Lord'? For he says," [see in section 2].
22   Those controlled by the sinful nature cannot please God. You, however, are controlled not by the sinful nature but *by the Spirit, if the Spirit of God lives in you*. And if anyone does not have the Spirit of Christ, he does not belong to Christ. [Or rather: Those who are in flesh cannot please God. But you are not in flesh but in spirit, if God's spirit lives (oikei') in you. And if anyone does not have spirit of Christ, he is not his.]
23   And he carried me away *in the Spirit* [in spirit] to a mountain great and high, and showed me the Holy City, Jerusalem, coming down out of heaven from God.
24   Therefore I tell you that no one who is speaking *by the [in] Spirit* of God says, "Jesus be cursed," and no one can say, "Jesus is Lord," *except by the Holy Spirit*. [if not in holy spirit].
25   And pray *in the Spirit* [in spirit] on all occasions with all kinds of prayers and requests. With this in mind, be alert and always keep on praying for all the saints.

with the state produced by Him". This is corroborated by Steyer (II 37K) where *en pneumati* is rendered as "im Geist, d.h. im Kraftbereich des Gottesgeistes": being in the power sphere of God's Spirit.

Therefore, spirit is factual, it is not a metaphor. Also, being in (the) spirit, is spatial (i.e., again, factual, not as a metaphor). It is added: "but approximates to the idea of a state," i.e., of one's being, a condition, a state of consciousness. This implies that it is not just a thought or a way of expressing. It is a reality: (the) spirit is in us, and at the same time 'us being in (the) spirit' is true as well.

En in NT Greek may be an instrumentalis (Steyer II, 34F): *by the spirit* rather than *in the spirit*. However, in the context of the above quoted pericopes it is unnecessary to interpret the *en* in this manner. Rather it is used "modal zur Bezeichnung des Zustandes, der Sphäre" (p. 31). Anyhow the instrumentalis is not the interpretation Oepke uses for *en pneumati*. At the end of the passage on *en pneumati* he says "There is a tendency towards the instrumental use", quoting R 14.7, 8.15; 1Cor 6.11, 12.9, 12.13; Eph 2.18, 3.5. Nevertheless, even for these pericopes no objection can be raised against a local interpretation: being in spirit, neither grammatically nor as to contents. Therefore we may conclude that some authors interpret the *en* with dative too easily and unnecessarily as instrumental. Facts point to a different conclusion: the local version. This is further corroborated by the analysis of 'in' in these and other pericopes.

> One is that in the baptism pericopes Lk has an instrumentalis for 'with water' (*hudati*). So does Mk according to some witnesses whilst other witnesses have *en*. Both have the parallel with 'spirit' with *en*. In 1 Cor 6:11 it is said that 'you were justified in (*en*) the name of the Lord Jesus Christ and in (*en*) the Spirit of God': a clear parallel in expression. A translation with 'in' is advisable in both cases. More cases will come up later. In 1 Cor 12:8-9 we find a sequence of different propositions: *dia, kata, en, en*, showing the difference between the instrumentalis and the *en*-form.[26] So both from the context and linguistically it seems appropriate to translate 'en' by 'in.'

Concluding, it is clear that there is no obstacle to the translation of *en* as 'in' as being the linguistically closest sense. This stands apart from arguments pro *en* from the point of view of contents.

WNT / BDAG[27]*:*

> The use of *en pneumati* is considered a formulaic expression. For example: *en pneumati ôn*[28], being under the special influence of a spirit. Or '*lalein en pneumati theou / hagiôi*, speaking under divine inspiration (or rather literally 'speaking (while being) in divine / holy spirit) 1 Cor 12:3.

---

26 NIV does not recognize this difference translating as through, by means of, by, by.
27 Lemma *en*: WNT sub I 5 (end, p. 524), BDAG 4c (p, 328, end).
28 WNT supposes the *einai*. See my argument supra.

> "The expr. *en pneumati einai* is also used to express the idea that *someone is under the special influence of the spirit*, even a demonic spirit", or rather: being in that spirit, referring to e.g. the pericopes Mt 22.43, Mk 12.36, Lk 2.27, presented above. Cf et Rev 17.3 (: the angel carried me being in spirit away into a desert), 21.10 (: …carried me being in spirit away to a mountain…).[29]

Also here the conclusion is that in the pericopes referred to here, *en pneumati* may be translated by '(being) in (the) (holy) spirit' without interfering with the meaning of the text.

A Few Comments

- Interestingly especially TDNT in its above quoted statement about 'we are in (the) spirit' and '(the) spirit is in us' justifies our variant translation.
- "The expression *en pneumati einai* is also used to express the idea that someone is under the special influence of the spirit, even a demonic spirit." (WNT, above). Interestingly, as is shown in the stories about expelling the impure spirit, it is clear that that spirit is inside the individual. So the influence comes from inside. Why should not the (pure) spirit be inside too? It disappears at death only (see later in this section), but it often needs to be renewed, or 'refueled', by the gift of God, of the Spirit, as grace. The places referred to at least open up this text as an alternative to the general doctrine that spirit is foreign to the human being.
- Interesting are the passages in the TDNT and the WNT (or BDAG, here like elsewhere) italicized by me: the *en pneumati* suggests a spatial concept; or it may refer to a state or condition of being, of consciousness. This may be the sense of R 8.8-9 also: *en sarki einai, en pneumati (einai)*. NIV translates the former as 'controlled by sinful nature'. Why not translate simply by 'being in flesh' and 'being in spirit'? After all, we *are* in flesh all the time. Why could we not be in spirit as well? This implies that spirit is something real: it can be experienced.
- Both the TDNT and the WNT, however, remain dualistic on the whole. Here however the 'inside' option is what *prima facie* the text is suggesting.
- What strikes one is the absence of major comments as regards content by either TDNT or WNT on the use or absence of the definite article. This seems an important issue in view of the question whether or not the text refers to the holy spirit or another definite spirit (like the impure spirits), or just to spirit or holy spirit in a general sense. We made it a point to be precise in this respect in our variant translations as presented. After all, the concept of the Holy Spirit in that particular sense came to bloom only much later.

---

29 Comparable are 1 Jn 5.19 *en tôi ponêrôi keisthai*, lying in the evil, R 3.19 *oi en nomôi*, who are in (the reach of) the law, 1 Cor 15.22 *en tôi Adam apothnêiskein*, like everyone being in Adam dies, so everyone being in Christ will be made alive. This proposal as an alternative (WNT, ibid.).

- Translating the expression by '*being* in spirit', as I do when it refers to a condition, may at first sight seem unjustified as the participium *ôn* is missing. In Greek this seems to be current practice, as illustrated by WNT's reference to "ἄνθρωπος ἐν πν. ἀκαθάρτῳ (ὤν)" (Mk 1:23) where the participium is added by way of clarification, suggesting that it is regular practice to leave it out. For further arguments see above. In any case the *en* is closer to the original than with *by*, e.g. in Mk 12:36.
- Significantly neither the WNT nor the TDNT discuss the pericopes around John's baptism. As we have seen, the relevant passages are generally translated by "by" instead of "in", whilst logic suggests that one would immerse in rather than by water (or spirit).
- The interpretation in both TDNT and WNT on *en pneumati* in the lemma *en* is different from what both dictionaries say about *pneuma* in the respective lemma *pneuma*.[30] See chapter 15.

In conclusion, neither the TDNT nor the WNT raise serious barriers against our hypothesis / proposal. On the contrary, they do offer materials sustaining it.

Other NT Texts

Therefore, spirit is an entity of a different dimension, different from matter, from psyche, from logic, from emotion. It is not material, it is essence. It is abstract and personal at the same time.[31] It can be inside one and at the same time can be outside (cf the kingdom in Th 3). In its definite and concrete appearance it manifests as the spirit (arthrous), in the abstract it is spirit (anarthrous), e.g.: '*pneuma ho theos*' (God Spirit, Jn 4:24, quoted above). From the variant translations it appears that both the concept of spirit inside one, and that of being in spirit are consistent with spiritual and mystical experiences as reported in literature. See chapter 2.

The text analysis in this chapter has highlighted pericopes exclusively with *en pneumati*. This section offers additional material about *pneuma* that will corroborate the conclusions reached so far.

---

30 In TDNT the authors are different: Oepke for *en pneumati*, Schweizer for *pneuma*
31 One might consider 'personal' and 'abstract' as opposites. This, however, is not logical: abstract is opposite to concrete, personal is opposite to impersonal. Personal is 'something' one can relate to in terms of love, attachment, communication. Spirit, as it appears in the NT texts referred to, is abstract in the sense that it is not visible, not sensual, not imaginable. Yet one can relate to it, love it, feel close to it, feel to be one with it, within it; and it may relate to you, you may feel its love, you feel drawn by it, you may feel it to be one with you, within you. *In spiritualibus* opposites are being transcended. One discovers that spirit is a spark of Spirit, spirit originating from and longing to unite again with Spirit.

In Jn abundant material is available about God in Jesus and Jesus in God, about Jesus in the disciples and disciples staying in Jesus. Here is one case about the spirit indwelling, Jn 14.17:

> ...the Spirit of [T]ruth. The world cannot accept him [it], because it neither sees him [it], nor knows him [it]. But you know him [it], for he [it] lives with you and will be [is][32] in[33] you.

The importance of this pericope resides in the statement that "you are in me, and I am in you" (Jn 14.20). Jesus (or his spirit) remains with the disciples and will be in them, or they in the spirit; all translations under review translate "in" (NRSV adds in a note 'or: among').[34]

Also at other places in the synoptic Gospels we find instances suggesting that the spirit is in the human being and is essential to being alive. See also the pericopes mentioned in the footnotes in the passage on *en pneumati* in TDNT (section 3.1).

> ...for it will not be you speaking, but the Spirit of your Father speaking in (NIV: through you (*en humin*) (Mt 10.20)

'The spirit of your Father is speaking inside you; it is the holy spirit which is speaking, not you yourselves': clear language which *prima facie* cannot be misunderstood: the spirit inside one is speaking in and through one.

Closely related are three texts about Jesus' death where spirit is mentioned explicitly[35]. For further details see next chapter.

> Mt 27.50: *aphêken to pneuma*: let go the spirit
>
> Lk 23.46: *eis cheiras sou paratithemai to pneuma mou*: into your hands I entrust my spirit.
>
> Jn 19.30: *paredôken to pneuma*, he entrusted / handed over the spirit

Which implies that Jesus had spirit inside him, which he surrendered in breathing it out when dying.

Also Paul states (R 8.9)

> ... spirit of God is dwelling in[36] you: *pneuma theou oikei*[37] *en humin*

---

32 Some reputed witnesses even say '*is* in you' (present rather than future mode!): P66* B D W and others; *estai* is supported by P66c, P75vid, S, A, q and others].

33 NRSV: 'among' instead of 'in'

34 Critics may remark that this spirit in John is not comparable to (the) (holy) spirit in the Synoptics. Let me have the benefit of the doubt in view of my extensive argument.

35 I.e. in all Gospels except Mark which has only *exepneusen*, breathed out.

36 NIV says: "...are controlled by ..."

The question to be asked is "why?": You are not in flesh but in spirit: *humeis de ouk este en sarki alla en pneumati*

Or

Don't you know that you are God's temple and that God's Spirit dwells in you?
Ouk oidate hoti naos theou este kai to pneuma tou theou oikei en humin?
1 Cor 3.16

For the reverse, us living in (the) spirit, there is a paucity of Pauline texts. See in the first place R 8:9a quoted above. Further:

... praying at all times (being) in [the] Spirit: *proseuchomenoi en panti kairôi en pneumati*
Eph 6.18

For in him (God) we live and move and are: *en autôi gar zômen kai kinoumetha*[38] *kai esmen*
Acts 17.28

Moreover the following texts, all from Lk, are relevant. We have met them before. There will be recognition. Holy spirit will come on Mary (in the annunciation, 1:35), Elizabeth was filled with holy spirit when meeting Mary (1:41), the same with Zechariah when prophesizing (1:67). With Simeon (2:25–27): Holy Spirit was upon him; revealed to him by the holy spirit; (being) in the spirit he went into the temple courts). Mary was pregnant *ek* holy spirit (Mt 1:18); John the Baptist will be filled by holy spirit, and acted in it (Lk 1:15, 17).

In these texts reference is made to different relationships of a particular human being to (the) (holy) spirit. All texts accentuate the nearness of spirit, or even some form of almost identity with it: it being inside one, one being in it, it coming upon one, it being upon one, being filled by it; and he acted in it.

In general logic we suppose that if a is in b, b cannot be in a: if the coffee is in the cup, the cup cannot be in the coffee. However, from the pericopes presented both above and earlier we find that both may be true: a human being may be in spirit / in the spirit / in the holy spirit / in holy spirit, and that—seemingly in contradiction to it—(the) (holy) spirit may be inside one. If I am in love, love is in me at the same time. Our hypothesis is affirmed.

---

37   The verb *oikein*, to dwell, is used (*oikos* is house). The verb is used "to describe inward psychological and spiritual processes". (TDNT V 135).
38   Zerwick 1996: pass., intr., hence 'are being moved'.

An Inquiry into Literature

Contrary to the results so far, most literature is of the view that there is a sharp division between on the one hand the Spirit of God and the Holy Spirit and on the other hand spirit and the human being in general. Moreover often a sharp division between NT and OT use is made, e.g. Ewert 1983, Barrett 1947, 1950, Batdorf 1950, Benjamin (1976), Montague (1976), Schweizer (1979, and in his article on *pneuma* in the TDNT), Westall (1977). The spirit of God would not be inherent to human nature (e.g. May 1957 when comparing *pneuma* with *atman*) nor is it to be obtained as a human quality. Dünzl (2000), alternatively, remarks that in some views the human being may possess *pneuma*, even as a gift from God.[39]

Moule (1971, 281) takes a middle position: "Both in the Old and New Testaments, the word 'spirit' sometimes denotes some aspect of man; but seldom without some indication that it is really the Spirit of God, on loan, *as it were* (italics, WvL), to man" [which does not match with many of the texts analyzed before]. Moule: during his ministry Jesus he was speaking and acting by [being in] the holy spirit but the Holy Spirit would come only after the resurrection and the glorification (the Paraclete). It is to be obtained through faith, more precisely through baptism, says Moule. Crump (1954) and others differentiate between "trinitarian use" and "OT use", as if there would not be anything in between. Crump—and rightly so, in my opinion—is criticized by Zerwick (1956) on the all too easy "hineininterpretierung" of church theology into the simple spiritual story of Mark (e.g., about baptism): his (Crump's) concept of the holy spirit breathes the OT view. A similar viewpoint we find in Kingsbury (1979). To what degree the impression is justified that mostly the meaning of (the) (holy) spirit in Gospel texts is interpreted in the light of the later trinitarian dogma and other doctrines is an open issue.

---

39 Dünzl differentiates between a theological and an anthropological pneuma concept. The latter implies "die natürliche Ausstattung jedes Menschen mit Pneuma" (11, n 1). He draws the attention of the reader to the fact that in the NT (like in the OT and the 'neben- und nachtestamentlichen Schriften'...) "auch der anthropologische Pneumabegriff verwendet wurde" (276): "ein von Gott geschenktes anthropologisches Pneuma" (Irenaeus, Tertullian) (295), or as a code for the divine ("für Gottes Sein oder Wesen, die göttliche Sphäre oder Dimension" (379). Here, it seems to me, the anthropological pneuma concept is similar to the pneuma concept found in the pericopes analyzed in Part IV. On the other hand Dünzl concludes that "Pneumabegabung jenseits der biblisch-kirchlichen Grenzen" is almost impossible (382). He also makes clear that the concept of *pneuma* did not evoke interest until Origenes. There was no pneumatology before Origen (11, 391). The developments since the 2nd century have altered the NT traditions (391). *Sic.*

In general what strikes one when reading this work is the lack of the differentiations I have brought to attention: spirit / the spirit / holy spirit / the holy spirit.

Over the past decades the general view on the roots of the NT shifts from Greek to Jewish tradition: the OT, culturally and theologically, is the main backdrop. It is found that the 'spirit' is quite frequent in the OT. Even 'holy spirit' is not absent.[40] On the other hand, I am in full agreement with those who underline the spiritual originality of the message of Jesus. The notion of spirit in the Gospels (and to a certain degree in the other books of the NT) is a fresh one, or more precisely, gets a deeper undertone.

What does one find as to the interiority of spirit? Younger (1967) suggests that the spirit of God is with and within (selected) human beings; to Paul the center of religious life was the experience: "an experience of the Spirit, of 'Christ in me.'" Westall (1977), though not being in agreement with the interiority quotes some scholars who maintain "that the Holy Spirit is at work at the natural level in man" (Lindsay Dewar 1959), or: that 'the Holy Spirit is speaking in men of all faiths' (Taylor 1972); Zaehner (1974) characterizes the Holy Spirit as "the God who is the inspiration of all religions and peculiar to none". Spirit is a universal notion in religion.

Some pericopes with *ruah* (or *pneuma* in the LXX) refer to the spirit in the human being or it being in the spirit. "The pervasive presence of the Spirit of God is everywhere assumed in the OT" (Ewert, 25). Schoemaker (1904) states that in Jewish writers *en pneumati* always refers to God's spirit: to be in spirit (*en pneumati*) meant to possess the spirit of God or to be possessed by that spirit." Burton (1918, p.71): *ruah* was used already very early as a religious term denoting the invisible power by which God operated in the world, or God himself operating, but not a hypostasis distinct from God. Lodahl (1992, 4), in a quotation from Killough:

"'Spirit' refers essentially to God: God experienced as inspiring, motivating, empowering, vivifying, indwelling, and acting in many ways which are...recognized by faith as modes of the personal active presence of God". It is "...referring to God's dynamic presence and activity". Crump (1954) makes clear that the concept of spirit, and even holy spirit, even before the baptism of Christ, was present—though not in the form of the Third Person. He quotes Knaben in his Gospel commentaries (1905) saying "the Holy Spirit is, as it were, a divine seed and soul, by which all living beings are fecundated and animated", very much in line with OT concepts (26). It reminds of his

---

40 Of these we quote three of the pericopes where it is clear that the spirit is within one (italics, WvL):
So the LORD said to Moses, "Take Joshua son of Nun, a man *in whom is the spirit* [who has spirit in him], and lay your hand on him (Num 27.18)
Create in me a pure heart, O God, and *renew a steadfast spirit within me*. Do not cast me from your [P]resence or take *your Holy Spirit from me*. (Ps 51.10-11)
Where is he who set *his Holy Spirit in them* (*en autois*) (NIV: among them) (Is 63.11)

contemporary, Harnack. Or Crump quoting another author, "God communicates a special energy" (27); we may interpret it "as the power of God in active exercise" (28).

If we then read the Gospel texts in the light of the OT tradition and in the variant translation of section offered in this chapter it is difficult to escape from the idea that the spirit of God or holy spirit is abundantly present.

Lodahl (1992) in his impressive work *Shekinah / Spirit: Divine Presence in Jewish and Christian Religion* works in a perspective different from the traditional view: "I believe that the concept of 'spirit' originally and best refers not to a distinct hypostasis either beside God or within the Godhead, mediating between God and the world, but to *God's own personal presence and activity in the world*" (41), a statement that I believe is fully supported by NT texts like the ones quoted.

See also some pericopes from the OT:

... and breathed onto his face breath of life, and the man became a soul having life[41].
Gen 2.7 LXX.[42]

Why not taking this phrase as a guideline when interpreting Bible texts about 'spirit'. [43]

There are a few more. We quote only the following ones:

But it is the spirit in a man, the breath of the Almighty, that gives him understanding ¨
Iob 32.8 NIV

Divine spirit[44] has made me, breath of the Almighty has taught me[45].
Iob 33.4 LXX

On these three places Schweizer says (TDNT VI, 453), "where the human *pneuma* (or its *pnoê*) is simply God's *pnoê* (or *pneuma*). Even where the meaning is simply the 'breath of life' (...) it is the breath given by Yahweh...", a statement close to mysticism.

---

41 The last words in the translation by Montague 1976, p.6
42 When Jesus breathed his last the Gospel texts implicitly refer back to the moment Adam was created: 'let go his spirit'; 'breathed out the spirit'; 'handed over the spirit'; see the next chapter.
43 Theologians have been perplexed by this Genesis text (cf R. McL. Wilson in Lindars/Smalley 1973, p. 348f) which, however, cannot be denied: the human being has divine spirit in him/her, whatever may have happened in and after paradise. For Christians, Benjamin (1976, 47) concludes his study of *pneuma* in John and Paul saying, "... the Holy Spirit is related to the perpetuation of Christ's presence with *and within* (emphasis added) his disciples...as well as the disciples of each successive generation and age".
44 NIV: the Spirit of God
45 NIV: gives me life

On the cross the life-giving spirit, which God breathed into Adam, leaves Jesus' body. His spirit as his essential being continues to live, as is also shown in the resurrection and the appearances.

Conclusions

In the previous chapter the concept of spirit in the Gospels was discussed. Spirit emerged as a concept with a much wider sense than usually is accorded to it. Its range reaches from the Holy Spirit to the spirit within an individual, from holy spirit as a supreme energy reigning all-over to spirit whose energy is to be grasped on the individual level. This chapter has tested this hypothesis with the pericopes with the phrase *en pneumati*, (being) in spirit. In so doing interesting cases of rendering the Greek into English crop up. Firstly in far the most translations and in comments the literal meaning of *en* is neglected. Secondly it was shown how lightly the article occurrence has been treated.

This chapter has investigated how these Gospel texts speak to us when we read them in a literal translation:

> *Jesus is full of holy spirit, rejoices being in the Holy Spirit, drives out demons being in God's Spirit, immerses you in holy spirit[46], being in the Spirit he went into the temple courts. David was in spirit or in the Holy Spirit. John the Baptist will go on before the Lord in spirit and power of Elijah.*

This offers a new perspective on the relationship to (the) (holy) spirit. Although this phrase *en pneumati*, is generally understood in the traditional way, the literature consulted is offering quite some space to support the view of this paper. This was further substantiated by other Bible texts.

There seems to be a reluctance to accept the suggestion given by the texts presented in this chapter that one may have spirit in one and that one may be in spirit; that in a way holy spirit may be in us and that one may be in holy spirit. Paul's famous words on pneumatic people *versus* psychic people (1 Cor 2:14-16) further corroborates our hypothesis; spirit essentially belongs to the human being (Dutch: 'is des mensen'). I refer also to 1 Cor 3:16: "Do you not know that you are the temple of God, and the spirit of God dwells in you?". On the other hand, the Church has developed this concept contrasting the human being and God as separated by a chasm, sometimes seen as insurmountable. I present my alternative option as a hypothesis for consideration.

After this rather technical treatise the next chapter will be an essay on the words on the cross. Its scope is to interpret these compact sayings from the wisdom gained so far.

---

46 In fact, John the Baptist tells that Jesus will immerse ('baptize') in holy spirit (Mt Mk Lk Jn)

ANNEX 5
The Texts Analyzed

John the Baptist about Jesus' baptism

Mt 3.11

Ἐγὼ μὲν ὑμᾶς βαπτίζω ἐν ὕδατι εἰς μετάνοιαν, ὁ δὲ ὀπίσω μου ἐρχόμενος ἰσχυρότερος μού ἐστιν, οὗ οὐκ εἰμὶ ἱκανὸς τὰ ὑποδήματα βαστάσαι· αὐτὸς ὑμᾶς βαπτίσει **ἐν πνεύματι ἁγίῳ** καὶ πυρί·[47]

I baptize you with water for repentance. But after me will come one who is more powerful than I, whose sandals I am not fit to carry. He will baptize you with the Holy Spirit and with fire.[48]

Notes[49]:
- in Greek without, in English with definitive article
- with Holy
- with preposition *en*; all witnesses according to NA27 agree; translated by *with*[50]
- *en hudati*: with preposition; witnesses according to NA27 agree; in both Greek and English without (definitive) article; translated as *with*

Pro27posal:

I immerse you in water for changing your mind[51]. *(...) But after me will come one who is more powerful than I, whose sandals I am not fit to carry. He <u>will immerse you in holy spirit and fire</u>.*

Comment:
without article: is literal rendering; fitting in theory of previous chapter

Mk 1.8

ἐγὼ ἐβάπτισα ὑμᾶς ὕδατι, αὐτὸς δὲ βαπτίσει ὑμᾶς ἐν πνεύματι ἁγίῳ.

I baptize[52] *you with / in water, but he will baptize you with the Holy Spirit.*

Notes:
- in Greek without, in English with definite article
- with Holy
- with preposition *en*; except some witnesses[53]; translated by *with*

---

47 Here and all other NT texts quoted: K. Aland et al. 1983
48 NIV unless stated otherwise.
49 Blass § 195 n.7 summarizes all baptism cases re *en* or dative.
50 Here and in the other three Gospels about the baptism all translate *en* by *with* except ASV by *in*. Some, however, refer to 'in' as an alternative.
51 See chapter 11 on *Metanoia*
52 Aorist. NSAV: I have baptized

- *hudati*: without preposition (except some major witnesses[54] who have *en*); in both Greek and English without (definitive) article; translated as *with*

Proposal:
I immerse you in water, but he will <u>immerse you in holy spirit</u>.

Comment:
- for most points, see ad Mt 3.11
- *hudati*: this dative grammatically suggests 'with water', but as to contents 'in water'

Mk, in contrast to the preferred text in NA27, has *en* in several witnesses (a [D] L W Q $f^{1.13}$ M it; the preferred text is witnessed by S B D and others. We prefer the other variant because of its consistency with ἐν πνεύματι ἁγίῳ.

Lk 3.16

ἀπεκρίνατο λέγων πᾶσιν ὁ' Ἰωάννης· ἐγὼ μὲν ὕδατι βαπτίζω ὑμᾶς· ἔρχεται δὲ ὁ ἰσχυρότερός μου, οὗ οὐκ εἰμὶ ἱκανὸς λῦσαι τὸν ἱμάντα τῶν ὑποδημάτων αὐτοῦ· αὐτὸς ὑμᾶς βαπτίσει **ἐν πνεύματι ἁγίῳ** καὶ πυρί·

John answered them all, "I baptize you with water. But one more powerful than I will come, the thongs of whose sandals I am not worthy to untie. He will baptize you with the Holy Spirit and with fire.

Notes:
- in Greek without, in English with definite article
- with Holy
- with preposition *en*: witnesses according to NA27 agree; translated by *with*
- *hudati*: without preposition; all witnesses agree; in both Greek and English without (definitive) article; translated as *with*

Proposal:
John answered them all, "I immerse you in water. But one more powerful than I will come, the thongs of whose sandals I am not worthy to untie. He will <u>immerse you in holy spirit and fire.</u>

Comment:
    See ad Mt 3.11

Jn 1.33

κἀγὼ οὐκ ᾔδειν αὐτόν, ἀλλ' ὁ πέμψας με βαπτίζειν ἐν ὕδατι ἐκεῖνός μοι εἶπεν· ἐφ' ὃν ἂν ἴδῃς τὸ πνεῦμα καταβαῖνον καὶ μένον ἐπ' αὐτόν, οὗτός ἐστιν ὁ βαπτίζων **ἐν πνεύματι ἁγίῳ**.

---

53 B L 2427 b t vg omit the *en*. This has been contested. See NA27.
54 A (D) L W (Q) *f1.13* M it

I would not have known him, except that the one who sent me to baptize with water told me, 'The man on whom you see the Spirit come down and remain is he who will baptize with the Holy Spirit.'

Notes:
- in Greek without, in English with definite article
- with Holy
- with preposition *en*; witnesses according to NA27 agree; translated by *with*
- *en hudati*: with preposition; in both Greek and English without article; translated as *with*. Note: some witnesses (among which P66, S) add the article.

Proposal:
I would not have known him, except that the one who sent me to immerse in water told me, 'The man on whom you see the Spirit come down and remain, <u>he is the one immersing in holy spirit.</u>

Comment:
- see ad Mt 3.11
- 'the one immersing' as literal rendering of *ho baptizôn*
- remarkable combination in one sentence of arthrous use ('the Spirit come down') and anarthrous use ('immerse in holy spirit'). This is a clear indication that this difference relates to the contents of the sentence.

* * *

Other pericopes with en pneumati:

Note: in all these pericopes the witnesses according to NA27 agree on the *en* unless stated otherwise.

Mt 12.28

[Jesus:]
εἰ δὲ **ἐν πνεύματι θεοῦ** ἐγὼ ἐκβάλλω τὰ δαιμόνια, ἄρα ἔφθασεν ἐφ' ὑμᾶς ἡ βασιλεία τοῦ θεοῦ.

But if I drive out demons by the Spirit of God, then the kingdom of God has come upon you.

Notes:
- in Greek without, in English with definite article: the Spirit of God
- *en* translated by *by* (all translations, except NCV: *if I use the power of God*)

Proposal:
But if I drive out demons <u>(being) in God's Spirit</u>, then the Kingdom of God has come upon you.

Comment:
- God's Spirit (or even: divine spirit) rather than the Spirit of God

- 'being in': the present participle *ôn* (ὤν) is silently understood. This omitting was current practice[55]
- in support: Mk 1.23 *en pneumati akarthatôi* indicates the condition of being in impure spirit. Blass etc § 203[56] suggests 'mit einem unreinen Geist in sich', which approximates my proposal
- the Lukan parallel (Lk 11.20) has 'by the finger of God' for the Greek *en daktulôi theou*. Here the *en* with dative is taken as an instrumentalis. The *en* in NT Greek often has an extended meaning (Blass etc 203, 218), and often replaces the instrumental dative (219). In the Lk case this is correct. Yet it is preferable to give priority to the first sense. Hence my rendering in Mt.
- which one is more original, Mt or Lk? Earlier scholarship tended to attributing it to Lk[57]. Nolland[58] argues convincingly on a variety of reasons for the primacy of Mt.
- this version is often considered more original than the Matthean text. Therefore the usual translation may be considered to be closest to the original

Mt 22.43

[Jesus:]
λέγει αὐτοῖς· πῶς οὖν Δαυὶδ **ἐν πνεύματι** καλεῖ αὐτὸν κύριον λέγων·

He said to them, "How is it then that David, speaking by the Spirit, calls him 'Lord'? For he says …[59]

Notes:
- in Greek without, in English with definite article
- *en* translated by *by*
- *in* or *in the* by Darby, ASV, KJ, Young;
- *under the inspiration of* by NLT;
- *by* or *by the power of* by NCV, NRSV
- without holy
- N.B. The LXX (Regnorum II = 2 Samuel 23:2):
πνεῦμα κυρίου ἐλάλησεν ἐν ἐμοί, καὶ ὁ λόγος αὐτοῦ ἐπὶ γλώσσης μου

The Spirit of the LORD spoke through [in] me; his word was on my tongue.
Therefore, my proposal 'speaking in spirit' is feasible

Proposal:
He says to them, "How is it then that David <u>(being) in spirit</u> calls him 'Lord'? For he says, …

---

55 Cf Mk 1.23; see WNT I 5 (end)
56 Quoting Langercrantz in *Glotta* 21 (1933) 11
57 Recently also by Wall, *NTS* 33 (1987) 144 (quoted by Nolland, see next note) and by Funk 1993, 330
58 Nolland 1993,, 639f
59 NSAV: How is it then that David by the spirit calls him Lord, saying …

Comment:
- translations vary
- there is no reason to read the text arthrously
- one can speak being in spirit; this makes sense

And its parallel:

Mk 12.36

[Jesus:] αὐτὸς Δαυὶδ εἶπεν **ἐν τῷ πνεύματι τῷ ἁγίῳ**·

David himself, speaking by the Holy Spirit, declared: …

Notes:
- in both Greek and English with definite article
- *en* translated by *by*
  o *in (the)* by Darby, ASV, Young
  o *under the inspiration of* by NLT
  o *by* by all others
- with holy

Proposal:
David himself (being) in the Holy Spirit declared: ….

Comment:
   - 'being in': see comment on Mt 12.28

Lk 1.17

[Angel:]
καὶ αὐτὸς προελεύσεται ἐνώπιον αὐτοῦ **ἐν πνεύματι** καὶ δυνάμει Ἡλίου, …

And he [John the Baptist] will go on before the Lord, in the spirit and power of Elijah, …

Notes:
- in Greek without, in English with definite article (except NCV)
- *en* translated by *in* (except NLT, NRSV: *with*)

Proposal:
*And he (John the Baptist) will go on before the Lord, **in spirit** and power (energy) of Elijah, …*

Comment:
He will go as being in a spirit that is related to Elijah

Lk 2.27

[Simeon] καὶ ἦλθεν **ἐν τῷ πνεύματι** εἰς τὸ ἱερόν

Moved by the Spirit, he went into the temple courts.

Notes:

- in both Greek and English with definite article
- *en* translated by *moved by*
  - ○ *in* by Darby, ASV, Young
  - ○ *by* by KJ, (NRSV: *guided by*; NLT, NCV: *the spirit led him*)

Proposal:
<u>Being in the Spirit</u> he went into the temple courts.

Comment:
Vs 25 tells that holy spirit was upon him. Being in that spirit he went into the temple courts.

Lk 4.1

Ἰησοῦς δὲ *πλήρης πνεύματος ἁγίου* ὑπέστρεψεν ἀπὸ τοῦ Ἰορδάνου καὶ ἤγετο **ἐν τῷ πνεύματι** ἐν τῇ ἐρήμῳ

Jesus, full of the Holy Spirit, returned from the Jordan and was led by the Spirit in the desert,...

Notes:
- in both Greek and English with definite article
- *en* translated by *by*
  - ○ *in* by ASV, Young
  - ○ *by* by all others (NCV: the Spirit led him)

Passage πλήρης πνεύματος ἁγίου·in Greek without, in English with definite article

Proposal:
Jesus, full of <u>holy spirit</u>, returned from the Jordan and <u>being in the Spirit</u> was led in the desert...[60]

Comment:
See previous pericopes.

Lk 10.21

[Jesus]
Ἐν αὐτῇ τῇ ὥρᾳ ἠγαλλιάσατο **[ἐν] τῷ πνεύματι τῷ ἁγίῳ** καὶ εἶπεν·

At that time Jesus, full of joy through the Holy Spirit, said, ...

Notes:
- in both Greek and English with definite article
- *en*'s authenticity discussed; it is translated by *through* in NIV
  - ○ *in (the)* by Darby, ASV, KJ, Young (NLT: *under the inspiration of*)
  - ○ *by (the power of)* by NCV, NRSV

---

60 Mk 1:12 says "at once the spirit sent him out into the desert": here the spirit is the actor whilst in Luke 4:1 the actor remains unmentioned. Cf the WNT, ἄγω, sub 3: "fig., of the working of the Spirit on man *lead, guide,* pass. *be led, allow oneself to be led*".

- Some witnesses have *tôi pneumati tôi hagiôi*, others *tôi pneumati* (without *hagiôi*), some others *en tôi pneumati*

Note: WNT says: the dative may indicate the one who causes the joy (here) or the cause; even without *en* it may mean *to rejoice in*.

Proposal:
At that time Jesus was full of joy <u>(being) in the Holy Spirit / the spirit</u>, and said, ……"[61]

Comment:
In the alternative without *en* the text says that Jesus was full of joy through (or under the inspiration of) the holy spirit (NIV, NLT). Otherwise the text tells that Jesus was in a state of consciousness where he experienced being in the holy spirit.

* * *

---

[61] As we have seen the witnesses are highly divided over the variants with/without ἐν and with/without ἁγίῳ. We agree with Aland (= text).

Chapter Seventeen

The Words from the Cross: A Scene of Serenity

Introduction

Over the centuries theology and the Church have been impressing people with the concept of 'passion': extreme sorrow, suffering, agony, distress (implying fear, anxiety and shame). This chapter will explore the scene at the cross and the words spoken by Jesus and see what is the role of spirit. Is it drama or rather serenity? Compared to the other chapters of this Part IV it is an essay rather than an analysis. It tries to offer a substantiated vision.

This chapter is a modest contribution that tries to take a perspective appropriate to this time. Many, both inside the Church and outside, try to find the essence of religion in their lives as well as for the world at large. Many are trying to retrace old traditions and to re-coin them in order to find a relevance for life today. What is the significance and the meaning of the words from the cross? Is it history? Does it lie in the verbal message? Is it symbolical? Is it possible we may find a hidden treasure? The scope of this chapter is to try if a 'psycho-spiritual' perspective—next to the literal and symbolical ones—offers additional value.

Spiritual refers to mysticism. Mysticism is the perennial hunger and thirst of the soul for the divine. When pure, it raises the consciousness to a level of light (enlightenment, illumination) and peace, in which one is aloof of worries (yet feeling fully responsible) and beyond distinctions and differences (yet in warm sympathy with one's fellow-creatures, whilst in the midst of the hustle and bustle of daily life). It is when spirit gets the upper hand.

The focus will primarily be on the three words from the cross in the Gospel of John in the framework of his passion narrative, with an *excursus* to the other Gospels. It will question the pervasive trend to view the passion as passion rather than seeing how the evangelist impresses the reader with the serenity and dignity of Jesus through the whole process of capturing, interrogation and crucifixion. It is important to note that the narrative never goes into describing Jesus' innumerable suffering, his unbearable pains, his death agony. What we do find is a story of someone who's spirit knows 'the why and for what' all this is inflicted on him. Of someone who has conquered himself, who is aloof of what is inflicted on him, who is capable of handling his body and psyche because he and his Father are one. His spirit inside, in union with the Holy Spirit, is master.

The issue of historicity of the text is left aside. The material is limited to the Gospels[1]; it does not take into account the Gospel of Peter, now considered an important source[2]. Neither does it discuss the abundant literature on the topic. Most of the publications in the field, however, either are directed on theological issues or focus on the narrative structure of the Gospel (for example Van Belle 2007).

The Scene at the Cross in John

In John's passion narrative Jesus speaks three times while on the cross (19:25–30)
- he speaks to his mother and to the beloved disciple
- he says that he is thirsty
- he says that it is finished.

then he bows his head and 'gives up his spirit.'

Here is the full text in English (NRSV) (Jn 19.25–30):

Meanwhile, standing near the cross of Jesus were his mother, and his mother's sister, Mary the wife of Clopas, and Mary Magdalene. When Jesus saw his mother and the disciple whom he loved standing beside her, he said to his mother, "Woman, here is your son." Then he said to the disciple, "Here is your mother." And from that hour the disciple took her into his own home.

After this, when Jesus knew that all was now finished, he said (in order to fulfill the scripture), "I am thirsty." a jar full of sour wine was standing there. So they put a sponge full of the wine on a branch of hyssop and held it to his mouth. When Jesus had received the wine, he said, "It is finished." Then he bowed his head and gave up his spirit.

The next words are selected for a closer analysis, with their Greek equivalent (NRSV)

A previous version has been read at SBL International Meeting, Groningen 2004, Section Johannine Literature

1. Aitken 2004 widens the field by including a wide array of texts. She understands the passion narratives as materials in which the early communities, each in their own way, reflected on the death, in a variety of ways. She widens the material beyond a strictly scribal use of *testimonia* (Helen Bond in *JSNT* 2006).
2. Bovon 2006.

- Woman, here is your son	*gunai, ide ho huios sou*
- Here is your mother	*ide hê mêtêr sou*
- I am thirsty	*dipsô*
- It is finished	*tetelestai*
- He bowed his head	*klinas tên kephalên*
- Gave up his spirit	*paredôken to pneuma*

We will examine the different possibilities of understanding and end up with a preference for what we call a 'psycho-spiritual' interpretation, with some follow-up as to an alternative translation.

Mary and the Beloved Disciple (Jn 19:26–27)

"Woman, here is your son." Jesus in his last moments takes loving care of his mother and establishes a direct family-like tie with his beloved disciple by 'nominating' him the son of his mother, and therefore his brother. It is a touching scene of humaneness, consideration, love and sympathy in view of his physical condition on the threshold of dying.

Dipsô (Jn 19.28)

"I am thirsty" is the usual rendering of *dipsô*. After uttering this word Jesus is given a sponge full of (sour) wine (or vinegar)[3] and he accepts it. The evangelist adds that this happened "when Jesus knew that all was now finished[4]". Indeed, what is more natural after all these sleepless hours of capture, waiting, interrogation, waiting again , condemnation, more waiting, crucifixion, that one would be thirsty? By the way, a quite modest last meal compared to the one offered to criminals on death row.....

Does this cry relate to the passion scene expressing the desolation, isolation and scorn described in Psalm 69?[5] Or would the evangelist want to transmit a covert other meaning, not excluding the literal one? It is a spiritual message rather than a symbolical one. Jesus, after having completed his task as messenger of the good tidings that the kingdom of God is here and now, after having given all that is his: body, psyche, spirit, after having delivered his message, he finally exclaims how desirous he is to quench the thirst of his soul, a thirst for the wine divine. What he gets, however, is sour wine. We find this metaphorical meaning elsewhere too. WNT calls it the thirst for an eternal drink (Jn 4.14, 6.35, 7.37). Metaphorically it means "to desire passionately a spiritual good without which one cannot live" (Mt 5.6) (TDNT I, 226). Quenching this thirst indicates "the

---

3   Comments on the word *oxos* vary among these meanings.
4   *Tetelestai*. See further in the next section, *Tetelestai*.
5   This is suggested for instance by Barrett 1978, 351. He refers to the parallel Psalm 22 quoted in the passion narratives in Mk 15.34 and Mt 27.46.

satisfaction of longing and therefore perfect felicity" (Jn 4.14). Symbolically it may refer to the cup in Gethsemane (Jn 18.11, Mt 26.39).

> But whoever drinks the water I give him will never thirst. Indeed, the water I give him will become in him a spring of water welling up to eternal life.
> Jn 4.14 NIV
>
> Then Jesus declared, I am the bread of life. He who comes to me will never go hungry, and he who believes in me (*puts his trust*[6] *in me*) will never be thirsty.
> Jn 6.35 NIV (italics added)
>
> If anyone is thirsty, let him come (to me[7]) and drink. Whoever believes in me (*puts his trust in me*), as the Scripture has said, streams of living water will flow from within him (*from his heart*).[8]
> Jn 7.37b-38 NIV (italics added)

Here we find an awareness of a spiritual thirst that is a living entity in him. In his last hour he testifies of this. He is looking over the threshold of death and feels a strong desire for quenching the thirst of his spirit. Would he really have taken it? Earthly drink is no longer his need or desire. He is craving for something more essential. Indeed, Mt and Mk do not say that Jesus actually takes the drink willingly: "gave it him to drink" (*epotizen auton*).

Proposed translation: I thirst.

A sober rendering, intransitive. Similar to the classic Dutch rendering: "mij dorst"[9] ('it thirsts me' [!]). Preferable to 'I am thirsty', as this refers too closely to physical thirst.

Tetelestai (Jn 19:30)

All major translations[10] say, 'it is finished'. Is this rendering the most close to the Greek original, *tetelestai*[11]? What does the *teleô* say?

> The usual meaning, also outside the NT, is 'to carry out', 'to execute', 'to bring to an end'. In the NT it retains this sense but often is considered to carry extra weight theologically.[12] The term can carry a lofty sound.[13]

---

6 *Ho pisteuôn eis eme.* See also chapter 6.
7 'To me' is not testified in most of the better witnesses (p66* S* D b e vg^{ms})
8 *Koilia.* WNT: apart from the physical sense (belly, stomach, womb) it stands for the innermost and most intimate inner part, hence heart. It adds that it must refer to the Savior, not to the believers. Sic.
9 Dutch translations since Statenvertaling 1637 through late 20th c.
10 NIV, ASV, RSV, NRSV, KJ, NewCentury.
11 Pf pass of *teleô*.
12 TDNT VIII 57–61 (here and all references with *tele**: Gerhard Delling).

The most narrow interpretation would indicate that it just refers to the passion itself: this indeed is finishing now. Yes, that is what 'finished' suggests: it is all over. The term is factual, it does not refer to the quality of what is finished. The *Webster's* confirms this: "finish may suggest full execution or resolution of the last steps or stages of a continued action or process."

Commentaries,[14] however, expand the action that is finished to the whole life of Jesus as the savior, his mission on earth. It is the fulfillment of all prophesies; as a positive statement: the work is done. Therefore the term has two senses: chronologically as 'ended' (German: 'beenden'), and theologically as 'achieved' (German: 'vollenden').[15]

> In a further step in the theological interpretation it came to carry extra weight when considered being "very thoroughly historicized and Christianized", like in this pericope (and in v. 28).[16] Also Beasley-Murray confirms this theological interpretation. The *tetelestai* refers to accomplishing an order. The verb "fundamentally denotes 'to carry out' the will of somebody", i.c. God's. The suffering would be the crowning conclusion and high point of the work that Jesus had performed in obedience. Hence his suggestion 'it is accomplished' next to the more matter of fact 'it is finished'.[17]
>
> Interestingly, both commentators relate the verb to ancient practices. Once it had been the concluding formula of a mystery ceremony.[18] Thus the term refers to completing an inner process. The same idea surfaces when, referring to Dodd,[19] Beasley-Murray says that the term also "conveys the notion of the completion of *rites of sacrifice and initiation*" (italics, original) in reference to the Hermetic literature where in the final stage of initiation the son of Hermes says "by thy will all things are completed (*tetelestai*)." The Gospel being written around the year 100, one may suppose that this sense could be present as an undertone.

My preference as an appropriate synonym therefore is the term 'to complete'. It indicates an ending marked by fulfilling, perfecting, leaving nothing undone, "to make whole, entire, or perfect"[20]. That seems to be more to the mark. "Le but est atteint."[21] The related verb *teleioô* is similar: to fulfill, to carry out, to come to entirety; it refers to wholeness, it is utterly complete. Basically it means 'to make *teleios*[22]

---

13 Ibidem, n.1: "*Teleô* is a very ancient…term, which in the post-classical period was increasingly supplanted by composites so that the simple form could have a lofty sound."
14 Barrett 1978 and Beasley 1999.
15 TDNT VIII *teleô*, sub C 1b, n 14.
16 Barrett 554 sub 30.
17 Beasley 352f.
18 Barrett, l.c.
19 Dodd, C.H., The interpretation of the fourth Gospel, Cambridge University Press 1968.
20 *Webster's* 'to complete' 2a.
21 Makambu 2007.
22 TDNT *teleioô* VIII (Delling*)*.

The Greek adjective *teleios* indicates synonymously: whole, without blemish (though not morally), complete in compass, nothing left outside that belongs to it,[23] perfect in the sense that there is nothing beyond that can still be reached. In the LXX[24] and in the Pauline corpus[25] (where it may also refer to 'mature') it has similar sense. 'Mature': referring to the completion of an inner(?) process toward its end. It may refer to spiritual development, well-known both inside and outside Christianity. TDNT for the Gospels refers to the general concept of 'totality,'[26] or, again, 'complete.' In the Greek mysteries it indicates the act of initiation, the completion of the process of becoming mature spiritually, and therefore complete. Maybe the logion 'Be perfect' is related to this[27]: to be complete, to be 'initiated' in the *mustêrion*? To 'learn' to see rather than looking, to hear rather than to listen. Another logion in Mt (19.21) is a clear case in point. Here eternal life (the search of the young man) is equalled (by Jesus) to being perfect, complete. I thus suggest to render *teleios* as 'complete.'

The perfect tense[28] in this text tells that Jesus knows that the whole process of spiritual development has been completed. He is ready to hand over his *pneuma*. The threshold to the goal is reached. *Telos* also signifies end or goal. The WNT says, *telos* means end or goal, apart from 'termination,' 'conclusion.'

The outcome is that the best translation is 'completed': Jesus looks back and sees that his work is complete, both out in the world and inside. Into the world he has brought the good message that the reign of God is present and he has brought the light of God, which is the salvation. Inside he has completed the work his Father gave him to do.

Proposed translation: It has been completed.

Klinas tên kephalên (19:30)

After this word *tetelestai* Jesus "bowed his head". What does this bowing mean? Is it hopeless surrender? Is it a natural consequence of energy flowing away?

Rather it may be a movement that accompanies being in the awareness of completion: all has been done. It may also be something happening naturally when the spirit is getting the upper hand, when it knows itself united with the

---

23 TDNT VIII *teleios* A1,2.
24 Unblemished, undivided, complete, whole, ibidem C1.
25 Ibidem D3.
26 Ibidem D1.
27 'Perfect', cf Mt 5.48 *esesthe oun humeis teleioi*, 'Be perfect, therefore' (NIV), You, therefore, must be perfect'(RSV). The quasi parallel (Lk 6.36) has *oiktirmonos*, merciful, compassionate. Generally Lk /Q is considered the original version (Robert H. Gundry, *Matthew*, Eerdmans, Grand Rapids 19942;,100; also Nolland , *Luke1-9-20*,300). An alternative is the hypothesis that both originate from independent traditions, retaining the *teleios*.
28 Makambu finds that v.30 is in aorist tense: it is a narrative. However, *tetelestai* is in the perfect tense, an indication that this word is an 'independent' logion, quoted within the narrative.

divine. Or: when one is ready to hand over one's spirit. In some religions it is the attitude of prayer. An alternative to 'bow' is 'to incline'. Of course, it may also be a physical reaction in the context of dying.

Proposed translation: Inclined his head.

Paredôken to pneuma (19:30)

In the chapter on 'Being in spirit,' it was found that *pneuma* may be seen as an attribute of the human being.

Paredôken is translated by 'gave up' in the same major translations. But does 'giving up' not associate too much with a hopeless situation: relinquish, surrender, forsaking, sacrifice, abandon[29]? Its main significance is 'handing over', both in positive and in negative situations. In relation to death it refers to willingness to die and/or self-sacrifice. It is also used when secret knowledge is transferred (Mt 11.27, Lk 10.22).[30] So we find that the verb is much richer than just 'giving up'. Rather it signifies taking an initiative actively. Handing over what one is having into the power of someone else (WNT). In this expression it conveys the willingness to die.[31] In the beginning of his 'career' Jesus had received the spirit, according to many at baptism, others maintain it was with him from the very beginning. (Even one may wonder whether it is not with everybody as his/her most intimate and essential being.) At death this spirit is returned, or handed over, i.e., to the Father. Jesus had been in the awareness of what was coming all the time since Gethsemane and even before, of course. He hands over his spirit in a full and positive resignation: all has been completed, he departs from physical life. All mental and physical hardships have been vanquished.

> Referring to the chapter on the psyche, especially the Gethsemane scene shows how annihilation in spiritual terms means transformation. Denying its dominating and autonomous nature the psyche is recognized as an instrument of the spirit: when we adhere to the autonomous nature of the psyche, we will lose our grip on it; when on the other hand we let it go and try to master it, then we gain it, or in another version: save it for eternal life.

This is the background of what we read in the passion narratives in all gospels.

Proposed translation: Handed over / rendered the/his spirit.

---

29 *Webster's* sub 1 and 4. But also sub 2, 'give up the ghost'. Although this latter meaning is valid here the *paredôken* may have a deeper bearing.
30 TDNT II 169ff.
31 Ibid., sub 4. It is also used when its object is teaching (sub 6). Also Makambu 262: "mort consciente et souveraine."

To give up is too passive, it is an active deed. And it suggests that by this act all is gone and finished. Cf *tetelestai*.

Complete proposed alternative translation Jn 19:28–30:
After (all) this—knowing that soon all would be completed so that the scripture would be fulfilled—Jesus said, "I thirst" ..... , , ... "it has been completed", and he inclined his head and handed over his spirit.

To sum up, the sequence of the narrative appears quite logical. After having taken care of his mother there remains one single desire: thirst for eternal life and re-uniting with the Father. He then realizes all has been completed and in physical and mental resignation he renders his spirit to the Father. He has vanquished: the cross as victory. The Jesus logia on the cross as well as the narrative as a whole is a story of dignity, serenity, and silent victory.[32]

From the argument we learn that a psycho-spiritual point of view may interpret a text differently, not necessarily as replacement but rather as an alternative view, an enrichment of insight and understanding.

The challenge of translation is to find a rendering that covers all interpretation in one term that is multi-interpretable, like the original Greek.

And in the Synoptic Gospels

It is interesting to see that in the passion narratives of the synoptic Gospels we find the same atmosphere, the same dignity and serenity as we found in Jn. The wordings are quiet and non-emotional.

Drinking (Mk 15.36, Mt 27.48)

In both Mk and Mt Jesus does not ask for drinking. And in neither narrative it is said that Jesus did take the sour wine. *Potizo* is ambiguous as it is also used for watering the cattle. We propose the NIV text '…gave it him to drink' as the correct translation. Jesus may or may not have taken it. Here even more than in Jn the scene may refer to Jesus being misunderstood by the bystanders: craving to quench his spiritual thirst he was given sour wine, for which he did not ask.

Forsaking (Mk 15.34, Mt 27.46)

"My God, my God, why have you forsaken me?"

How Jesus could die with this cry of despair, in a feeling of complete dereliction? It is a quotation from Psalm 22, its very first line. For a correct understanding it is necessary to take the complete Psalm into consideration.

---

32 E.g., Makambu 2007, 254–55, 258, though placed in a different theological context.

Hooker (1997, 375-6) recognizes this but considers this cry as central to the understanding of the death of Jesus. He argues Jesus is sharing human despair to the full, it shows the oneness of Jesus with humanity. This text taken *per se* comes as a shock to the reader of Mark, rather than fitting in the whole narrative (Hooker). Another view is to see this cry of dereliction on the cross as references to Jesus as the dying Messiah-King[33]

Here we propose a different view. Throughout these Gospels one has come to know Jesus being closely related to the Father, in whatever circumstances and conditions. Only in Gethsemane he was found in a moment of grief and loneliness, with his dearest disciples forsaking him. Yet it does not touch his spirit, it is his psyche that grieves (*perilupos estin hê psuche mou*, Mt 26.38 / Mk 14.34). He is united in prayer with the Father and surrenders to His will. During the whole passion narrative following this, Jesus is staying aloof of what is happening. He is completely himself. How are we to understand this cry at the cross?

Jesus as a rabbi of course knew the psalm by heart. He must have had the complete text at his heart. Also in circles around Mark and later, or Matthew for that matter, it must have been understood that the phrase does not stand on itself but serves as reference to the contents of the complete psalm. One easily imagines Jesus quoting, or even singing, the complete psalm, maybe just for himself as his physical powers were diminishing.[34]

The psalm text as a whole is revealing: a sign of the complete surrender of Jesus to his fate and to God's will. Here are a few lines, illustrating the transformation the psalmist is describing as the spiritual process: (verses 1a, 3a, 4, 5a, 6, 9ab, 11ac, 13, 15a, 19a, 21a, 23a, 24,

> *My God, my God, why have you forsaken me?*
> *Yet you are enthroned as the Holy One*
> *In you our fathers put their trust; they trusted and you delivered them.*
> *They cried to you and they were saved.*
> *But I am a worm and not a man, scorned by men and despised by the people.*
> *Yet .. you made me trust in you.*
> *Do not be far from me... there is no one to help.*
> *Roaring lions tearing their prey open their mouths wide against me.*
> *My strength is dried up like a potsherd.*
> *But you, o Lord, be not far off,*
> *Rescue me from the mouths of the lions.*
> *You who fear the Lord, praise him!*
> *For he has not despised or disdained the suffering of the afflicted one,*
> *He has not hidden his face from him but has listened to his cry for help.*

---

33   Hannan 2006, 223.
34   Also: Bradley 2007, 162.

Suffering severely yet his connection to God remains firm and strong. Then the psalm continues with further praises.

Discussion with the two criminals (Lk 23.32–43)

Jesus shows himself the compassionate, the master of the situation, and above all master of his emotions and his ego.

Commending the spirit (Lk 23.46)

Here Jesus himself mentions about his spirit. *Paratithêmi* is more than commending: it is literally to put it in God's hands.[35] It closely resembles Jn's pericope and the *paradidômi*, and affirms it.

In Mk 15.37 Jesus *exepneusen*, breathed out. The verb *ekpneô* is related to *pnoê* and hence to *pneuma*. It suggests Jesus is returning his spirit that he had received at baptism (or at birth).[36]

Evaluation and Conclusions

The cross scenes in the synoptic Gospels appear to be in line with Jn. The one single contradiction ('forsaking') has been cleared as a pseudo-contradiction.

Over the centuries theology and the Church have been impressing us with the concept of 'passion': extreme sorrow, suffering, agony, distress (implying fear, anxiety and shame). Art has sometimes shown the drama rather than the serenity and dignity of the passion narrative. What strikes one is the objective way the evangelists describe the capture, the interrogation, the condemnation and the execution. No drama, no Grünewald, no Mel Gibson. No word about how terribly Jesus was suffering. It is a story about dignity, about someone being aloof of what was being inflicted on him.

This is corroborated by the words from the cross. In the situation of utter despair, of extreme suffering, of being totally left to himself, when energy and strength are flowing away—in this situation of deepest humiliation, the words by Jesus on the cross again show a dignity beyond words. Here spirit is speaking. Here is one who is totally in control of both the situation and himself. The one word of desperation (forsaking) has been cleared as to signify the reverse: a process of change from hopelessness and despair to hopefulness, trust and confidence.

---

35 TDNT VIII sub 1 gives this as a standard phrase in Greek 'to give someone something in trust'. See also ψ 30.6 (LXX) from which it is a citation. Note, most English translations render it as 'I trust in the Lord' (*sic*) (NRSV, NIV, NAS). The French Maredsous (1950) keeps to the literal 'Je remets mon âme entre vos mains', like the new Naardense Bijbel.

36 See the footnote on Hanhart in chapter [spirit 1], section on The spirit.

What is the result? That the cross is victory rather than defeat. And that resurrection is the natural consequence. Spirit prevails over body and psyche.

Chapter Eighteen
Rendering *ekstasis* in the NT

Introduction

An absolutely paralyzed man is lying on his mat. Suddenly he rises, takes his mat and goes home, just on being told so. Would a spectator be amazed or rather completely taken in rapture? Would one just be astonished when a girl of twelve years thought dead stood up and walked around, just on being told so, or rather be 'rapt in great rapture'?

Once I attended an Orthodox Easter celebration somewhere in Greece, the gospel of Mark recited in a beautiful singsong way. On the point when the women exit the grave—the very heavy stone already rolled away, a young man in shining white robe telling them Jesus is risen and no more here—they are overcome by tromos *and* ekstasis. *This last single word being recited in a long extemporisation, enveloped in breathtaking silence all around– it was ecstasy itself.*

Is ecstasy so foreign to our culture, is the awe for the Other so gone, now being understood as fear? Ecstasy (or rapture) now are interpreted as terror and amazement (NRSV), or trembling and bewildered (NIV)? Is ecstasy to be out of mind? Or a function of the spirit coming free? This made me wonder, and caused me, decades later, to take up the challenge.

In the previous chapters some aspects of the phenomenon of the spirit have been discussed. One of the remaining questions is, how does spirit manifest? What has been found, is a spirit that is intangible, invisible, inaudible, yet perceivable. But, then, in what way can it be perceived, if not by the senses? When it does manifest, it mostly happens indirectly, in a hidden way, it seems. Associated to it is a state of inner transformation. In Part II, on the Kingdom of God, these aspects were touched already: perception on different levels, and transformation. Transformation was discussed in Part III also: transformation of the psyche in relation to spirit. Sometimes, however, this transformation is not limited to inner change: it manifests to view. Ecstasy is one of its principal expressions. Rapture is a variant. Reversely, the inner expression may be called 'enstasy'.[1] Or, on the other hand, is ecstasy an irregularity of the mind, a fault in the brain?

This is a revised text of a paper read at the SBL International Meeting, Groningen 2004.
1   See chapter 2 and below in the Excursus.

The issue is: does one find the concept of ecstasy or rapture in the NT? Is the Greek term *ekstasis* an equivalent? In the NT *ekstasis* occurs in 23 pericopes. When consulting English translations of the NT one does not find *ekstasis* (or the verb *existêmi*[2]) rendered by ecstasy. As a matter of fact this single term in Greek is translated variously into five different terms (NIV): amazement (10 times), astonishment (7), trance (3), out of one's mind (2), and bewildered (1). Thus on the one hand *ekstasis* is interpreted as an ordinary general human experience: astonishment, amazement. On the other hand it is presented as something negative, or undesirable: bewildered, out of one's mind, trance. This latter interpretation fits well with a concept of ecstasy as a state close to the abnormal, cases of a psychiatric nature. In the realm of spirituality and mysticism, on the contrary, ecstasy is a special and positive phenomenon, a culmination in the seeking of the divine. Obviously in NIV and other translations this is not considered to be the case. What to do? The handbooks will help us out further down.

> *The object of this chapter then is to have a closer look at the NT pericopes with* ekstasis, *as it occurs in the Synoptics (*deest *in John), in Acts, and in the Epistles (only once). The first question to be posed is: to what extent the concept is close to the English term 'ecstasy'? Is it appropriate to translate it one-to-one as 'ecstasy'? Related is the question: what is ecstasy?*

Among the variety of meanings of ecstasy the spiritual or mystical one springs to the fore, as in the NT we are dealing with spiritual literature. From this vantage point we will have a critical look at the *ekstasis* pericopes and see whether any may be interpreted in this light. Then the issue of translation is coming up. Do the current translations do justice to the spiritual interpretation? What alternative may be offered? In this way the chapter intends to offer a humble contribution to the understanding of NT spirituality.

> A word of caution. Spirituality in the NT is not limited to the word *ekstasis*. Manifestations of the spirit are described in other terms also[3]. Especially Paul in his Epistles makes one share in his spirituality and occasionally his mysticism, especially in his visions and revelations (2 Cor 12.2–4).[4]

---

2 In this chapter the two forms, noun and verb, will be taken together as *ekstasis*.
3 Johnson indicates indeed that religious experience in early Christianity is a missing dimension in NT studies. His book intends to start and fill the gap. However, at two issues the gap continues: *ekstasis* is not found in the index, and more important he does not cover the Gospels.
4 Lietaert Peerbolte (2008) refers to the ecstasy of Paul as a practice that was not limited to Jewish apocalypticism but was also part and parcel of the ancient world (168). Paul's faith is essentially experiential in character; understanding this is a clue to his theology (176).

The study of the pertaining literature[5] suffers from the fact that as far as I could reach no study is to be found relating *ekstasis* in the Gospel pericopes and in the NT as a whole to the concept of ecstasy. The general view seems to be that the Greek *ekstasis* should not be translated by 'ecstasy' or equivalents. This chapter takes up the challenge to see if this relationship is to be found, and if so, is justified.

The chapter is organized as follows.

The first section focuses on the concepts behind the terms ecstasy and *ekstasis*. Is *ekstasis* ecstasy? A concept of ecstasy is developed which will help us to understand the NT texts which speak of *ekstasis*. The latter are then presented in the next section, both in Greek and as translated in some current English translations (with some reference to other western languages). Included is a proposal for an alternative rendering, for each of the cases. The final section contains an evaluation and the conclusions.

Ecstasy: Term and Concept, Greek and English

The section will discuss the concept of ecstasy, as far as expressed in this term. This will be by first looking at the English term, then checking the Greek term, and finally examining the concept in mysticism and spirituality as far as possible within the framework given.

The English Term 'Ecstasy'

For English 'ecstasy' *Webster's* gives various meanings, both on the level of the psyche and of the spirit. Psychologically it refers to emotions: "a state of being beyond reason and self-control through intense emotional excitement, pain, or other sensation"[6]. The second meaning includes, but is not limited to, the spiritual dimension: "a state of exaltation or rapturous delight either demonstratively...or in *a profound calm or abstraction of mind*" (italics, WvL). And the third meaning refers to an extreme form of experience: "a trance state in

---

5 The literature search focused mainly on the word group *ekstasis* in the University of Amsterdam Library systems, on the ATLA data base, on references in the literature, and various other sources. One of these is F. Neirynck c.a. (eds.), *The Gospel of Mark 1950–1990: a cumulative bibliography*, Peeters, Leuven 1992.

6 Holm (1992, 9) writing on the psychological aspects of ecstasy, classifies ecstasy in the category of 'altered states of consciousness'. Following Ludwig (1968) "Altered states of consciousness", in R.Pronce, *Trance and Possession States*, Montreal 1968) he says that these altered mental states are induced by various physiological, psychological or pharmacological maneuvers or agents that cause deviations from the normal alert waking consciousness. Thus he excludes the spiritual dimension where the alert and waking consciousness is raised to a higher and more refined state of perception. N.G. Holm, "Ecstasy research in the 20th century, an introduction", in: Holm 1982.

which intense absorption in divine or cosmic matters is accompanied by loss of sense perception and voluntary control". In the synonym section *Webster's* says, "ecstasy, rapture and transport agree in designating a feeling or state of intense, often extreme, mental and emotional exaltation." Then it refers to two sides of ecstasy, one at the level of the psyche, the other spiritual. The former resembles trance, making one oblivious of all else, the latter "an overmastering exalted joy or similar intense emotion". Rapture, according to *Webster's*, "implies intense bliss or beatitude, sometimes connoting an accompanying ecstasy". Summing up *Webster's*, ecstasy refers either to an emotional state of being or to a profound calm where the mind is on another level of functioning ('abstraction'). Rapture may be considered a synonym for ecstasy. In this chapter, however, rapture is taken as a grade of ecstasy characterized by a lower degree of intensity. Often, one could suggest, rapture is triggered by an outside stimulus whilst genuine ecstasy may be a spontaneous event on the purely spiritual level. The sensory effect of both rapture and ecstasy will happen as the case may be physically, mentally, emotionally or spiritually, or combinations of these.

Ecstasy and rapture in this chapter will be used in the sense of a functioning of the spirit that leads to a heightened state of consciousness and a sharpened and refined way of perception and cognition. Rapture indicates a degree of lower intensity, more down to earth, ecstasy indicates a higher degree of intensity. This implies a critique on some current points of view, like Holm's (just quoted), who limits the understanding of ecstasy to the psychological dimension. See also below when Evelyn Underhill's view is discussed.

The Greek ekstasis / existêmi

The question now is whether, and if so to what degree, the Greek term *ekstasis* (including the verb *existêmi*)[7] refers to the concept of ecstasy. Here the lexicographical meaning will be explored, later the contextual sense in the NT will be looked at. When interpreting these texts from the NT one needs to bear in mind that in the rational western culture the concept of ecstasy is hardly accepted, let alone as a spiritual phenomenon.

> As to Greek in general Lidell Scott says the meaning of *ekstasis* is displacement, but also astonishment, entrancement, trance[8]. Or in German similarly 'aussersichgeraten', 'Entsetzen', 'Verzückung' (rapture, exaltation)[9], deep emotion ('diepe ontroering')[10]. As to the verb: to put out of its place, to drive mad, to astonish, to stand aside from, to

---

7   Unless stated differently in this text *ekstasis* will include the verb *existêmi* and its synonym *existamai*. In koinê the latter word gradually replaces the former. In the pericopes treated here both forms exist next to one another without differences of meaning.
8   The Little Liddell 2007, *ekstasis*.
9   Langenscheidt, *ekstasis*.
10 Muller 1926, sub 3.

make way for. Muller: 'displacing something that is standing somewhere' ("alles wat staat of staande gedacht wordt zijn plaats elders geven"[11]), or: "removing oneself from a given place"[12], "standing outside oneself"[13].

WNT/BDAG[14]: *ekstasis* is 1. distraction, confusion, astonishment, terror, lit. being beside oneself, 2. *trance, ecstasy, a state of being brought about by God* (emphasis, WvL), in which consciousness is wholly or partially suspended. As to the verb (intransitive[15]): become separated from something, lose something of spiritual and mental balance, lose one's mind, be out of one's senses, be amazed, be astonished, the feeling of astonishment mingled with fear, caused by events which are miraculous, extraordinary, or difficult to understand. In my interpretation this refers to awe, "reverent wonder with a touch of fear inspired by the grand or sublime" to which the *Webster's* adds 'esp. in nature and art', as if religion can be excluded.[16]

In the introductory section to this lemma TDNT[17] speaks about *ekstasis* outside the NT. In a condensed description it is rendered as a "beneficial apprehension and infilling by a higher power which may sometimes be experienced as an impersonal substance and sometimes as a personal being...as when a god puts man in a state of ecstasy, not by entering into him but by breathing upon him."[18] This seems a fair general description applicable to the NT as well.

Ekstasis in the NT means, according to TDNT : astonishment, terror at numinous revelations, apart from the general meaning: confusion of spirit, alienation (often as convulsive excitement), but also: *ecstasy* (emphasis, wvl) (II 450). It rejects Jesus being an ecstatic on the premise that ecstasy is an abnormal state from which one does not easily recover. It opposes ecstatic and pneumatic. We will see that this is a false opposition. Yet it acknowledges that the baptism (Mk 1.10f par), the temptation (Mt 4.1 par), the cry of jubilation (Mt 11.25ff par), and the transfiguration (Mk 9.2ff par) "may with greater or lesser justice be described as ecstatic" (II 456f) thus acknowledging the divine nature of real ecstasy.[19] For the verb *existêmi* TDNT does not offer additional insight. So it appears the verb is dealt with only summarily, allowing but not making explicit, the spiritual meaning. The noun is treated one-sidedly, neglecting but not excluding its positive religious and spiritual meaning.

Ekstasis, therefore, in specific contexts carries the same meaning as the English ecstasy. *Ekstasis*, in spiritual texts, may thus be translated as rapture, ecstasy,

---

11 Muller 1926.
12 Holm 2002, 8.
13 P. Tillich, *Systematic theology I*, Chicago 1951, 111, quoted by T. Kurtén 2002, 245
14 WNT (in abridged English translation, Logos Systems 2.1). Also BDAG.
15 The transitive use is found in three out of the 24 pericopes only.
16 *Webster's* sub 3d.
17 Albrecht Oepke, in TDNT II 449-460.
18 TDNT II sub A 1, p.451.
19 Cf Bernoulli, 1928: "... nach der Seite einer religiös höchstpotenzierten Bewusstseinsinhaltes hat Jesus den Zug nach Süden...als antiker Ekstatiker angetreten." Although this may sound ambivalent Bernoulli adds a few lines later, "Der...als religiöse Triebfülle in ihm erbrausende Lebensinhalt bestand in der Gewissheit, der Sohn eines lebendigen Gottes zu sein,...weil er das Pneuma...in sich aufgenommen hatte." (266).

amazement, trance; this is apart from uses like displacement, astonishment, confusion, 'aussersichgeraten', 'Entsetzen', standing outside oneself, awe (rather than terror). As said *supra,* it may be experienced as an impersonal substance and sometimes as a personal being.

Before coming to the NT texts we need to look at how ecstasy is understood in literature. Literature almost exclusively focuses on ultimate forms: high stages of spiritual awareness. In the NT passages theses forms hardly exist. a survey is presented in the Excursus below. It serves as a background for the analysis of the NT passages with *ekstasis.*

It may be noted that the notion of ecstasy is not a central concept in the NT. It is infrequent and is absent in the Jesus logia. The motivation yet to include it is the wish to do justice to the phenomenon of rapture and ecstasy, and to critically analyze the understanding and interpretation of it in the NT texts.

Excursus into the literature: ecstasy in mysticism and spirituality

What is the understanding of ecstasy in literature? On the one hand, it is said to belong to psychiatry and forms of eccentric esotericism. On the other hand ecstasy is related to mysticism. Is it triggered from outside, an action? Or an emotion caused by perception? Or is it rather an energy inside, coming into action when receiving a glimpse of the other world? What mysticism is in this work has been presented in chapter 2. A short summary is given below. As a start a synopsis of the topic in two recent influential handbooks is presented.[20]

> In his excellent *Spiritualiteit* Kees Waaijman[21] makes some important statements about ecstasy. In ecstasy God powerfully draws the soul totally into himself (Jean de Saint-Simon). Both the initiative and the act are by God, provided one is ready to let it be done. It is a process of loving and be loved. 'Positive' and 'negative' fuse and become one in terms of consciousness. It is not the soul leaving the body (Dutch: 'uittreding'), it is love by which one is drawn out of oneself, at the same time remaining oneself and fusing with the Other[22]. Maybe *ek-stasis / existêmi* can be understood to mean to step out of oneself, to rise above one's limited self. To lose oneself in the Creator is supreme delight (Baal Shem Tov). "In rapture and in experiencing divine fire the commandments are fulfilled" (669). The book contains a riches of inspiring and enlightening insights.

---

20   This review is to be seen in conjunction with what was treated in chapter 2 on mysticism. Some overlaps are unavoidable if not wanted.
21   Waaijman 2000, 466-469, 669, 674-675. Also available in English *Spirituality, Forms, Foundations, Methods,* Peeters, Leuven 2002.
22   "Ecstasy comes only when the heart is tuned to that pitch of love which melts it, which makes it tender, which gives it gentleness, which makes it humble" (Khan 1990, 191). For 'humble' cf Mt 18.4, *tapeinos.;* see chapter 9, section 'as a 'little child').

In the equally excellent Dutch language *Encyclopedie van de mystiek*[23] (Encyclopedia of mysticism) Waaijman describes ecstasy "as a mystical phenomenon, like visions, stigmata, the faculty of tears, indicating that human perception is incapable as to the divine, and therefore is disordered by the divine Presence" and completely caught up by it, thereby losing the self. It is prayer void of any desire for self-expression. There is an intense focus of the psyche, an ineffable bliss or rapture of the heart, an insatiable joy of the spirit (Cassianius (ca. 365-ca. 433), *Collationes 10,11*, quoted in this Encyclopedia). It is also fiery love, a complete 'entering into'. This glowing bliss prevails over prayer, and one enters into *pardes*, into the sphere of mystical transformation (61-62). Otgar Steggink says that in the negative theology of Pseudo Dionysius ecstasy implies rising above human faculties (in my terminology: human limitations), and union (*henosis*) with God and deification (*theosis*) (323). Cassianus, continues Steggink, describes the character of ecstasy as deep impressive silence, a silent prayer, *per excessum mentis*, without image or voice it expresses the inexpressible rapture of the heart and the insatiable joy of the spirit (324). According to Steggink (323-4) ecstasy as a genuine religious experience is of all times and of all cultures. It expresses the eternal longing to rise above oneself and to unite with the divine. It is an extreme form of the basic structure of the human. It is *ek-stasis*: to 'stand out of (oneself)', i.e. to rise to another dimension of perception, to another reality. And one has to add± essentially also toward one's fellow-men, because ecstasy awakens one to one's being human, also in our relationships.

This amounts to an understanding that ecstasy is a genuine phenomenon of religion and part of mysticism. In the chapter on mysticism it was noted that the mysticism of Jesus in the Synoptics remains almost unnoticed. The same obtains for ecstasy. McGinn's thorough history of Western Christian Mysticism spends hardly a word on ecstasy in the Gospels[24]. The term *ekstasis* remains almost unnoticed by NT scholars. Does one deny this term to indicate ecstasy, maybe relying on current translations? In the next sections some light will be thrown on this issue.

Gradually in the western culture of today ecstasy is being accepted more and more by both psychology and theology as a genuine human experience of the 'beyond'.[25] It is getting integrated also conceptually into these fields, in the framework of mysticism. We have to differentiate between on the one hand extreme forms in which it may be expressed and on the other the essence of ecstasy. Its essence contradictorily might be called 'en-stasy'[26]: the absorption of

---

23 Baers, *Encyclopedie van de mystiek* 2003
24 McGinn, *Foundations*, 66-69. The concept of ecstasy is discussed amply throughout the period covered (to the fifth century) but a definition is lacking. However, much insight is gained.
25 Cultural anthropology has always taken interest in this phenomenon but with differing viewpoints. See e.g. I.M. Lewis, *Ecstatic religion*, Penguin 1971.
26 The term *enstasis* in this sense originates from Plotinus. In modern times it was taken up by Mircea Eliade who equated it to yogic samadhi (*Yoga*, Princeton / Bollingen 1969^2 , reprint

the energy created by entering into the realm of the divine rather than the expression of energy in physical or psychic forms. This absorption of energy helps to transform body and psyche into instruments of the spirit and 'purifying' them, rather than making them forces in themselves. The case of ecstasy of Jesus quoted above from TDNT (the transfiguration) is an example of this 'enstasy'. If ecstasy is defined as 'to step out of one's self, enstasy may indicate the potential to find one's inner self, the *pneuma*. See references by Clément, below.

Underhill in her classic *Mysticism*[27] (1911 numerous reprints, also recently) offers valuable insights into the nature of ecstasy. She differentiates among three types (or levels) of ecstasy: physical (= trance), mental (complete unification of consciousness) and spiritual: exalted act of perception. It represents, she says, the greatest possible extension of the spiritual consciousness in the direction of Pure Being", resulting in "a profound experience of Eternal Life" (367). The latter form is to be seen as the 'real' mysticism, in which the 'real' ecstasy may occur.

> Resuming from chapter 3 she defines mysticism as "the nature and development of man's spiritual consciousness" (the subtitle of her book). So it belongs to human nature, yet needs to be developed, like other faculties, in a process of transformation. Or, in her more elaborate definition (xiv), "[Mysticism is] the expression of the *innate tendency* (italics, wvl) of the human spirit towards complete harmony with the transcendental order; whatever be the theological formula under which that is understood ..."; "....and in the experience called 'mystic union', it attains its end". "... this is a genuine life process and not an intellectual speculation...".

The mystic union is the ultimate ecstasy. However, on the long road of mysticism, ecstasy may occur in grades of intensity, and on any stage of development. The crux of mysticism is the innate faculty to experience the divine in oneself, at the same time experiencing a feeling of unification. If the experience is more inward, it may better be called enstasy (Clément, see below).

> Underhill rightly does not consider ecstasy to be an aberration, nor as something particular to specific natures. It is a basic human potential. However, aberrations do occur, and seemingly more often than the genuine ones, but this is because they are the more conspicuous cases compared to the more frequent hidden and silent experiences. Moreover those whose bodies and psyches are stronger can keep their balance physically and emotionally, even under the impact of such an overwhelming experience of the soul.

1990, French original Paris 1954). See also the work of Herman Dooyeweerd, *De wijsbegeerte der wetsidee* where the concept is developed philosophically.

27 Underhill, *Mysticism* 1911. Quoted here from University Articlebacks / Methuen, London 1960

Heiler relates ecstasy to prayer. Ecstasy (in the sense of enstasy) is a higher stage of prayer. He shows how prayer, ecstasy and meditation form one whole in a long series of stages of development, in a way culminating in ecstasy.[28]

RGG supports the spiritual meaning as referring to it as generally a presence of God in man, and an "Entleerung des Selbsts."[29]

Sometimes the mystic experience occurs all of a sudden, God's grace descending. It is a 'peak experience.' Thus mystical texts are often reflections of such an experience.

However, mostly mysticism is a gradual process, a process of transformation, of development (Underhill, quoted above), a process of alternating phases of light and shade, in various intensities. Then ecstasy (in the form of enstasy) becomes a state of (sub)consciousness rather than a momentary experience. Mysticism covers all phases of this inner development. In many religious movements spiritual development is a central theme by which one is helped along on this path of transformation.

> Augustine (354–430) expresses it as "*Tu autem, Domine, eras interior intimo meo et superior summo meo*" (But you, Lord, were more within me than my innermost being, and higher than my highest being, transl. WvL). Clément adds about Augustine's ecstasy at Ostia "God who is inaccessible and quite suddenly perceptible to the heart with an overwhelming immediacy .... glimpsed as an 'abyss of inner joy' and as the Other, as my Creator, in whose presence I am and who is speaking to me" (Clément, pp. 231–232).
>
> For Philo of Alexandria (ca. 20 BC–ca. 50 AD) ecstasy is "von einem vollkommenen Finden und Schauen Gottes, von vollkommener eingemischten Freude, von einem plötzlich hereinbrechenden Erlebnis."[30] But ecstasy is not limited to the field of religion or psychology. Artistic and other forms of creativity often have the same root.[31] The phenomenon also relates to certain human efforts and acts, which are characterized by inspiration. Inspiration is induced neither psychologically nor sensually, yet conversely it does affect the psychological state of being and perception.
>
> Then there is the issue of the relation between ratio and ecstasy. The definition by Paul Tillich is doing justice to both: "'Ecstasy' ('standing outside of one's self') points to a state of mind which is extraordinary in the sense that the mind

---

28 Heiler 1923 is a goldmine of statements and a rich array of quotations on ecstasy embedded in the chapter on prayer in mysticism (as set apart from prayer 'in der prophetish-evangelisher Frömmigkeit', both in the book proper 248–55, 284–346 and in the rich supplement 584–98. To select just one statement: "Die entscheidende Erfahrung der Ekstatiker ist das Bewusstsein einer ganz unmittelbaren, realen Berührung mit der göttlichen *Wirklichkeit*" (original emphasis) (587).

29 H. Betz et al. (ed), *Religion in Geschichte und Gegenwart (RGG)*, Band 2, Tübingen: Mohr Siebeck 1999. The precise reference is untraceable.

30 H. Windisch, *Die Frömmigkeit Philos und ihre Bedeutung für das Christentum; eine religionsgeschichtliche Studie*, Leipzig 1909, pp. 60–62.

31 A. Geels, "Mystical experience and the emergence of creativity", in: Holm 1982, 26–62

transcends its ordinary situation. Ecstasy is not a negation of reason, it is he state of mind in which reason is beyond itself, that is, beyond its subject-object structure. In being beyond itself reason does not deny itself. 'Ecstatic reason' remains reason; it does not receive anything irrational or antirational—which it could not do without self-destruction—but it transcends the basic condition of finite rationality, the subject-object structure."[32]

From all this we may conclude that there is more under the sun than the many current ideas about ecstasy, preponderantly placing it in the realm of psychology and extremes. Only rarely is it admitted that there may be a genuine spiritual dimension to it. Yet in phenomenology and the history of religion, in both Christian and other spiritual traditions, it is impossible to ignore the other dimension, which is based on genuine experience, as we have tried to demonstrate only too briefly.

Last remark. Most of the literature quoted stresses the qualities of ecstasy in its full state. Like so many human qualities ecstasy appears in grades and shades, depending on the condition of the individual, or his/her stage of spiritual development, and on the circumstance that induces the ecstasy.[33] As a matter of fact the pericopes with *ekstasis* will demonstrate different grades of ecstasy as experienced by the individuals indicated.

This chapter, therefore, analyzes *ekstasis / existêmi* in the NT, and assesses whether it expresses aspects of genuine ecstasy, in different grades.

Ekstasis in the NT: A Presentation

Here is a presentation of pericopes with *ekstasis / existêmi* or *existamai*.[34]

---

[32] P. Tillich, *Systematic theology I*, Chicago 1951, 111, quoted by Tage Kurtén, "Ecstasy—a way to religious knowledge: some remarks on Paul Tillich as theologian and philosopher," in Holm 1982, 254.

[33] Dag Hammerskjöld, once Secretary General of the UN, is an example of a mystic who lived a full, worldly life and at the same time living a genuine spiritual life. His *Markings* (Vägmärken, 1963, and Faber, London 1964) is a remarkable witness of his inner life characterized by ecstatic experiences in full integration with his life in the world.

[34] The noun occurs 7 times, the verb 17. This is the distribution over the NT books:

	verb	noun	total
Mt	1	0	1
Mk	4	2	6
Lk	3	1	4
Jn	0	0	0
Acts	8	4	12
2Cor	1	0	1
	---	---	---
Total	17	7	24

No occurrence in the other books

The pericopes are numbered 1–24 in the right margin.
Translation: NIV.

The line in bold italics contains alternative renderings proposed by the author.

Mt
12.23 All the people were astonished (*existanto*) and said, "Could this be the Son of David?" ***All the people were enraptured....*** Context: After healing, in context of Sabbath celebration.   **1**
Mk
2.12 He got up (*êgerthê*), took his mat and walked out in full view of them all. This amazed (*existasthai*) everyone and they praised God, saying, "We have never seen anything like this!" ***This enraptured everyone....*** Context: After healing a paralytic. Law teachers oppose. People praising God. Comment: *êgerthê*, he rose, like in Mk 16.6: he has risen   **2**
3.21 When his family heard about this, they went to take charge of him, for they said, "He is out of his mind (*exestê*)." ***He is in a trance.*** Context: Family tries to keep Jesus from serving the masses and from healing.   **3** Comment: one may rightly doubt if the family of Jesus really can perceive Jesus' condition as rapture. But the use of rapture can be defended as the family perceives the extraordinary condition of Jesus, naming it by the same term but in its negative connotation. We have preferred, however, to use the term 'trance', which may indicate more adequately how the family perceived the situation.
5.42 Immediately the girl stood up and walked around (she was twelve years old). At this they were completely astonished (*exestêsan ekstasei megalêi*). ***...they were rapt in great rapture.*** Context: After healing.   **4, 5**
6.51 Then he climbed into the boat with them, and the wind died down. They were completely amazed (*lian existanto en heautois;* some mss add *kai ethaumazon*); ..... ***Inwardly they were in deep rapture (and amazed);*** ..... Context: Storm on the lake.   **6** Comment: some mss add *kai ethaumazon*, and they were amazed. Obviously the *existanto* cannot and should not be the amazed of the NIV rendering.
16.8 Trembling and bewildered (*eichen autas tromos*[35] *kai ekstasis*), the women went out and fled from the tomb. They said nothing to anyone, because they were afraid (*ephobounto gar*).

---

35 Some witnesses have *phobos*: D W *pc* it sa[ms]

> ***Quivering and overcome by rapture the women went out and ran away from the tomb ….. because they were in a state of awe***
> *Context*: women at the tomb on Easter Sunday. Have been told by young man in white robe that Jesus is not here, he has risen (*êgerthê*, cf 2.12). **7**
>
> See the Excursus
>
> **Lk**
>
> 2.47 Everyone who heard him was amazed (*existanto*) at his understanding and his answers.
> ***…was enraptured…***
> *Context*: The boy Jesus in temple participating in discussions **8**
>
> 5.26 Everyone was amazed (*ekstasis elaben*) and gave praise to God. They were filled with awe (*phobou*) and said, "We have seen remarkable things (*paradoxa*) today."
> ***…rapture took them…***
> *Context*: After healing **9**
>
> 8.56 Her parents were astonished (*exestêsan*), but he ordered them not to tell anyone what had happened.
> ***…were enraptured…***
> *Context*: After healing. **10**
>
> 24.22 In addition, some of our women amazed (*exestêsan*) us. They went to the tomb early this morning …
> ***…caused us to be in a state of rapture…***
> *Context*: two disciples answering the risen Jesus about the women who went to the tomb. **11**
>
> *Comment*: here the meaning is close to 'astonishment' or 'amazement' because the disciples may have found the message too incredible as it was conveyed second-hand only.

RENDERING *EKSTASIS* IN THE NT 311

Acts

2.7 Utterly amazed (*existanto de kai ethaumazon*), they asked: "Are not all these men who are speaking Galileans?
They were enraptured and amazed...
Context: On Pentecost when the Spirit manifested **12**

Comment: *existêmi* together with *thaumazô* [!]

2.12 Amazed (*existanto*) and perplexed, they asked one another, "What does this mean?"
Enraptured and perplexed...
Context: Same. **13**

Comment: perplexed (*diêporoun*), literally completely at a loss

3.10 they recognized him as the same man who used to sit begging at the temple gate called Beautiful, and they were filled with wonder and amazement (*thambous kai ekstaseôs*) at what had happened to him.
...they were filled with wonder and rapture...
Context: Peter heals a crippled beggar. **14**

8.9–13 Now for some time a man named Simon had practiced sorcery in the city and **amazed** (*existanôn*) all the people of Samaria. He boasted that he was someone great,and all the people, both high and low, gave him their attention and exclaimed, "This man is the divine power known as the Great Power."They followed him because he had **amazed** (*exestakenai*) them for a long time with his magic.But when they believed Philip as he preached the good news of the kingdom of God and the name of Jesus Christ, they were baptized, both men and women.Simon himself believed and was baptized. And he followed Philip everywhere, astonished **(enraptured)** (*existato*) by the great signs and miracles he saw.
My proposal printed in bold italics. Twice the same as NIV, once different
Context: Philip in Samaria **15, 16, 17**

9.21 All those who heard him were *astonished* (*existanto*) and asked, "Isn't he the man who raised havoc in Jerusalem among those who call on this name? And hasn't he come here to take them as prisoners to the chief priests?"
[no change proposed]
Context: Paul preaching in Damascus. **18**

Comment: They were astonished to see Paul preaching in favor rather than against Christians.

10.10 He became hungry and wanted something to eat, and while the meal was being prepared, he fell into a trance (*egeneto ep'auton ekstasis*) (later texts: *epepesan*, fell)
...he fell into ecstasy.
Context: Peter went up to the roof to pray. He gets a vision. **19**

10.45 The circumcised believers who had come with Peter were astonished (*exestêsan*) that the gift of the Holy Spirit had been poured out even on the Gentiles. ***...were in a state of rapture...*** *Context*: Peter at Cornelius' in Caesarea. Holy Spirit manifests to people while Peter is speaking.	20
11.5 I was in the city of Joppa praying, and in a trance (*en ekstasei*) I saw a vision. I saw something like a large sheet being let down from heaven by its four corners, and it came down to where I was. ***...and in ecstasy I saw a vision....*** *Context*: Peter tells what happened.	21
12.16 But Peter kept on knocking, and when they opened the door and saw him, they were astonished (*exestêsan*). ***...they were amazed...*** *Context*: Amazement and happiness when seeing Peter escaped from prison.	22
Comment: here the rapture is out of happiness and amazement rather than spiritual.	
22.17–18 When I returned to Jerusalem and was praying at the temple, I fell into a trance (*genesthai me en ekstasei*) and saw the Lord speaking … ***...that I fell into ecstasy*** *Context*: Paul tells what happened	23
2Cor 5.13 If we are out of our mind, it is for the sake of God; if we are in our right mind, it is for you (*eite gar exestêmen, theôi; eite sôphronoumen, humin*). ***For if we are in a state of ecstasy, it is for God; if we are in a state of reason, it is for you*** *Context*: Paul explains different levels of understanding.	24

Comments

As to the other major translations we find a fairly great *communis opinio* with NIV concerning the English rendering of *ekstasis* (e.g., KJ, NRSV). But it is remarkable that over the past decades practically no critical attention has been paid by scholars to the meaning of *ekstasis* in the various pericopes. An analysis of *ekstasis*, ecstasy, rapture, and trance in the database ATLA in September 2004 did not result in a single publication focusing on this issue for any of the above mentioned texts. Since, Peerbolte (2008) published his significant article on *ekstasis*; the results have been mentioned.

Reviewing the translation of *ekstasis* in the 24 places where the term is used in the NT we find it is almost exclusively used in a positive sense, as against many instances in the LXX.[36] There the Greek *ekstasis* is a hyponym used to translate different Hebrew terms, conveying various meanings, fairly often including negative ones. In the majority of these cases it is used more positively than in LXX. Further the single word *ekstasis* is rendered in five quite different English words (in NIV and various other English translations).

It is interesting to note that we never find 'ecstasy' in NIV as translation. In 17 cases it is translated by 'astonishment' or 'amazement', rather neutral and even pale terms, compared to what ecstasy stands for in our overview in section 2. In three places it is rendered by 'trance', a term that is not incorrect in itself but suggests the abnormalities that we try to exclude from what we found genuine mysticism to be, and its expression in ecstasy. The same goes for the two places where we find 'out of one's mind' and the one pericope at the grave, 'bewildered'.

We do find a difference in what happens to the subjects who experience *ekstasis*. In some cases it is triggered by an external event, like a miraculous healing. In other cases it just happens to the subject, resulting e.g. in a vision.

It is remarkable that when *ekstasis* is described or mentioned, it is never accompanied by 'abnormal' signs. This is underlined by Clark[37] who finds that in NT we find "emphasis on self-control and clear-headedness". "(…) the uncontrollable physical manifestations (…) were reserved largely for those who stood in opposition to the Spirit". In the new covenant, Clark continues, "the presence of the Spirit is now an on-going *inner reality*"(emphasis added). Referring to Paul, "when he is in *ekstasis* it is part of his relationship with God."

The different English words for *ekstasis* seem too far apart in meaning as to represent the one Greek word. 'Amazement' and 'astonishment' refer to a common human reaction on the psychological rather than spiritual level. Trance[38], a term generally referring to a phenomenon of psychiatric nature and therefore considered by many as abnormal, occurs in Acts only and clearly indicates a different meaning. Cf Underhill in section 2 above. Bewilderment and out-of-one's-mind are translations referring to a state characterized by a lack of control over the psyche. At first sight a translation of *ekstasis* as 'ecstasy' seems to have a too extreme connotation. So it is appropriate to inquire in what situations *ekstasis* does occur in the NT.

---

36 Lust et al., *Greek-English Lexicon of the Septuagint* 2003: illusion, terror, dismay, entrancement, astonishment, torpor, and only once as ecstasy (Ps 30/31.23).

37 M. S. Clark, "Ekstasis in New Testament Christianity," *Cyberjournal for Pentecostal-charismatic research*, 1997, 1.

38 *Webster's:* 1: state of partly suspended animation, or of inability to function; 2: a somnolent state such as that of deep hypnosis appearing also in hysteria and in some spiritualistic mediums and characterized by limited sensory and motor contact with the surroundings and subsequent lack of recall, 3: a state of profound abstraction or absorption accompanied by exaltation.

The majority of pericopes with *ekstasis* (18x) describe the effect of some miracle:

(Numbers refer to the numbered pericopes listed above)

- healing (1,2,4,5,9,10,14), temple discussion (8), storm scene (6), tomb scene (7,11), Holy Spirit (12,13,20), Simon and Philip (17), magic (15,16), escaped from prison (22).

Other pericopes (6x) describe states of changed consciousness:

- trance or vision (19,21,23) and 'out-of-one's mind situations (3,24), while one case only (18) it is astonishment only.

In all cases (except one) where NIV says 'astonishment' or 'amazement' the text refers to miracles. The tomb scene in Mk, if viewed as a miracle, is translated differently (bewildered). 'Out of one's-mind' we find in the scene when Jesus' family wants to take him with them as they do not recognize the miracle. And in Paul's pericope 2C 5.13 to which we will come back.

So we see that in most cases the *ekstasis* is triggered by an act of healing or by another miracle performed by Jesus (Synoptics), or later by the apostles (Acts). Trance only occurs in Acts.

This variety of English terms solicits a closer look questioning whether or not this variety is necessary or reasonable. It is amazing and astonishing [!] to see how quite miraculous occurrences are reduced in significance using the much weaker terms 'amazing' and 'astonishing'. The healing scenes (7 pericopes), for example, in reality are more than astounding: here something is happening that cannot be. Here the 'beyond' becomes manifest, even to an average bystander. Yes, admittedly: bystanders of ordinary understanding would become critical and derisive, even angry because Jesus 'obviously' is working for Beelzebub (cf the Pharisees in Mt 12.24, Mk 3.22 par). However, people open to the 'beyond', and those under the spell of Jesus' overpowering charisma must have experienced it as a true miracle. And of course the evangelist will render that reaction rather than the more neutral astonishment. Otherwise, why would the authors of these narratives not have used the usual and current Greek words for astonishment and amazement? The same, *mutatis mutandis*, goes for the other cases that arouse *ekstasis* where it is described.

An Alternative Rendering

So what we need is an English term (with both a noun and a verb form) that renders the Greek term adequately, in the perspective we have just drawn. The prime alternative would be 'ecstasy.' However, we find that ecstasy is too strong a term for some of the cases for the *ekstasis* raised by the occurrences described.

There we propose 'rapture' as an alternative.[39] Earlier we have already seen that rapture is ecstasy but on a lower level of intensity, often triggered by an external event. Other pericopes refer to an experience of a higher intensity, where the *ekstasis* just seems to occur to the subject, without a trigger from the outside world. There we use 'ecstasy' rather than rapture. This solution will turn out to be a satisfying alternative. Rapture is also a satisfying term because it helps to bridge the gap that ordinarily exists between the 'worldly' and the 'spiritual'. Rapture indeed is experienced in art and nature as well as in religion. Its working culminates in mysticism.

Having selected rapture and ecstasy as satisfying renderings, what does it amount to?

What do we find? See the presentation of the texts we have discussed already. Here is a summary.

> *People are enraptured when a totally paralyzed man rises, takes his mat and goes, just on Jesus saying so. At another situation spectators are rapt in great rapture when a girl considered dead came back to life. The disciples got into deep rapture inwardly when Jesus climbed in to the boat and the storm abated. The women at the grave were overcome by rapture and in a state of awe. The pouring out of the holy spirit caused people standing around to be enraptured and amazed. When people found Peter returned they were amazed. Peter went up to the roof to pray and fell into ecstasy. At another time Peter was praying and in ecstasy saw a vision. Paul relates ecstasy to God, reason to man.*

The proposed alternative opens up new views on the text, and new insights into the meaning. Apart from a new translation for *ekstasis / existêmi* a few other suggestions for translation have been made above that seem to be closer to the original. The result may be interpreted as leading to a more spiritual understanding and opening up new perspectives for the significance of the NT at the present time. But above all: it may lead to an open discussion on the subject of spirituality in the NT.

* * *

Some Issues

Three issues need further attention and will be treated in this *excursus*. Mk 16.5–8 requires a fuller treatment. The terms amazement, astonishment, wonder

---

39 Literature about rapture and NT is scarce. Zwiep uses the term quite differently, interpreting it as the German *Entrückung*: "a bodily translation into the 'beyond' as the conclusion of one's earthly life without the intervention of death" (in: *Auferstehung*, the 4th Durham-Tübingen research symposium, Tübingen 1999, 323–49). In the dictionaries we consulted (see above) this meaning was not given.

having been largely rejected will be looked at more closely. The term *phobos* is intriguing; a few words will be given.

The Scene at the *mnêmeion* (Mk 16.5-8): A Closer Look

My alternative in the text at the pericope at the *mnêmeion* (grave) invites to a closer look at the narrative of Mk 16.5–8, not only about *ekstasis* but also about the *ekthambein* (NIV: alarmed) and about the women being afraid (*phobos*) at the grave.

> The women are coming to the grave and they find the big stone rolled away. Upon entering the *mnêmeion* they find a young man in white *stola,* sitting inside. Still unaware of the grave being empty they *exethambêthêsan,* and the young man tells them not to do so. Many translations say they were alarmed[40]. The Greek has *ekthambeô,* its basic meaning being utter wonder or amazement.[41] Generally, however, in NT studies it is associated with fear, alarm, etc. Rather, in my opinion, the women were struck with utter wonder. They are completely overwhelmed by a situation they cannot explain. Yet being aware of the sacred place they are in, close to the (supposed) body of their beloved Master they fall into rapture. Miracles seem to continue, it appears, even after his horrible death! They run away (rather than fleeing) from the *mnêmeion* taken by *tromos* (or *phobos,* as some authoritative witnesses say [42]) and *ekstasis.* This is usually translated as (e.g. NIV:) 'trembling and bewildered'. Also Paulsen views the combination as "die auffallende Verstärkung in den Termini der Furcht."[43] What is the sense of this pericope? Is it bewilderment and fear? Or is it something that overtakes them, confronted with a grand miracle that they may sense but do not and cannot understand? Current interpretations and translations almost invariably refer to the concept of fear.[44]

This chapter has opened with a reference to me experiencing another understanding than that of alarm, fear and bewilderment. It was rapture, awe and being filled with wonder. What was it that happened at the *mnêmeion* in the story by Mark?

---

40 NRSV, NIV. Others: ASV has 'amazed' and KJ 'affrightened'. German translations (original Luther, Elberfelder 'entsetzen', French (NEG) 'épouvanter'. In Dutch 'verbaasd' (Staten), ontzetten (Luth), ontstellen (Leids, Brouwer, Canisius, NBV), schrikken (Willibrord).
41 J. Luzarraga ("Retraducción semítica de *fobeomai* en Mc 16,8 », *Biblica: Commentarii* 50 (1969) 497–510) is the only author we found to discuss the meaning of *phobos* in Mk 16. Related to this is the meaning of *thauma* and *thambos.* He affirms that they possibly are interrelated: « Los conceptos pueden tener cierta relación mutua. » (p. 506, n. 5) in the sense of wondering, being amazed, etc.
42 D W *pc* it sa^{ms} (NA 27)
43 H. Paulsen 1980, 152. There is no discussion on the meaning of the terms. Luzarraga sees the terms as mutually reinforcing (503).
44 E.g., Stacy 1979 (not obtainable in Holland), Güttgemans 1972, 89, Hooker 1991, 387, Thimmes 1989, 139-147 (not obtainable in Holland), Thurston 1985, 305-319 (not obtainable in Holland).

Let us first look at the *tromos*. Some witnesses say *phobos*. In my view the difference is not essential: *tromos* is a sign of their psyche being vehemently moved by the spirit by what is happening with them, then and there. Obviously something great has occurred: the Master is not there anymore, he has gone somewhere. He is not dead! After all that they have experienced that with Jesus anything may happen. They feel that this is a moment of tremendous importance. It is awe (*phobos*)[45] that fills their hearts rather than fear or anxiety. Their souls leap upward (*ekstasis*) in an overwhelmingly deep experience of wonder: a rapture, or even an ecstasy, that they can neither explain nor understand. Physically it causes trembling. Even their souls are shaken. They are quivering for rapture. The moment is so grand that they cannot stand the situation and they run in anxious wonder, thinking how to explain this supernatural phenomenon to the disciples, as instructed by the young man. However, they keep silent. What else can one do when experiencing this extraordinary event? They have to, maybe until their psyche has recovered its balance again. They waver between complete incomprehensibility and an unexplainable awareness of something extremely beautiful and joyous that is there, struck by a deep feeling of awe, that they cannot put into words.[46] When looking at the parallel text in Mt (28.8) we find a striking confirmation: "the women hurried away from the tomb, afraid and yet filled with joy" (NIV) (*meta phobou kai charas megalês*). Cassian speaks of ecstasy as "spiritual tenderness that overwhelms the soul". This feeling "is rendered unbearable by its very intensity". "The suddenness of the light stupefies it [the soul] and robs it of its speech. All its senses remain withdrawn in its inmost depth or completely suspended".[47] So they could not tell anything to anybody because of this state of awe. They were struck with silence.[48] This interpretation answers a lot of questions raised in the discussion about the sudden ending of Mark's Gospel. Anyhow it solves the puzzle for what the women were in fear of.[49]

---

45 Luzarraga argues that *phobos* is a translation from the Hebrew/Aramaic root *bhl* which means both to fear and to walk quickly (*el sentido de 'temer' y también el de 'marchar aprisa'*) (501). In my view this is not a plausible solution. It is pity Luzarraga does not offer a complete translation of the pericope.

46 I find support in C.F.D. Moule who suggests in a short note in NT Studies (2,1 (1955/56), 58-59) that their silence is only for the moment. They want to keep their experience intact till their meeting with the disciples.

47 John Cassian, *Confessiones* IX 27, quoted in Clément 1982, 255.

48 A promising publication is Focant, "Un silence qui fait parler [!]" 2002, 79-96, in: A. Denaux, *New Testament textual criticism and exegesis*, Festschrift J. Delobel, Peeters/University Press, Leuven 2002, 79-96). Although it does not go into the matter further it touches the silence of the women. Focant interprets it for its meaning for the abrupt ending of the Gospel.

49 The sudden ending of Mark has given rise to an abundance of interpretations. Rarely the issues raised in this section are connected to it. One of the publications where it is done is by Boomershine and Bartholomew 1981, 213-23. Their interpretation is traditional, but their argument how to view the short sentence *ephobounto gar*, is convincing and is applied to our interpretation.

Astonishing, Amazing, Wondering

As we have seen the terms *ekstasis / existêmi* are often translated with amaze / astonish. One should be amazed with this rendering as the Greek provides adequate terms for this concept: *thaumazô*, and also to a certain extent *thambeô, ekthambeô* [50]. In e.g. Acts 3.10 people are filled with both *thambos* and *ekstasis* where obviously different emotions are indicated: amazement and rapture.

But is *ekthambeô* wondering? WNT (abridged): "*ekthambeô*, aor. pass. *exethambêthên*, in our lit. only in Mk and only pass.: *be amazed*, Mk 9:15; *be alarmed* 16:5f; *be distressed* w. *adêmonein* 14:33." I wonder why it translates the one Greek term into three English words, ranging from a positive amazement to alarm and distress. Let us see what NIV does with it. It translates Mk 9.15 (when Jesus comes to the crowd after the transfiguration) as "overwhelmed with wonder," 14.33 (Gethsemane) as "deeply distressed," 16.5,6 "be alarmed" (at the tomb). In Acts 3.10 (healing) people are "filled with wonder" (*thambos*) (see above). Hooker, in his commentary on the Gospel of Mark, translates 'astounded' in v. 5 and 'alarmed' in v. 6[51] (sic: different terms for the same concept). And when the women 'flee' it is with 'trembling and terror'. And he adds, "This is precisely how many other characters in the story have reacted…when confronted with the powers of God" (385–87).

> We understand the Gospel completely different. For healthy people (healthy, physically, mentally as well as spiritually) a confrontation with the numinous (Rudolf Otto) is a positive experience. It may be staggering and destabilizing, but it is positive and full of light, peace and joy, yet—and that is important—inexpressible.

> We therefore suggest as standard translation for *ekthambeô* 'overwhelmed with wonder.' In Mk 9.15 people are overwhelmed with wonder when they see Jesus as he returns transfigured[52]. The women at the *mnêmeion* are equally overwhelmed by the grave being open and by the young man in white sitting there at the right side. So far, so good. But what about the feelings of Jesus in Gethsemane (Mk 14.33–34 NIV) where we find the same *ekthambeô*? When taking some disciples with him he began to be deeply distressed (*ekthambeô*) and troubled (*adêmoneô*) (be embarrassed, be in anxiety, be distressed, restless[53]), saying "my soul is overwhelmed with sorrow to the point of death." How is this to be understood? We suggest the following. Jesus is overwhelmed (*ekthambeô*) and

---

50 See the earlier note on being alarmed.
51 Marcus 2009, 1079 has astounded in both v. 5 and 6.
52 Luzarraga (1969, 506) provides us with the different interpretations (and concomitant translations) some commentators present. One, Turner, "suggested that something of the glory of the Transfiguration could still be seen upon the face of Jesus." Luzarraga does not support this view but I think Turner's is a correct interpretation, and it supports the NIV translation.
53 Among dictionaries a great divergence is found: LidellScott: to be in great distress, anguish. WNT: in Angst sein, in Unruhe sein. EWNT: in Unruhe sein. Langenscheidt: unruhig sein, verlegen sein. Muller: in verlegenheid of onrust zitten.

embarrassed (*dêmoneô*) saying 'my soul is deeply sad until death' (*perilupos estin hê phuchê mou heôs thanatou*). He is aware of something grand and grandiose to happen, though suffering with the prospect of death. At the same time he is overwhelmed with wonder and awe at what is there, beyond the threshold of Gethsemane. And when addressing God, what else can consciousness be filled with but wonder and awe? He then prays that the cup will be taken from him, yet he resigns to God's will, in which he has always stayed and felt at home.

Phobos: Fear or Awe?

About the word group *phobos*. Generally understood as fear, and rendered so. In classical antiquity the term exhibited various shades. *Phobos* describes encounters with force expressed as terror and anxiety but also honor and respect.[54] This concept of terror, fear and anxiety has haunted much of Christianity as it referred to the fear of God and his punishment. It is often seen as a heritage from the OT; we will see in a moment that the OT fear often exhibited more the concept of awe. In the Gospels the feared 'fear of God' does not figure at all, but surfaces in the Epistles and is continued in early Christianity[55]. But the OT picture of fear is not so bleak. In various layers of the OT fear refers to other connotations. TDNT (Günther Wanke, the author for the OT part) is quite clear on this issue, if read meticulously. Apart from meaning fear and being afraid it also carries connotations of having someone in honor (B I 1), of respecting (B I 2), feeling reverence, holding in respect (B II 1a,b): "man treats with fear and reverent awe especially persons and places that stand in a special relation to God" (B II 2). My interpretation is that it implies an awareness of distance. The OT formula 'fear not' expresses a reassurance and assistance in everyday life (B II 4) and thus diminishes this distance: communication is open. (*mê phobeisthe*) it means that this distance is removed: communication is possible. Fearing God should be along with loving God. Then there is not even room for fear of the punishment of Yahweh (B II 3b). In the Wisdom literature the fear of Yahweh changes face and is equated with knowledge, insight and wisdom (II B 3c). 'God-fearing' refers to people whose conduct is orientated to the will of God (B II 3a). It also refers to fear for punishment that constantly is lurking around the corner. Yet Psalm 2.11 LXX speaks of 'serving the Lord *en phobôi* and rejoice in him *en tromôi*. Should it be 'in fear' and 'in trembling'? But why tremble when rejoicing? It refers to a quiver as is experienced in utmost joy. Therefore: serving while in awe, and rejoicing while in a spontaneous quiver.

---

54 Balz in TDNT sub A4.
55 Balz in TDNT sub E: "the word group is a favorite one in the post-apostolic fathers. In distinction from the NT the fear of God is increasingly used in formulae."

How to interpret *phobos* in the Gospels? Where it refers to an encounter with the sacred one's reaction is that of awe, a condition of being totally impressed with something grand, unattainable and distant, the *mysterium tremendum* of Rudolf Otto (cf G. van der Leeuw in RGG II 1180–82). Yet this overriding confrontation with the sacred evokes an awareness of being connected, of belonging. This reaction is completely different from a confrontation with hostility and threat or intimidation. In first instance the confrontation with the sacred is startling, a momentary emotion, it is a shock. When one then is told 'don't be shocked' a connection is established. Distance diminishes, communication starts. When the disciples are confronted with a miracle (e.g. Mk 4.41 par) they do not fear but are startled and stand in awe. The transfiguration cannot evoke fear, it is utter awe (Mk 9.6 par).

Evaluation and Conclusions

Resuming the question raised at the beginning of this chapter:

An absolutely paralyzed man is lying on his mat. Suddenly he rises, takes his mat and goes home, just on being told so. Would a spectator be amazed or rather completely taken in rapture? Would one just be astonished when a girl of twelve years thought dead stood up and walked around, just on being told so, or rather be 'rapt in great rapture'?

Therefore, a more precise understanding of the word ekstasis *opens a new perspective on how humans react to an extraordinary event, an event that touches one's very existence: stilling a storm, resuscitating a dying person, witnessing the holy spirit, getting a vision. It is not just amazement that is evoked, the event triggers the spirit to rise, and it takes thought and emotion into a different layer of consciousness. Paul relates ecstasy to God, reason to man. This is what the term* ekstasis *represents. The events at the grave cause a rapture to the effect of quivering and being silent, where emotion and questioning are expected. Why? 'Because they were in a state of awe'. The singsong rendering in a religious meditation (referred to in the Introduction) is a true way of reflecting on such event. The stories referred to convey that other dimension evoking the spirit inside: ecstasy need not be foreign to our culture, the awe for the Other has not gone but went into hiding. The deeper level of an extraordinary emotion may be recognized and admitted.*

People are enraptured when a totally paralyzed man rises, takes his mat and goes, just on Jesus saying so. At another situation spectators are rapt in great rapture when a girl considered dead came back to life. The disciples got into deep rapture inwardly when Jesus climbed in to the boat and the storm abated. The women at the grave were overcome by rapture and in a state of awe. The pouring out of the holy spirit caused people standing around to be enraptured and amazed.

The English word ecstasy does not occur in the current translations, e.g. in NIV as a rendering of the Greek *ekstasis*. A short survey of dictionaries and literature has disclosed that the English term ecstasy or its equivalent rapture are fair renderings of *ekstasis* in many of the 24 cases in which it appears in the NT. It is found to be a positive phenomenon, an expression of the spirit, quite different from being out of one's mind. 'Rapture' indicates a mild form of ecstasy triggered by an impression from outside whilst 'ecstasy' refers to a deep inner experience of some presence.

When applying this rendering to the NT cases the result is that a translation by 'rapture' or 'ecstasy' in most cases is satisfying. It can safely replace in almost all pericopes all the words used in current translations: amazement, astonishment, trance, out of one's mind, bewildered. At some places, however, the usual terms meet the condition better. My proposal is not a one-to-one rendering. But the commonly applied translations do not do justice to the Greek of the narrative. The scene at the *mnêmeion* in Mk 16, again, is one of ecstasy, awe and wonder rather than fear, bewilderment and alarm.

Ekstasis is not a central concept in the NT. The outcome of this study is not of an essential nature on the literary level. Yet what we have found does contribute to the results of this Part IV: the spirit does play an impressing role in the Gospels and even wider. A spiritual view on the pericopes in question changes the perspective, offering a fresh understanding in terms of mysticism and spirituality in view of the sacred character of the NT and especially of the Gospels.

The proposed translation and concomitant interpretation is offered for consideration. It may serve as an alternative to the current ones. Further research and testing is recommended.

Concluding, *ekstasis* is a term found in the NT, offering additional insight in spirit, that alas hwas mostly been neglected. One finds it used mostly in a positive sense: inspired by God or the holy spirit.

Concluding Part Four

Explorations in the Field of *pneuma*, Spirit

What is spirit? The explorations in this Part have highlighted different aspects, *capita selecta* of this vast field, so hard to get a grip on. What has been found?

Spirit is a neglected field in NT studies, and possibly even more so in theology and doctrine. It has all focused on the Holy Spirit. A simple grammatical analysis has resulted in discerning spirit from the spirit, holy spirit from the Holy Spirit. Through the ages the focus on the latter has relegated all else to metaphoric understanding or to the impalpable arena of miracles. An impressive array of texts in the NT, however, is testimony of the genuineness of the phenomenon of *pneuma* and its variety of meanings. Evidently spirit is related to the human, evidently too it is of another dimension. It is a presence, abstract yet personal. Is it a human capacity? If not inborn, yet within reach. It seems rather to be a matter of consciousness. It may happen to you, it may not. When discussing the Kingdom the same issue was at the table, and with similar questions and optional answers. Spirit is a potentiality, external, internal. Revealing is the new insight of being in spirit, and of spirit being in you, emerging from a simple grammatical exercise. Rapture or ecstasy have been removed from the extraneous, the abnormal, the psychiatric and eccentric. *Ekstasis* is a true expression of the spirit inside one, triggered from outside, *enstasis* being triggered from inside.

Summary of outcomes

Chapter 15 deals with question what spirit is, definite or indefinite, holy or not. In the Gospels spirit emerges not only as the spirit and the Holy Spirit, but even as holy spirit, and finally as just spirit. The remarkable thing is that current translations neglect the difference between the definite spirit and an indefinite one, adding in English the article where it is absent in Greek. Yet the phrases with 'spirit' rather than 'the spirit' are quite sensible. As to holy spirit the pronouncements are revealing. Traditional views are challenged.

Here are the passages where spirit is described as something indefinite:

- Mary is pregnant out of (*ek*) holy spirit (Mt 1.18)
- Joseph is told by the angel that Mary conceived out of (*ek*) holy spirit (Mt 1.20)
- Zachariah is told that he will be filled with (gen.) holy spirit (Lk 1.15)
- Zachariah indeed is filled with (gen.) holy spirit (Lk 1.67)
- Mary is foretold that holy spirit will come upon (*epi*) her (Lk 1.35)
- Elizabeth filled with (gen.) holy spirit (Lk 1.41)
- John the Baptist going in (*en*) spirit and power of Elijah Lk 1.17x)
- And the child grew and became strong in (dat.) spirit (Lk 1.80)
- Holy spirit was upon (*epi*) Simeon (Lk 2.25)
- John the Baptist foretells that Jesus will immerse in (*en*) holy spirit (and fire, Mt and Lk). All four canonical Gospels report this remarkably consistently: Mt 3.11, Mk 1.8, Lk 3.16, Jn 1.33.
- ... unless he is born out of (*ek*) water and spirit nobody can enter the Kingdom of God (Jn 3.5)
- What is created out of flesh is flesh, and what is created out of the spirit is spirit (Jn 3.6)
- ... praying to the Father in (*en*) spirit and truth (Jn 4.23)
- God is spirit and his worshipers must worship in spirit and truth(Jn 4.24)
- the words that I have spoken to you are spirit and are life. (Jn 6.63)
- Jesus full of (gen.) holy spirit (Lk 4.1a)
- Spirit of the Lord is upon (epi) me (Lk 4.18) (quotation from Isa 61.1)
- ... how much more the Father will give from heaven holy spirit to those who ask for it Lk 11.13)
- If I drive out demons being in divine[1] spirit, then the Kingdom of God has come upon (*epi*) you (Mt 12.28)
- David speaking in spirit (Mt 22.43), i.e. being in spirit

Another remarkable point is that in the Gospels 'the spirit' obviously sometimes refers to the spirit of a person, or the spirit inside one, contrary to the widespread *communis opinio* that the spirit does not belong to the individual unless donated as a grace, at baptism.

Clearly this is the case when *pneuma* comes with a personal pronoun:

- Jesus knew by his (*autou*) spirit (dat.) what they in their hearts were thinking (Mk 2.8)
- My (*mou*) spirit rejoices in (*epi*) God (Mary) (Lk 1.47)
- Her spirit (*to pneuma autês*) returned (daughter of Jairus) (Lk 8.55)
    i.e. she returned from death when her spirit had departed, and it came back to the effect that she was alive again
- Jesus commits his spirit (*to pneuma mou*) (cit. Ps 31.6) in God's hands (Lk 23.46)

But also with the definite article:

- The spirit is willing, but the flesh is weak (Mk 14.38, Mt 26.41)
- Jesus gave up his (*to*) spirit Mt 27.50
- Jesus hands over his (*to*) spirit (Jn 19.30)

---

1 *En pneumatiu theou*: with an implied *ôn*: being in. The noun *theos* without the article is indefinite and is therefore rendered as an adjective, 'divine.'

- Jesus returned to Galilee in the power of his (*tou*, gen.) spirit (Lk 4.14)
- Simeon went to the temple being in his (*en tôi*) spirit (Lk 2.27)

Paul, of course, is of the same opinion: the spirit of God is inside.

The concept of 'spirit' originally and best refers not to a distinct hypostasis either beside God or within the Godhead, mediating between God and the world, but to God's own personal presence and activity in the world" (Lodahl).

Chapter 16 has further demonstrated that this presence even is hidden in the individual, sometimes manifesting. Or one may be in spirit, or even in holy spirit. Here too new insights developed when having a close look at the phrase *en pneumati*, being in spirit. Here too the crux lies in the precise rendering. Here too the presence of the article (where it fails in Greek) tends to lead astray. Moreover the preposition *en* ('in') generally is not translated as 'in'. Here is what was found:

- Being baptized turns out to be enveloped and purified in holy spirit;
- when driving out demons Jesus is in spirit rather being prompted by it from outside;
- Jesus was in the spirit when being led in the desert;
- he returned to Galilee being in the power of the spirit rather than being guided from outside.
- spirit is not outside but rather within.
- David was speaking in spirit or even in the holy spirit rather than being prompted from outside;
- one can be full of holy spirit.

This suggests that apart from being in spirit, spirit may be inside one.

In chapter 17 the essay on the words from the cross underlines the serenity of the scene at the cross as narrated by the evangelists. The passion narratives tell about scenes of dignity and serenity rather than dramas of suffering, agony, and distress. Spirit permeates the scene. The words spoken by Jesus are testimonies of the spirit. The psalm Jesus recites—with the misleading opening line 'why have you forsaken me'—is one of complete surrender to his fate and to God's will. Finally he entrusts his spirit into the hands of God, and when 'it' is completed hands over his spirit.

Finally, chapter 18 on ecstasy has found that ecstasy is a moment when the spirit manifests, when it comes out of the person as it were, it seems to 'stand out' (*ekstasis, existêmi*). Generally it is translated as amazement, astonished, in trance, out of mind, never by ecstasy or its synonym rapture. Time and again, when Jesus performs a miraculous healing people English bibles tell us people are just amazed or astonished. Imagine, seeing the daughter of Jairus returning from death, Jesus stilling a storm, a blind and deaf person healed even on Sabbath, a paralytic taking his mat and walking home. Rather, would one not be enraptured, taken by the spirit? Rapture took people when the young boy Jesus displayed such understanding. The women at the grave were overcome by rapture (rather than bewilderment) and awe (rather than fear), finding the grave open and a young man clothed in white telling them Jesus not being here. When seeing the daughter of Jairus walking around people 'were rapt in great rapture'. Although the word *pneuma* is not used it is clear that an agent other than the usual mental function of amazement and bewilderment is acting.

Therefore, what is the relationship between spirit and the human being? There is no concluding evidence for *pneuma* to reside in the individual. Or that one is in spirit by one's very nature. Yet many pericopes in the New Testament testify to it, or at least present indications for it. Spirit is given to a person, or it may happen to one, it may be upon one, it may be inside one, or a person may be in (the) spirit. Spirit may be holy, there is the Holy Spirit. Does it refer to the Kingdom of God? Being present, being inside one? What transpires unmistakably in the Gospels that *pneuma* plays a far greater role than generally is thought of. This is due on the one hand to the dramatic shift to the Holy Spirit as Person in the one God. On the other hand modernity exacts its toll: spirit is non-existent materially, empirically, logically.

> *This Part then causes one to rethink the concept of spirit. Spirit in by far the most cases does not refer to the Holy Spirit, let alone as part of the Trinity. Spirit is found both in the human being and all-around, as a Presence, a presence that is found in the Kingdom of God. It manifests in the atmosphere at the scene of crucifixion as it did during the passion. Spirit is what appears as ecstasy in the women at the mnêmeion, and at so many other occasions. In the course of this Part it has been brought up as an alternative to the current notions, successively in each of the chapters. The proposals offered are presented as an additional layer of understanding adding to the present interpretations.*

PART FIVE
What It Was About

Conclusions

Now that the expedition has completed its explorations, like in all Bible research: preliminarily, it is time to summarize the diary. Much attention is given to the organization: 'Approach'. The 'Analysis' reports the findings of the various explorations in the fields of the Kingdom of God, of the land of transformation, the vicissitudes of the psyche, and the blessings of the spirit. Some findings are reported in a schematic form. In 'Evaluation' the overall results are viewed with an excursion on what mysticism in the Gospels implies. Included are a few suggestions for continued research that I hope will be taken up.

For the Synthesis the expedition returns to the explored land in a balloon surveying its conclusions.

Finally, the Annex provides summaries of the outcomes of each of the case studies: the Kingdom of God: *hê basileia tou theou,* transformation: *metanoia,* self / psyche / mind-and-heart: *psuchê,* spirit: *pneuma,* and rapture / ecstasy: *ekstasis.*

Approach

The book has developed along two lines, one bottom-up, the other top-down. The bottom-up line analyses various words and sayings of Jesus, the logia, in a semantical approach. The top-down approach starts from the question if Jesus was a mystic, or a messenger of God, or maybe both, and then asks if this can be traced in his sayings: what is his message? Initially I followed the first line only, fascinated as I was by the meaning of some specific words by Jesus. Soon, however, the other line proved necessary when the question became urgent how alternative meanings would fit in an over-all frame, other than offered by theology and Church doctrines. Here mysticism presented itself. Jesus' message, centering around the Kingdom of God, offers such framework if viewed as a perspective on an inner reality. Would such top-down approach offer solutions for open questions and riddles raised in the bottom-up analysis? Constant watching was practised against implying preconceptions, even unaware. Yet, much may have escaped attention.

As to the bottom-up, questions were tabled that had made me wonder already for some time. What about the commandment to lay down one's life, like the shepherd is supposed to do?, or the disciples, out of love for one another? What is the implication of losing life in order to save it? Did Jesus call for repentance, implying penitence and the like, and sin? His call was to 'hear' and 'see' a new perspective in the expectations for the Kingdom of God. This kingdom was a hot issue in his time: the end of time was near, some thought and predicted, the Kingdom of heaven would descend on earth. Others hoped for an earthly Kingdom where God would re-establish the Davidic kingship of righteousness and peace. Neither had happened. What was Jesus' intent? What does kingdom mean, when understood spiritually? Jesus announced its arrival, here and now. He even told people that it was not to be expected here or there, it is to be found inside the human being. Then, I wondered, is this corroborated in the sayings and parables? In the scholarly profession as well as in most Christian denominations this is often denied. But at the same time there is confusion because the end of time had not come, the *parousia* (Jesus' second coming) did not happen. The earthly Davidic rule with peace, righteousness and the like turned out to be an utopia. What did Jesus intend when announcing God's Kingdom? Had it something to do with spirit? What about the role of the spirit? Did John the Baptist announce that Jesus will baptize by the Holy Spirit, or immerse in holy spirit, words originating from elsewhere and referring to a different concept? Is spirit foreign to the human being? And, to name another case, what did the spirit work out on the women at the grave of Jesus, the *mnêmeion*: fear, trembling and bewilderment? Or was it awe and rapture?

Inevitably during my research work on these topics the question arose in what way these logia fit in the overall message Jesus was delivering. What is this message, after all? Thus I started the top-down line. My a priori question was the following. Often one finds mysticism in religion. Do we find it in the Gospels? Most scholars say no. One of the reasons is that Christian mysticism is supposed to have started not earlier than in the 5th c. Collections of mystical literature, therefore, do not contain texts by Jesus in far the most cases. Is this correct? Moreover, the development in Christian doctrine has moved in a direction often contrary to what mysticism stands for. In order to try and get a picture the first question arising was, what is mysticism? The next one: what indicators do we find in order to analyze the relevant logia on traces of mysticism.

How to tackle that job? The general approach in NT criticism is to take the Gospels as literary units. The logia, sayings by Jesus are part and parcel of that text, it is composed as a whole. The logia are not independent units. While belonging to the narrative genre they have to be treated accordingly. My approach has been different from the outset. Often the acts of Jesus and what was said about him have been taken as the message, with a strong emphasis on the (post-)Easter accounts. Would it not be plausible to take the words of Jesus as the message? Yes, that is being done too, but contextualized in the narrative, colored by eschatological and Christological perspectives, and put into the scenario of the later developing doctrines. The logia, however, form specific elements in the narrative. They can arguably taken as the oldest and probably most authentic tradition, handed over as the sacred words of Jesus, orally and later also in writing. The sayings collections of Q and Th, 'sayings Gospels' are a case in point. Some voices suggest that apart from these two, other sayings (maybe even with Gospel status?) may have circulated. The logia we now find in the canonical Gospels may plausibly be seen as selections each evangelist has made out of the existing sayings traditions. One cannot exclude that some of these may have been more sizeable than what has been conserved in our scriptures.

The main thing is that these sayings must have been considered sacred, and naturally so because originating from Jesus himself. On the one hand it is improbable that such tradition would be able to conserve a sayings collection literally. What must be assumed, on the other hand, is that disciples and other followers, initiates maybe, have been quite particular in keeping these sayings intact, handing them over from one person to another, in communities, saving the words if not literal yet as integral as possible. Ancient societies had skills to do so. Moreover, these words were considered sacred, each of them to be kept in the sanctuary of the heart, as an invocation, or included in a prayer, maybe repeated as a 'mantra', guarded and conserved both individually and in communities. Thus, is my assumption, early in time, prior to the writing of the Gospels, saying traditions had formed, orally and soon also in written form.

Parallel to this the acts of Jesus and stories about him were remembered, told and retold among members of a group, and also as a mission to others, outside of the tradition. Variations grew and were conserved, each answering the sharp contours of story telling tradition. At some point in time a scribe took up the task to write down such narrative. Or did it happen in a gradual process? Thus a Gospel was formed. In each of the Gospel traditions sayings were incorporated, or parallel to this, sayings were conserved in a so-called sayings Gospel. The best known case is Th. Another is the reconstructed Q. In this way different narratives formed around these sayings, developing into different Gospels. Much later some were recognized as canonical, others remained extra-canonical. In this course, the sanctity particular to the saying, the logion, was transferred to the narrative. Consequently attention shifted from the word in itself to the context created by the narrative. What is seen as essential in this project is to differentiate between the logia as found in the Gospels and the narrative. And to view the logion as an entity to be studied per se, as the sacred word, supposedly spoken *by* Jesus. The narrative is the story told *about* Jesus.

In terms of methodology it appears necessary, therefore, to introduce another genre, the logia genre, as a specific approach within NT criticism. Logia are not narrative. Logia have been incorporated in narratives, but must be considered to stand in a tradition of its own. The incorporation in narratives must be seen as contextualization. In order to analyze logia they have to be de-contextualized. In this book this is done preliminarily and tentatively by just taking them as a text *per se*.

What is peculiar in this genre? The main point is the sanctity of a word delivered by Jesus. Mystics, prophets, messengers speak a language different from normal language. Though they use the same words the sense of it may be different. Their language points to a reality different from the usual. Jesus speaks about the *mustêrion*, he speaks as a mystic. Therefore what is said may have more than one meaning at the same time. It may be literal, it may be symbolical, it may refer to an inner reality: it is sacred. 'Kingdom' then refers to an inner reality, 'Kingdom of God' to a Presence in and around. At the same time the same pronouncement may be understood as referring to a worldly reign, or to an eschatological event where God will rule as King. There is a *double entendre*. Such a text is different from normal literature, a bit like poetry. Critical analysis of poetry needs to recognize the peculiarity of poems.

> The methodological chapter suggested the option of de-contextualization. Like close-focus in photography: the context does not matter as the object is sufficient in itself. Four ways have been discerned. The first one was in the formal step of taking the logion per se. Next, by understanding its contents irrespective of what the preceding and following pericopes tell. The third was to detach it from the context of later interpretations, of its embedding in systematic theology and Church doctrine. A fourth way we did not include: to 're-contextualize' the text as a logion, in the understanding that the phrasing, indeed, may have been influenced by its being placed inside, and therefore being part of, a narrative. For example, logia with eschatological wordings or context need to be examined from the point of view that they may not be eschatological. In other cases eschatological logia presented in imagery forms of apocalyptic nature may be interpreted as depicting actual visions / trances of mystical nature that do not refer to eschaton but to inner processes in the subject having these apocalypses.

Apart from Jesus speaking sacred words as a mystic, Jesus was a Messenger of God, bringing the new message, the *euaggelion*, the good Message. He was a Jew, spoke and acted as a Jew, was part and parcel of Jewish culture and religion. But because of his mission as a messenger of God his words must be understood as having a bearing far beyond what (other) teachers, rabbis, exorcists, healers, or wandering sages were telling. When speaking of the Kingdom of God he spoke about something far beyond what people understood as such. They saw an earthly kingdom, the Davidic state re-established, where oppressors and opponents were removed and justice and righteousness ruled. Also something quite different from the expected eschaton where all world would be destroyed and Heaven would descend on this elect people. Therefore, to understand what

CONCLUSIONS

Jesus was saying usual practices of interpretation cannot be sufficient. Tracing his words to Hebrew and Aramaic roots is necessary but not enough. Understanding Jesus as part and parcel of the Judaism of that period is needed but does not do suffice. He reminds people of the divine, of the spirit, of spirit. He awakens them to a Presence that he announces because people have forgotten. He calls for transformation of the self, not just to repent for sin in a moral or ritual sense. We must be aware: are we, people of this time, able to retrace such sense in the logia? What a messenger does is charging current language with new dynamics, with a new spirit, that in its roots is universal. Christendom has claimed unicity among the world religions. But religions have as their core the message that the human being is related to God, that one strives for God, that one desperately desires his presence, that one needs to transform to meet the divine. That unique figures are sent to remind the human race of their inner being. Mysticism in this sense is universal.

Analysis

In this sense some crucial logia and terms have been analyzed. Let us summarize the work done. An alternative interpretation for many logia and specific terms is found feasible, if not plausible. It does not pretend to be *the* valid rendering and is not applicable in all cases but the solutions found are offered for serious consideration. Typically sometimes a different understanding has come about by a semantic analysis, a different interpretation and thus a new translation, of just a single word. Examples are *psuchê, êggizô, entos, metanoeô, pneuma, ekstasis*, and some more.

The Kingdom of God (Part II) is the core message of Jesus, that is *communis opinio*. Yet serious discussions continue to be held where the Kingdom is situated and when it will come. (Chapters 6 and 7) Here Mk 1.14-15 is seen as telling it *has* approached, *êggiken*, and therefore is within reach, it is present. Mostly it is understood as being near but not yet present, or in theological terms, not yet fully. But then, in Lk 17.20-21, Jesus being asked when the Kingdom will come, answers by saying, 'see! the Kingdom of God is inside you'. He adds, you need not hunt for it searching, dramatically saying it is not to be seen here or there, no, it *is*. The *entos humin*, inside you people, has been discussed over and over again as not fitting in the doctrine of the Church, yet has been confirmed in this study both as to grammar, and as to content. Is this sufficient evidence for the Kingdom as an entity inside the human being? (Chapter 8) Studying the parables that refer to the Kingdom of God one finds that time and again images are used of something that is hidden inside, like a treasure. And where does reside its energy? It is the *dunamis*, its strength, its energy that is inside, and it wants to express and expand. The minimal mustard seed will grow out, the leaven will raise the bread, the treasure hidden in the ground must be found, the pearl that is the only thing worthwhile, the seed that needs fertile soil in order to grow. Is that what a kingdom is? It is a *mustêrion*, it is to be discovered. What is it? Nowhere in literature anyone wants to define it. Neither does Jesus. Most authors think of the kingdom as a reign or rule based on power and authority. The king as sort of dictator or autocrat, to appear at the end of times, or at the miraculous restoration of the Davidic kingdom. Scripture has nourished this image, here or there. What have democrats to do with a king indeed?

What we have found is quite different. The Kingdom of God is a Presence, manifesting to the individual or a community, creating an atmosphere of glory together with intimacy, of grandeur together with a feeling of belonging, of being at home, of security and safety.

If this Kingdom is an inherent reality why was it necessary to announce its arrival? Jesus had to break the concept of a Kingdom to come at the eschaton. What he did was proclaiming its Presence that he was about to disclose.

Another characteristic we found is Transformation, both as an effect and as a condition for it to come about. Both presence and transformation were found to be indicators of mysticism. Both are found in respect of the Kingdom of God. Transformation as a condition to be part of it, transformation as an effect of its presence. One of the conditions is worded in one of the so-called Beatitides (Mt 5.3). It tells that it is the *ptôchoi tôi pneumati* whose is the Kingdom of God. A *ptôchos* is someone in basic need, a mendicant, here as someone desirous of the Spirit, craving for it. Being in spirit means that one belongs to the Kingdom. It is not about poor in spirit. Another logion says that a condition to the belonging is to become like little children (chapter 9), their receptivity, their innocence, their confidence. Thus is the idea of transformation.

When Jesus announces the Kingdom, he says: *metanoeite!*, chapter 11. Usually it is interpreted as repentance or *Busse*. Or could it be a call for a transformation of the self, of one's life conduct in mind and heart, of one's psyche? It seems that the Message of Jesus is not only a moral call, let alone to repent, but rather a call for opening up to the spirit. The Kingdom in essence is neither eschatological nor ethical, though these dimensions remain valid: spiritual transformation implies moral transformation. This *metanoeite* refers to that same transformation: to become desirous of spirit, to become attuned to the atmosphere of the Kingdom as Presence. Nowhere Jesus connects this *metanoia* with sin (*hamartia*), a remarkable fact, contrary to what one might think as influenced by theology and Church doctrine. Besides, *hamartia* refers to having missed the target rather than to sin, and does not necessarily convey a moral value, or breaking law. As to *metanoia*, John the Baptist had made the connection with sin in his announcement of the Kingdom. Jesus does not. Rather he makes a direct connection between transformation and confiding oneself to the good Message (traditionally 'to believe in the Gospel'), to that glorious Presence, the Kingdom.

That transformation we meet again with when Jesus speaks about the *psuchê*, though not in the same terminology (chapter 10). Jesus often connects this word with an act implying transformation. This is a relative novelty of interpretation as *psuchê* mostly is rendered as 'life', whilst the primary meaning of the word was and is self or psyche or soul. Does the shepherd really lay down his life for the sheep (Jn 10.11) (chapter 12)? Or does he rather dedicate his self to the sheep? Like when Jesus calls on his disciples to dedicate heart-and-soul to one another, out of love, rather than asking them to lay down their lives (Jn 15.12 and 13.34). Another central logion is found in Mk 8.35 par, including a variant in Jn, where Jesus speaks about losing and saving the *psuchê* (chapter 13, also 14). Generally this is understood as life, referring to the eschaton or martyrdom. The solution proposed in this book is close to other spiritual traditions, to classical mysticism: when losing the (limited or 'false') self one gains the (real) Self. And it goes without saying that this is a process of transformation. This rendering, by the way, is close to other sayings of Jesus propagating asceticism and the like. Well understood, my understanding of this process of transformation does not require asceticism but stands for a spiritual attitude towards body and mind.

One more central concept in the Gospels is related to the term *pneuma*. Reading English versions of the NT one gets the impression the Gospels tell us about the Spirit and the Holy Spirit (chapter 15). Remarkably, the Greek text speaks about spirit as well as the spirit, about holy spirit as well as the holy spirit, obviously deliberately differentiating between the words with and without the article. The most striking case (chapter 16) is where John the Baptist, in the current translations, announces that Jesus will baptize not only *with* water but also *with the Holy Spirit*. But what does one find? All Synoptics write that Jesus will 'immerse' (*baptizô*) *in* water and *in holy spirit*. A remarkable statement, indicative of the spirituality of his message. What was it that Jesus did, 'immersing in holy spirit'? Was it maybe his presence that was understood as spirit, his healings and exorcisms that were prompted by spirit? This statement brought me to further investigating the use of the term *pneuma* throughout the Gospels. It turns out that Scripture does differentiate between what is called arthrous and anarthrous use: with or without the (definite) article. Analyzing the texts with the term *pneuma* one finds that the concept *pneuma* is much closer to the human level than thought of usually. Moreover, the way the term is used suggests that spirit and the spirit are different entities, like maybe holy spirit and the holy spirit.

It therefore is cautiously suggested to read these texts as 'to be in spirit', or even 'in holy spirit', without implying a direct reference to the Spirit, or to the

Holy Spirit. It is also found that a human being may have spirit, like he has body, mind and heart. A rather revolutionary view.

Within the sphere of 'spirit' the last term to be discussed is *ekstasis* (chapter 18), generally rendered as amazement, astonishment, and the like. However, scouting all pericopes in the complete NT it is found that in most cases something more is happening than amazement. What happens to individuals in the situations described is rapture, occasionally even ecstasy. A clear case is in Mk 16.8 where the women, visiting the grave or *mnêmeion* of Jesus, fall into rapture (rather than bewilderment or fear) at the miracle they are confronted with. They do not utter a word, not out of fear, but in awe for what they witnessed.

In conclusion then, the focus on some terms has turned out to be fruitful. Some terms bear an additional special or new significance, different from the usual one. Let us have a look at the relevance of all these terms. The term Kingdom of God, *basileia tou theou,* was kept in this wording, though with a rather different meaning than usual. The term *pneuma* was understood as spirit, or as the spirit, depending on the presence or absence of the definite article. Transformation was found to be the better rendering of *metanoeô*. Rather revolutionary was the argument for translating *psuchê* in some crucial cases as self, or psyche, or mind-and-heart, rather than life. *Ekstasis* turned out to be more than just astonishment in most cases: it transmits the idea of rapture or even ecstasy. During my exploration many interesting and challenging discoveries followed. Unexpectedly some other terms turned out to be important, like *entos humin* and *eggizein*. Others appeared as of special interest, like *euaggelion, kêrussein, pisteuein*. During the study it has become clear that in some instances a different translation followed from the logic of the argument. This has led me to fascinating trips through dictionaries, handbooks and other literature. Sometimes a 'spiritual' interpretation had to be rejected, in some other cases forgotten translations revealed hidden meanings. In quite a few cases a 'new' translation was a logical outcome in order to do justice to the new interpretation. Here are some of the major cases:

Presentation of some important terms

Guideline to the presentation:
Greek word   a current translation   proposed translation (concise)
     Sample phrase in which it occurs

Entos humin   among you,...   inside you
     The Kingdom of God is inside you
Êggiken   at hand, near, ...   has approached > has arrived > is present
     The Kingdom of God has arrived

CONCLUSIONS

Psuchê	life (mostly)	self / psyche / mind-and-heart
	The shepherd dedicates his self to the sheep	
	To lose one's self and to save one's Self	
Metanoeô	repent (mostly)	change mind / mentality, transform
Metanoia	repentance	transformation
Pisteuô	believe	confide
Euaggelion	Gospel, good news	(good) message
	Transform! and entrust yourself to the (good) Message	
Kêrussô	preach	proclaim
	Proclaiming [the arrival of] the Kingdom of God	
Ekstasis	amazement, ...	rapture, ecstacy
	the women ran from the grave quivering and in ecstasy	
Pneuma	the Spirit (mostly)	spirit
	Jesus will immerse in holy spirit and fire	
Pneuma hagion	the Holy Spirit (mostly)	holy spirit
To pneuma hagion	the Holy Spirit	the Holy Spirit
Ptôchos tôi pneumati	poor in spirit	craving for the spirit

Besides, some terms suggested understandings different from the current ones
  - 'seeing' next to seeing, 'hearing' next to hearing
  - child as a young person versus innocent, pure, receptive
  - *mustêrion* rather than secret, or mystery
  - the concept of unworded words
and others.

We have arrived at the end of this analytical expedition through some aspects of the Message of Jesus in search of its mysticism. We have explored the field of the Kingdom of God, and what it means to inner life. The worlds of *psuchê* and *metanoia* have been examined resulting in some insight in the self or psyche, and its transformation. Another crucial term, *pneuma*, has been investigated tentatively, finding a more varied use in the Gospels than is usually understood; it tells about the nature of the human being. All these terms that have been studied, often in-depth, refer to concepts that cohere and deepen the sense of the Kingdom of God and of the human being.

What, now, is the purport of these findings, is this the mysticism we have been tracing? The Synthesis below tries to answer to that question. But first an evaluation.

Mysticism

The canonical Gospels contain many instances of mysticism. They are found especially in the words by Jesus, the logia, and in many parables. The Jesus mysticism thus emerging does not compare to esoteric mysticism, or apocalyptic mysticism. Its character is intimate, silent, dynamic, *pneuma* oriented, inviting to grow and mature and blossom. It is dynamic in two senses. One is its transformational powers manifesting in natural growth (Seed, Mustard seed, Leaven). The other is its *dunamis*, its silent and loving power, strength rather than dominating power: energy. It is a potential that can either be dormant or become active and influential. The Kingdom of God is an accommodation where God has his domain. A domain beyond our dimensions of location and time. A domain, an atmosphere, an accommodation where humans are welcome, where they may enter, be enveloped by its atmosphere of peace, joy, comfort. Then the reverse process may take place, then one may experience how the enveloping presence becomes an inner presence: the Kingdom enters the human being.

This Presence triggers a transformation in the psyche of such a person, by which he or she becomes open, innocent, receptive, natural, energetic, in a rhythm of peace and silence. It may also happen to someone who is craving for spirit, that is for this Presence, a presence which in this process of transformation may be discovered inside. When this grows and matures it turns out one to be part of that Kingdom, receiving all blessing. This transformation of the psyche is the alchemy of the spirit: spirit acting as the agent causing this process of change, of *metanoia*: a change in mentality, of mind-and-soul. Then one is prepared to dedicate one's self to one's beloveds, to one's neighbors, to one's dependents. Then one is prepared to lose one's self and to save one's Self. To take one's cross, to follow Jesus on the path of mysticism. Then one may be able to remain serene, entrusting oneself to this good Message, even when suffering, sorrow and other forces tend to overpower one's self. One then may realize that this Kingdom, his Presence is inside one, and at the same time all around.

Evaluation

What does all this amount to? A new view has been developed on some issues that do matter in NT criticism, in NT theology, and in Church doctrine. Although sometimes radical the outcomes do not pretend to be the single correct interpretation, far from that. An important argument of this book rather is that the logia contain multiple truths, related to different levels of consciousness. What I present is an alternative vision on concepts of the Message of Jesus, and to some extent on its purport. Jesus is viewed as the Messenger and the mystic calling humanity to discover the Kingdom of God as an inner Presence and to transform one's *psuchê* in order to find *pneuma*.

What emerges is an indication of an anthropology where the human being appears as an indivisible whole, yet characterized by well-defined aspects. HeShe is a being with a body, with a psyche, and with traces of spirit. Jesus' teachings

CONCLUSIONS

are about this human being, and they focus on the call to start and discover the *mustêrion* of that being: being Being. Presence and transformation have emerged as central concepts in an understanding of that 'being' and of its relationship with the divine.

This interpretation of the logia analyzed builds a new bridge between the canonical Gospels and the Gospel of Thomas. In the field of historical Jesus studies it suggests a new line of interpretation. It offers an alternative between the secular Jesus and the 'confessional' Jesus. It may mean a renewal of the significance of Christian faith in this changing world of dominating Modernity, tracing new ideals for the development of humane qualities that tend to be drowned in materialism and commercialism. A new kingdom.

From what started as disparate studies of isolated terms the work has resulted in a more or less consistent and interconnected view on aspects of the Gospels, on Jesus and on his Message connecting to the ongoing enduring search for the historical Jesus.

All these results, together as well as individually, must be regarded as preliminary, as a stimulus to further research, a need in order to widen the scope and deepen the analysis.

Here are some recommendations to work on the development of:

- aspects of a methodology for the study of logia as a *genre* of its own
- criteria by which texts are discerned as logia
- methods for de-contextualizing a logion from the context of the narrative and of theology and doctrine
- criteria for identifying a text as sacred
- further work on discriminating eschatological logia from *hic et nunc* logia
- option of re-contextualization a logion as an identity of its own:
- comparative studies on the contents of logia in other major religions: Jesus logia as expressions of the universal wisdom as divine message.

Synthesis

The Kingdom of God has approached, right now and right here: and therefore is present. As what? As a permanent presence of the Spirit. One need not look here or there, one need not expect it eagerly. It is present indeed. Where? It is to be found inside oneself out of all places, and—in quasi-contrast—spread out as well. Therefore, it is accommodating, offering safety, protection, peace, livelihood, love and care. It is available to all souls, provided one is seeking, one feels a desperate desire, it is considered as the one precious pearl. Provided one is ready to lose one's self, gaining the Self. Provided one is ready to dedicate one's self to one's friends. The shepherd is caring.

This is in a nutshell the mysticism of Jesus: presence and transformation.

Is the Kingdom visible or audible, can one perceive it with one's senses? It can be 'sensed' when one is in a state when one can 'hear' and 'see', it is 'yours' when one 'craves for spirit', or when one has become pure in heart, open, accommodating, humble, 'innocent', qualities similar to that of a little child. It is a state of consciousness, in its culmination approaching the so-called near-death experience. One is conscious of another reality than one is accustomed to.

The message is: entrust yourself to the (good) Message of that Kingdom—and it is yours. It is inside yourself, and at the same time outside: spread out over the world: omnipresent, all-pervading. What is at stake is to be prepared and ready to receive as fertile soil the blessings of the Sower when one is prepared to give up anything in order to acquire what is essential in value, when one has changed one's mentality and has entrusted one's self to that good message that is as a kingdom, an atmosphere of presence, an accommodation that is peace-giving, protecting, life-giving. One feels, yes, I am belonging. One is donated with that kingdom when one is ready to 'lose' one's self in order to 'save' one's Self. When one is ready to dedicate one's self for one's friends whom one loves, and for one's dependants who are entrusted to one. That is what is called 'following Jesus'. It is the spirit of God that is around, inside, everywhere. It is the spirit, its dunamis, *that guides, that enlivens, that creates joy, that is life's fulfilment. It is that spirit that carries one through life's dangers, physical, mental, emotional that may be like the cross we have to take up and carry till the very end: to the goal* (telos) *in order that we may be complete* (teleios) *and our work may have been completed* (tetelestai). *Spirit victorious over psyche: in the words of Paul from* (sarkikos through) *psuchikos to transform into* pneumatikos: *expanding consciousness. It is spirit that was in Jesus (and who handed over his spirit when dying), and it was Jesus who was in spirit, like what happened to Simeon, to Mary, and what may happen to every human being maybe? Being in spirit, spirit being in one. Isn't this a perspective for and a promise to all human beings who may find the Kingdom inside and all around: to become* pneumatikos? *Is this what it is to be like a child? To crave for spirit? Who*

CONCLUSIONS

have entrusted themselves to the Message? To experience the protective, loving, caring atmosphere of the glorious kingdom? This is the immersing in holy spirit that was promised, and that is it what Jesus did and does to human beings, that is what we found throughout his sayings. In rapture and ecstasy the spirit springs out and lifts the psyche to a higher consciousness. Though for short moments maybe, the transformative impact on the psyche may be enduring.

Thus it turns out that the disparate terms and concepts like transformation, metanoia, psuchê, pneuma merge into one over-all concept, the Kingdom of God: the realm of the Spirit, manifesting as spirit in and around the human being. Through it one is capable of transforming the self: losing it to the effect of gaining the Self. Through it one is capable of dedicating one's self in mind-and-heart to one another, out of love – the energy (dunamis) of the Spirit. Rapture, or ecstasy, is a sign of spirit rising and springing forth

This is the Message of Jesus: becoming aware of the Presence through transformation of the self, either self-induced or affected by the Spirit as grace. And at the same time transformation, self-induced or by grace, working out into an awareness of the Spirit, the Kingdom.

This is the mysticism of Jesus. This is what has been found in our explorations. A tentative new view on Jesus and his spoken message has emerged. The logia of Jesus have opened new insights of wisdom. They contain mysticism, in the sense of 'presence' and 'transformation', two terms that were identified as keywords for mysticism. Presence of the Spirit, presence as a kingdom to feel safe, protected and belonging, experiencing an atmosphere of peace and happiness, an accommodation to feel at home and uplifted together. Transformation as a process, a necessary precondition to experience this Presence. Transformation also as an inherent consequence of the discovery of that Presence, leading to deeper transformational processes and deeper discoveries of Truth.

A mysticism, therefore, that is in the here and now, that is practicable in daily life, that seeks integration with life in the world, that is humane, that supports the development of the psyche, that triggers the hidden powers of the spirit, that makes the personality humane. A mysticism that creates by itself the wonderful world of that kingdom everybody idealizes as a utopia but which makes one aware that now it may be realized.

ANNEX 6
Summaries of the Outcomes of the Case Studies

The Kingdom of God

What is the Kingdom of God? Interpretations have varied greatly without solving contradictions and inconsistencies. Here some simple questions have been asked about the Kingdom: the when and where issues, about what it is and for whom it is destined. Traditionally it has been interpreted as other-worldly: it is heaven and will arrive at the eschaton. Some take it as this-worldly, as the future utopia of righteousness, peace and welfare on earth. Here an alternative view has been analyzed, asking whether some of the logia display a measure of inner-worldliness: the Kingdom is inside the human being. After an in-depth analysis of all relevant logia it is found that the Kingdom alternatively may be viewed as inner-worldly rather than as this-worldly or other-worldly. Jesus may hav indicated that it is to be seen as multi-dimensional. Eschatology apart, in Jesus' words it is not far away, it is not of the future. Rather 'it has arrived' because 'this is the moment': it is here and now. At the same time it is not 'here' or 'there', 'it is not to be observed by one's senses, for 'it is inside you people'. Thus it is an inner reality, "a silent, strong divine power in the heart, says the great NT scholar Von Harnack. He adds: "It grows surely and silently like a seed and it brings forth fruit". So, it is not an occurrence at the eschaton? Harnack maintains both is true, the future Kingdom and the present inner one.

It is a *mustêrion*, a hidden reality to be discovered through the ability to 'hear' rather than to hear, to 'see' rather than to see. When one has become a *teleios*, someone in search, someone who is able to transform, who may complete his journey. The Kingdom of God is an accommodation for the Presence of the one who reigns, who 'waltet' with and in his being, where his qualities are radiating, where the spirit is alive, penetrating all and everybody coming into its Presence.

And consequently it is an accommodation where human beings may enter into, know to be at home when they have turned or rather: transformed, their mentality changed toward being like a little child, out of a deep craving for the spirit. That spirit is a powerful agent for transformation. It is by such expansion of consciousness that one becomes aware of a process of transformation (*metanoia*): becoming aware of being more than just a psyche, and therefore finding one's true being in that Presence of the Spirit, by realizing one is spirit in essence. That spirit then enlivens the psyche and the physical being, making the human being humane. Then one may have a glimpse of the glorious, silent, subtle Presence.

That presence is like a small seed in fertile soil with an inner potentiality to grow, mature, blossom, and to welcome the angels from heaven to dwell in the grandiose tree that has developed. That presence is like the pearl for which one gives up anything in order to acquire it, as the treasure in the field. The nullity of the mustard seed silently growing and blossoming as a mighty tree accommodating the angels of heaven. The unbelievable potentiality of the leaven affecting the dough to produce a perfect piece of bread.

'That glorious, silent , subtle Presence': in this sense it is true: the Kingdom of God is the *eschaton*, the ultimate state of consciousness, the condition mystics have testified to as the utter reality. The *teleios* has been transformed from *sarkikos* to *psuchikos*, and from *psuchikos* into *pneumatikos*. *Sômatikos:* identifying with one's body where perception is just by the physical senses only. *Psuchikos*: identifying with one's thoughts and emotions through one's mind and heart, using the *sôma* as an instrument. *Pneumatikos*: identifying with the spirit using both the *psuchê* and the *sôma* as one's instruments, having transformed into 'such one', becoming as a little child, having found the nutrition in one's craving search for spirit, having bought the pearl, having discovered the treasure, offering the fertile soil to receive the seed from the Sower, accepting the leaven to produce good bread.

This interpretation of the Kingdom of God as an inner reality stands in stark contrast to the view that the Kingdom will occur at the eschaton, often described in terms of an apocalypse.

Harnack has maintained that both views may be valid at the same time. Let it be so. In my view this could be so if we interpret the apocalyptic images as visions of the glorious light of Truth.

Metanoia

Right at the beginning of his Message Jesus calls for *metanoia*, for *metanoeô*, to change (*meta*) one's mind (*noos*), for a transformation (Mk 1.14-15). Is this the same process with the same end as the one we just saw in regard of the Kingdom, and which we will see in the next section regarding the *psuchê*? Does the *pneuma* have to do with it? To be 'craving for the spirit'? The transformations the Kingdom requires are certainly involved: this call for *metanoia* is pronounced in the same logion where the arrival of the Kingdom of God is announced.

The traditional renderings of *metanoia*, however, have a different tone. 'Repent' is the usual term in English translations, *Busse* in traditional German Bibles, conversion in many different languages (with the side connotation of changing faith, or rather accepting the right faith). *Metanoia* is associated with penance, penitence, remorse, sin, to turn to God. 'Repentance' is the act of turning from sin out of penitence for past wrongdoings toward the intention to amensd one's life, to receive spirit. Often the act of penitence has overshadowed the bright horizon of being immersed in spirit. This is largely due to the Latin version deplored by both Tertullianus and Lactantius who say that only the Greek can render *metanoia* properly, indicating that penitence refers to the confession of the *delictus* whilst *metanoia* refers to the *demutatio animae*.

This book has challenged these interpretations. What is this change of mind? This process either grow out of an individual's past behavior, sort of natural process in the mind, 'alternation'. Or it is 'conversion', characterized as rejection of past convictions and affiliations for an affirmed present and future. However, there is a third type of change: transformation. This happens when a new way of perception forces the radical re-interpretation of the past in a new understanding of God and the world, in an altered perception (Gavender). In this logion the altered perception is caused by the perspective of the discovery of the presence of the Kingdom of God, It is not looking back but forward to as bright future, to the wonderful Message, the good news. It is a sweeping occurrence full of light. Transformation may either be anthropological (change of mentality) or spiritual. If anthropological the agent causing the change comes from outside or from the psyche, whilst the spiritual one originates in the spirit. In an image: the former is bottom up trying to climb and reach, the latter is top down where the inspiration flows freely. It is 'not to cover the inner light under a bushel but rather to let it shine out (Mt 5t.15-16); to contemplate Jesus 'as the great light that is seen', 'light that has dawned' (cf Mt 4.16, a text immediately followed by Jesus' announcement of the arrival of the Kingdom). This transformation creates a new awareness, it causes a breakthrough into a new consciousness where spirit takes the lead and the *psuchê* follows. It brings about a new mentality and consequently a new conduct in life.

What about the relationship of *metanoia* with sin and forgiving? Remarkably, Jesus does not call for *metanoia* because of sin. He does not relate the two. John the Baptist does: he "preaches a baptism of repentance for the forgiveness of sins" (Mk 1.4), whilst Jesus' call is "Repent and believe the good news" (Mk 1.15), or in my rendering: Transform and confide yourself to the Message. Also in other pericopes there is never a call for transformation related to sin. Sin is not an issue to Jesus: the word does not occur in the Gospels in the framework of his teaching the Message. No doctrine of sin is given neither to his disciples nor to the generality.

What is 'sin', what is 'to sin'? The basic meaning of *hamartanô* ('sinning') is 'not to hit, to miss, to err, to fall short morally, to do wrong'. A *hamartêma* ('sin') therefore is a shortcoming. It is a condition or fact of failing to reach an expected or required standard e.g. of character or of performance; it is a defect, an imperfection (*Webster's*). It is an inadequacy. Who is a 'sinner'? The term 'sinners' in the Gospels refers to categories (profession, class and its implied behavior) rather than to individuals for individual conduct: sinners and collectors are mentioned together. Maybe one could see a parallel with today's down-trodden, those who 'did not make it', the deprived, the underclass: a category rather than a group of individuals showing joint individual conduct? It is they whom Jesus calls upon!

A *hamartolos* ('sinner') is the one who acts like that. If this is structural it refers to someone who is inferior, intellectually or morally, in the eyes of the dominant society.

If sinning is a shortcoming, failing to reach the goal, falling short of the ideal or task or standard of values the what is forgiving?

In regular Greek usage forgiving means to release, to let go, to let be, or concepts like pardon, send off, let alone, remit, forgive, to become free of. In the logia with 'sin' only twice 'forgiving' is found (of which one in a post-Easter pericope, and therefore remaining outside my scope). Remarkably, this one single remaining logion (Lk 15.7,10) with both sin and forgiving is about the day-to-day conduct among the disciples. There is no trace of any serious offence, let alone a reference to rules and regulations. This means that what was found for *metanoia* is valid for 'forgiving' also: the theological implications of sin and forgiving is not yet present in these logia. This is a wonderful perspective on the freedom of the Message of Jesus.

Therefore, *metanoia* is a concept that builds a bridge between the Kingdom logia and the ones on *psuchê* in a way that adds to the meaning of both word groups. *Metanoia* is not just change of mind, it implies a transformation of the psyche that will be illustrated further in the next section.

Psuchê

The psyche is an important concept in the Gospels though generally unrecognized, because in all important cases the term *psuchê* traditionally is translated as life rather than as psyche, or self. There are two major instances in the Gospels where the term *psuchê* bears an meaning that is essential for interpreting two major logia. One is in about dedicating one's self to one's friends rather than laying down one's life for one another. The other about losing one's self or saving the Self rather than saving or losing one's life. Quite a difference!

Dedicating the self

In the Gospel of John Jesus calls his disciples to dedicate their selves to one another, out of love for one another and, implied in it, out of love and sincerity for Jesus. Earlier the evangelist had depicted Jesus as the excellent and devoted shepherd who dedicates his self to the sheep.

This interpretation stands in sharp contrast to the usual translation 'to lay down one's life'. Is that what the shepherd does, laying down his life for the sheep? Is that what Jesus asks his disciples to do: to love each other, and the greatest love is to lay down one's life for one's friends?

The two passages are closely related by using the same Greek expression, *tên psuchên tithêmi*, which does not occur elsewhere in the NT (apart from 1 Jn, where it has the same meaning). *Tithêmi* does not have the meaning 'to lay down' elsewhere. *Psuchê* though generally rendered as life has as its usual meaning 'psyche' or 'self'. The combination of the two terms invites an alternative interpretation and translation. The outcome 'to dedicate the self' appears plausible, if not more reasonable. Laying down his life does not comply with the task of the shepherd, it would result in a mere disaster for the sheep. Laying down their lives for one another does not seem an appropriate advice for Jesus to give to his disciples. Should he, on the verge of completing his life, suggest to his disciples to do the same to each other -- out of love for one another?

Rather what these logia convey is the transformative power innate in the human being, and to waken it, because it often is in a sleeping state. In this interpretation the logion is a call to follow the example set by Jesus to feel responsible for one's friends, one's beloveds, one's co-workers and dependents. The shepherd dedicates his self to the sheep. like the disciples dedicate themselves to one another wholeheartedly.

What is the psyche? It stands for the qualities in a human that are neither physical nor spiritual. Roughly speaking the psyche contains thoughts and feelings, also the greater part of the will, memory, the 'ego'; let us say: mind and heart. It is also the entity with which one tends to identify with. Let us have a look at the other instance where the *psuchê* plays a prominent role.

Saving or losing the self

In the heart of Jesus' message we find a set of powerful and radical logia that put us at the cross-roads. All Synoptics put it somehow in the center of their narratives whilst John refers to it in clear language. What do these logia say? They either refer to following Jesus in martyrdom and death, *psuchê* meaning 'life', or they sound a call for psycho-spiritual transformation, *psuchê* meaning self.

At first sight the logia present a riddle. Jesus informs his disciples that to save one's *psuchê* means to lose it. Rather, he adds, lose your *psuchê* and as a happy consequence save it. Does this refer to life implying death and an unclear alternative life to be gained or saved? Let us see what the alternative offers where *psuchê* is translated as 'self' or 'Self':

- saving the self is losing the self
  - whilst losing the self is saving and finding the Self
- wishing to acquire the self is losing the self
  - whilst losing the self is making the Self alive
- 'hating' the self is protecting it for unlimited life.

Hating to be understood as disregarding the self, a de-identification of the self.

Traditionally these logia are seen as a call to follow Jesus into his suffering and death: it is either saving one's life or losing it. Seeking it and therefore losing it, or rather: losing one's life and finding it. However, the alternative option is a plausible and attractive one to be considered. The following argument is in support of this:

> These logia are preceded in Mk by Jesus saying, in my interpretation, follow me, take up the hard duties of your cross, deny yourself. For if you want to save your 'self' you will lose it. Gaining the whole world does not profit you when it implies to damage (to harm) your 'Self', your heart and soul?
>
> What is this losing? The Greek word *apollumi*'s meaning is to ruin, to destroy. It suggests getting rid of, to forsake, to annihilate. In Buddhism this latter meaning stands for transforming the self into the Self: the Phoenix arising from the ashes of the self. Also like the caterpillar and the butterfly. It is losing something that one had identified with, a thing one now really speaking wants to get rid of. Because one has discovered a bright new perspective, a view on a new reality of one's Self. Or in the words by John: "who loves his self will lose it, but who 'hates' his self in this world, will keep it for unlimited life. I understand these logia to call on a potential inherent in the human being: to give up one's identification with the self or ego (de-identification), and to transform it into the true Self, a Self that is created in the image of God, with the spirit of God breathed unto the body and *psuchê* (Gen 2.7).

These logia form probably the single strongest case calling for transformation of the psyche, within the unity of body, *psuchê* and *pneuma*, in the spirit of Paul's call 'to keep these three blameless at the coming' of the Kingdom of God ('of our Lord Jesus Christ') whilst praying that 'God sanctify you through and through' (1Thess 5.23).

This transformation is a fine case of the spiritual psychology of the Jesus logia. Especially in one's relation to the Kingdom of God the psyche is at stake. The process of becoming like a little child, or to become a *ptôchos* of spirit requires an intensive transformation especially of the self. It also implies to prepare one's soil (the heart) for the Sower to receive the seed of the Kingdom. To be prepared to take the tiny mustard seed in one's care in full trust of its inherent capacity. To be ready to accept the leaven so that the bread may attain the desired quality for nutrition. It is a call on the psyche to wake up, and it is a call on one's consciousness to expand so that one becomes aware of a process of transformation (*metanoia*): becoming aware of being more than just a psyche, and therefore finding one's true being in that Presence of the Spirit, by realizing one is spirit in essence. That is the theme of the next section: *pneuma*.

Pneuma

What is spirit? Or should one say 'the spirit'? What about holy spirit and the Holy Spirit? Is spirit a person, an entity, a living entity, or is it a 'something'? And what about its holiness? And we are faced with a problem of method: there are only a few Jesus logia on *pneuma*. Nevertheless, what is mysticism without spirit? In this section we will therefore analyze all pericopes with the word *pneuma* in the NT. An exception is made for such as the unclean spirits; these passages will be left out.

Three topics come to the fore: the phrase *en pneumati* raises questions about the identity of spirit in the Gospels. The words by Jesus on the cross raise questions about passion and spirit. Finally it may be asked if the double meaning of *pneuma*, spirit and breath, can be traced in the Gospels.

The expression *en pneumati* used in the NT, read at close view, offers a new perspective on the concept of 'spirit'. This is corroborated by other pericopes where *pneuma* occurs, either as a term, or as a concept in different wordings.

Pneuma, according to John the Baptist, is the 'stuff' Jesus would use when 'he will be 'baptizing'': "[He] will immerse in holy spirit (and fire)", rather than *with the* Holy Spirit. Time and again these two errors remain consistent in current translations. What could it mean, to be immersed in holy spirit? This is what may have happened: 'holy spirit' obviously was in Jesus and with him all the time. And the ones close to Jesus would sense that spirit, and on special occasions knowing to be immersed, resulting in awareness of being 'born again', being 'born anew'. And the 'fire' of his radiance and love would cleanse people spiritually, in their minds and souls. Consequently they would follow Jesus, or be healed, or just be amazed by what they saw, or coming in touch with that spirit radiating from Jesus they would rather come into a rapture (*ekstasis*). Others would rather react negatively, even hostile, as not being able to understand, to feel, to react adequately, and thus be seized by 'the evil'.

Is spirit inside or outside? The Kingdom being both inside and outside one would expect the same for spirit and for the spirit. Here are some samples. Jesus would 'drive out demons being in God's spirit'. He could be 'full of holy spirit', or 'in the power of the spirit'. He is reported to be 'full of joy being in the holy spirit'. By some working of the spirit he could perceive what others were thinking. Also of others we learn that they could be 'in the spirit and power of Eliah' (John Baptist), or 'being in the spirit' (Simeon). Jesus refers to David as 'speaking in spirit', or declaring something 'being in holy spirit'. And 'worshipping the Father in spirit and truth', the spirit of truth. 'The spirit is willing but the flesh is weak' indicates a presence inside. This is also the case of a dead person who rises to life when Jesus says 'rise', and 'her spirit returned', the returning indicating that it was there previously also. And earlier Jesus told about people 'craving for the spirit'. Concluding, we find spirit both inside and outside human beings, whilst holy spirit and especially the Holy Spirit remain outside normal humans. By the way, holy spirit remains indefinite throughout the Synoptics except for a few cases (the Holy Spirit speaking through the disciples, David being in the Holy Spirit declared, Jesus was full of joy being in the Holy Spirit).

What strikes in all these passages is the nearness, the directness, the presence of spirit.

Sometimes when reading of the Kingdom and trying to come in touch with its meaning one may sense that it refers to what we quoted as 'spirit', or even 'holy spirit', sometimes more definite (with article), sometimes more general (without). "The Kingdom of God is inside as well as spread out". Is it maybe something all humans share? But are not fully aware of?

Spirit is something the human being is in need of, should even be 'craving for' (rather than being 'poor in spirit', *sic*). This obviously is of paramount importance for humanity, as 'theirs is the Kingdom of God', as soon as one fulfills the requirements. Or is it a basic human quality, though mostly undeveloped and hidden? Jesus refers to humans 'whose is the Kingdom of God'. He mentions the children as typical examples. But it is wider, encompassing anybody who is 'such as the child'. Could it be that the quality of the 'such ones' is that they have been touched by spirit? Or even are possessing spirit? Is that not what is behind the usual characteristics of 'the' child? Is that not, therefore, what Jesus calls humans to become, like little children. And thus to develop these qualities in their selves?

Jesus of course is the paramount 'model' of being in spirit, especially when we observe him in his words when he is on the cross an example of dignity and grandeur. None of his words express any suffering, any agony. He is master of the situation, master of the self, in immediate contact with the spirit. His thirst is his soul's, his mission is completed as his Message, he inclines his head in reverence, he hands over his spirit by breathing it out, he has shown compassion to his fellows on the other crosses. And his cry of 'being forsaken' is a recitation of Ps 22 expressing full trust in God who is conceived to be near, saving him from he roaring lions.

Summarizing, *pneuma*, spirit, the spirit, holy spirit, the holy spirit, as these terms appear fresh from our analysis they convey a sense of nearness, of a divine element that is not foreign, that one might discover in oneself, or in the atmosphere around.

Summing up, spirit is a clear entity though neither defined nor definite. Spirit is an important element in the Gospels where a bridge is built and a path shown between the physical and the spiritual, the two not being separate but rather as parts of a whole: the Kingdom of God, maybe?

Ekstasis

Ecstasy is sometimes seen as connected with mysticism. It may be one of the many expressions of the mystic state, or as an inner experience of a raised consciousness.

In the NT 23 places are found where the Greek word for ecstasy (either as a verb, *existêmi,* or as a noun, *ekstasis*) occurs. However, nowhere in the current translations it is rendered as ecstasy. On the contrary, we find amazement (10), astonishment (7), trance, out of one's mind, bewildered. Here, as with *pneuma*, there are no pericopes with *ekstasis* that contain logia by Jesus. Yet the phenomenon is so important to mysticism, both in the negative sense and in the positive value of it, that we need to have it included in this study.

The first question to be answered is whether the terms *ekstasis* and *existêmi* convey something that relates to ecstasy and to mysticism? In the handbooks primary meanings set a negative tone as something abnormal, even as being psychiatric phenomena. Yet both BDAG and TDNT acknowledge that *ekstasis* also means ecstasy, in a positive sense. What does it mean? In English, ecstasy and rapture are quasi synonyms. Rapture is ecstasy on a less intense level, connoting intense bliss or beatitude. It is often triggered by an outside stimulus. Ecstasy refers to different states of consciousness and concomitant mind-sets. On the one hand ecstasy may express itself in joy, song and dance, in a heightened state of emotion. On the other hand it refers to a state that might also be called *en*stasy, a profound calm where the mind is on another level of functioning and emotions are levelled out as there is need of them, as the self is ' craving for the spirit'. This ecstasy may be triggered from outside but basically it is a spontaneous event on the purely spiritual level of consciousness. In rapture, and even stronger in ecstasy, the spirit drowns as it were both the senses and the voice of the psyche: glimpses of the transcendent are perceived and the spirit inside comes to life immanently, bringing about the experience of enstasy, a form of ecstasy that remains inside and is not expressed physically or emotionally. It is spiritual, an expression of the *pneuma*. It may be said to be as a deep impressive silence, a silent prayer, *per excessum mentis*. Or in the words of Augustine: "*Tu autem, Domine, eras interior intimo meo et superior summo meo*", an excellent expression of transcendence and immanence together, real mysticism. In English: "You, Lord, you are more inside than my most intimate being, and you are more supreme than my highest being".

CONCLUSIONS

Yet it is important, in line with Evelyn Underhill, to realize that ecstasy, like mysticism and its ways of expression, manifests in a scale of degrees. Therefore I discern rapture from ecstasy, rapture being the adequate translation of *ekstasis* in most cases. A few examples. Sometimes it obviously is just happy astonishment. People are 'enraptured when witnessing a healing'. The disciples 'inwardly are in deep rapture at the stilling of the storm on the lake, Jesus climbing into the boat': *kai lian ek perissou en heautois existanto*. Ecstasy, on the other hand, is experienced by the women at the grave as they sense the exceptional occurrence they have heard from the exception figure in white: Jesus is alive, and they 'run away from the tomb quivering and in ecstasy'. Whilst Luke reports that 'the disciples were enraptured by the story of the women having visited the grave'. Peter, on two occasions, 'falls into ecstasy while praying'. The same happens to Paul in Jerusalem. His explanation of 'ecstasy' makes clear it 'is related to God', it is not an emotional or physical phenomenon: "For if we are in a state of ecstasy, it is for God; if we are in a state of reason, it is for you", says Paul to the Corinthians.

Summing up, rapture and ecstasy are reported as positive experiences in view of the spirit operating either outside or inwardly in one's consciousness.

Bibliography

Aagard, A. M. "Die Erfahrung des Geistes." In O. A. Dilschneider, *Theologie des Geistes*, Gütersloh: Gerd Mohn, 1980 11–24.

Adams, J. R. *The Essential Reference Book for Biblical Metaphors: From Literal to Literary.* Cleveland: Pilgrim 2005.

Aitken, E. B. *Jesus' Death in Early Christian Memory: The Poetics of Passion.* Göttingen: Vandenhoeck & Ruprecht 2004.

Aland, B. "Seele, Zeit, Eschaton bei einem frühen christlichen Theologen: Basilides zwischen Paulus und Platon." In Ψυχη;—*Seele-anima, Festschrift für Karin Alt*, ed. J. Holzhausen. Stuttgart / Leipzig, 1998 255–78.

Aland, K., and Aland, B. *Der Text des Neuen Testaments*, Stuttgart: DBG 1989.

Aland, K. *Synopsis of the Four Gospels.* Stuttgart: DBG 1993.

Aland, K., Black, Matthew, Martini, Carlo M., Metzger, Bruce M., and Wikgren, Allen. *The Greek New Testament, Stuttgart*: DBG 1983.

Allison, D. C. *The Jesus Tradition in Q*, Harrisburg: Trinity 1997.

Ambrozic, A. M. *The Hidden Kingdom: A Redactional-Critical Study of the References to the Kingdom of God in Mark's Gospel. Catholic Biblical Quarterly* (CBQ) Monograph Series II, Washington DC, 1972.

Argyle, A. W. "God's 'Repentance' and the LXX." *Expository Times* 75s 1964.

Aulén, G. *Jesus in Contemporary Historical Research.* Philadelphia: Fortress 1976.

Baers, J., Brinkman G., Jelsma A., and Steggink, O. *Encyclopedie van de mystiek: fundamenten, tradities, perpsectieven*, Kampen: Kok, 2003.

Bailey, K. "The Shepherd Poems of John 10 and Their Culture." *Irish Biblical Studies*, 15 1993.

Bailey, K. "Middle Eastern Oral Tradition and the Synoptic Gospels." *Expository Times* 1995.

Bailey, K. E. "Informal Controlled Oral Tradition and the Synoptic Gospels." *Asia Journal of Theology* 5 1991 34–54.

Barrett, C. K. *The Gospel according to St.John: An Introduction with Commentary and Notes on the Greek Text.* London, SPCK, 1978.

Barrett, C.K. *Holy Spirit and the Gospel Tradition.* London: SPCK 1947, 1977.

Barrett, C. K. "The Holy Spirit in the Fourth Gospel." *Journal of Theological Studies*, N. S., 1,1 1950 1–15.

Barton, J. *The Nature of Biblical Criticism.* Louisville: Westminster John Knox 2007.

Batdorf, I. W. *The Spirit of God in the Synoptic Gospels: An Historical Comparison and a Reappraisal.* Princeton Theological Seminary, 1952.

Bauckham, R. *Jesus and the Eyewitnesses: The Gospels as Eyewitness Testimony.* Grand Rapids: Eerdmans, 2006.

Bauckham, R. "Eyewitnesses and Critical History: A Response to Jens Schröter and Craig Evans." *JSNT* 31, 2 2008 221–235.

Bauer, W., Aland K., and Aland A. *Griechisch-deutsches Wörterbuch zu den Schriften des Neuen Testaments und der früh-christlichen Literatur*, Berlin: De Gruyter, 1988.

Bauer, W., Gingrich F. W., and Danker F. W. *A Greek-English Lexicon of the New Testament and Other Early Christian Literature.* Chicago: University of Chicago Press, 1979.
Beasley-Murray, G. R. *John,* World Biblical Commentary 36. Nashville: Nelson 1999.
Beavis, M. A. "The Kingdom of God, 'Utopia' and Theocracy." *JSJH* 2.1 2004.
Beelzen, J. A., and Geels, A. *Mysticism, a Variety of Psychological Perspectives.* Amsterdam: Rodopi 2003.
Behm, J. "Metanoia—ein Grundbegriff der neutestamentischen Verkündigung, *Deutsche Theologie* 7 1934, 75–86.
Beilby, K., Eddy, P.R. (eds) *The Historical Jesus: Five views.* London: SPCK 2010
Bendemann, R. von. Review of Frankenmölle H. *Sünde und Erlösung im Neuen Testament,* 1996. *Theologische Literaturzeitung* 122 (1997): 7/8, 670–73.
Benjamin, H. S. "Pneuma in John and Paul: A Comparative Study of the Term with Particular Reference to the Holy Spirit." *Biblical Theology Bulletin* 6,1 1976 27–48.
Bennema, C. "Spirit-Baptism in the Fourth Gospel: A Messianic Reading of John." 1.33. *Biblica* 2003.
Berkhof, H. "Die Pneumatologie in der niederländischen Theologie." In O. A. Dilschneider, *Theologie des Geistes.* Gütersloh: Gerd Mohn, 1980.
Bernoulli, C. A. *Jesus wie sie ihn sahen; eine Deutung der drei ersten Evangelien.* Basel 1928.
Bieringer, R. "Traditionsgeschichtlicher Ursprung und theologische Bedeutung der ὑπερ-Aussagen im Neuen Testament." *The Four Gospels.* Festschrift, ed. F. van Segbroeck. Leuven: Peeters, 1992, vol. 1 219–248.
Bird, M. F. "The Criterion of Greek Language and Context: A Response." *JSHJ* 4.1 2006 55–67.
Black, C. C. "Mark as Historian of God's Kingdom." *The Catholic Biblical Quarterly* 71 2009 64–83.
Blair, H. A. "Spirit-Baptism in St. Mark's Gospel." *Church Quarterly Review,* 155, 1954 153–66.
Blanc, R. « L'emploi des mots 'psuché' et 'pneuma' dans le Nouveau Testament.» *Positions luthériennes,* 44 1996.
Blass F., Debrunner A., and Rehkopf F. *Grammatik des neutestamentlichen Griechisch,* Göttingen: Vandenhoeck & Ruprecht, 1990.
Boda M., and Smith, G. *Repentance in Christian Theology.* Collegeville MN: Liturgical 2006.
Bohlen, M. "Die Einlasssprüche in der Reich-Gottes-Verkündiging Jesu." *ZNW* 99 2008 167–84.
Bond, H. K. Review of E. B. Aitken. *Jesus' Death in Early Christian Memory, JSNT* 28,5 2006 30.
Boomershine, Th. E,. and Bartholomew, G. L. "The Narrative Technique of Mark 16:8," *JBL* 100,2 1981 213–223.
Borchert B., *Mystiek: geschiedenis en uitdaging* ('Mysticism: history and challenge'). Haarlem: Gottmer, 1989.
Borg, M. J. *Jesus: Uncovering the Life, Teachings, and Relevance of a Religious Revolutionary,* San Francisco: Harper San Francisco, 2006.
Borg, M. J. *The Heart of Christianity: Rediscovering the Life of Faith,* San Francisco: Harper San Francisco, 2003.
Borg, M. J. *The God We Never Knew.* San Francisco: HarperSanFrancisco 1997.
Borg, M. J., ed. *Jesus and Buddha: The Parallel Sayings.* Berkeley: Ulysses 1997.
Borg, Marcus. *The Lost Gospel: The Original Sayings of Jesus.* Berkeley: Ulysses 1996.
Borg, M. J., and Wright, N. T. *The Meaning of Jesus: Two Visions:* San Francisco: Harper San Francisco, 1989.

Bos, A. *Hoe de stof de geest kreeg,* Zeist: Christofoor, 2008 (the evolutionary relation between matter, mind and spirit).
Boucher, P.-M., » Γενηθηναι ἄνωθεν: la valeur de l'adverbe ἄνωθεν en Jn3,3 et 7, 1ére partie : La réception chrétienne », *Revue Biblique* 115,2 2008, 191–215.
Boucher, P.-M. » Γενηθηναι ἄνωθεν: la valeur de l'adverbe ἄνωθεν en Jn3,3 et 7, 2ième partie: Les acceptations du terme ἄνωθεν en grec classique et koinè non sémitisé», *Revue Biblique* 115,4 2008, 568–95.
Bovon, F. *Les derniers jours de Jésus: texts et événements,* Genève: Labor et Fides 2004.
Bovon, F *The Last Days of Jesus.* Louisville: Westminster John Knox, 2006.
Bovon, F. *Studies in Early Christianity.* Grand Rapids: Baker, 2005.
Bowden, J. *Christianity: The Complete Guide.* London: Continuum, 2005.
Boyd, J. H. "The 'Soul' of the Psalms Compared to the 'Self' of Kohut." *Journal of Psychology and Christianity,* 19 2000.
Branden, R., C. *Satanic Conflict and the Plot of Matthew.* New York: Peter Lang, 2006.
Bradley, M. C. *Matthew: Poet, Historian, Dialectician.* New York: Peter Lang 2007.
Braun, W. *It's Just Another Story: The Politics of Remembering the Earliest Christians,* London: Equinox, forthcoming.
Breck, J. *Spirit of Truth: The Origins of Johannine Pneumatology.* Crestwood, NY: St Vladimir's Seminary Press 1991.
Brown, R. *The Death of the Messiah.* New York: Doubleday 1994.
Brown, S. "'Water-baptism' and 'Spirit-baptism' in Luke-Acts. *Anglican Theological Review* 59 Apr 1977 135–51.
Buber, M. *Ich und Du.* Stuttgart: Reclam 1995.
Buber, M. *Königtum Gottes,* Heidelberg: Schneider (1932) 1956
Bütler, R. *Die Mystik der Welt,* Bern: Scherz Verlag 1992.
Bultmann, R. *Jesus and the World.* New York: Scribers 1958.
Bultmann, R. *Theologie des Neuen Testaments.* Tübingen: Mohr Siebeck 1948/1984.
Burkett, D. *Rethinking the Gospel Sources: From Proto-Mark to Mark.* New York: T&T Clark 2004.
Burkett, D. "The Return of Proto-Mark: A Response to David Neville." *Ephemerides Theologicae Lovanienses* 85,1 2009 117–34.
Burridge, R. A. *What Are the Gospels? A Comparison with Graeco-Roman Biography,* Grand Rapids: Eerdmans 1992, 2004.
Burton, E. D. *Spirit, Soul, and Flesh: The Usage of πνεῦμα, ψυχή, and σάρξ in Greek Writings.* Chicago: Chicago UP 1918.
Čabraja, I. *Die Gedanke der Umkehr bei den Synoptikern; eine exegetisch-religionsgeschichtliche Untersuchung,* St. Ottilien: EOS 1985.
Cameron, R., and Miller, M. P., eds. *Redescribing Christian Origins.* Leiden: Brill 2004.
Carey, G. *Sinners : Jesus and His Earliest Followers.* Waco TX: Baylor UP 2009.
Carlson, S.C. "A Stimulating Step back from the Jesus Quest." *Expository Times* 118 (Nov 2006) .
Carmignac, J. *Le mirage de l'eschatologie: royauté, règne et royaume de Dieu—sans eschatologie.* Paris: Letouzey 1979.
Casey, M. *The solution to the 'Son of Man' problem,* New York: T&T Clark 2007.
Casey, M. *The solution of the 'Son of Man' problem,* review by P.Owen, *RBL* 2/9/2009.
Catechism of the Catholic Church, London: Burns & Oats 1994/2003.
Catechismus. De nieuwe, Hilversum 1966.

Chancey, M. *Greco-Roman Culture and the Galilee of Jesus.* Cambridge: Cambridge UP 2007.
Charlesworth, J. H. *Jesus' Jewishness*, New York: Crossroad 1991.
Charlesworth, J. H. Pokorný P. *Jesus Research: An International Perspective.* Grand Rapids: Eerdmans 2009.
Chilton, B. *Pure Kingdom: Jesus' Vision of God.* Grand Rapids: Eerdmans 1996.
Cho, Y. *Spirit and Kingdom in the Writings of Luke and Paul: An Attempt to Reconcile These Concepts.* Waynesboro: Paternoster 2005.
Clark, M. S. "Ekstasis in New Testament Christianity." *Cyberjournal for Pentecostal-Charismatic research,* 1997, 1.
Claus, D. *Toward the soul: an inquiry into the meaning of ψυχή before Plato,* New Haven / London: Yale 1981.
Clément, O. *The Roots of Christian Mysticism: Text and Commentary.* London: New City 1993, 1994.
Comfort, P. W. "Light from the New Testament Papyri Concerning the Translation of *pneuma.*" *The Bible Translator* 35,1 1984N 130–33.
Commentary on Holy Scripture: A New Catholic -. Westminster: Nelson 1969/1981.
Concordance to the Novum Testamentum Graece. Berlin: De Gruyter 1987.
Conzelmann, H., and Lindemann, A. *Arbeitsbuch zum Neuen Testament.* Tübingen: Mohr Siebeck 1991.
Coppens, J. *La royauté - le règne - le royaume de Dieu; cadre de relève apocalyptique.* Leuven: Peeters 1979.
Cothenet, E. « Chair et esprit en Saint-Jean », in: Triacca, A.M., A. Pistoia, *Liturgie éthique et peuple de Dieu,* Roma, C.L.V. Edizioni Liturgiche, 1991 81–96.
Crossan, J. D., *The historical Jesus: the Life of a Mediterranean Jewish Peasant,* San Francisco: HarperSanFrancisco 1991
Crossan, J. D. *Four Other Gospels: Thomas, Egerton, Secret Mark, Peter.* Sonoma: Poleridge 1992.
Crossan, J. D. *The Essential Jesus: What Jesus Really Taught.* San Francisco: Harper San Francisco 1994.
Crossan, J. D. *The Birth of Christianity: Discovering What Happened in the Years Immediately after the Execution of Jesus.* San Francisco: HarperSanFrancisco 1998.
Crossley, J. G. "The Semitic Background to Repentance in the Teachings of John the Baptist and Jesus." *JSJH* 2,2 2004.
Crump, F. J. *Pneuma in the Gospels.* Washington, D.C.: The Catholic University of America Press 1954.
Danker, F. W. A *Greek-English Lexicon of the New Testament and Other Early Christian Literature (BDAG).* Chicago: Chicago UP 2000.
Dantine, W. "Die ethische Dimension des 'pneuma hagion.'" In O. A. Dilschneider, *Theologie des Geistes,* Gütersloh: Gerd Mohn 1980.
Dautzenberg, G. "Seele (näfäs - psyche) im biblischen Denken sowie das Verhältnis von Unsterblichkeit und Auferstehung." In *Seele: ihre Wirklichkeit, ihr Verhältnis zum Leib und zur menschlichen Person,* ed. K. Kremer. : Leiden: Brill 1984 186–203.
Dautzenberg, G. *Sein Leben bewahren:* Ψυχή *in den Herrenworten der Evangelien,* München: Koesel 1966.
de Marquette ,J. *Introduction à la mystique comparée.* Paris: Adyar 1956.
De Vries, L. "Bible Translations: Forms and Functions." *The Bible Translator* 52,3 2001 306–319.

De Witt Burton, E. *Spirit, Soul and Flesh: The Usage of* pneuma, psuchê *and* sarx *in Greek Writings and Translated Works from the Earliest Period to 180 A.D.* Chicago: Chicago UP 1918.

DeConick, A. *The Original Gospel of Thomas in Translation.* New York, T&T Clark 2007.

DeConick, A. *Recovering the Original Gospel of Thomas: A History of the Gospel and Its Growth.* London / New York: T&T Clark 2005.

DeConick, A. D. *Voices of the Mystics.* London / New York: T&T Clark International 2001.

Denaux, A. *New Testament Textual Criticism and Exegesis*, Festschrift J. Delobel, Leuven: Peeters/University Press 2002.

Denney, M. "Delight: A Discourse upon the Spiritual Function of the Psyche." *The Journal of Pastoral Care*, 54 2000 187–193.

Dirksen, A. H. *The New Testament Concept of metanoia.* Washington, DC: Catholic Univ. of America 1932.

Dirksen, A. H. "New Testament *metanoia* in Current English Uage. *The Classical Bulletin*, 1933.

Dodd, C. H. *The Parables of the Kingdom.* London: 1936.

Doran, R. M. *Theological Foundations: Intentionality and Psyche*, vol. 1. Marquette: Marquette UP 1995.

Dörrie, H., "Platons Begriff der Seele und dessen weitere Ausgestaltung im Neoplatonismus." In *Seele: ihre Wirklichkeit, ihr Verhältnis zum Leib und zur menschlichen Person*, ed. K. Kremer. Leiden: Brill 1984 18–45.

Dschulnigg, P. *Der Hirt und die Schafe (Joh 10,1–18), Studien zum Neuen Testament und seiner Umwelt* 1989.

Du Plessis, P. J. Teleios*: The Idea of Perfection in the New Testament.* Kampen: Kok 1959.

Du Toit, A. B. "Romans 1,3–4 and the Gospel Tradition: A Re-assessment of the Phrase *kata pneuma hagiôsunês.*" In Van Segbroeck , *The Four Gospels 1992: Festschrift Frans Neirynck.*Leuven: Peeters 1992 249–256.

Duintjer, O. D. "De innerlijke weg: hoezo?", in Th van Leeuwen, H. Muijen (ed), *De innerlijke weg*, Kampen: Ten Have 2007,18-34 (:the inner path, why?)

Dünzl, F. "Pneuma: Funktionen des theologischen Begriffs in frühchristliecher Literatur", *Jahrbuch für Antike und Christentum*, Ergänzungsband 30, 2000.

Durr, H., and C. Ramstein, eds., *Basileia*, Festschrift E. Buss, Basel: Simson 1993.

Dunn, J. D. G. *Jesus Remembered*, vol. 1 of *Christianity in the Making.* Grand Rapids: Eerdmans 2003a.

Dunn, J. D. G. "Jesus and the Kingdom: How Would his Message Have Been Heard?", in *Neotestamentica et Philonica*, D.E. Aune, T, Seland (eds), Festschrift P. Borgen, Leiden: Brill 2003b.

Dunn, J. D. G. *A New Perspective on Jesus: What the Quest of the Historical Jesus Missed*, Grand Rapids: Baker Academic 2005.

Dunn, J. D. G. "Eyewitnesses and the Oral Tradition." *JSJH* 6 2008 85–105.

Durken, D. *Sin, Salvation, and the Spirit.* Collegeville MN: Liturgical Press 1979.

Dussaud, R. « La *néphesh* et la *rouah* dans le 'Livre de Job' » *Revue de l'histoire des religions*, 129 1945.

Ehrman, B. D. *The Orthodox Corruption of Scripture.* Oxford: Oxford UP 1993.

Ehrman, B. D. *Lost Christianities: The Battles for Scripture and the Faiths We Never Knew.* Oxford: Oxford UP, 2003.

Ehrman, B. D. *Misquoting Jesus*, San Francisco: HarperSanFrancisco 2005.

Ehrman, B. D. *Jesus Interrupted*, San Francisco: HarperSanFrancisco 2009.

Ekem, D. "Another Look at the Ttranslation of Matthew 16.19." *The Bible Translator* 55,1 2004 119–124.
Elmer, M., Hoppe R., and Schmeller, Th.. "Der 'historische' Jesus aus der Sicht Joseph Ratzingers." *Biblische Zt NF* 52,1 2008.
Etzioni, A., and Carney, D. E. *Repentance: A Comparative Perspective.* Lanham: Rowman & Littlefield, 1997.
Evans, C. "Assessing Progress in the Third Quest of the Historical Jesus." *JSHJ* 4,1 2006 35–54.
Evans, C. "Implications of Eyewitness Tradition." *JSNT* 31,2 2008 211–219.
Ewert, D. *The Holy Spirit in the New Testament.* Scottdale, PA: Herald Press 1983.
Feifel, E., ed. *Busse, Busssakrament, Busspraxis.*, München: Don Bosco 1975.
Ferguson, E. *Baptism in the Early Church: History, Theology, and Liturgy in the First Five Centuries.* Grand Rapids: Eerdmans 2009.
Ferguson, E., ed. *Encyclopedia of Early Christianity.* New York: Garland 1990.
Fitzmyer, J. A. The Gospel According to Luke: A New Translation with Introduction and Commentary, 2 vols. New Haven / London: Yale UP1970, 1985.
Flannery, F., ed., *Experientia vol. I, Inquiry into Religious Experience in Early Judaism and Christianity.* Leiden: Brill 2008.
Flowers, H. J. "Ἐν πνεύματι ἁγίῳ καὶ Πυρί." *Expository Times* 64 1953 155–56.
Focant, C. «Une christologie de type ‚mystique' (Marc 1.1–16.8*).*» *New Testament Studies* 55 2009.
Focant, C. *L'Évangile selon Marc.* Paris: Cerf 2004.
Focant, C. "Un silence qui fait parler." In A. Denaux, *New Testament Textual Criticism and exegesis.* Festschrift J. Delobel, Leuven : Peeters/University Press, 2002, 79–96.
Francis, D. *The Holy Spirit: A Statistical Inquiry. Expository Times* 96,5 1985 136–137.
Frankenmölle, H. *Sünde und Erlösung im Neuen Testament.* Freiburg: Herder 1996. Review by R. Von Bendemann, *Theologische Literaturzeitung* 122 (1997), 7/8, 670–673.
Freed, E. D. « Psalm 42/43 in John's Gospel. » *New Test. Studies*, 29 1983.
Fuente : Juan de la Cruz 1591-1991, Amsterdam: D'Arts 1991.
Füglister, N., "Die biblische Anthropologie und die postmortale Existenz des Individuums." *Kairos* 22, 3-4 1980 129–145.
Funk, R. W., and Hoover, R. W. The Jesus Seminar. *The Five Gospels: the Search for the Authentic Words of Jesus.* New York: Poleridge Press / Macmillan 1993.
Funk, R. W. / The Jesus Seminar, *The Acts of Jesus.* San Francisco: HarperSanFrancisco 1998.
Gaventa, B. A. *From Darkness to Light: Aspects of Conversion in the New Testament.* Philadelphia: Fortress 1986.
Geels, A. "Mystical Experience and the Emergence of Creativity", in: Holm, N. G. *Religious Ecstasy.* Stockholm: Almqvist&Wiksell 1982.
Gerber, U., and Güttgemans E., *'Linguistische' Theologie.* Bonn: Linguistica Biblica, 1972.
Getty-Sullivan, M. A. *Parables of the Kingdom: Jesus and the Use of Parables in the Synoptic Tradition.* Collegeville, MN: Liturgical 2007.
Giesen, H. *Herrschaft Gottes—heute oder morgen?: zur Heilsbotschaft Jesu und der synoptischen Evangelien.* Regensburg: Pustet 1995.
Gnilka, J. *Das Evangelium nach Markus,* 2. Zürich: Benzinger 1989.
Goldhahn-Müller, I. *Die Grenze der Gemeinde: Studien zum Problem der Zweiten Busse im Neuen Testament unter Berücksichtigung der Entwicklung im 2. Jh. bis Tertullian.* Göttingen: Vandenhoeck&Ruprecht 1989.

Goodacre, M., and Perrin, N., eds. *Questioning Q: A Multi-Dimensional Critique*. Downers Grove: InterVarsity 2004.
Gordley, M. Review of Peter J. Leinhart, *Deep Exegesis*, RBL 3/12/2010.
Gorman, M. *Elements of Biblical Exegesis*, Peabody: Hendrickson 2009.
Görg, M. "Vom Wehen des Pneuma." In Görg, M., *Biblische Notizen: Beiträge zur Exegetischen Diskussion*. Bamberg 1976 5–9.
Gregg, B. H. *The Historical Jesus and the Final Judgment Sayings in Q*. Tübingen: Mohr Siebeck 2006.
Gribbin, J. *Q Is for Quantum: Particle Physics from a to Z*. London: Weidenfeld & Nicolson 1998.
Güttgemans, E. "Linguistische Analyse von Mk 16, 1–8." In U. Gerber and E. Güttgemans (eds.), *'Linguistische' Theologie*, Linguistica Biblica. Bonn 1972 89.
Gundry, R. H. *Matthew: A Commentary*. Grand Rapids: Eerdmans 1994.
Hägerland, T. *Jesus and the Rites of Repentance*. New Testament Studies 52 2006 166–187.
Hammerskjöld, D. *Markings (Vägmärken)*, 1963 (and Faber, London 1964).
Hannan, M. *The Nature and Demands of the Sovereign Rule of God in the Gospel of Matthew*. London: T&T Clark 2006.
Happold, F. C. *Mysticism: A Study and an Anthology*. Harmondsworth: Penguin 1963.
Harland, P. A. *Dynamics of Identity in the World of Early Christians: Association, Judeans, and Cultural Minorities*. New York: T&T Clark 2009.
Harnack, A. von. *Das Wesen des Christentums*. Leipzig: Heinrichs'sche Buchhandlung 1900. Also in a later reprint: Siebenstern, München / Hamburg 1964.
Harnack, A. von. *Ueber die jüngst entdeckte Sprüche Jesu*, 1897 / London 1908 (*The Sayings of Jesus: The Second Source of St. Matthew and St. Luke*).
Harvey, A. *Teachings of the Christian Mystics*. Boston: Shambala 1998.
Hatina, T. R. "Who Will See 'the Kingdom of God Coming with Power' in Mark 9,1—Protagonists or Antagonists?" *Biblica* 86,1 2005.
Hays, R. B. *Seeking the Identity of Jesus: A Pilgrimage*. Grand Rapids: Eerdmans 2008.
Heaney, J. J. *Psyche and Spirit: Readings in Psychology and Religion*. New York: Paulist Press 1984.
Heikkinen, W. "Notes on 'epistrepho' and 'metanoeo.'" *Ecumenical Review* 19 1967 313–316.
Heiler, F. *Das Gebet: Eine religionsgeschichtliche und religionspsychologische Untersuchung*. München: Reinhardt, 1923.
Helminiak, D. A. *The Human Core of Spirituality: Mind as Psyche and Spirit*. Albany: State of NY UP 1996.
Hendriks, W. M. A. "Brevior lectio praeferenda est verbosiori." *Revue Biblique* 112,4 2005 567–595.
Hicks, P. "Fathoming the Unfathomable." In Partridge and Gabriel, *Mysticisms*, 2003.
Hodges, Z. C. "Water and Spirit—John 3:5: Problem Passages in the Gospel of John." Part 3, *Bibliotheca Sacra and Theological Review*, 1978 206-21.
Hoffer, M. *Metanoia (Bekehrung and Busse) im Neuen Testament*. Review in *Theologische Literaturzeitung* 1950, 10.
Holm, N. G. *Religious Ecstasy*. Stockholm: Almqvist&Wiksell 1982.
Holmén, T. "The Alternatives of the Kingdom; Encountering the Semantic Restrictions of Luke 17,20–21 (ἐντὸς ὑμῶν)," *Zt. für die neutestamentliche Wissenschaft*, 87 1996 204–229.
Holzhausen, J. "Die Seelenlehre des Gnostikers Herakleon." In Ψυχή—*Seele-anima, Festschrift für Karin Alt*, ed. J. Holzhausen. Stuttgart / Leipzig 1998 279–300.

Hood, R. W. Jr. *Dimensions of Mystical Experiences: Empirical Studies and Psychological Links.* Amsterdam: Rodopi 2001.

Hooker, M..D. *The Gospel according to St. Mark, Black's NT Commentaries.* London: Black 1991/1997.

Horsley, R. A. et al., eds. *Performing the Gospel: Orality, Memory, and Mark.* Minneapolis: Fortress 2006.

Huffmon, H. B. et al., eds. *The Quest for the Kingdom of God.* Winoma Lake: Eisenbrauns 1983.

Hur, J. "A Dynamic Reading of the Holy Spirit in Luke-Acts." Supplement Series 211, *Journal for the Study of the New Testament,* Sheffield: Academic Press 2001.

Hurtado, L. W. *Lord Jesus Christ: Devotion to Jesus in Earliest Christianity.* Grand Rapids: Eerdmans 2003.

Isaacs, M. E. *The Concept of Spirit: A Study of* pneuma *in Hellenistic Judaism and Its Bearing on the New Testament.* London: Heythrop, 1976 391–407.

Iverson, K. R. "Orality in the Gospels: A Survey of Recent Research." *Currents in Biblical Research* 8,1 2009 71–106.

James J., *The varieties of religious experience: a study in human nature,* Longmans, Green, and Co. 1902 / 1985

Johnson L.T., *Religious Experience in Early Christianity: a Missing Dimension in New Testament Studies,* Minneapolis: Fortress 1998

Kamp G. C. v. d. *Pneuma-Christologie: een oud antwoord op een actuele vraag? (An old answer to a current question),* Amsterdam: Rodopi 1983.

Kanagaraj, J. J. "Jesus' Message of the Kingdom of God: Present and Future Tensions Revisited." In B.J. Oropeza et al., *Jesus and Paul,* Festschrift James D.G. Dunn, T&T Clark, London 2009.

Katz S. T. *Mysticism and Religious Traditions.* Oxford: Oxford UP 1983.

Keener C. S. *The Spirit in the Gospels and Acts: Divine Purity and Power.* Peabody, MA: Hendrickson 1997.

Khan, (H.) I. *The Sufi Message.* Delhi: Motilal Banarsidass Dass, 13 vols, Delhi 1989–1991.

Khan, (H.)I. *Philosophy, Psychology, Mysticism.* Vol. XI of *The Sufi Message.* Delhi: Motilal Banarsidass 1990. Also by Barrie&Rockliff, London 1964

Khan, (H.)I., *The Dance of the Soul,* Delhi: Motilal Banarsidass 1993, also: *Gayan, Vadan, Nirtan,* London: Barrie and Rockliff

Kiefer, O. *Die Hirtenrede, Analyse u Deutung von Joh 10,1–18.*Stuttgart 1967.

Kilgallen, J.J., *Twenty parables of Jesus in the Gospel of Luke,* Roma: Pontificio Istituto Biblico

Kingsbury, J.D. "The Spirit and the Son of God in Mark's Gospel." In D. Durken, *Sin, Salvation and the Spirit.* Collegeville, MN 1979. 195–202.

Kittel G., and Friedrich G., *Theological Dictionary of the New Testament,* 10 vols., Grand Rapids: Eerdmans, 1964–1976, reprint 1991.

Kloppenborg, J. S. *Apocalypticism, Anti-Semitism and the Historical Jesus.* London: T&T Clark 2005.

Kloppenborg, J. S. "Associations in the Ancient World." In A.-J. Levine et al., *The Historical Jesus in Context.* Princeton: Princeton UP 2006, 323–338.

Kloppenborg, J. S. *Q: The Earliest Gospel: An Introduction.* Louisville: Westminster John Knox 2008.

Kloppenborg, J. S. "Q, Eschatology, and Christian Origins." *Expository Times* 118, April 2007.

Kloppenborg, Verbin J. S. *Excavating Q: The History and Setting of the Sayings Gospel.* Minneapolis: Fortress, 2000.
Kloppenborg, J. S. "Variation in the Reproduction of the Double Tradition and an Oral Q?" *Ephemerides Theologicae Lovanienses* 83,1 2007 53–80.
Koester, H. "The Apostolic Fathers and the Struggle for Christian Identity." In P. Foster, *The Writings of the Apostolic Fathers*, London: T&T Clark 2007 1–12.
Koester, H. *Ancient Christian Gospels: Their History and Development.*Philadelphia: Trinity 1990.
Kornhaber, A. *Spirit: Mind, Body, and the Will to Existence.* New York: St. Martin's Press 1988.
Kowalski, B. *Die Hirtenrede (Joh 10,1–18) im Kontext des Johannesevangelium.*, Stuttgart: KBW 1996.
Kraus, T. J. "Der Artikel im Griechischen: Nutzen einer systematischen Beschäftigung anhand von ausgewählten Syntagmata (Hab 1,12; Jud 17; Joh 6,32*).*" *Revue Biblique*, 107 2000, 262–272.
Kremer, K. "Zur Einführung: die Problemlage." In *Seele: Ihre Wirklichkeit, ihr Verhältnis zum Leib und zur menschlichen Person*, ed. K. Kremer. Leiden/Köln: Brill 1984 1–17.
Kuhn, K. G. "Jesus in Gethsemane." *Evangelische Theologie* 12/NF 1952/53 260–285.
Kuitert, H. M. *Jesus: The Legacy of Christianity.* London: SCM 1999.
Kuitert, H. M. *Voor een tijd een plaats van God.* Baarn: Ten Have 2002.
Kurtén, T. "Basic Trust: The Hidden Presence of God." *Studia Theologica* 48 1994 110–124.
Kurtén, T. "Ecstasy—A Way to Religious Knowledge: Some Remarks on Paul Tillich as Theologian and Philosopher." In Holm 2002.
Kvalbein, H. "The Kingdom of the Father in the Gospel of Thomas." In *The New Testament and Early Christian Literature in Greco-Roman Context*, ed. J. Fotopoulos Festschrift D. E. Aune. Leiden: Brill 2006, 203–228.
Ladd, G. E. "The Kingdom of God: Reign or Realm?" *JBL* 81,3 1962 230–238.
Langenscheidt Taschenwörterbuch Altgriechisch. Berlin: Langenscheidt 1993.
Laurin, R. "The Concept of Man as a Soul." ,*Expository Times* 72 1961 131–134.
Leezenberg, M. *Rede en religie, een verkenning (Ratio and religion)*, Amsterdam: Van Gennep 2007.
Légasse, S. "L'autre 'baptême' (Mc 1,8; Mt 3,11; Lc 3:16; Jn 1,26.31–33)." Van Segbroeck c.a., *The Four Gospels 1992:* Festschrift Frans Neirynck. Leuven: Peeters, 1992 257–273.
Leisegang, H., *'Pneuma Hagion': Der Ursprung des Geistbegriffs der synoptischen Evangelien aus der griechischen Mystik,* Leipzig: Hinrich, 1922 (also Hildesheim / New York: Olms 1970)
Leithart, P. J. *Deep Exegesis: The Mystery of Reading Scripture.* Waco: Baylor UP 2009.
Lê-Minh-Thông, J. « Aimer sa vie' et 'haïr sa vie' (Jn 12,25) dams la Quatrième Évangile. » *Revue Biblique* 115,2 2008 216–244.
Levinsohn, S. H. "Anarthrous References to the Holy Spirit: Another Factor." *The Bible Translator*, 44,1 1993 138–144.
Lewis, I. M. *Ecstatic Religion.* Harmondsworth: Penguin 1971.
Lewis, K. M. *Rereading the 'Shepherd's Discourse': Restoring the Integrity of John 9.39–10.21.* New York: Peter Lang 2008.
Liebenberg, J. *The Language of the Kingdom and Jesus: Parable, Aphorism, and Metaphor in the Sayings Material Common to the Synoptic Tradition and the Gospel of Thomas.* Berlin: De Gruyter 2001.
Liddell and Scott's Greek-English Lexicon Abridged: The Little Liddell. Simon Wallenberg Press 2007.
Lightfoot, R. H. *St. John's Gospel, a Commentary.* Oxford: Clarendon 1956.

Limbeck, M. "Jesu Verkündigung und der Ruf zum Umkehr." I O. Knoch *Das Evangelium auf dem Weg zum Menschen.* Frankfurt a .M.: Knecht 1973 35–42.

Lindars, B., and Smalley, S. S. *Christ and Spirit in the New Testament,* Cambridge: Cambridge UP 1973.

Lodahl, M. E. *Shekinah / Spirit: Divine Presence in Jewish and Christian Religion.* New York: Paulist Press 1992.

Lohse, E. *Die Entstehung des Neuen Testaments.* Stuttgart: Kohlhammer 1991.

Loubser, J. A. *Oral and Manuscript Culture in the Bible: Studies on the Media Structure of the New Testament—Explorative Hermeneutics.* Stellenbosch: Sun 2007.

Lundström, G. *The Kingdom of God in the Teaching of Jesus: A History of Interpretation from the Last Decades of the Nineteenth Century to the Present Day.* Edinburgh: Oliver and Boyd 1963.

Lust, J. et al. *Greek-English Lexicon of the Septuagint.* Stuttgart: DBG 2003.

Luttikhuizen, G. *De veelvormigheid van het vroegste Christendom,* Delft: Eburon 2002 (the pluriformity of earliest Christianity).

Luzarraga, J. "Retraducción semítica de *fobeomai* en Mc 16,8.» *Biblica: Commentarii* 50 1969 497–510.

Lys, D. *Nèphèh: histoire de l'âme dans la révélation 'Israël au sein des religions proche-orientales.* Paris: PUF 1958.

Lys, D. "Israelite Soul according to the LXX." *Vetus Testamentum* 16 1966 181–226 Ap

MacDonald, D. R. *The Homeric Epics and the Gospel of Mark.* New Haven / London: Yale UP 2000.

MacDonald, D. R. "Imitations of Greek Epic in the Gospels." In A.-J. Levine et al., *The Historical Jesus in Context.* Princeton: Princeton UP 2006, 372–384.

Mack, B. L. *The Lost Gospel: The Book of Christian Origins.* SanFrancisco: HarperSanFrancisco 1993.

Makambu, M. A. *L'ésprit-pneuma dans l'évangile de Jean: approche historico-religieuse et exégétique.* München: Echter 2007.

Maloney, E. C. *Jesus' Urgent Message for Today: The Kingdom of God in Mark's Gospel.* New York: Continuum 2004.

Maly, E. H. "Sin and Forgiveness in the Scriptures." In D. Durken (ed.), *Sin, Salvation, and the Spirit.* Collegeville, MN: Liturgical Press 1979 40–48.

Marcus, J. "Entering into the Kingly Power of God", *JBL* 107,4 1988 663–75.

Marcus, J. *The Anchor Bible, vol. 27: Mark 1–8.* New Haven: YUP 1999.

Marcus, J. *The Anchor Bible, vol. 27A: Mark 8–16,* New Haven: YUP 2009.

Matzkow, W. *De vocabulis quibusdam italae et vulgatae christianis: quaestiones lexicographae.* Berlin: Pilz & Noack 1933.

May, D. "'You Cannot Hide the Soul': 1 Thessalonians 5:12–22." *Review and Expositor,* 96 1999 277–285.

May, P. "The Self and the Spirit." *Indian Journal of Theology* 6 1957 131–142.

Mayotte, R. A. *The Complete Jesus.* South Royalton VT: Steerforth Press, 1997.

McGinn, B., and McGinn P., *Early Christian Mystics: The Divine Vision of Spiritual Masters.* New York: Crossroad 2003.

McGinn, B. *The Foundations of Mysticism: Origins to the Fifth Century.* Part 1 of a four-volume series *The Presence of God: A History of Western Mysticism.* New York: Crossroad 1991.

McIntyre, J. *The Shape of Pneumatology: Studies in the Doctrine of the Holy Spirit,* Edinburgh: T&T Clark 1997.

McKenzie, S. L., and Haynes, S. R. *To Each Its Own Meaning: An Introduction to Biblical Criticisms and Their Application.* Louisville: Westminster John Knox 1999.
Meeks, W. A. *Christ Is the Question.* Nashville: WJK 2006.
Merklein, H. "Die Umkehrpredigt bei Johannes dem Täufer and Jesus von Nazaret." *Biblische Zeitschrift* 25 1981 29–46.
Mettayer, A. « L'ésprit descendit du ciel tel comme un colombe ou lorsque le déplacement détermine le choix de la métaphore », *Studies in Religion / Sciences Religieuses* 24, 1 1995 433–439.
Metzger, B. *A Textual Commentary on the Greek New Testament.* Stuttgart: DBG 1994.
Meyer, M. *The Gospel of Thomas: The Hidden Sayings of Jesus.* San Francisco: HarperSanFrancisco 1992.
Michaels, J. R. "Almsgiving and the Kingdom Within: Tertullian on Luke 17:21." *Catholic Biblical Quarterly*, 60,3 1998 475–483.
Michiels, R. « La conception lucanienne de la conversion. » *Ephemerides theologicae lovanienses* 41 1965 4278.
Miller, R. J. *The Complete Gospels* (annotated scholars version). San Francisco: Harper 1994.
Moltmann, J. *The Trinity and the Kingdom of God: The Doctrine of God.* London: SCM 1981.
Montague, G. T. *The Holy Spirit: Growth of a Biblical Tadition: A Commentary on the Principal Texts of the Old and New Testaments.* New York: Paulist Press 1976.
Moule, C. F. D. *An Idiom Book of the New Testament Greek.* Cambridge: Cambridge UP 1968.
Moule, C. F. D. "The Holy Spirit in the Scriptures." *The Church Quarterly* 1971 3 279–287.
Mowery, R. L. "The articular references to the Holy Spirit in the Synoptic Gospels and Acts," *Papers of the Chicago Society of Biblical Research*, Amsterdam: 1957, and *Biblical Research* Chicago: 31 1986 26-45.
Muller, Jzn, F. *Grieksch woordenboek,* Groningen: Wolters 1926.
Mundhenk, N. A. "Translating 'Holy Spirit'", *Bible Translator* 48 1997 201–207.
Nasr, S. H. *Knowledge and the Sacred.* SUNY 1981.
Nathan, E. "Truth and Prejudice." *Ephemerides Theologicae Lovanienses* 83,4 2007 281-318.
Nave, G. D. Jr. *The Role and Function of Repentance in Luke-Acts.* Leiden: Brill 2002.
Nave, G. D. Jr. "'Repent, for the Kingdom of God Is at Hand': Repentance in the Synoptic Gospels and Acts." in Boda et al. 2006.
Neirynck, F. C. A. *The Gospel of Mark 1950–1990: A Cumulative Bibliography.* Leuven: Peeters 1992.
Nel, G., and Van Aarde, G. "Die Koninkryk van God by Jesus: 'n apokalipties-eskatologiese of eties-eskatologiese begrip?" *Hervormde-teologiese-studies.* 58,3 (2002) 1113–1133.
Nestle-Aland, *Novum Testamentum graece et latine,* Stuttgart: DBG 1984.
Neyrey, J. H. "The 'Noble Shepherd' in John 10: Cultural and Historical Background." *JBL* 120 2001 2 267–91.
Nodet, E. *The Historical Jesus? Necessity and Limits of an Inquiry.* New York: T&T Clark 2008.
Nolland, J. *Luke 1–9:20.* Word Biblical Commentary 35A. Dallas TX: Word Books 1989.
Nolland, J., *Luke 9:21–18:34,* Word Biblical Commentary 35B. Dallas TX: Word Books 1993.
Nolland, J. *Luke 18:3–24:53.* Word Biblical Commentary 35C. Dallas TX: Word Books 1993.
Oakman, D. E. *Jesus and the Peasants.* Eugene: Cascade 2008.
O'Donnell, J. "In Him and over Him: The Holy Spirit in the Life of Jesus." *Gregorianum*, 70, 1 1989.
Oropeza, B. (ed.), *Jesus and Paul, Festschrift James D.G. Dunn*, London: T&T Clark 2009 24–34.

Osei-Bonsu, J. "Anthropological Dualism in the NT." *Scott. J of Theology* 40 4 1987 571–90.

O'Toole, R. "The Kingdom of God in Luke-Acts." In Willis (ed) *The Kingdom of God* etc. 1987, 147–62.

Otto, R. *Mysticism East and West.* New York 1932.

Otto, R. *Reich Gottes und Menschensohn: ein religionsgeschichtlicher Versuch.* München: Beck'sche 1954.

Oussoren, P. *De Naardense Bijbel.* Vught: Skandalon 2004.

Owen, P. Review of Maurice Casey. *The Solution to the 'Son of Man' Problem. RBL* 2/9/2009.

Pagels, E. *Beyond Belief: The Secret Gospel of Thomas.* New York: Random House 2003.

Pagels, E. *The Gnostic Gospels.* New York: Vintage Books 1981.

Pagels, E. *The Gnostic Paul: Gnostic Exegesis of the Pauline Letters.* Philadelphia: Trinity Press International 1992.

Painter, J. "Tradition, History and Interpretation in John 10." *The Shepherd Discourse of John 10 and Its Context.* Studies by the Johannine Writings Seminar, ed. J. Beutler and R. T. Fortna. Cambridge: Cambridge UP1991 53–74.

Pannenberg, W. *Theology and the Kingdom of God.* Philadelphia: Westminster 1969.

Parratt, J. K. "The Holy Spirit and Baptism, Part I: The Gospels and the Acts of the Apostles." *Expository Times* 82 May 1971 231–35.

Partridge, C., and Gabriel T. *Mysticisms East and West: Studies in Mystical Experience.* Carlisle: Paternoster, 2003.

Paulsen, H. "Mk XVI 1–8." *Novum Testamentum,* 22, 1980, 152.

Pearson, B. A. *The* pneumatikos-psychikos *Terminology in 1 Corinthians: A Study in the Theology of the Corinthian Opponents of Paul and Its Relation to Gnosticism.* Society of Biblical Literature, Dissertation Series, Number Twelve, 1973.

Peerbolte, L., Bert, Jan. "Paul's Rapture: 2 Corinthians 12.2—4 and the Language of the Mystics." In Frances Flannery, *Experientia, vol. 1: Inquiry into Religious Experience in early Judaism and Christianity,* Leiden: Brill 2008.

Perdue, L. G. *Scribes, Sages, and Seers: The Sage in the Eastern Mediterranean World,* Göttingen: Vandenhoeck & Ruprecht 2008.

Perrin, N. *The Kingdom of God in the Teaching of Jesus.* London: SCM 1963/1975.

Perrin, N. *Rediscovering the Teaching of Jesus.* New York: Harper & Row 1967.

Pesce, M. *Le parole dimenticate di Gesù.* Verona: Mondadori 2004.

Phillips, P. "Casting out the Treasure: A New Reading of Matthew 13.52." *JSNT* 31,1 2008 3–24.

Pike, N. *Mystic Union: An Essay on the Phenomenology of Mysticism.* Ithaca: Cornell UP 1992.

Plisch, U-K. *Das Thomasevangelium: Originaltext mit Kommentar.* Stuttgart: DBG 2007.

Pohlmann, H. *Die Metanoia als Zentralbegriff der christlichen Frömmigkeit.* Leipzig: Hinrichs 1938.

Porsch, F. *Pneuma und Wort: Ein exegetischer Beitrag zur Pneumatologie des Johannesevangeliums,* Frankfurt a. M.: Knecht 1974.

Porter, S. E. "Jesus and the Use of Greek in Galilee." In *Studying the Historical Jesus: Evaluations of the State of Current Research* (B. Chilton, C. A. Evans). Leiden: Brill, 1994, 123–154.

Porter, S. E. "The Criterion of Greek Language and Its Context: A Further Response." *Journal for the Study of the Historical Jesus* 4.1 2006 69–74. Powell, E. *The Myth of the Lost Gospel,* Las Vegas: Symposium Press 2006.

Prieur, A. *Die Verkündiging der Gottesherrschaft: exegetische Studien zum lukanischen Verständnis von βασιλεία του θεου*, Tübingen: Mohr Siebeck 1996.
Pronce, R. *Trance and Possession States.* Montreal 1968.
Proulx, P., and Schokel, L. A. "Heb. 6,4–6 : εἰς μετάνοιαν ἀνασταυρουντας. *Biblica : Commentarii* 56 1975 193–209.
Quarles, Ch.L., « Jesus as merkabah mystic. » *JSHJ* 3,1 2005 5–22.
Rahlfs, A. *Septuaginta.* Stuttgart, DBG 1979.
Rajak, T. *Translation and Survival: the Greek Bible of the Ancient Jewish Diaspora*, Oxford: Oxford UP 2009.
Ramelli, I. "Luke 16:16: The Good News of God's Kingdom Is Proclaimed and Everyone Is Forced into It." *JBL* 127, 4 2008 737–58.
Ramelli, I., and D. Konstan, *Terms for Eternity: αἴνια and a'διoσ in Classical and Christian Texts.* Piscataway NJ: Gorgias 2007.
Ramsey, M. *Holy Spirit: A Biblical Study.* London: SPCK / GrandRapids: Eerdmans 1977.
Ratzinger, J. "*Metanoia* als Grundbefindlichkeit christlicher Existenz." In E. C. Suttner, *Busse und Beichte.* Regensburg: Pustet 1972.
Rêgopulos, G. C. "Jesus Christ, 'the Good Shepherd', An Interpretative Approach." *Deltio biblikôn meletôn*, 8 1989 5.
Reiser, M. "Die Prinzipien der biblischen Hermeneutik und ihr Wandel unter dem Einfluss der Aufklärung." In M. Mayordomo (ed), *Die prägende Kraft der Texte*, Stuttgart: SBS 2005.
Renard, P. *Jezus spreekt.* Amsterdam: Karnak 1983.
Richards, L. O. *Expository Dictionary of Bible Words.* Grand Rapids: Zondervan 1991.
Richter, S. *Metanoia; von der Busse und Beichte des Christen: Überlegung und Einübung*, Luzern / Stuttgart: Räber 1964.
Rienecker, F. *Sprachlicher Schlüssel zum griechieschen Neuen Testament.*Giessen: Brunnen 1992.
Riesenfeld, H. *The Gospel Tradition and Its Beginnings, The Gospel Tradition.* Philadelphia: Fortress 1970.
Roberts, J. M. "The Divine King and the Human Community in Isaiah's Vision of the Future." In Huffmon 1983.
Roberts, A., et al. *The Ante-Nicene Fathers.* Logos: Oak Harbor 1997.
Robinson, J. M. *The New Quest for the Historical Jesus.* London: SM Press 1959.
Robinson, J. M. *Kerygma und Historischer Jesus.* Zürich / Stuttgart Zwingli 1960.
Robinson, J. M., P. Hoffman, and J. S. Kloppenborg, eds. *The Critical Edition of Q.* Minneapolis: Fortress 2000.
Robinson, J. M. *The Gospel of Jesus: A Historical Search for the Original Good News.* San Francisco: HarperSanFrancisco 2005.
Robinson, J. M. *Jesus according to the Earliest Witnesses.* Minneapolis:Fortress 2007.
Rodd, C. S. "Spirit or Finger." *Expository Times* 72 1961 157–158.
Rogerson, J. W., and Lieu, J. M. *The Oxford Handbook of Biblical Studies.* Oxford: Oxford UP 2006.
Rollins, W. G. *Soul and Psyche: The Bible in Psychological Perspective.* Minneapolis: Fortress 1999.
Rowe, R. D. *God's Kingdom and God's Son: the Background to Mark's Christology from Concepts of Kingship in the Psalms.* Leiden: Brill 2002.
Rüegger, H.-U., "Hermeneutische Prinzipien traditioneller und kritischer Bibelauslegung." *Biblische Zt* NF, 51,2 2007 235–248.

Rüstow, A. "ENTOC YMWN ECTIN; Zur Deutung von Lukas 17:20–21." *Z. f. neutest. Wisschaft u. die Kunde der älteren Kirche* 51 1960 97–224.
Sabbe, M. "John 10 and Its Relationship to the Synoptic Gospels." *The Shepherd Discourse of John 10 and Its Context.* Studies by the Johannine Writings Seminar, ed. By J. Beutler and R. T. Fortna. Cambridge: Cambridge UP 1991.
Sanders, E. P. *Jesus and Judaism.* Philadelphia: Fortress, 1985.
Sasson, V. R. *The Birth of Moses and the Buddha: A Paradigm for the Comparative Study of Religions.* Sheffield: Sheffield Phoenix 2007.
Schaper, J. *Textualisierung der Religion.* Tübingen: Mohr Siebeck 2009.
Schaper, J. "'Scriptural Turn' und Monotheismus." In J. Schaper (ed), *Textualisierung der Religion.* Tübingen: Mohr Siebeck 2009 (b), 275–91.
Scharbert, J. "Fleisch, Geist und Seele in der Pentateuch-Septuagint." In J. Schreiner, ed., *Wort, Lied und Gottessspruch,* Festschrift. München: Echter 1872.
Schenke, L. *Das Rätsel von Tür und Hirt: Wer es löst, hat gewonnen! Trierer theologische Zeitschrift.*—105 1996.
Schlosser, J. *Le règne de Dieu dans les dits de Jésus,* 2 vols. Paris: Gabalda 1979.
Schmid, J. "Der Begriff der Seele im NT." In *Einsicht und Glaube,* Festgabe G. Söhngen (J. Ratzinger, ed.), 1962 12–31.
Schmidt, K. L. "Pneuma, Wind, Geist", *Theologische Zeitung* 4,5 1948 398.
Schnackenburg, R. *God's Rule and Kingdom,* Freiburg: Herder 1963.
Schneider, B., "Kata pneuma hagiôsunês", *Biblica: Commentarii* 48,3 1967 359-87
Schoemaker, W. R. *Use of* ruach *in the Old Testament and of* pneuma *in the New Testament: A Lexicographical Study,* Menominee, MI 1904.
Schröter, J. *Von Jesus zum Neuen Testament: Studien zur urchristlichen Theologiegeschichte und zur Entstehung des neutestamentlichen Kanons.* Tübingen: Mohr Siebeck 2007.
Schröter, J. "The Gospels as Eyewitness Testimony? A Critical Examination of Richard Bauckham. *Jesus and the Eyewitnesses. JSNT* 31,2 2008 195–209.
Schuon, F. *The Transcendent Unity of Religions.* Quest 1984.
Schweitzer, A. *Die Mystik des Apostel Paulus.* Tübingen: UTB 1980.
Schweitzer, A. *Von Reimarus zu Wrede.* 1906. English: *Quest of the Historical Jesus,* 1910.
Schweizer, E. "With the Holy Ghost and Fire." *Expository Times,* 65 1953 29.
Schweizer, E. "What Is the Holy Spirit? A Study in Biblical Theology." *Concilium: Theology in the Age of Renewal,* 1979, 128 ix-xvii.
Schweizer, E. *The Holy Spirit,* London: S.C.M. Press 1980 (German ed. 1978)
Schweizer, E. "The Kingdom of God and the Kingship of Christ in the Fourth Gospel." In *Neotestamentica et Philonica,* ed. D. E. Aune and T. Seland, Festschrift P. Borgen. Leiden: Brill 2003 215–232.
Segal, A. F. "The Afterlife as Mirror of the Self." *Experientia vol. 1, Inquiry into Religious Experience in Early Judaism and Christianity,* Leiden: Brill 2008.
Seligson, M. *The Meaning of* nephesh meth *in the Old Testament.* Diss. Helsinki 1951: Review in *J of Am Oriental Society* 74 1954 97.
Shedinger, R. F. "Kuhnian Paradigms and Biblical Scholarship: Is Biblical Studies a Science?" *JBL* 119, 3 (2000) 453–471.
Shepherd, W. H., Jr. *The Narrative Function of the Holy Spirit as a Character in Luke-Acts.* Atlanta, GA: Scholars Press 1994.
Sholem, G. *Major Trends in Jewish Mysticism.* New York: 1961.

Siffer-Wiederhold N., *La présence divine à l'individu d'après le Nouveau Testament*. Paris: Cerf 2005.

Simonis, A. J. *Die Hirtenrede im Johannes-Evangelium; Versuch einer Analyse von Johannes 10:1–18 nach Entstehung, Hintergrund und Inhalt* Roma 1967.

Simonis, W. *Jesus von Nazareth: Seine Botschaft vom Reiche Gottes und der Glaube der Urgemeinde: Historisch-kritische Erhellung der Ursprünge des Christentums*. Düsseldorf: Patmos 1985.

Smith, D. A. "Matthew and Q: the Matthean Deployment of Q and Mark in the Apocalyptic Discourse." *Ephemerides Theologicae Lovanienses*, 85 2009 99–116.

Smith, H. *Forgotten Truth*. San Francisco: HarperSanFrancisco 1976.

Smith, M. *The Secret Gospel*. Middletown CA: Dawn Horse 1984.

Snodgrass, K. *Stories with Intent: A Comprehensive Guide to the Parables of Jesus*. Grand Rapids: Eerdmans 2008.

Soesilo, D. "Translating 'the Kingdom of God' in the Malay Bible." *The Bible Translator* 52, 2002.

Sölle, D. *Mystik und Widerstand*. Hamburg: Hofmann u. Campe 1997.

Soulen, R., and Soulen, R. K. *Handbook of Biblical Criticism*. Louisville: Westminster John Knox 2001.

Spencer, R. A. *Orientation and Disorientation: Studies in Literary Criticism and Biblical Literary Criticism*. Pittsburgh: Pickwick 1980.

Spitaler, P. "Welcoming a Child as a Metaphor for Welcoming God's Kingdom: A Close Reading of Mark 10.13–16", *JSNT* 31,4 (2009), 423–446.

Staal, F., *Exploring Mysticism*. Harmondsworth: Penguin 1975.

Stacy, R. W. *Fear in the Gospel of Mark*, PhD diss., Louisville 1979.

Staten, H. "How the Spirit (almost) Became Flesh": Gospel of John, *Representations*, 41, Winter 1993.

Stettler, C. "Purity of Heart in Jesus' teaching: Mark 7:14–23 par, As an Expression of Jesus' Basileia Ethics." *J. Theological Studies*, NS, 55,2 2004 467–502.

Steyer, G. *Handbuch für das Studium des neutestamentlichen Griechisch , Band I, Formenlehre*, Berlin: Evangelische Verlagsanstalt 1963

Steyer, G. *Handbuch für das Studium des neutestamentlichen Griechisch, Band II, Satzlehre*. Berlin: Evangelische Verlagsanstalt 1992.

Stonehouse, N. B. "Repentance, Baptism and the Gift of the Holy Spirit." *The Westminster Theological Journal* 13n 1950 1–18.

Strobel, A. *Erkenntnis und Bekenntnis der Sünde in neutestamentlicher Zeit*. Stuttgart: Calwer 1968.

Suttner, E. Chr. *Busse und Beichte*. Regensburg: Pustet 1972.

Swanson, J. *Dictionary of Biblical Languages with Semantic Domains, Greek: New Testament*, Logos Research Systems, Inc., 1997.

Swartz, S. "The Holy Spirit: Person and Power: The Greek Article." *The Bible Translator*, 44,1 1993.

Swete H. B. *The Holy Spirit in the New Testament: a Study if Primitive Christian Teaching*. London: Macmillan 1910

Swetnam, J. "Bestowal of the Spirit in the Fourth Gospel." *Biblica: Commentarii*, 74, 4 1993 556–576.

Taeger, J. W. *Der Mensch und sein Heil: Studien zum Bild des Menschen und zu Sicht der Bekehrung bei Lukas*, Gütersloh: Mohn 1982.

Teilhard de Chardin, P. *The Divine Milieu*. New York: Harper & Row 1960.

Theissen G., and Winter D. *The Quest for the Plausible Jesus: The Question of Criteria*, Louisville / London: WestminsterJohnKnox, 2002, Original German: *Die Kriterienfrage in der Jesusforschung*. U.P Fribourg, Fribourg.

Thiagarajah, D. S. "The Image of the Good Shepherd in the Fourth Gospel." *Christian Conference of Asia / Commission on Theological Concerns, CTC Bulletin*, 17,1 2001 28–30.

Thimmes, P. "Fear as a Reaction to Jesus in the Markan Gospel." In *Proceedings of the Eastern Great Lakes and Mid-Western Biblical Societies*, 1989.

Thompson E. F. METANOEW *and* METAMELEI *in Greek Literature until 100 a.D., including Discussion of Their Cognates and of Their Hebrew Equivalents*. Chicago: Chicago UP 1908.

Thümmel, H. G., ed. *Pneuma. Funktionen des theologischen Begriffs in frühchristlicher Literatur. Gnomon:* kritische Zeitschrift für die gesamte klassische Altertumswissenschaft. Berlin: Weidmannsche 1925.

Thümmel, J. P. *Pneuma*, review of Dünzl, *Pneuma*, 2000, *Gnomon*, Bd 75 2003 262-65.

Thurston, Bonnie. "Faith and Fear in Mark's Gospel." *The Bible Today* 23 (1985).

Tillich, P. *Systematic Theology* I, Chicago 1951.

Todoroff B. *Een verlangen naar eenheid*, Budel: Damon 2006.

Tragan, P. R. « La parabole du 'pasteur' et ses explications : Jean 10 :1–18. » *StudAns*, 67, Roma 1980.

Tuckett, C. M. *Q and the History of Early Christianity: Studies in Q*, Edinburgh: T&T Clark 1996.

Turner, J. D. "The History of Religions Background in John 10." *The Shepherd Dscourse of John 10 and Its Cntext*. Studies by the Johannine Writings Seminar (J. Beutler, R. T. Fortna, eds). Cambridge: Cambridge UP 1991 33–52.

Underhill, E. *Mysticism: A Study of the Nature and Development of Man's Spiritual Consciousness*. London: Methuen, 1911.

Underhill, E. *The Essentials of Mysticism and Other Essays*. Oxford: One World, 1995.

van Belle, G. *The Death of Jesus in the Fourth Gospel*. Leuven: Peeters, 2007.

van de Kemp, H. "The Tension between Psychology and Theology: The Etymological Roots." *J of Psychology and Theology* 10 Summer 1982, 105–12.

van de Kemp, H., "The tension between psychology and theology: an anthropological solution." *J of Psychology and Theology* 10 Fall 1982, 205–211.

van der Leeuw G. *Phänomenologie der Religion*, 1933.

van der Walt, T. *Die Koninkryk van God—naby!* Kampen: Kok, 1962. (The Kingdom of God—at hand!).

van Lohuizen, W. "Transformatie van emotie in gevoel" (Transformation of emotion into feeling), in: *De Soefi-gedachte*, 50 Sep 1996 Sep, 17–19.

van Lommel, P. *Near-death Experiences in Survivors of Cardiac Arrest: a Prospective Study in the Netherlands*, The Lancet 358, 2039-45 2001.

van Lommel, P. *Consciousness Beyond Life*, New York: HarperOne, 2010 (forthcoming in German, French and others). Originally Dutch: *Eindeloos Bewustzijn*. Kampen: Ten Have 2007.

van Oyen, G. "Marcus 10.13–216: als was men een kind." *Nederlands Theologisch Tijdschrift* 57 2003.

van Ruysbeek, E. *Mystiek en mysterie*, Deventer: Ankh-Hermes, 1992.

Vanhoozer, K. J. *Theological Interpretation of the New Testament: A Book-by-Book Survey*. Grand Rapids: Baker, 2008.

Vena, O. D. *The parousia and Its Rereadings: The Development of the Eschatological Consciousness in the Writings of the New Testament*. New York: Peter Lang, 2001.

Verhoeven, C. "The Meaning of metanoia." *Metanoia*, Spring 1994.
Verma, G. *Searching for the Real Jesus*. London: SCM 2009
Waaijman, K. *Spiritualiteit: vormen, grondslagen, methoden*, Gent / Kampen: Carmelitana / Kok 2000. Also available in English: *Spirituality, Forms, Foundations, Methods*. Leuven: Peeters, 2002.
Walter, Gingrich, F. Wilbur, and Danker, F. W. A *Greek-English Lexicon of the New Testament and Other Early Christian Literature*. Chicago: University of Chicago Press 1979.
Webster's Third New International Dictionary, 3 vols, Encyclopedia Britannica, Chicago 1981.
Weier, W. "Geist und Psyche in tiefenpsychologischer und phänomenologischer Perspektive." *Freiburger Zeitschrift für Philosophie und Theologie*, 41 1994 155–87.
Weren, W. "Portetten van Jezus in de Evangeliën: een pleidooi voor pluraliteit", *Tijdschrift v Theologie*, 48 2008 (Portaits of Jesus in the Gospels: a plea for plurility) 367–75.
Westall, M. R. "The Scope of the Term "Spirit of God" in the Old Testament." *Indian Journal of Theology* 26 1977 29–43.
White, V. *Soul and Psyche: An Enquiry into the Relationship of Psychiatry and Religion*. New York: Harper, 1960.
Witherington, B. III. *The Jesus Quest: The Third Search for the Jew of Nazareth*. Downers Grove IL: InterVarsity Press, 1995.
Wikgren, A. *The Greek New Testament*. Stuttgart: Bibelgesellschaft, 1983.
Willis, W. *The Kingdom of God in 20th century interpretation*. Peabody: Hendrickson, 1987.
Windisch, H. *Die Frömmigkeit Philos und ihre Bedeutung für das Christentum; eine religionsgeschichtliche Studie*. Leipzig: 1909 60–62.
Wolff, H. W. "Das Thema 'Umkehr' in der alttestamentlichen Profetie." *Z. f. Theologie u. Kirche* 48 1951 129–48.
Woods R. *Understanding Mysticism*. Garden City NY: Image Books / Doubleday 1980
Wrede, W. *Das Messiasgeheimnis in den Evangelien*. Göttingen: Vandenhoeck & Ruprecht 1901.
Wrede, W. "Μετάνοια Sinnesänderung?" *Z. f. die neutest. Wissenschaft u. die Kunde des Urchristentums* 1 1900 66–69.
Wyrwa, D., "Seelenverständnis bei Irenäus von Lyon." *Ψυχή—Seele-anima, Festschrift für Karin Alt* (J Holzhausen, ed.), Stuttgart / Leipzig 1998 301–34.
Young, F. W. "Luke 13:1–9." *Interpretation*, 31 (Jan. 1977) 59–63.
Younger, P. "A New Start towards a Doctrine of the Spirit." *Canadian Journal of Theology*, 13 1967 123–33.
Zerwick, M., and Grosvenor M. A *Grammatical Analysis of the Greek New Testament*. Roma: Pontifico Istituto Biblico 1996.
Zimmerman, R. *Kompemdium der Gleihnisse Jesu*, Gütersloh: Verlagshaus 2007.
Zmijewski J. *Die Eschatologiereden des Lukas-Evangeliums : eine traditions- und redaktionsgeschichtliche Untersuchung zu Lk 21,5–36 und Lk 17,20–37*. Bonn: Hanstein 1972.
Zwiep, A. W. "Assumptus est in caelum." *The Fourth Durham-Tübingen Research Symposium on Resurrection, Transfiguration and Exaltation in Old Testament, Ancient Judaism and Early Christianity*, Tübingen, September 1999, Tübingen: Mohr Siebeck 2001. 323–49.

Index

Agathos, 132–33n38, 222
Aphiêmi, see Forgiveness
Aphorism, 9, 9n11, 10, 75, 151
Apollumi, 183, 208, 225, 229–30, 230n21, 230n22, 238, 347
Aramaic (language), 76–78, 180–81, 333
'As a little child.' *See under* Child/children
Assumptions (of this study), 4, 4n3
Augustine, 36–37, 43, 44, 307, 350

Awe, 42, 45, 45n71, 96n10

Bach, xvi
Baptism
    and the article, 252n11
    and early Christians, 44, 147
    and ecstasy, 303
    and *en* or dative, 281nn49–50
    of fire, 267, 267n4, 268
    and immersion, 20, 21, 198, 267, 269n12, 269n13, 323
    and the Holy Spirit, 20, 268, 277
    of Jesus, 254, 257, 259, 260n27, 266, 278, 294, 297
    in the pericopes, 267, 268, 272
    and *pneuma,* 258n23
    of repentance, 196, 197
    scrutiny of texts on, 269
    and 'self,' 223
    spirit, 268n11
    See also John the Baptist; Matthew
Basileia tou theou See under Kingdom of God
Beatitudes, the, 21, 50, 148–49, 151, 153–55 passim, 203
'Became a living being,' 26–27n12
Being in spirit, see *En pneumati*
Belonging. *See under* Child/children
Bible
    exegesis, present-day, 46
    as human construct, 49
    Jesus logia in, 53
    metanoia in, 202, 343
    psuchê in, 172, 180, 184, 224, 226
    See also Criticism, biblical
Bios/zôê, 66, 66n51, 176, 176n14, 177n15, 177n18, 178n21
Buber, Martin, 39
Buddhism, 72, 230, 347

Child/children
    'As a little child,' 139–40
    and Belonging, 140–42
    Characteristics of, 142–43
    and *hôs to paidon,* xvn1
    Jesus on, 99, 139–48, 165
    and the Kingdom, 140n2
    newborn, 149n30
    and *paidion/pais,* 139n1
    and 'Receiving and Entering,' 146–48
    slaughter by Herodes, 236
    and 'The Such Ones,' 140n4, 141n5, 144, 159
    and 'Turning,' 145–46
Christians, earliest, 8, 8n10
Clairvaux, Bernard de, 37
Clementina, 191
Clement of Alexandria, 61n32, 196, 238n9
'Cloud of unknowing,' 31, 31n26
Consciousness, 34 (defined)
    and ecstasy/*ekstasis,* 20, 301n6, 302–7 passim, 319, 320, 341, 350, 351
    inner, 84
    of Jesus, 20, 124, 235, 287
    and Jesus' message, 124
    and Kingdom, 21, 89, 99, 156, 161, 162, 340, 343
    and knowing, 25n8
    and knowledge and experience, 30–31
    level(s) of, xv, 24, 70, 70n54, 71, 75, 202, 338
    of limitation/smallness, 263

and *metanoia,* 194, 343, 348
and mind, 29
mystical, xv, 19, 24–25, 32, 35
Origen on, 26n11
and parable of the fig tree, 208
pathological, 36
pericopes on, 314
and *pneuma,* 85, 266, 272, 273, 322
and Presence, 35, 257, 262, 265
and *psuchê,* 176
raised/raising, 34, 263
and religion, 28–30, 49
and the 'sacred,' 50
and sacred texts, 52, 68, 69
of self, 32, 228n20
self vs. expanded, 32
and *sola scriptura,* 32
spiritual, 19
transforming, 23, 99, 195, 203, 343
See also Mysticism; Near-death experience
Continuity, 196–200 passim, 63, 65, 185, 189 *See also* under Metanoia
Conversion, 195 (defined)
and change and transformation, 200–1, 243, 343, 344
and the Kingdom, 101
and *metanoia,* 170, 187, 190–92, 201–2
and participation, 45, 45n73
Criticism, biblical, 47–78
deconstructive (poststructuralist), 48, 72, 73
form, 74–75
form, source, and redaction, 62
implications of, 68–74
literary, 48
and logia as sacred text, 59
of NT, 330, 331, 338
Q as instrument of, 54
reader-response, 75
redaction, 75
source, 74
structural, 75
See also Method
Cross, words from the, 288–98 passim
Cruz, Juan de la, 17, 37

Davidic kingdom, 85, 95, 97, 101, 105, 124, 166, 197
Decontextualization, 67–68, 71, 119, 332, 339
Dechomai, 147n27
Didômi, 125n3, 183, 214n2, 216
Disciples
as audience, 32, 114, 149
attitude of, 57
and the Beatitutdes, 154–55
and the children, 140, 144, 147
at the Cross, 289–90
and *entos humin,* 121
and fasting, 198
forsaking Jesus, 296
and healing, 108
and the Holy Spirit, 349
'inward heart' of, 149n31
Jesus in, 275
and Jesus' words, 61, 61n33, 64
and the Kingdom, 112, 113, 114n2
and laying done one's life, 170, 181, 224, 329
and love one another, 21, 41, 213–18 passim, 224, 329, 335–46 passim
and *metanoia,* 188
and the *mustêrion,* 125–31 passim
names of, 78
and *psuchê,* 346
and *ptôchos,* 151
and rapture, 315, 317, 320, 351
and self, 234, 243
and Sermon on the Mount, 107
and sin, 205, 209, 344, 345
and spirit, 45
and transformation, 45, 46, 84
Dunamis. See *Energy*

Eckhart, Meister, 38
Ecstasy, 299–315 passim, 320–25 passim
and apocalyptic writing, 95
interpretations of, 299
in mysticism and literature, 304–8, 350–51
in the NT, 308–12
and Paul, 300n4, 320
the term, 301–4

INDEX

See also *Ekstasis;* Entasy; Rapture;
Transformation
Êggiken, 103–11 passim, 203, 333, 336
Ekstasis, 299–321, 350–1
   as spirit inside, 20
   literary descriptions of, 95
   and the NT, 22, 299–322 passim
   and 'spirit,' 336
   as term and concept, 248
   translation of, 337
   See also Ecstasy; Rapture
En pneumati, 264–87 passim
   as 'in spirit,' 20, 248
   case with preposition, 251, 255, 263
   in the NT, 265–80
   and the Spirit, 258, 348
   in text analysis, 284
Encyclopedie van de Mystiek, 46
Energy/*dunamis*
   as Holy Spirit, 252, 258, 340, 341
   and the Kingdom of God, 85, 97, 99, 156, 210
   as potential, 210n67
   as strength, 97–98, 333, 338
   and transformation, 203
   and words of Jesus, xvii, 9–10
Enlightenment, 33, 49
Enstasy, 36, 300, 306–8, 350
Entolê, 215, 219, 221, 222
Entos (humin), 114–24 passim, 116, 116n5, 120, 120n23, 120n24, 121, 126n4, 333
Enstasis, 305n26, 322
Eschatology, 84n4 (defined), 81–93 passim
   apocalyptic, 58n22
   futuristic, 86n9
   interpretations of, 86, 91–93, 117n11
   and Jesus, 12, 12n35, 13, 56, 88, 101, 119
   Jewish, 85n7
   as Last Day, 81
   and Mark, 90, 197
   and Matthew, 134n45
   'realized,' 91, 112, 118, 119
   and Sower parable, 131n29
   and transformation, 211
   See also *Psuchê*
Eschaton

   and fire, 267n6
   and Jesus, 163
   and Jesus' contemporaries, 95
   and the Kingdom of God, 81–90, 100–23 passim
   and the NT, 95
   See Model, eschatological
Euaggelion
   found in the logia, xv, xvi, 3, 8, 59
   as divine message, 10, 59, 104, 104n11, 113, 133, 359
   as good message, 8, 14, 104, 337
   in the presence of the Kingdom, 188
Exousia, 97, 98, 215, 219, 222
Exegesis, 46, 47n1, 48, 48n2, 72, 87. *See also* Criticism, biblical
Experience(s)
   and believe and trust, 17
   contemplative, 43
   and consciousness, 29, 124
   deciding, 163
   and destruction, 230n21
   divine, 17, 38, 43, 44, 198, 256
   and ecstasy, 301, 305, 308, 321, 350, 351
   of *ekstasis,* 300, 303, 313–17 passim
   and enstasy, 306, 350
   existential, 5
   of God as king, 92, 107
   as gradual awakening, 29
   inner, 51, 95, 119, 266, 350
   and inward/outward presence, 20
   Jesus', 18, 287
   of the Kingdom, 99, 119, 124, 125, 163, 338
   and knowledge and consciousness, 30–32, 126
   of loss, 228n15
   and *metanoia,* 189
   pasquale, 10n13
   as *psuchê,* 174n7(3)
   religious, 57, 97, 300n3
   and sacred texts, 68
   of spirit, 273, 278
   and spirituality, 17
   See also Mysticism; Near-death experiences

'Faith is a hindrance,' 5, 5n4
Forgiveness/*Aphiêmi*, 92, 101, 136, 170, 192, 196–98 passim, 204–9 passim, 243, 344
Forsaking, 294–97 passim

Geenna, 186, 237, 238–39
Genre. *See under* Method
Gnosis. See *Knowledge*
Gnostic Gospels, The, xvi, xviii
Gnostic Paul, The, xv, xvi, xviii
Good Shepherd pericope, 213–23 passim
Gospel of John. *See* John, Gospel of
Gospel of Luke. *See* Luke, Gospel of
Gospel of Mark. *See* Mark, Gospel of
Gospel of Matthew. *See* Matthew, Gospel of
Gospel of Peter. *See* Peter, Gospel of
Gospel of Q. *See* Q, Gospel of
Gospel of Thomas. *See* Thomas, Gospel of
Greek (language), 76–78, 178–80 passim, 302–3
Gregory of Nissa, 37

Hamartêma, hamartanô, hamartia, See under Sin
Hammerskjöld, Dag, 38
Handbooks, the, 33–34
Hasmonaeans, 105
Hebrew (language), 179–81, 184–85, 313, 333
Hellenism, 30, 43, 77, 178–80, 185, 195
Herodes, 236
Holy Spirit
    and Baptism, 264, 267, 268, 269n13, 281–87, 330, 335
    blasphemy against, 204
    body as temple of, 271n19
    as Counselor, 247
    and David, 269, 349
    dunamis of, 98
    and *ekstasis*, 312, 314
    and fire, 268n10
    and holy spirit, 265, 322, 330
    in the individual, 262, 349
    and Jesus, 270, 289
    and the Kingdom, 136, 137
    at Pentecost, 256
    as Person, 252, 253, 325
    and *pneuma*, 249n1, 251n8, 252–53, 256, 257, 279n43, 335, 337, 348
    and the Spirit, 259
    and spirit, 261n28, 262, 266, 277, 278, 280, 322
    traditional interpretation of, 256, 256n20
    and the Trinity, 250, 258, 261
    See also *pneuma*

Idou, 123, 123n27
Ignatius of Antioch, 37
Immanence, divine, 263, 350
Inner Strength, 97–99
Isaac of Niniveh, 37

James, King, 116
Jesus
    as Christ, 5
    the Church on, 92
    on conversion, 45n73
    'contextual,' 12
    and Continuity, 196–200
    eschatological, 11–15
    following, 228, 228n12
    grieving, 235, 235n6
    life of, 15, 15n44
    as *merkabah* mystic, 28n17
    Message of, xv, xviii, 6, 53, 59–60, 164, 242, 334, 341, 345
    as messiah, 8, 12, 18, 59, 92, 127
    as messenger, 7, 13–16
    as mystic and messenger, 4, 8, 13–16, 30, 42, 42n63, 43, 43n65
    native tongue of, 76, 76n65
    quest for, 8, 10–17
    research of vertical vs. horizontal, 16–18
    and seeing and hearing, 95, 95n5, 129, 129n17, 133n35
    words of as sacred, 4, 7
    See also Child/children; *Euaggelion,* Jesus Seminar; Kingdom of God; Logia; Mysticism; Poor, the; Poor in spirit, the

INDEX

Jesus Seminar, 12, 64, 67, 127, 135n46, 210
John, Gospel of
    and the Good Shepherd, 213–23
    and 'laying down life', 213–23
    and Greek and Jewish culture, 179
    on Jesus as mystic, 43
    on 'knowledge,' 31
    life/self, 225, 227
John the Baptist
    on baptism, 106, 255, 269–70, 281, 281n46, 330, 335
    on the Kingdom, 170
    on repentance, 106, 189, 197
    and the Spirit, 254, 323, 330, 334
Jonge, H. J. de, xvi, xviii
Judaism
    to Christianity, 198
    contemporary (to Jesus), 102, 186, 333
    and the evangelists, 176
    and first-century Palestine, 77
    and Greek-Hellenistic influences, 178–79
    later, 185
    mysticism in, 30, 43
    See also under Continuity

Kairos, 103n6, 105, 105n12, 106, 187n1
Kalos, 132–33n38, 222, 222n15
Kerugma, 11n17
Kêrussô, 104, 104n9, 106, 337
Kêrussôn, 106, 106n14
Khan, Inayat, 23, 42
Kingdom, 94–95, 99. *See also* Davidic kingdom; Kingdom of God
Kingdom of God, 81–164 passim, 342–3
    alternative views of, 81–82, 91–95 passim, 95n2, 100, 117–20
    Basileia tou theou
        as foundational concept, xxi
        as inner potential, xv
        as a kingdom, 82
        and the logia, 22, 81, 110n25
        and mysticism, 5, 10, 81, 82
        in NA27, 103, 115, 141, 150
        and the poor, 149
        relevance of, 336
    in the Synoptics, 82n3, 100n2
    as eschatological, 68, 86n9
    as eschaton/inner reality, 83–93
    glory of, 94–9
    as inner potential, xv, 343
    as inner strength, 97–9
    'is inside,' 116–17
    inside, or in the midst of, 120–21
    introduction to, 81–83
    and Jesus, 14, 17, 18, 100–1
    in Jewish community, 100
    and mysticism, 5
    and the *mustêrion,* 126–30 passim
    other-worldly view of, 93
    parables on, 134–37
    partaking, 99
    and *paratêrêsis,* 122–23
    and not recognizing, 211n69
    and the Sower parable, 131–34
    as a term, 94n1
    this-worldly view of, 93
    and *waltet/walten,* 95, 95n4
    what, 94–99 passim, 125–38 passim
    when, 100–113 passim
    where, 114–24 passim
    for whom, 139–161 passim
    See also Eschaton
Kingship, 96–97
Knowledge/*gnosis,* 30n25 (defined)
    as altered state, 25n8
    of the disciples, 126
    and ecstasy, 308n32
    and experience and consciousness, 30–32
    experiential, 34
    inner, 9, 25n8, 123
    of Jesus, 15, 57
    Matthew on, 108
    and *Metanoeô/metanoia,* 190, 190n6
    and *mustêrion,* 127
    and mysticism, 24, 36
    and *Paredôken,* 294
    and religion, 48
    required to enter the Kingdom, 157
    search for of Jesus, 11, 15
    and the Synoptics, 108
    transmittal of, 62, 75
Koilia, 291n8

Lactantius, 191, 193, 199, 344
Lambanô, 215, 219, 221–22, 221n14
Last Judgment, 84n4, 101
Latin Vulgata,
Law, William, 38
'Laying down life', *see under* Good Shepherd
Logia, the, xv–xvi, 3n1
   absence of eschaton in, 92
   authenticity of, 60–61, 65n47
   and children, 139–46 passim
   comparative study of, 69, 69n53, 74–75, 75n61
   and criticism, 75–76
   as disciple-directed, 154
   as genre, 8n9 19, 53–68 passim
   and Gospel of Paul, xv, 128
   and Gospel of Thomas, 88–89
   as independent sacred message, 8–10
   as individual text units, 67–75
   and inner perceiving, 129–30
   interpretation of, 47, 47n1
   Kingdom of God in, 94, 100–6, 134–37, 161, 342
   as meaning beyond the word, 47–76
   Jesus as mystic in, 15–16
   language of, 76–77
   and mysticism, 3–7, 23–46 passim, 337–38
   and narrative, 3n1, 4, 7–10 passim, 19, 47–71 passim, 153, 199, 209, 219, 220, 231, 232, 330–32 passim, 340, 346
   as oldest remembrance of Jesus, 60–62
   and the Other, 207–11
   and poor in spirit, 148–155 passim
   as sacred text (message of Jesus), 7, 59–60, 70, 70n54
   as sayings, xv–17 passim, 25, 43, 47, 53–59 passim, 64–69 passim, 71–77 passim, 88n10, 93n28, 146, 225–26, 228, 329–31 passim, 347
   with 'self' instead of 'life,' 227
   on sin and forgiveness, 204
   verticality in, 16–18
   See also *Metanoia; Psuchê*

Lord's Prayer, 46, 87, 106–7
Luke, Gospel of
   and ecstasy, 351
   entos humin in, 121
   on the Kingdom, 151, 157
   on life/self, 224–32
   on the nature of humans, 206
   and *pneuma hagion,* 257
   and the rich man, 239
   and the Sermon on the Mount/Plain, 149
   and the Spirit, 256
   and the transfiguration, 45

Mark, Gospel of
   ending of, 317, 317n49
   and the Kingdom of God, 89, 89n14, 147
   on life/self, 224–32
   and the logion, 231
   on the *mnêmeion,* 316
   narrative of, 65n46
   use of *pneuma* in, 257
   and *pushên/tithêmi,* 216
   and the transfiguration, 45, 45n72
Matthew, Gospel of
   and Jesus' cry, 296
   and the Kingdom, 81n1, 157
   on life/self, 224–32
   and *pneuma,* 251, 259
   and the 'poor in spirit,' 149
   and *psuche,* 236
   and the Sermon on the Mount/Plain, 149
   and the Spirit, 256
Message of Jesus. See *Euaggelion*
Metanoia/metanoeô, 187–211 passim, 19, 67, 105, 170,, 242, 343–5
   and continuity, 196–204
   in the logia, 187–9, 207–11
   and sin and forgiveness, 204–7
   as term/concept, 189–96
Method/methodology
   bottom up/top down, 5, 6–7, 329, 344
   deconstruction, 73
   (de)contextualization, 67–68, 71, 119, 332, 339

and exegesis, 72–74
and genre, 7, 19, 53–55, 66, 66n50, 68–9, 71–2, 74, 331–32, 339
implications of, 68
lines of approach to, 7–8
revisited, 74–76
and 'sayings Gospels,' xvii
task of, 51–52
See also Criticism, biblical
Middle Ages, 46
Min
  active, 29
  change of, 21, 99, 103, 105, 159, 187, 281, 344, 345
  and ecstasy, 299, 300–10 passim, 313–14, 321, 324, 341, 350
  as element of human being, 69n1
  and-heart
    and the Kingdom of God, 16, 132, 329, 334
    and *psuchê*, 20, 26, 169, 170n1, 173, 182, 183, 216–26 passim, 233–38 passim, 258, 336–37, 346
    transformation of, 19, 25, 38, 95, 144, 156–61 passim, 188, 194n23, 208, 243
  and Jesus' words in, 61
  and matter and spirit, 32n32
  medical, 35
  and the Message, 242
  open, 53, 68, 242
  as psyche, 27, 170, 173
  and receiving, 147
  and self, 213–23, 224–32
  and spirit, 32n32
    See also *Metanoia/metanoeô*; *Psuchê*; Psyche; Repentance
Model, eschatological, 90–91
Modernism, 11, 12n25, 33, 59, 60, 60n28, 116
Mozart, W. A., 1, 1n1
Mustêrion, the. *See under* Kingdom of God
Mysticism, 23–46 passim, 337–38
  apex, 18
  categories of, 19
  Christian, 17, 33, 43, 44, 45, 165, 305, 330
  classical, 335
  defined, 5, 18–19, 24–25, 27–34 passim, 288
  and ecstasy, 300–7 passim, 313, 350
  God, 43
  in the gospels, 42–46
  gradual, 35, 35n41
  ineffability of, 34, 36
  and 'inner path,' 46n75
  of Jesus, 3, 17–18, 116, 341
  key concepts of, 3–6, 15, 46, 50, 81, 163, 165, 334, 339
  and the Kingdom of God, 100, 164
  and knowledge, 36
  Paul on, 43, 52
  pure, 123
  and rapture, 315
  in realization, 42, 50, 53
  and the senses, 130
  as spiritual closeness, 25n6
  and spiritual duality, 43, 43n66
  and spirituality and religion, 46
  and testimonies, 24–25, 31–32, 36–38, 156, 160
  texts on, 32
  and the transfiguration, 45, 45n70
  words in, 3
  worldly, 96
  See also Consciousness; Experience; Presence; Texts, types of; Testimonies; Transformation
Mustêrion. See under *Kingdom of God*

Nag Hammadi Library, 53
Near-death experiences (NDE), 31, 50n5
Nephesh, 169, 172–86 passim, 216n7
Nova Vulgata, 191
Numinous (defined), 25n9

Orality/oral tradition, 62–68 passim
  and Clement of Alexandria, 61n32
  of Jesus' words, 61, 62, 62nn34–37, 63n40, 331
  and lost sheep parable, 209n60
  and pericopes, 163
  and priority of, 10
  and criticism, 74
  and sacred words, 64n43

and 'sayings Gospels,' xviii, 64n44
and Thomas, 54
Origen, 26, 26n11, 44, 196, 238n9

Paenitentia/poenitentia, 191, 193, 194
Paidion, 139n1
Palestine, first-century
    bilingual, 77
    Hellenistic, 77, 178, 185
    and Jesus' message, 75
    literacy in, 64
    orality in, 62
    and the 'timeless now,' 106
    and vertical versus horizontal, 16
Palin, 220n11, 221n14, 222
Parables, 123, 135, 137, 142–3, 157, 165, 207–10, 333, 338, 343
    as evangelists' message, 59n27
    hard to understand, 129
    and inner teaching, 130
    and Jesus texts, 59n27, 60–1, 61n29, 125–26
    and Jesus Seminar, 64
    and the Kingdom, 19, 134–37
        as clue to, 125
        as explanation of, 20, 67, 137–38
        and inner reality, 88–89
        inside, 116, 123, 330, 333
        Matthean, 157–58
        and the merchant, 136n48
        and not recognizing, 211n69
    of the lost sheep, 98n19, 209
    Lukan, 207–10
    mustard seed, 143
    and the *mustêrion,* 82, 126, 128–29, 133
    mysticism in, 337
    and the oral tradition, 63, 209–60
    and Paul, 128
    self-evidence of, 106
    and the story of Jesus, 87
    See also Sower parable
Paradigm, 13, 180–81, 201
Partaking, 99
Paratêrêsis, 122, 122–23n26
Paratithêmi, 297, 297n35
Parousia, 21, 44, 85, 85n7, 101, 166, 330

Pascal, Blaise, 38
Paul
    *arrhêta rhêmata*3, 52, 52n8, 133n41
    and *ekstasis,* 300n4, 313–14, 315, 320
    and the Kingdom, 87, 101, 347, 351
    mysticism of, 30, 44, 52, 124, 300
    on pneumatic versus psychic, 280
    on the spirit, xv, 275–76, 278, 300, 340
    on suffering, 101
    and the 'unutterable,' 52, 52n8, 133n41
    writings of, 57
    See also Gnostic Paul, The
Penance, 190–202 passim, 343
Penitence, 19, 21, 170, 180–203 passim, 211, 242, 243, 330, 343–44
Peter, 213–14, 218, 223, 231, 311–12, 289, 351
Philip, 41, 78, 311, 314
Philo of Alexandria, 307
Pisteuein, 107, 107n18
Pisteuete en tôi euaggeliôi, 103, 105, 106, 107–8, 203
Pisteuô, 108, 337
Pistis, 108, 108n20
Phobos, 45n71, 309, 316, 316n41, 317, 318n45, 319–20
Pneuma, 247–322 passim, 333–41, 348–50
    (an)arthrous use, 20, 249–58 passim, 261n28, 265, 266, 268n10, 271, 274, 283, 285, 335, 337
    concept of, 249–63, 322–5
    four forms of, 258–62 passim
    literature on, 252–53
    as Spirit, xv, 249–60 passim
    translation of, 254–58
    See also under En pneumati,, Pneumatikos, Holy Spirit
Pneumatikos/psuchikos, 184, 220–1, 340, 343
Poor, the, 82. *See also* Poor in spirit, the
Poor in spirit, the, xvii, 82, 139, 148–55 passim, 165, 337, 349. *See also* Poor, the
Presence, passim
    inner, xvii
    divine, 10, 15, 18–20

inside the human being, 164
Jesus on, 333, 341
and Jesus' contemporaries, 95
as key concept, 3–6, 18–20, 46, 339
and 'Kingdom,' 332, 334–35, 342–43
and the logia, 10
as *mustêrion,* 127
and mysticism, 3–6 passim, , 23–46, 165
and the parables, 138
as a present, 156, 160
and Receiving, 147–48
as salvation, 204
and Sufism, 145
triggers transformation, 338
Protestantism, 11, 194
Psalms, Book of, 43, 124, 152
Pseudo-Dionysius the Areopagite, 37, 74
Psuchê, 169–241 passim, 213–42, 345–8
and another paradigm, 180–82
classification of use in the Bible, 183–84
dictionaries on, 173–74
emotional aspects of, 233–36 passim
in the Epistles, 26–28, 154
as human being, 20–21n51
as life/self, 172–86
interpretations of, 173nn4–6, 177n13
literature on, 174–76, 184–86, 216n7
losing/saving, 20, 169, 180–83 passim, 215, 215n6, 224–32 passim, 243, 263, 330, 335, 341, 345–47 passim
meanings of, 173–74n7, 216–21, 224–32
physical aspects of, 236–41 passim
and self in pericopes, 169–89, 213–32
and transformation, 172–85 passim, 233–41passim
translations of, 173n4
See also under Mind-and-heart, Psyche
Psuchikos, see *pneumatikos*
Psyche
and *airô,* 222
and ecstasy, 301, 302, 305, 307
and Geenna, 239
and Gethsemane, 294, 296
in the gospels, 183, 233, 236–37, 239
and Jesus, 172, 219
and manifestation of mysticism, 25
and 'self,' 223
and *soma,* 179, 186
totality of, 200
and transformation, 35, 46, 144, 196, 203
and Paul's 'trichotomy,' 43
See also *Metanoia*; *Psuchê*
Psycho-spirituality
and the Beatitutdes, 204
and Gospel of Thomas, 53
interpretation of texts, 290, 295
and *lambanô,* 221n14
and mysticism, 27
path toward God, 27
and the pericopes, 180
and *praus,*153
process, 25
and *psuchê,*181, 224
and Sower parable, 131n27, 132, 134
transformation, 229–31 passim, 346
view of Jesus' Message, 6, 25
Ptôchos, 149, 151–53, 154, 334, 347
Psuchên tithêmi, 20, 170, 213–23 passim

Q, Gospel of
and the eschaton, 56, 58, 58n22
and the Kingdom, 92–93, 93
logia missing in, 65n28
and the logion, 153
and Mt and Lk texts, 238
project, 13n55
reconstructed, 331
scholars of, 62
and Thomas, 54–59, 65–66, 71, 74–75, 92–93, 331
word for *sin* in, 206
Quest, 8, 10–18 passim, 60n28

Rapture, 247, 299–300, 302 (defined), 304, 310–12, 315–21 passim, 351.
See also Ecstasy; Ekstasis
Receiving and entering. See under Child/children
Religion, 48–49 (defined)
and consciousness, 28–30

and conversion, 195
and *ekstasis,* 303, 305, 307, 308, 315
and faith, 108
Greek, 221
history of, 14, 75n61
as human construct, 49, 49n3
inner schools of, 155
and Jesus Quest, 60n28
and Jewish culture, 12, 196
and mysticism, xvi, 7, 24, 25n7, 40, 46, 74, 180, 330
and spirit, 248, 278
'traditional,' xvi, 16
Repentance, xvi, 19, 21, 93, 106, 170, 182, 187–211 passim, 242, 281, 330, 334, 337, 343, 344
See Conversion, *Metanoia*
Rumi, Jelaluddin, 17, 37

Sacred, 4, 7–10, 20–22, 32,, 42, 47–76 passim, 320–1, 330–1
Saving/losing life, 224–32 passim
Sayings. *See under* Logia
Saying versus narrative, 66–67
Second Coming, 21, 81, 85, 101, 330
Second Temple period, 43
'Seeing and hearing.' *See under* Jesus
Self, *see under* Mind, *Psuchê*
Semantics, 9, 9n12
Sermon on the Mount/Plain, 21, 46, 101, 107, 149, 187
Septuagint, 43, 49, 97, 110, 121–2, 124, 173, 175–8, 180, 184, 189, 190, 205, 216, 234, 266, 271, 278–9, 284, 293, 297, 313, 319
Sin, 21, 170, 187–210 passim, 242, 330–34 passim, 343–45 passim
Skopos, 104, 104n8
Sôizô, 183, 219, 225, 229, 230, 230n24, 231
Sola fide, 32
Sola scriptura, 32
Song of Songs, 43
Sower parable, 131–34
Soul, *See under* psuchê
Spirit. See under *Pneuma,* Holy Spirit
Spirituality, 25n10
and daily life, 22
dynamic, 88
and early Christians, 43
and ecstasy, 300, 301, 304
en pneumati, 265
hidden, 242, 243
and Jesus, 13n40, 335
and the Kingdom of God, 89
and *metanoia,* 192n15, 242
and mortification, 221n14
and mysticism, 10, 19, 25n10, 29, 42, 43, 46, 50, 72
and NT, 300, 315, 321
and the pericopes, 180
and *psuchê,* 182
and the psyche, 25–26, 248
and *ptôchoi,* 150n34
and 'spirit,' xvii
universal nature of, 127
in Western/contemporary culture, 14, 17, 87, 181
Straphête, 141n7, 145, 145n21
Strephô, 141n7, 146n21, 159
'Such ones, the.' *See under* Child/children
'Sublime commonness,' 39, 39n57
Sufism, xix, 53, 144, 230
Suniêmi, 128n14, 129, 130, 261
Synoptic Gospels, periscopes in, 82n3, 264–81 passim
Synoptic Problem, 54–55

Teilhard de Chardin, 39
Teleios, 292, 292n22, 293, 293n27
Teleô, 291, 292n13, 340, 342, 343
Tense, 109–10, 117n11, 122, 293, 293n27, 293n28
Teresa of Avila, 17, 27n16, 35, 39
Tertullian, 179n25, 191, 193, 193n20, 199, 277n39, 344
Text, types of, 32
Thelêi, 230n25
Theology, kerygmatic, 11
Thomas, Gospel of
and bridge to canonical gospels, 339
consists exclusively of logia, 54
discovery of, 53
and eschatology, 54, 54n9
and Kingdom of God, 88–89, 93, 99, 164, 210n61, 274

INDEX

merit of, 153
and Q, 54, 54n10, 55–59, 63, 65–66, 71, 74–75, 92–93, 331
and the sayings gospel, 9, 53, 55
Tithêmi, 217
Tithêmi tên psuchên, 213–32
Tôn Toioutôn/Toioutôn, 140, 140n4, 141n5, 145n19
Trance, 313, 313n38
Transcendence, 97, 263, 350
Transfiguration, 45, 303, 306, 318, 318n52, 320
Transformation, passim
    155–61, 169–243
    and annihilation, 294
    and the Beatitudes, 155
    and 'becoming like a child,' 148n30, 165
    and change mind/heart, 105
    character of, 85n7
    and ecstasy, 299
    gradual, 25
    inner, 148, 300
    and the Kingdom, 83, 87–89 passim, 95, 140, 155–61, 334–48 passim
    and the logia, 25
    and losing and saving, 224
    and *metanoia*, 186–211 passim, 194n23
    and mind, *see* Mind
    and mysticism
        as key concept of, 1, 5–6, 42, 46, 47, 165
        of Jesus, 4, 50
        and the logia, 1, 4, 10, 15
        and *pardes*, 305
        of the soul, 42
    necessity of, 162
    and the pericopes, 156–57, 228
    and the parables, 134, 138
    as a process, 34, 35, 306, 307
    and the psalms, 296
    and *psuchê*, 16, 172–86 passim
    and the psyche, 1, 20, 25, 144, 170, 242
    psycho-spiritual, xxi, 134, 229–32
    of the self, 17, 23, 163, 165, 170–86 passim, 333

spiritual/moral, 334
and turning, 145
See also Consciousness; Logia; Mysticism; Presence
Turning. *See under* Child/children
Two Document Hypothesis, 54–55
Two Source Hypothesis, 54–55

'Understand what is in front of you,' 90, 90n20, 90n21
'Unutterables,' 52, 52n8, 133n41

Vaticanum II, 39
Vulgate, 191

Waltet/walten, 95, 95n4, 98, 98n15, 342
Word (as concept), 7, 7n7

Studies in Biblical Literature

This series invites manuscripts from scholars in any area of biblical literature. Both established and innovative methodologies, covering general and particular areas in biblical study, are welcome. The series seeks to make available studies that will make a significant contribution to the ongoing biblical discourse. Scholars who have interests in gender and sociocultural hermeneutics are particularly encouraged to consider this series.

For further information about the series and for the submission of manuscripts, contact:

> Peter Lang Publishing
> Acquisitions Department
> P.O. Box 1246
> Bel Air, Maryland 21014-1246

To order other books in this series, please contact our Customer Service Department:

> (800) 770-LANG (within the U.S.)
> (212) 647-7706 (outside the U.S.)
> (212) 647-7707 FAX

or browse online by series at:

> WWW.PETERLANG.COM